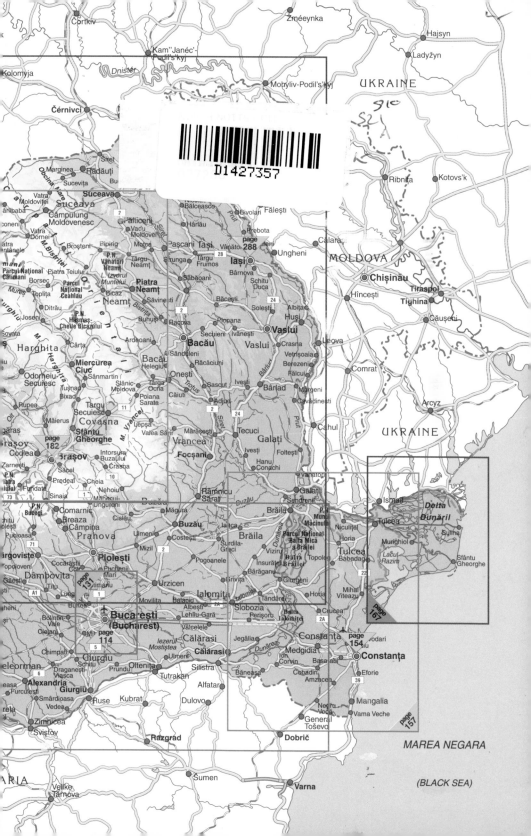

☀ INSIGHT GUIDES

ROManIa

APA PUBLICATIONS

Part of the Langenscheidt Publishing Group

✳ INSIGHT GUIDE

Romania

Editorial
Editor
Tom Le Bas
Principal Photographer
Gregory Wrona
Editorial Director
Brian Bell

Distribution

UK & Ireland
GeoCenter International Ltd
Meridian House, Churchill Way West
Basingstoke, Hampshire RG21 6YR
Fax: (44) 1256 817988

United States
Langenscheidt Publishers, Inc.
36–36 33rd Street 4th Floor
Long Island City, NY 11106
Fax: 1 (718) 784 0640

Australia
Universal Publishers
1 Waterloo Road
Macquarie Park, NSW 2113
Fax: (61) 2 9888 9074

New Zealand
Hema Maps New Zealand Ltd (HNZ)
Unit D, 24 Ra ORA Drive
East Tamaki, Auckland
Fax: (64) 9 273 6479

Worldwide
Apa Publications GmbH & Co.
Verlag KG (Singapore branch)
38 Joo Koon Road, Singapore 628990
Tel: (65) 6865 1600. Fax: (65) 6861 6438

Printing

Insight Print Services (Pte) Ltd
38 Joo Koon Road, Singapore 628990
Tel: (65) 6865 1600. Fax: (65) 6861 6438

©2007 Apa Publications GmbH & Co.
Verlag KG (Singapore branch)
All Rights Reserved

First Edition 2007

ABOUT THIS BOOK

The first Insight Guide pioneered the use of creative full-colour photography in travel guides in 1970. Since then, we have expanded our range to cater for our readers' need not only for reliable information about their chosen destination but also for a real understanding of the culture and workings of that desti-nation. Now, when the internet can supply inexhaustible (but not always reliable) facts, our books marry text and pictures to provide those much more elusive qualities: knowledge and discernment. To achieve this, they rely heavily on the authority of locally based writers and photographers.

Insight Guide: Romania is struc-tured to convey an understanding of the country and its people as well as to guide readers through its wide range of attractions:

◆ The **Features** section, indicated by an orange bar at the top of each page, covers the natural and cultural history of Romania in a series of informative essays.

◆ The main **Places** section, indicated by a blue bar, is a complete guide to all the sights and areas worth visit-ing, organised by region. Places of special interest are coordinated by number with the maps. At the end of each Places chapter is a list of recommended restaurants.

LEFT: rural life in much of Romania remains largely untouched by the modern world.

section on the Danube Delta and much of the Székely Lands chapter.

A veteran travel writer, **David St Vincent** (www.sohoscribbler.com), discovered Romania travel in 1986 and has been an irregular visitor or resident ever since. In the 1990s he was a founder member of ACCEPT, one of Romania's key human rights organisations. He wrote the chapters on Bucharest, Wallachia, the Black Sea coast section of Dobrogea, Moldavia and Transylvania, plus the features on Food and Architecture, and helped to compile the Travel Tips.

Craig Turp, the other major contributor, is the publisher of *In Your Pocket*, a Europe-wide series of locally-produced city guides. He lives with his family in Bucharest. Turp wrote the History section, the People feature, chapters on The Banat, Crişana, Bukovina and Maramureş, and compiled much of the Travel Tips.

Romanian film historian, writer and lecturer **Rolland Man** wrote the Arts and Culture chapter, while **Padre Ambrogio**, an Orthodox priest working in Italy, supplied the Religion chapter. **Ben Le Bas**, a naturalist with a special interest in Romania, wrote the chapters on Geography and Wildlife.

Pam Barrett helped with the copyedit, **Sylvia Suddes** proofread, and **Helen Peters** indexed the book.

David St Vincent would like to thank Paco Morado Santín for his support, Virgil Mager for his kindness and hospitality, Simona Kessler and Mircea Toma for their entrée to Vama Veche, and the late Baroness Auguszta Kemény for inspiration. Tom and Ben Le Bas would like to acknowledge Calin Hodor and Andrei Blumer, authorities par excellence on Romanian natural history.

Map Legend

▬▬ - ▪ -	International Boundary
▬ ▬ ▬	Province Boundary
▬ ▪ ▬ ▪	National Park/Reserve
▬ ▬ ▬	Ferry Route
⊖	Border Crossing
✈✈	Airport
✝✝✝	Church (ruins)
✝	Monastery
▉▉	Castle (ruins)
∴	Archaeological Site
∩	Cave
★	Place of Interest
◤	Beach
❈	Viewpoint
Ⓜ	Metro
❶	Tourist Information
☾	Mosque
✡	Synagogue
⚲	Statue/Monument
⚑	Lighthouse

The main places of interest in the Places section are coordinated by number with a full-color map (e.g. ❶), and a symbol at the top of every right-hand page tells you where to find the map.

◆ The **Travel Tips** listings section, with a yellow bar, provides all the practical information you will need for a trip to Romania. It is divided into five key sections: transport, accommodation, activities, and an A–Z listing of practical tips, and a language and further reading guide. An easy-to-find contents list for Travel Tips is printed on the back flap, which also serves as a bookmark.

The contributors

The book was commissioned and edited by Insight managing editor **Tom Le Bas** – a Romania enthusiast ever since an eventful motorbike trip there in 1988. He also wrote the

horse-drawn transport at
Cotanari, Moldavia

Maps

A map of Romania is on the
front inside cover;
a map of Bucharest is on
the back inside cover

Travel Tips

THE BEST OF ROMANIA

Setting priorities, unique attractions, top beaches...
here, at a glance, are our recommendations, plus some
tips and tricks even the locals won't always know

TOWNS AND CITIES

● **Braşov**
Handsome, tourist-friendly and with a beautiful setting, Braşov makes a perfect base for exploring Transylvania. *See page 181.*

● **Timişoara**
Awash with glorious Secessionist architecture and a buzzing nightlife. *See page 272.*

● **Sibiu**
The European City of Culture for 2007 is a seductive blend of pastel-hued Saxon townhouses, lively bars and cafés, and historic sights. *See page 204.*

● **Sighişoara**
Lost in a medieval time-warp, sleepy Sighişoara is energetically promoted by the tourist industry and comes close to matching the hype. *See page 213.*

● **Cluj-Napoca**
Usually known simply as Cluj, this is a sophisticated and proudly independent city. *See page 233.*

● **Constanţa**
An ancient city that has one of the best museums in the country, Roman and Greek ruins and a beach. *See page 153.*

● **Iaşi**
This cultured provincial city was briefly the capital of Romania, and is home to its oldest university. *See page 285.*

● **Bucharest**
The Romanian capital takes a while to appreciate, but there is plenty to see here and some fantastic restaurants and nightlife. *See page 113.*

BEST CASTLES

● **Peleş**
Fantastical, fairy-tale *schloss* built by Romania's first king high above the Carpathian resort of Sinaia. The sumptuous decor inside comes close to matching the extraordinary exterior. *See page 195.*

● **Corvin (Hunedoara)**
This spiky Gothic pile is absolutely breathtaking at first sight. Although the interior is clumsily restored in places, it is still fun to explore. *See page 249.*

● **Bran**
Tourists flock to this 'fake' Dracula castle, but arrive early and there is much to admire (regardless of any bogus links with the fanged one). *See page 191.*

● **Poienari**
This ruined hilltop castle has stronger links to Vlad the Impaler than Bran. It's a stiff climb, but worth the effort. *See page 142.*

● **Raşnov Citadel**
With sweeping views across to the Carpathians, Raşnov rewards exploration. *See page 191.*

ABOVE: Peleş Castle. **LEFT:** central Sibiu.

BEST SCENERY, HIKING AND WILDLIFE AREAS

● **Danube Delta**
Unlike anywhere else in Romania, the Delta is a watery wonderland sheltering a fabulous array of wildlife. *See page 166.*

● **Bucegi Mountains**
Easily accessible from Sinaia and Bușteni by cable car, this spectacular range offers a superb range of walks across a high plateau. *See page 197.*

● **Făgăraş Mountains**
Romania's highest chain of mountains, this long east-west ridge rises dramatically from the Transylvanian basin. The amazing Transfăgărașan Highway runs right through the middle of the range, close to its highest peaks. Walking the length of the Făgăraş (allow 4–6 days) is the holy grail for local hikers, but there are plenty of short walks too. *See page 203.*

● **Retezat National Park**
These rocky heights are punctuated with mountain lakes and there are plenty of hiking opportunities. *See page 251.*

● **Rodna Mountains**
In the north of Romania near the Ukrainian border, these wild mountains harbour bears, wolves and lynx. *See page 329.*

● **Padiş Plateau**
This limestone plateau in the Apuseni Mountains west of Cluj features some incredible caves. *See page 242.*

● **Ceahlău Massif**
Visible for miles around, the Ceahlău Massif was sacred to the Dacians and has been dubbed Romania's Olympus. The forests surrounding the crags are teeming with wildlife. *See page 301.*

● **Lake Razim**
Lakes Razim and Sinoe, to the south of the Danube Delta, offer tremendous bird-watching, particularly during the spring and autumn migrations. *See page 171.*

● **Iron Gates**
A series of gorges where the mighty Danube has forged its way through the mountains between Romania and Serbia. *See page 277.*

ABOVE: Transylvanian sunflowers. **BELOW:** exotic-looking bee-eaters are a common sight in summer.

BEST MUSEUMS AND ART

● **Peasant Museum, Bucharest**
A must for anyone interested in Romanian culture, with imaginative displays on various aspects of rural life. *See page 128.*

● **Village Museum, Bucharest**
Laid out as a real village, this collection is one of the largest of its kind in Europe. *See page 128.*

● **Astra Open-Air Museum, Sibiu**
Another museum covering Romanian ethnography, the Astra benefits from a beautiful setting south of Sibiu, and some extraordinary examples of home-spun technology. *See page 210.*

● **Museum of Arrested Thought, Sighetu Marmației**
This poignant museum and memorial occupies the former prison, right on the old Soviet border, and remembers the victims of communist oppression. *See page 325.*

● **Brancuşi Ensemble, Târgu Jiu**
A stunning outdoor collection showcases the work of Romania's best-known artist, and features the *Endless Column* (pictured right). *See page 146.*

● **The National History and Archaeology Museum, Constanța**
Well-arranged displays of Roman and Greek relics from the Dobrogea region, including some fabulous statuary. *See page 154.*

CHURCHES AND MONASTERIES

● **Voroneţ painted monastery**
Perhaps the most spectacular of the famous painted monasteries of Bukovina, Voroneţ features especially fine frescoes. Other fabulous painted monasteries include **Moldoviţa**, **Humor**, **Suceviţa** and **Putna**. The latter has a beautiful natural setting and contains the tomb of Stephen the Great; pilgrims flock here on his feast day in July. *See pages 309–315.*

● **Biertan fortified church**
Looming massively over a small Transylvanian village, Biertan fortified church represents the apogee of these remarkable structures, built by the Saxon settlers to combat the threat from the steppe warriors. *See page 212.*

● **Timişoara Orthodox Cathedral**
A masterclass in Byzantine extravagance, with some superb frescoes. *See page 273.*

● **Wooden Church on the Hill, Maramureş**
In the heart of the rural time-warp that is Maramureş, this is the oldest of the region's distinctive wooden churches. *See page 328.*

● **Church of the Holy Cross, Prejmer**
Just north of Braşov, Prejmer is an impressive example of a Saxon fortified church. Within the formidable walls, store rooms and living quarters could sustain the entire village through long periods of siege. *See page 188.*

● **Cozia Monastery**
This harmonious 14th-century building marks the emergence of Byzantine architecture in Romania. It is set in gorgeous scenery. *See page 143.*

● **Curtea de Argeş Monastery**
Elegant architecture in the midst of a lovely park makes this monastery a pleasure to visit. The town is nice too. *See page 141.*

BEST DRIVES

● **Transfăgăraşan Highway**
Romania's highest road cuts its way across the highest section of the Făgăraş Mountains. Only open in summer. *See page 142.*

● **Gheorgheni to Bicaz**
A beautiful route through the Eastern Carpathians passing Lacu Roşu and the Ceahlău Massif. *See pages 225, 301.*

● **Sighetu Marmaţiei to Vatra Dornei**
The remote forested backwaters of northern Romania are traversed by this fantastic stretch of road. *See pages 328–9.*

● **Băile Herculane to Râmnicu Vâlcea**
Route 67 follows the scenic Cerna Valley before heading east to Târgu Jiu, and then shadowing the Southern Carpathians past Horezu Monastery. *See pages 144, 277.*

● **Along the Danube**
The road from Moldova Nouă to Turnu Severin follows the gorges leading to the Iron Gates. *See page 277.*

ABOVE: driving the Transfăgăraşan Highway. **LEFT:** detail of a fresco from Voroneţ. **BELOW:** Moldoviţa painted monastery

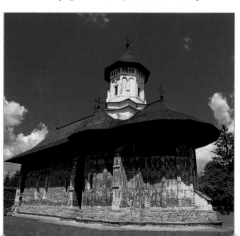

BEST RESORTS AND BEACHES

● **Mamaia**
Very lively and blessed with a terrific 8-km (5-mile) beach, Mamaia may be the brashest Black Sea resort but it is also the most fun. *See page 164.*
● **Vama Veche**
Very different to Mamaia, this is a laid-back, bohemian kind of place, unique in Romania. Campaigners aim to keep it that way. *See page 163.*
● **Sfântu Gheorghe**
Most definitely *not* a resort, this remote village in the Danube Delta lies close to a beautiful beach and is a good base for exploring the Delta. *See page 171.*

BELOW: Mamaia beach. **RIGHT** traditional *ciorbă*.

A TASTE OF ROMANIA

● **sarmale**
Derived from the Turkish *sarma*, these spicy rice and meat rolls wrapped in cabbage (or vine) leaves are delicious. Usually served with *smântână* (similar to crème fraîche). *See page 61.*
● **mămăligă**
Everywhere you go in Romania you will come across the versatile polenta-like *mămăligă*. *See page 60.*
● **mici**
Small spicy rissoles made with seasoned pork and beef, usually served as a hot starter with garlic sauce and beer. *See page 60.*
● **ciorbă**
Traditional Romanian sour soup, *ciorba* comes with a wide variety of ingredients. Tasty and cheap. *See page 61.*
● **Cabernet Sauvignon**
Romanian wines are underrated; Cabernet Sauvignon and Merlot are the best varieties. *See page 63.*
● **ţuică**
This potent plum brandy is the traditional start to a meal. *See page 62.*

TRAVELLERS' TIPS

● **Information**
Information can be hard to come by – even Bucharest has no tourist information office. Make friends with hotel receptionists, as they can be extremely helpful with local information.
● **Service Mentality**
In common with many ex-communist countries, customer service is not Romania's strong point. In the old days, access to information, goods or services was a privilege, and old-style attitudes linger.
● **Vegetarians**
It can be tough being a vegetarian in Romania, although the Orthodox tradition offers some solace: many restaurants offer a year-round fasting menu *(meniu de post)* to cater to the devout.
● **Opening Hours**
Opening hours are fickle and places can close temporarily without notice. Last entry is often half an hour before the official closing time *(see page 365).*
● **Restaurants**
Anyone looking for authentic dishes in a rustic environment with live folk music should seek out a *han* or *restaurant rustic*.

COMING IN FROM THE COLD

One of Europe's least familiar countries, Romania has
a huge amount to offer, and at last appears poised
to receive the recognition it so richly deserves

When Romania joined the European Union on 1 Jan 2007 it became its fifth-most populous member, but at the same time one of its least known. To the extent that people have heard of Romania at all, it has been from relentlessly negative publicity about orphans, AIDS epidemics and poverty. Or, of course, from Dracula films. Yet those who actually go there tell a different story, returning with accounts of fairy-tale medieval architecture, fantastic mountain scenery, lively towns and some of the most hospitable and fun-loving people in Europe.

Certainly Romania's recent history has not been easy. Under Nicolae Ceauşescu's dictatorship, it suffered perhaps more than any other Warsaw Pact country, and following its bloody revolution, the transition from communism was also fraught with difficulties. However, starting in the early 2000s, with the carrot of European Union entry dangling, it has made swift progress towards reform, while the economy has grown at an impressive rate. Things are definitely looking up.

With its profile raised enormously by EU membership, and the advent of budget flights from western Europe, tourism is set for rapid take-off. And there is certainly no shortage of reasons to visit. Much of the country is outstandingly scenic, from the wild Carpathian Mountains to the gentle rolling landscapes of Transylvania. The extent of unspoiled forest, coupled with traditional farming methods, has ensured that wildlife has survived here as practically nowhere else in Europe. Rural folk traditions are still much in evidence in the quiet backwaters of Maramureş and elsewhere. Then there

are the amazing painted monasteries of Bukovina, the sandy beaches along the Black Sea, and an increasingly sophisticated entertainment and restaurant scene. So much that has disappeared from the western side of the continent is still alive and well in Romania. A memorable experience awaits the curious. ❑

PRECEDING PAGES: Transylvanian landscape – the village of Măgura west of Bran; frescoes at Suceviţa painted monastery, Bukovina; Gypsy wedding near Sibiu.
LEFT: ornate Secessionist facade in Arad.

DACIANS, ROMANS, MAGYARS AND TURKS

Shrouded in myth and legend, the origins
of Romania and the Romanian people
continue to provoke fierce debate

When a casual reader comes across
phrases in Romanian history books
such as "Michael the Brave's short-
lived unification of the Romanian lands [in
1600] inspired the Romanians to struggle for
cultural and political unity," a sense of despon-
dency takes hold. The very idea that in 1600
the average peasant – or even nobleman –
would have been troubled by such abstract
notions as pan-Romanian national identity is
as insulting to the reader as it is downright daft.
Yet this kind of nonsense was, until recently,
common currency in Romania, where history
was for a long time written, taught and interpreted by a class of historian used to the notion
that "the past must reflect the present".

Old habits die hard, and in some circles the
mutability of history remains a key part of an
historian's armoury. We shall therefore place a
rider at the beginning of this brief history of
Romania: we shall concentrate only on what
we know: proven facts, or assumptions agreed
on by historians of all nationalities. The many
alternative histories (such as the Daco-Roman
Continuity Theory, *see page 52)* we shall leave
to the historiographers.

The Geto-Dacians

Although most of the Carpathian Mountain
region has been peopled since Paleolithic times,
around 60,000 years ago, there are very few
traces of early human activity on Romanian
soil. Cave paintings at Cucialat, in Sălaj county,
and the scant remnants of a Stone Age settlement near Botoşani, are all that remains.

The first real long-term inhabitants of the
lands that form present-day Romania are considered to be the Thracians, an Indo-European
people who settled most of central and southern
Europe over a 2,000-year period from around
3500–1500 BC. The Thracians were not by any
stretch of the imagination a united people. In
his *Histories,* Greek writer Herodotus wrote
with barely disguised desperation that "if only
the Thracians could unite under a single leader
they would be the greatest nation on earth."
Instead of uniting, however, the Thracians
tribes appear to have splintered into a number
of distinct peoples by around 1200 BC, some
integrating with Greeks and Persians, others
pursuing a more solitary existence.

LEFT: images of the Dacian wars on Trajan's column
in Rome. **RIGHT:** Decebal, Dacian king AD 87–106.

The two Thracian tribes considered to be the forefathers of the Romanians, the Getae and the Dacians – generally referred to as a collective bunch, the Geto-Dacians – fell into the latter bracket. Occupying the land north of the Danube (it is thought that the Getae occupied the Banat and Crişana, the Dacians the Wallachian Plain), they had limited contact with Greeks, Macedonians and Persians, and their society developed more slowly than that of other Thracians; development was also arrested by constant attacks from Barbaric tribes to the north.

By the mid-7th century BC, however, Greek trading colonies had spread along the Black Sea

coast as far north as the Danube, and the commercial settlements of Histria (Istria), Tomis (Constanţa) and Callatis (Mangalia) were buzzing communities. The superior culture of the colonists had a great impact on the Geto-Dacians, and progress in all fields of their development was rapid. There was a great deal of integration: matrimonial alliances were common, and by and large co-existence was peaceful. Although the Geto-Dacians came into contact with other relatively advanced civilisations in the same period, including the Scythians and the Celts, the Greek culture probably had the deepest impact.

Geto-Dacian society reached its zenith during the 1st century BC, when the legendary King Burebista (ruled c. 70–44 BC) succeeded in bringing about the political unity of the Geto-Dacian tribes from around 70 BC. Aware that the Thracian tribes south of the Danube had lost their independence to the rapidly advancing Roman Empire, he assembled a formidable army to defend his new kingdom. At its height, around 50 BC, Burebista's domains stretched from the Pannonian Plain to the Black Sea, and from the northern Carpathians to the Hemus Mountains in present-day Bulgaria. Burebista supported Pompey in his civil conflict with Julius Ceasar, who, it is said, was planning to invade Dacia at the time of his assassination in 44 BC. Burebista was himself assassinated the same year; his kingdom did not survive him, dissolving into general chaos shortly after his death. However, with Rome itself weakened, there was no invasion. Instead, Rome entered into commercial alliances with various Dacian rulers.

Roman Dacia

It was not until AD 87 that the Dacians were once again united under a single leader. This was Decebal (ruled 87–106), a warrior king who believed that attack was the best form of defence and that Rome, by now resurgent under Domitian (ruled 81–96), could only be stopped by pre-emptive attack. Decebal twice crossed the Danube (in 87 and 88) and defeated Roman armies in Moesia (present-day Bulgaria), but after a heavy defeat at Tapae, in the Banat, in 89, he signed a punitive peace treaty that made Dacia a Roman protectorate. But when Emperor Trajan (ruled 98–117) claimed the Roman throne, he was anxious to avenge the two defeats suffered by the Roman armies under Domitian, and hellbent on total military defeat of Decebal.

After careful preparation Trajan launched his offensive against Dacia in the late summer of 101. His army of around 150,000 crossed the Danube at Bersobis (Berzovia), and though it met fierce resistance, by the winter Roman armies had closed in on Sarmizegetusa, the Dacian capital, close to the present-day city of Deva. The next spring the Dacians went on the offensive but failed to halt the Roman advance, and Decebal was forced to sue for peace.

Under the terms of the treaty Rome stationed a garrison in the Dacian capital, and built a remarkable bridge across the Danube at Drobeta (Turnu-Severin; *see page 278)* to link

Dacia with the rest of the empire. However, Decebal failed to comply with the terms of the treaty, and peace lasted just three years. In 105 Trajan again attacked Dacia, conquering Sarmizegetusa the following spring. Decebal committed suicide. The epic story of the Dacian Wars is told on Trajan's Column in Rome. There is a plaster-cast copy in Bucharest's National History Museum *(see page 122)*.

Dacia – comprising almost all of modern-day Romania – now became a fully fledged province of the Roman Empire. The political structures of the old Dacian kingdom disappeared and were replaced by Roman adminis-

mined and transported back to Rome on a network of stone roads built by the conquerors.

The history of Roman Dacia ends in 271. The conquest of these lands had marked the outer limits of Roman ambition, the point that Edward Gibbon refers to in *The Decline and Fall of the Roman Empire* when speaking of an empire that "comprehended the fairest part of the earth, and the most civilised portion of mankind". North of Dacia were a number of Barbarian tribes, notably the Carps and Sarmatians, and by the time of Aurelian (ruled 270–5), despite its mineral deposits, the province was no longer considered worth defending.

tration. A large number of Latin-speaking colonists were brought to the province. The Dacians were lucky in that the Roman conquest came at a time when the empire was seeking to integrate and assimilate – rather than enslave – its various ethnic groups. Those Dacians who had survived the war and had not fled north or west, benefited from rapid Romanisation.

Dacia's primary attraction to Rome had always been its mineral deposits, and in the 170 years of Roman rule these were fully exploited. Gold, silver, copper and especially salt were all

LEFT: marble bust of Trajan.
ABOVE: Dacian relic from the 3rd century BC.
RIGHT: Roman remains at Denşus.

The Dark Ages

Nobody is entirely certain as to what happened in the aftermath of Roman withdrawal. Probably, in the initial period the people of what was Roman Dacia (hereafter Proto-Romanians) did little except get on with their lives. By the third century, however, Barbarian invaders – primarily the Goths, who had hounded the Romans out of much of northern Europe, had occupied most of Dacia. The Proto-Romanians fled south of the Danube, to Moesia (which became Dacia Augustus), and subsequently to Thracia.

Of the early conquerors of the land left in their wake, the most influential were the Slavs and the Bulgars. The original Slav homeland was in eastern Ukraine, from where they migrated south along the coast of the Black Sea, first settling – in the 6th century – on the Wallachian plain, before moving to the eastern and southern Balkans half a century later. After early skirmishes, the Byzantine authorities that controlled land south of the Danube – buoyed by the Slav attraction to Christianity – allowed the Slavs to settle throughout their empire. They quickly became the most powerful people in the Balkans, although their hegemony did not last: in the second half of the 6th century another tribe, the Bulgars, arrived.

Politically astute and brilliant horsemen, the Asian Bulgars pitched up south of the Danube

in 680. Led by Khan Asparuh they then conquered Dacia Augustus and part of Thracia, and these territories were recognised as an independent state under a treaty signed with Byzantine emperor Constantine IV Pogonatus in 681. The state was called the *Parvo Bulgarsko Tsarstvo* (the First Bulgarian Kingdom), but its population almost certainly contained a large number of Proto-Romanians.

As the Bulgarian kingdom expanded northwards over the next two and a half centuries, so the Proto-Romanians returned to the lands they had abandoned after the Roman withdrawal. Some had already migrated west, to the Adriatic coast: these groups would become the Istro-Romanians of Croatia (of which just a

handful now remain) and the Aromanians of Macedonia and Albania. At its height, achieved during the reign of Simeon the Great (ruled 893–927), the Bulgarian kingdom stretched from Mount Olympus to the Dneipr River, and from the Black Sea to the Adriatic. It comprised almost all of modern Romania, and within its boundaries the Proto-Romanians adopted Christianity (along the Black Sea coast Christianity had for centuries been the primary religion) and the Slavonic liturgy. Over the centuries these people became the Romanians, known at the time as *Vlachs*.

Medieval Transylvania

The Magyars, a nomadic, pagan, Finno-Ugric tribe whose original homeland is thought to have been somewhere east of the Urals, arrived in central Europe around 895, and occupied the land west and north of the main Carpathian chain, which would become known as Transylvania (meaning The Land Across the Forested Mountains) a century or so later. According to Hungarian historians the Magyars found a sparsely populated land; Romanian historians, on the other hand, insist that the area was inhabited by Vlachs (ie Proto-Romanians), who had remained there continuously since the Roman withdrawal. While it is doubtful that either version is entirely correct, it is now generally assumed that there were no large Vlach populations in Transylvania at the time of the Magyar conquest. It is, however, just as safe to assume that there were at least some Vlachs living north of the Carpathians – by 920 the Bulgarian kingdom stretched almost to Pest (Budapest) and it is highly unlikely that Vlachs did not settle to some degree in Transylvania. Anonymous P., the notary and chronicler of Hungarian King Béla III (ruled 1172–96), wrote in the *Gesta Hungarorum (The Deeds of Hungary)* that at the time of their arrival in Transylvania, the Magyars "found Bulgars, Vlachs and Slavs".

The Magyars did not initially include Transylvania in the Kingdom of Hungary. Instead, the region was briefly ruled as the personal fiefdom of the mysterious Gyula, said to be a grandson of Árpád, the first Magyar king, who had his capital at Alba Iulia. After falling out with his nephew, King István (St Stephen, ruled 997–1038), he attacked Hungary, only to be defeated and captured in 1003; Transylvania was made part of Hungary, and colonised, initially with Hungarians. The Magyar system of administration, based on counties *(comitat)* replaced the Byzantine *voievode*. After the Christian church split in the Great Schism of 1054, Roman Catholicism replaced Eastern Orthodoxy among the Magyar nobility.

In 1224 King Andrew II of Hungary, concerned that steppe warriors from the east would meet little resistance in under-populated Transylvania, granted non-Magyars the right to settle there. Large numbers of Germans (the Saxons; *see page 55)* populated the southern areas (some had arrived a century earlier at the

beginning to emerge as states in their own right. Hungary – led by Károly Róbert – was defeated by Wallachian prince Basarab (ruled 1310–52) at Posada, in 1330. This confirmed Wallachia as an independent principality (it had hitherto paid an annual tribute to Hungary), and Basarab entered into treaties with Serb and Bulgar rulers to the east and south to consolidate his position. The Battle of Posada was a turning point in Hungarian and Wallachian history: it marks both the birth of a fully independent Wallachia, and the end of Hungary's ambition to extend its kingdom to the Black Sea.

behest of King Géza II), and were given land and various privileges in return for their military dues. Despite these efforts, the Mongols devastated much of Transylvania during their brief and bloody European sortie in 1241, but by the end of the century the Saxon migrations had given new impetus to the economic development of the area.

Foundation of the principalities

While Transylvania was developing as a recognisable entity, albeit within the Hungarian Empire, the rest of the Romanian lands were

---

LEFT: Arpad, the first Hungarian king. **ABOVE:** the Mongol invasions brought death and destruction.

Basarab's son, Nicolae Alexandru (ruled 1352–64), sought *rapprochement* with Hungary, and allowed Hungarian Catholic missionaries to operate in the principality, although he also created the first Romanian patriachate, the Wallachian Mitropolate. The first capital of Wallachia was at Câmpulung, in Argeş county.

It was a similar story in Moldavia. After defeat at Posada, Károly Róbert had turned northeast in his quest to expand Hungary and spread the word of the Catholic Church. Under the compliant Vlach prince Dragoş, Moldavia was a Hungarian vassal state created primarily as a bulwark against the threatening Mongols. It was a Vlach from the Maramureş, Bogdan of Cuhea (ruled 1359–65), who won Moldavia's independence, after crossing the northern Carpathians to defeat the Hungarians in a number of battles during the winter of 1364–65. The first Moldavian capital was at Siret.

The Ottoman invasions

No sooner had Wallachia and Moldavia emerged as independent states than they were threatened by the emergence of a new menace to the south: the Ottoman Turks. The Turks first crossed the Bosphorus in 1352, and after defeating the Serbs at Kosovo Polje in 1389 launched a campaign against Wallachia, ruled by Mircea the Old (ruled 1386–1418), who

Sultan Bayazid and starting a civil war. It was more than a decade later that Turkish attacks against Wallachia recommenced, but they quickly made up for lost time: facing total annihilation in 1417, Mircea agreed to make Wallachia a Turkish tributary, paying Sultan Mehmet I 3,000 gold coins a year.

Moldavia's first military contact with the Turks came in 1420, at Cetatea Alba, now the Ukrainian city of Bilhorod-Dnistrovsky in the Odessa region. The battle, in which the Moldavians were led by Alexandru cel Bun (Alexander the Good, ruled 1400–32), ended in stalemate, but the Turks were deterred from

had sent an army to fight alongside the Serbs at Kosovo. The Ottomans captured Mircea close to Argeş, and held him until he agreed to pay tribute.

Not content for long, the Turks attacked Wallachia again in 1394, although they were defeated at the Battle of Rovine. The following year Mircea formed an alliance with Sigismund of Hungary in an attempt to decisively defeat their common enemy, but the campaign was an utter failure. The Turks routed Sigismund's forces in 1396 at the Battle of Nicopolis in present-day Bulgaria. Mircea hung on to power however, by hook or by crook, until a year before his death. The Mongols had attacked the Turks from the east in 1402, killing

further Moldavian incursions for the next decade. It was only after the death of Alexandru in 1432 that they again moved north, bolstered by victories against Venice for Salonika (1430) and southern Albania (1432). Alexandru Aldea (ruled 1432–36) did not command Moldavia with anything like his predecessor's authority, and fearing heavy defeat he moved to find a negotiated peace with the Turks, under Sultan Murad II (ruled 1421–51). He negotiated badly, however, and besides having to pay the sultan an annual tribute, he was obliged to send Moldavian troops to serve under Ottoman commanders when required.

The greatest resistance to the Turks initially came from Transylvania. The principality had been ruled since 1441 by the high-born János Hunyadi, known in Romania as Iancu de Hunedoara. Hunyadi's origins are disputed: both Romanians and Hungarians claim him, but the chances are that he was of Serb lineage.

Hunyadi was taken under the wing of Holy Roman Emperor Sigismund (King of Hungary 1387–1437) at an early age, and accompanied the emperor on diplomatic and military missions. He distinguished himself in battle against the Turks at Semendria (Serbia) in 1436, and after Sigismund's death he took part in the Hungarian civil war of 1438–40, supporting the candidature to the Hungarian throne of Vladislaus III of Varna, King of Poland.

He was rewarded by Vladislaus with great swathes of land in Transylvania, and made its ruler. He defeated the Turks near Sibiu in 1442, and after serving as Regent of Hungary from 1448–50 he concluded a pact with Bogdan II of Wallachia in 1450, returned to the battlefield and again routed the Turks, this time at the Iron Gates. His last victory came in 1456, at the Battle of Belgrade, shortly after which he died of bubonic plague. His son, Mátyás Corvinus (Matei Corvin) would become Hungary's greatest king.

Stephen the Great

Although Mátyás did not directly control Wallachia and Moldavia, the alliances his father had put in place briefly made him kingmaker over the two Romanian principalities. He supported Vlad III Dracul (ruled 1456–62) in Wallachia, and after originally attempting to occupy Moldavia militarily, he formed an alliance in 1467 with its prince, Stephen III, known as Ştefan cel Mare (Stephen the Great).

Stephen is regarded as the finest medieval Romanian leader. Like his Hungarian contemporary he was a Renaissance man who encouraged culture, the spread of Christianity and – where possible – peaceful coexistence. To these ends he originally pursued a conciliatory policy vis-à-vis the Turks, but after the Ottomans ousted Radu the Handsome (ruled 1462–73) from the Wallachian throne in 1474, he invaded Wallachia to claim the throne for himself. The Turks responded by invading Moldavia, only to be beaten by Stephen's armies at Vaslui in March 1475. The Turks invaded again the next year, led personally by Sultan Mehmed II (The Conqueror), and reached Suceava, where they defeated the Moldavian forces in a battle from which Stephen was lucky to escape. Moldavia was saved by an outbreak of plague, which severely depleted the Ottoman Army and forced a retreat. A peace treaty was signed, and Moldavia agreed to pay the sultan a modest tribute in exchange for its continued independence.

Stephen died in 1504 after reigning for 54 years. His greatest legacy remains the artistic treasures of the Bukovina: the painted monas-

teries at Voroneţ, Humor and Putna, where he is buried. Following his death, succession battles for power weakened Moldavia and it was eventually and inevitably conquered by the Ottomans.

The 16th century

After the Turks occupied Budapest in 1541, Transylvania was made an autonomous province within the Ottoman Empire, which was keen to ensure that the principality did not become a hotbed of Habsburg-sponsored resistance. Instead, they encouraged local Hungarian and Saxon nobles to preserve their traditions and system of administration. The province was ruled by a prince, elected by

LEFT: the siege of Constantinople in 1453 as depicted at Moldoviţa Monastery, Bukovina. **RIGHT:** statue of Stephen the Great, Moldavian king, at Iaşi.

noblemen. The Protestant Reformation spread rapidly in Transylvania following Hungary's collapse, and the region soon became one of Europe's Protestant strongholds. Transylvania's Saxons adopted Lutheranism, and many Hungarians converted to Calvinism. However, although the Protestants printed and distributed religious texts in the Romanian language, they converted only a handful of Romanians from Orthodoxy.

Throughout the 16th century Wallachia and Moldavia fell increasingly under the Sultan's reach, as the collapse of the Kingdom of Hungary made both principalities vulnerable to

Ottoman invasion. Princes were required to pay heavier and heavier tributes to the sultan, and their thrones became little more than expensive commodities that could be bought from the Sublime Porte (the Ottoman court). One such transaction took place in 1572 when Ion cel Viteaz (John the Brave) purchased the Moldavian throne for 200,000 galbens.

Mihai Bravu (Michael the Brave), who ruled Wallachia from 1593–1601, Transylvania from 1599–1600 and Moldavia briefly in 1600, came to the throne of Wallachia in the same way, by bribing the Sublime Porte with the assistance of the Greek banker Andreas Cancacuzino. Early in his reign, however, he developed a fierce anti-Ottoman policy, and joined Spain, Venice and the Papal States in their wars against the Sultan. He signed treaties with Sigismund Bathory, Prince of Transylvania, and Aron Vodă (ruled 1591–95) of Moldavia, and together they initiated a campaign against the Turks in 1594, conquering several citadels near the Danube, including Giurgiu, Brăila, Hârşova and Silistra. At Călugareni, Michael led a 100,000-strong army to victory over the Turks, a battle still regarded as Romania's greatest military victory. By the end of 1595 the Turks had been expelled from Wallachia, and Michael continued the war south of the Danube, briefly occupying Vidin and Pleven.

After Sigismund created a political crisis in Transylvania by resigning in 1598 then immediately changing his mind, Michael crossed the Carpathians to claim the Transylvanian throne. He defeated Sigismund's armies at Şelimbar, near Sibiu and was proclaimed Prince of Transylvania at Alba Iulia on 1 November 1599. The next summer he sought to strenghen his hold over Wallachia and Transylvania by invading Moldavia, which, under the poor leadership of Ieremia Movila had become a vassal state of Poland. In July 1600, Michael was crowned Prince of Moldavia at Iaşi, and proclaimed himself "by the grace of God, the ruler of Wallachia, Transylvania and Moldavia". Purely out of personal ambition he had created the first Romanian state.

It lasted less than three months. Transylvanian nobles formed an army to defeat him at Miraslau in September 1600, while the Poles invaded Moldavia at the same time to restore Ieremia Movila to the throne. Michael was killed the following year on Câmpia Turzii, near Turda, while trying to topple the Magyar nobles of Transylvania with an army backed by the Habsburg Emperor, Rudolph II (ruled 1576–1612).

The decline of the Ottomans

After the death of Michael the Brave, all three states quickly returned to the Ottoman sphere of influence. As before, however, Transylvania fared better than Wallachia and Moldavia. The principality's independence was generally respected, and under enlightened leaders including Gábor Bethlen (ruled 1613–29), Transylvania experienced a brief period of growth and development, as Bethlen promoted agriculture, trade and industry, and sent students abroad to Protestant universities.

After the Turkish defeat at the Gates of Vienna in 1683, however, Ottoman influence throughout Europe began to decline. Transylvania was restored to Hungarian (now Habsburg) rule, in 1687, while Moldavia and Wallachia became increasingly difficult places for the Turks to control. They responded by installing Greek Phanariots *(see below)* to rule in their stead, no longer trusting local princes, who had spent much of the 17th century fighting each other.

One exception to the list of incompetent rulers was Constantin Brâncoveanu, Prince of Wallachia from 1688–1714. Despite increasingly

The Phanariots

The Phanariots were members of prominent Greek families residing in Phanar, the Greek quarter of Istanbul. Phanariots traditionally dominated the administration of the Greek patriarchate and frequently intervened in the selection of prelates, including that of the patriarch himself. From the beginning of the 18th century, they began to occupy high political and administrative posts in the Ottoman Empire, and in 1711 they were handed control of the Danubian principalities (Wallachia and Moldavia). Although initially a modernising influence, with an interest in developing commerce and agri-

harsh financial demands from the sultan, he managed to implement fiscal reform in 1701, and to keep the peace in the principality by cleverly playing off the Turks against the Habsburgs. Unfortunately, when the new power in the region, Russia, attacked Turkey in 1711 (the First Russo–Turkish War), Brâncoveanu remained neutral, angering the sultan (Ahmed II). He was taken to Istanbul and held until 1714, when he was executed. His achievements (and architectural legacy *(see page 83)*, coupled with his martyr's death, turned him into a national hero.

LEFT: a miniature of Mehmed II (Mehmed the Conqueror). **ABOVE:** the Battle of Câmpia Turzii in 1601 at which Michael the Brave was killed.

culture, the Phanariots soon became appalling rulers, who heavily taxed the local noble and peasant populations.

Their rule lasted until 1821, when Tudor Vladimirescu, a landed peasant who had fought with the Russians in the Russo–Turkish War of 1806–12, led a revolt against them, and Turkish hegemony over the principality in general. Although the uprising failed (Vladimirescu was captured and killed), it did persuade the Turks to remove the Phanariots and restore the rule of local princes over both Wallachia and Moldavia. This was an important step towards their eventual unification, and Vladimirescu was soon being proclaimed as a national martyr *(see page 30)*. ❑

THE BIRTH OF MODERN ROMANIA

Although Transylvania did not become part of Romania
until 1918, it was here that the birth of the country –
and of Romanian national consciousness – took place

The birth of the modern Romanian state, which officially – albeit without Transylvania – came into being in 1878, was in part a result of the gradual erosion of Ottoman power, the manoeuvrings of the great European powers and, above all, the rise of French-inspired romantic nationalism which swept through the Balkans in the latter half of the 19th century. The origins of the coming together of Wallachia, Moldavia and Transylvania, however, can be detected as early as the 17th century.

The rise of nationalism

A significant move towards Romanian national consciousness was set in motion by the creation of the Uniate Church in Transylvania at the end of the 17th century. This ecclesiatical initiative had been a compromise, brought about by the stubborn refusal among Transylvania's Orthodox Romanian population to convert to Catholicism. Rome changed tack, insisting that total conversion was no longer necessary: recognition of the Pope as head of the Church would suffice, and the Byzantine/Slavonic liturgy could stay. As further inducement, members of the new Uniate Church that this created were promised the same rights as Hungarians and Saxons in Transylvania, regardless of their social status.

Despite this, over the next century less than a quarter of Romanians in Transylvania joined the new church. It would become most popular among intellectuals, who felt that it could create direct contact between the Romanians and Rome, their spiritual home. It was this tiny

LEFT: nationalist revolutionaries, 1848. **RIGHT:** Habsburg Emperor Leopold I granted Uniate priests in Transylvania equal rights to their Catholic counterparts.

minority of Uniate Romanian intellectuals who would assume a leading role in the emancipation of all Romanians in Transylvania at the end of the 18th century.

Initially, the Uniate clergy themselves were the most influential forces in improving the rights of Romanians. With their political and religious influence in Vienna and Rome (cities to which many travelled and returned home with progressive ideas), they began to investigate the origins of the Romanian people. The Uniate Church's seat, at Blaj, became a centre of Romanian culture. There the Latin alphabet was adapted to the Romanian language (the Romanian Orthodox Church continued using Cyrillic until 1860), and the first Romanian grammars and prayer books were published (a Romanian Bible had first appeared in Bucharest in 1688).

From 1729 until his death in 1768, Inocenţiu Micu Klein, a Uniate priest and member of the Transylvanian Diet, submitted repeated petitions to the Diet and to Vienna requesting that the feudal obligations of Romanians be reduced, that expropriated land be restored to Romanian peasants, and that feudal lords should be barred from depriving Romanian children of an education. His efforts were not entirely successful, and despite an imperial decree establishing a legal organisation for Transylvania's Romanian Orthodox commu-

nity, they remained second-class citizens under Habsburg/Hungarian rule.

After witnessing Klein's failure to achieve more than token reform by peaceful means, three outlaws, known as Horia, Cloşca and Crişan, launched an uprising against the Habsburgs in November 1784 from a base in the Apuseni Mountains. The revolt spread quickly, and garnered widespread support among the Romanian peasantry. It was not fully crushed until February 1785, when its leaders were captured near Alba Iulia, and later executed

After the repression of the uprising, the increasing number of Romanian Uniate intellectuals in Transylvania who had attended university in Vienna, again took up a peaceful

struggle for Romanian improvement. This élite became known as the Şcoala Ardeleană (Transylvanian School), and was led by the teacher and polymath Gheorghe Şincai *(see also page 50)*. In 1791 the school published *Supplex Libellus Valachorum*, a petition demanding equal political rights for the Romanians of Transylvania and loosely based on the groundbreaking French *Declaration of The Rights of Man and of the Citizen*. It centred on the School's claim that Romanians, rather than Hungarians, were the original inhabitants of Transylvania – and as such can be seen as the origin of the Daco-Roman Continuity Theory *(see page 52)*. The petition was sent to Emperor Leopold II, who referred it to the Transylvanian Diet. Dominated by Hungarians, the Diet rejected the proposals and findings out of hand.

The road to unification

The Turks had replaced the Phanariots *(see page 27)* with Romanian princes in 1821, and after the Second Russo–Turkish War (1829–30) the two principalities of Wallachia and Moldavia became all but independent, albeit with considerable Russian influence. A token tribute still had to be paid to the Sublime Porte, but autonomy was notionally guaranteed by Russia, which was officially named "protector state of Wallachia and Moldavia".

Romanian cultural life in this period flourished. While the 1821 revolt *(see page 27)* was ultimately a failure in its attempt to rid Romania of the Turks for good, by the 1840s its executed leader Tudor Vladimirescu had become a legend, and something of an embodiment of what was beginning to be perceived as the Romanian national struggle. Journals such as *Dacia Literară* and *Arhiva Românesca* mythologised Vladimirescu and Michael the Brave, and focused on the Roman and Dacian roots of the Romanian people: not just of Wallachia and Moldavia, but of Transylvania too.

In 1835 the Moldavian prince Michael Sturdza set up the Mihaileanu Academy in Iaşi, the first Romanian seat of higher education, and soon its graduates were teaching at Romanian schools throughout Wallachia and Moldavia. It would not be long before their liberal teachings had an impact on local populations and, from this point onwards, notions of equality and liberty gained much support in the principalities.

A great wave of revolutions hit Europe in

1848, as the ideas of the Enlightenment were manifested as political ideals and revolutionary movements. In March 1848, news of the European revolutions reached Moldavia, and posters appeared in Iași criticising the one-man rule of Prince Sturdza and calling for political reform. Although the prince met the leaders of the protest movement, he feared Russian intervention should he give in to any of their demands, and exiled the reformers to Bukovina. A year later Sturdza's seven-year term was not renewed, and the Sultan of Turkey (who still made the princely appointments) named Grigore Ghica as Prince of Moldavia. Ghica

formed the executive of the Wallachian Revolutionary Movement, founded in May. By June they were ready to strike and, given support by the Wallachian Army, they organised a mass rally at Islaz, in Oltenia, on 21 June. Declaring a provisional government, they called for an end to serfdom, an elected prince to replace the incumbent, George Bibescu, freedom of the press and the emancipation of the Jews. On 25 June the revolutionaries marched to Craiova, where they were warmly received. Fearing a nationwide revolution Bibescu resigned and agreed to the revolutionaries' terms. Neither Russia nor Turkey was happy, however, and in

recalled the reformers from exile and gave them places in his administration. As Sturdza had feared, the Russians duly occupied the principality, concerned about far-reaching reform spreading into and destabilising their domains.

Revolution in Wallachia

In Wallachia revolution broke out in June 1848. It was led by Romanians who had been in Paris during the French Revolution four months earlier and who had rushed home full of revolutionary fervour. Nicolae Bălcescu and Ion Ghica

October they acted. Turkey sent its troops to occupy Bucharest, a feat they managed only after meeting fierce resistance. Russian troops simultaneously attacked other parts of Wallachia, and the status quo was restored.

Russian and Ottoman forces remained until 1851. The sultan named Barbu Știrbei as Prince of Wallachia, and confirmed Grigore Ghica in Moldavia. Both were reformers, and Ghica, especially, was an advocate of Wallachian and Moldavian unification. In the chaos of the Crimean War, whose outbreak in 1853 had ended the peace between Russia and Turkey, the nationalist movement grew in strength. Supported by French intellectuals, writers and politicians (who wanted a united state to form a

---

LEFT: Nicolae Bălcescu, a leader of the 1848 Wallachian revolution. **ABOVE:** the Battle of Plevna in 1876, a victory for Russia against the Turks.

barrier between the Russians and Constantinople), the nationalists managed to get union on the agenda of the Crimean Peace Conference, held in Paris in 1856. The outcome was a compromise: the principalities could elect small parliaments, which would in turn elect the princes.

In elections held in 1858 both Wallachia and Moldavia returned unionist majorities. On 17 January 1859 Wallachia's parliament elected Alexandru Iona Cuza as prince. On 4 February, Moldavia's parliamentarians did the same. Russia and Turkey were not happy, but the election did not violate the terms of the Paris agreement. In December 1861, having garnered

French and British support over two years of painstaking diplomacy, Cuza declared himself Prince of the United Romanian Principalities. Still weak after the Crimean War, neither Russia nor Turkey raised objections.

Transylvania and the Hungarian revolutions

Transylvania's revolution of 1848 took place in the context of the wider Hungarian revolution – which in itself was part of a French-inspired revolutionary wave that swept through Europe in that year. The Hungarian revolutionary programme, which sought full independence from Habsburg Austria and promoted political liberties and the rights of man, was

initially viewed favourably by Romanians in Transylvania, but it soon became apparent that although the Hungarians managed to obtain such liberties and rights from the Austrians, they had little intention of passing them on to the Romanians. The Saxons of Transylvania were also concerned that Hungarian independence woud see them lose their privileges. Both groups set about preventing Transylvania becoming part of an independent Hungary.

Civil war was inevitable, and in October Romanians swallowed hard and fought alongside Habsburg and Saxon armies, having been promised that their reform agenda – which the Hungarians had dismissed – would be given a fair hearing in Vienna. Hungarian forces initially held the upper hand, but by March 1849 the last flames of their revolution had been put out, and Transylvania was placed under the direct rule of Vienna.

After the failure of the revolution, Hungarians realised that any independence, in the short term at least, would have to be a compromise. The Hungarian political élite, led by diplomat Ferenc Deák, began negotiating with Vienna and by 1866, when Austria had become somewhat isolated after the disastrous Austro–Prussian War, Vienna was more than ready to strike a deal. In a process known as the Ausgleich, the Habsburg Empire agreed to transform itself into a federation comprising Austria and Hungary. The two parts of the federation would be equal and separate, with the emperor at once Emperor Franz Joseph of Austria, and King Ferenc Joszef of Hungary taking on the dual roles of monarch. There were two crowns, two parliaments, two governments and two cabinets. Only foreign affairs, defence and finance remained under joint control. Transylvania subsequently became part of the Kingdom of Hungary.

Independence and a foreign king

As talented a diplomat as Alexandru Ioan Cuza turned out to be, he was a failure in office and, after flirting dangerously with the idea of ruling as an absolute monarch, he was persuaded by his brilliant first minister, Ion C. Bratianu, to resign in 1866. Bratianu replaced him with a foreigner, the young German prince Karl Friedrich de Hohenzollern. Although the Great Powers objected (realising that a foreigner, with no local friends or enemies, would cement the union of the two principalities), Hohenzollern's position was rubber-stamped by Romania's now-unified parliament. He became Prince Carol on 22 May 1866, and one of his first acts was to marry a Romanian of Saxon origin, Elizabeth von Wied.

Though Wallachia and Moldavia remained united, and were now led by a prince of the finest European stock, the principalities were still technically part of the Ottoman Empire. Fortunately for Romanian unity, Sultan Abdulhamid II was dragged into a disastrous war against Russia in 1877–78, in which Turkey lost great swathes of territory. The Ottomans were all but thrown out of the Balkans and forced to sign the humiliating San Stefano Peace Treaty (1878), which recognised Romanian independence. Romania had, in fact, with tacit Russian approval, unilaterally declared its independence on 21 May 1877. Four years later Romania declared itself a kingdom, and Prince Carol became King Carol I.

During Carol's long reign (until 1914) he did much to bring about the modernisation of Romania. He paid special attention to the army, and allowed his talented politicians, especially Ion C. Bratianu, and later his son, Ion I.C. Bratianu, to consolidate Romania's position as a modern state. Carol patronised the arts, and personally oversaw preparations for a successful exhibition – held in Bucharest in 1906 – which did much to portray Romania to the many foreign and local visitors who attended as a progressive, modern country. He was not above hubris: the fairy-tale Peleş Castle in Sinaia was built on his orders from 1875–1914, and the boundless luxury Carol demanded for the interior almost bankrupted the country.

And despite the efforts to modernise, much of the country remained backward and poor, with huge tracts of land owned by wealthy landlords and a miserable, exploited peasant underclass. In 1907 desperate poverty in the Moldavian countryside sparked a full-scale peasant revolt, which spread south into Wallachia. Details have remained sketchy because the king ordered documents destroyed, but certainly the army was involved and several thousand peasants died as the revolt was quelled. Rural poverty and anti-Semitism encouraged mass emigration from Romania in these pre-war years.

LEFT: a romantic 19th-century portrayal of Wallachia.
RIGHT: German prince Karl Friedrich von Hohenzollern (Carol I) ruled from 1866 until 1914. He was said to have never heard of Romania before being appointed.

World War I

After brief involvement in the Second Balkan War of 1913, which finally brought an end to the Ottoman Empire in the Balkans and led to the temporary annexation (until 1940) of southern Dobrogea at Bulgaria's expense, Romania remained neutral at the outbreak of World War I. The king's German ancestry, and a number of mutual-assistance treaties, countered the Romanian people's overwhelming sympathy for the French. Carol died late in 1914, and as he had no male heir he was succeeded by his nephew, Ferdinand, whose English wife, Marie, was the granddaughter of Queen Victoria.

By 1916, neutral or not, much of Romania was occupied by the Axis Powers, and the king committed his country to war on the side of the Allies, seizing what he saw as an outstanding opportunity to wrest Transylvania from the disintegrating Habsburg Empire. The war was initially disastrous for Romania. German troops occupied Bucharest and the king and his government had to flee to Iaşi. By March 1918, with no breakthrough on the western front in sight, Romania was forced to negotiate a humiliating peace with Germany. Only the collapse of the Axis Powers in September 1918 allowed Romania to re-enter the war – just two months before the end of the war – and reclaim some territory.

Transylvania and Romania unite

In Transylvania, the national movement advocated unification with Romania, for which it garnered wide public support. The Kingdom of Hungary tried to negotiate a federal arrangement, based on the Swiss model, but the Romanians refused any compromise. Woodrow Wilson's speech guaranteeing self-determination to the peoples of Europe in October 1918 fuelled Romanian ambitions, and on 1 December the Romanian National Party organised a meeting of Romanian representatives from all over Transylvania. They voted for independence from Hungary, and unification with Romania. On

National Liberal Party of Bratianu, favoured by the urban élite, and the National Peasant Party, led by Iuliu Maniu, whose support base was primarily made up of smallholders.

Until 1929 the two parties traded office on a regular basis, and Romania's economy grew apace. Life was good for most people, especially the new urban middle class and those who had done well out of pre-war land reform. The problems began in 1929, when the international stock-market crash required Romania to repay its loans almost instantly. Inflation hit the roof and industrial output was hindered by strikes by workers furious at reductions in pay.

28 December a meeting of Saxons at Mediaş passed a similar vote. The union was approved at the Treaty of Versailles (1919), and legalised by the Treaty of Trianon the following year.

Towards World War II

Romanian territory expanded enormously with the addition of Transylvania, and there were also gains in the east: Bessarabia declared its independence from Russia and was assimilated into Romania. What became known as Greater Romania (Romania Mare) adopted a model liberal Constitution in 1919, which allowed for near-universal suffrage (military cadres were banned from voting), and a parliamentary democracy. There were two political parties: the

The industrial action sometimes became violent, the worst incident taking place in the mines of the Jiu Valley in November 1929, when the authorities fired on protesting miners.

As living standards continued to fall, many Romanians sought answers in fascism (not communism – local communists enjoyed almost no native support whatsoever during the 1930s). The situation was not helped by the succession crisis that had followed Ferdinand's death in 1927. His eldest son and heir, Carol II, had renounced his right to the throne after a series of scandals and gone into self-imposed exile. From 1927–30 Romania's head of state was Carol II's young son (born in 1921), Michael (Mihai). In 1930, however, Bratianu –

seeking continuity in difficult times – persuaded Carol to return and take up the throne.

By 1937 the two traditional political parties had lost much of their support. Nationalist groups such as the Agrarian Party, the League of Christian Defence and the National Legionary Movement (Iron Guard), were able to dominate parliament. The Prime Minister, Ion Duca, tried to disband the Legionary Movement in 1933, but was shot at Sinaia railway station by an Iron Guard assassin.

Carol distrusted the nationalist parties, and after elections in February 1938 had left the Iron Guard as the largest political party, he back to Michael, who in turn deferred almost all political decisions to the leader of the army, the English-educated Marshal Ion Antonescu.

Taking sides

Caught between the Soviets and the Nazis, Antonescu tried to keep Romania out of the war for as long as possible. His hand was forced, however, by the wish to reclaim northern Transylvania and Bessarabia. Subtle German promises of its return saw Romania join in Operation Barbarossa in 1941, invading Bessarabia side by side with the German Army, and quickly retaking the territory it had lost to the Russians.

refused to sanction a government containing its members. He declared a Royal Dictatorship, banned all political movements, and had Corneliu Zedrea Codreanu, the Iron Guard leader, imprisoned and later shot.

Carol was a dreadful leader, however. After two years of utter misrule, which had seen Romania fall increasingly within the German sphere of influence, he was forced by the military to abdicate in 1940, after having agreed to Hitler's demands that he award the northern part of Transylvania to Hungary, and Bessarabia to the Soviet Union. Carol passed the crown

LEFT: King Carol II and his son, Michael (Mihai), in 1939.
ABOVE: villagers welcome the Red Army in 1944.

It was only when Antonescu committed Romanian troops to continuing into pre-war Soviet territory that the Allies declared war on the country. Meanwhile, Romania, which had been enacting harsh anti-Semitic legislation since the mid-1930s, declared a dirty war on its Jewish residents. It is thought that up to 286,000 Romanian Jews were murdered during World War II.

After the defeat of the Axis powers at Stalingrad, where tens of thousands of Romanians lost their lives, the end for Antonescu came swiftly, ousted by King Michael in a palace coup on 23 August 1944. Romania rejoined the war on the side of the Allies three days later. It was too little too late, however: the Soviets occupied the country early in September. ❏

ROMANIA SINCE 1945

More than 40 years of communism have left an indelible mark on the Romanian soul, but there are hopes for a brighter future now that the country has become a member of the European Union

Romania, like almost every country in central and eastern Europe that found itself under Soviet occupation in 1945, was treated as a defeated nation. This was despite the not-unfounded claim that Romania's joining the Allies in August 1944 had shortened the war considerably (the country's switch of des had denied Germany its precious oil). The Soviets had installed Petru Groza as prime minister in March 1945, despite Groza's Ploughmen's Front and the Romanian Communist Party performing poorly in elections. Through him the Soviets controlled the Interior Ministry – and with it the army and security apparatus – and the Justice Ministry, and placed its officials in high-ranking positions in all other ministries.

The facade of democracy was preserved until the summer of 1947, when the pre-war political parties, which had been harrassed and persecuted since 1945, were all banned. Iuliu Maniu was arrested and interned in the notorious prison at Sighetul Marmaţiei *(see page 325).*

He died there in 1953, a short while after Gheorghe Bratianu, son of Ion I.C. Bratianu, who had taken over from his father as the leading figure in the Liberal Party. King Michael was given an ultimatum in December 1947: exile or arrest. He chose exile, and abdicated on 30 December.

The regime of Gheorghiu-Dej

With all instruments of the old democratic system swept away, Romania's communist leaders – completely subservient to the Kremlin – set about the total transformation of the country into a Stalinist satellite. From 1948 until the end of the 1950s, economic, social, political and cultural life in Romania followed the model

and directives of the Soviet Union, passed through its local agents based at the enormous Soviet Embassy on Kisellef Boulevard in Bucharest (today the Russian Embassy and Consulate).

Opposition was dealt with swiftly. Those members of the pre-war governments who had not yet been arrested were rounded up, along with intellectuals, Uniate priests, former Iron Guardists, journalists, writers, actors and even sportsmen: anyone who failed to recognise the absolute authority of the new regime. Smallholders were targeted as agriculture was collectivised, with most landowners stripped both of their property and of their liberty. For many, death came on the Canalul Morţii (Canal of

Death), an attempt to build a canal from the Danube to the Black Sea, begun in 1949 but abandoned in 1953 (and later resumed, *see page 161*). It cost the lives of at least 40,000 people.

Although Petru Groza remained prime minister until 1953, overseeing all was the brutal Gheorghe Gheorghiu-Dej, General Secretary of the Romanian Workers' (Communist) Party. Dej was a barely literate former railway worker who had led strikes on the Romanian railways in the 1930s. He was the leader of a group of communists who had remained in Romania during the war, and which by the late 1940s had defeated another communist group, led by Ana

Czechoslovakia. Aided by the fact that Soviet troops were no longer stationed in Romania (the last left in 1953), Dej began to carve out a relatively independent path, and unilaterally proceeded with rapid industrialisation. He also gradually de-Stalinised Romania: many political prisoners were granted an amnesty in 1962, Russian street names were changed, and Stalin City returned to its original name, Braşov.

Life for most people remained tough, however: the need to pour resources into industrialisation meant that the production of consumer goods was neglected, and there were perennial shortages of foodstuffs. The rights of workers

Pauker, who had spent the war in Moscow. By 1954, Dej's only rival for power was the moderate and popular Lucreţiu Patraşcanu, who supported a policy of de-Stalinisation. Dej had him shot as a traitor and his supporters arrested.

Although initially an obedient disciple of the Soviet Union, by 1958 Dej had become impatient with the Soviet refusal to assist Romanian industrialisation. The USSR had decided in late 1955 that Romania, Bulgaria and Hungary should become agricultural feeder states for the industrial Soviet Union, East Germany and

were non-existent, and conditions in the factories – many of which had been built hastily – were generally awful. In the countryside, collectivisation of agriculture had reduced most farmers to a status little better than serfs, although in some remote regions (including parts of the Apuseni and Maramureş), opposition to collectivisation had been so strong that local party cadres simply gave up trying to implement it.

The Ceauşescu years

Dej died in 1965, just two months before the Ninth Congress of the Romanian Communist Party. This created a problem: who would deliver the keynote address? The task fell to the

LEFT: Gheorghe Gheorghiu-Dej (left).
ABOVE: queuing for food was a familiar trial in Ceauşescu's Romania.

The Ceaușescus

Of the great villains of the 20th century, few have had worse posthumous press than Nicolae Ceaușescu. It was not always so. Detested at home for much of his 25-year period in office, during which Romania was transformed from a hard-line, Soviet-controlled orthodox socialist state into a giant maze of contradictions – a destitute kleptocracy, a dynastic communist republic – he was fêted abroad, until near the very end, by naïve foreigners who took his loud anti-Soviet rhetoric at face value.

Ceaușescu was not the first Romanian communist to preach the anti-Soviet line; his predecessor Gheorghe Gheorghiu-Dej had done so since the late 1950s, angered at the USSR's desire to confine Romania to the status of agricultural backwater. In 1968 Ceaușescu took the policy to new levels, when he publicly declared his opposition to the Warsaw Pact invasion of Czechoslovakia. It was his finest hour, and for a brief period the adulation of the crowds was genuine.

Yet, unlike the Czech regime he so vigorously defended, Ceaușescu did not follow words with deeds. Romania remained a closed society: there was no Bucharest Spring. Only after the high profile visits of US and French presidents Richard Nixon (1969) and Charles de Gaulle (1970) did Romani-

ans witness any loosening of the state's grip on their lives. But the reprieve was little more than illusory, and it was to be temporary.

Few historians agree on much when it comes to Ceaușescu – mystery surrounds him in death as it did in life – but most consider that his state visit to North Korea and China in 1971 was the catalyst for the devastation he later unleashed on Romania. Ceaușescu was impressed at the order of North Korean society, its unflinching worship for its leader, Kim Il Sung, and the scale of the capital, Pyongyang. Elena Ceaușescu – who had until then taken a back seat – couldn't help noticing the leading role taken by Jiang Ching, Madame Mao, in the running of China. Elena's rapid ascent up the party ranks to claim the de-facto number-two position began shortly after the couple's return.

Still riding a wave of popularity and enjoying the benefits of the pre-OPEC oil boom, Ceaușescu named himself President of Romania (a post created for the purpose) in 1974. Now unquestionably the sole leader of the country, the cult of personality was about to go into overdrive (see pages 74–5). Economically, too, Ceaușescu began calling his own tunes, and rapid industrialisation replaced the production of consumer goods as the economic priority. Living standards – relatively good throughout the 1960s and early 1970s – declined quickly. But things were about to get even worse.

The Systemisation Policy – which, if completed, would have seen 7,000 villages destroyed – was little less than an attempt to industrialise the countryside. Even Stalin did not attempt this. Urban agricultural centres would replace the collective farms (themselves bad enough) and systemise food production. Even the cities did not escape: houses were declared redundant and vast swathes of them were replaced with tower blocks, nowhere more so than in the capital, where the Uranus district was razed to the ground to make way for the Parliament Palace and the Centrul Civic (see pages 116–118). Fortunately, the full horror of Systemisation was never meted out on the Romanian people. The end, when it came, was swift. Arrested on 23 December 1989, the Ceaușescus, loyal to each other until the end, were shot two days later – almost certainly on the orders of Ion Iliescu – after being tried by a kangaroo military court. The image of their lifeless yet strangely youthful faces remains a vivid one. Like the memories of 25 years of misrule, they will take decades to fade. ❏

LEFT: Nicolae and Elena.

relatively youthful Nicolae Ceaușescu (he was 47) who, to the astonishment of his audience, denounced the abuses of the Dej years. The Congress confirmed Ceaușescu as general secretary of the party, and most delegates left full of promises of a more liberal and open society. Initially their hopes were fulfilled. Small-scale private enterprise was encouraged, American films were again shown in cinemas, foreign books translated and foreign plays staged. Russian disappeared from the school curriculum, and was replaced with French and English.

The early benefits of Ceaușescu's liberal reforms, therefore, were mainly cultural. Economically, the country struggled to meet internal demand for consumer goods, and living standards did not noticeably improve. Yet Ceaușescu – no intellectual – was a clever political operator and in 1968 he pulled off a political masterstroke by condemning the Soviet invasion of Czechoslovakia, a move that secured him superstar status at home, in Washington, in Paris and in London. His reward was billions of dollars in foreign loans, which were spent on consumer goods and on industrialisation. The problem with this largesse was that the loans had been granted on a political nod and a wink, with barely a glance at the country's books. Romania was already heavily in debt, and its capacity to repay its loans had been based on overly optimistic export projections. When exports failed to meet desired levels, the country was in trouble.

Economic pressures

Macro-economic policy was a disaster: in 1976 Romania invested heavily in its oil refining capacity, requiring it to import oil to keep the refineries burning – all this while the international price of oil was steadily climbing, culminating in the massive price hikes of 1978. Romania needed to borrow more and more money, and by 1981 the country's external debt reached $10.2 billion (from $3.6 billion in 1977). In February 1982 the International Monetary Fund (IMF) demanded that Romania reduce its level of imports. By then, however, Romania was already importing food to feed its people. What angered Ceaușescu was that a foreign organisation could dictate economic policy to him. In December 1982 he announced that, in

order to preserve its independence, Romania would repay its entire foreign debt by 1990. At the beginning of 1983 rationing was introduced in some provinces for flour, bread, sugar and milk. By the end of the year only the capital was free of rationing. Other restrictions were placed on the consumption of petrol, electricity (there were constant power cuts throughout the 1980s) and gas. From 1986 onwards many homes, even in the capital, went unheated.

The revolution

By 1989 Romania was a failed country. It had a leader and a government, but little else.

Schools closed early in winter for lack of heating, people did not have time to work as they spent all day queuing for basic foodstuffs, and a rampant black market saw speculators and shadowy middle-men make small fortunes.

Yet even as late as November, when the Communist Party held its four-yearly congress, electing Ceaușescu as president (unanimously, as usual) for another four-year term, there was no real sign that the regime was in trouble, even as communist regimes crumbled all over Eastern Europe. Then came Timișoara.

Always a city whose people were better informed than the rest of the country (they could watch Yugoslav television), the population of Timișoara staged their first demonstra-

RIGHT: Ceaușescu, with Erich Hönecker, waves to the crowds on a state visit to East Germany in 1980.

tion on 16 December, initially in protest at the demotion of a local Hungarian priest, László Tőkés. The demonstrations quickly became political, and spread widely. On 17 December tens of thousands gathered in front of the city's Orthodox Cathedral. Ceauşescu ordered the army to fire on the protestors, which it did, shortly after nightfall. The demonstrators dispersed and the next day the city was calm, with soldiers and secret policemen everywhere; Ceauşescu proceeded with a planned two-day state visit to Iran.

He returned from Iran on 20 December, and the next day a rally in Bucharest was organised

Salvation Front (FSN). It officially declared itself the new government on 23 December. On Christmas Day, Ceauşescu and his wife were shot in the town of Târgovişte.

To this day it is not known if the shots fired at demonstrators during the revolt came from Ceauşescu loyalists or from forces loyal to the new regime, which – it has been suggested – needed martyrs to give itself credibility in the eyes of the general public. What is generally agreed, however, is that the FSN had been organised long before December 1989, perhaps as early as the previous winter. We also know that, of the official revolution death toll of

to reassure the population that he was still in control. He wasn't. He was booed off the balcony of the Central Committee Building in Bucharest, and the crowd that had been brought in to cheer him ended up spending much of the evening of 21–22 December on the streets around Piaţa Universităţii fighting security forces. The next day protestors – not hindered by the army – entered the Central Committee Building where Ceauşescu and his wife Elena had spent the night; the couple fled by helicopter from the roof.

Inside, a new government was already being formed. Ion Iliescu, who until the early 1980s had been one of Ceauşescu's most loyal henchmen, formed a group calling itself the National

1,104, just 162 were killed before Ceauşescu fled. The vast majority, 942 people, died in the fighting that occurred after the seizure of power by the FSN.

Post-revolution Romania

Despite initially promising that the FSN would be a purely transitional government, the organisation fielded candidates in the April 1990 elections. Although they were nominally free and fair, the fact that the FSN had absolute control of the media (there was just one television and radio station) and all state apparatus, meant that anything other than a resounding victory for the organisation and for Iliescu – who ran for president – was never in question.

Soon after, in June 1990, students and workers in Bucharest – appalled at the apparent replacement of one authoritarian regime by another – demonstrated against the new government, demanding that the FSN remove itself from politics, and that Iliescu step down. The demonstration was brutally suppressed by miners loyal to the regime, who were brought in by Iliescu to do the job the secret police would have done in the old days. More than 100 demonstrators died in what became known as the *mineriada*. Further demonstrations and a second *mineriada* in 1991 finally brought down the government, although Iliescu hung

on, appointing a technocrat, Teodor Stolojan, to oversee the writing of a new Constitution and to organise new elections in 1992. Although better organised, the opposition was still soundly defeated. Iliescu remained president and his PDSR (the renamed FSN) formed a new government that became a byword for theft, corruption and economic stagnation. There was no privatisation, with Iliescu memorably stating: *"Noi nu vândem țara"* ("We will not sell the country").

LEFT: tanks on the streets of Bucharest in 1989. **ABOVE:** Adrian Nastase, Romania's Prime Minister 2000–2004. **RIGHT:** Romanians have welcomed European Union membership.

From the moment Ceaușescu fled, day-to-day life for ordinary people greatly improved. All restrictions on private ownership of land, housing and businesses were lifted, and the posession of foreign currency legalised. Romania was swamped with cheap imported consumer goods, and inflation was rampant. The country benefited from a great deal of international goodwill, as charity workers, in many cases woefully misguided, came to offer their (usually wholly unqualified) assistance. Moved by the infamous pictures of the country's orphanages under the old regime, they built luxurious children's homes in villages where most houses had no

running water, thereby encouraging local people to dump their children in the new institutions.

Iliescu was temporarily removed from power in 1996, only to be re-elected in 2000, having had the Constitution changed in order to be able to run for a third term. Unable to change the Constitution a second time, he was finally forced to step down in 2004. His anointed successor, Adrian Nastase, was easily defeated by the popular, populist Traian Basescu, erstwhile Mayor of Bucharest. Basescu appointed a new government, most of whose members were relatively untainted by corruption and the 15 years of economic stagnation since the revolution. He also initiated a campaign to weed out all remaining members of the secret police from public life.

Into the European Union

On 1 January 2007, following years of negotiation, Romania was formally admitted into the European Union. Two massive celebrations – the biggest since the fall of Nicolae Ceauşescu – were held in Bucharest to mark the occasion, and other events were organised in cities across the country, and on the border with Hungary. As many as two million people spent the night quite literally dancing in the streets.

The mood is upbeat, with most Romanians firmly of the opinion that this is the best thing that has ever happened to their country. Following on from NATO membership in 2004, it represents a decisive break with the past. What's more, the economy appears to be in good health. Indeed, some sectors could even be described as booming. The advent of budget airline flights from western Europe in 2007 and significant foreign interest in buying up Romanian property is expected to create a boom in tourism.

Yet it is easy to get the impression that people were expecting more. There are still homeless children on the streets of Bucharest, there is still dreadful poverty in much of the countryside, as anyone who has visited a typical country village, with its horse-drawn transport and rutted lanes, will know. These brutal realities are unlikely to

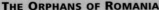
disappear any time soon. Lucian Boia, a contemporary Romanian philosopher, has suggested that this is because Romania is still "a prisoner of the eastern model, either of the Turks or of its own making, where there will always be enormous discrepancies between the haves and the have-nots. In this regard the notion of national unity must be seen as nothing more than empty words, for in reality it does not exist."

Modern Romania is indeed full of contrasts, where the latest sports cars race past old women eking out a living selling turnips. The divide between rich and poor is wider than anywhere else in the EU, and the gap between urban and rural living standards is equally enormous. After nearly two decades of democracy and market economics, the question is: will Romania ever bridge the gap between the haves and have-nots?

Lucian Boia may suggest that the answer is no, but others are more positive. The usual response is a reasonable one: you are asking the wrong question. Most Romanian sociologists prefer to ask: will life ever be tolerable for the whole population? They, in turn, like to answer that, by and large, it already is.

The new safety net

For anyone who visited before 1989, it is clear on even the most superficial level that life for everyone in Romania is unquestionably better

than it was before. The freedom of movement craved for so long has been realised, as has the flow of funds for massive infrastructure projects, such as the country's long-overdue network of motorways (still a long way from being built, it should be pointed out). Even for first-time visitors, the images that they see will be far less horrific than the pictures of orphanages, interminable queues and revolutionary chaos they remember from news bulletins. For no matter how poor some Romanians may still be, the EU safety net now exists to protect

FAR LEFT: relic of an unlamented age.
LEFT: Maramureş honey. ABOVE: former King Michael.
RIGHT: a promising future in the European Union.

them. Crucially, the will and ability to aspire to better things has led to a dynamic entrepreneurial spirit that the country has never before possessed.

The economy is, in fact, booming, with an annual growth of around 6 percent in 2005–6. Foreign companies are attracted by favourable tax rates and cheap labour. Romania is currently the poorest of the EU states (GDP is around a third of the average, wages around a sixth), but the gap is expected to narrow quickly. There are negative stereotypes to overcome – some argue that the decision by the British Government to prevent Romanians entering the UK to

work in the same way that, for example, Poles did after their EU accession in 2004, is an indication of this (although it has been suggested that the affinity that many Romanians feel with the Latin countries of southern Europe, and an antipathy to the north, would make large-scale movement to the UK unlikely, anyway).

To thank for this sea change is the EU. For all its flaws, for any initial disappointment at its failure to deliver instant wealth, it has had a positive impact. It is too easily forgotten that the country's starting point was a long way behind that of its neighbours. It seems that, at last, Romania can be said to have put its fatalism to good use: things will get better; the glass is no longer half empty, it is half full. ❏

Decisive Dates

THRACIANS, DACIANS & ROMANS:

c. 650 BC Thracian tribes – at the time populating much of present-day Bulgaria – cross the Danube and settle on the Wallachian Plain to the north.

430 BC In his *Histories* (c. 430 BC), the Greek Herodutus provides the first recorded mention of the Dacian tribe living on present-day Romanian lands. The Dacians are thought to have fought with other Thracians in the Persian wars of 514–13.

400–300 BC Dacians move north to occupy the southern part of Transylvania.

c. 200 BC Dacians defeat Celtic tribes to occupy much of the Carpathian Basin.

113–09 BC A series of disastrous alliances and subsequent wars against the Romans.

70–44 BC The fortunes of Dacia revived during the reign of Burebista, who created an empire stretching from the Pannonian plains to the Black Sea.

AD 106 After two short wars, the Dacians, led by Decebal, are defeated by the Roman Empire under Emperor Trajan. Dacia becomes a province of Rome.

271 Facing attacks by Barbarian tribes on Dacia's northern borders, Rome abandons the province.

THE DARK AGES

271–c. 400 Dacia ceases to exist as a recognisable state and is occupied by various tribes of Goths and Visigoths. Dacians probably retreat south of the Danube to Byzantium, though the subject is the most hotly disputed in Romanian history.

450–800 Avars, Bulgars, Pechenegs and Slavs all occupy the Carpathian basin at various times but none settles permanently. In the south, much of the Wallachian plain and Dobrogea form part of Khan Asparuh's First Bulgarian Kingdom.

927 By the time of the death of Simeon the Great, all of present-day Romania is part of the Bulgarian Kingdom. The Vlachs (the contemporary name for descendants of the Dacians, still living mainly south of the Danube) have adopted Christianity, the Slavonic liturgy and the Cyrillic alphabet.

1003 The Magyars, led by Stephen the Great, settle in the Carpathian basin. Transylvania is incorporated into the Kingdom of Hungary as a quasi-autonomous principality.

WALLACHIA, TRANSYLVANIA AND MOLDAVIA

1224 The Golden Bull issued by King Andrew II of Hungary grants Saxons (Germans) privileged rights to Transylvanian land in exchange for defending Hungary's eastern frontiers (the first Saxon settlers having arrived some 80 years earlier).

1250–1300 As the Byzantine Empire collapses, the principalities of Wallachia and Moldavia emerge as recognisable states, both ruled by Vlach leaders known as *voivodes*.

1418 On the death of Mircea the Old, who kept the Turks at bay for almost 20 years, Wallachia and Moldavia become vassal states of the Ottoman Empire, paying annual tribute to the Sublime Porte.

1475 Stephen the Great leads a Moldavian revolt against the Turks, defeating them at the Battle of Vaslui. Moldavia is briefly independent but, weakened by succession battles after Stephen's death (1504), is gradually reeled back into Ottoman control.

1541 The Turks capture Pest and install a pasha to rule over central Hungary. Transylvania becomes a principality, but with a fair amount of autonomy: native princes rule the territory until 1690, but must pay a large annual tribute to Constantinople.

1600 Michael the Brave, Prince of Wallachia, invades Moldavia and Transylvania, uniting the three principalities for six months before he is betrayed and killed by Hungarian noblemen.

1687 Transylvania returned to Hungarian (now Habsburg) rule as the Ottomans are thrown out of central Europe. Moldavia and Wallachia remain Ottoman territories, ruled by Phanariots, Greek trustees who bid for the right to rule principalities. Provinces are highly taxed and economic development retarded.

TOWARDS INDEPENDENCE

1812 After defeat in the First Russo–Turkish War, the Ottoman Empire is forced to cede the eastern part of Moldavia, known as Bessarabia, to Russia.

1821 Tudor Vladimirescu leads a revolt of Wallachian peasants, which, while easily defeated, persuades the Turks to end Phanariot rule and to appoint Vlach princes to rule in their place.

1829 The Treaty of Adrianople, ending the Second Russo–Turkish War, makes Moldavia and Wallachia Russian protectorates. The Russian Army withdraws in 1834, making both independent in all but name.

1859 Alexandru Ioan Cuza elected Prince of Wallachia and Moldavia. Three years later the union of the two principalities is formalised: the name Romania is used for the first time.

1877 Moldavia and Wallachia declare formal independence, recognised by the Great Powers at the Treaty of Berlin the following year.

1881 Romania becomes a constitutional monarchy: Prince Karl of Hohenzollern-Sigmaringen becomes King of Romania, and takes the name Carol I. Ion C. Brătianu is his first prime minister.

MODERN TIMES

1907 Peasant Revolt in Moldavia and Wallachia.

1919–20 After the defeat of Austria-Hungary in World War I, Transylvania is awarded to Romania by the Treaty of Trianon, and unified with Wallachia and Moldavia to form Greater Romania. Bessarabia is also returned to Romania; the country thus doubles in size and population.

1938 Carol II disbands parliament and forms a Royal Dictatorship with a pro-German approach. The first anti-Semitic legislation soon appears.

1939 Molotov–Ribbentrop Pact awards Bessarabia to the Soviet Union, and Northern Transylvania to Hungary. Carol abdicates in favour of his son Michael (1940), but real power goes to Marshal Ion Antonescu, head of Romania's armed forces.

1941 Antonescu reluctantly takes Romania into war on the side of the Axis powers, ostensibly to recover Bessarabia. Deportation of Jews begins.

1944 King Michael's palace coup deposes Antonescu and withdraws Romania from the war; it re-enters three days later on the side of the Allies.

1944–47 Occupied by the Soviet Union, King Michael is forced to abdicate in 1947, and the country is declared a People's Republic. Gheorghe Gheorghiu-Dej is the first leader.

LEFT: sultan Suleyman the Magnificent (1494–1566).
RIGHT: at home with Nicolae and Elena Ceauşescu.

1955–56 A staunch Soviet ally, Romania is a founding member of the Warsaw Pact and COME-CON. Romania assists in the invasion of Hungary.

1965 Gheorghiu-Dej dies, and Nicolae Ceauşescu is named head of the Romanian Communist Party.

1968 Ceauşescu refuses to allow Romanian troops to take part in the Warsaw Pact invasion of Czechoslovakia, openly condemning the invasion in a famous speech in front of thousands.

1970s–80s Ceauşescu is fêted in the West for his independent stance from the Soviet Union. However, the US later (1983) revokes Most Favoured Nation status over concerns about his mistreatment of the Hungarian minority.

1977 Devastating earthquake kills over 1,500.

1989 Ceauşescu is shot on Christmas Day after a popular revolution, of which the full details have yet to emerge. Backed by the army, Ion Iliescu, a former Ceauşescu henchman, names himself leader.

1990 Elections confirm Iliescu as president. Bucharest University students occupy Bucharest's central square, but are dispersed by miners brought in from the Jiu Valley. With full government support the miners kill more than 100 students.

1996 Amid plummeting living standards, Iliescu and his PDSR party are defeated in elections by a centre-right coalition. But the coalition is weak, and in 2000 Iliescu and his renamed PSD return to office.

2007 Romania becomes a member of the European Union on New Year's Day. ❑

A MIXED POPULATION

All the way back into the distant past, the lands that now comprise Romania have been a melting pot of the Balkan and the Latin, the Magyar and the Slav. Today, the country's ostensibly homogenous people represent an array of very different races, nations and traditions

The ethnography of Romania's population has shown a steady trend towards homogeneity since the end of World War II. Before the mass extermination of the Jews in the Holocaust, and the exodus of Hungarians and German Saxons at the end of the war, the country was a rich tapestry of Romanians and Ruthenians, Saxons and Magyars, Gypsies and Macedonians, Jews and Russians. Though more than 21 distinct ethnic groups are currently recognised by the Romanian authorities, more than 90 percent of the population declared themselves ethnically Romanian in the 2002 census. In 1930, before war, holocaust and communism, just 70.9 percent claimed Romanian ethnicity.

Yet for all its statistical homogeneity, in reality Romania remains a hotchpotch of peoples. Walk along any street of any city in the country and you will see a collage of faces, races and traces. Most Romanians have a swarthy complexion, but there are many pale faces in the crowd. Any myths of racial or national purity are blown apart simply by walking down a Romanian street.

To define just who is and is not a Romanian is therefore a wilfully difficult thing. Nicolae Ceausescu's policy of assimilation made it so. Integration of the minorities was in most cases forced, making everyone a Romanian whether they considered themselves to be so or not. Hungarians – historically the rulers of Transylvania and still a large ethnic minority there – were especially targeted. Yet while a policy removing minority identities would inevitably

PRECEDING PAGES: playing the pipes at a folk festival near Sibiu. **LEFT:** faces of the future.
RIGHT: shepherd with *coaja* cheese and fleece coat.

result in a more homogenous society, it should be noted here that the dictator's real purpose was to entrench his own power. The ethnic Romanians of Transylvania, traditionally a disadvantaged minority, were the natural supporters of his nationalist policies.

Ethnic Romanians

So what is a Romanian? The modern term usually refers to all those who feel bonded together by the Romanian language, state, citizenship and culture, but the idea of being *Romanian* has meant many different things over the years. In fact, the word is a relatively new invention. Until the end of the 18th century Romanians were known to themselves and to the Slavs, Turks and

Magyars who surrounded them, as *Vlachs*, or Wallachians. That term, first used by Slavs, is still in use today – mainly by historians – to refer to all people traditionally considered to be of Romanian descent, including the Istro-Romanians of the Croatian far northwest and the Aromanians of Albania and Macedonia.

The fact that the Vlachs (hereafter Romanians) descended from the Romanised peoples of ancient Dacia and Thrace is disputed by no-one – the language, the only Latin-based tongue in the Balkans, is evidence enough. Exactly *how* they developed as a distinctive people is the subject of bitter dispute, however.

The name Romania was not given to a political entity until 1859, when the principalities of Wallachia and Moldavia elected the same prince, Alexandru Ioan Cuza, and united to form a proto-state (formal independence from the Ottoman Empire was not achieved for a further 19 years). The name was chosen to reflect the Roman origins of the Romanian people. Perversely, at the beginning of the 1950s the local spelling of the country's name was changed by the communist regime of Gheorghe Gheorghiu-Dej – at Soviet insistence – from *România* to *Romînia*, precisely in an attempt to "Slavicise" the language and people, and to

The notion of Romanianism can be traced back to the Uniate Church (*see pages 29–30*) and, particularly, to the work of the 18th-century Şcoala Ardeleana (Transylvanian School), a group of humanist nobles led by the Cluj-based teacher and polymath Gheorghe Şincai – who were influenced by the Enlightenment and who sought scientific answers to the questions of the origins of the Romanian people. In 1791 they published *Supplex Libellus Valachorum* (loosely based on the French *Declaration of the Rights of Man and of the Citizen*), demanding equal political rights for the Romanians of Transylvania. What we term modern Romanian culture, and the national consciousness, have their roots in that document.

obfuscate their true origins. By the end of the 1960s, the more nationalist regime of Nicolae Ceauşescu had not only returned the local spelling to *România*, but was also heavily lobbying the United Nations (UN) and the English-speaking world to adopt *Romania* and *Romanian* in preference to the older *Rumania* (a spelling still seen in some old encyclopedias and text books). These may seem like fickle points, but such things count in a country whose past is riddled with myth and falsehoods. The campaign to have the UN change the country's name, for example – finally successful in 1971 – marks the point where Romania had rediscovered pride in its people's Roman roots and Latin origins, after years spent denying them. By the 1980s however the regime had changed its mind again, and began promoting local values over foreign.

The Magyar Question

Romania's biggest minority remains the population of 1.5 million Hungarians who live in Transylvania ("Erdely" in Magyar), where they account for around one fifth of the population. In the area of eastern Transylvania known as the Székelyföld (Székely lands), comprising the counties of Covasna, Harghita and parts of Mureş, Hungarians form a majority (one school of thought defines the Székely

Transylvania long before the Magyars (one version of this is the Daco-Roman Continuity Theory, *see opposite*), while Hungarians insist that when the Magyar tribes settled the Carpathian Mountains around 1000 AD – a century after they had arrived in central Europe – they found the land empty. Whichever is true, Hungary – in one guise or another – then ruled the region for the best part of 1,000 years; Transylvania only became part of Romania after the Treaty of Trianon was signed in 1920.

From the signing of the treaty to the outbreak of World War II, more than 300,000 ethnic Hungarians chose to leave Romania. Many were rel-

as a separate ethnic group from other Hungarians). Other counties with large Magyar populations include Satu Mare, Bihor and Salaj. Most of Romania's Hungarians are Roman Catholics, although there are a large number of Calvinists and Unitarians, too.

The presence of such a large minority is a legacy of Romania's, and Transylvania's, much-disputed past. Even today few Romanians and Hungarians agree on the region's history. In brief, Romanians believe that they populated

atively well-off landowners who lost much of their wealth in the land reform of the early 1920s. Others fled the often overt discrimination that saw Hungarians and Jews reduced to second-class citizens in matters of commerce and banking: areas in which they had long been in the ascendancy. In 1940, the Second Vienna Award gave northern Transylvania (present-day Maramureş plus the counties of Mureş and Harghita) back to Hungary, which held it until 1944. Now it was the Romanians in the region who found themselves persecuted in daily life, a factor that led to the notorious anti-Hungarian campaign of autumn 1944. More than 40,000 Hungarian men were arrested and sent to internment camps, while there were a number of

FAR LEFT: Romania has high marriage rates compared with other European countries.
LEFT: engraving (1840) of a Wallachian in a warm winter coat. **ABOVE AND RIGHT:** rural and urban youth.

The Daco-Roman Continuity Theory

On 5 July 1980, Romanians enjoyed a national holiday to celebrate "the 2,050th Anniversary of the Founding of the First Independent and Unified Dacian State on the Territory of Romania." The highlight was a mass-participation spectacular involving 150,000 perfectly coordinated members of the Bucharest public. It portrayed Nicolae Ceaușescu as the rightful heir of Dacian King Burebista, who had formed that first Dacian Kingdom in 70 BC, and Romania as the sole heir of the

Dacia, which comprised almost all of present-day Romania, including, most importantly, Transylvania.

The event was the vulgar, kitsch, physical manifestation of the Daco-Roman Continuity Theory, originally devised by 19th-century Romanian nationalists but used to far greater effect by Ceaușescu, primarily to justify Romania's claim to Transylvania. The theory has since entered the public consciousness (one oddity arising from it is the number of Romanians called Octavian and Traian, another is the ubiquitous Dacia, the local make of car), and though it is to a certain extent popular for the opportunity it gives to look West (the desire to be identified as Latin rather than Slav or – God forbid – Balkan) and goes some way to explaining the Romanian

affinity for all things Latin (French, especially), it is providing a pro-Romanian answer to the Transylvania Question that remains its *raison d'être*.

The idea behind the theory is simple: modern Romanians are the direct descendants of "Romanised" Dacians who lived in the Roman province of Dacia from AD 101–271. After the Roman withdrawal the "Romanised" Dacians retreated to the caves and peaks of the Carpathians where they preserved their Latin language and racial purity, only repopulating the Carpathian Basin after it was safe to do so, hundreds of years later, and after – for here lies the rub – the Magyars had settled it.

The problem with the theory is that there is no evidence whatsoever to prove it, despite great efforts to find some. In reality the "Romanians" are thought to have withdrawn from Dacia completely by the end of the 3rd century AD, seeking refuge south of the Danube. Communists will be communists, however, and the facts were not allowed to get in the way of a good theory. And just as Ceaușescu was given blind support by naive Western politicians who applauded his anti-Soviet stance while his people were treated as slave labour, so the vast majority of Western historians were prepared to go along with his view of Romania's origins. In August 1980 more than 2,000 of them (from 50 countries) attended the 15th International Congress of Historians, dedicated that year to the subject of Daco-Roman Continuity. Those few dissenting (mainly Hungarian) historians who had spoken out against the theory in the past refused to attend.

Through the 1980s the theory became part of a strategy intended to remove all traces of Hungarian territorial identification. Bilingual inscriptions were removed, and streets – and in some cases, cities themselves – were renamed to emphasise Roman roots. Turnu Severin became Drobeta-Turnu Severin, and Cluj was renamed Cluj-Napoca *(for more on the oppression of the Hungarians, see opposite).*

Though now widely discredited by foreign historians, the theory remains the preferred explanation of the Romanian people's origins among the vast majority of the country's academics. It's importance may have diminished (Romania and Hungary are both members of the EU and NATO, two organisations that in theory forbid any territorial disputes between member states), but it has not gone away. That will only happen when the Romanian nation is ready to objectively investigate its origins. ❏

LEFT: most Romanian cities feature a Romulus and Remus statue, a very visible reminder of the Roman link.

mini-pogroms, especially in remote villages where the brutalities of a world war were used to excuse the actions of the lynch mobs.

As it gained power after the war, Romania's Communist Party included a large number of Hungarians (and other ethnic minorities, especially Jews) in its upper echelons. Though most were purged in the early 1950s, Romania's communists paid lip service to the Marxist notions of national freedom and equality by creating the Hungarian Autonomous Province in 1952, comprising most of Harghita, northern Covasna and eastern Mureş counties (roughly the area covered in the Székely Lands chapter on pages 219–31). According to a census taken in 1956, 76 percent of this region's population was Hungarian. In reality, any idea of autonomy was a sham, as control over the lives of every Romanian citizen, ethnically Hungarian or otherwise, was centred firmly and squarely on Bucharest. Indeed, the real attitude of the Romanian Government towards the Hungarian question was better displayed in 1959 when it began a programme to merge Hungarian schools with Romanian, and closed the Hungarian Faculty at Cluj University. The Hungarian Autonomous Province was disbanded in 1968.

Villages bulldozed

The worst discrimination against the Hungarian minority was carried out from the late 1970s onwards, when Ceauşescu and his regime encouraged the idea that Hungarians were to blame for the country's economic woes. Schoolbooks were rewritten to depict Hungarians as unpatriotic. Those who did not attempt to flee (which was difficult), attempted to assimilate as best they could, often changing their names and speaking Hungarian only within the confines of their own homes. Ceauşescu's Systemisation Programme, which involved the bulldozing of Transylvanian villages, was set to worsen the minority's already abject situation, but then came the 1989 revolution (sparked to some extent by the outspoken Hungarian priest, László Tőkés), and, eventually, better times.

One of the first things that Ion Iliescu's 1990 government did was to scrap the discriminatory policies against the Hungarian minority. Nonetheless, with law and order across the country

RIGHT: women of the Csángó Hungarian minority in Ghimes, close to the border of Transylvania and Moldavia.

reeling in the immediate aftermath of the revolution, inter-ethnic conflicts flared up, culminating in the events in the divided city of Targu Mureş in March 1990. After Romanian youths attacked the offices of the UDMR – a political party created in January 1990 to defend the rights of Hungarians in Romania – Hungarians retaliated and a full-scale riot (which the police did little to stop) broke out, lasting three days.

Hungarian-Romanian relations

Fortunately, the Targu Mureş riot was as bad as things got. Since then, thanks in no small part to the UDMR, which has been a small but

effective coalition partner in every Romanian government since 1996, the Magyar question has eased. To all intents and purposes it was answered in 1995, when Hungary and Romania signed a bilateral treaty in which Hungary renounced all territorial claims to Transylvania and Romania reiterated its respect for the rights of its minorities. Given that both countries are now members of the European Union (EU), any ongoing or future disputes will be resolved in a European framework.

Minor points of quarrel remain. One is the continued failure of the Romanian authorities to create an exclusively Hungarian-language university in Cluj-Napoca, despite repeated promises to do so. Another is the interminable delay in returning property confiscated by the communist regime from the Catholic Church, whose congregation is overwhelmingly Hungarian. The UDMR also occasionally brings up the question of granting some kind of autonomy for the Székely areas. Other disputes, such as the right of Hungarians to take their driving tests in their mother tongue, have been resolved by EU membership and the adoption of EU-wide legislation covering such issues.

Romania's Jews

At Romania's 2002 census, just 5,780 people declared themselves ethnically Jewish; a further

1,200 attested to being members of the Jewish faith. At the outbreak of World War II there were as many as 750,000 Jews in Romania, representing nearly 6 percent of the population.

The Romanian Holocaust began in the summer of 1941, with the deportation of Moldavia's Jews to Transnistria and to German-held territory in the Ukraine. At least 100,000 were shot by the Romanian Army at Odessa, in October 1941. In Wallachia, many Jews were spared deportation but were subjected to forced labour and faced miserable living conditions. Transylvania's Jews survived deportation until the summer of 1944, when the vast majority were taken directly to Auschwitz. In all, at least half of Romania's pre-war Jews (between 300,000 and 400,000 people) were killed in the Holocaust.

Most Jews left in Romania at the end of the war fled to Israel: more than 200,000 departed between 1945 and 1950. Those who remained suffered unofficial persecution, especially after 1952, when the Romanian Communist Party – whose upper ranks had until then been largely dominated by Jewish members – carried out an anti-Jewish purge. During the latter years of communism the Ceauşescu regime actively promoted a policy of "cash for Jews", under which Israel would purchase exit visas for Romania's Jewish population. As many as 50,000 emigrated this way.

Romania's few remaining Jews maintain a low profile: none currently occupies a cabinet post or holds an elevated position in any of the political parties. There are still 33 functioning synagogues in the country, however, many of

WHERE THE JEWS CAME FROM

Jews have been present on Romanian territory from the Roman invasion of Dacia onwards. Many Jewish traders arrived on Roman coat-tails, and there is a history of Jewish-dominated commerce on the Black Sea coast throughout the Middle Ages. Large-scale settlement, however, did not take place until the mid-19th century, when huge numbers of Ashkenazi Jews emigrated to Moldavia to escape persecution in Russia. There were over 250,000 Jews living in Romania by 1850. A second wave of Jewish migrants arrived in Moldavia from Bessarabia in 1905, fleeing widespread pogroms.

By the mid-1930s Jews could be found in the highest echelons of Romanian society, and became a target for the increasingly influential and popular fascist National Legionary Movement (or Iron Guard) led by Corneliu Codreanu. In 1938, shortly after King Carol II declared himself absolute ruler, he enacted a number of anti-Jewish measures in an attempt to appease the Iron Guard (Carol's mistress was, ironically, a Jewess).

After the declaration of the military-dominated National Unitary State in 1940, led by Marshal Ion Antonescu, anti-Semitism became state policy. A pogrom in Bucharest in January 1941 saw 120 Jews killed as the police stood by; in July the same year an estimated 10,000 Jews were killed in the worst Romanian pogrom, in Iaşi.

which are historic monuments – and with funds from wealthy Jews living abroad they are being renovated to past glories. Unlike Poland and Germany, however, there has yet to be any large-scale return of Jewish migrants, at least in part because of a lingering anti-Semitism (only in 2005 did Romania officially recognise its role in the Holocaust).

The Saxons

The term Saxons (Romanian *Saşi*) is used to describe a people of German origin who settled in Transylvania from the 12th century onwards. The colonisation of Transylvania by Rhenish

privileges and the right to choose their own judges and priests. These were exceptional allowances for that day and age, and were to remain in place for over 600 years. This in turn encouraged further waves of settlers.

By the end of the 13th century, seven great fortified cities, Bistritz (Bistriţa), Hermannstadt (Sibiu), Klausenburg (Cluj-Napoca), Kronstadt (Braşov), Mediasch (Mediaş), Mühlbach (Sebeş) and Schässburg (Sighişoara) had developed to accommodate them. Collectively, the seven cities were known as the *Siebenbürgen*. To protect themselves against the threat of the steppe warriors, the Saxons built massively fortified

Germans (the generic term "Saxon" applies to all of these German migrants) was initiated by King Géza II of Hungary in the 12th century, and for centuries the main purpose of encouraging these settlers was to defend Hungary's sparsely populated southeastern borders. Saxons were also brought in for their knowledge of mining and other areas of expertise. In 1224, following the Teutonic Knights episode *(see page 189)*, Saxons were rewarded for their loyalty to the Hungarian throne with a charter consolidating their rights, which included trading

LEFT: László Tőkés, the Hungarian priest who helped set the events leading up to the 1989 revolution.
ABOVE: village people.

churches, taking full advantage of their skills in stonework and their right to build in stone. *For more on these churches, see page 212.* Together with the Széklers *(see page 231)* and Hungarian nobles (as part of the Union of Three Nations *(Union Trium Nationum)*, the Saxons controlled Transylvania politically and economically.

They continued to enjoy a privileged position during the years of Habsburg ascendancy over Transylvania, though their standing fell after Hungarian independence in the mid-19th century, and many emigrated to Germany and Austria. There were further migrations at the end of World War II, and throughout the communist period: as with the Jews, Saxons were sold exit visas for hard currency. This time Germany paid. After 1989 most remaining Saxons left (Germany considered them *Auslandsdeutsche* – foreign Germans – and granted them citizenship). In doing so they left entire villages abandoned; there are many of these settlements around Făgăraş, their stone dwellings and churches crumbling into oblivion. Some 60,000 Saxons remain, however, and though this is a far cry from the 800,000 who lived in Romania in 1930, the number is once again climbing: many Saxons who fled for Germany decades ago are returning to Romania, to their old villages, to retire – encouraged by their generous German pensions and the low Romanian living costs.

Viideanu flatly denies the claims, somewhat compounding the problem.

The Gypsies are believed to have originated from the Punjab and Rajasthan regions of India. They began their migration to Europe and North Africa via the Iranian plateau around 1000, fleeing the Indian caste system, at which they found themselves at the bottom. While their traditional language is *Romani* (Romany), an Indo-Aryan language, most speak Romanian.

Though Gypsies have suffered a long history of persecution (they were freed from slavery in Romania only after the unification of Wallachia and Moldavia in 1859, and suffered

The Gypsies

Romania has easily the largest Gypsy (also known as Roma, and Ţigani to the Romanians) population in Europe, but arriving at a precise figure is difficult. According to the 2002 census, they number 535,140 people or 2.5 percent of the population, but estimates made by the International Roma Congress (IRC) place the number closer to 2 million. The IRC claims that fear of persecution leads Gypsies to disguise their true identity. There are certainly few recognised Gypsies in public life: one high-profile Gypsy politician, Marian Vanghelie, is mayor of Bucharest's largest sector, and though it is often whispered that the general mayor of the city, Adrian Viideanu, is himself a Gypsy,

terribly in the Holocaust), they are – at least in comparison with the other nations of central and eastern Europe – fairly well integrated into Romanian urban society, and almost no nomadic Gypsies remain. Like the districts of Ferentari and Colentina in the capital, most major towns have readily identifiable Gypsy slums, but just as many live in the same ordinary housing blocks as Romanians. And though Gypsies claim to be the most socially disadvantaged group in the country, the problems they encounter on a day-to-day basis, such as lack of running water or heating in winter, are the same as those faced by all Romanians of limited means. In Romania at least, Gypsies do not have a monopoly on poverty. On the other hand, they do still suffer discrimination and although, as mentioned, there is a degree of integration, culturally they remain distant from the rest of society. In wretchedly poor villages across the country, Gypsy women are still subservient to the men. Traditionally, the most respected Gypsies are musicians *(see page 76)*.

EU membership, which demands full human rights and protection for minorities, should improve the lives of the Gypsies. It is hoped that a long-standing distrust of formal institutions will fade, and this will allow social issues, such as abandoned babies, to be tackled.

both Serbs (22,000) and Croats (9,000), and some 17,000 Slovaks in the northwest.

Of newer populations, the largest influx has been by Turks. Though a Turkish minority of variable size has existed in Dobrogea for centuries, Turks have been coming to Romania in significant numbers since 1989, mainly as small businessmen. There are now more than 30,000 throughout the country. Greeks too have been returning in their thousands to a land they colonised 2,000 years ago, while in and around Timişoara a sizeable Italian community – now more than 5,000 – has developed. In Bucharest there are 2,500 Chinese. ❏

Romania's other minorities

There are 60,000 Ukrainians living in Romania, most along the northern border of the country, and in towns such as Suceava and Rădăuţi, where they account for 7 percent of the urban population. In the Danube Delta there is a sizeable Russian-speaking minority, the Lipovani, a people who migrated from Russia in the 18th century to avoid religious persecution *(see page 69)*. They still speak Old Russian, the language of the Kyivan Rus and begetter of modern Russian, Ukrainian and Belarussian. In the west of the country there are sizeable communities of

LEFT: the bride leaves the family home at a Gypsy wedding. **ABOVE:** most Gypsies still live in poverty.

THE EXPATRIATE COMMUNITY

There are also in Romania more than 13,000 people of "other ethnicity" – mainly the growing number of Western expatriates who have come to work in the country on short contracts, and who have stayed on. Many are active in the real-estate market, buying houses and land in the capital and throughout Romania. Prince Charles became the owner of a vast estate around Viscri *(see page 213)* in Transylvania in 2006. Interesting to note, however, is that foreigners are still technically disqualified from owning land here: many buy houses which then have to sit on land held in trust by Romanian friends or companies until legislation changes to bring it in line with the rest of the EU.

FOOD AND DRINK

Eating out is one of the great pleasures of a visit to Romania – local food is fresh, often delicious and remarkably cheap. The beer and wine is good, too.

In recent times, few countries' cuisines have yo-yoed in critical esteem quite so dramatically as Romania's. In the 1930s visitors wrote of the amazing variety and deliciousness of its restaurants, with some of Bucharest's considered among Europe's finest. By the late 1980s, thanks to the policy of exporting almost anything worth exporting, standards had sunk so low that Romania was eastern Europe's laughing stock. Visitors were well advised to bring enough food to last the trip plus almost any kind of the most basic provisions for Romanian friends.

While Romanians never lost their love of food, cooking traditional specialities required increasing ingenuity, while finding many staple ingredients meant resorting to the black market, growing them yourself or barter (Ceauşescu once said the reason for the shortage of food in the country's shops was due to people hoarding provisions in their freezers). In 1989, the food shortage was a main rallying cry among protestors. One of the new government's first acts was to reverse the food-export policy.

Times have changed. These days, international supermarket chains are making inroads in the larger cities, and a growing sophistication has helped spur a growth of pride in Romanian products. Adverts boast: "Romanian produce, European Union standard." If you stay in the countryside, more likely than not the chicken in your pot will have travelled no further than the backyard or a neighbour's garden. Even in cities, many have rural relatives who provide some produce. And for the rest there are plenty of what those in the West call farmers' markets.

LEFT: a rustic restaurant in Borşa, Maramureş.
RIGHT: *papricaş* (spicy stew) is a common winter food.

Economic circumstances, however, mean that even if food is widely available, many can only afford a basic diet. On the other hand, it's often in Romanians' houses you enjoy the best cooking. As guest of honour you're unlikely to see much evidence of shortages.

Influences

It doesn't take an expert to trace the origins of many favourite Romanian dishes. The Turks are behind the Romanians' love of sugar-laced pastries and desserts such as *baclava (bakhlava)*, *rahat* (Turkish delight) and dishes such as *frigărui* (kebabs), *sarmale* (stuffed cabbage or vine leaves), *ciulama* (white sauce stew), *pilaf*, *salată de vinete* (char-grilled aubergine salad).

From Austria come *şniţel* (schnitzel), *ştrudel* and *covrigi* (pretzels); from Hungary *gulaş* (goulash), *papricaş* (spicy stew) and many pastries; from Bulgaria *zacuscă* (roasted aubergine, red pepper and onion relish).

Romanian cuisine has a good deal in common with that of neighbouring countries, which share many of these influences. Within the country, regional variations exist even if they aren't always apparent in restaurants. Hungarian dishes are particularly popular in Transylvania, where the food tends to be heavier than elsewhere. In the Delta look for fish soup *(ciorbă pescărească* or *ciorbă de peşte)*, which

porridge, but at the opposite end of the scale it resembles a very thick Italian polenta. In poorer households *mămăligă* can be a meal's main ingredient, often mixed with *brânză* (cheese) and *smântână* (similar to crème fraîche, but sourer) or stirred into *lapte* (milk). *Mămăligă* is highly versatile and, despite its peasant origins, graces even the swankiest restaurant menus.

First courses

Cold starters *(gustări reci)* often mean a platter of cheese, olives and salami, or – in summer – fresh vegetables. Another first course is a selection of cold cuts *(mezeluri,* from Turkish *meze)*,

usually comes served bones and all. In Moldavia, *borş* (borshch) is more common than elsewhere and invariably excellent.

Romanian staples

A century ago, Romania was one of Europe's leading grain exporters, and bread *(pâine)* remains a vital staple. Recipes, sizes and shapes vary by region, the commonest form being white, large and circular, with a thick crust and soft chewy middle. Special knotted loaves are baked for special occasions.

Another staple is *mămăligă* (or *mămăliguţă)*, a yellow cornmeal mush made by stirring cornmeal, boiling water and salt in a special pot called a *ceaun*. More watery versions look like

perhaps including salami *(salam)*, ham *(jambon)*, cured ham *(şuncă)*, pastrami *(pastramă)* or *slănină* (salted pork belly).

Hot starters *(gustări calde)* include sausages *(cârnaţi)*, frankfurters *(cremvurşti)* and *cabanos* (thin dry spicy sausages), often fried. The most famous are *mici* or *mititei* – "little ones" – small spicy skinless rissoles made with a highly-seasoned mixture of pork and beef, served with garlic sauce and beer. *Cârnaţi de Pleşcoi* are a fiery version of mutton sausage. The less squeamish can try *creier pané* – brains in breadcrumbs – or *drob de miel*, Romania's answer to haggis and traditional at Easter (note that despite the presence of, or similarity to, certain French words in Romanian, *miel* is lamb, not honey).

Salads are also a mainstay, although in winter pickles *(muraturi)* reign supreme. In summer, *salată de vinete*, made from char-grilled aubergines, is traditional.

Soup comes in three varieties: *supă* (from French *soupe)*, *ciorbă* (from Turkish *çorba)* and *borş* (from Ukrainian borshch). The second two are sour soups, while a *supă* is a simple broth or cream soup. *Ghiveci* and *tocană* are types of stew, normally served as main courses.

At its simplest, *borş* is a mildly vinegary amber liquid obtained by fermenting wheat bran, cornflour, a sprig of cherry tree, thyme and basil in small water vats. However a *borş*

including *ciorbă de pui* (chicken sour soup), *ciorbă de potroace* (giblet sour soup) and *supa de pasăre*, chicken bouillon, often served with dumplings *(găluşte)* or noodles *(tăiţei)*. *Borş de miel* (sour soup with pieces of lamb, head often included) is a traditional Easter dish.

Main courses and desserts

A characteristically Romanian dish, especially in winter, is *sarmale* (from Turkish *sarma)*. A spicy rice-and-meat mix wrapped in sour cabbage rolls *(sarmale în foi de varză)* or vine-leaves *(sarmale în foi de viţă)*, it's a classic companion to *mămăligă* and *smântână*.

can also be any highly flavoured soup soured with this liquid. Although the word derives from Ukrainian, the tradition of making *borş* goes back to ancient Moldavian times; the Romanian type is fermented from bran rather than sugar beet. A *ciorbă*, on the other hand, is a vegetable-based soup soured with lemon juice or vinegar. Sour soups are often dressed with *smântână*

Traditional at Christmas, *ciorbă de perisoare* is a seasoned sour vegetable soup with rice-and-meat balls. *Ciorbă ţărănească* is a hearty beef-and-vegetable sour broth flavoured with parsley. Chicken soups are also common,

Stews include *iahnie de fasole*, a thick bean cassoulet with garlic sauce, often livened up with pork or smoked bacon. Another favourite is *tocană* (also known as *tocaniţă* or *tochitură)*, a casserole flavoured with onions or spices. *Tocană de legume* is a vegetable stew, while *ghiveci* is a Romanian ratatouille.

Romanians adore fried cuts of meat, especially pork *(carne de porc)* and beef *(carne de vacă)*, depending on season. Lamb *(carne de miel)* is traditional at Easter and pork at Christmas. Beef cuts, usually fried with chips, include the French export *filet châteaubriand* (tenderloin), *escalop* (escalope), *muşchi de vacă* (sirloin) and *muşchi filet* (fillet). Veal is most commonly found in *şniţel de carne de viţel* (Wiener schnitzel).

LEFT: smart dining at the Lloyd in Timişoara.
ABOVE: *ciorbă* (soup) is a staple food.

One French-inspired meat dish not for weight watchers is *şniţel cordon-bleu*, a breaded pork or beef escalope with ham and cheese. Other traditional gut busters are *muşchi ciobănesc*, pork stuffed with ham and cheese under a rich sauce, and *muşchi poiana*, beef stuffed with mushrooms, bacon and peppers in a tomato sauce. A *mixt grill* is a meat-lover's feast, comprising *mici*, fried sausages, braised chicken liver, beef and mutton, served with a garlic sauce.

Turkish influences are apparent in *pilaf de post* (rice with vegetables or mushrooms), *frigărui de porc* (grilled pork kebabs), and *chiftele* (fried minced meatballs – from Turkish *köfta*). *Pâr-*

joale are a larger, flatter, highly spiced type popular in Moldavia, often served with garnishes.

Chicken *(pui)* is popular, often spit-roasted whole over an open fire *(pui la cuptor)* or roasted with garlic sauce *(pui cu mujdei)*. Two traditional chicken dishes are *ciulama de pui*, chicken in a white wine sauce with herbs, and *găină umplută*, roast chicken stuffed with egg, liver, breadcrumbs and herbs. Many Moldavian recipes are chicken-based.

Hunting has a long tradition, and game dishes include *potarnichi cu smântână* (roast partridge with *smântână*) and *pulpă de căprioară la tavă* (venison marinated in wine and vinegar). Bear is a tough meat, sometimes made into salami.

Fish dishes – often spicy – are popular, particularly carp, trout, pike and perch. In the Delta, dishes include the unappetising-sounding *frigărui de crap* (carp kebabs) and *saramură de peşte* (spicy fish stew with hot paprika and salt), one of the few dishes truly approaching fieriness.

Seafood is rare. Romanians do, however, have a tradition of eating fish roe, especially in *salată de icre* (taramasalata). Although many associate it with the Caspian Sea, sturgeon also inhabit the Black Sea, and in the 1930s Romania produced 23 tons of caviar annually. In 2004, when overfishing led to bans on most Caspian countries' exports, Romania became the largest beluga exporter. In decreasing price order, *icre negre* is caviar, *icre de Manciuria* keta roe, *icre de păstrăv* trout roe, and *icre stiucă* pike roe.

Desserts include *baclava*, *clătite* (crepes, usually stuffed with sugar and jam), *înghețată* (ice cream), *papanaşi* (fried cottage-cheese dumplings), *plăcintă* (flaky pastry pie), *prăjitură* (small torte), *salată de fructe* (fruit salad) and *ştrudel cu mere* (apple strudel).

Drinks

Beer, traditionally a Pilsener-style lager *(bere)*, is popular. The Saxons brought their love of beer to Romania and the country's oldest surviving brewery opened in Timişoara in 1718, two years after the Ottomans left. It still produces *Timişoreana*, a moderately-regarded Pilsener.

Until the late 1990s, Romanian beer drinkers usually stuck to local brands, but in the past few years Romania has quickly gone the way of much of the rest of the world, with a few global conglomerates dominating the beer market. Nevertheless, a few small independent breweries still produce interesting beers for a largely local market. These include Satu Mare and Azuga's eponymous breweries as well as Sibiu's *Trei Stejari* and Râmnicu Valcea's *Alutus*. A few breweries still produce unpasteurised beer, including Iaşi's *Şapte Coline*.

Probably the best and most famous Romanian brand is *Ursus*, brewed in Cluj since 1878. Other beers worth trying include Reghin's porter-like *Silva Strong*, Azuga's *Valea Prahovei*, Miercurea Ciuc's *Ciuc Premium* and Baia Mare's *Bergenbier*, all crisp Pilsener-style lagers.

You're unlikely to travel far without being offered *ţuică*, plum brandy. It's difficult to generalise about its bouquet, strength or dryness as recipes vary so widely. Traditionally no meal starts without a glass – theoretically just one – and no glass without a toast.

Romanians are fond of infusing vodka or other spirits and show no lack of imagination in their choice of ingredients. Examples include *caisată* (apricot brandy), *vişinată* (sour cherry brandy), *lichior de nuci verzi* (green-walnut liqueur), *lichior de izmă* (peppermint liqueur) and many others. Naturally, many enjoy claimed medicinal properties.

Visitors to Romania are often pleasantly surprised by the variety, complexity and quality of Romanian wine. Surprised, because Romanian wine undoubtedly has an image problem

ducer. Transylvania and the Banat supplied wine to the Habsburgs and other royal courts, while until the 1930s Cotnari *(see page 296)* was one of Europe's highest-prized dessert wines. EU entry looks likely to lead to increased investment and know-how – and a wider export market.

Romania's best-known wines internationally are varietals already recognised globally, including Cabernet Sauvignon and Merlot. Pinot Noir, a notoriously difficult variety to grow well, thrives in Romania and enjoys acclaim abroad. However, some of the finest are indigenous tongue twisters including *Busuioacă de Bohotin*, *Tamâioasa Româneasca* and *Grasă de Cotnari*.

abroad. Under communism, quotas overruled quality and nearly all wine was produced for sweet-toothed domestic and Soviet customers. More recently, obsolete technology, under-investment and New World competition have kept Romanian wine firmly at the lower end of the market. In the late 1990s, when Romanian winemakers first tried to enter the mass market, a run of poor vintages scuppered their plans.

Yet Romania has produced wine since at least the 7th century BC, has a climate suited to almost any grape and is the world's ninth-largest pro-

Thanks to Ottoman influences, a traditional home-made drink is *şerbet* (sherbet), commonly made from flower petals, fruit, nuts or vanilla. Another traditional soft drink is *socată* (elder-flower cordial). With more than a third of Europe's mineral and thermal springs, Romania produces hundreds of varieties of mineral water.

Coffee is traditionally Turkish *(cafea turcească* or *cafea naturală)*, served black with sugar in small cups. An ersatz substitute for instant coffee, known as *ness*, is also popular. A legacy of the lean years when real coffee became near-unobtainable, it derives from vegetable extracts. Herbal teas are quite easy to come by, but those desiring English-style tea are advised to bring their own supplies from home. ❑

LEFT: there is a long history of beekeeping in Romania. **ABOVE:** the Ottomans gave Romanians their love of sweet sticky cakes. **RIGHT:** local wines can be good.

RELIGION IN ROMANIA

Religion remains important, with the Romanian
Orthodox, Roman Catholic, Uniate and
various Protestant denominations attracting
consistently high church attendances

Romania is one of the most religious nations in Europe, with its mixed population practising Orthodox Christianity, Roman Catholicism and various Protestant faiths including Lutheranism and Calvinism. The Uniate Church, also known as Greek-Catholic, is unique to Transylvania. There are also small numbers of Muslims and Jews.

The Spread of Christianity

An old Christian tradition attributes the first evangelisation of Romania to the mission of St Andrew the Apostle, although historians date the arrival of Christianity to the Roman conquest of Dacia in AD 106; some Roman soldiers were covert Christians, and with the opening up of much of present-day Romania to what could loosely be termed Mediterranean influences, Christianity gradually made inroads into the region. A similar development took place in the Greek colonies along the Black Sea coast, settlements that were often the destination for deportees, including persecuted Christians.

In time, Christianity outgrew the remnants of the local Geto-Dacian religion, assimilating its strong emphasis on the immortality of the soul (this can still be seen in the frequent recourse to memorial services for the dead in Romanian Orthodoxy). The Romans departed in AD 271, but remained in Dobrogea, which later became part of the eastern Roman (Byzantine) Empire. Oppression of Christianity came to an end with the conversion of Emperor Constantine in the 4th century.

LEFT: Romanian Catholics light candles for Pope John Paul II in 2005. **RIGHT:** an Orthodox priest.

The Balkan peninsula was now open to more systematic efforts at Christian evangelisation. Given its geographical position, closer to Asia Minor than to Italy, and with natural access to the Black Sea, it is easy to see how the future Romanian lands of Wallachia and Moldavia came under the influence of the Eastern (ie Greek Orthodox) Church in Constantinople (Byzantium) rather than the Western Church in Rome, despite linguistic ties to the latter. The entire Carpatho-Danubian area remained firmly Orthodox following the great schism (1054) between Western and Eastern Christianity.

Under the Byzantine Emperor Justinian, in 535, the archdiocese of Prima Justiniana was founded to oversee the lands north of the

Danube, and over the next few centuries the regional power of the Bulgarian Empire meant that these territories adopted the old Slavic tongue as a liturgical language. Even when Romanian gradually replaced Slavonic, it continued to be written in Cyrillic characters until the second half of the 18th century, and it wasn't until 1863 that Romanian became the exclusive language of the Romanian Orthodox Church.

With the formation of the Romanian principalities of Ungro-Wallachia (Muntenia) and Moldo-Wallachia (Moldavia) in the 14th century, the Patriarchate of Constantinople established metropolitan Sees at Curtea de Argeș

and had closer contacts with Orthodox Russia.

It should be pointed out that despite controlling – directly or indirectly – much of the region, the Ottomans were essentially tolerant of the Christian faith. Christians may have been heavily taxed and excluded from the upper echelons of Ottoman society (the Greek Phanariots were an exception), but there was no forced conversion to Islam. And whilst it is true that in those parts of the Balkans under direct rule from Constantinople, subject peoples would often convert to improve their circumstances, this was rarely the case in the semi-autonomous Romanian lands.

(1359), Suceava (1401), Targoviște (1517) and Bucharest (1668).

With the Turkish invasion of the Balkans following the fall of Constantinople in 1453, the various fates of the conquered lands had an impact on religious life. Muntenia (present-day eastern Wallachia) saw its Orthodox Church subjected to a more direct (and sometimes quite oppressive) supervision by the Patriarchal See of Constantinople, with the Ottomans appointing Phanariot *(see page 27)* ecclesiastical overseers, who worked to bring the Romanians more and more under the Greek sphere of influence. Further north, Moldavia managed to retain its independence a little longer, thanks to the efforts of Stephen the Great (1433–1504),

The rise of the nation state of Romania following the unification of Wallachia and Moldavia between 1859 and 1878 strengthened the local Orthodox Church, and after a few years of conflict with the See of Constantinople, it managed to fulfill its wish for autonomy: in 1885 the Patriarchate of Constantinople formally approved the autocephaly (ecclesiastical independence) of the Romanian Orthodox Church, and in 1925 granted it the rank of an independent patriarchate.

Part of Romania's elevation to patriarchal status was the adoption of the new calendar (a reformation of the old Orthodox calendar, created to bring it more in line with the Gregorian calendar used in the West). This change was received with considerable hostility, especially among the monastics, and resulted in the creation of a schismatic old-calendar Orthodox Church, which still claims the sympathy of hundreds of thousands of Romania's 17 million Orthodox Christians.

Orthodoxy under communism

Under communist rule, Romania followed a somewhat unusual approach to relations between church and state. Early attempts at Soviet-style atheism were replaced from the 1970s onwards with tolerance of the church, in large part because Ceauşescu saw it as a useful,

Whereas the Polish Catholic Church was fundamental in toppling the Polish communist regime, the Romanian Orthodox Church remained silent throughout even the harshest period of communism, eager to retain its limited autonomy. The revolution may well have started with the persecution of a priest, László Tőkés, but he was a Hungarian prelate of the Uniate Church. Under Ceauşescu, religious minorities, including Catholics, enjoyed less freedom than the Orthodox Church. The Uniates *(see page 69)* were actively oppressed, forced to choose between full assimilation into Latin Catholicism or entering the Romanian Orthodox Church.

nationalist tool. From this point on, the Romanian communists followed a policy of heavy control and infiltration (paradoxically, the government never enacted a formal separation of church and state). Churches remained open and very well attended, although a firm grip was held on every aspect of church life. Under the watchful eye of the state, the Orthodox Church was also able to retain seminaries and centres of biblical and theological studies. Almost the only places that were subjected to restrictions were the monasteries, which were the only hotbeds of religious dissent.

LEFT: crosses and icons for sale at an artisans fair.
ABOVE: Orthodox nuns at Easter midnight mass.

ORTHODOX ORTHODOXY

It is difficult to pinpoint distinctive traits of Romanian Orthodoxy, despite its attempt to characterise itself as a unique "Latin" Orthodox phenomenon. In fact, except for the use of the Romanian language in worship, there are few variations from the religious practices of neighbouring Orthodox countries. Iconography, for instance, lacks a definite Romanian style, and the best wooden icons and frescoes generally follow the Greek style. Liturgical chant also is mainly a development of the Greek musical style (an older form of local polyphony still survives in Transylvania, around the town of Alba Iulia). The tradition of Christmas carols is shared with western Ukraine and central European countries.

Its cosy arrangement with the Ceaușescu regime left the Orthodox Church tainted in the eyes of many, and it endured a difficult period following the revolution. Yet while the institution itself was diminished, faith remained strong and Romanians continued to observe the church's holidays and perform its rituals. In recent years the Orthodox Church has recovered its status to a large degree, and be it disappointment with the liberal social climate brought on by EU membership, a need for identity, or simple crises of faith in a turbulent world, recent years have witnessed many Romanians fall back into the fold. Romanians

remain religious and visitors are often surprised to see locals furiously cross themselves while passing a church or on public transport.

Besides its staunch opposition to a great deal of EU social policy – it opposes the idea of equal rights for homosexuals and women, for example – the church has won admiration for being one of the few Romanian institutions to genuinely get down to a bit of soul searching since 1989. In 2006 its cooperation with the so-called *Doseriada* (a campaign to rid Romanian public life of former collaborators of the communist secret police, the Securitate) won it much admiration, and placed it in stark contrast with the many politicians and political parties who did not. If the church – and the Romanians who support it – could become just a little more flexible, and a little more liberal, a rejuvenated Romanian Orthodox Church may find itself one of few institutions strong enough to preserve the country's traditions. For ultimately, if the church can take a hard look at itself in the mirror, there is no reason why the rest of Romanian society cannot either.

Catholics and Protestants

Transylvania has a history quite different to that of Wallachia and Moldavia. As part of the Hungarian Kingdom, and never fully under Ottoman rule, Magyar language and culture was dominant. Embedded into this culture was Roman Catholicism, which today is traditionally seen as the religion of Romanians of Hungarian descent, although the presence of Magyarised Romanians and of Romanised Hungarians makes the ethno-religious mosaic quite difficult to evaluate.

From the mid-16th century onwards, the Reformation swept through Transylvania, and large numbers converted to Protestant denominations – primarily Calvinist among the Hungarian community and Lutheran among the Saxons. Later on a significant Unitarian minority developed, notably among the Hungarian Székely people. These days some are in decline – particularly the Lutheran churches catering for the Saxon minorities of Transylvania, most of whom have returned to Germany. At the same time, evangelical new denominations from western Europe and the US, more aggressive in their proselytism, are making inroads. Yet despite the influx, this remains a largely Orthodox country: according to the 2002 cen-

A DEVOUT NATION

A recent study by the Open Society Foundation raised fears of a religious decline in Romania. Its main statistic, that only 39 percent of urban Romanians attend church once a week or more, could, if taken out of context, lead to that conclusion. However, the figures only reflect the urban population, where religious observance is always lower than in rural areas, and still shows a rate of church attendance double that of the most religious countries in the Christian West, and considerably higher than that of most neighbouring Orthodox lands. Faith remains a central part of community life across the country, as anyone visiting at Easter – when villages go into religious overdrive – can see for themselves.

sus, 86.8 percent of Romania's total population, and 94 percent of ethnic Romanians, identified themselves as Romanian Orthodox. The next largest group, Roman Catholics, comprise only 5 percent, while 1 percent of Romanians declare themselves to be Uniates *(see below)*. Except for the Reformed churches (3.7 percent), no Protestant group comprises more than 1 percent of the population.

The Uniate Church

Until Transylvania became part of Romania in 1920, its ethnic Romanian peasantry were a low-status majority under Hungarian (and Habsburg) rule. In earlier centuries they had held onto their Orthodox Christianity as one safeguard of their identity in the face of increasingly determined efforts by Catholic (and to a lesser degree Protestant) missionaries to convert them.

When Transylvania was incorporated into the Habsburg Empire after 1683, Rome – confronted by this stubborn disinterest – encouraged the formation of the Uniate Church (also known as Eastern Rite Catholic and Greek Catholic), which permitted the Orthodox/Slavonic rite but demanded recognition of the Pope as the head of the Church. The incentive was that this offered a way to escape the lesser social status of the Orthodox, but it was not particularly successful and most of the peasantry remained Romanian Orthodox. The Uniates did better in the higher ranks of society, however, and, somewhat ironically, this hybrid church became a focus for the first stirrings of Romanian nationalism *(see page 29)*. Remaining confined to Transylvania, it retains the Orthodox ceremonial rite to this day, having survived a period of oppression during the Ceausescu era.

Minorities

Romania's history has bequeathed a variety of minorities. Some of these are quite tiny, such as the Jews, once very numerous but decimated in the Holocaust and then further reduced by large-scale emigration to Israel. Other small minorities include the Armenians, and some Muslim communities – mainly in Dobrogea – the last remnants of Turkish domination, with

their centre in the city of Constanta. In recent years their numbers have been bolstered by an influx of migrants from Turkey.

A unique minority is that of the Lipovani, or Russian Old Believers. Persecuted by the Russian emperors (especially Peter I) for their wish to keep ancient Russian traditions after a liturgical reformation in the middle of the 17th century, they emigrated to Romania during the following century from northern Russia and the Ukraine. They settled mainly in the Danube Delta, where they established enclaves of old Russian Orthodoxy, which co-exist peacefully with the existing Romanian culture.

The majority of Romania's Gypsies are Orthodox Christians, with a noticeable growth of membership in the independent Pentecostal churches, which seem to relate more easily to the Gypsies' free lifestyle.

These days Romania is a generally welcoming place for all religions, and takes an active role in ecumenical and inter-religious dialogue. It is the first eastern European Orthodox country to host both a visit from the Pope, in 1999, and a European Assembly of the World Council of Churches (in Sibiu in 2007). On the other hand, a recent law approved by Traian Basescu requires religious denominations to include a minimum of 20,000 members before they can receive official recognition. ❏

LEFT: the villagers of Săliștea de Sus, Maramureș, welcome their new bishop. **RIGHT:** the interior of the fortified Lutheran church at Biertan.

ARTS AND CULTURE

After the difficult years under communism, the
Romanian cultural scene is recapturing
its former effervescence

Before starting to discuss different aspects of Romanian culture, a few general observations may be helpful. While many may not be unique to Romania, they help paint an overall picture of the country.

One thing that is unique is the geographical and linguistic situation: Romania is the only country in eastern Europe with a Latin language, and of that linguistic group of countries (France, Spain, Italy, Portugal), it is the only one where the Orthodox religion is dominant.

This situation may help explain Romania's isolation from its neighbours. It may also account for the strong bonds that Romania's elite has formed with more distant nations, some of which were seen almost as "cousins". French influence and French models, in particular, have proved very strong. This Francophone identity continues to play a leading role in Romania's cultural and political life.

The brain drain

The conflict between tradition and modernity in Romania is an ongoing cultural issue. As in many small or medium-sized countries, resistance to new art forms encouraged innovative artists to emigrate to larger capitals of culture, in the hope of finding kindred spirits. Often absorbed by their adopted cultures, many of them are no longer recognised as Romanian. Such is the case of the sculptor Constatin Brâncuşi and the essayist and philosopher Emil Cioran, both commonly perceived as French.

This exile of brilliant minds became more serious under communism. Nonetheless, there is a paradox in that communism's official tenets and demands were contradicted by the huge success of many serious works of art at this time. Literary novels were published and sold on a large scale. More often than not, cinemas, theatres and concert halls sold out well in advance for highbrow events. It is only recently that the number of books and tickets sold has started to plummet. Have Romanians finally lost their appetite for culture?

Many cultural pundits blame the problem on the recent availability of other, lighter forms of entertainment. Cable TV is now a fixture in Romanian homes – not a luxury but an "essential" (cable services in Romania are relatively

LEFT: a Csángó ethnic Hungarian with a *gardon* cello.
RIGHT: footballers as heroes of Socialist labour: Communist-era mural outside Targovişte stadium.

cheap compared to those in the West). However, such mindless entertainment (as many call it) cannot be held wholly to blame.

Culture was heavily subsidised by the state under communism and was thus affordable to the average consumer. Since 1989, the decline in the spending power of most Romanians means they now have far less to splash out on entertainment – be it highbrow or lowbrow.

While the communist regime tried to impose a set of cultural values, however faulty, the upheavals in Romanian society today offer no such values at all. There are now as many value systems as there are political or cultural groups.

Many Romanian artists are still judged primarily by the concessions they made or did not make to the communist regime, rather than by the actual value of their work – and any list of "leading artists" is bound to cause a riot on one side or another. It will take years for the dust to settle.

Literature

The first printed texts in Romania were Slavonic religious books which appeared at the beginning of the 16th century, and for the following three centuries, religious and historical texts made up the majority of works published. Modern literature in the Romanian language began to crystallise in the 19th century, and contributed to the formation of a strong sense of national identity.

Many intellectuals had studied abroad – mainly in Germany, France and Italy – and were familiar with both classical and modern literature. Literary criticism and artistic debate soon become central to Romanian cultural life, with diverse schools of thought spreading around the country, from adepts of traditional forms to fervent modernists. However, even the latter tried to incorporate elements of oral folk traditions in their work.

Mihai Eminescu (1850–99) is Romania's national poet. His style combines influences from German philosophy, Romantic literature and folk traditions in a distinctive lyrical voice. His poem *Luceafarul (Hyperion)* is praised as the highest achievement of poetry in the Romanian language. However, in common with many other writers of his generation, Eminescu did not confine himself to poetry, also writing prose, drama and acute pieces of cultural and political journalism.

Another pioneer was Eminescu's contemporary and friend, **Ion Creanga** (1837–89). A natural storyteller, he collected popular folk tales and re-told them with a good-natured humour that made him very popular. His own book of recollections from his childhood is still one of the best-selling children's books.

By the end of the 19th century, all major artistic currents of the age could be detected in Romania's now-vibrant cultural scene. This continued to flourish and by the interwar period is considered by many to have reached a high point, particularly in the literary field. The creation of the unitary state in 1920 allowed ideas to circulate freely between the historically separate provinces that made up the new Romania.

The arrival of communism was a setback for literature. In the 1950s many intellectuals were imprisoned. Some writers chose to collaborate with the regime in order to survive, while others were virtually banned from publishing, and had to earn a living in other ways. Some went into exile, notably the writer, philosopher and religious historian **Mircea Eliade** and the leading essayist and philosopher **Emil Cioran**.

By the mid 1960s, the situation started to return to normal. New writers emerged, formal experiments were no longer forbidden and translations of world literature were printed on a large scale. Hopes of an artistic renaissance were high. These were soon shattered by Ceausescu's renewed extremism in the late 1970s and 1980s.

The new generation of iconoclastic writers who emerged at this time found it a serious struggle to publish their work. Novelist **Augustin Buzura** managed to survive, and his contribution to the Romanian canon of post-World War II literature is unequalled. His *tour de force* remains *Refugii (Places of Refuge)*, written in 1984 – ironically the year that Romanian reality began to outweigh Orwellian fantasy. Its publication cost the regime's censor her job.

Officially censorship did not exist; in reality, of course, books were banned outright, or cuts were demanded by editors in order for a work to appear. These invisible censors worked in

many writers entered politics or journalism and had little time to devote to literary careers.

All this meant that fewer original titles by Romanian authors were published in the 1990s than in the previous decade. As the number of publishing houses exploded in the free market, more commercially viable books came to dominate. In recent years, however, the situation seems to have stabilised. New authors and new works are emerging all the time. At the same time, Romania has a long tradition of cultural magazines that try to polarise public opinion and champion new writers. For the time being, that tradition looks set to continue.

mysterious ways, making it much more difficult to fight them. It was impossible to appeal to the censor when, according to the rulers of the country, no censors existed.

Given this situation, one might have expected many so-called "drawer-books" (books that were written but never submitted to a publisher) to appear after 1989. In fact, surprisingly few emerged. This seems to suggest that a lot of writers learned to live with the realities of communism, and practised a dangerous form of self-censorship. In the post-communist era,

LEFT: statue of Mihail Eminescu, Romania's national poet. **ABOVE:** modern theatre explores issues from the immediate past.

Theatre

Although theatre in Romania started to develop rather late (not counting traditional folk forms), it rapidly became one of the most popular forms of entertainment. The first documented performance of a play in Romanian dates from 1755; the first Romanian theatres appeared in the early 1800s, and drama schools and national theatres soon followed in Bucharest and Iaşi. The birth of state-subsidised theatres encouraged playwrights to produce substantial bodies of work.

The first notable playwright was **Vasile Alecsandri** (1821–90), also a major poet. Although he wrote in all genres, it is his lively comedies that are still popular today. The enduring popularity of comedies, which satirise all kinds of social mores, is a testament to the saying that Romanians laugh so as not to cry.

Further proof is offered by the comedies of **Ion Luca Caragiale** (1852–1912), still universally acknowledged as the most important Romanian playwright. *A Lost Letter*, his mordant and effervescent satire of political mores and human hypocrisy, has been a fixture in theatres all over the country for more than a century.

In parallel with quality writing, drama schools provided good actors, directors and technicians, enabling Romanian theatre to achieve a high standard, and by the time of

World War II, it had embraced a wide diversity of forms from traditional staging to avant-garde experiment, from light, frothy comedies to heavy philosophical dramas.

As in the other arts, communism meant a stifling of creativity – at least in the first decade after the war. Among the many artists who chose exile over communism, one of the most notable was **Eugène Ionesco**. One of the founders of the Theatre of the Absurd, he found his fame abroad rather than at home.

By the mid-1960s, an ideological thaw allowed a new generation of directors, actors and writers to breathe new life into the theatre, albeit, of course, under state control. For decades, the Romanian public was faithful to

those stage artists it believed in. Even complex and difficult works remained in the repertory for years, often selling out well in advance.

For many Romanians, going to a serious play (like reading a good book or seeing an exhibition by a great artist) was one way of resisting the official indoctrination of communist ideology – a silent opposition through culture. Not all theatre was on an elevated level, and the same company might well stage a "subversive" reading of a classical text alongside a light comedy or a play by an "official" playwright.

One characteristic of theatre in the last days of communism was the recurrence of *sopirle* (lizards). These were references to contemporary problems, meant to make the public laugh, or at least smile, and feel they were watching a truly subversive performance. Sometimes, a few words might be added to a play; at others, a mere vocal inflection might give a line some alternative meaning. In the 1980s, when fuel and electricity were in short supply, lines like "It's so cold!" or "It's too dark in here!" (if spoken with the right inflection) were guaranteed a round of applause.

The Ceauşescu extravaganzas

In the late 1970s and 1980s, Romanians enjoyed another type of entertainment – if one can call it that. Mass rallies and parades had traditionally been reserved for special occasions such as May Day or National Day on 23 August. Now they became more frequent, more lavish, more extravagant and, ultimately, more kitsch. The inspiration seems to have been a visit to China and North Korea by Nicolae and Elena Ceausescu in the early 1970s.

The communist leader and his wife became obsessed with what they saw as perfect cultural organisation, with gargantuan displays of disciplined obedience in all walks of life. After a decade of relative liberalisation, party leaders thought the time was ripe for a mini-Cultural Revolution. Starting with a few hints to writers and artists to get closer to the masses, Romania descended little by little into a new form of socialist realism.

By the mid 1970s, such deranged visions had become a day-to-day reality. The devastating earthquake of 1977 became a pretext to demolish many old buildings, to be replaced by giant monstrosities in neo-Stalinist style, which in turn became the settings for a new type of show.

Two national competitions were launched: in culture, the National Festival Cintarea Romaniei (Praise to Romania); in sport, the Daciada – a sort of national Olympics. In theory, these offered amateur artists and athletes a chance to display their talents, yet they soon merged into extravagant rallies. Thousands of people were forced to take part, whether or not they had any interest or talent. Some were quite happy to participate, and even welcomed the break from a boring day-to-day routine. Others, with health problems or large families to support, were less enthusiastic, but were required to join in regardless.

These shows – often held in stadiums or large squares – included songs in praise of the country, the Communist Party, Ceauşescu and his wife. They employed choirs and soloists, both professional and amateur, as well as actors and hundreds upon hundreds of extras of all ages. In a sort of socialist-realist answer to Busby Berkeley, the crowds formed letters and symbols with their bodies, made human pyramids and ran in formation about the stadium.

Extravagant floats circled the crowd, displaying allegorical messages. At key moments, the participants held huge panels above their heads. The images they formed were meant to please the audience or, at any rate, the leader: portraits of Ceauşescu and his wife, the Romanian flag and other national emblems.

With minor variations, these spectaculars spread all over the country and were broadcast on state TV, which in the 1980s was limited to only two hours a day in order to save energy. These two hours included extensive coverage of the big shows, in between news bulletins that lauded the great visions of the leader and his wife. The Ceauşescus' personality cult, blown up to a grand scale, became the new form of showbusiness.

After 1989, Romanian theatre continued to be interesting, varied and alive. Plays and authors banned under communism appeared on the bill. Among the authors who had emigrated, and whose plays were now staged with success, one of the most outstanding was **Matei Visniec**, who had started out as a poet in the 1980s. His plays mix his own brand of theatre of the absurd with social and political comment.

As new theatres continued to open and new private companies emerged, the quality of productions remained high. Yet the theatre as a whole ran into serious problems. State subsidies decreased, forcing theatres to limit their repertory to commercially viable plays. The number of spectators has fallen dramatically, from around 7 million in the 1980s to about a million in recent years. However, new talents have emerged, with directors such as **Silviu Purcarete** and **Mihai Maniutiu** often touring their productions abroad. Artistically at least, the Romanian theatre is in good health.

Classical music

In the work of many Romanian composers, there are two major sources of influence. One is the Byzantine school of religious music, as practised in the Orthodox churches and based on the human voice, often with no instrumental accompaniment. The other is Romanian folk music, which varies from one region to another, and has been exhaustively researched since the beginning of the 20th century, thanks mainly to ethnomusicologists such as **Constantin Brailoiu**.

By the second half of the 19th century, composers were attempting to interweave these influences with Western patterns, thus creating a national school. The creation of music conservatories in Cluj, Bucharest and Iaşi helped

LEFT: the playwright Eugène Ionesco, exiled from the communist regime. **RIGHT:** portrait of George Enescu, Romania's best-known composer.

this process. Among composers of this time, **Ciprian Porumbescu** (1853–83) is the best remembered, for both his orchestral and choral works. He wrote the Romanian national anthem, and also composed one of the first Romanian operettas, *Crai Nou (New Moon)*, which is still popular today.

Romania's greatest and best-known composer is **George Enescu** (1881–1955), one of the most original talents in modern classical music. His *Romanian Rhapsodies* are among the most popular pieces of music in the country, combining traditional folk rhythms with ingenious modern orchestration. His opera *Oedipus* has won inter-

original *Tosca* – to current operatic superstar **Angela Gheorghiu**.

There are professional symphony orchestras in all Romania's major cities, with regular seasons offering both classical and contemporary music. Since 1989, the traditional George Enescu International Festival has been revived, bringing some of the best-known names in classical music to Bucharest.

Folk music

No wedding would be complete without them; neither would any self-respecting three-day festival. They can play infectious tunes that set

national praise as one of the outstanding works of the 20th century. Enescu was also an illustrious teacher, whose pupils included the violinist Yehudi Menuhin (1916–99). According to the press of his day, Enescu was himself a brilliant and charismatic violinist, and it is even said that Marcel Proust based his famous Vinteuil sonata from *In Search of Lost Time (Remembrance of Things Past)* on a concert given by Enescu.

Romanian musicians who have made their name internationally include pianists **Clara Haskil**, **Dinu Lipatti** and **Radu Lupu**, and conductors **Ionel Perlea** and **Sergiu Celibidache**. In opera, the Romanian school is world-renowned, with a string of charismatic divas from Haricleea Darclee (1860–1939) – Puccini's

everyone's feet to dancing, or heart-rending ballads that bring a tear to the most hardened eye. They are *lăutari*, traditional Romanian folk musicians.

The word *lăutar* is derived from *lăuta* (lute). A group of these musicians is organised in a *taraf*. The structure of such a band is very loose, but it usually includes violins, accordion, double bass and dulcimer. Sometimes the players are also vocalists; at other times they have one or more singers. Many *lăutari* are Gypsy musicians, based in the countryside or outer suburbs. They have preserved strains of folk music distinct from the folklore sanctioned by the Communist Party, while incorporating elements from different regions or even from neighbouring countries. In this way, they have contributed to the development (some critics would say the decline) of folk culture.

Some *lăutari* have gone down in legend, such as **Zavaidoc**, whose songs of the 1930s and '40s are still performed. A number of today's *tarafuri* have won international renown. The best known, **Taraf de Haidouks**, were filling concert halls and releasing best-selling albums in the West long before achieving popularity at home.

Fine arts

Byzantine painting was a major influence on early Romanian art, and the 16th-century murals on the outer walls of the monasteries in Bucovina offer some of the finest examples in the world. The detail is exquisitely realised, the colours vibrant and well-balanced. Yet by the 19th century, Western influences and models had become more important. Romanian artists travelled throughout Europe and studied at foreign art schools, notably in France and Germany.

The most popular Romanian painter is probably **Nicolae Grigorescu** (1838–1907). He spent his formative years in France and brought home the *plein air* techniques of the Barbizon School. His best-known paintings depict scenes of rural life and lyrical landscapes in warm, soothing colours.

Since then, all the major schools and trends will have found disciples (and detractors) in Romanian art. Yet Romania's artists have done more than imitate Western models. Some have innovated and formed a school of their own. **Constantin Brâncuşi** (1876–1957), who left Romania for Paris in 1904, initially working as Rodin's assistant, is considered one of the fathers of modern sculpture. His style, which became almost abstract, aimed at the simplest, the most elemental and most archetypal forms. His celebrated *Bird in Space*, for instance, is a vertical shaft of polished metal, at once highly-stylised and supremely minimalistic. In Romania, he is best known for his monumental group of open-air sculptures in Târgu Jiu (*see page 146*), dedicated to the soldiers who died in World War I.

Brâncuşi was not the only avant-garde artist to become famous abroad. **Victor Brauner**

(1903–66), who also settled in France, is one of the major figures of surrealism. His work, like that of other modern artists, was not appreciated in Romania at the beginning of the communist period, which was dominated by socialist realism. Many artists tried – with varying degrees of success – to subvert the official line. Others made compromises in order to survive. At the height of Ceauşescu's personality cult, many respected painters and sculptors made portraits of the leader and his wife.

The 1970s also saw the birth of "sculpture camps", of which Magura Buzaului is probably the best known. Every year, a group of

sculptors was selected to work for a few months on a project of their own. The result is an open-air museum of modern sculpture.

Artistic life since 1989 has been varied. Galleries in major cities exhibit the most diverse works of art, from traditional painting and sculpture to multi-media installations.

Cinema

While the first cinema projection took place in Bucharest only months after the famous 1895 Lumière projection in Paris, it took more than a decade for any native production to develop. Lack of funding and proper organisation meant that the first film of real importance in the history of Romanian cinema appeared only in

LEFT: Taraf de Haidouks have enjoyed success in the West and are Romania's best-known Gypsy band.
RIGHT: Anghela Gheorghiu in full flow.

1912. *Independenţa României (Romanian Independence)*, directed by Grigore Brezeanu and Aristide Demetriade, was a big epic involving most of the artistic community and hundreds of extras – a huge financial, artistic and logistical effort. The film was a big success, although this did not lead to an organised film industry.

Cinema later received special attention as a powerful tool for propaganda. In the 1950s, a state-of-the-art studio was built in Buftea, near Bucharest. Word has it this was a present from the premier, Gheorghe Gheorghiu-Dej, to his daughter Lica – who fancied herself as an actress. She was duly cast in several big productions.

at the Cannes Film Festival with *The Forest of the Hanged* – a bleak, uncompromising and powerful adaptation of a classic Romanian novel about World War I, by Liviu Rebreanu.

The 1970s brought a new generation of directors. Their cinema was at once more metaphorical and more direct. Branded the '70s Generation (with spectacular lack of imagination), they would hold centre stage in Romanian cinema for the next two decades. In their constant battle with the censors, some had to emigrate, for either political or artistic reasons. Given the social, political and economic conditions, it is surprising how many interesting

Despite the nepotism, ideological bias and a plethora of films where everybody laughs, dances and sings (to paraphrase the title of a Soviet musical that did good box office in Romania), some skilled directors, actors and technicians were involved. In 1950 a National School of Theatre and Cinema opened in Bucharest. Among its young graduates were Manole Marcus and Iulian Mihu. Together, they made two of the most interesting films of that period, *The Apple Thief* (1956) and *Life Does Not Forgive* (1958). Innovative in both form and content, neither film was well received by cultural officials.

The biggest international success of the time came from a director trained in the theatre. In 1965, Liviu Ciulei won the Best Director prize

and personal works were made. As in all the arts, to avoid censorship or an outright ban, filmmakers developed a special metaphorical style, and the public soon learned to read between the lines, interpreting symbols that expressed what could not be said directly.

In the first years after the fall of communism, two main trends arose – the presence on screen of sex and profanity, hitherto banned, and the denunciation of communist atrocities. While both were inevitable after decades of strict censorship, state funding soon started to dry up. With the poor state of the economy, production declined to only a handful of films a year.

But, little by little, things have improved. Private producers learned to navigate in a capitalist free market, while the state slowly stepped up its investment. Romanian directors began to win regular prizes at international festivals. Veterans like Lucian Pintilie (*The Oak*, financed, as always, by French producers) were joined by new talents such as Cristi Puiu *(The Death of Mr Lazarescu)* and Cristian Mungiu *(Occident).*

Location, location, location...

The local film industry has been boosted by Romania's reputation as a film-shoot location *par excellence*. Film makers have long been taking advantage of the country's skilled (and cheap) technicians and actors – not to mention

Rome (1968) and Pope Joan (1972) brought international names like Orson Welles and Maximilian Schell. Yet for every film shot, several others fell apart in the planning stage – due to intractable bureaucracy, ideological headaches or logistical woes. Among those films that had to move, Pasolini's *Oedipus Rex* (1967) shifted its location to Morocco, but managed to keep some ancient Romanian folk songs on the soundtrack.

Once the communist regime fell, films like *Subspecies* (1991) lavished straight-to-video audiences with bloodthirsty monsters and vampires in "authentic" Transylvanian locations. Yet over the next decade, the infrastructure

its beautiful, varied (and cheap) locations. In the 1950s and '60s the French came, mainly left-wing film makers invited to work here. Some were based on classics of Romanian literature and featured a Franco-Romanian cast. Although now forgotten, films like *Ciulinii Bărăganului (The Burs of the Field*, 1957), *Codin* (1963) or *Steaua fără nume (The Star without a Name*, 1967) were big news at the time.

In the late 1960s and early '70s, Romania was a handy location for big international projects. Shot at Buftea studios, films like *The Battle of*

improved sufficiently to attract more prestigious projects, such as *Cold Mountain* (2003). If stars like Nicole Kidman or Jude Law did not always curry favour with the local press, they did not tire of telling international journalists about the natural wonders of Romania. In a rather different vein, Romania was used as a substitute for "Kazakhstan" when the opening scenes of *Borat* were shot here in 2006.

The villagers of Glod, a small and impoverished settlement in the mountains southwest of Sinaia, weren't too pleased when the film was released, aiming accusations of exploitation and ridicule at the film's makers (they had been told the film was a documentary). Legal action on their behalf began in December 2006. ❑

FAR LEFT: portrait by Grigorescu. **LEFT:** Constantin Brâncuşi. **ABOVE:** Romania is a major location for film shoots, such as 2003's big-budget *Cold Mountain.*

FOLK FESTIVALS

In many parts of Romania, fastidiously observed traditions and folk festivals ensure a strong link with the past

Almost every Romanian city, town and village, no matter how big, small or otherwise insignificant, comes alive at least once every year to the sights, sounds, smells and traditions of its local festivals. Unusually, and to the chagrin of its workforce, Romania has very few public holidays. May Day and the National Holiday aside (1 December, marked by a sombre military parade in Bucharest), religious holidays are the only chance that Romanians get to celebrate without worrying about work the next day. Partly as a result, both Christmas and Easter are major events, with Easter (*Paşte*) – usually celebrated a week or two later in Romania than in western Europe – the most important event of the year. There are a number of traditions that surround Easter, such as the painting of eggs, sacrificing the Easter lamb, and attending mass on Easter Day. Lent is still strictly observed throughout the country, and as such spring festivals have to wait until after fasting is over. One such event is the *Stâna*, the Measurement of the Milk Festival, held across the Carpathians.

A number of fairs take place on or around May Day, including the *Târgul Fetelor* (Girl Fair), held throughout Mureş county, though the best known is at Gurghiu. In the past, girls of marriageable age were brought to the fair with part or all of their dowries (*zestre*) as bait for boys of similar age. Today the fair is merely a pageant and involves much younger girls and boys. There is another similar event in the Apuseni region in July. Another rite of passage takes place in Braşov: the *Juni* Festival sees the city's bachelors take part in an elaborate and colourful procession.

Autumn is famous in Romania for its *Zilele Orasului* (the Days of the Town, or Village): a chance for towns and villages to showcase the best that they have to offer, be it enormous vegetables from a bumper harvest, cakes and other sweet treats, handicrafts, combat skills or complicated local dances. *Zilele Orasului* are one of the few chances that many people – often entire villages – get to shine.

For a list of festivals, see page 358.

ABOVE: brightly dressed young boys wait their turn to view this year's "offerings" at *Târgul Fetelor* (Girl Fair), in Gurghiu, Mureş county. Purely a pageant today, in the past the fair was a genuine wedding market.

ABOVE: Sighişoara's Medieval Arts Festival is a colourful three-day multimedia event featuring pop and rock concerts, handicraft exhibitions, craft fairs and street theatre. It is usually held over the last weekend of July.

RIGHT: The *Juni* (unmarried men) of Braşov are split into seven distinct groups for their annual parade, held in early May. Every aspect of the Juni costume, from hat and jacket to boots and breeches, depends on which group the bachelor belongs. This horseman is a member of the *Roşiori* (Mounted Red Bachelors).

MUSIC FESTIVALS

Big name rock and pop acts tend to give Romania a wide berth, but in recent times a number of music festivals, mainly featuring local bands, have been popping up in an effort to fill the void. The biggest such festival is the now celebrated Stufstock, a rock festival held in summer at the bohemian seaside resort of Vama Veche *(see page 163)*. In August the kitsch but enjoyable Callatis pop music festival is held at Mangalia. A Romanian version of Italy's celebrated San Remo Festival, it often attracts foreign acts, mainly from Latin countries. A similar festival takes place up the road at Mamaia, also in August.

A September fixture for almost 40 years, the Golden Stag Festival in Braşov has recently suffered from a lack of funding and organisational chaos. Now held (usually) in July, this three-day-long amateur song contest takes place in the superb setting of Piata Sfatului, and is often closed by a reasonably well-known international star.

Also in September, the Bucharest Opera and Atheneum are host to the George Enescu Music Festival, a three-week-long extravanganza of classical music.

ABOVE: as part of the *Zilele Oraşului* of any town or village, you can expect to see lively dances performed by locals in traditional costume. Folk groups rehearse for weeks in advance to make sure that everything goes according to plan. Putting on a poor show at *Zilele* is said to doom a village to a bad harvest the following year.

RIGHT: intricately painted eggs are a feature of Romanian Easter *(Paşte)*. Romania, which follows the Julian calendar to date religious events (except, strangely, Christmas), celebrates Easter a week or two after Western Europe.

LEFT: the Girl Fairs of Mureş county are not the only festivals of their kind in Romania. On the weekend preceding 20 July a similar event takes place on Mt Gaiăna in the Apuseni Mountains.

BELOW: a shepherd strains curds during a *Stâna* (Measurement of the Milk Festival) in late April or early May. After being strained, the curds will be hung up to dry to make a ceremonial cheese known as *caş*. The curds used to make the cheese are usually those of the most successful shepherd in a village: a title won after each shepherd's flock has been milked, and the yield quite literally measured. The festival marks the time of the year when the shepherds would leave for the mountains with their flock in the traditional transhumance – largely a thing of the past since the 1950s.

ROMANIAN ARCHITECTURE

An array of styles and influences from East and West enlivens the country's architecture – be it ecclesiastical, urban or domestic

One of the most pleasant surprises for the average visitor to Romania is to see just how many lovely old buildings have survived. In Transylvania, some towns and villages remain almost untouched from the Middle Ages, even if decades of neglect have taken their toll. And many cities, particularly in western Romania, are crammed full of handsome examples of Secessionist architecture.

Of course, it is also true that few towns escaped the communist era unscathed architecturally – even some villages were transformed into agglomerations of tower blocks in a madcap process of "systematisation" *(sistematizare)*. In places such as Ploieşti and Hunedoara, little remains from pre-communist times, the result either of wartime bombing or ideological zeal.

The religious dimension

For much of Romania's history, two distinct religious and cultural influences have inspired its architecture. The effects remain very apparent to this day. In Transylvania, the Catholic tradition led to a succession of Romanesque, Gothic, Renaissance and Baroque styles. In the Middle Ages, Saxon colonists built fortified stone citadels to protect inhabitants from siege. Inside the citadel the towns were laid out around a church in a square, from which there radiated narrow paved streets lined with stone houses. Many Transylvanian towns and villages preserve their original citadels more or less intact. In smaller settlements, the fortification was the church itself *(see page 212)*.

In Moldavia and Wallachia, Orthodox Christianity – and to a lesser degree Islam – brought a strongly Byzantine influence, in which gradual evolution was more typical than radical innova-

tion. While rulers built monumental structures – palaces, castles, churches and monasteries – the majority of townspeople lived in adobe houses on mud streets in *mahalas* (variously translated as slum, district or suburb). Bucharest is a perfect example of this: unlike most European capitals, it evolved from a series of disparate communities rather than radially from a distinct centre.

In the Middle Ages, the most original buildings were the Moldavian churches built in the reign of Stephen the Great (1457–1504), notable for their stylistic unity and harmonious proportions. One of the finest examples is Neamţ Monastery. The tradition evolved with the development of exquisite exterior painting seen in the famous painted monasteries of Bukovina.

It was in the 17th century that the first distinctly Romanian architectural style came into existence, the so-called Brâncoveanu *(Brâncovenesc)* style named after Constantin Brâncoveanu. A harmonious fusion of Oriental and Baroque influences, it incorporated beautifully ornate stone carvings and lavish painting. Some of the best surviving examples are the Three Ierarchs Church in Iaşi, Horezu Monastery and Brâncoveanu's palace at Mogoşoia.

Baroque arrives

The 18th century saw a flourishing of the Baroque style in Transylvania, one example being Sibiu's Brukenthal Palace. Meanwhile in Moldavia and Wallachia, Phanariot rule brought a more obvious Oriental influence and a decline in Christian religious architecture. In the 19th century increasing urbanisation and Westernisation saw the development and expansion of many cities along neoclassical and Romantic lines. Romanian architects often studied in Paris, bringing back a taste for the French Eclectic and Rococo styles still evident in many towns.

In the west of Romania, notably in the cities of Crişana and the Banat, as well as in places such as Cluj, Satu Mare and Târgu Mureş, the Secessionist style (similar to Art Nouveau and better known internationally as Jugenstil) was particularly common at the turn of 20th century. Originating in Vienna as a reaction against or "secession" from existing architectural traditions, the style spread throughout the Austro-Hungarian Empire, with local adaptations incorporating traditional folk motifs. It is characterised by sharp lines and colourful floral or geometric decorations, often incorporating ceramics, One of the finest examples is Târgu Mureş's gloriously exuberant Palace of Culture, but wonderful Secessionist buildings can be seen in abundance in Timişoara, Oradea and Arad.

The Bauhaus influence

In the late 19th century the influential architect Ion Mincu led a rebellion against the Western trend, promoting a revival of traditional Romanian folk styles. Right up until the communist era, the modernising and the traditionalist so-called neo-Romanian camps fought for dominance. In the 1930s Bauhaus became an

important influence, especially in Bucharest, as did Soviet brutalism.

In many ways the communist years were a rejection of traditional Romanian styles. While nationalism was promoted in other aspects of public life, adherence to Stalinist blueprints took precedence in architecture (as, of course, did cost-effectiveness). At first, large new residential quarters full of identikit tower blocks were largely restricted to the outskirts of towns. However after his visit to Pyongyang, Ceauşescu became increasingly obsessed with systematisation and the building of gargantuan civic centres, not only in urban centres but in villages.

Recent years have brought foreign investment alongside Western architectural concepts. As adverts for new housing demonstrate, the dream of many Romanians is to live in US-style ranches, many of which can be seen in well-to-do residential quarters. Meanwhile, many of the largest new buildings are international-style mirror-glass office blocks.

There are wide regional variations in domestic architecture, such as the colourful pastel-hued, oddly-shaped small dwellings found in Transylvanian villages, the massive carved wooden gateways of Maramureş and the Székely lands decorated with traditional motifs, and the vibrantly painted houses with reed roofs and fences of Dobrogea. ❏

LEFT: Secessionist facade on Timişoara's Piaţa Unirii.
RIGHT: typical rural dwellings in Moldavia.

GEOGRAPHY AND THE ENVIRONMENT

Romania is blessed with some of the most beautiful
and unspoiled landscapes in Europe, and its vast
forests and rolling pastures are home to an
outstanding diversity of plants and animals

Romania is a country packed with interest for the traveller with a passion for the natural world. With almost the same surface area as the UK, the country's plentiful wildlife *(see pages 92–99)*, its protected areas, its many spectacular landforms and, not least, its timeless pastoral landscapes, will undoubtedly be among the highlights of a visit for many tourists.

In contrast to the positives, Romania also has some undesirable environmental issues. Several decades of extreme pollution from communist-era industrial sites has left an insidious legacy for many years to come, and, in 2000, two successive cases of near-catastrophic river pollution *(see page 89)* made the headlines worldwide.

The lie of the land

Geographically, Romania is dominated by the striking arc of the Carpathian Mountains. Effectively an eastward extension of the Alps, the mountains are similarly young in geological terms, merely 35 million years old, and extend for almost 1,500 km (900 miles) in a giant loop from Austria to Serbia via Slovakia, Ukraine and Romania.

Two-thirds of the chain lies in Romania, where it is divided for convenience into two main parts, the Eastern and Southern Carpathians, with an offshoot to the west forming the Apuseni Mountains. The eastern range runs from the Rodnei Massif just south of the Ukrainian border to the Vrancea Mountains – Romania's earthquake epicentre – east of Brașov. There the mountains

make a dramatic turn to the west, with a series of massifs including Bucegi, Piatra Craiului, Făgăraş and Retezat, forming the well-forested Southern Carpathians, also known as the Transylvanian Alps. It's here that they reach their highest point, where the summit of Moldoveanu (2,550 metres/8,365 ft) in the crystalline Făgăraş Mountains is an attainable goal for reasonably fit and well-equipped walkers. The Apuseni Mountains are lower, mostly below 1,000 metres (3,300 ft). Primarily limestone, they are the country's most extensive area of karst scenery, with deep water-eroded gorges, sinkholes and many caves. The country as a whole is underlain by an estimated 12,000 caves, only half of which are considered to be completely explored.

LEFT: the Ceahlău Massif. **RIGHT:** carpets of wild crocus appear with the melting of the mountain snows.

The Transylvanian plateau lies in the crook of the Carpathian curve. It's an area of rolling hills, forest and farmland. Sparsely populated, the region has a strong sense of the medieval about it, not least in its wealth of plants and animals.

To the south and east of the mountains, a broad half-circle of often fertile plain stretches south to the Danube and east towards the Black Sea. The Danube itself forms the greater part of the southern boundary of the country, cutting through the Carpathian chain at the Iron Gates but suddenly changing its easterly course where it meets the ancient eroded mountains

of bushy dwarf mountain pine and various shrubby willows. The upper pastures and rocky heights hold many of Romania's endemic flowers, including pinks and hawkweeds, alongside orchids, gentians, primroses, bellflowers and a great many more.

Although these largely natural elements of the country's vegetation are impressive, it is the traditional agricultural habitats of lower altitudes that really stand out in a European context. Here, without the mechanisation or chemicals of farming systems elsewhere in Europe, hectare after hectare of farmland with an outstandingly rich flora has survived. Arable

(Europe's oldest) of Dobrogea near the Black Sea coast, at which point it swings north and finally reaches the sea via its huge delta along the Ukrainian border.

Forests and meadows

The lower slopes of the heavily forested Carpathians, as well as extensive parts of Transylvania, support woodlands full of lime, oak and hornbeam. As the altitude increases, so does the percentage of beech and, at around 1,400 metres (4,500 ft), it forms distinctive mixed stands with silver fir and sycamore. Surmounting this, Norway spruce becomes dominant, sometimes with Arolla pine or larch, merging with the alpine zone through a blanket

fields can be studded with larkspur and poppies, but it's the grasslands – both meadows and pastures – that are the true gems, crammed with flowers both abundant and rare. Southeastern Transylvania is particularly renowned for such splendour, but the Apuseni, and indeed every area where traditional agriculture remains dominant, is a delight from May to July.

Much of the natural steppe vegetation of eastern Romania survived until as recently as the 1950s, when huge areas disappeared under

ABOVE: as Patrick Leigh Fermor puts it in *Between the Woods and the Water*, "a kind of spell haunts wooded slopes like these". **RIGHT:** farming methods remain traditional. **FAR RIGHT:** pelicans in the Delta.

the plough. Only fragments remain, some designated as nature reserves for their plants and, especially, their birds.

Patterns of land use

The marvellously rich landscapes and biodiversity of Romania are, at least in part, a result of the inefficiencies of the communist era. Fifty years of communist rule led the agriculture of Romania, a relatively undeveloped area before World War II, down a route entirely unlike that of western European countries over the same period. The implementation of collective farming policies was tardy in comparison with other eastern bloc countries, but by 1962, following much coercion, they were in place just about everywhere. Their inefficiencies, such as near-zero investment in individual farms as profits were taken by the state to pay off foreign debt, and the fact that machinery was managed in separate state-run concerns, resulted in agricultural improvements generally being limited to the better farmland areas. Many marginal areas, although collectivised, remained in low-fertility, low-production systems.

After the 1989 revolution, 80 percent of farmland returned to private hands, although frequently there was much difficulty in estab-

HAYRICKS

The traditional hayrick – *căpiţă de fân* – is a common and picturesque sight throughout rural Romania away from the southern plains. It is built on a bed of dry leaves, the grasses and herbs cut by scythe (or, increasingly, by mower) then built up in layers around a central wooden pole. One person stands on top, packing each layer down, and others throw more hay up with pitchforks. The final layers are inclined, then combed to create a watertight roof. Ricks are used to dry the hay rather than to store it; before the autumn rains begin, the stacks are toppled into waiting horse-drawn carts for transport to the barns, from which the fodder will be taken to the livestock during the long winter months.

lishing true ownership. The average size of a private farm is now about 2.5 hectares (6 acres), often managed in conjunction with other sources of income, such as forestry. With such small parcels, themselves often fragmented, fields are too small to be practical for tractors, and so horse- or oxen-drawn ploughs are still commonly seen. Crucially, the economics and practicalities also work against the use of chemical fertilisers, a single application of which would be enough to see a drastic reduction in the floristic diversity of the grasslands.

Some "associations" have appeared, in which farmers work the land together, but the very word "co-operative" is, understandably, off-putting to the Romanian people, and a high proportion of farms remain as small-scale (but still economically viable) individual units.

Fully 27 percent of Romania is forested, with large tracts of woodland present in low-lying areas as well as in the mountains. This vast expanse of forest, and its amazing biodiversity, can also, in part, be attributed to the system of management under communist and preceding regimes. As well as a timber resource, the country's woodlands have long been valued for hunting and for their role in protecting water resources. The communists ensured that detailed 10-year plans covered all state-owned – and therefore almost all – woodland. With such huge areas at their disposal, clear-fell zones were well separated and natural regeneration could be used to full effect (although conversison to planted spruce forest was the goal for many areas). Romania's post-revolution governments have undertaken to dismantle years of state control and to restore areas of woodland to their former owners (who could be from wealthy or poor backgrounds). Several methods have been tried, but the ownership issue remains messy, and partly as a result, much uncontrolled logging is taking place. The favoured way forward seems to be to reinstate 10-year forest plans. It remains to be seen how effectively EU membership

assures the protection of this priceless national asset, although initiatives such as the the Natura 2000 network *(see page 90)* are already in place.

Conserving the environment

Environmental conservation is one of Romania's greatest challenges. Under communist rule, the country's development was promoted with no heed at all for the environment (even if the inefficiencies of that period have inadvertently benefited the landscape and ecology of the country in other ways; *see page 87 and above*). Large tracts of the countryside were heavily polluted, one of the worst areas being around Copşa Mică. The Danube was canalised (by the infamous Danube–Black Sea Canal), blocked (by the Iron

GEOLOGICAL HOTSPOTS

On the southeastern edge of the 90-degree turn made by the Carpathians, near the towns of Focşani and Buzău, are several unusual geological phenomena. At the geological reserve of Focul Viu (Living Flame), natural gas issues from the ground and ignites spontaneously in 30–50-cm (1–1½ft) flames. At nearby Pâclele Mari and Pâclele Mici, another geological reserve protects a landscape of bubbling mud pools also formed from natural gas *(see page 302)*. To the north, more volcanic landforms and numerous hot springs are in evidence in the Harghita Mountains. Lac Sfântu Ana (St Anne's Lake), just east of the spa resort of Băile Tuşnad, is Europe's only volcanic crater lake *(see page 221)*.

Gates Dam), overloaded with nutrients, contaminated with chemicals, and lost hectare after hectare of its associated wetlands and floodplains.

Today, those legacies remain, but the list of threats is expanding: inappropriate tourism developments in the Carpathians and the Delta; detrimental logging; new roads cutting across the territories of the large carnivores; EU-led agricultural reform that could see huge changes to the small family farms that are so important in maintaining the fabric of the countryside; a continuation of the demographic changes that have been ongoing for years – rural depopulation and an ageing farming community; under-grazing

The large open-cast gold mine at Rosia Montana in the Apuseni Mountains is an indication that industrial threats are still very relevant today. However, this project is a test case for forward-looking environmental protection. Substantial private backing allows for a proper assessment of its environmental impact.

Looking on the bright side

On the positive side, Romania's conservation movement is ever-growing. In total, more than 5 percent of the surface of the country is protected for its bio- or geodiversity, a figure comparable to that in many western European countries.

and abandonment of land, and conversely, in some areas, over-grazing, causing a reduction in biodiversity and more conflicts with wolves.

The worst recent catastrophe was the spillage of cyanide and other toxins from mining-waste lagoons at Baia Mare into the Tisza river system in the winter of 2000, which had a serious impact on 1,000 km (620 miles) of aquatic ecosystem downstream, especially in neighbouring Hungary (the effects on the Delta were not as serious as originally thought, however, and there has been little lasting damage here).

LEFT: bubbling mud pools at Pâclele Mari.
ABOVE: the bare crests of the Retezat Mountains emerge from a forest of dwarf mountain pine.

Romania's national and natural parks are becoming much better organised, too. Although some of these date from the first half of the 20th century, most have simply been "paper parks" and hunting preserves, with no staff, little regulation and almost non-existent infrastructure until recent years, when administrations have been appointed. By 2006, the country had 27 national and natural parks (the difference between the two being the extent of human influence within the park boundary: natural parks are generally more developed than national ones). In addition, there are numerous nature reserves for smaller areas of exceptional flora, fauna or geology, and nature monuments, which can be for individual features – rare trees or flowers, for example.

EU membership brings with it a sophisticated system of biodiversity protection measures in the form of the Natura 2000 network; this brings significant protective measures, as well as funding, for many of the best wildlife areas and most important species. More areas are being designated all the time.

Protecting wildlife

Non-governmental conservation organisations have been blossoming in recent years. These include Milvus, a bird-protection charity (although concerned with far more than just birds), and the Mihai Eminescu Trust, which

but also a payback to the environment. Expertly supported by the Romanian Ecotourism Association (AER), and based on Australian and Swedish models, ecotourism is certainly playing, and will continue to play, a key role in the future of the "big three" carnivores (bears, wolves and lynx) as well as many other species and habitats. Tourists hoping to view bears in the Piatra Craiului region, for instance, already make a significant contribution to the local economy by using the services provided.

In agriculture, there is some optimism regarding environmentally-friendly organic production. The Arnica Project in the Apuseni

aims to conserve the traditional elements of the Transylvanian landscape, including its grasslands and woodlands.

The international bodies are present in strength, with the World Wildlife Fund initiating the major Danube-Carpathian Programme. One product of that programme is the multistate Lower Danube Green Corridor Agreement, signed in 2000 and billed as "the most ambitious wetland protection and restoration project in the world." Romania has also signed the Carpathian Convention, a multi-state programme encouraging protection and sustainable development of the entire mountain chain.

A growing ecotourism industry offers not only access to wild areas and the wildlife within them,

Mountains is a great example of how livelihoods can be improved while biodiversity is maintained. *Arnica montana*, a yellow wildflower with homeopathic properties, is found in the meadows of the region and is much in demand. Although there is a history of harvesting, this has been recently harnessed by a World Wildlife Fund partnership project, which has brought together local farmers and a German processing company, resulting in a better-quality product and a much-improved income for locals. The project has also established a conservation charity for the meadows themselves, and harvesting is very much along sustainable lines. ❏

ABOVE: a shepherd in the mountains north of Târgu Jiu.

The Growth of Tourism

There's no denying Romania's tourism industry is rich in potential. With everything from Bucharest's nightlife and the Black Sea beaches to Transylvanian castles, painted monasteries and some of Europe's most spectacular wilderness, Romania lacks neither attractions nor diversity. As ecotourism becomes increasingly fashionable, it offers a growing network of bed-and-breakfast accommodation in unspoilt locations, where organic food comes as standard. The country also appeals to many niche markets, from budget skiers to railway buffs to bird-watchers and speleologists, while its Dracula association is an obvious selling-point.

But despite all this, the tourism industry has, to date, struggled to fulfil its potential; perhaps surprisingly, both visitor numbers and spending levels have been in decline in recent years (annual visitor numbers are around 6.5 million). While tourism has flourished in some other former Warsaw Pact countries since 1990, relentlessly poor publicity about poverty, orphans, AIDS and stray dogs has helped deter all but the most adventurous from visiting Romania. Additional obstacles have been the sluggish pace of privatisation and investment, with poor service and inadequate facilities the norm.

Things are at last on the turn. Anyone who last visited in the 1990s or earlier will be struck by the huge improvement in hotels and restaurants, while Romania remains one of Europe's cheapest destinations. In many places, increasing awareness of tourism's importance has led to greater competition. With EU entry, Romania is at long last beginning to attract investment as well as better publicity. A crucial development has been the advent of low-cost flights from western Europe, with new routes from London to Bucharest and Timișoara starting up in 2007. In 2006 the World Travel & Tourism Council (WTTC) published a report predicting that the number of visitors to Romania would increase dramatically in the next ten years. At present, Romania is 162nd out of 174 countries in terms of the amount tourism contributes to GDP.

Progress has, however, been patchy, with most investment in well-established tourist centres along the coast and in parts of Transylvania, where the rapid transformation of Sibiu and Brașov are signs of what could be achieved elsewhere. Elsewhere there has been a shortage of money to invest, poor

RIGHT: British tourists in Retezat National Park.

cooperation between rival operators and an absence of strategy, marketing or "joined-up government", including the peculiar decision to downgrade the tourism ministry to a portfolio of the Ministry of Transport, Construction and Tourism. The country's top tourism official, Ovidiu Iuliu Marian, quit in 2006, exasperated with the situation.

All of this means that the levels of tourist infrastructure are primitive compared with most of the rest of Europe. In 2007 Bucharest still lacked a tourist office, while most ecotourism options remain badly-publicised. Getting to attractions can be difficult, with public transport inconvenient or non-existent. Another issue is that the seasonal nature of

most tourism in Romania, poor pay and training have discouraged the ablest from working in the sector.

Some development has been of dubious merit, such as Mamaia's infamous telegondola and the proposed Dracula theme park. In the Danube Delta and elsewhere, ecotourism objectives to keep benefits of tourism within the local community and to limit inappropriate developments struggle in the face of vested interests from Bucharest.

But few will disagree that Romania has many unique advantages as a destination. If it can capitalise on these, the industry's future looks bright. As the WTTC report concluded: "It is widely agreed that Romania's differentiating factor with respect to its competitors is its culture and heritage, and this is where the focus of development must lie." ❑

ROMANIA'S WILDLIFE

Europe's largest population of brown bears, and healthy populations of wolves, lynx and other mammals, coupled with spectacular birdlife – notably in the Danube Delta – make Romania an unmissable destination for anyone interested in the natural world

Romania, with its huge swathes of relatively undisturbed forest, traditional patterns of land use and lack of intensive agriculture – away from the southern plains – is one of the best places to see wildlife in Europe. Apart from the magnificent riches of the Danube Delta, the Carpathian Mountains harbour more large carnivores – brown bears, wolves and lynx – than any other European country.

Bears in the woods

Between 40 and 60 percent of Europe's brown bears live in the woodlands of Romania. This rather impressive statistic is the result of the remarkably intact woodland ecosystem and traditional land-management practices but, surprisingly, can also be attributed to the hunting preferences of Nicolae Ceauşescu. The dictator so loved to hunt the animals (he's said to have shot some 4,000) that he ordered a nationwide programme of feeding stations to ensure that the stock was always plentiful and suitably large for the trophy cabinet. From 1975, bear hunting became illegal for anyone but Ceauşescu and other top party officials or invited guests. From a low of 1,500 individuals in the 1960s, the bear population soared to more than 8,000 in the 1980s, an unsustainable level that led to increased attacks on livestock. Since then, various estimates put the population at between 4,000 and 6,000 animals.

The brown bear is a sizeable creature, up to 2 metres (6½ ft) in height if standing on its hind legs, and is omnivorous: although it will take meat (including livestock), berries, fruits, nuts, grasses and, of course, honey make up a good proportion of its diet. It has a poor digestive

system, and one sign of being in bear territory is finding their characteristic droppings, which contain large amounts of undigested food. You may also find their territorial scratch marks on trees, three to five parallel gouges, which, if fresh, may be accompanied by rich brown hairs snagged on the bark.

Local advice is that the bear is generally not a danger to the public. Almost all incidents involving bears attacking humans are when shepherds are defending their flocks. A bear will usually see a human before the human sees it, and will quickly move off into dense cover. They will also retreat in the face of noise.

Of the three large carnivores of Romania, bears are the most likely to be seen, although that's not to say it's easy. They tend to steer clear of the more popular hiking areas, but there is always a chance of coming across them in the quieter forests of the Carpathians. Several "bear hides" have been set up, including two within striking distance of Zărneşti, near Braşov, and others are likely to be developed; an evening visit to these provides the best opportunity to see wild bears.

Whether the population is stable or in decline is keenly debated. Some parties believe that the pressures of hunting – now permitted but regulated – are too great; others think that 6,000 bears, if that is an accurate assessment, is an

bit of a spectacle and some bears are being fed by hand *(see page 188)*.

Howling wolves

While seeing a bear in Romania is a possibility, wolf observations are far less likely. That's not to say that wolves aren't fairly numerous: 3,000 individuals, perhaps 35 percent of the European population (including European Russia), inhabit the Carpathians and other less-developed areas of the country. But their huge territories and mainly nocturnal habits, coupled with their avoidance of man, ensures that even experienced naturalists consider themselves

unsustainable population for the habitat available, arguing that 4,000 is nearer the natural carrying capacity. Hunting is on the increase, a pastime not only for rich foreigners (King Juan Carlos of Spain recently shot nine bears on a single visit) but also Romania's wealthy élite.

In Răcădău, a suburb of Braşov, bears have been raiding rubbish bins since the 1980s, and the number doing so is increasing. They are becoming more and more fearless of people, especially since the nightly event has become a

LEFT: European bee-eaters, a colourful summer visitor.
ABOVE: one of Romania's c.4,000–6,000 brown bears.
RIGHT: wolves are also present, but more elusive.

fortunate to come across them. An expert eye is required to differentiate their tracks from those of large dogs. They do tend to take very direct routes, unlike dogs, and often follow one another in Indian file, each placing their feet in exactly the same position as the animal in front. It's only when the pack meets an obstacle that one sees that there are a number of individuals travelling together.

Hunting mainly in packs of two to seven animals, they feed on small mammals, insects and plants. They are more prone than the bear to take domesticated animals, a fact that has inevitably led to their persecution. They are a very real and current threat to the livelihoods of the shepherds of Romania's hill country. Sheep are gathered in well-built folds for the night and the shepherd sleeps close by in a makeshift shelter, guarded by dogs. Electric fencing is a relatively recent, and often effective, development. Hunting is controlled and the wolf population is considered to be stable, having recovered from state-sponsored elimination campaigns, using poison in addition to shooting and snaring, in the 1950s and 1960s.

The elusive lynx

The lynx, like the wolf, is a very rare sight, despite the fact that the forests of Romania support about 35 percent of the total European

population. The country's count of about 2,000 animals seems all the more remarkable when it is compared with census data from neighbouring countries: the Ukraine estimates that it has about 250 lynx, Serbia and Montenegro 80, while there are thought to be only a few individuals remaining in Hungary and Bulgaria. The vast Carpathian forests provide this shy member of the cat family with the range – a male has a territory of about 250 sq. km (100 sq. miles) – and the habitat it requires. Its prey ranges from rodents to roe deer, which it stalks or ambushes at dusk or during the night. Outsize paws and a short tail with an obvious black tip are two of the features that stand out to those lucky enough to catch sight of one.

The Carpathian ark

Bears, wolves and lynx are not only important in their own right: they are significant barometers of the overall condition of the woodland ecosystem. With such good numbers of all three species, it's clear that the Romanian Carpathians are in relatively good health.

There are good populations of roe deer and the larger red deer. In higher areas, chamois is one of the more visible mammals, sharing its rocky habitat with alpine marmots. A piercing whistle from among the screes is often the first indication of the presence of the latter species, which was re-introduced in the 1970s (although perhaps never having been native). Wild boar are common in both upland and lowland areas, where their extensive grubbing for roots leaves telltale signs of their passage. They are a major quarry species for Romania's hunters.

Wildcats are fairly common and most likely to be seen a dusk and dawn. Pine martens are frequent in extensive forest areas, while their close cousins, the beech martens, often find their homes in houses and barns in lower country districts where they store their prey items in noxious "larders". On the Olt River north of Braşov, beavers have been introduced from southern Germany.

Carpathian birds

The forests hold an equally spectacular array of birds. The capercaillie, a goose-sized member of the grouse family, needs undisturbed tracts of large conifers, sometimes mixed with broad-leaved trees, with glades holding berried plants such as bilberries. It's in these glades that as many as 20 males gather at first light on spring mornings for their elaborate display and courtship rituals, involving a strutting march, feather fanning and an extraordinary series of vocalisations likened to sticks being tapped together, followed by a quiet drum roll, the sound of a cork popping out of a champagne bottle and finally a *saw-whet*.

A second grouse species, the hazel grouse, is also to be found. Partridge-sized, but with a longer tail, it too requires relatively intact forest with enough plant diversity to provide for its various dietary needs throughout the year within a relatively small area. As a result of these exacting demands, it is suffering a widespread decline across Europe. A very shy bird, it has the ability to create underground burrows in deep snow to help it survive the hard winters of its mountainous habitat.

Owls contribute to the fairy-tale atmosphere. Alongside the widespread tawny and long-eared owls, the much larger and fearsome Ural owl is present: the female will defend her nest aggressively against human intruders. The tiny pygmy owl, little bigger than a sparrow, and Tengmalm's owl are also at home here. Golden and lesser spotted eagles are the two larger raptors most likely to be seen in the Carpathians; the latter, much the commoner of the two, is generally seen at lower altitudes than the former. Some experts consider that all Romania's eagles except the white-tailed eagles of the Delta are in decline.

The far-carrying drumming of the large black woodpecker can be heard in the spring as this distinctive bird marks out its large territories – at least 300 hectares (750 acres) – with 20 or so hammer-like blows on dead timber in two-second bursts. The three-toed woodpecker is unmistakable, the only member of this family in Europe with a yellow crown to its head. It has a preference for steep, inaccessible slopes with plenty of ageing spruce trees. The white-backed woodpecker also depends on ancient woodland with plenty of rotting timber, and is an excellent indicator of the ecological health of these forests. The colourful wallcreeper is an attractive sight in gorges and on mountain crags, and alpine accentors inhabit the highest areas.

In the hay meadows of the Carpathians and other less-developed quarters of the country, corncrakes are still faring well – in contrast with the rest of Europe where it has suffered as a result of mechanised, early-season grass cutting.

PROTECTED AREAS

There is a whole series of protected areas along the Carpathian arc, accounting for almost three-quarters of Romania's national and natural parks. *For a listing of these parks see page 363.*

The Southern Carpathians

Retezat National Park lies towards the western extremity of the Southern Carpathians (Carpatii Meridionali; also known as the Transylvanian Alps). A pristine area of high-altitude habitats with all the major wildlife elements of the Romanian mountains, it has one of the best-

LEFT: lynx favour forested areas with rocky outcrops.
RIGHT: chamois can be seen on high mountain ridges.

developed park infrastructures in the country. This has resulted in it recently acquiring PAN park status, a designation given to a small, select series of European national parks meeting the exacting standards of conservation and visitor management set by the World Wildlife Fund. Its northern areas offer a granitic landscape shaped by past glaciation, studded with 80 alpine lakes, screes and cirques. Little Retezat to the south is a limestone massif with attendant gorges, caves and sinkholes. The park is a prime area for butterflies, with species such as Balkan heath, scarce fritillary, clouded apollo, large blue, Sudeten ringlet and large heath. There are a number of

accommodation options around the park's periphery, as well as the Vila Rotunda, one of Ceausescu's hunting lodges, within the park boundary.

The sizeable **Hațeg Geopark**, linking Retezat with Grădiștea Muncelului Cioclovina Natural Park, is a fine area for butterflies and hay meadows. Its unique claim to fame, though, is that several well-preserved clutches of dinosaur eggs have been found here, dating from the Cretaceous period, 68 million years ago *(see pages 249, 250)*. These are attributed to *Telmatosaurus transsylvanicus*, a duck-billed herbivore which, alongside a group of other dinosaurs, were isolated on an island in the ancient Tethys Ocean and evolved as an assemblage of dwarf species. Fossils of the largest flying reptile *Hatzegopteryx* *thambema* (taking its generic name from Hațeg county), which had a wingspan of 14 metres (46 ft), have also been found. Some eggs are on display at the park's centre in Hateg, but there are plans to develop a much larger facility to interpret the region's palaeontological story.

Abutting Retezat to the south is the even larger **Domogled-Valea Cernei National Park**, with an outstanding and unspoiled karst landscape of cliffs and gorges, topped by the 1,100 metre (3,600 ft) Mount Domogled. The park is particularly well known for its butterflies, with populations of species such as Russian heath and black ringlet. Its warm microclimate favours plants

with Mediterranean preferences such as downy and Turkey oaks. It also supports the local form of Austrian pine, known as Banat pine, which grows into sculptured, graceful forms on the broken limestone slopes. The spa resort of Băile-Herculane lies on the park's doorstep.

Near the towns of Reșița and Anina, 75 km (45 miles) southeast of Timișoara, more karst is protected in the neighbouring **Cheile Nerei-Beușnița** and **Semenic-Cheile Carașului national parks**. *Cheile* is the Romanian word for gorge, and the wild Nerei Gorge is the country's longest. The Carașului gorges make for exciting hiking and this park also has some spectacular caves, but it's the vast virgin beech forests that are its chief *raison d'être*.

Cozia National Park is in the central sector of the Southern Carpathians, lying on the approaches to the higher Făgăraș range. Its 17,000 hectares (40,000 acres) are dominated by forest whose character is influenced by the area's somewhat milder climate: oak woodland attains an unusually high altitude here. Cozia is also called the Mount of Flowers, due to the rich plant life that includes edelweiss and martagon lily. The well-known and much-visited Cozia Monastery *(see page 143)* lies within the park.

The country's highest and longest limestone ridge forms the backbone of **Piatra Craiulu National Park**. The 20-km (12-mile) edge is a classic but serious hike, with the high Făgăraș range dominating the superb views. Caves – more than 700 of them – are also a feature, including Avenul din Grind, which descends to 540 metres (1,800 ft) below the surface and is the country's, indeed southeastern Europe's, deepest pothole. The endemic Piatra Craiulu pink is the park's symbol.

Craiului is a fabulous hiking area and Carpathian carnivores are also present in numbers here. There's a bear hide in Bârsa lui Bucur Valley, just outside the park, 15 km (9 miles) southwest of Zărnești. The park and other organisations have encouraged the sensitive development of small-scale tourism facilities and the area stands out as a centre of exemplary ecotourism in Romania.

The **Bucegi Massif**, with a natural park of the same name, has a well-developed system of footpaths serving the many visitors based at the adjacent resort towns of Sinaia and Bușteni. The park is essentially a plateau with very steep slopes along its eastern edge, which drop down to the Prahova Valley 1,200 metres (4,000 ft) below. Each town has a cable car to reach the heights with a minimum of exertion. Two sets of wind-eroded rocks, head-shaped Sfinxul and mushroom-esque Babele, are a popular draw, but there's much harder hiking to be had, including long walks to Bran and summits such as Omu, standing at 2,500 metres (8,000 ft). The wildlife is richer towards the less-disturbed western fringes of the park, where there are bears, capercaillie and lynx.

The Eastern Carpathians

The Eastern Carpathians (Carpatii Orientali) comprise some of the wildest mountains in the country, and are appropriately well-endowed with protected areas. **Cheile Bicazului-Hăşmaş National Park**, on the borders of Transylvania and Moldavia, presides over the dramatic Bicaz gorges, cut through limestone by the eponymous river. Huge bare cliffs and vertical pillars provide excellent habitat for wallcreepers. The park is also known for lady's slipper orchid and the apollo butterfly. Lacu Roşu, a curious natural lake created in 1837 by a huge landslip that blocked the Bicaz River, lies within the boundary; long-dead pine trees still stand in the water. The gorges are traversed by the Gheorgheni to Piatra Neamţ road and are therefore relatively easy to visit. There is an information centre and

remote, wild place. The area is known for its caves, in particular for some of the strange features they contain, such as limestone spheres, rare minerals and stalactites made from gypsum. The park is home to black grouse, and rare butterflies including three similar species of ringlet: blind, water and Sudeten. However, its most celebrated wild species is *Lychnis nivalis*, a small pink alpine flower the size of a buttercup, found nowhere else in the world.

The Apuseni Mountains

Significantly lower and less alpine in character than the other Carpathian protected areas, the

a network of paths. Not far away, the **Ceahlău Massif**, also with national park status, provides fantastic hiking amid towering crags.

The **Rodna Massif** in Maramureş shows signs of a glacial past, unusual in the Carpathians. The national park here holds the highest of the peaks of all the eastern ranges, reaching 2,300 metres (7,500 ft) in the permanently snowcapped Mount Pietrosul. Waterfalls such as Cailor, some 80 metres (250 ft) high, and more than 20 beautiful glacier lakes like Iezer and Lala, add to the appeal of visiting this

Apuseni Mountains (Munţii Apuseni) west of Cluj comprise, nonetheless, a remote and beautiful region of traditional land management, with plenty of forest cover and large expanses of flowery pasture and meadow. The tranquil "Lost World" area within the **Apuseni Natural Park** is remarkable for the effect its microclimate has on the vegetation: it traps cold air, resulting in an inversion of the usual pattern of forest zones, with conifers filling the depression while deciduous trees line the slopes above them. A limestone area, the Apuseni has more than its share of spectacular caves and other karst features.

In Valea Rea cave, 19 km (12 miles) long, 35 different minerals have been found, making it one of the most mineral-rich in the world. There

LEFT: a lesser spotted eagle. **ABOVE:** the vividly coloured fire salamander is not hard to spot on rainy spring and summer days in the Carpathian valleys.

are five caves with perennial ice deposits, the most famous of which is Ghețarul de la Scărișoara, which contains 75,000 cubic metres (2.5 million cubic ft) of ice dating back 3,500 years. Peștera Urșilor (Bear Cave) is not only known for its giant cave-bear skeletons but for its fantastic displays of stalactites and stalagmites. Romania's longest cave is to the northwest of the Apuseni, in the Pădurea Craiului Mountains. Peștera Vântului (Wind Cave) is a tortuous 50 km (32 miles) in length. The area also has gorges; Cheile Turzii (Turda Gorge) in the east has cliffs 300 metres (985 ft) high, which host raptors and an important assemblage of plants.

tation known as *plaur* consist of reeds and roots combined with organic matter, creating a buoyant carpet at least 1 metre (3 ft) thick. Only 9 percent of the area is permanently above water. The river itself flows in three principal channels: Chilia to the north, Sfântu Gheorghe in the south and the much-altered Sulina between the two.

At more than 7,500 sq. km (3,000 sq. miles), this is by far the largest protected area in Romania and has a long list of conservation accolades: Biosphere Reserve, World Heritage Site and Ramsar Site (indicating that it is a wetland of international importance for birds). There are many strictly protected areas in the reserve

Delta airways

East of the mountains, exotic birds, including bee-eaters, rollers, hoopoes and lesser grey shrikes, fly up from roadside wires during the summer months. But this is just a prelude to the **Danube Delta** and the coastal strip of Dobrogea, where the bird life is among the richest in the whole of Europe.

The Danube Delta claims the title of the world's largest reed bed, as well as Europe's largest continuous wetland. A vast complex of open water, reed beds, dunes, sandbanks, marshland, wooded areas and farmland, it is constantly evolving due to the deposition and reshaping of millions of tons of sediment carried by the river each year. The unusual floating islands of vege-

to which access is restricted.

More than 300 bird species have been observed in the Delta. The largest white pelican colony in Europe is on Lacul Rosca near the Ukrainian border, while the much rarer Dalmatian pelican (which has pale, not black, flight feathers) nests on *plaur* in the Sacalin Zătoane Strictly Protected Area. Most of Europe's pygmy cormorants are here, along with other specialities like glossy ibis, collared pratincole and paddyfield warbler. There are many heron species, some nesting in colonies: little and great egrets, grey, purple, squacco and black-crowned night herons, and little bitterns. Waders include avocets, black-winged stilts and marsh sandpipers. Raptors such as the white-tailed eagle (up to 10 pairs), red-footed falcons and marsh harriers breed in good numbers. Large gull and tern colonies are also a spectacle, Mediterranean gulls and whiskered terns among them.

The whole area becomes even more hectic during the spring and, especially, the autumn migration period, from early August to October, as vast numbers of Europe's breeding birds, including many from the Arctic such as broad-billed sandpipers and ruff, make it a stopover on the way to their African wintering grounds.

Letea and Caraorman are the Delta's two rather extraordinary forests, growing in 10-metre (30-ft) wide bands along parallel sand dunes. Oak and various ash species dominate the canopy, with a tangled under-storey of traveller's joy, wild hops and other climbers including the world's most northerly lianas. Spur-thighed tortoise and the very rare Orsini's viper are associated with these areas.

Day of the jackal

Most people would be surprised to know that there are jackals in Europe, but in recent years increasing numbers have spread northwest from Turkey, and are present in the Delta region. The Delta is also home to otters and the European mink. Indeed, the *plaur* are one of the mink's last refuges, as the species is suffering a drastic decline across the continent, being replaced by American mink, its non-native relative that has escaped from fur farms and established very successfully. The uncommon marbled polecat is also found in adjacent steppe areas, for instance at Capul Doloşman where it preys on souslik, a ground squirrel that lives in colonies.

Amphibians and reptiles are plentiful in this watery paradise. Marsh frogs create a cacophonous chorus in summer months, while various lizards and snakes, including the fish-eating dice snake, can also be seen.

Fish, of course, are much in evidence in the Delta, where the wels, or European catfish, can grow to 4 metres (13 ft) and will seize waterfowl as they nonchalantly swim on the surface. But it's the sturgeon that is Romania's most noted fish. Sadly though, of the six species that once swam in the Danube and Black Sea, one is extinct, another nearly so and the remaining four are seriously declining. The giant beluga sturgeon, for example, which was formerly to be found in the Danube by the thousand, with specimens of 8 metres (26 ft) or more, has been relentlessly fished for its roe and is now drastically reduced. The Iron Gates Dam has blocked the migration route of several species.

Many bird-watchers head straight for the Delta proper, but for all the ecological interest there, arguably the best bird-watching in Romania is in some of the southern reaches of the Biosphere Reserve around Lake Razim and Lake Sinoe. Here, the marshes, reed beds, lakes and channels are probably the highlight, as nearly all the birds of the region can be seen with relative ease.

Almost the entire world population of the handsome red-breasted goose passes the early part of the winter in the arable fields and unfrozen lakes of the lagoons, retreating to Bulgaria when the weather turns worse. About two thirds the size of a domestic goose, it is easily told from all other species by its elaborate pattern of black and white with a chestnut-red breast.

Inland, there is a wooded steppe area in the hills just west of the Delta, between Badadag and Măcin, which has a reputation as the best place in Romania to see birds of prey, including species such as the rare levant sparrowhawk, and imperial and booted eagles that have disappeared from other parts of the country. Part of the area is in the Muntii Măcinului National Park. ❏

FAR LEFT: tracking bears at Vrancea. **LEFT:** avocets in the Delta. **RIGHT:** sousliks can be seen in steppe areas.

PLACES

A detailed guide to the country with
the principal sites clearly cross-referenced
by number to the accompanying maps

Romania rewards exploration. As a visitor you are spoiled for choice, with an abundance of glorious scenery, an extraordinary array of architecture, folk festivals, romantic castles, lively resorts and intriguing cities competing for your attention. To help make sense of it all, we have divided this part of the book into four sections covering the historic regions that comprise modern Romania.

The capital, Bucharest, is not immediately appealing and rarely receives more than a brief visit, but there are some excellent museums, restaurants and nightlife. The southern region of Wallachia lacks the dramatic scenery of areas further north, but is not without interest, while Dobrogea has long been Romania's favourite summer destination. As well as seaside resorts, it also has some fine archaeological sites, while the unspoiled Danube Delta is one of Europe's most special places.

Romania's highest road leads from beautiful Curtea de Argeș in Wallachia, past the 'real' Dracula castle at Poienari and into Transylvania. Enclosed by the wild Carpathian Mountains, this part of the country is a scenic treat, its towns and villages dripping in Gothic, Baroque and Secessionist architecture, a fascinating testimony to the Saxon and Hungarian communities, and its Habsburg rulers.

Crişana and the Banat have a more Western look and feel, thanks to a long, relatively benign period of Habsburg rule, and there is much to enjoy in the lively city of Timişoara.

Moldavia's capital Iaşi rivals Bucharest as a centre of culture, religion and learning, all strongly reflected in its impressive monuments. While many head north for Bukovina's fabulous painted monasteries, parts of Moldavia can compete with Transylvania for natural beauty. Finally, nowhere in Romania has preserved its traditional peasant culture as well as Maramureş. In parts resembling a land from some remote pre-industrial age, it also has some unusual festivals and the chance to look on the bright side of death at its Merry Cemetery. ❑

PRECEDING PAGES: Sirnea village and the Bucegi mountains in autumnal frost; Biertan is typical of many Transylvanian villages; the view across Sighişoara from the clock tower. **LEFT:** the Bocicoel road from the Iza Valley to Vişeu de Sus, Maramureş.

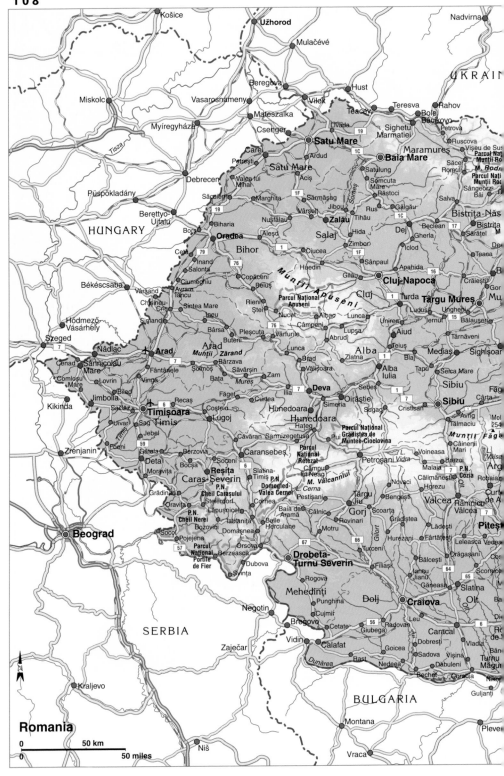

Romania

0   50 km

0   50 miles

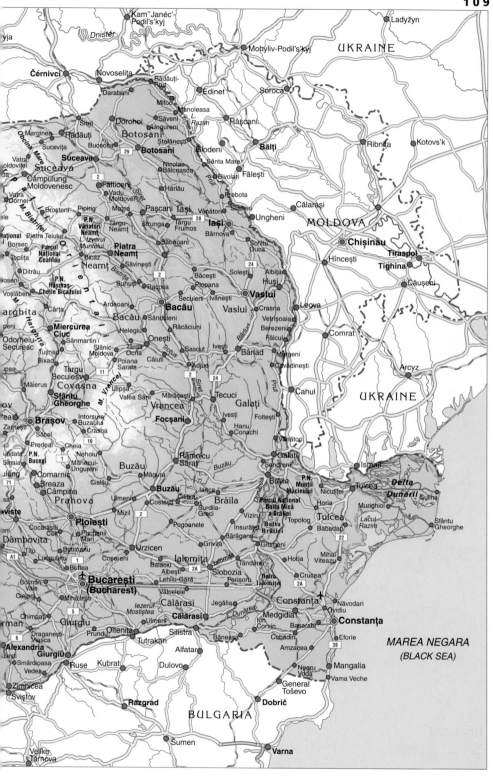

THE SOUTH: BUCHAREST, WALLACHIA AND DOBROGEA

Sunny beaches, classical ruins and one of the world's largest wetlands are the main draws, although much-maligned Bucharest rewards exploration, too

Many visitors to Romania don't venture south of the Carpathians, except for a dash through Bucharest or perhaps a trip to the Black Sea coast. But for those who do make it, the reward is having some of Romania's most enticing attractions largely to oneself.

Bucharest bears heavy scars from the communist era, and first impressions of the city are rarely favourable. Yet anyone who allows time to get lost in the northern backstreets will find that a surprising amount of the prewar city survives behind the Ceauşescu-era showpiece tower blocks. Certainly, much is in need of more than the odd lick of paint, but Bucharest is fast regaining the reputation for hedonism it once enjoyed in the 1930s. While it may no longer be the Little Paris nor yet the new Prague, it certainly repays investigation.

Romania's first principality to escape Hungarian rule, Wallachia fell under Ottoman suzerainty in the 15th century. In 1859 it united with Moldavia, and Bucharest became the capital of the new Romania. Although much of Wallachia is flat and agricultural, it has many areas of scenic interest, including Romania's highest road, the Transfărăşan Highway, the Argeş Valley and the Danube itself. It also has some superb monasteries, of which the most notable is Horezu, a sublime masterpiece of the Brâncoveanu style. The charms of smaller towns such as Curtea de Argeş are readily apparent.

Dobrogea has long been the mainstay of Romania's mass tourism industry. While Mamaia is brash and mass-market, pleasantly laid-back resorts lie further south, including Vama Veche and Doi Mai. To the north, the Danube Delta, Europe's largest and best-preserved wetland, is a joy for even the most amateur of naturalists. Dobrogea also preserves archaeological sites aplenty and has Romania's richest mix of nationalities, with Turkish, Bulgarian, Lipovani, Ukrainian and Greek communities, among others; it's also home to most of Romania's Muslims, a legacy of Ottoman rule, with all but one of the country's 91 mosques situated here. ❑

LEFT: a white pelican takes to the air in the Danube Delta.

BUCHAREST

Scruffy and chaotic, this is not a city in the usual European mould. Yet look a little deeper, and Bucharest can be an enjoyable experience

Bucharest (Bucureşti) is a strange city. Much of it is ugly and haphazard, the result of World War II bombs, communist planning and a lack of money. Today, bureaucracy and corruption tend to limit improvements and, although some modern growth and sprucing-up is evident (it was far worse ten years ago), the city is still remarkably scruffy compared to most other European capitals.

Unlike many large cities, Bucharest developed on a haphazard plan rather than systematically and radially, and this presents something of a problem to visitors, as it lacks any coherent centre. The old city quarter of Lipscani has a claim, as does the rather featureless Piaţa Universităţii, the geographical and academic hub at that district's northeastern corner. A little to the south by the Dâmboviţa River, Piaţa Unirii is a concrete mishmash, typically communist in its gargantuan bleakness, with huge boulevards reaching a crazed climax at the gigantic Palace of Parliament.

But there are a few greener, older corners, remnants of the early 20th century and a time when Bucharest merited its "Little Paris" sobriquet – particularly to the north of Piaţa George Enescu and the Athenée Palace Hotel, where some glorious prewar villas overlook pleasant squares shaded by walnut trees. Although many of these buildings are in poor shape, others have been lovingly restored and

show what much of Bucharest could look like with a bit of money and attention. Places of interest are spread out all over the sprawling city and, with the heavy traffic, can take some time to explore properly.

Around University Square

Piaţa Universităţii **Ⓐ** (University Square) is an incongruous jumble of periods, styles and proportions, reflecting the fact that, historically, Bucharest evolved as a series of distinct *mahalas* – districts or suburbs.

Maps
on pages
114, 117

LEFT: a reminder of the events of 1989.
BELOW: an EU luminary is immortalised at Herăstrău Park.

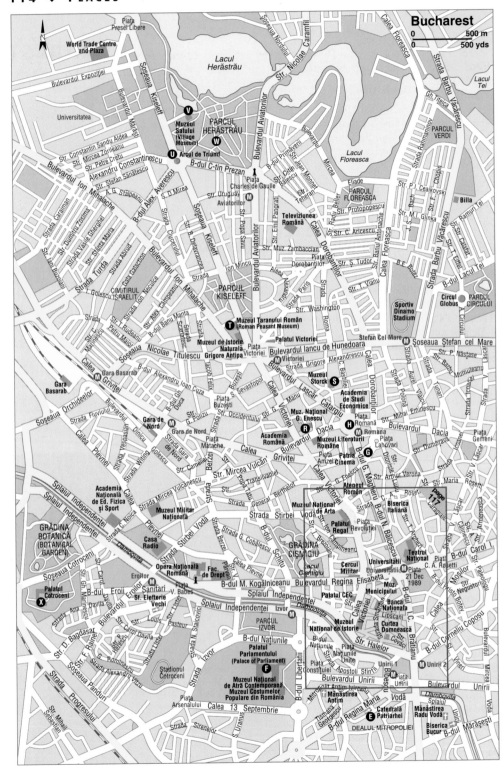

Bucharest

0   500 m

0   500 yds

Lacul Tei

Lacul Herăstrău

World Trade Centre and Plaza

Piața Presei Libere

Universitatea

Bulevardul Expoziției

Șoseaua Kiseleff

Bulevardul Mărăști

Muzeul Satului (Village Museum) **V**

W

PARCUL HERĂSTRĂU

PARCUL VERDI

Billa

Arcul de Triumf **U**

B-dul C-tin Prezan

Bulevardul Aviatorilor

B-dul Primăverii

Lacul Floreasca

PARCUL FLOREASCA

Str. Constantin Sandu Aldea
Str. Mircea Zorileanu
Str. Patru Cretu
Bulevardul Ion Mihalache
A.G. Stălpeanu
Alexandru Constantinescu

Piața Charles de Gaulle

Str. Uruguay
Aviatorilor

Televiziunea Română

Str. Muz. Zambaccian

Piața Dorobanților

Calea Dorobanților

PARCUL KISELEFF

Str. Washington

Muzeul Țăranului Român (Roman Peasant Museum) **T**

Palatul Victoriei

Sportiv Dinamo Stadium

Circul Globus

PARCUL CIRCULUI

Muzeul de Istorie Naturală Grigore Antipa

Piața Victoriei

Bulevardul Iancu de Hunedoara

Șoseaua Ștefan cel Mare **M**

Gara Basarab

CIMITIRUL ISRAELIT

Șoseaua Nicolae Titulescu

Bulevardul Alexandru Ioan Cuza

Muzeul Storck **S**

Academia de Studi Economice

Gara Basarab **M** Griviței

Gara de Nord

Gara de Nord **M**

Academia Română

Muz. Național G. Enescu **R**

Muzeul Literaturii Române

Patria Cinema

Ateneul Român

H Piața Romană **M** Romană

Piața Lahovari

G

Academia Națională de Ed. Fizica și Sport

Muzeul Militar Național

Casa Radio

GRĂDINA BOTANICĂ (BOTANICAL GARDEN)

Opera Națională Română

Fac. de Drept

Muzeul Național de Artă

Palatul Regal

Piața Revoluției

Biserica Italiana

page 117

Palatul Cotroceni **X**

B-dul Eroii Sanitari
Sf. Elefterie Vechi

B-dul M. Kogălniceanu

GRĂDINA CISMIGIU

Lacul Cismigiu

Cercul Militar

Universității

Teatrul Național

Bulevardul Regina Elisabeta

Palatul CEC

Muz. Municipiului

Piața 21 Dec 1989

Banca Națională

Splaiul Independenței

PARCUL IZVOR

Muzeul Național de Istorie

Curtea Domnească

Stadionul Cotroceni

B-dul Națiunile

Palatul Parlamentului (Palace of Parliament) **F**

Piața Națiunile Unite

Piața Constituției

Str. Halelor

Bulevardul Unirii

Muzeul Național de Atră Contemporană, Muzeul Costumelor Populare din România

Mănăstirea Antim

Catedrală Patriarhei **E**

Unirii 1

Unirii 2 **M**

Mănăstirea Radu Vodă

Biserica Bucur

DEALUL MITROPOLIEI

Calea 13 Septembrie

B-dul Regina Maria

B-dul Mărășești

On the square's northeastern side, the 22-storey **Intercontinental Hotel** (Hotelul Intercontinental; Str. Nicolae Bălcescu 4) towers above its neighbours. Erected in 1970 at a time when Ceauşescu was the darling of the West – and popular at home – it was then Bucharest's tallest building, and an important symbol that Romania was part of the outside world.

Standards were never staggeringly high in communist times. In the late 1980s foreigners who stayed there reported having to pay extra for heating – although there was no additional charge for bugging – while ordinary Romanians were only allowed access to the showcase soft-currency snack bar. The panoramic Luna Bar on the hotel's 21st floor offers one of Bucharest's best viewpoints.

Behind a fountain just northwest of Piaţa Universităţii, the **Architecture Faculty** building is a fine example of the neo-Romanian style that became officially encouraged after World War I. An early 20th-century reaction against modernism, the style fuses Brâncoveanu *(see page 83)* and other traditional Romanian elements with Mediterranean, Oriental and Balkan influences. The new wing is a less distinctive addition. During the so-called Mineriad of June 1990, student protestors barricaded themselves here against miners bussed in from the Jiu Valley by Iliescu.

Facing Bulevardul Regina Elisabeta on the west side of the square, the colossal neoclassical **University Palace** dates from 1857–59, although Bucharest University (www.unibuc.ro) wasn't founded until 1864. It was then the newly unified Romania's second university after Iaşi. Stalls outside sell second-hand books. The **National Bank of Romania** opposite occupies an imposing French neoclassical building faced with Corinthian columns. Dating from 1883, it sits on the site of the former Şerban Vodă Inn, which had been one of Bucharest's most famous buildings before being demolished to make way for the bank. Statues outside represent Agriculture, Industry, Justice and Commerce.

Not clearly delineated from Piaţa Universităţii, the square with a fountain outside the National Theatre is **Piaţa 21 Decembrie 1989** ❸ (21 December 1989 Square), commemorating the beginning of the 1989 revolution. These days it's a popular rallying point for good-natured groups of football fans celebrating victory.

On the eastern side of the square, behind a poorly lit concrete concourse, the gigantic **National Theatre** (Teatrul Naţional; http://tnb.kappa.ro), dating from 1973, is a clumsy example of the communist-style neoclassicism beloved of Ceauşescu. Originally, the facade was inspired by the style of a traditional Moldavian monastery, but the current, stockier design is the result of a heavy-handed makeover in 1984. It is formally known as the I.L. Caragiale National Theatre, after the famous Romanian satirical author and playwright. Such was his love of poking fun at politicians it is unlikely he would have been so honoured had he lived in

Maps on pages 114, 117

The Intercontinental Hotel is still one of the city's top hotels.

BELOW: the University Palace and Bulevardul Regina Elisabeta.

The 1977 earthquake devastated Bucharest and other places in the east of the country. The epicentre was in the Vrancea region of the eastern Carpathians. Over 1,500 people were killed.

BELOW: a hot summer's day in Piața Unirii.

communist times. Hidden behind scaffolding to the southeast, **Colțea Church** (Biserica Coțea; B-dul. Bălcescu 1) dates from 1701–2 but sits on the site of a much older building.

Opposite, the often-overlooked **Bucharest Municipal Museum of History and Art** ● (Muzeul de Istorie și Artă al Municipiului București; B-dul. Ion Brătianu 1; open Tues–Fri 10am–6pm; admission charge) is one of Romania's best local-history museums, although there are no English labels. A guided tour (book in advance) is recommended. The museum occupies a palace built for fabulously rich nobleman Costachie Șuțu by Viennese architects Konrad Schwinck and Johann Veit in the 1830s. The exterior is neo-Gothic, with four towers giving it castle-like pretentions. Its many innovations included a sundial with a cannon, whose gunpowder was ignited by the heat of the sun at noon. Inside, the 10-sq. metre (108-sq. ft) mirror over the staircase came from Venice. If you can understand the labels or have a guide, the collection is a fascinating explanation of important devel-

opments in Bucharest's history, including the establishment of the fire brigade and police, the introduction of electricity and the mains-water supply, and the public-transport system. (Much of this civic improvement came about in the 1830s and 1840s during the period when Russia assumed the role of "protector" of the Danubian Principalities, ie Wallachia and Moldavia.) The museum also showcases many finds from the Princely Court *(see page 124).*

Piața Unirii and the Centrul Civic

South of Piața Universității, **Piața Unirii** ● (Union Square) has a communist wasteland feel. When Ceaușescu came to power in 1965 Bucharest largely retained its prewar architectural atmosphere, with new developments mainly at the edges. A visit to North Korea in 1971 enamoured the leader with grandiose boulevards and tower blocks and, following the earthquake of 1977, the re-creation of a new-look Bucharest began in earnest. Determined to make a suitably grand archi-

tectural and political statement, Ceaușescu chose one of Bucharest's few hills as the focal point of a new civic centre. Its creation meant the demolition of a famous Art Deco stadium, a historic monastery, churches, and even a hospital.

It was only because of relentless opposition abroad – and muted objections at home – that some churches survived. Thanks to a method pioneered by the architect Eugen Iordăchescu, several were, incredibly, moved by rail on giant platforms to less conspicuous locations – and often ended up sandwiched between tall buildings, all but invisible.

The **Unirea Shopping Centre** (www.unireashop.ro) on Piața Unirii is Romania's largest department store. In communist days, Bucharest's equivalent of Moscow's GUM offered a bigger choice than anywhere else, though there wasn't a lot to choose from. Even in the mid-1990s shoppers had to put up with such absurdities as attendants who would let you take the lift up but not down. Nowadays, with Unirea increasingly resembling a US-style shopping mall, the range of

goods is better, although the profusion of tiny shops over four floors can make finding what you want a time-consuming process.

Bulevardul Unirii stretches east and west from Piața Unirii, and stands as one of Bucharest's most disastrous examples of town planning. On the east side it hosts a scruffy market as well as a few shops and office buildings. In the other direction it leads lifelessly to the Palace of Parliament, with a procession of monumental disused fountains and little else. Originally intended to provide a clear view of the palace all the way from Piața Unirii, and to house many of the political elite, the project was never completed, and most of the buildings remained empty. It continues to be a monumental waste of space. Plans are afoot to revitalise the area east of Piața Unirii with a radically ambitious Manhattan-style development, **Esplanada**, complete with buildings up to 80 storeys high.

Even Ceaușescu baulked at the idea of demolishing the headquarters of the Romanian Orthodox Church, but the Centru Civic was deliberately designed

Map below

TIP

Pedestrian unfriendly and badly lit, Piața Universității is best avoided after dark, as it attracts street hustlers and ne'er-do-wells. The underpass has shops and the main metro station, Universității. From 1989 the concourse was allowed to decay, but in 2006, EU entry beckoning, the city authorities decided to stage a long-overdue refurbishment.

BELOW: Radu Voda Monastery.

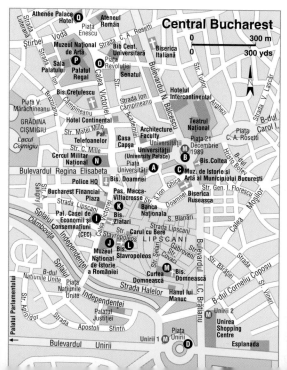

The Palace of Parliament is Ceauşescu's most visible legacy in Bucharest.

BELOW: the Palace of Parliament is home to some 4,500 crystal chandeliers.

to reduce its architectural profile. Thus the **Metropolitan Hill** (Dealul Mitropoliei) no longer dominates the surrounding area as originally intended. Nonetheless it remains a fine assembly of religious architecture. Its centrepiece, the **Patriarchal Cathedral** ❺ (Catedrala Patriarhei) is a surprisingly modest little building, largely remaining faithful to its original 1654–58 design, based on that of Curtea de Argeş Monastery Church *(see page 141)*. More grandiose, and guarded by soldiers, the Patriarchal Palace next door dates from 1708 and is the residence of the supreme leader of the Romanian Orthodox Church, currently Patriarch Teoctist, who is also the Bishop of Bucharest.

The nearby **Radu Vodă Monastery** (Mănăstirea Radu Vodă; Str. Radu Vodă 24A; open daily 8am–8pm; free; www.bisericabucur.com) was founded by Alexandru II Mircea in the 16th century. Originally intended as the Metropolitan Church, it was built, like the cathedral, in the style of Curtea de Argeş Church with later neoclassical additions from 1714 and 1859–63.

Next to Radu Voda, **Bucur Church** (Biserica Bucur; Str. Radu Vodă 33) was, according to legend, founded by Bucur the Shepherd, who gave his name to Bucharest. However, as in many of the best legends, there is extremely scant evidence to support either theory.

At the intersection of Bulevardul Unirii with Strada Justiţiei, **Antim Monastery** (Mănăstirea Antim; Str. Mitropolit Antim Ivireanu 29), from 1715, is a fine example of the Brâncoveanu style despite the Centru Civic buildings hemming it in. The beautiful statues are the work of one of Romania's leading sculptors, Karl Storck (1826–87), father of Frederic *(see page 128)*. The monastery now houses just seven monks.

The Palace of Parliament

For sheer insanity, few buildings can compete with Bucharest's **Palace of Parliament** ❻ (Palatul Parlamentului; Calea 13 Septembrie 1; guided tours daily 10am–4pm; admission charge). A grotesque tribute to a grotesque ego, it required the destruction of around a fifth of old Bucharest, including most

of the historic quarter of Uranus, and starved Romania of resources at a time when living standards were becoming increasingly desperate. The scheme also inadvertently created the city's notorious stray-dog problem *(see page 125)*. Since 1994 the building has housed the Parliament and since 2004 the Senate. It also hosts exhibitions, conferences, concerts and other events. Be aware that as a working government building it is sometimes closed.

A visit is an unmissable, if disturbing, insight into Ceaușescu's folly. Visitors are likely to feel a mixture of revulsion at the building's sheer pointlessness – as well as the gaudiness of much of the interior – with admiration at the skill of the craftsmen who worked under such harsh conditions. The entrance is on the southern side of the building.

The Palace also contains the **Museum of Romanian Folk Costume** (Muzeul Costumelor Populare din România; open daily 10am–6pm; admission charge); and the **National Museum of Contemporary Art** (Muzeul Național de Artă contemporană; open Wed–Sun 10am–6pm; admission charge).

North of Piața Universității

Maps
on pages
114, 117

Leading north from Piata Universității to Piața Romana, what could be termed Bucharest's main street starts off as **Bulevardul Bălcescu** and then changes its identity to become **Bulevardul Magheru ⑥**. Even Bucharesters often confuse the two, lumping them together as Magheru. The strip is mainly a place to shop (and incidentally is the best place in town for books, old or new, in English or Romanian), visit the obligatory casino or gentlemen's club, change money or buy an air ticket or holiday package. This being Bucharest, it's still far from resembling any other cloned high street, and here and there the odd hole-in-the-wall lighter repair shop or antiquarian bookshop casts one back to an earlier time. However, these oddities are becoming increasingly outpaced by Body Shop, McDonald's, KFC and the rest. If you are looking for Roberto Cavalli shades, a Bulgari watch, or a plasma TV, your chances of finding it here are higher than anywhere else in Romania. A few plaques and crosses along the street commemorate victims of the 1989 revolution.

The 45-minute guided tours of the Palace of Parliament take in just a few of the gilt-and-marble-clad rooms, but it's difficult not to be impressed by the scale and audacity of everything.

LEFT: the view along Bulevardul Unirii to the Palace.

Roll-call of Megalomania

Originally built as the House of the People (Casa Poporului) to house government offices, the Palace of Parliament is the world's second-largest building after the Pentagon for surface area, and third after Cape Canaveral in volume. Its exterior measures 270 metres by 240 metres (885 ft by 785 ft), its 12 storeys towering 84 metres (275 ft) above ground. Another eight floors underground – only four complete – reach a depth of 92 metres (300 ft). Ornately decorated with purely Romanian materials, its 1,100 rooms vary in size from 100–2,600 sq. metres (1,075–28,000 sq. ft). The largest, Unification Hall, features a sliding roof wide enough to allow a helicopter to land. Construction began in 1984, and required more than 4,000 architects and 20,000 builders, while the secret tunnels were the work of death-row prisoners. Slaving around the clock to the whims of increasingly impatient and demanding patrons, workers lived in daily terror of site inspections by the Ceaușescus. Unreasonable deadlines, combined with woeful safety precautions, led to numerous accidents and shoddy workmanship. When the regime fell, the palace was near completion but no longer served any obvious purpose. One plan, to blow it up, proved unfeasibly expensive. Another scheme, to convert it into a museum of communism, lacked political will.

Bucharest in the 1930s

Many Romanians, including those who are much too young to have experienced it, recall the interwar period as a golden age for Romania, and especially for Bucharest. Foreign travellers wrote in praise of the richness of Bucharest's cultural and social life and the excellence of its restaurants, with their enormous helpings and low prices, as well as describing the intrigue and debauchery. "Bucharest was delightfully depraved," Cyrus Leo Sulzberger, a *New York Times* foreign correspondent, wrote in his memoirs, *A Long Row of Candles*. In the West, the Bucharest of the 1930s is probably best known through Olivia Manning's *Balkan Trilogy*. Depicting the city as a hotbed of decadence, debauchery and espionage full of colourful characters, the work was only partly fiction. She based it on her experiences living there at the outbreak of World War II, with much of the action taking place in the legendary Athenée Palace Hotel and especially its English Bar, the axis of the city's social life, where it appeared everyone was spying on everyone else.

In the 1920s, the newly-enlarged Romania enjoyed a flourishing economy, in large part thanks to its grain exports, while government policies encouraged foreign investment in Romanian industry. But the global financial crisis following the Wall Street Crash of 1929 caused grain prices to plummet, leading to an agricultural crisis and high unemployment, even if investment in new industries, particularly after 1934, helped to soften the blow.

Yet throughout the 1930s Bucharest enjoyed rapid growth and unprecedented property development, partly because of government policies encouraging construction and partly to cope with the influx of new residents. Investors considered property investment a shrewd way to protect their capital from devaluation. The pace of urbanisation was rapid, with Bucharest's population leaping from 383,000 in 1918 to 870,000 in 1939.

At the same time as this boom in urban growth there was an increasing interest in the Modern Movement among Romanian architects, giving rise to some strikingly avant garde buildings such as the ARO building (currently the Patria cinema on Bulevardul Magheru) and Băneasa railway station. Many of Bucharest's finest neoclassical buildings were also built at this time, ranging from the Arch of Triumph and the new Royal Palace to residential blocks along tree-lined boulevards inspired by French models.

Bucharest's taste for French architectural styles, which dates back to the end of the 19th century, was largely the result of the fashion among the upper classes – and its architects – for studying in France. But if it was fashionable to hire Romanian architects trained in Paris, it was even grander to appoint French architects, such as Paul Gottereau, who designed the Royal Palace. Although there is some uncertainty as to how the name arose or when, prewar Bucharest enjoyed the epithet Little Paris (micul Paris), as much for its cultural life as its architecture.

In intellectual and artistic realms too, Bucharest enjoyed a boom in the 1930s, with luminaries such as Enescu, Eliade and Brâncuşi achieving international fame, and its educated classes becoming known for their increasingly progressive ideas. For the hedonist with cash to spare, the city offered no shortage of pleasures, illicit or not, and Calea Victoriei boasted some of the finest shops, restaurants and hotels in southeastern Europe.

The 1930s were certainly an exciting time to be in Bucharest for many, but while people recall the opulence and cultural flourishing, they tend to overlook the many negative aspects of the period, such as the rise of fascism, political instability and lack of any real democracy, as well as the huge disparities in wealth. But of all the places to be rich in the 1930s, Bucharest was surely one of the most fun.   ❏

LEFT: Calea Victoriei in 1930.

One of the few tourist attractions on Bălcescu-Magheru, the red-brick **Italian Church** (Biserica Italiană; B-dul. Nicolae Bălcescu 28; open daily 9am–7pm; free) caters to one of Romania's least-known minorities. Encouraged to migrate here during Carol I's reign, tens of thousands of Italians came to Romania in search of a better life. Many worked in construction. In 1948 Bucharest alone had 1,200 Italian families. Nowadays – Italy's economy long having overtaken Romania's – migration is in the opposite direction.

Despite its strikingly modernist appearance, the block at Magheru 12–14 now housing the **Patria Cinema** – originally the Aro building – dates from 1931–35. It's one of the earliest and best-known works of influential architect Horia Creangă, grandson of novelist Ion Creangă. From the beginning, the building was known for the luxury and modernity of its vast, 1,200-seat marble hall, originally used both for concerts and films. Recently renovated, the Patria remains Bucharest's most splendid cinema.

At Magheru's northern end, **Piața Romană** ❸ (Roman Square) commemorates the Romanians' supposed Latin ancestry. Reinforcing the message, Romulus and Remus suckle beneath the square's **She-Wolf of Rome monument** (Monumentul Lupoaica Romei). These days, Piața Vodafone might be a more appropriate name for the square, thanks to the colossal advertising billboards.

The **metro station** beneath Piața Romană owes its impossibly cramped design to the fact it would have been impossible to build it any wider without digging up and rebuilding the entire square *(see margin)*.

Southern Calea Victoriei

Parallel to the west of Magheru, **Calea Victoriei** (Victory Avenue) was once Bucharest's most aristocratic street, lined with boyars' (important landowners) palaces. Constantin Brâncoveanu built it in 1692 to link the royal palace

on the bank of the Dâmbovița with his Mogoșoia estate. Laid out on wood rather than the usual mud prevalent elsewhere in the city, it became the pride of Bucharest, not least because it did not turn into a swamp in winter. Later the thoroughfare became known for the quality of its shops and restaurants, and remained highly aristocratic until communist times. In fact it still retains a leafy, aloof air today. The name dates from 1878 when Romanian troops returned victorious from the Russo-Turkish War (known to Romanians as the War of Independence) and made their triumphal entrance to the city along the avenue.

Approaching from the Dâmbovița River in the south, the first impression of Calea Victoriei, overshadowed by a concrete tower block, isn't very prepossessing, but it soon improves. At Nos 11–13, the genuinely palatial CEC **Palace** ❶ (Palatul Casei de Economii și Consemnațiuni; www.cec-sa.ro) stands as a surprising temple to capitalism that survived the communist era as the HQ of the only bank allowed to stay in existence. Designed in an eclectic

Maps on pages 114, 117

TIP

One story tells how Ceaușescu, informed by engineers that a metro station at Piața Romană was impossible, insisted it be built anyway. Another version is that he originally refused to let it be built because there were other perfectly good stations 15 minutes' walk away and he didn't want Romanians to get fat – but later changed his mind.

BELOW: typically old-fashioned store in a Pasajul.

The CEC Palace is not open to the public, although it does still function as a bank. Security guards may stop you entering unless you have business there.

BELOW: the elegant Pasajul Macca-Villacrosse.

style by Paul Gottereau, it dates from 1894. Decorated with serpents, caryatids and heraldic devices beneath a vast glass dome, the interior is even more lavish than the exterior.

Immediately north of CEC, the brand spanking new marble-and-glass facade of the **Bucharest Financial Plaza** reflects the old buildings nearby. Typical of a post-communist breed of building, the plaza, despite being Bucharest's tallest building, doesn't overwhelm the CEC palace or other historic buildings in the vicinity, with the space left between allowing them to retain some dignity. A post-Brâncuşi, post-Stalinist take on the *Angel of the North*, the striking bronze *Bird in Flight (Pasare in Zbor)* sculpture outside was a 1997 work by Gheorghe Iliescu-Călineşti.

Opposite, at No. 12, the **National History Museum of Romania** ❶ (Muzeul Naţional de Istorie a României; open Tues–Sun 10am–6pm, Oct–Mar until 5pm; admission, photo and video charge; free entry on the last Fri of the month; www.mnir.ro) is in a building occupied until 1970 by the

Postal Palace (Palatul poştei). Built from 1894–1900 in a French-eclectic style on the site of the former Constantin Vodă Inn, its architect was Alexandru Săvulescu. Guided tours in English, French or Romanian can be booked 24 hours in advance.

The central hall has a **lapidarium** arranged around a plaster cast of **Trajan's Column** (Columna din Traian). The Roman Senate commissioned the original, completed in AD 113, to commemorate Trajan's victory over the Dacians; it still stands in Trajan's Forum in Rome. Arranged in an ascending spiral pattern around the column, a 200-metre (650-ft) relief depicts the two military campaigns against the Dacians (AD 101–2 and 105–6), culminating in King Decebal's capture and suicide. In the museum, 125 numbered tablets laid out over two floors reproduce scenes from the original.

Romania had to pay more than 6 million lei for the copy, made from 1939–43 by Vatican craftsmen. However, thanks to World War II and then the Cold War, there was a long period of diplomatic wrangling before it even-

tually reached Romania in 1967. The former Postal Palace was then specially converted to accommodate it.

The museum's most valuable section is the **Romanian Treasury** (Tezaurul Român), guarded by soldiers. As well as a collection of gold items dating back to the 5th millennium BC, the treasury contains coronation crowns and other regalia belonging to the Romanian royal family. An additional photography charge applies here. Other rooms house temporary exhibitions.

Next door, the **Zlătari Church** (Biserica Zlătari; Calea Victoriei 12) dates from 1637 with many subsequent renovations. It is mainly of interest for the interior paintings (1853–56) by Gheorghe Tattarescu, although these are badly in need of restoration.

At Nos 16–20, two interconnecting passageways form Bucharest's most picturesque shopping arcade. With two curving branches joining under a central glass dome, **Pasajul Macca-Villacrosse** , originally built to link the National Bank of Romania with Calea Victoriei, dates from 1890–91 Roofed with glass and wrought iron, it retains its original symmetrical form. These days, smart shop façades share space with some of Bucharest's most atmospheric bars and cafés. On the other side of Calea Victoriei, the **Police Headquarters** was the scene of mayhem during the *mineriada* of June 1990 when demonstrators seized it and threw files from the windows *(see page 41).*

Further north at No. 28, the **Doamnei Church** (Biserica Doamnei) dates from 1683 and takes its name from its founder, Princess (Doamna) Maria, second wife of Şerban Cantacuzino. Built of stone, it features ornate floral sculptures on the doors and columns.

Lipscani – the old city

One of Bucharest's main tourist attractions, the district of **Lipscani** lies east of Calea Victoriei and south of Bulevardul Elisabeta, taking its name from the main street, Strada Lipscani. With a maze of cobbled streets dating back to the Middle Ages, this was originally the merchants' quarter. Later it became a largely Jewish neighbourhood, and in recent times has been populated with Gypsies. It remains the heart of old Bucharest and escaped systematisation under communism, but not severe neglect. Many buildings, both residential and commercial, are in an advanced state of dereliction. Some have balconies or facades so crumbling one fears to walk underneath them.

Although there are some recognised attractions, half the point in visiting Lipscani is to take in the ramshackle mix of shops where facades – and sometimes contents – seem unchanged since the Ceauşescu years. This is also one of the best places in Romania for small specialist shops selling anything from old coins and violins to camera equipment, or to get almost anything repaired. Retaining its raw edge, Lipscani also has some of Bucharest's liveliest bars, cafés and restaurants. It is worth remembering that sights many foreign tourists see as quaint, such as Gypsies hanging washing from their balconies, and their children playing

Maps on pages 114, 117

Geto-Dacian helmet at the National History Museum.

BELOW:
Strada Lipscani has been partially pedestrianised – it's just about the only place in downtown Bucharest that has – which makes it a pleasant place for a stroll.

Lipscani is one of the best areas for eating out in Bucharest.

BELOW: the remains of the Princely Court.

football in the street, are an embarrassment to some Bucharesters.

While there were signs of a revival of Lipscani in the 1990s and early 2000s, there has been little progress since 2004. Many buildings are for sale, but few investors are willing to agree to the City Hall's stringent conditions, preferring to buy properties elsewhere that do not need restoration. In addition, continuing uncertainty over property ownership (some properties may be returned to a former, pre-communist era owner) has scared away investors.

One of Bucharest's architectural highlights, the tiny **Stavropoleos Church ●** (Biserica Stavropoleos; Str. Stavropoleos 4; open daily 8.30am–6pm; free) lies on the attractive street of the same name. Founded from 1722–24 by the Greek monk Ioanichie, it is one of the finest examples of Brâncoveanu architecture – combining Byzantine elements with aspects of the late Renassisance and Romanian folk art – as well as one of Bucharest's oldest churches. Delightful icons, wooden and stone sculptures inside and a garden outside complete the picture.

Also on Stavropoleos, at Nos 3–5, wrought-iron dragons and lamps announce the entrance to the delightfully old-world **Carul cu Bere**. One of Bucharest's best-known beer halls, it dates back to 1875 and has a lavish neo-Gothic interior. Once a favoured meeting place for writers and businessmen, it went into decline in the communist and post-communist period, and has acquired a reputation as a tourist trap. Closed for restoration in 2006, it may once again revive its sparkle.

A few minutes' walk towards the river at the western end of Strada Franceză, and watched over by a modern statue of Vlad Țepeș, the ruins of the **Princely Court ●** (Curtea Domnească; open daily 9am–8pm; admission charge) mark the oldest surviving part of Bucharest. In the late 14th century a brick fortress stood here, but archæological evidence suggests the site was inhabited much earlier. From 1458–59, Vlad Țepeș enlarged the fortress and surrounded it with stone walls. Succeeding *voievodes* (princes) enlarged and strengthened the building but it was abandoned at the end of the

18th century when Alexandru Ipsilanti moved to the New Court in Dealul Spirii. It subsequently fell into ruin, although the surrounding district continued to flourish as Bucharest's commercial district. The current ruins are the result of excavations in the 1950s and late 1960s. There is no longer very much to see except some pieces of wall and a few arcades, as well as fragments of masonry scattered around the site.

The **Princely Church** (Biserica Domnească) nearby, built by Mircea the Shepherd in 1546 in traditional Wallachian style, is Bucharest's oldest church. Its intricately carved wooden door was an 18th-century addition.

Across the street, the long, white wall and distinctive grey, fish-scale-tiled roof belong to Bucharest's best-preserved old inn/caravanserai, **Hanul lui Manuc** (Str. Iuliu Maniu 62). It dates from 1808 and once belonged to a rich Armenian merchant called Emanuel Marzaian or Manuc-bey. A large structure with galleries built around a courtyard, it still resembles an Oriental caravanserai and offers accommodation. The restaurant, however, is best avoided.

Bulevardul Elisabeta to Piața Enescu

At the intersection of Calea Victoriei with Bulevardul Elisabeta, the imposing **National Military Circle**  (Cercul Militar Național; Str. Constantin Mille 1) is a French neoclassical masterpiece dating from 1912. The interior is closed to civilians, but the exterior terrace is open to all.

Once a symbol of the Romanian high life in the days when Bucharest was famous for its cuisine, **Casa Capșa** (www.capsa.ro), at No. 36 was reopened in 2003 and is again one of the top restaurants and hotels in town. The 1930s **Telephone Palace** (Palatul Telefoanelor) at No. 37 is one of Bucharest's boldest prewar stabs at modernism, and was Romania's tallest building until 1970, when the Intercontinental stole its crown. With lofty ceilings and mouldings, the **Hotel Continental** (www.continentalhotels.ro) at No. 56 was constructed in 1828 in the German Renaissance style, and recently renovated.

A short distance further north, the attractive **Crețulescu Church** (Biserica Crețulescu) dates from 1722 and

Maps on pages 114, 117

Periodic efforts at tackling the stray dog problems have been accused of brutality.

BELOW: watch out for stray dogs.

The Dogs of Bucharest

Bucharest's authorities have never dealt properly with the estimated 100,000 stray dogs that roam the city, a problem that originated with the clearing of old housing following the 1977 earthquake, and Ceaușescu's grandiose Palace of Parliament scheme. People were rehoused in tiny apartments unsuitable for their pets, and so a significant number were simply left to fend for themselves on the streets. This population of strays quickly grew until packs of aggressive feral dogs were becoming a safety hazard across the city.

With thousands of people requiring treatment for dog bites at Bucharest's hospitals each year, the government took action in 2001 with a major cull which has certainly improved the situation – in the city centre at least. Yet, incredibly, in 2006 a Japanese businessman died after being bitten by a stray dog outside his apartment building in Piața Victoriei. Animal-rights campaigners have argued for the strays to be neutered rather than put down.

Visitors should take care to avoid dogs when walking in the city. A dog alarm (which emits a high-pitched noise to scare them off) is a wise investment. Never approach a stray: cross the road to avoid them if you have to, and don't walk alone in areas known to be populated by them. If you are bitten, a rabies shot is required.

Memorial for those who were killed in the mineriad *of 1990, when miners were brought in from the Jiu Valley to break up anti-Iliescu protests. Iliescu has always denied the charge, but is currently standing trial over the matter.*

BELOW: Piața Revolutiei in late December 1989.

was built by Boyar Iordache Crețulescu in a Brâncoveanu style. Damaged in 1989, it was subsequently restored. Inside, some fragments remain of frescoes by Gheorghe Tattarescu. Opposite the church, Calea Victoriei widens into **Piața Revoluției** (Revolution Square), historically the political – and once royal – centre of Bucharest. As the name indicates, it also played an important part in the events of 1989 (prior to this it was called the Piața Republicii). Nowadays, however, it is a regular location for events as revolutionary as a Barbie Festival.

The **Senate Building** (Senatul; www.senat.ro) on the square's southeast corner once housed the Central Committee of the Communist Party. Its balcony was famously the scene of Ceaușescu's last public speech on 21 December 1989. The burnt-out shell opposite, which housed an "underground house" where the Securitate questioned and tortured people, has been left largely in ruins as a memorial (a newer glass structure perched uncomfortably on top is the headquarters of the Romanian Union of Archi-

tects). Today the ruined section contains a small café, its walls and bar area covered in pictures and memorabilia of the events of 1989. Unfortunately, protestors also burnt down the Gottereau-designed **Central University library** next door, wrongly thinking it was also a Securitate building. It has been painstakingly restored (Biblioteca centrala universitara; open Mon–Fri 8.30am–8pm; www.bcub.ro).

On the western side of the square, the former **Royal Palace** (Palatul Regal) houses the **National Art Museum of Romania** (Muzeul Național de Artă al României; Calea Victoriei 49–53; open May–Sept Wed–Sun 11am–7pm, Oct–Apr 10am–6pm; admission charge; http://art.museum.ro). The palace was built in 1870 for Carol I by Paul Gottereau but largely destroyed by a fire in 1926, then later rebuilt by Carol II. The only part of the original to survive the fire was the grand marble staircase leading to the Throne Hall, today called the Stairs of the Voivodes. The palace was nationalised in 1948, seriously damaged in 1989 and is undergoing extensive long-term renovation. Nonetheless, it

has a fine collection of Dutch Old Masters, as well as works by Monet, Rubens, El Greco, Durer, Tintoretto, Renoir and Delacroix, and local talents Brâncuşi, Tonitza and Grigorescu.

Built as a suitably grand venue for Communist Party congresses, presumably with acoustics to amplify the mandatory standing ovations, the UFO-like **Palace Hall** (Sala Palatului) is now one of Bucharest's top concert and exhibition venues.

A few minutes' walk west of the Royal Palace brings you to the pleasant **Cişmigiu Gardens** (Grădina Cişmigiu), the city's most central and oldest public garden, landscaped by Carl Meyer in 1854.

On the other side of Piaţa Enescu – a northern extension of Piaţa Revolutiei – the **Romanian Athenæum** (Ateneul Român; Str. Franklin 1; open Tues–Sat noon–7pm, Sun 6–7pm; http://fge.org.ro/ateneul-roman) is one of the city's prettiest buildings, as well as its most highly rated musical venue. Built from 1886–88 in neoclassical style with a 40-metre (130-ft) Baroque dome and Ionic columns, it resembles a giant temple. It is home to the highly regarded George Enescu Philarmonic Orchestra and is the best place in town to hear classical music.

The **Athenée Palace Hotel** **Q** (Str. Episcopiei 1–3; www.hilton.co.uk/bucharest) was built in 1914 and recently restored to its former imposing grandeur by the Hilton chain, which wisely retained the original name. As headquarters of the Romanian and German forces in World War II, it was once known as a hotbed of intrigue.

North to Piata Victoriei

Of interest more for the building than the contents, the **George Enescu National Museum** **R** (Muzeul Naţional George Enescu; Calea Victoriei 141; open Tues–Sun 10am–5pm; admission charge) occupies the former **Cantacuzino Palace**, completed in 1900. Guarded by two stone lions, this huge French-Baroque masterpiece with its exuberant clam-shaped *porte-corchere* was, among other things, briefly home to Romania's national composer George Enescu, it belonged to his wife, Maria Cantacuzino. Today

Maps on pages 114, 117

*As well as bullet holes deliberately left in place, several monuments around Piaţa Revolutiei commemorate the events of 1989. The largest and most controversial of these is popularly known – for reasons that will become blindingly evident when you see it – as the **Speared Potato** (cartoful intepat).*

BELOW LEFT: the Senate Building.
BELOW: exhibition outside the Peasant Museum.

The Triumphal Arch was built in 1878 to mark Romania's official recognition as a nation state. The original was made out of wood; the stone Parisian replica was not commissioned until the 1930s.

BELOW: mirror glass at the Financial Plaza.

the building houses an exhibition of limited interest devoted to Enescu.

Some of Bucharest's most gorgeous pre-war villas line the streets either side of this northern end of Calea Victoriei, in varying states of repair. Some of the best are in Strs. N. Iorga, G. Manu, G. Patrichi, Moxa and Sevastopol.

Calea Victoriei ends at Piaţa Victoriei, mainly notable for the **Victoria Palace** (Palatul Victoriei), a Soviet-style building dating from 1937–44. It houses the offices of the prime minister and his cabinet.

Tucked away to the southeast, the little-known **Storck Museum** ⑤ (Muzeul Storck; Str. Vasile Alecsandri 16; open Tues–Sun 9am–5pm; admission charge) has a worthwhile exhibition of sculptures by Frederic Storck (1872–1924) and paintings by his wife Cecilia (1879–1969).

Şoseaua Kiseleff

North of Piaţa Victoriei, one of Bucharest's leafiest and grandest streets, **Şoseaua Kiseleff**, leads past parks, embassies and villas. Legend has it Ceauşescu offered a villa here to the driver he flagged down on his escape from Bucharest in December 1989.

The excellent **Grigore Antipa Museum of Natural History** (Muzeul de Istorie Naturală Grigore Antipa; Şos.Kiseleff 1; www.antipa.ro; open Wed-Sun 10am–6pm; entry fee) at the southern end of Kisseleff has a particularly fine aquatic collection as well as a famous skeleton of a Deinotherium giganteum, a huge prehistoric elephant, discovered near Vaslui.

Next door, the **Romanian Peasant Museum** ⑦ (Muzeul Ţaranului Român; Şos. Kisseleff 3; open Tues–Sun 10am–6pm; admission charge; www.itcnet.ro/mtr) has one of Romania's most valuable ethnographic collections and is a must-see for anyone interested in Romanian culture. Some 20,000 costumes, six wooden churches, thousands of traditional wooden and iron objects, 18,000 items of pottery, textiles, pictures, photos and videos portraying rural customs, are all imaginatively arranged and labelled.

The museum was originally founded in 1905 as the Ethnographical and National Art Museum, but only completed in 1935. In 1953 the collection was moved elsewhere and the building became a museum dedicated to the history of the Communist Party. It was not until 1990 that the original collection returned. In keeping with its communist links, the museum has a basement gallery dedicated to the horrors of collectivisation as well as busts of communist leaders and a vase dedicated to Stalin. The museum shop is one of the best places in Romania to buy handicrafts.

Further north, the **Triumphal Arch** ⑪ (Arcul de Triumf) stands on an island in the middle of a busy traffic roundabout and is a copy of the one in Paris but with Romanian emblems.

Continuing north on Kiseleff, the **Village Museum** ⑫ (Muzeul Satului; Şoseaua Kiseleff 28; open Mon 9am–4pm, Tues–Sun 9am–7pm, Apr–Nov until 4pm; admission, film and video charges; www.muzeulsatului.ro) contains

a breathtaking collection of wooden houses, churches, windmills and other buildings from villages around the country. Some of the buildings were originals, painstakingly moved here and reassembled, others are reconstructions. Laid out as in a real village, this collection is one of the largest of its kind in Europe. Festivals and folk-music performances are an occasional extra draw. Guided tours are possible in Romanian and English for an extra charge.

On the left, just before Piața Presei Libere, there is the **World Trade Centre**, which houses the Sofitel, Bucharest's first modern luxury hotel back in the 1990s. Part of the same complex, the **World Trade Plaza** is a mostly up-market shopping centre where you can buy furs, furniture, a teddy bear or even a car. There is also an expensive bar where businessmen discuss deals. There's also the Vegas-style Casino Napoleon.

Bordering the upper stretch of Kiseleff to the east is **Parcul Herăstrău** , Bucharest's largest park, laid out around a lake. The circle of statues of luminaries from the history of the EU, presum-ably a condition for EU funding of the park's renovation, is a curious sight.

South of the river

One of Bucharest's few obvious attractions south of the Dâmbovița River, **Cotroceni Palace** ✪ (Palatul Cotroceni; B-dul. Geniului 1; open Tues–Sun 10am–5pm; admission charge; www. presidency.ro) now houses presidential offices and can only be visited on a guided tour, booked in advance. However, it's worth the effort. The palace was built by Carol I between 1893 and 1895 and housed the royal family until Michael's abdication in 1947. It then became the Pioneers' Palace, where generations of young Romanians underwent indoctrination about the joys of communism and, no doubt, the evils of the monarchy. The 1977 earthquake seriously damaged the building, and after restoration work its next incarnation was, on Ceaușescu's orders, as a protocol guesthouse for visitors. The restoration took 10 years and never served Ceaușescu's intended purpose. He did, however, have a room specially prepared for the British Queen in a

Maps
on pages
114, 117

TIP

To reach the Peasant Museum from the city centre, take the Metro to Piata Victoriei. The Village Museum and Herăstrău Park are a further stop north at Aviatorilor – or a pleasant 2-km (1¼-mile) stroll along the tree-lined Șoseaua Kiseleff.

BELOW AND BELOW LEFT: the Village Museum is one of the best in the country.

Eating al fresco in the Lipscani district. The city authorities, waking up to the area's tourism potential, are encouraging small independent businesses to open here.

BELOW:
weekenders at
Snagov Lake.

feminine style he thought would be to her taste. Her Majesty never visited.

Although some effort has been made to redecorate the interior, most of the original fittings have disappeared. Officially, much of the furniture was destroyed in the earthquake, but wholesale theft seems an equally plausible explanation.

Opposite the palace, the **Botanical Garden** (Grădina Botanică; open summer daily 8am–8pm; admission charge) enjoys some architecturally challenging buildings related to the university, as well as three industrial cooling towers on its southern edge. Apart from that, it makes a pleasant respite in summer. It has a **museum** (open Tues and Thur 8am–3pm, Sat–Sun 9am–1pm) and glasshouses (open Tues, Thur and Sat 9am–1pm).

Trips out of town

With a shoreline of 18 km (12 miles), **Lake Snagov ❶** (Lacul Snagov) – 40 km (25 miles) north of Bucharest – attracts water-sports enthusiasts and is a popular weekend retreat. Once a notorious haunt of brigands, the thick surrounding woodland is one of the few remaining vestiges of Codrii Vlăsiei (the Forests of Wallachia) that encircled Bucharest until the 19th century.

Snagov's other attraction is **Snagov Monastery** *(*Mănăstirea Snagov; open daylight hours; admission charge), housing just three monks on a tiny island in the northern part of the lake (hire a rowing boat from the jetty near Complexul Astoria on the lake's southern edge). It was founded in the 14th century by Mircea the Elder (1386–1418). Later Vlad Țepeș fortified it as a prison and torture chamber, building a defensive wall and a bridge from the shore.

The oldest surviving building is the church, built during the reign of Neagoe Basarab (1512–21) in a Mount Athos style. The original frescoes, dating from 1563, are particularly fine. Constantin Brâncoveanu enlarged the monastery and the famous publishing house he established here helped consolidate Snagov's reputation as a leading cultural centre.

Evidence to explain the exact circumstances of Vlad Țepeș' death and burial here is somewhat shaky. Accord-

ing to the best-known legend, he met his come-uppance in late 1476 or early 1477 following a conspiracy by a group of boyars loyal to Basarab Laiotă the Elder, the Ottomans' favoured candidate to succeed him. Decapitating Vlad in the woods near Snagov, the plotters sent his head as a gift to the sultan, who impaled it on a spike. The monks who found Vlad's body buried it in the church crypt, where it lies to this day under a simple tomb. Clearly Vlad left a good impression, for successive generations of monks erroneously claimed him as the monastery's founder.

The finest domestic example of the Brâncoveanu style, **Mogoșoaia Palace** ❷ (Palatul Mogoșoaiei; open Tues–Sun 10am–7pm, winter 9am–5pm; admission charge) serenely dominates a park on the edge of Lake Mogoșoaia, 14 km (8 miles) north of Bucharest. Built from 1692–1702, it shows a characteristic combination of traditional Wallachian elements with Byzantine, Baroque and Renaissance influences. The most distinctive exterior feature is a Venetian-style loggia; the interior was once richly decorated with stucco and murals depicting the princely family. Alas, soon after building the palace, Brâncoveanu fell out with the sultan, who deposed him and then imprisoned him with his four sons in Constantinople. Given the choice between all five converting to Islam or being beheaded, Brâncoveanu chose the latter. The Romanian Orthodox Church canonised them in 1992. The Turks subsequently converted Mogoșoaia into a *han* (inn) and it soon fell into disrepair.

However, in 1860, after the end of Ottoman rule and a propitious marriage to Zoe Brâncoveanu, last of her line, the palace became the property of the princely Bibescu family. Many of the building's most flamboyant touches show the hand of Princess Martha Bibescu (1889–1973), socialite, politician and writer of some famously raunchy novels. Mogoșoaia held some of Romania's most glittering parties. The palace **museum** has a valuable collection of pictures, sculptures, rare books and manuscripts. Outside, an unusual **sculpture park** features toppled statues of communist leaders, brought from around the country. ❏

Maps
on p114
& below

Casinos have become a feature of the Bucharest nightlife scene in recent years (see page 356).

BELOW:
Mogoșoaia Palace.

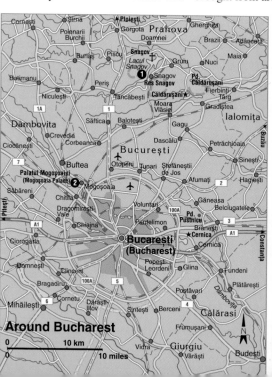

Around Bucharest

RESTAURANTS AND CAFÉS

Restaurants

Romanian

Casa Doina
Șos. Kiseleff 4
Tel: 021-222 3179
The oldest and most famous restaurant in the city. It serves classic Romanian dishes in a more refined and better-presented way than anywhere else, and prides itself on the standards of its service. A must for any visit to Bucharest, and great value. €€

Count Dracula
Spl. Independentei 8A
Tel: 021-312 1353
Good Romanian food at good prices on the embankment of the Dâmbovița River, but what people love about

this kitsch place is the Dracula chap who dims the lights halfway through your meal and does a round of the tables. €€€

La Taifas
Str. Gh. Manu 16
Tel: 021-212 7788
Modern versions of Romanian classic dishes in a great atmosphere, with live music of some sort – sometimes a band, sometimes just a girl on the cello – most evenings. Lively terrace in summer and great prices. €€

Rossetya
Str. Dimitrie Bolintineanu 9
Tel: 021-805 9199
Great Romanian food at knockdown prices close to the city centre. While

there are no surprises on the menu it is a treat and a rarity to find such refined versions of local classics, such as *mama-liga cu branză*. €€€

International

Arcade
Str. I. Cantacuzino 8
Tel: 021-260 2960
Outstanding contemporary European cuisine in a wonderful villa in the residential north of the city that attracts a smart crowd. The terrace is great in summer, and there's a nightly barbecue too. €€€€

Avalon
Calea Dorobantilor 5–7
(Howard Johnson Grand Plaza Hotel)
Tel: 021-201 5030
This place serves some of the most adventurous cusine in the city. Try the divine asparagus cappuccino and the duck blinis, then attempt to choose a dessert without drooling. €€€€€

Café & Terrace
Str. Franklin 12
Tel: 021-310 1017
The best-located terrace in Bucharest serves only average food at rather high prices, but there is nowhere better to enjoy the summer in the city than here. The service is often atrocious, however. €€€€

Casa di David
Downtown
Str. Lascar Catargiu 56
Tel: 021-317 4551
Wonderful modern European food served in a beautiful villa. The somewhat stiff prices make it popular with local poseurs. The terrace is great, however. €€€€€

Balthazar
Str. Dumbrava Rosie 2
Tel: 021-212 1460
The best restaurant in the city, and it knows it. This is where the Bucharest jetset eat, spending small fortunes on giant prawns in chilli sauce, warm foie gras with cranberries and some of the best wines ever produced. €€€€€

Barka Safron
Str. Av. Sănătescu 1
Tel: 021-224 1004
Relaxed atmosphere, indifferent service and decent-value fusion-esque food. It is the vibe and cocktails that people come for, though. €€€€

Bistro Atheneu
Str. Episcopiei 1–3 (Athenée Palace Hilton Hotel)
Tel: 021-313 4900
Great-value food chosen from a varied menu that is chalked up on a blackboard every day. There is always Transylvanian food, often something with lamb and plenty for vegetarians. €€€

LEFT: Bistro Atheneu at the Athenée Palace Hotel.

Cupola

Calea 13 Septembrie 90
(JW Marriott Grand Hotel)
Tel: 021-403 1903
Flagship fusion restaurant of the JW Marriott, a wonder of invention and taste sensations. You may not expect to find new flavours in Bucharest, but here you can. Prices are high. €€€€€

Esperanto

Str. Eremia Grigorescu 17
Tel: 021-211 3646
Fashionably tatty kind of place. The owner is also the chef and he knows his stuff: expect no more than four dishes on the menu at any one time: all will be adventurous and good. €€€€

La Mandragora

Str. Mendeleev 29
Tel: 021-319 7592
Expensive and pretentious it may be but there is no faulting the fantastic fusion cuisine. The great location makes it very popular. €€€€€

American

Champions

Calea 13 Septembrie 90 (JW Marriott Grand Hotel)
Tel: 021-403 1917
Great burgers and ribs in enormous portions at rather high prices. The 30 screens showing live sports ensure that you will never miss a kick. €€€€

French

La Provence

Str. Barbu Vacarescu (Fosta Baza Cutezatorii)
Tel: 021-243 1777
Wonderful, exclusive Parisian eatery in the grounds of the wonderful, exclusive Bucharest Tennis Club. Two French chefs keep standards high, making the astronomical prices entirely justifiable. €€€€€

La Villa

Str. Al. Constantinescu 65
Tel: 021-224 1505
Cheaper than you would think, this French restaurant retains a charm and elegance difficult to find elsewhere in Romania. Excellent wine list. €€€€

German

Die Deutsche Kneipe

Str. Stockholm 9
Tel: 0722-284560
Tiny little *kneipe* where bratwurst and sauerkraut are served in enormous portions. All the sausages are made on the premises by the German couple who own the place. Closed Sundays. €€

Hungarian

Kiraly Csarda

Calea Dorobantilor 177
Tel: 021-230 4083
Decent Hungarian food and wine, including the dessert wine Aszu, in a lovely two-level villa on the smartest street in Bucharest. The best tables are upstairs. €€€

St. George

Str. Franceză 44
Tel: 021-317 1087
The best Hungarian restaurant in the country. Nowhere comes close to matching the various goulash soups served here, nor the selection of Aszu and Tokay wines. Super terrace in summer. €€€€

Italian

Byblos

Str. N. Golescu 14–16
Tel: 021-313 2091
Great Italian restaurant (not a pizza in site) with a decent selection of seafood dishes and a wine list to die for. Not as pricey as its reputation suggests. €€€

Roberto's

Str. Episcopiei 1–3 (Athenée Palace Hilton Hotel)
Tel: 021-303 37 77
Changes its menu every month to offer the cuisine of just one region of Italy at a time. A high-quality experience. €€€€

Japanese

Benihana

Calea Dorobantilor 5–7
(Howard Johnson Grand Plaza Hotel)
Tel: 021-201 5030
Benihana is the only real Japanese deal in the city. You can enjoy tepanyaki cuisine every evening, with sushi available all day. It all costs a small fortune. €€€€€

South American

Churrascaria Carnivore

Str. Garlei 1
Tel: 021-233 5555
Probably the best steak in the city at this meat-fest of a restaurant out in the Baneasa woods (you will need to take a taxi here). €€€€

Thai

Thai Moods

Str. Petre Crețu 63
Tel: 021-224 6851
Using only the finest, mainly imported, ingredients, how this place keeps quality so high and prices so low is a mystery. Gorgeous garden at the back. €€€€

Cafés

Amsterdam Grand Café

Str. Covaci 6
Tel: 021-313 7580
This was the place that kick-started the Lipscani revolution. Still as good as new, the place oozes class, simple but decent food and is everything to everyone, be it pub, café or restaurant. €€€

Caffe & Latte

B-dul. Schitu Măgureanu 35
Tel: 021-314 3834
Italian trattoria and coffee house opposite Cișmigiu Gardens. Small and friendly, it is always busy with regulars. €€

Festival 39

Str. Franceza 64 (Entrance on Piata Unirii)
Good café with great views of Piata Unirii. The terrace is tempting in summer but it is close to one of the city's very busiest roads. €€€

PRICE CATEGORIES

Price categories are per person for a three-course meal with wine:
€ = under 30 lei
€€ = 30–45 lei
€€€ = 45–60 lei
€€€€ = 60–75 lei
€€€€€ = over 75 lei

WALLACHIA

With large expanses of featureless plain stretching south to the Danube, most of the interest in Wallachia is in its northern third, where historic monasteries shelter in the Carpathian foothills

Wallachia is the Romanian homeland, its name derived from the word *vlach,* the old term for ethnic Romanians. This region forms the southern third of the country, and is traditionally divided into two by the Olt River: Muntenia to the east and Oltenia to the west.

Not a priority on most visitor's itineraries, Wallachia lacks the natural drama of the lands further north, although there are still some places of interest, particularly in the northern parts: Curtea de Arges is a delightful town, from where the Arges Valley leads up into the mountains and Transylvania. Further west are the magnificent monasteries of Cozia and Horezu. It should be noted that the mountain resort of Sinaia is in Wallachia, but is included in the Transylvania section because of its proximity to Brasov, that region's largest city. Few tourists venture south into the largely featureless flatlands that run all the way to the Danube and the Bulgarian border.

Ploieşti

Many people skip through **Ploieşti** ❶ (pop. 227,000; www.ploiesti.ro), a major railway and road junction, en route to the more enticing resort towns of the nearby Prahova Valley, which is understandable but not entirely fair: Ploieşti may be humdrum, but there are a couple of sights of interest.

The town started life when Michael the Brave established his court here in 1597. It then continued to flourish quietly and unspectacularly, thanks to its strategic location on important trading routes. In the second half of the 19th century its fortunes were to improve drastically with the discovery of oil. Romania claims to have the world's oldest petroleum industry, dating back to 1857, and Ploieşti was to become one of the globe's top oil extraction and refinery centres.

An earthquake took a heavy toll in 1940, and then later in World War II the region became Nazi Germany's

Map on pages 136-7

LEFT: the wide-open spaces of southern Wallachia, Romania's great plain.
BELOW: miner from the Jiu Valley.

The Moreni-Prahova oilfield at Ploieşti in its 1930s heyday (the first oil was extracted here back in 1857). Oil production remains important to the economy.

main source of oil. At first it escaped bombing by the Allies because it was out of range of their bombers. However, by 1943 this was no longer the case, and the city underwent massive aerial bombardment from the USAF.

In the postwar years the oilfields were speedily nationalised and received massive state investment. Since 1989, the investment has come from foreign companies, including Lukoil, BAT, Unilever, Coca-Cola and Interbrew, which has helped to compensate for the long-term decline in oil production. Four refineries remain in use.

The **National Petroleum Museum** (Muzeul Naţional al Petrolului; Str. Dr Bagdasar 8; open Tues–Sun 9am–5pm; admission charge) is one of those places it just seems rude not to visit. It is Romania's only such museum and one of only a few in the world. As your guide will tell you, this one is the best. While the collection could definitely do with a make-over, the hugely enthusiastic guide goes a long way towards bringing the exhibits to life. Tracing the history of oil extraction from ancient times, it

has a weird and wonderful array of exhibits with captions you probably wouldn't understand even if they were translated into English. There's a particular focus on World War II and the bombardment.

Another collection unique in Romania, the delightful **Nicolae Simache Clock Museum** (Muzeul Ceasului Nicolae Simache; open Tues–Sun 9am–5pm; admission charge) is perhaps a more surprising find. In a 19th-century historical monument, it contains about 4,000 horological treasures, guarded by soldiers. Exhibits include not only clocks but watches, pianolas, symphonions and musical boxes. If you ask the staff nicely they will demonstrate some of the cuckoo clocks and musical items for you.

In the **old town** around the Clock Museum, look out for some unexpectedly lovely, if crumbling, old villas – many occupied by multiple Gypsy families.

Câmpina

Thirty-two km (49 miles) north along the main Braşov road – past a flock of

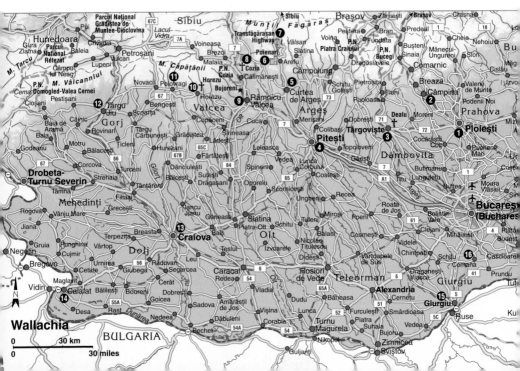

Map
below

giant metal woodpeckers better known as oil derricks – **Câmpina** ❷ (pop. 38,000; www.primariacampina.ro) is another petroleum town. It also has one of Romania's most unusual monuments – **Haşdeu Castle** (Castelul Haşdeu; B-dul. Carol I 199; open Tues–Sun 9am–5pm; admission charge), 1.5 km (1 mile) north of the centre.

Bogdan Petriceicu Haşdeu (1838–1907) was a leading scientist and writer. In 1888, his 19-year-old daughter Iulia, one of the first women to study at the Sorbonne, died of tuberculosis. Devastated by her death, he increasingly turned to spiritualism, communicating with his daughter through séances. As a result, he decided in 1893 to build this stone, wood and iron castle as a temple to her, according to plans he believed were passed on to him from beyond the grave. The project was blessed by the Bishop of Argeş, and Haşdeu lived here from 1897 until his death, withdrawn from the outside world and communicating to Iulia in a language no-one else understood.

As well as an altar to Iulia, the museum contains photographs, paintings and furniture belonging to the family. The interior frescoes and marble mouldings are particularly fine. While foreigners may see the project as bizarre, even creepy, Romanians revere it as a celebration of spirituality and fatherly love.

Along the same road, the **Nicolae Grigorescu Memorial Museum** (Muzeul Memorial Nicolae Grigorescu; B-dul. Carol I 108; open May–Aug Tues–Sun 10am–6pm, Sept–Apr 9am–5pm; admission charge) commemorates one of Romania's best-loved artists. Grigorescu *(see page 77)* adapted Impressionism to Romanian themes, and became known as the father of modern Romanian painting. The great man spent the last three years of his life in this house, choosing the location for its clean air and fine views. There is a small collection of his paintings and sketches, as well as some personal belongings. Although Câmpina's air is no longer the cleanest, the views of the Prahova Valley remain superb.

Târgovişte

Although clearly touched by the communist era, **Târgovişte** ❸ (pop. 88,000; www.pmtgv.ro) retains its pretty old town and has more than its fair share of monuments.

In 1396 Mircea the Elder moved Wallachia's capital here from Curtea de Argeş, a status it held until Constantin Brâncoveanu's time, when the court shifted between Târgovişte in summer and Bucharest in winter. After Brâncoveanu's death in 1714, Bucharest became the sole capital and Târgovişte's decline began.

Midway between Ploieşti and Piteşti in the Carpathian foothills, Târgovişte and the surrounding county became heavily industrialised in the communist period. However, local authorities and businesses have now started latching onto the potential of tourism. The Dracula connection *(see page 200)*

The Salt Mountain (Muntele de Sare) at Slănic Prahova, 30 km (18 miles) north of Ploieşti has been created by five centuries of salt mining in the area. The mine is open to the public, and is used for treating respiratory ailments as at Praid salt mine in Transylvania (see page 224).

Uniforms at the Romanian National Police Museum in Ploieşti.

BELOW: an old wall drawing of Vlad Tepeş.

does no harm, of course. On Christmas Day 1989 Târgovişte hit the world's headlines when Romania's modern-day Dracula – Nicolae Ceauşescu – and his wife Elena were executed at the military barracks here after a kangaroo-court hearing.

A walk along Calea Domnească from the centre is a good start. Lined with glorious old villas sporting flower-filled window boxes, and old ladies sitting doing their knitting in the doorways, it seems largely unscathed by the communist era. It also has many of Târgovişte's main attractions.

At the first left, **Stelea Monastery** (Mănăstirea Stelea; Str. Stelea 6) is an impressive complex of buildings for a community of only six monks. Built in 1582 on the orders of Stelea, commander-in-chief of the *voievode*'s court, it was rebuilt in 1645. Nine years later it suffered fire damage and was not repaired until the 1940s, when it became a parish church. It reopened as a monastery in 1993 and is now undergoing further restoration.

Behind the (closed) Art Museum, the **Romanian National Police Museum** (Muzeul Naţional al Poliţiei Român; Calea Domnească 187; open Tues–Sun 9am–5pm; admission charge) is – like Ploieşti's Petroleum Museum – one of those places you feel you have to visit. The collection starts off with various Ottoman torture implements from the 18th century and goes up to the present day. Unlike most Romanian museums, this one covers the communist era. Perhaps the highlight is the room full of mothballed police uniforms and helmets donated from forces worldwide.

Visiting the nearby **History Museum** (Muzeul de Istorie; Calea Domnească 233; open Tues–Sun 9am–5pm, until 6pm in summer; admission charge) is a somewhat depressing experience, unless you enjoy having the attendant follow you around turning the light on and off in each room you pass through.

Further up the road, the **Princely Court** (Curtea Domnească; Str. Justiţiei 7; open Tues–Sun 9am–7pm; admission and photo charges) was Wallachia's royal seat of power for three centuries. Today it is one of Romania's best-preserved such com-

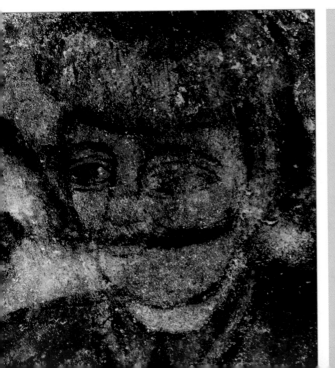

The Lad Tepeş

Vlad Ţepeş was just 11 years old when he and his younger brother Radu Mircea were removed from the court at Targovişte to become hostages of the Ottomans. During the five years they were held captive, they witnessed at first hand the everyday use of terror. While Radu – whose angelic looks gave rise to the epithet Radu the Handsome – agreed to convert to Islam, Vlad refused to renounce Christianity and was repeatedly whipped as punishment. He had much to fear, as other hostages had been blinded with red-hot pokers. It was an experience which left him brutalised and bent on revenge. After Wallachian boyars murdered his father and elder brother Mircea, he briefly became ruler in 1448, only to be ousted by János Hunyadi; he returned to power from 1456.

Map on pages 136-7

plexes. As you enter, the stone building on the right is the **Great Princely Church** (Biserica Mare Domnească), founded by Petru Cercel in the late 16th century, when it was Wallachia's largest religious building. The original paintings inside date from 1696–98. Next on the right there are some ruins linked with rickety metal walkways, which children love using as an adventure playground.

The tallest part of the Princely Court is the well-preserved **Chindia Tower** (Turnul Chindia). It was constructed in the late 15th century, probably by Vlad Ţepeş. A narrow spiral staircase (121 steps) leads to the top, with various items relating to Ţepeş on the three landings. From the top there are excellent views over the town and a close-up view of the roof of the church, which resembles lizard skin.

North of the Princely Court, **Chindia Zoo** (Parcul Zoo Botanic Chindia) is the sort of place that makes one think of setting up a Romanian chapter of the Animal Liberation Front. The plants are better looked after than the animals.

Four km (2½ miles) east of Târgovişte, **Dealu Monastery** (Mănăstirea Dealu; Viforâţa village; open daily 10am–6pm) was founded by Radu the Great in 1501. It contains paintings by one of Romania's most celebrated religious artists, Dobromir of Târgovişte, and also houses six royal tombs. It is the site of one of the country's first printing presses for the production of religious texts, which went into operation in the early 16th century. The collection of old religious works is particularly valuable.

Piteşti

An industrial city perhaps best known for its car factory and linked to Bucharest by one of Romania's two existing motorways, **Piteşti ④** (pop. 167,000; www.primariapitesti.ro) is a surprisingly lively and pleasant place to visit.

On Strada Victoriei, more a town square than a street, the **Princely Church** (Biserica Domnească; free) was built in 1656 by Constantin Şerban and his wife Bălaşa. Saturday is a good time to visit, as every wedding

The Dacia car plant at Piteşti was built in 1968, and until the advent of the Logan model in 2004 all of the cars it produced were based on 1960s and 1970s Renault designs. Until very recently, these ageing throwbacks were just about the only cars on the road in Romania.

BELOW: much of Romania's industry is in need of modernisation, but the sector still contributes around 30 percent of national GDP.

Hats off to the Piteşti city authorities for transforming what was a somewhat grim centru civic *area into a pleasant place to while away a few hours. Post-communist public art includes three curious water installations, one with giant rotating yellow blades. All look like works by Brâncuşi – but aren't.*

BELOW: the Piteşti Experiment Monument Complex.

party in town poses for photos outside.

The **County Museum** (Muzeul Judeţean Argeş; Str. Armand Călinescu 44; open Tues–Sun 10am–6pm; admission charge) has an unedifying collection of stuffed beasts on the ground floor. The history section upstairs claims to have the original of the first document written in Romanian (1521), but as it's sellotaped to a window the claim seems unlikely.

Romanians seem reluctant to commemorate the bad aspects of communist days. Few history museums, for instance, seem to have any idea how to deal with anything happening after King Michael's abdication in 1947. The **Piteşti Experiment Monument Complex** (Complexul Monumental Experimentul Piteşti; Str. Negru Vodă), north of the centre, is a poignant exception. While the location – surrounded by apartment blocks – may seem strangely inconspicuous, it marks the site of a former political prisoners' camp, of which nothing remains. Although there were detention camps throughout Romania, only a few such monuments exist.

The monument has four parts. From the left, the first is a big upright block of white stone, partly chipped off, symbolising heavy labour. The second is a simple white marble cross with an inscription in memory of those political prisoners who died from 1949–52. An incomplete list of names ends "and others". Second from right there's a more complex monument, with a mosaic depicting a prisoner reaching upwards for freedom. A white diagonal cross protrudes slightly at the right. The inscription commemorates all the victims of the communist dictatorship who died in prison. Last in the quartet, is a free-standing wall, an eloquent encapsulation of the prison experience. It has a miniature guard tower, barbed wire, barred windows and a heavy door with many bolts and locks.

A map shows the locations of political detention camps around Romania. There's also a plaque explaining that, in the absence of a museum dedicated to the Piteşti Experiment, this complex will have to suffice.

Curtea de Argeş

When Queen Marie visited **Curtea de Argeş** ❺ (pop. 32,000; www.primaria-curtea-de-arges.ro) in October 1914, she wrote: "When I arrived in Curtea de Argeş together with my daughters, everything was brilliant. Never have I seen anything more beautiful, there was a background of golden yellow birds, gentle blue hills and above the brilliant sky, without clouds, a blaze of azure."

The years have changed Curtea de Argeş since then but it remains one of Wallachia's most beautiful and verdant cities. It's a fine base for exploring the Argeş Valley or just taking in its superb views. With the definite air of a mountain resort on the up, it's a bit like Sinaia *(see page 193)* but without all the tourists. It also, like Sinaia, has impeccable royal connections. Were every town in Wallachia like this, it would give Transylvania a run for its money. Although it has the inevitable low-rise horror here and there, Curtea

Map on pages 136-7

de Argeș has survived the Ceaușescu period less visually battered than most places. Located at the end of a branch line from Pitești served only by *personal* (ie very slow) trains, it does, though, feel a bit out on a limb.

Originally built by the *voievode* Seneslau during the 13th century, the **Princely Court** (Curtea Domnească de la Argeș; open daily 10am–6pm; admission charge) was the Wallachian rulers' first capital. Early in the 14th century Basarab I (1330–52) founded the Princely Church, while a palace and house were 16th-century additions. Built from river stones in the shape of an inscribed Greek cross, the church retains some original paintings from the 14th century, remarkably vibrant despite the gloominess of their surroundings. Some fragments of frescoes also remain from the 16th and 19th centuries. Despite various restorations, little else remains to be seen in the farmyard-like grounds. Most of the ruins are a little above ground level or a few metres below.

Opposite, the **Municipal Museum** (Muzeul Municipal; Str. Negru Vodă 2; open Tues–Sun 9am–4pm; admission charge) has the usual collection labelled in Romanian only and more or less stopping at 1947. Dracula fans may be interested in Vlad Țepeș's coat of arms.

Curtea de Argeș Monastery (Mănăstirea Curtea de Argeș; B-dul. Basarabilor 1; open daily 8am–7pm; admission charge) is one of Romania's finest religious ensembles, perfectly set off in a glorious French-style park. As well as being a major Orthodox pilgrimage site and the Bishop of Argeș 's seat, it houses the royal crypt.

Built by Neagoe Basarab (of the important Wallachian noble family who gave their name to Bessarabia) from 1512–17, the monastery was intended to show the world how cultured, rich and powerful he was. It clearly had the intended effect, because the Patriarch of Constantinople himself attended the opening in 1517 and observers compared it favourably with the greatest monasteries of the age. It was later restored under Matei Basarab (1632–54) and later by French architect Jean Lecomte de Noüy (1842–1923).

While not enormous, the monastery overwhelms visitors with the intricacy and quality of the stone sculptures. Designed like several layers of the cakes you find in Romanian patisseries, the exterior shows a use of colour, abstract geometrical patterns and almost indecipherable calligraphy that show a clear Oriental influence.

Inside, the hand of Lecomte de Noüy, famous for his fake-Moorish taste, is apparent. Some columns are decorated with giant geometrical floral motifs while others are gilded and twisted like barley sugar. Everywhere gold and bright colours predominate. Behind the altar the stained-glass window could almost be a neon sign in Piccadilly Circus. Some would call the décor exuberant, others would say gaudy.

The monastery complex is also rich in royal symbolism. It contains the graves of Neagoe Basarab, Radu of Afumați, kings Carol I and Ferdinand

Matei Basarab, voievode of Wallachia 1632–54. An enlightened ruler, he has been compared to Moldavia's famous Ștefan cel Mare.

BELOW: Queen Marie and her daughters were enchanted by Curtea de Argeș.

Manole's Well. As the story goes, Neagoe Basarab removed the scaffolding from the church Manole was working on so that he could not repeat anything so splendid. Manole attempted to escape using makeshift wings, but crashed to the earth. A spring then emerged from the ground.

BELOW: Curtea de Argeș Monastery.

and queens Elizabeth and Marie, an inscription on the last recording her birth at Eastwell, England. The enormous 12-candled candelabra in the *pronaos* (the inner portico) and even bigger one in the naos resemble crowns, while smaller candelabra in the church look like doffed boyars' caps. Facing the altar, two royal thrones sit empty, awaiting a restoration of the monarchy.

Laid out by de Noüy's brother, the lovingly tended gardens are a work of art in themselves. The urge to sit down on one of the benches and write a postcard should not be resisted.

Other buildings include the ivy-clad Bishop's Palace – surely one of Romania's best occupational perks – and a more recent cathedral. If you ever wondered how the Romanian Orthodox Church finds the money to build so many new churches, just watch the speed at which it sells religious trinkets to punters here.

Walk 100 metres/yds downhill from the monastery, past an almost Celtic-looking statue of Neagoe Basarab. Set in yet another park, **Manole's Well** (Fântâna Mesterului Manole) commemorates the spot where the legendary craftsman Manole – hero of many a ballad – met his end *(see margin, left)*. Drinking from the water fountain on the site requires some dexterity.

The Argeș Valley

Twenty-five kilometres (15 miles) north of Curtea de Argeș, on a crest above the village of Arefu, the real Dracula's castle awaits the determined and the fit. Unlike Bran *(see page 191)*, **Poienari Castle ❻** (Cetetea Poienari; open daily 9am–5pm; admission and photography charge) isn't particularly accessible and is largely ruined, thanks partly to a mudslide in 1888. On the other hand, the sense of achievement and – dare one say – smugness, in being one of the few to see it is hard to beat. The views over the Argeș Valley from the castle are another reward.

The structure originally dates back to the early Basarab rulers in the 14th century, who chose the location because it was at the top of an impregnable mountain guarding the Argeș River gorge. Vlad Țepeș subsequently rebuilt it, using material from an older castle in the nearby village. According to legend he made the local nobles carry the building materials in punishment for their disloyalty, but when the Turks besieged Poienari in 1462, Vlad escaped with the help of Arefu villagers: following an old woman's advice, he left a false trail by fleeing on a horse shod back-to-front (making the Turks think the horse was going in the opposite direction).

At Arefu's northern edge, a sign indicates whether the **Transfăgărașan Highway ❼** to the Făgăraș Mountains in Transylvania is open or not – usually not. Peaking at 2,042 metres (6,700 ft), it is usually only fully open from July to early September. This amazing route is Romania's highest, and runs between the country's two loftiest peaks, Moldoveanu (2,544 metres/8,346 ft) and Negoiu (2,535 metres/8,316 ft). Ceaușescu was obsessed with building

it because, following the Soviet invasion of Czechoslovakia in 1968, he was afraid the same might happen to Romania – the idea being that the Transfăgărașan would allow the Romanian army to cross the Carpathians quickly and repel an attack from the north. The highway was built in under five years and cost at least 38 soldiers their lives.

Above Arefu, the road winds past Vidraru Lake into the high mountains There is no pass as such, just a short tunnel at the top; once through onto the northern side, the change in scenery is dramatic (the approach from the north is far steeper). It's best to allow at least five hours to drive from Curtea de Argeș to Sibiu, but an entire day if you want to stop and fully appreciate the scenery.

Along the Olt to Cozia

While the Transfăgărașan Highway follows the Arges Valley into the mountains, further west the larger River Olt carves a broader and more accessible route into Transylvania. Three kilometres (2 miles) north of Călimănești, midway along the main road between Pitești and Sibiu, the 14th-century **Cozia Monastery** ❽ (Mănăstirea Cozia; open daily 8am–6pm; admission charge) marks the beginning of the Byzantine style in Romania. A model of harmonious proportions, the main church, founded by Mircea the Elder from 1386–88, is richly decorated with frescoes going back to 1390, some still in good condition. The oldest are in the *naos* (inner chamber) and depict Mircea the Elder and his son, also called Mircea. Alongside these there's a later portrait of Șerban Cantacuzino, who restored and enlarged the monastery from 1706–7. Mircea the Elder is buried in the pronaos alongside Mother Teofana, who took holy orders after the death of her son, Michael the Brave. The **museum** (no fixed hours; admission charge) has a valuable collection of books including an epitaph from 1396. The monastery has a community of 30 monks.

West to Horezu and Târgu Jiu

The undistinguished town of **Râmnicu Vâlcea** ❾ lies on the western banks of the River Olt, marking the border

Map on pages 136-7

Forced into exile in 1940, King Carol II, eventually settled in Portugal. He died in 1953, but it was 50 years before his remains returned to Romania, alongside those of his third wife – and former mistress – Princess Elena. They were buried in the grounds of Curtea de Argeș Monastery, but outside the cathedral that is the usual royal burial site. His estranged son, King Michael, attended neither funeral.

BELOW: the ruins of Poienari Castle.

Turnul Roşu, the Red Tower, at the mountain pass of the same name. Situated by the River Olt, the tower marks the traditional border between Wallachia and Transylvania.

BELOW: ascending the Transfăgărașan Highway.

between the two halves of Wallachia. Just to the north, the **Bujoreni Open-air Museum** (open Tues–Sun 10am–6pm; admission charge) is, however, well worth a visit. The complex recreates a typical village from the region with various structures dating from the 18th to early 20th century.

From Râmnicu, Route 67 twists and turns its way across 100 km (60 miles) of Oltenian foothills to reach Târgu Jiu. With the mighty Carpathians just to the north, this is one of the most scenic and unspoilt routes in Wallachia. All you see along the road are mountains, trees, small farms and cottages, and horse-drawn carts.

Around a third of the way to Târgu Jiu is the town of **Horezu** ⓾, renowned for its pottery, which comes in a panoply of different colours and styles. With its breezy hill-top location and range of accommodation, Horezu makes a fine base for exploring rural Wallachia at its most picturesque.

There are plenty of tranquil villages along the main road, many with trails over the Carpathians into Transylvania, used mainly by shepherds and cowherds. For less hardcore hikers who prefer their creature comforts, there are plenty of small hotels and restaurants as well as a burgeoning agrotourism industry. Look for signs along the main road offering rooms (*cazare* or *camer*).

The main attraction, however is **Horezu Monastery** (Mănăstirea Horezu, 3 km (2 miles) north of Horezu near the village of Români de Sus; open daylight hours; admission charge). It's a masterpiece of the Brâncoveanu style and it doesn't take an art historian to see why it is on the UNESCO World Heritage List. With its breathtaking mountainous setting, Horezu is simply one of the most serene monasteries in Romania. Even the most unspiritual may feel just a little bit closer to God here. And you'll probably have it more or less to yourself – except for the 60 nuns who live there, of course. If you find it hard to tear yourself away from all this tranquillity, overnight accommodation is available. Although simple, the rooms were good enough for the Prince of Wales to spend a night here in 2005 on a private visit.

Built from 1690–97 by Constantin

Brâncoveanu, Horezu was originally intended to be a necropolis for himself and his family, but it was never to be. In 1714, Brâncoveanu was beheaded in Constantinople on treason charges, together with his four sons.

With a sublime sense of proportion and extraordinary sculptural detail, it is widely considered to be the finest and most complex example of the architectural style he created. The original paintings inside, of religious scenes as well as portraits of the Brâncoveanus, Basarabs and Cantacuzinos, are also of exceptional quality.

Just east of Horezu, 2 km (1¼ miles) north of the main road, the village of **Costeşti** hosts the colourful **Roma Festival** (first week in September). Four km (2½ miles) further north, **Bistriţa Monastery** (Mănăstirea Bistriţa; accommodation available; *note there is another Bistriţa Monastery in Moldavia, see page 298*) was the site of Wallachia's first printing press. The oldest church and the hospital date from 1520–21. The paintings inside the church are the work of renowned Romanian artist Gheorghe Tăttărescu.

A vertiginous path from the monastery leads to **Bistriţa Cave** (Peştera Bistriţa), containing two chapels.

You won't have to look hard to find Horezu pottery. There are stalls outside people's houses as well as a big Ceramica shop opposite the bus station. The road leading up to the monastery is another place to find pottery stalls.

North of the village of **Polovragi** ⓫, 20 km (12 miles) west of Horezu, a forestry road leads to **Polovragi Monastery** (Mănăstirea Polovragi). The small monastery dates back to at least 1505 and was renovated under Constantin Brâncoveanu. The *bolniţă* (hospital) church, from 1736, preserves many outstanding original frescoes. Further on, **Polovragi Cave** (Peştera Polovragi; guided tours daily 9am–5pm; admission charge) was, according to legend, home of the Dacian god Zamoixes and is famous for its stalactites, supposedly formed by his tears after the Roman conquest.

Târgu Jiu

Târgu Jiu ⓬ (pop. 97,000; www.targu jiu.ro) is a major educational centre

Map on pages 136-7

According to legend the name Horezu derives from the word huhurezi (owls), because the builders worked only at night for fear of the Ottomans. A more mundane theory is that the region was particularly abundant in owls at the time.

BELOW: donations in the well at Cozia Monastery.

BELOW: Brâncuşi's *Endless Column.*

and home to Romania's best-known sculptural ensemble, the work of the internationally famous Constantin Brâncuşi, who was born in the nearby village of Hobiţa in 1876.

Sadly, the small **Art Museum** (Muzeul de Artă; open Tues–Sun 9am–8pm; admission and photography charge) at the north of Brâncuşi Park contains nothing by the great man. It does, however, have some rather fun wooden statues in Native American style by Rodica Popescu (1932–67), including totem poles, which make it worth a visit.

The sculpture outside by Tatsumi Sakai, with two blocks hollowed out into the shapes of female breasts and waist, is just one of many homages to Brâncuşi throughout the town. Another – *Homage to Constantin Brâncuşi* – by Gheorghe Iliescu-Călineşti lies within the museum.

The history section of the **Alexandru Ştefulescu County Museum** (Muzeul Judeţean Alexandru Ştefulescu; Str. Geneva 8; open Tues–Sun 9am–5pm; admission and photography charge) has a particularly good collec-

tion in the first room, including palaeolithic finds from two caves at nearby Baia de Fier. The Cotofeni culture (who?) is also well represented here. More recent items include a petrified chainmail shirt from the Geto-Dacian era and the remains of a Roman underground heating system. One room is dedicated to local hero Tudor Vladimirescu *(see page 27)*. Another covers Târgu Jiu's role in World War I. The final room has photographs of the restoration of the Brâncuşi Ensemble *(see panel, below)*.

Three km (2 miles) north of the centre, the **Ecaterina Teodoroiu House Museum** (Casa Memorială Ecaterina Teodoroiu; B-dul. Ecaterina Teodoroiu 270; open Wed–Sun 8am–4pm; admission charge) commemorates the World War I soldier's birthplace. Befitting her national heroine status, her burial place is in a more prominent location, right outside the prefecture. Fringed with bas-reliefs depicting her bravery, the 1936 **Ecaterina Teodoroiu Mausoleum** (Mausoleul Ecaterinei Teodoroiu) is the work of Miliţa Petraşcu, a pupil of Brâncuşi's in Paris.

The Brâncuşi Ensemble

Constantin Brâncuşi (1876–1957; *see also page 77)* is widely regarded as a founding father, even *the* father, of modernism in sculpture, and while many of his works grace leading museums, or exchange hands for astronomical prices, his most famous ensemble is outdoors in Târgu Jiu. Commissioned as a tribute to Romania's World War I heroes, it dates from the late 1930s, was restored from 1998–2000, and comprises several works laid out in parks at opposite ends of Calea Eroilor (Heroes' Road), traversing the town centre. At the eastern end, the 29m-tall Endless Column *(Coloana Infinitului* or *Coloana fără Sfârşit)* is a shimmering stack of 17 cast-iron rhomboids seemingly tapering into infinity. At the other end, the *Gate of the Kiss (Poarta Sarutului)* heralds the entrance to Brâncuşi Park (Parcul Brâncuşi), leading to a pathway lined by the *Alley of Chairs (Aleea Scaunelor)* to the *Table of Silence (Masa Tăcerii)*.

While in a characteristically stylised Brâncuşi form, the pieces also pay homage to local architectural motifs such as funerary pillars. Although the communist authorities mooted destroying the ensemble as a symbol of bourgeois art, and scarred the Heroes' Road with some architectural horrors, the local authorities have now redressed matters by planting Brâncuşi-inspired sculptures all around Târgu Jiu.

The area around Târgu Jiu is rather bleak and short of obvious tourist appeal – the Jiu Valley is Romania's major coal-mining centre. The communist regime lauded the Jiu miners as proletarian heroes. In the early 1990s Iliescu relied on them as bully boys to intimidate the opposition, mobilising thousands of them on special trains to Bucharest to break up student protests.

Craiova

At first sight **Craiova** ⑬ (pop. 304,000; www.primariacraiova.ro) isn't the easiest city to like. Not so much scarred as mutilated by some of the most brutalist architecture imaginable, and in the midst of the vast dusty plain that extends right across southern Wallachia, Craiova is not near the top of many people's must-see lists. With endless rows of identical high-rise horrors flanking what appears to be an urban motorway, Craiova would win few awards for town planning. As pedestrian-friendly as a Formula I race track for most of the day, its centre is eerily quiet at night.

Thanks to its heavy industry, this is a city you smell before you see it. You name the industry, Craiova probably has it. The most famous, the gigantic Electroputere factory, has since 1941 been the main supplier of electric locomotives for Romanian railways, also exporting to Bulgaria, Poland and China. Unfortunately for train buffs, its steam-engine repair unit is closed to visitors. Although Romanian steam trains have enjoyed a revival thanks to enthusiasts, and operate on special tourist routes –visit www.turismferoviar.ro for details – they no longer operate on regular railways (you sometimes see retired ones in sidings).

But it's not all about rusting industry and disastrous town planning: Craiova had an important part in Romanian history. Because of its strategic location at the crossroads between the Carpathians, the Black Sea and the Danube, the region has been on important trading routes for millennia. As a visit to the **History Museum** (Muzeul de Arheologie si Istorie; Str. Madona Dudu 44; open Tues–Sun 9am–5pm; admission charge) will confirm, one of the earliest south European civilisations of

Map on pages 136-7

MAI MULT CARBUNI
MAI MULT FIER...
MAI MULTE TRACTOA

The Jiu Valley miners were glorified in communist propaganda.

BELOW: the Brâncuși Museum at Hobița, the town of his birth near Târgu Jiu.

Craiova's University is one of the country's premier educational institutions.

BELOW: most of Romania's steam trains were built at Craiova; some still function.

Neolithic times was in the region. The nearby camp of Pelendava was one of the most important Dacian-Getic settlements in the area, falling to the Romans in AD 102. More recently, Craiova had pride of place among Wallachian towns as seat of its first king, Michael the Brave. The city also has one of Romania's largest universities.

Perhaps Craiova's main attraction is the **Art Museum** (Muzeul de Artă; Calea Unirii 15; open Tues–Sat 10am–5pm, Sun 9am–5pm; admission charge). It is housed in a magnificent palace dating from 1900, which originally served as the seat of nobleman Constantin Mihail and his family. It is in the eclectic French Academic style then hugely fashionable among Romania's upper classes. The French architect, Paul Gottereau, was also responsible for Bucharest's Royal Palace.

Alas, Mihail Palace wasn't to remain a family house for long. When his line died out with him in 1936, Constantin's son Jean left the palace to the state. Subsequently, at various times King Carol I, President Ignacy Moscicki of Poland and Marshall Tito briefly lived here. In World War II it was the site of the signing of two peace treaties – between Romania and Bulgaria in 1940 and Bulgaria and Yugoslavia in 1944.

In 1954 the palace became Craiova's art museum, and today houses one of Romania's largest art collections. The genesis of the collection goes back to 1908, when a body of paintings and sculptures was bequeathed to the city by local art collectors and philanthropists Alexandru and Aristia Aman.

The building is worth visiting just to marvel at the sumptous, silk-lined interior, especially the ground-floor hall decorated with gold ornaments, Venetian mirrors and crystal candelabra. The Carrara marble staircase is another indication that Constantin Mihail was then high on Romania's rich list.

The art collection is divided into Romanian and foreign sections. In the first, seven sculptures by Brâncuși, including *The Kiss* (Sărutul), are the main draw. There are also works by Nicolae Grigorescu, Gheorghe Tăttărescu and Theodor Aman, Stefan Luchian, Nicolae Tonitza and others. The foreign art section has 17th-century paintings from the Dutch, Flemish, French and Italian schools.

Another escape from Craiova's general grimness is **Bănia's House** (Casa Băniei; Str. Matei Basarab 14; open Tues–Sun 9am–5pm; admission charge), housing the ethnography museum. Built by Constantin Brâncoveanu in 1699, it is Craiova's oldest domestic building and one of Romania's oldest houses.

St Dumitru Cathedral (Catedrala Sfântu Dumitru; Str. Matei Basarab) was founded by Matei Basarab in 1652 but largely destroyed in the 1840 earthquake. Subsequently rebuilt in 1889 by Lecomte de Noüy, it shimmers with one of his characteristically exuberant gilded interiors.

The **old town** is in the vicinity. While you're here, it would be a mistake not to check out the **Green House Hotel** (Str. Frații Buzești 25; tel: 0251-411352). Restored to its original Art

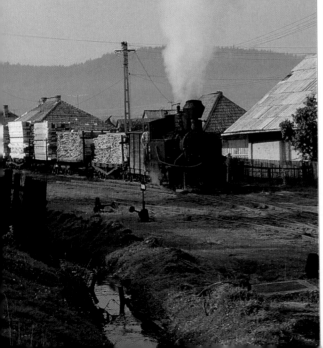

Deco splendour, this hotel shows what could be done with so many similar villas in Romania with a bit of love and money. Here you may decide that Craiova isn't such a bad place after all to spend the night – or at least stop for a meal in its blissful gardens.

With all its pollution, Craiova needs some lungs. Doing its bit, the 120-hectare (295-acre) **Romanescu Park** (Parcul Romanescu), at the south edge of town, is one of Romania's largest and most impressive. The design was considered so innovative at the time it was created that it earned its French landscaper Edouard Redont a gold medal at the 1900 Paris Exposition. Its many features include a lake with islands, a ruined castle, 35 km (22 miles) of paths, a small zoo and even a hippodrome.

Calafat

Another Danubian town, **Calafat ⑭** (pop. 19,000; www.municipiul-calafat.ro) was colonised by Genoese merchants in the 14th century. It's only visited en route to or from Bulgaria, but offers anyone temporarily stranded here an **Art and Folk Art Museum** (Muzeul

de Artă și Artă Populară; Str. 22 Decembrie 6; open Tues–Fri 10am–4pm, Sat 8am–12.30pm; admission charge) and two monuments commemorating what Romanians call the War of Independence (1877). Ferries carry cars and foot passengers to Vidin, Bulgaria, round the clock in summer and 5.30am–midnight in winter.

Giurgiu and around

Surrounded by marshes, the dusty Danube port of **Giurgiu ⑮** (pop. 69,000; www.primaria-giurgiu.ro) is mainly of interest as the principal crossing point into Bulgaria, lying as it does on the main route south from Bucharest to Istanbul. Although you'd never suspect it, the town actually dates back to the 14th century. One theory is that its founders were Genoese traders and the name Giurgiu derives from San Giorgio, the patron saint of Genoa. Most long-distance Danube river-cruise vessels stop here while passengers make an excursion to the capital.

Whatever the truth, the 14th-century ruins of **Giurgiu Fortress** (Cetatea Giurgiu; open access), on a small island

Map on pages 136-7

The Danube plain is one of the best habitats in Europe for dragonflies and damselflies.

BELOW: welcome to Romania: the bridge over the Danube at Giurgiu.

ROMANIA

Map on pages 136-7

The 1980s Danube Flood Plain drainage project destroyed most of southern Wallachia's reed beds.

BELOW: the striking blue plumage of the roller is a common sight on roadside telegraph wires in summer.

in front of the town, are the sole reminder of Giurgiu's origins. Although it was once heavily fortified, with five towers and a moat, there's no longer very much to see. Thanks to its strategic importance, Giurgiu fell into Ottoman hands in 1420 and was subsequently fought over in many battles. The stone **clock tower** (Turnul Ceasornicarului) in the centre of town dates from 1700 and was originally built by the Turks so that they could observe Romanian troop movements below. The clock itself is a later addition.

The commune of **Comana** ⑯, 32 km (20 miles) northeast of Giurgiu, has one Dracula monument you might not expect to find – a house of God. At least outside Romania, Vlad Ţepeş is little known for his pious nature. He did, however, take time out from impaling people to found **Comana Monastery** (Mănăstirea Comana; open daylight hours; admission charge) in the mid-15th century. The monastery was rebuilt in the 17th century by Radu Şerban, whose grave lies alongside those of many members of the illustrious Cantacuzino family. One of the largest wetlands in Wallachia is situated close by.

Lovers of the surreal are in for a treat at **Călăraşi** ⑰ (pop. 69,000; www.municipiu.ro). Surrounded by a gargantuan gauntlet of rusting, abandoned steel mills stretching to the horizon, it may lead visitors to think the body-snatchers got there first. A legacy of the traditional communist obsession with developing heavy industry at any cost, the metallurgical plant ceased serving any purpose soon after the fall of COMECON, when the low-grade steel it produced was no longer saleable. After just 11 years, full production ended in 1992. Since then the only future for this rusty elephant is recycling for scrap – or perhaps as a set for post-apocalyptic sci-fi flicks. In its way it's every bit as telling a testimony to Ceauşescu's folly as Bucharest's Palace of the People.

Apart from this unlikely tourist attraction, Călăraşi's **Museum of the Lower Danube** (Muzeul Dunării de Jos; Str. Progresului 4; open Tues–Sun 10am–6pm; admission charge) covers the region's archaeology and ethnography. Mainly of interest to historians, the largely ruined **Vicina Citadel** (Cetatea Vicina; open access), 10 km (6 miles) to the southeast on the island of **Păcuiul lui Soare**, was a Byzantine regional capital from the 10th–13th century.

Călăraşi itself still depends mainly on industry. The surrounding countryside, however, is largely agricultural. To hunters, Călăraşi county is the Perla Dunării (Pearl of the Danube) for its abundance of wild boar, deer, foxes, rabbits and other game. The extensive **Ialomiţa Swamp** ⑱ (Balta Ialomiţei), accessible by boat along the Danube from Călăraşi, attracts anglers and nature lovers.

Otherwise, the main reason to pass through this southern corner of the country is to reach the Bulgarian border, 12 km (7 miles) to the south. The main road from Silistra (Bulgaria) to Feteşti (DN3B in Romania) crosses through Călăraşi and skirts the Danube for much of its scenic route before joining the main road to Constanţa. ❑

RESTAURANTS

Restaurants

Craiova

Green House Hotel
Str. Frații Buzești 25
Tel: 0251-411352
A totally unexpected oasis of tranquillity in the old town, this lovely restaurant recalls an age of Art Deco elegance that makes you feel like donning a Panama hat and linen suit. In summer everyone heads for the thoroughly enchanting terrace, candlelit at night. Superb repertoire of Romanian and international dishes. €€€

Curtea de Argeş

Iancoviç (Restaurantul Sârbesc)
Str. Cuza Vodă
Tel: 0248-729016
In a unprepossessing location in one of the few modern parts of Curtea de Argeş, this villa restaurant offers honest Serbian fare (not dissimilar to Romanian) at keen prices. The *cârnați de caprioară* (venison sausages) are excellent. €€

Posada
Hotelul Posada,
B-dul. Basarabilor 27–29
Tel: 0248-721451
On the ground floor lobby of Curtea de Argeş' main hotel, this agreeably old-fashioned restaurant combines touchingly sweet service with the best Romanian

food in town. You can't go wrong with the *sarmale*. Often booked up at weekends. €€

Montana
B-dul. Basarabilor 72
Tel: 0248-722364
Cheap and cheerful place on the main street offering Romanian basics and pizza, as well as the "chef's surprise" *(surprisa bucatorului)*. Most people come here to drink. €

Pitești

Calabria
B-dul. Eroilor 5
Tel: 0248-217178
Lively and likeable Italian restaurant opposite the County Museum. Despite the location next to a busy road, the traffic noise cannot compete with the music and conversation. The menu goes beyond the usual pizza and pasta dishes. Efficient service. €€

Matteo
Str. Bălașa 13
Tel: 0248-223390
Opposite the Princely Church, this is a fine place to watch Pitești's fashion victims catwalking past or newlyweds posing for photographs. While it may look like a typical fast-food joint, the illustrated menu features a substantial range of Romanian and Italian dishes, as well as *pui indian* (Indian chicken) and *pui shang-*

hai (Shanghai chicken). Not the swiftest service. €€

Ploiești

Bulevard
Str. Golești 25
Tel: 0244-521500
Dating from 1885, this grand old dame opposite the Clock Museum was restored in 2004 to its former glory and is Ploiești's finest restaurant by far, with attentive service and top-notch Romanian and international cuisine. €€€

Hanul Găzarilor
Str. Mihai Bravu 45
Tel: 0244-597577
Despite its location beside a stadium in one of Romania's grimiest towns, this colourful inn does a surprisingly good job of recreating a traditional *han*. The extensive menu features rustic dishes such as roast suckling pig *(purcel la rotizor)*, as well as plentiful vegetarian and even a few low-fat dishes. €€€

Targoviște

Casa Domnească
Str. Arsenalului 14
Tel: 0245-613173
In what is generally a culinary wasteland, this is one of Târgoviște's few places serving traditional Romanian food. At times the atmosphere can be a bit hushed, but the professional service compensates. €€

Casa V
Str. Revoluției 36
Tel: 0245-217021
A lively bar-cum-restaurant in the old town. People come for a pizza, drinks or both, but the place also makes a competent stab at pasta dishes and the usual Romanian staples. Open later than most. €

Târgu Jiu

Europa
Str. Calea Eroilor 22 (colt cu Popa Sapca)
Tel: 0253-211810
The best place to eat in Târgu Jiu, with good Romanian food and international dishes such as steaks. As the one classy place in town, it is a popular wedding venue and can therefore often be closed at weekends. €€€

Quattro Stagione
Str. Eroilor 9
Tel: 0253-222224
Italian restaurant with astonishingly cheap prices considering the quality. The menu offers little more than standard trattoria fare but the service is friendly. The pizzas are good. €€

DOBROGEA

This southeastern corner of Romania has brash seaside resorts, classical ruins, lively music festivals and a remarkable river delta teeming with wildlife

I n the distant past, the Black Sea coast and hinterland that comprises Dobrogea (sometimes spelled Dobruja or Dobrudja) was by far the most developed area of what is now Romania. Greeks and Romans settled here, building sizeable towns, as the region became a well-established trading centre.

The maritime location has ensured a cosmopolitan history, with Genoese and Venetians mixing with Greeks, Jews and Russians, while the proximity to Turkey and centuries of Ottoman rule have left a tangible whiff of the Orient, with a sizeable Turkish minority still in residence. Dobrogea continues over the border into Bulgaria (southern Dobrogea); between 1913 and 1940 the entire region lay within Romania.

Today, the long sandy beaches attract the bulk of foreign tourists to Romania, most of whom arrive on package tours. It's also the place where many Romanians head for their summer holidays. And while no-one is going to force you out of your deckchair, anyone who makes the effort will be rewarded with a heady mix of Roman, Byzantine and Ottoman remains, some great music festivals and, last but not least, Romania's most ethnically diverse population.

Further north lies the Danube Delta, a fascinating region where the great river splits into three channels before flowing through a gigantic wetland. This is one of Europe's best-preserved natural environments.

CONSTANŢA

Romania's main port and the Black Sea's busiest, **Constanţa ❶** can trace its origins back to the 6th century BC when Greek settlers founded the citadel of Tomis. In 29 BC it became a sleepy backwater of the Roman Empire, hosting the poet Ovid on his unhappy exile here. The curmudgeonly Ovid had little love for Tomis, writing mournful poems about its miserable weather and frozen wine.

Were he to return these days, however, Ovid would find much to like

Maps on pages 154, 157

LEFT: Jupiter Beach.
BELOW: coffee the Turkish way.

The Roman wolf that suckles the twins Romulus and Remus is seen in all large Romanian cities.

BELOW: the Roman poet Ovid was banished by Emperor Augustus to Constanţa (or Tomis as it was then called). He lived in the city from AD 8 until his death nine years later.

about Constanţa and would certainly have better things to do than write supplications to the emperor begging to be allowed to return to Rome. For one thing, the climate would appear to have improved considerably since Roman times (although winters are bleak and cold – sometimes *very* cold; *see picture on page 156*). For another, Constanţa is a lively port city with fine hotels and restaurants where wine is never served frozen. It also has some of the best museums in Dobrogea as well as an impressive portfolio of Roman remains.

After a difficult spell in the 1990s with the collapse of COMECON and the blockade on Yugoslavia, Constanţa's fortunes look set to rise with Romania's EU membership and the improved investment and transport links that this will bring (the city is at the eastern end of one of the EU's ten Pan-European Corridors, designated priority transport routes).

The oldest part of Constanţa lies on the headland between the marina and the port. With Gypsy children playing in the street, washing hanging from

balconies and buildings so derelict that some have signs warning of the danger of collapse, Constanţa's ramshackle old town is reminiscent of Bucharest's Lipscani quarter, but possibly even scruffier.

Archaeological treasures

An appropriately mournful statue of Ovid dominates **Piaţa Ovidiu**, the old town's central square. Italian sculptor Ettore Ferrari worked on it from 1883–84, and it was placed in its present location in 1887.

The large neo-Brâncoveanu building on the southern side of the square houses the **National History and Archaeology Museum** Ⓐ (Muzeul de Istorie Naţională şi Arheologie; Piaţa Ovidiu 12; open May–Sept daily 8am–8pm, Oct–Apr Wed–Sun 9am–5pm; admission charge). One of the finest museums of its kind in Romania, this one shines not just because of the wealth of archaeological finds it contains but also because of the visitor-friendly approach to labelling. It has a particularly rich collection of statues and reliefs of Greek

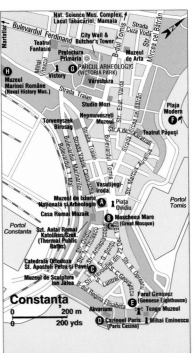

and Roman deities, from the 2nd and 3rd centuries AD, which were buried in the 4th century when Christianity became the official religion. The most famous is an extraordinary statue of the snake god Glykon with long hair and an anthropomorphic face. Although, as usual in Romania, the collection grinds to a halt in 1947, a delightful collection of 19th-century tobacco pipes helps to compensate.

In a modern concrete shell behind the museum, the **Roman Mosaic Building** (Edificiul Roman cu Mozaic; open summer daily 8am–8pm, winter 9am–5pm; admission charge) offers a viewing platform over a mosaic from the 3rd–4th century AD, discovered in 1959. Originally forming the terrace of a Roman commercial building, the well-preserved mosaic was originally 102 metres by 20 metres (335 ft by 66 ft) in extent, of which about 850 sq. metres (3,000 sq. ft) survives. Made of stone and marble cut and laid in layers of Roman mortar (hydraulic lime), the mosaic combines different geometric patterns and floral motifs and is one of the longest Roman mosaics ever

found. A terrace behind the building leads to the remains of the **thermal public baths**.

A short walk south of Piaţa Ovidiu, the **Great Mosque ❸** (Moscheea Mare; Str. Crângului 1; open summer daily 9am–6pm; admission charge) was inspired by the Konya Mosque in nearby Turkey, the designer Paul Constantinescu combining Byzantine and Arab elements in the 47-metre (154-ft) minaret and dome with Romanian elements in the rest of the building.

Curiously, it was the first building in Romania to be made of reinforced concrete. The steel soon began to rust and the building needed extensive repair in the 1950s. Inside the mosque, Romania's largest Oriental carpet, measuring 144 sq. metres (515 sq. ft), which originally belonged to Sultan Adbul Hamid, was brought here from Ada Kaleh *(see page 278)* in 1965. The 140-step minaret, open to visitors, offers one of the best views in town. The mosque is the seat of Romania's mufti, head of a community of 55,000 Muslims.

Constanţa's second mosque, the **Hunchiar Mosque** (Geamia Hunchiar;

Map on page 154

The Great Mosque dates from 1910. Built with state money, it was originally known as the Carol I Mosque.

BELOW LEFT: the Archaeological Museum. **BELOW:** the famous mosaic.

Frescoes at Constanta's Orthodox Cathedral.

B-dul. Tomis 39) was built from 1867–68 in a Moorish style and has a 24-metre (78-ft) minaret.

Further south, the **Orthodox Cathedral of SS Peter and Paul** (Catedrala Ortodoxa Sfintii Apostoli Petru şi Pavel; Str. Lahovari 18), was built from 1883–95 in Greco-Roman style by Ion Mincu, but the neo-Byzantine paintings inside date only from 1959–61. More remains of ancient Tomis lie south of the cathedral. The nearby **Ion Jalea Sculpture Museum** (Muzeul de Sculptură Ion Jalea; Str. Arhiepiscopiei 26; open Wed–Sun 10am–6pm; admission charge) has a small exhibition of works by this local sculptor.

On the waterfront

On the promenade by the waterfront, Constanța's most famous landmark, the **Paris Casino** (Cazinoul Paris) is a gloriously exuberant example of Art Nouveau, replete with giant clam shells and stained-glass windows. Built from 1904–10 by architects Daniel Renard and Petre Antonescu (who also designed Bucharest's Arcul de Triumf), the building was restored in 1985–87. At one time the former casino had one of the most noted restaurants in Romania, but these days it is a shadow of its former self, clearly overdue for privatisation. However, it is a fine place to enjoy a drink overlooking the Black Sea.

The **Aquarium** (B-dul. 16 Februarie 1; open daily summer 9am–8pm, winter 9am–4pm; admission charge) opposite is every bit as woeful inside as out. Further along the promenade, the 8-metre (26-ft) octagonal **Genoese lighthouse** (Farul Genovez) was the work of the British Danube and Black Sea Railway Company in 1858–60, but is so named to commemorate the Genoese traders who plied the coast in the 13th century.

Behind the lighthouse, the **statue of Mihai Eminescu** looking out to sea honours a wish he made in his famous poem *One Wish Alone Have I* (*Mai am un singur dor*). It dates from 1930 and the sculptor was Oscar Han.

While it doesn't compare with Mamaia or other resorts further south, Constanța's sandy **beach** is pleas-

ant despite – or perhaps because of – its current lack of commercial development. Building work is afoot, however. With a characteristically Romanian disregard for health and safety, the builders and carpenters wear flip-flops.

Back in town at the corner of Bulevardul Ferdinand and Bulevardul Tomis (the edge of the new town), **Victoria Park** features remains of ancient Tomis, including a 3rd-century **city wall**, rows of amphorae and the 6th-century, Byzantine **Butchers' Tower**. The huge **statue of Victory** in the park is a treat for lovers of socialist-realist kitsch, with its procession of happy workers striking heroic poses beneath a flowing banner held aloft by Victory.

South of the park on Strada Traian, the **Naval History Museum** (Muzeul Marinei Române; open summer Tues–Sun 9am–5pm, winter 10am–6pm; admission charge; www .fortele-navale.ro) covers the evolution of civil and military navigation as well as the history of the Romanian Navy and the commercial fleet.

THE BLACK SEA RESORTS

South from Constanța

While the 43-km (26-mile) stretch of coastline from Constanța south to Mangalia appears to be more or less one continuous development, in fact it comprises different resorts, each with a more or less distinctive character and clientele. All are backed by cliffs 15–30 metres (50–100 ft) high.

Ten km (6 miles) south of Constanța, the commune of **Agigea** (pop. 5,400; www.primaria-agigea.ro) has a famous tuberculosis sanatorium and is known for its impressive sand dunes, measuring up to 8–10 metres (26–33 ft) in height. Heading south, the main road passes through a narrow strip of land between Techirghiol Lake and the Black Sea, entering Eforie Nord at the northern tip. Although administratively a single unit, **Eforie** (pop. 9,500; www.primaria-eforie.ro) is effectively two small resort towns 5 km (3 miles) apart, and with quite different atmospheres.

Eforie Nord ❷, the second-biggest spa on the Romanian coast, has been

Maps on p154 & below

The Genoese lighthouse dates from the mid-nineteenth century.

BELOW: by the beach at Constanța.

flourishing since 1894, when a fashionable sanatorium opened there. Many people still come throughout the year for health treatments based on concentrated saltwater or warm mud from **Lake Techirghiol** – celebrated as Romania's most therapeutic.

With a more established character than most other resorts, Eforie retains some architectural splendours from its genteel heyday in the late 19th century. These days, however, it is equally popular as a bucket-and-spade resort for families – mostly Romanian – attracted by its fine 3-km (2-mile) beach beneath a 30-metre (100-ft) cliff. One indication that visitors to Eforie Nord are less well-heeled than those in nearby Neptun-Olimp *(see page 159)* is that most restaurants are *autoservire* (self-service). To a casual observer the implausibly high number of stalls selling seashells, corals and inflatable knick-knacks all along the main road to the beach would suggest that the souvenir industry is the mainstay of the local economy.

Attached to the Europa Hotel, the **Ana Aslan Health Spa** (www.hotel-europa.ro) is Romania's largest health and recreation centre. Named after the founder of the anti-ageing cream Gerovital, it offers luxurious pampering as well as a yacht club and a private beach.

At the other end of the strip, **Eforie Sud** was Romania's first Black Sea resort and has an altogether sleepier, even rural, feel compared with its twin to the north. A hypochondriac's dream, Eforie Sud offers heliomarine and mud treatments for everything from rheumatism to rickets. Otherwise, the main draw is the 2.5-km (1½-mile) beach.

It is not necessary to go to a hotel or health spa to enjoy a mud treatment, though. There is plenty to spare in Lake Techirghiol itself and nude sunbathing there is a time-honoured tradition, as anyone going past on the train is likely to notice. However, the lake beach is not particularly clean except between Eforie Nord and Sud. The best place to sample the mud is at the **cold baths** (băile reci; open June–mid-Sept daily 9am–5pm; admission charge), 300 metres/yds south, and across the railway line, from Eforie

BELOW AND BELOW RIGHT: mud treatment for all ages.

Nord train station. Inside, signs point to two tiny, single-sex nudist beaches – *bărbaţi* for men and *femei* for women – surrounded by high walls. The mud stands ready in buckets. Slap it on all over, or ask someone else to help smother the hard-to-reach bits, then lie down and wait an hour or two for the sun to do its work, enjoying the strains of Irish folk music from the loudspeakers. Beware, though: the mud is very sticky and smelly and takes much longer to get off than to put on, especially if not completely dry. To wash it off there is a choice between the sea and outdoor showers with warm seawater. Facilities are extremely basic, even derelict, with no towels, lockers or beach mats provided, but for most the mud, the beach and the sea are enough. Dry and mud massages are available for an extra fee.

One unusual place to stay is in the small town of **Techirghiol** (pop. 7,000; www.primaria-techirghiol.ro), 5 km (3 miles) west of Eforie Nord. Originally set up in 1928 as a sanatorium for priests from all over Romania, **St Mary's Monastery** (Mănăstirea Sfânta Maria; Str. Ovidiu 5; www.sfanta-maria.ro) now offers comfortable accommodation, hydrotherapy treatments and spiritual cleansing in summer in a tranquil setting on Lake Techirghiol's northern shore. The 17th-century wooden church was transplanted here from Transylvania in 1951.

Costineşti & Neptun-Olimp

Costineşti ❸, 11 km (7 miles) south of Eforie Sud, started life in 1949. It has always been primarily a youth resort, although some people have remained loyal into middle age. Meanwhile, older visitors may be attracted by its cures for rheumatism. Facing eastwards, Costineşti's 5-km (3-mile) beach is arguably Romania's best. A modern youth holiday complex and an international student camp, together with a packed calendar of cultural and entertainment events, help keep the young crowd occupied when they are not sunbathing. In former times socialist indoctrination came as part of the package. Since 2002, however, Costineşti has had a church known as the Youth Cathedral (Catedrala tineretului) to cater for visitors' spiritual needs.

Seven kilometres (4 miles) further along, on the sand strip between the sea and Comorova Forest, **Neptun-Olimp ❹** has an air of leafy sophistication not found in the other resorts. In communist times it was largely the preserve of the *nomenklatură* and members of the Writers' Union, which had – and still has – many properties here. Ceauşescu had a luxury villa in Olimp, which is still heavily guarded and used as a holiday retreat for Romania's president. Nowadays the resort is popular with a slightly older, wealthier Romanian crowd, as well as foreigners on package holidays.

Accommodation and facilities are swankier than elsewhere, with prices to match. Neptun-Olimp is particularly well-equipped for families, with many hotels offering kindergartens or organised activities for children. Other pur-

Map on page 157

Colourful cocktails in one of the dozens of bars found in every resort along the coast.

BELOW: dancing the samba on stage at Mamaia.

suits include tennis, riding, volleyball, mini golf, basketball, water skiing and surfing.

Overall, while Neptun-Olimp is a good place for a quiet break, the main Steaguri beach can get very crowded and anyone under 50 may find the nightlife somewhat subdued.

Further south, Jupiter, Cap Aurora, Venus and Saturn are fairly low-key, low-rent modern resorts without a great deal to distinguish between them. In part because of its enormous camp site, **Jupiter** attracts a young, low-budget crowd. Its 1-km (½-mile) beach is very good, and there is a picturesque golf course.

In a pretty setting on the cape of the same name, **Cap Aurora** is the whippersnapper among Black Sea resorts, dating only from 1973. Lovers of modern architecture will appreciate its bold pyramid-shaped hotels laid out in the style of an amphitheatre. Continuing Jupiter's planetary theme, **Venus** and especially **Saturn** – practically a suburb of Mangalia – have little to recommend themselves except cheap accommodation (in high-rise blocks).

BELOW: volleyball on the beach at Neptun-Olimp.

Mangalia

Despite its brash modern appearance, **Mangalia ❺**, like Constanța, traces its origins to Greco-Roman times. Known originally as Callatis, it was founded in the 6th century BC by Greeks from Pontic Heracleea, who established a fortress. It continued to flourish under Roman occupation in the 2nd–4th century AD and was revived in the 13th–14th century by the Genoese, who called it Pangalia.

Nowadays, Mangalia is Romania's second Black Sea port and depends only partly on tourism, although the city authorities have been energetic in promoting it as a conference destination.

During the construction of the President Hotel (Str. Teilor 6; www.hpresident.com) builders unearthed some remains of the southern perimeter of the **ancient Callatis Fortress**. Rather than covering them in concrete, the authorities decided to build the hotel around the remains, which are stylishly on display near the entrance and in the basement of the restaurant at the back of the hotel. There are fragments of an urban settlement and part

of the southern gate. The wall, which was rebuilt in the 2nd century, is of large blocks of carved stone and is almost 2 metres (6 ft) thick. More **ruins** of Callatis, including a Roman-Byzantine basilica from the 5th–6th century, and sarcophagi, are to be found in Parcul Stadionului, just north of the centre.

Behind the park, other remains from the citadel are on show at the **Callatis Archaeological Museum** (Muzeul de Arheologie Callatis; Șoseaua Constanței 23; www.muzeulcallatis.ro; open summer daily 8am–8pm, winter 8am–6pm; admission charge), including ancient columns, aqueduct pipes and fragments of stone sarcophagi. However, it's not a patch on Constanța's archaeological museum.

Built in the Moorish style in 1525 by Esmahan, daughter of Sultan Selim II, Mangalia's **Esmahan Sultan Mosque** (Geamia Esmahan Sultan; Str. Oituz 1; open summer daily 9am–6pm) is the oldest mosque in Romania, and remains in use. In the cemetery, some of the gravestones are recycled fragments of buildings from ancient Callatis.

Discovered in a mine shaft in 1986,

the 300-metre (985-ft) **Movile Cave** (Peștera Movile) 1 km (½ mile) west of Mangalia immediately attracted interest from scientists around the world because of its unique ecosystem. Instead of relying on sunlight and photosynthesis, the 46 species of plant living there are specially adapted to survive on chemosynthesis, chemical energy created by the oxidising of hydrogen sulphide, methane and ammonia. Cut off from the outside world for more than 5 million years, all the animals living there – 31 are unique to the cave – have evolved with no, or reduced, eyes and with loss of pigmentation. They include a blind leech, a sightless water-scorpion and many arthropod species. To protect the fragile ecosystem, only professional researchers are allowed to visit the cave. It is possible, however, to watch a documentary about the cave at the Laboratory of the Group for Underwater and Speleological Exploration (Laboratorul grupului de explorări subacvatice și speologice) on Mangalia beach.

Three kilometres (2-miles) north of Mangalia, the 588-hectare (1,455-acre)

Map on page 157

The Aqua Magic Waterpark at Mamaia.

BELOW: the Danube–Black Sea Canal.

The Black Sea Canal

One of communist Romania's costliest and most controversial engineering achievements, the Danube-Black Sea Canal (Canalul Dunăre-Marea Neagră) was built to enable inland navigation all the way from Rotterdam to Constanța – a plan first hatched in the 1840s. While the Delta also links the Danube to the sea, it's difficult to navigate and before the canal most shipping circumvented it. Work lasted from 1949–1987, with a gap from 1953–76.

In the 1950s, thousands of political prisoners, including some of the cream of prewar society, served forced labour on it. Many perished, hence the name "Death Canal" (Canalul morții). Many question if it merited the huge human and economic cost. Each of its three arms presents navigational hazards and at current rates it'll take centuries to become profitable.

Originally set up as a one-off protest (see panel, below), Vama Veche's Stufstock has since become a four-day annual music festival attracting home-grown and foreign acts. It was free, but so many people crowded the beach in 2006 that it is now likely to become a ticket-only event.

BELOW: president of the campaign

Mangalia Stud Farm (Herghelia Mangalia; open daily 8am–6pm; admission charge) has been breeding pure-bred Arab horses since it was founded in 1926. The farm has 350 horses, of which about 50 are usually for sale. They are particularly popular with foreign buyers because prices are knock-down by European standards. However, you don't have to visit with fistfuls of cash and a horsebox in tow. You can take guided tours of the farm, with riding lessons in its equestrian centre or carriage rides along the shore. Attached to the farm, **Mangalia Hippodrome** used to be famous as the only course in Romania with horse-racing. Alas, the weekly summer races stopped in 2006 for financial reasons and it is unclear when or if they will resume.

Doi Mai and Vama Veche

Because of its proximity to the Bulgarian border and, equally importantly, the Turkish coast, the final stretch of coast south of Mangalia was deliberately left undeveloped in communist times. Outsiders were forbidden to buy property and access to Vama Veche, a stone's throw from the Bulgarian border, was officially only for employees of the famously nonconformist Cluj University *(see page 237)*.

Partly as a result of this, it became popular with a bohemian crowd attracted to the unspoilt beaches and simple comforts. While the rule restricting access to Vama Veche to university staff was never very rigidly enforced – regular visitors reported that a bottle of vodka to the guard was enough to secure entry – luggage inspections were extremely rigorous. Anything that might be used to escape, even inflatable life rafts, would be confiscated.

These days, although its beach lies in the shadow of the massive yellow cranes of Daewoo Mangalia Heavy Industries, **Doi Mai** (2 May), 14 km (8 miles) south of Mangalia, remains a pleasant, sleepy fishing village popular with old-timers, who valiantly keep up the tradition of nude sunbathing on the beach. Traditionally residents throw open their houses to paying guests in summer, with meals included, and many visitors have been staying with the same families every summer for 30

The Save Vama Veche Campaign

Immured by decades of oppression, Romanians sometimes appear a somewhat supine lot. However, when in summer 2003 gun-toting special forces acting on the orders of Romania's tourism ministry raided Vama Veche beach to clear it of "illegal" tents – camping had long been a tradition alongside nude bathing – they weren't dealing with just any Romanians. Since the 1950s Vama Veche and Doi Mai have been favoured summer retreats for Romania's intellectual élite. Spared development under communism because of their sensitive border location, the resorts remained relatively undeveloped. To old-timers, that's just the way they wanted to keep them.

Fearful the government intended to turn Vama Veche into another Mamaia, the so-called *vamaioți* – many with impeccable media connections, decided to fight back. Their chosen weapon was a rock concert. Named Stufstock (*stuf* means reed in Romanian; www.stufstock.com) after Vama Veche's distinctive foliage, the concert took place on the 44th anniversary of Woodstock. Meanwhile supporters help publicise the cause through websites such as www.salvativamaveche.ro. Rapidly the campaign became one of Romania's highest-profile lobbying groups and now the local authorities consult it about any new developments.

years or more. As a result, there are few restaurants in Doi Mai, although there is one hotel, the Hellios Inn, the only traditional Balkan-style *han* (traditional inn) on the coast. It is also easy to find accommodation in houses wherever there is a sign advertising rooms *(cazare* or *camere)*.

Most of Doi Mai's permanent residents are Lipovanis whose ancestors were forced to flee Russia in the 17th century. To this day they speak Russian, retain the old calendar and worship at a very Russian-looking church with a double cross.

Vama Veche ⑥, just shy of the Bulgarian border (the name means old customs post), has a more diverse population, with around 100 Gagauz (a christian Turkic minority) as well as smaller numbers of Turks and Lipovanis. Nowadays, however, the native population is far outweighed in summer by visitors from all over Romania. Foreigners are a rare sight. So distinctive is the typical Vama Veche visitor that the term *vamaiot* is a badge of honour among a bohemian, alternative crowd. Older people, though,

complain that it is no longer what it used to be and that it has become too well known for its own good. Even the tradition of nude sunbathing has been eroded. Some long-term visitors even talk of starting up a new Vama Veche in a remote part of the Danube Delta.

Even so, Vama Veche remains less spoilt and commercialised than most Black Sea resorts and it is easy to avoid the crowds by visiting midweek. One interesting development since 2002 has been the success of the high-octane Save Vama Veche Campaign *(see panel on page 162)* in restricting the pace of building and mass tourism. While bars and low-key clubs fringe the beach at Vama Veche, there is a refreshing lack of high-rise architecture and new structures have to comply with a development plan. The Save Vama Veche Campaign also stages one of Romania's most enjoyable music festivals, **Stufstock**.

North of Constanţa

On the road between Constanta and Mamaia, **Lake Tăbăcăriei** (Lacul Tăbăcăriei) is a popular destination for

Map on page 157

To this day, despite increasing numbers of hedonistic weekend trippers, attracted by the best nightlife on the coast, Doi Mai and Vama Veche retain an ambience not found elsewhere in Romania.

BELOW: Stufstock in full swing

families. On the southeastern shore of the lake the **Natural Science Museum Complex** (Complexul Muzeal de Ştiinţele Naturii; B-dul. Mamaia 255; open daily summer 9am–8pm, winter 9am–4pm; admission charge) contains an aquarium, planetarium and astronomic observatory as well as Romania's only dolphinarium. However, none is in particularly good shape.

West of Constanţa, the famous vineyards of **Murfatlar** are only open to organised groups.

Mamaia ❼, 6 km (4 miles) north of Constanţa, is the liveliest and brashest Black Sea resort and a favoured destination for package holidays. On a narrow strip of land between the sea and Lake Siutghiol, this Romanian Benidorm has a terrific beach, some 8 km (5 miles) long and pleasantly cooled by sea breezes. It also has some of the best facilities on the coast for water sports enthusiasts as well as a wide range of land-based pursuits.

However, its other charms are less obvious. Although the resort started life in 1906, very little, apart from the stately Rex Hotel, remains from earlier days. Most of the hotels are high-rise communist blocks and since 1989 developers have built funfairs, fast-food joints and amusement arcades, while long-term investment has proved elusive.

In a resort with no canals and a maximum altitude of 8 metres (26 ft), Mamaia's Telegondolă – combining elements of a gondola and chairlift – constructed in 2004, is a much-derided but popular attraction. The architecturally distinctive four-star Iaki Hotel, belonging to Romania's footballing legend Gheorghe Hagi, is arguably a more welcome development.

In communist days Mamaia largely attracted older holiday-makers, but these days it seems to be aimed at the lowest common denominator. Certainly older travellers will find the relentless pop music a deterrent, while young people will find better nightlife at Vama Veche.

Accessible by boat from Mamaia, nearby **Lake Siutghiol** (Lacul Siutghiol) is a good place for water sports, and motorboat cruises are available. **Ovidiu Island** (Insula Ovidiu) on the

Vama Veche is a great place for eating out; restaurants are cheap and relaxed.

BELOW: inviting-looking water at Vama Veche.

lake takes its name from the poet Ovid and many believe he was buried there.

On the banks of Lake Sinoie (Lacul Sinoie), 8 km (5 miles) east of the village of Istria, are the remains of **Histria** ❽ (open daily, summer 9am–8pm, winter 9am–5pm; admission charge), the earliest and most important Greek settlement on the western Black Sea coast. The first town to exist anywhere on present-day Romanian territory, it was founded by settlers from Miletus in the mid-7th century BC and remained continuously inhabited until the 7th century AD, becoming a Roman settlement about halfway through its existence. When invading Avars and Slavs destroyed it, Histria was already in decline as encroaching silt had begun to restrict access to the sea. The remains include various Greek temples and Christian basilicas as well as defensive walls and the ruins of a paved residential quarter. Near the site entrance the **Histria Archaeological Museum** (Muzeul de Arheologie Histria; same hours) has a collection of Greek, Roman and Byzantine finds from Histria and the surrounding area. Maxitaxis run from Constanța to Istria.

More ancient ruins can be seen just north of the village of **Adamclisi**, 64 km (40 miles) west of Constanța, where there stands a remarkable marble reconstruction of **Tropaeum Traiani**, a triumphal monument erected by Trajan from 106–9 AD to commemorate his victory over the Dacians. Bas-reliefs around the base depict scenes from the battles, as well as the richness of Dobrogea's agriculture. The carving is somewhat lumbering, and the monument appears to have been intended as a symbol of Roman might to the local population rather than a work of high art. Around the monument there lie the remains of the Roman settlement also founded here by Trajan, while back in the village the **Adamclisi Archaeological Museum** (Muzeul Arheologic Adamclisi, open daily summer 8am–8pm, winter 9am–5pm; admission charge) has fragments of the original column and other local archaeological finds. Daily buses between Constanța and Ostrov stop at Adamclisi.

Map on page 157

A quiet rural road near Babadag between the Black Sea resorts and the Delta.

BELOW:
the ruins at Histria.

TIP

Three daily hydrofoils
operate between
Tulcea and Sulina,
taking around 1 hour
30 m. Catamarans (2
hours) and slower
ferries (4 hours) also
run daily, and on the
Tulcea-Sf Gheorghe
route. There are fewer
boats in winter. For full
details and ticket
information visit
www.navrom.x3m.ro

BELOW:
white pelicans.

THE DANUBE DELTA

Romanians tend to regard the **Danube Delta** (Delta Dunării) as a foreign land, and it is true that this spectacular region is completely different from other parts of the country. Romania has no shortage of remote, wild places, but the Delta is unique, a roadless wilderness that comprises Europe's largest wetland and the world's biggest reed-bed. Its watery labyrinth has acted as a sanctuary not just for a tremendous array of wildlife (notably birds) but also for fugitives fleeing persecution from Russia and the Ukraine.

The best time to visit depends on what you want to see. Overall, May is about as good as it gets, with plenty of migratory birds and most of the summer migrants in residence, pleasant weather, flowers in abundance and an amazing evening chorus of marsh frogs. The summer months are also good, but it does get very hot and the mosquitoes can be troublesome in the evening. The various migratory bird species pass through at different times, but in general spring (late Mar–mid-May) and autumn (early Sept–early Nov) are favourable times to visit. Disadvantages are the lack of colourful summer species, and occasional wet and cold weather. Even the depths of winter offer interest for bird-watchers and fans of Stygian gloom, but you'd have to be hardy – temperatures are usually below freezing and the piercing wind makes it impossible to stay out for long.

Nature and ecotourism

For most people, visiting the Delta is all about connecting with nature. A vital stopover for migrating birds en route to the Middle East and Africa in autumn, or northern Europe in spring, the reed beds, mud flats and coastal waters sustain huge numbers of waders, herons, egrets, ducks, geese and other waterfowl as well as various birds of prey and assorted finches, thrushes, buntings, tits, woodpeckers, owls, shrikes and warblers (amongst others).

The A-list celebrities in this avian land of plenty are the pelicans (white pelicans, of which there are around 8,000 individuals, and the rare Dalmatian pelican). Other glamorous species are the glossy ibis and the white-tailed

Map below

eagle. Less glossy, but of great interest to bird-watchers, are the red-breasted geese that can be seen from November to early March and pygmy cormorants (most abundant in summer). Raptors include white-tailed eagles, marsh harriers, red-footed falcons and hobbys. Kingfishers, squacco herons, night herons, great and little egrets are everywhere in the warmer months, with colourful summer migrants such as the bee-eater, roller, golden oriole and hoopoe also present in abundance.

Mammals include Europe's largest population of mink, other semi-aquatic species such as otters, a growing number of golden jackals, and the unusual raccoon dog *(for a full account of the birdlife, and other wildlife, of the Delta, see pages 98–99).*

It almost goes without saying that this is a fragile ecosystem, and efforts are made to minimise the impacts of tourism upon it. The principals of ecotourism also attempt to ensure that it is local communities, rather than businessmen from outside, that benefit; the emphasis is firmly on *pensiones* and homestays rather than hotels. The reserve is managed by the Administratia Rezervatiei Biosferei Delta Dunării (ARBDD) in Tulcea; in theory you are supposed to buy a permit (1 euro) from their office on the Tulcea waterfront before entering the reserve, but as most people visit as part of a tour this is handled by the agency on their behalf. The area has been a designated UNESCO Biosphere Reserve since 1990; in tandem with this, environmentally responsible tourism has been highlighted via schemes such as the Landscape of the Year programme run by the International Friends of Nature for 2007/8, and the Association of Ecotourism in Romania (AER).

Many Romanians visit the Delta to fish – aquatic life is rich and plentiful and fishing has been the mainstay of the local economy for as long as people have lived here.

The decreased flow of water since the 1972 completion of the giant Iron Gates Dam hundreds of miles upstream resulted in a serious decline in fish stocks, with such species as sturgeon disappearing almost entirely. These days the numbers of fish have largely

An unforgettable experience for anyone visiting the Delta in the summer is the remarkably loud chorus of marsh frogs, tree frogs (pictured) and fire bellied toads.

BELOW: great egrets are one of the Delta's most graceful birds.

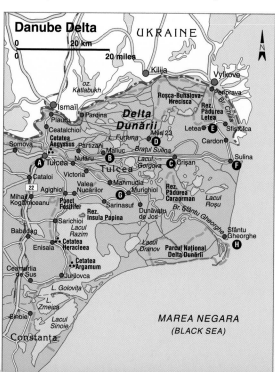

TIP

Try to avoid taking a
Delta tour on one of
the larger vessels –
you won't see much
wildlife on account of
the engine noise.
Arrange your trip with
one of the responsible
agencies listed on
page 362.
Independent travel
can be tricky – but
fine if you only want a
brief taste of the
Delta. You can take a
public ferry to Crişan
or Sfântu Gheorghe,
for instance, and then
try to arrange trips
into the backwaters
once you are there.

BELOW: waterlilies
carpet the surface
of some of the
Delta's lakes.

stabilised and are sufficient to sustain other wildlife and fishing communities, although there is some concern about overfishing. The much-discussed poisoning of the Tisza and Danube from the gold mine accident at Baia Mare in 1990 was not, in fact, very harmful this far downstream, and the 2006 floods have helped cleanse the water.

In the Ceauşescu years some areas in the north of the Delta were drained for agriculture, but these reclamations have long since been scrapped. Unfortunately that is not the case across the border in the Ukraine (home to around one sixth of the Delta), where the construction of a canal is set to have a serious impact. Romania has officially objected to these proposals but it does seem depressingly likely that they will continue.

One thing you may notice as you explore the backwaters is the unwelcome presence of bits and pieces of rubbish – mainly bottles and plastic containers – washed up seemingly in the middle of nowhere. Much of this detritus is simply carried down the Danube and ends up here, although some of it is caused by local litter louts.

Tulcea

To visit the Delta you will almost certainly pass through the regional centre of **Tulcea** Ⓐ, from where ferries run to various locations within the reserve. It's not a particularly pleasant or interesting town, but apart from the ferries it is home to the office and visitor centre of the **Danube Delta Biosphere Reserve Administration** (ARBDD; open Mon–Fri 8am–4pm; www.ddbra.ro) – a useful source of information, and the place to buy a permit if you are visiting independently. Also on the city's waterfront are a number of tour operators – some good, some not.

There isn't much else to do in Tulcea. A short walk from the Piața Republicii, behind the Delta Hotel, is a moderately diverting **Art Museum** (Muzeul de Artă, open Tues–Sun 9am–5pm; admission charge). Carry on in the same direction along Strada Sahia and you'll reach the **Azizie Mosque** (Moscheea azizie), a reminder of Ottoman times and focal point for the town's Turkish community. Past the mosque there are some Roman remains and the **History and Archaeology**

Museum (Muzeul de Istorie şi Arheologie; open Tues–Sun 9am–5pm; admission charge).

Close to the Art Museum, on Strada 9 Mai, the **Ethnographic Museum** (Muzeul Etnografic; open daily 10am–6pm; admission charge) has a series of rooms depicting the costumes worn by various local minorities, while the **Danube Delta Museum** (Muzeul Delta Dunării; open Tues–Sun 9am–5pm; admission charge) on Strada Progresului is a musty old place filled with stuffed animals.

Into the Delta

The Danube splits into two upstream from Tulcea, and then the southern arm divides again further down. There are thus three main channels (known as *bratul)* through the Delta: the **Chilia arm** in the north forms the border with the Ukraine and is rarely visited by tourists; the **Sulina arm** in the centre, which runs directly east to the eponymous coastal town; and the **Sfântu Gheorghe arm** in the south. The latter two have tourist facilities.

Although the Sulina arm is largely artificial, having been straightened in the 1870s with British involvement (19th-century geopolitics made Britain keen to improve access from central Europe to the Black Sea) and handles a fair amount of commercial shipping, many visitors base themselves along its shores, either in the main tourist hub of Crişan, in smaller Maliuc, or in Sulina itself, the Delta's only real town beyond Tulcea. The meandering Sfântu Gheorghe arm has had some straight sections added but is still the quietest of the three, and the coastal fishing village of the same name is remote and beautiful – even if it's under threat from a slightly improbable gentrification, with a trend for people from Bucharest to buy second homes there.

The Sulina arm

The floating hotel moored beside the tiny community of **Maliuc B** is used by tour groups, and is within reach of

Lake Furtuna, renowned for its birdlife. Further along the Sulina arm, the long thin village of **Crişan C** has places to stay *(pensiones* and one hotel) as well as a bar. It is possible to arrange bird-watching trips from here along the smaller channels. Inconveniently on the other side of the channel from Crişan there is an ARBDD tourist information centre (theoretically open in summer Tues–Fri 10am–4pm, Sat–Sun 10am–2pm, winter Mon–Fri 10am–6pm). The original course of the Danube (Dunărea Veche) meanders along to the north, and the village of **Mila 23 D** lies on its banks (the name comes from the number of nautical miles from the sea along the original course). Another excursion from Crişan that follows the old course of the river is to the large village of **Letea E** and the unique inland sand dunes and oak forest beyond (the forest is a strictly protected area and access is limited). Letea is a good place to see traditional wooden houses.

Both Mila 23 and Letea are home to Lipovani people, the Russian Old Believers who fled their homelands in

Map on page 167

Some of the oak trees in Letea Forest are 600 years old – about as old as the land itself. Many are covered in writhing lianas, the world's most northerly outpost of this subtropical plant.

BELOW: fishing remains important.

As a result of the inexorable eastward expansion of the Delta (40 metres / yards per year), Sulina's old lighthouse is now over 2 km (1¼ miles) from the sea.

BELOW:
on the lookout
on Lake Furtuna.

the 17th and 18th centuries after they rejected liturgical reform in the Russian Orthodox Church and were persecuted. Most of them were fishermen in Russia, and they thrived in their new home. In the 18th century a wave of Ukrainian fugitives also arrived. There was some conflict between the two, but these days they live peacefully side by side (Letea has a large Ukrainian population). Together the descendants of these migrants make up the majority of the Delta's 15,000 population (this figure excludes Tulcea).

As the waterway nears the sea, **Sulina ❼** rears up out of the reeds. This is the only proper town in the Delta, with streets and cars. These days it has a woebegone, end-of-the-world feel, but a century ago it was a significant port through which much of Romania's lucrative grain harvest was exported – having benefited from the straightening of the channel and its status as a free port. Prosperity was fleeting, though, with the vagaries of global economics, problems with silting and, later, the advent of the Black Sea Canal consigning Sulina to something resembling a

ghost town. These days, subsidies and tourism have helped perk things up a bit. There is an ARBDD tourist office close to the main ferry dock.

The main sight is the old **lighthouse** (open Mon–Fri 2–6pm; admission charge) in the centre of town, dating from 1802 and protruding some 50 metres (165 ft) from the surrounding flatness. Another defunct 19th-century lighthouse lies across the channel from the town. The **International Cemetery**, a reminder of the years when Sulina was home to the Danube European Commission (the international body that was responsible for maintaining the channels from Brăila to Sulina), and had a lively maritime trade, is also of interest. The long-disappeared cosmopolitan port is recalled by the gravestones of the Greeks, the pre-eminent business community, several British engineers and administrators, and sailors from various countries. The sandy **beach** is a further 1 km (½ mile) to the east.

There is a range of accommodation in Sulina and the town makes a reasonable base from which to explore the Delta – several operators offer excursions.

The Sfântu Gheorghe arm

Access along this southern branch is good – apart from the ferries and hydrofoils from Tulcea *(see margin, page 166)* it is possible to get as far as **Murighiol** Ⓖ by bus (the village has accommodation and at least one restaurant). The stretch from Nufaru to Mahmudia and Murighiol lies at the southern edge of the Delta and is flanked by hills. Further downstream the channel passes close to the Caraorman Forest – this and neighbouring wetlands offer excellent bird-spotting.

The mainly Ukrainian fishing village of **Sfântu Gheorghe** Ⓗ is a picturesque place close to a fine beach and within easy striking distance of some of the best bird-watching areas; it is becoming the most popular place to stay in the Delta. The village was once famed for its caviar, but production has drastically declined in recent years.

Coastal areas to the west of Sfântu Gheorghe, particularly around Lake Razim and Lake Sinoie, are prime territory for observing migrating birds, notably red-breasted geese and various species of wader.

The Măcin Mountains

To the west and southwest of Tulcea, Dobrogea is hilly, and within this expansive, sparsely populated and rather un-European landscape of wooded steppe and craggy summits, the small **Munţii Măcin National Park** Ⓝ (Parcul Naţional Munţii Măcinului) protects one of the continent's best places to observe raptors (birds of prey), with numerous migrating species passing overhead in spring and autumn. There are also numerous reptiles including Mediterranean spur-thighed tortoises, Balkan wall lizards and nose-horned vipers. The highest point is only 467 metres (1,536 ft).

There is no visitor centre or other facilities in the park, it's simply a case of finding your way here by car; a few kilometres southeast from the village of Măcin, shortly after the quarry, turn left onto a dirt road which leads to the park – the pathway is easy to spot as it climbs into the hills. From the rocky summits you can gaze down to the Danubian flatlands, the giant chemical works at Galaţi, and across to the Ukraine and a small wedge of Moldova. ❑

The ancestors of the Delta's Ukrainian population arrived in the 18th century.

BELOW: steppe vegetation on the Măcin Mountains. The range is one of the world's oldest.

Maps on pages 157, 167

RESTAURANTS

Restaurants

Outside Constanţa many restaurants are only open in summer. Some establishments do not possess a street address.

Constanţa

Acropolis
Str. General Manu 1
Tel: 0742-692234
A Greek restaurant not afraid to place Italian olive oil on the table is a great place indeed. The food is authentically Greek, with plenty of *meze* to choose from, and there are some memorable lamb dishes too. Gets very busy at weekends, so book a table. €€€€

Au Coq Simpa
Str. Ştefan cel Mare 19
Tel: 0241-614797
French and Romanian food served in a charming little restaurant on Constanţa's main street. Posesses the best wine list in the city, with as many international wines as there are local on offer. €€€€

Beirut
Complexul Dacia,
B-dul. Tomis 235

PRICE CATEGORIES

Price categories are per person for a three-course meal with wine:
€ = under 30 lei
€€ = 30–45 lei
€€€ = 45–60 lei
€€€€ = over 60 lei

Tel: 0241-558815
Ignore the unpromising location in what appears to be a *palat al foamei* (palace of hunger) on a major traffic intersection, as this place offers authentic Lebanese food at reasonable prices. For the indecisive – or cash-strapped – the daily set menus are a sound choice. €€€

Cazinoul
Faleza Cazino
Tel: 0241-617416
Glorious Art Nouveau casino that was once the pride of Constanţa, now long overdue for privatisation. Still, few places on the coast offer a finer location to soak in the sea views over a drink, or a meal, if you can get anyone to serve you. €€€

Davia Brau
Str. Smârdan 18
Tel: 0241-619477
Lively Romanian take on a bierkeller, although nothing particularly German about the food or drink. Dishes so beautifully presented they look like a food photographer's portfolio. Erratic service. €€€

El Greco
Str. Decebal
Tel: 0722-414010
Superb Greek restaurant though they overdo the Greek theme, with mini-Acropolis ornaments and pictures of Olympian athletes at every turn. The food is great however, and the

very sweet range of desserts is not to be passed over. €€€

Irish Pub
Str. Stefan cel Mare 1
Tel: 0241-550400
Not exactly an Irish pub as you may know it, but it does serve Guinness alongside some great pub food. Long tables make it a friendly, busy place where getting a seat can be tough. In summer the terrace serves terrific ice cream. €€€€

Kleyn
Hotelul Kleyn,
Str. Primăverii 63A
Tel: 0241-656622
In a well-to-do residential quarter near Lake Tăbăcăriei, this intimate contemporary restaurant feels a bit like the dining room of a modern-art lover. It's worth coming here just to take in the surrounding villas of Constanţa's nouveaux riches. But the fine food, attentive service and friendly atmosphere are equally good reasons. Children receive a warm welcome. Excellent value. €€

La Fattoria
B-dul. Tomis 235–237
Tel: 0241-542466
Wildly popular and ludicrously affordable Italian restaurant that is hard to fault in any way, with the possible exception of the decor. Unlike most Italian restaurants in Romania, this one

has the courage of its convictions to offer a totally Italian menu – except the pickles and drinks – and gets it mostly right. At busy times – ie weekends and almost any evening – reservations are advisable. Superb. €€

La Scoica
Str. Aprodu Purice 5
Tel: 0241-614164
Pizza, pasta and salads line up on the menu at this bright restaurant alongside a smart selection of seafood dishes. Choose from *saramura de crap* (the best Romanian fish dish: carp marinated in pepper water), mussels, squid and simple grilled pike. €€€

Mao-Lin
B-dul. Mamaia 68 (behind Restaurantul London).
Tel: 0241-613535
Good place for vegetarians but otherwise run-of-the-mill Chinese restaurant with mustardy decor so kitsch you cannot decide between screaming and slapping a preservation order on it. €€€

New Safari
Str. Karatzali 1
Tel: 0722-322461
Swish and intimate seafood restaurant resembling a cross between a loft apartment and a minimalist Japanese restaurant. Popular with the nouveaux riches, who probably don't mind that the waiters try to

steer diners towards the most expensive dishes and wines. The exposed terrace offers superb sea views but is frequently too windswept for comfort. Quite pricey, although sauces, *smântână*, bread and chilli peppers are free. Better for fish than seafood. **€€€€**

On Plonge
Portul turistic Tomis
Tel: 0241-601905
While not the seafood wonderland it could and should be, this long-time favourite does serve a couple of good fish dishes, and offers outstanding views out to sea from its upper level. **€€€**

Royal
B-dul. Mamaia 191
Tel: 0241-545570
In the basement of the hotel of the same name, Constanța's finest restaurant offers delectable Greek and Romanian dishes and flawless service in a plush and intimate venue. The place doubles as a 24-hour bar for hotel residents, but it's rarely raucous. Try the *tochitură dobrogeană*, Dobrogean stew. **€€€€**

Eforie Nord

Rubin Center
B-dul. Republicii 12
Tel: 0744-289670
Bedecked with more flower boxes than many florists' shops, this pleasant terrace offers pizza and Romanian sta-

ples at low prices, and some of the cheapest beer in town. Inoffensive pop music helps keeps the atmosphere lively. Service can be slow. **€€**

Mamaia

La Fattoria
no street address
Tel: 0241-831010
Tasteful if pricy beachside offshoot of Constanța's restaurant of the same name, offering a sophisticated menu and polished service. Amazingly for Mamaia, where blaring pop is the norm, it has a refreshingly music-free atmosphere. It also runs a café bar and ice-cream parlour opposite.
Summer only. **€€€€**

Rex
no street address
Tel: 0241-831595
A rare touch of class in a resort lately famed for tack, the Rex has been oozing Art Deco elegance and exclusivity since opening in 1936. Its best feature is the impossibly romantic restaurant terrace overlooking the hotel's private beach and swimming pool. Reservations are a good idea. Summer only. **€€€€**

Neptun-Olimp

Insula
Neptun (no street address)
Tel: 0241-731306
Legendary seafood restaurant that somehow manages to live up to its reputation. If a

better place exists in Romania for a romantic tête-à-tête than this ivy-clad Robinson Crusoe fantasy, we have yet to discover it. As the name suggests, the restaurant occupies an island in Lake Neptun. Reservations advisable.
Summer only. **€€€**

Mediterraneo
no street address
Tel: 0241-701107
A successful formula of tasty food at reasonable prices in a central location keeps the punters coming back. Mostly pizza, prepared from scratch and cooked in brick ovens in front of you, although other Romanian and Italian classics are also on offer. While unobtrusive, the disco lights and lively upbeat music also make this an excellent

pre-club choice in a resort that is short on clubs. Summer only. **€€**

Tulcea

Select
Str. Pacii 6
Tel: 0240-51030
Tulcea's top restaurant has some good fish dishes. Expect carp and trout. Served grilled with boiled potatoes and crushed garlic they are mouth-watering. **€€€**

Vama Veche

Papa la Șoni
No address or tel.
Legendary beach-side hang-out that is – according to Vama Veche old timers – the only place to go. Lashings of hearty Transylvanian food, Goa-hippy-style décor and live music make this unforgettable. **€€**

RIGHT: when ordering fish, check if the price is by item or by weight – if the latter, it can get expensive.

TRANSYLVANIA

Many people in the West are unsure whether Transylvania actually exists or not, and some of the scenery, both urban and rural, can seem almost unreal. This beautiful region is at last waking up to its tourist potential

For many non-Romanians, Transylvania's biggest surprise is that it exists at all. Famed throughout the world (although not in Romania itself) as the playground of vampires, werewolves and ghosts, it may seem to fans of popular culture about as real as Ruritania.

In fact, Transylvania is the best-known and most visited of Romania's three historical principalities. Its history is immersed in obscurity and controversy, its long-resident Romanian and Hungarian communities both claiming to have settled it first. *(For more on the controversy, see pages 51–54.)*

However, of all Transylvania's peoples, the Saxons, medieval émigrés from northwestern Germany, left the most disproportionate mark. For many visitors, no Romanian trip is complete without seeing the medieval Saxon towns of Braşov, Sibiu and Sighişoara, quite rightly, as their architecture intoxicates. Inevitably touted by some as the new Prague, Braşov is Romania's most tourist-friendly city. In the mountains to the south, two castles – fairy-tale Peleş above the resort town of Sinaia, and touristy but picturesque Bran – are on most tourists' itineraries.

Anyone who found Sibiu's selection as European City of Culture 2007 surprising only need go there to see why it was chosen, while impossibly romantic Sighişoara is the Middle Ages on a golden platter. And those with a taste for more of the same will find no shortage of fortified Saxon churches in the villages. These Saxon areas are covered in the first two chapters of this section of the guide.

For something different, the Székely lands are a crucible of Hungarian culture, while further west the other great Transylvanian city, Cluj, is a major draw. To the south lies dramatic Corvin Castle, Roman Sarmizegetusa and Alba Iulia, a beacon of Romanian unity. All are described in the latter two chapters of this section.

And if all these symbols of national identity get too much, take a hike. Transylvania's Bucegi, Craiului, Făgăraş, Retezat and Apuseni mountains are wonderfully unspoiled, and offer some of the best trekking in Europe. ❏

PRECEDING PAGES: springtime in the Bucegi Mountains. **LEFT:** Sighişoara passageway.

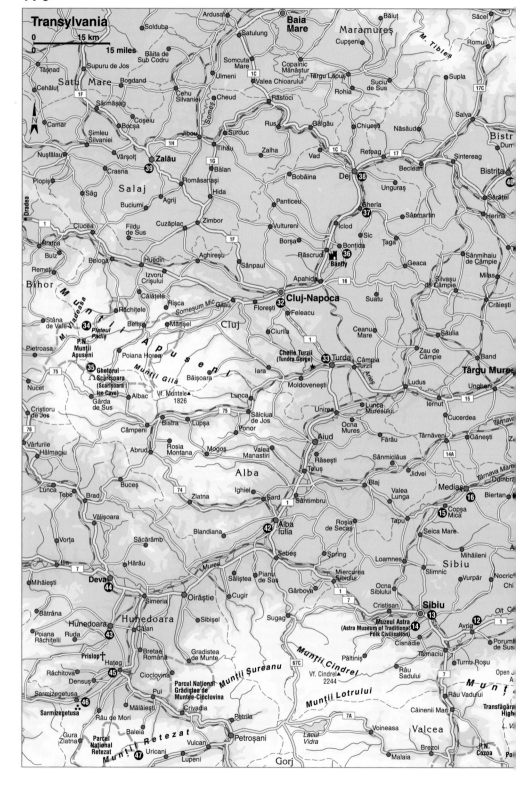

Transylvania

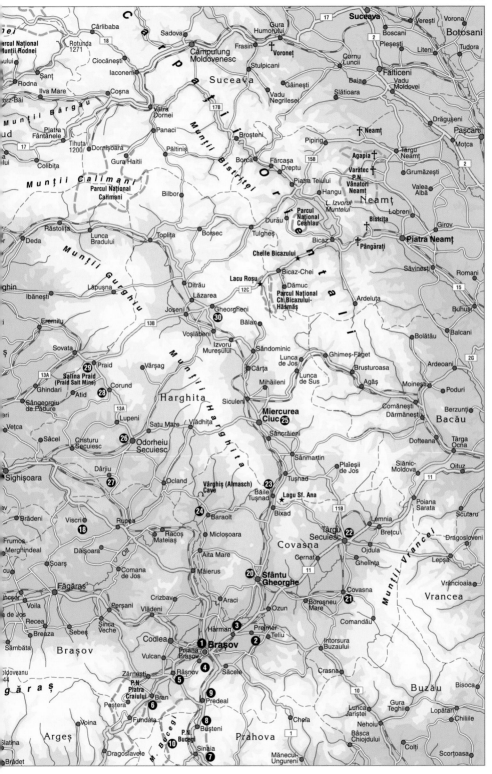

BRAŞOV AND THE EASTERN SAXON LANDS

The first taste of Transylvania for most visitors, Braşov is hard to beat. What's more, it lies on the edge of a magical, mountainous region with some of the country's most alluring destinations

asily accessible from Bucharest and with the best tourist infrastructure in Romania, this southeastern corner of Transylvania is on almost every visitor's itinerary. Within these old Saxon lands are the country's most enjoyable city, its most popular skiing resorts, fabulous mountain scenery and many of its most impressive citadels. (Sinaia, technically in Wallachia, is included here as it lies so close to Braşov, both geographically and logistically.)

The Saxons first began arriving in these parts (mainly the area around Braşov known as the Burzenland) in the early 13th century, and although their numbers are now greatly reduced, their legacy remains in the architecture and culture of the region. Not that they were the only inhabitants – as elsewhere in Transylvania, Magyars and ethnic Romanians co-existed, not always harmoniously, with their Germanic neighbours. The more westerly Saxon lands are covered in the next chapter *(see page 203)*.

BRAŞOV

Visit **Braşov ❶** (Brassó, Kronstadt) and you may conclude that all is right with the world – and with Romania. The most important Saxon town in Transylvania, the centre of Braşov still looks as if the Saxons never moved out. If you haven't developed a strain in your neck after a day exploring, you aren't paying attention. With one of the

largest and most intact medieval town centres in Romania, and one its finest town squares, Braşov is a superb place to brush up on your architectural vocabulary and feast your eyes. It also feels closer to nature than most Romanian cities, with the imposing Tâmpa Mountain looming large over the old town.

Few cities in Romania are quite so geared up to deal with tourism, and few are better for hanging around in cafés or wandering through back streets. Braşov also has the most devel-

Maps on pages 178, 182

LEFT: Piata Sfatului (Council Square, or Marktplatz), the Saxon heart of Braşov.
BELOW: happy musicians.

St Catherine's Gate dates from 1559 and bears the city's original coat of arms.

oped restaurant scene outside Bucharest, friendly people and a far more relaxed air than the capital. Unusually for Romania, the train station even has announcements in English and French. The place also has an ordered, law-abiding feel to it, although local cynics say that is partly because of the very visible police and security-guard presence, even on Tâmpa trails. On the downside, it can be crowded with tourists, especially in summer, and the nightlife is not a patch on the capital's.

Brașov, called Kronstadt by the Saxons for whom it was one of the seven cities *(Siebenbürgen)* of Transylvania, developed as a trading colony in the 13th century and soon grew prosperous because of its strategic location. While the Saxons lived within city walls they built to defend themselves from the Mongols and Turks, the Romanians were confined, in an early version of apartheid, to Șchei, outside the city walls. While the Romanians have long been free to move between the two, the districts still have a very different feel, the citadel crowded with imposing Teu-

tonic burghers' houses, while Șchei has a more rural atmosphere. During the communist era, when Brașov was briefly renamed Orașul Stalin (Stalin City), heavy industry and endless apartment blocks (the city sprawls for miles) arrived, but systematisation did not encroach on the old town or Șchei.

Piața Sfatului

Surrounded by Saxon merchants' houses painted in fetching pastel shades, the pedestrianised **Piața Sfatului Ⓐ** (Council Square) is the heart of Saxon Brașov and one of Romania's most imposing town squares. Not only is the architecture enchanting, but the mountainous backdrop adds natural drama. This was the commercial centre of the city in the Middle Ages and regular fairs would take place here, hence its Saxon name of Marktplatz. Late in summer it is the venue for the Cerbul de Aur (Golden Stag) music festival. Terraces lining the square provide a perfect excuse to sit down and absorb its medieval spendour. It's also worth exploring some of the residential passageways lining the square.

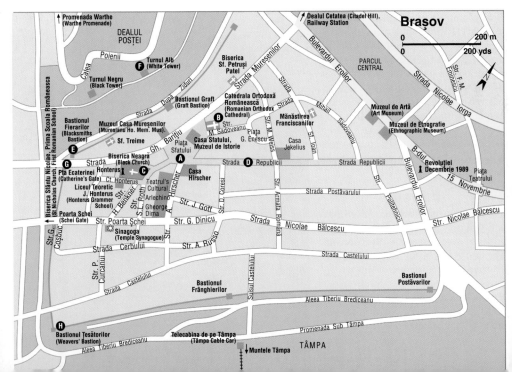

The focal point, the sturdy **Council House** (Casa Sfatului, Rathaus) is, despite its name, not an enlightened piece of social housing, but the original home of the city hall. With Gothic, Renaissance and Baroque elements, it dates from 1420 or earlier, although the tower, upper floor and Renaissance-style loggia were added later (16th–18th century), and much of the building was rebuilt after a fire in 1689. The facade bears the coat of arms of Braşov, which was originally the sign of the Honterus printing press.

Dominating the building, the somewhat top-heavy 48-metre (156-ft) **Trumpeters' Tower** is so named because heralds poised on top would warn the people of invasion or other imminent danger. According to one version of the Pied Piper legend, the children of Hamelin emerged here at the end of their subterranean journey.

Nowadays the building houses the tourist office and the moderately absorbing **History Museum** (Muzeul de Istorie; open Tues–Sun 10am–6pm; admission, photo and video charge), with collections of medieval weapons, old books and items relating to the guilds of Braşov dating back to the early 15th century. More labels in English would enhance the collection. The museum gives access to a balcony overlooking the square.

At No. 14, the imposing **Hirscher House** (Casa Hirscher) is a fine example of the Transylvanian Renaissance style, although damaged by two fires in the 17th century. Still bearing the coat of arms of the Hirscher family, it was built from 1541–7 as a present to the city from Apollonia Hirscher, widow of mayor and merchant Lukas Hirscher, to be used as a commercial centre for the Saxon merchants. It is also known as the Merchants' Hall (Casa Negustorilor) or less officially as High-Boots' Bridge (Podul Batusilor), because of its loggia and the fact that the first floor was a footwear market. Nowadays the building houses a famous, if highly overrated, restaurant, Cerbul Carpatin.

At No. 25, the **Mureşianu House Memorial Museum** (Muzeul Casa Mureşenilor; open Tues–Fri 9am–5pm, Sat–Sun 10am–5pm; admission charge

Map on page 182

Two useful websites are www.poiana-brasov.ro for hotels, www.poiana.info.ro for general tourist information.

BELOW:
the prosaically named Council House dominates Piaţa Sfatului.

Braşov is Romania's most touristy town and, together with Sibiu, it has the best facilities in the country.

BELOW: folk festival in Braşov.

except Sat–Sun; www.muzeulmuresenilor.ro) was originally the home of the influential Mureşianu family, highly active in politics and journalism in the 19th century. One of its most famous members, Andrei Mureşianu (1816–63) was author of Romania's current national anthem. The quirky collection inside is one of the largest family archives in Romania, donated in 1968.

Hidden at the end of a Baroque passageway in the middle of the merchants' houses on the square's northern side, the lovely **Romanian Orthodox Cathedral** Ⓑ (Catedrala Ortodoxă Românească) provides a dash of exoticism in contrast to the sturdy Germanic feel of the square. If other Orthodox cathedrals in Transylvania seem calculated to overpower their surroundings, this one seems almost apologetic. Built in 1896, the cathedral is based on a Greek Orthodox design, the tower a later addition, added in 1972, following an earthquake in 1940. Particularly vibrant frescoes inside, of a Byzantine, almost Liberty style, liven up an otherwise gloomy interior.

If the Romanian Orthodox cathedral underwhelms with its subtle proportions, the austere 89-metre (292-ft) long **Black Church** Ⓒ (Biserica Neagră, Fekete templom, Schwarze Kirche; open Mon–Sat 10am–5pm; admission charge), towering just south of the square, does quite the opposite. Still catering to Braşov's 1,700-strong Saxon community, it is often claimed to be the largest Gothic church in southeastern Europe and is one of the most important Lutheran churches in Romania.

Built from 1383–1477, it started life, like many Lutheran churches in Transylvania, as a Roman Catholic place of worship. Inside, the nave overwhelms with its staggeringly lofty proportions. The church is not black at all: the name comes from its appearance after a fire in 1689. Thanks to the tradition of Saxon merchants donating Turkish carpets from their travels, the 120-strong collection of rugs from the 17th–18th century lining the interior is one of the richest in Europe. The column nearest the western door still bears bullet marks from the 1989 revolution. At a

Map on page 182

height of 66 metres (216 ft), the bell tower is claimed to be the largest in Europe, and its bell, weighing 7 tons, is the heaviest in Romania.

Two side chapels have exhibitions relating to Johannes Honterus and the history of the church. The largest mechanical organ in Romania was added in 1836–39 by Buchholz of Berlin and has around 4,000 pipes – the biggest of which measures 11 metres (35 ft) – as well as 63 sounding registers and four manuals and pedals. Organ concerts take place here at 6pm every Tuesday.

Lined with parish and school buildings, the close around the church, Curtea Johannes Honterus, still feels very much like a Saxon enclave. The prestigious **Honterus Grammar School** (Liceul Teoretic Johannes Honterus; Johannes Honterus Lyzeum; www.honterus.xhost.ro) takes its name from its founder and first rector, Johannes Honterus (1498–1549). A geographer, publisher and scholar, Honterus is best remembered as the Lutheran reformer of Transylvania's Saxons, although he is also famous for his contribution to cartography. While the school is still one of the five in Romania where the main medium of teaching remains German, the pupils in their neat uniforms are as likely to be Romanian or Hungarian as Saxon. The school has functioned since 1544. A stern-looking **statue of Honterus**, the work of German sculptor Harra Magnussen, stands between the school and the church, and was unveiled in 1898 to mark the 400th anniversary of Honterus' birth.

A former catacomb of the Black Church on Piața Sfatului is now the Bella Muzica restaurant *(see page 198)*.

At Strada Poarta Șchei 29, 100 metres/yds south of the Black Church, the restored **Temple Synagogue** (Sinagoga; Str. P. Șchei 29), which looks Moorish in parts, dates from 1901 and caters to Brașov's 280-strong Jewish community.

Around the old town

Brașov's main street, the pedestrianised **Strada Republicii** D, leads north off Piața Sfatului towards Bulevardul Eroilor and is the main shop-

Signs around the Black Church warn visitors not to stand too close to the walls because of the danger of falling masonry.

BELOW: the view from Mount Tâmpa.

BELOW: the Festival of the *Juni* takes place in early May.

ping strip. However, as Braşov is a relatively conservative place, few shops in the centre stay open late at night. In summer the street comes alive with pavement cafés and street entertainers, and you are almost as likely to hear English or German as Romanian.

In a neo-baroque building (1902) at Bulevardul Eroilor 21A, the **Art Museum** (Muzeul de Artă; www.mab.ro; open Thur–Sat 10am–6pm; admission charge) has works by Romanian and international artists from the 17th century onwards. Almost any leading Romanian artist has works on show here, with Theodor Pallady, Ştefan Luchian and Nicolae Grigorescu particularly well represented, as well as local artist János Máttis-Teutsch (1884–1960). The basement has a fine collection of Oriental art and European porcelain.

The **Ethnographic Museum** (Muzeul de Etnografie; open summer Tues–Sat 10am–6pm; winter 9am–5pm; admission charge; www.etno brasov.ro) next door has a small but worthwhile collection of textiles and folk costumes from the Braşov region.

Fortifications

Now housing Braşov's state archives, the **Blacksmiths' Bastion** **E** (Bastionul Fierarilor; Str. Bariţiu 34) originally guarded the northwest side of the citadel and dates from 1529 or earlier. At first it bore the shape of a pentagon, although almost all of the current structure is the result of rebuilding in 1668 and 1709. The valuable collection includes the earliest document in Romanian, a letter from Neacşu of Câmpulung, dated 1521.

Behind the Blacksmiths' Bastion a road leads to the best-preserved part of the old city walls, with a stream running alongside overlooked by a cliff. Known as **Strada După Ziduri** (Beyond the Walls Street), the pathway between the walls and the stream feels so rural it is hard to imagine you are near the centre of town, although speeding cyclists and skaters can remind you of the fact with a jolt. From here a path leads up to the square **Black Tower** (Turnul Negru; open Tues–Sun 10am–6pm; admission, photo and video charge), built in 1494. Like the Black Church, it is not black at all but so named because of a fire, in 1599. Although the tower houses a small **museum**, there is not much to see inside and better views are available for free from the **Warthe Promenade** (Promenada Warthe) higher up the hill. A popular place with lovers as well as those merely enamoured with Braşov, the viewing platform provides a superb view of the Black Church and most of the city. From here you can appreciate just how intact Braşov's old city is.

Closer into town up a flight of 200 steps, the semicircular **White Tower** **F** (Turnul Alb), which *is* white, is another of the seven bastions guarding the 15th-century wall and also dates from 1494. Beneath the White Tower is the rectangular **Graft Bastion** (Bastionul Graft). After all that climbing, you may feel the need to sit down for a drink. Fortunately the Graft Bastion doubles as one of

Braşov's most atmospheric cafés, Cafeneaua Graft. The **museum** (open Mon noon–7pm, Tues–Fri 11am–7pm, Sat–Sun 10am–7pm; admission charge) upstairs has an interesting collection of old weapons and items related to Braşov's mediaeval guilds. It is also a good place to buy souvenirs.

Another stretch of city walls runs southeast past **Catherine's Gate ⓖ** (Poarta Ecaterinei), a gloriously spiky construction that represents exactly what many Westerners think of when imagining Transylvanian architecture. The original outer tower, with four small pinnacles around a central tower, is the only original medieval city gate still preserved, and dates from 1559. The facade bears the city's original coat of arms. Next to it the baroque **Şchei Gate** (Poarta Şchei) resembles a triumphal arch. It dates from 1828, although built on the site of an earlier gate. From the 13th–17th century this was the only entrance Romanians living in Şchei could use to reach the Saxon citadel.

Further along, the imposing **Weavers' Bastion ⓗ** (Bastionul Ţesătorilor; open Tues–Sun 10am–6pm; admission, photo and video charges) is the largest and best-preserved of the city's original seven, dating from 1421–36 and rebuilt from 1570–73. Inside the courtyard, with four levels of wooden loggias linked by walkways, it is still easy to imagine its original use as an emergency storehouse for food. The ground floor also has the remains of an old stone doorway and some Saxon funerary tablets. The small **museum** inside the bastion has some military relics from the 14th century onwards but the most impressive exhibit is a remarkable 19th-century scale model of Brasov's old town as it was in 1600.

Above the bastion, a bracing trail through the thickly wooded foothills of Mount Tâmpa (Muntele Tâmpa) leads to the **Tâmpa cable car** (telecabina de pe Tâmpa; open Mon noon–5pm, Tues–Fri 9.30am–6pm, Sat 9am–7pm, Sun 9.30am–6pm). Whisk-ing passengers to the peak (960 metres/3,150 ft), the chairlift offers access to one of the best views in town, although if you are fit you may prefer to walk instead. Now topped with a TV antenna, the Tâmpa peak was the site of Braşov's original citadel until Vlad Ţepeş stormed and destroyed it in 1458–60. The base station has a good game restaurant with a terrace.

Visible from the main square and much of the town, a huge sign near the peak of Mount Tâmpa has spelled out the name Braşov in large white capital letters, illuminated at night, since 2006. While the homage to Hollywood is obvious, there is another precedent. From 1950–60 Braşov was known as Oraşul Stalin (Stalin City) and the Soviet leader's name was etched out of fir trees on the same spot.

Above Citadel Hill (Dealul Cetăţii), the ruined 16th-century **citadel** (cetatea) houses a touristy complex of restaurants and bars.

Şchei district

In the days of Saxon hegemony, Romanians were not allowed to live in

Map on page 182

Paid for by the Romanian Women's Assembly, this 1939 statue on Piaţa Unirii in Braşov's Şchei district dates commemorates soldiers killed in World War I.

BELOW: in the heart of Şchei district.

*Near the Şchei Gate, linking Strada Cerbului with Strada Poarta Şchei, the 80-metre (87-yard) long **Strada Sforii** (Rope Street) is, according to whom you ask, the narrowest street in Braşov, Romania or Europe.*

BELOW: do not feed the bears.

the citadel and could only enter on special occasions, including the annual Juni Festival (*see page 80*). The quarter where they were allowed to live, Şchei, lies southwest of the medieval city walls, originally linked only by the Şchei Gate. To this day, Şchei retains a very different air from the old town, the architecture more simple and almost rustic. The further uphill you climb the more rural it feels. While there are few monuments as such, the district richly rewards a stroll.

Şchei's highlight, the dream-like **St Nicholas Church** (Biserica Sfântu Nicolae) is a fairy-tale Transylvanian construction with absurdly pointy spires, seemingly imitating the TV antenna atop Mount Tâmpa. Built in stone in 1495 on the site of an earlier wooden church, it was Transylvania's first Orthodox church. The neo-Byzantine frescoes help brighten up the gloomy interior (where photography is banned). Behind the church lies the grave of Nicolae Titulescu (1882–1941), a prominent Romanian politician and diplomat who was twice president of the League of Nations (1930

and 1931). Later falling out with Carol II, he died in exile and was only returned for burial in Romania in 1990.

The grounds of the church contain the site of the **First Romanian School** (Prima Şcoală Românească), also dating from 1495 although rebuilt in 1760–1. Now a museum (open daily 9am–5pm; admission charge), it has a re-creation of an old classroom replete with abacus on the ground floor, while upstairs there is a valuable collection of early books in Romanian. Multilingual guides are available on request: you may even get a priest to show you around. Some of Şchei's prettiest houses lie on narrow winding roads uphill from the church.

Prejmer and Hărman

The village of **Prejmer** ❷ (Prázsmár, Tartlau; pop. 8,000; www.geocities.com/primaria_prejmer) is conveniently close to Braşov, 16 km (10 miles) away in the middle of the large plain that lies to the north of the city, and can be reached by maxitaxi from there several times a day. The massively fortified **Church of the Holy Cross** (Biserica Sfânta Cruce,

The Bears of Braşov

In Răcădău, a suburb of Braşov, bears have been raiding rubbish bins since the 1980s. The number doing so is increasing, and they are becoming more and more fearless of people, especially since the nightly event has become a bit of a tourist spectacle and some bears are being fed by hand. Conservationists fear a backlash against bears if these urban scavengers increase and get out of hand.

From a low of 1,500 individuals in the 1960s, Romania's bears recovered to more than 8,000 in the 1980s (partly because Ceauşescu's passion for hunting led them to be protected), an unsustainable level that led to increased attacks on livestock. Since then, estimates put the population at 4,000–6,000 animals, which equates to 40–60 percent of the entire bear population of Europe.

Szent Kereszt templom, Kreuzkirche; open Tues–Fri 9am–5pm, Sat 9am–3pm; admission charge) is the reason to visit, and is located just off the main Braşov–Buzău road. There are plaques in English explaining the history of the church and its fortifications, as well as a small museum on site.

The church was built by the Teutonic knights (from 1218), brought here by Hungarian King Andrew (András) II to strengthen the defence of this eastern border region (the Burzenland) against the ever-present threat from the steppe warriors. The knights were given land around Braşov, but when they attempted to make this land independent and effectively hand it over to the Pope in Rome, they were sent packing by a Magyar army (it was bad timing; just 16 years later the Mongols swept through Transylvania). The church was later extended by the Cistercians, before being massively fortified by the Saxons against further invasions in 1421, to include some 270 rooms inside on three or four levels for the villagers' refuge in case of attack or siege. It has been on the UNESCO World Heritage list since 1999, and has undergone major renovation work in recent years. Together with Biertan and Viscri, further west in Transylvania, this whitewashed fortress is the most rewarding of the Saxon churches to visit; walking around the inner circle it's not difficult to imagine the place teeming with the local population sheltering from the rampaging Tatars.

In a large valley even closer to Braşov, the equally scruffy **Hărman ❸** (Szászhermány, Honigberg; pop. 4300; www.primaria-harman.ro) is another Saxon village, its German name meaning honey castle. Behind seven strong bastions, the circular 16th-century **fortified peasant citadel** at its heart successfully withstood numerous sieges by various invaders, although not one by the Turks in 1421. Wooden ladders in the courtyard still lead to the rooms where the populace stored food and other supplies. Inside the delightful Romanesque church (open Tues–Sun 9am–noon, 1–5pm; donations requested), built by Cistercian monks, dates from 1280 with later Gothic

Map on pages 178-9

The Teutonic Knights, evicted from this part of Transylvania (Burzenland) by the Hungarian king in 1225, moved north to establish a longer-lasting power base in Prussia.

BELOW: the inner wall of Prejmer fortified church.

BELOW: winter
landscape near
Râşnov.

modifications. As elsewhere, four pinnacles on the 52-metre (156-ft) tower
indicate that Harman once had the
right to hold trials and execute people.

SOUTH OF BRAŞOV

Poiana Braşov

Officially a district of Braşov but 12
km (8 miles) south geographically and
a world away in atmosphere, **Poiana
Braşov ❹** (alt. 1,030 metres/3,378 ft;
www.poiana-brasov.ro) sits on the slopes
of the dramatic Postăvaru Massif.
Romania's most popular skiing resort,
it is a common destination for Westerners on bargain package tours, as
well as Romanians. While it certainly
competes favourably in price with
Klosters and Aspen and is a good place
for beginners, not least children, more
advanced skiers may find the slopes a
little too easy. Many will also find the
après-ski a bit subdued compared with
the Alpine resorts. However, the blissfully tranquil and sheltered setting is a
major plus and skiing is possible here
longer than in most places in Romania.
The tourist office in the centre is a good

source of information on skiing and
hiking possibilities. Poiana Braşov has
some rustic restaurants and a wide
range of accommodation.

The town lacks architectural monuments, although buildings have to be
in an alpine chalet style and there are
few monstrosities to mar the skyline.
Even the bus shelter, in wooden Maramureş style, is a work of art and probably the most beautiful in Romania.

There are two cable-car lines running
from Poiana Braşov. One to the peak of
Mount Postăvaru (1,800 metres/5,908
ft) runs only in summer, while the less
dramatic but still impressive other line,
to Kanzel, runs all year round. Many
facilities close down outside the skiing
season (Dec–Mar), although lots of
people come in summer to enjoy the
cool weather, pure air and fine views.
In summer, Poiana Braşov is also popular with motorcylists and cyclists.
Bicycle hire is available from Casa
Vinga near the centre.

Râşnov

Continue along the mountain road
from Poiana Braşov and you will end

up in **Râşnov** ❺. While Bran, just 12 km (8 miles) further south, gets all the tourists – especially package tourists – Râşnov is well worth a stop.

The **Castle** (Castelul Râşnov; open daily summer 7am–8pm, winter 7am–6pm; admission and photo charge) is at first sight so imposing, and visible from so far away, it would be easy to confuse it for the much better-known Bran Castle. Built as a peasant citadel in the 13th century, it was one of the main defences of the Burzenland. While there is no longer a huge amount left to see of the structure itself, which is less well-preserved than Bran, the ethnographic folk art exhibits help bring it to life and the views are stupendous. At the top of a stony climb, the 360-degree panorama at the highest point offers fine vistas over Râşnov town, the Bucegi Mountains and Piatra Craiului. The castle is so big and sprawling that it is easy to miss some sections – although the best-preserved parts are near the entrance, as well as the external wall and a couple of towers. At the other end the ruins remain rather difficult to distinguish. The paths and signs are not very good,

but children will love it. It has one of the most picturesque taverns in Romania – but beware of the dogs outside. The well of the castle (146 metres/480 ft deep) was the work of Turkish prisoners who were promised their freedom when the job was finished. Starting in 1623, it took them 17 years.

Although slightly scruffy, the nearby town of **Râsnov** (Barcarozsnyó, Rosenau; pop. 15,000) repays visitors with some well-preserved Saxon architecture around the centre.

Bran

On a rocky outcrop above the village of **Bran** ❻ (Törcsvár, Törzburg; pop. 5100; www.primariabran.ro), 30 km (18 miles) south of Braşov, the perennially popular **Bran Castle** (Castelul Bran; www.brancastlemuseum.ro; open daily summer 9am–6pm, winter 9am–4pm; admission charge) is a fixture of most organised tours of Romania. So closely linked is Bran Castle in many visitors' minds to the Dracula legend that it has become an essential stop. Certainly the eerie Gothic turrets and sharp sloping roofs would make a fitting home for a

Map on pages 178-9

Wild fruit is often gathered for home use, although Romania is developing this resource on a larger scale and becoming a leading exporter of fruit to western Europe.

BELOW: the view from Raşnov Castle.

A crowded courtyard at Bran Castle. Arrive early to avoid the hordes of visitors.

BELOW: looking along the Bârsa Valley from Bran. For years this was the main route between Transylvania and Wallachia.

vampire, and there are enough pointy architectural features to delight any impaler.

In reality, though, the Dracula connection is tenuous at best. Vlad the Impaler, on whom the Dracula legend was loosely based, never even lived here, let alone built it, although he may have spent two nights here hiding from the Turks, or may have besieged the castle at one point. In reality, Vlad was a prince of Wallachia, not Transylvania, and it is to Wallachia you should head for real Dracula associations. However, it is possible that Bram Stoker based Dracula's castle on Bran, and many film companies set Dracula movies here. Incidentally, the "real" Dracula's castle at Poienari *(see page 142)* gets a tiny fraction of the visitors Bran does, the mandatory 1,000-step ascent being a deterrent to many.

However, notwithstanding the lack of Dracula credentials and the slight Disneyland-meets-Hammer-House-of-Horror feel to the place, Bran Castle is definitely worth a visit. The Romanian royal family lived there, and many of the rooms display homely touches of Queen Marie's taste. On the other hand, if you only have time to visit one castle in Romania, Corvin *(see page 249)* or Peleș *(see page 195)* might make better choices.

Saxons built the castle around an inner courtyard in 1377 to defend the Bran Pass: for centuries, until it was superseded by the road along the Prahova Valley, this was the main route between Transylvania and Muntenia (eastern Wallachia). Bran thus protected nearby Brașov against invasion from the south, and also served as a customs post. In 1920 the city of Brașov gave the castle as a present to Queen Marie, who decorated it according to her very individual style. It became her favourite residence.

While the castle itself may be rather overrated, the countryside surrounding it is some of Transylvania's loveliest and there are plenty of agrotourism options hereabouts.

Sinaia and around

The narrow Prahova Valley, along which the resort towns of Sinaia, Busteni and Predeal sprawl for miles,

cuts through the mountains forming a natural route into Transylvania from the Wallachian plain.

The former summer retreat of Romania's royal family, **Sinaia** (pop. 12,000; www.primariasinaia.ro) ❼ has Romania's most spectacular castle and retains an unruffled aristocratic air barely withered by decades of communism. It developed as a mountain resort in the 19th century, with the construction of Peleş Castle in the cool conifer forests above the town. (At the time, the Hungarian border lay just to the north, at Predeal; this is still the border of Wallachia and Transylvania – Sinaia and Busteni lie within Wallachia but are included here for convenience.)

At an altitude of 800 metres (2,620ft), the town has a wonderful location at the foot of the Bucegi Mountains in the Prahova Valley, and makes a popular base for walkers and skiers – or simply a place to relax. Beware, though: it is extremely popular over Christmas and New Year and many places to stay are booked up months ahead. Year round the main attractions can get terribly crowded at weekends.

In fact, this is probably Romania's top resort after the Black Sea beaches, and unlike these it is a year-round destination, it's popularity bolstered by the fact that it is so accessible from Bucharest – just a couple of hours by car or train.

If you are arriving by train, the most direct access to the centre is up a steep staircase from the station to the main road, Bulevardul Carol I. However, there's also a longer road leading right from the station, which may be a safer bet in winter. The station is of interest in its own right, not only because it once had a royal waiting room, but because it was the site of the murder of Romanian prime minister, Ion Duca, by the Iron Guard in 1933.

The main drag, **Bulevardul Carol I**, is an odd assortment of concrete horrors such as the large Hotel Sinaia, and the fantastical spired and turreted architecture from earlier times. The street is lined with all the ephemera you'd expect in a popular resort; souvenir shops, exchange bureaux, internet cafés, hotels, restaurants and bars, extending into the smaller streets leading up the hill side.

Map on pages 178-9

A Bavarian/alpine style is apparent in some of Sinaia's older buildings.

BELOW: classic rock – the Sphinx (Sfinxul) in the Bucegi Mountains during the 1999 total eclipse.

Some of the mountain trails are badly littered, particularly those lying close to the cable cars at Sinaia and Buşteni.

BELOW: the road up to Kota 1400 from Sinaia.

The **Dimitrie Ghica Park** (Parcul Dimitrie Ghica) at the northern end of the strip has a fine ensemble of neo-Brâncoveanu buildings, including the splendid **Hotel Caraiman**, built in 1880 and rebuilt in 1924, and a **casino**, dating from 1912–13. A secret tunnel linking it with the nearby Hotel Palace was built so that successful gamblers could go back to their beds without being mugged. At the turn of the 20th century Sinaia was an important stop on the Orient Express and the Caraiman and Palace hotels were built to cater for passengers. A small stone bench in the park, dating from 1905, was the work of Carol I and is known as the king's bench. So elegant is the setting that when Romanian mineral-water company Biborţeni shot a much-aired fin-de-siècle-style advert promoting the refinement of their product, this park was chosen as the setting.

Founded by Mihail Cantacuzino, the serene if sometimes overcrowded **Sinaia Monastery** (Mănăstirea Sinaia; open daylight hours; admission charge) dates from 1690–5. A short walk uphill from Ghica Park, a com-munity of 20 monks live within its neat, whitewashed cloisters decorated with flower pots. There are two churches. The original, smaller church, on your left through a finely carved stone doorway as you enter, is currently closed for restoration. The larger, modern church dates from 1843–6. Enamelled bricks and painted alcoves lavishly embellish the exterior. A curious fusion of political and religious symbolism, the three intertwined green bands around the church represent both the Holy Trinity and the Union of the Romanian Principalities.

Inside, the vibrant neo-Byzantine frescoes are the work of Danish artist Aage Exner. Underlining Sinaia's royal connections, portraits of its founder and various members of the Romanian royal family line the walls. One of Carol I symbolically has his hand resting on a column missing a corner, indicating that Romania was incomplete without Bukovina, Transylvania and Bessarabia (eastern Moldavia). A small **museum** (open July–Aug Mon–Sat daylight hours; admission charge) in the grounds has a collection of religious art.

Peleş Castle

In a large, landscaped garden high above Sinaia (a stiff 30-minute walk from Bulevardul Carol I), the fairy-tale **Peleş Castle** (Castelul Peleş; open Wed 11am–5pm, Thur–Sun 9am–5pm, last ticket 4pm; admission charge; www.peles.ro) is the town's main attraction and Romania's most romantic fortress. Built as King Carol I's summer home from 1873–83 in a spectacular German Renaissance style, it resembles a Bavarian *schloss* and is better preserved than other royal palaces in Romania. One explanation is that the communist authorities used it as a guesthouse for important visitors, although it was also intermittently open to the public. The difference between Peleş and Cotroceni *(see page 129)*, for example, is striking. Here, almost all the original fittings remain in place whereas in Cotroceni most are gone.

Although many of the castle's 160 rooms are surprisingly small, it's the quality and intricacy of the decor that astounds, from the Murano crystal chandeliers to the carved teak and German stained-glass windows. While the exterior represents the German high culture with which King Carol was most comfortable, the interior is more eclectic and in places even homely. The hand of Carol's wife Elizabeth is everywhere apparent. Better known by her nom de plume Carmen Sylva (Song of the Forest), she was a lover of all things Celtic and Scandinavian, and filled the palace with Celtic crosses, Norwegian chairs and wood and leather panelling. Many of the features, including a whole staircase, are purely decorative.

The castle is also impressive for its high-tech appliances, including a vacuum cleaner from 1901 and an electric food elevator from 1912, still in use. One room decorated by a young Gustav Klimt served as the royal cinema.

Although the castle was the royal family's private property rather than the state's, negotiations to return it to King Michael have been protracted. While all agree the castle should remain open to the public, there are some concerns that the king lacks the financial means to maintain or restore it. The subject is a hot topic among Romanians.

Map on pages 178-9

TIP

Without the right contacts, visiting Peleş Castle is possible only as part of a group. At busy times the tours can seem a bit rushed, and many rooms are off-limits. Note that there is a separate entrance for foreigners, and that there are no toilets available in the building.

BELOW:
Peleş Castle has a lavish interior, and an extraordinary exterior.

Cable cars operate at Bușteni and Sinaia. Sinaia also has a chair lift on the upper section, mainly for the use of skiers but also open at weekends at other times of year when the cable car is closed for maintenance (around one month each year).

BELOW: Predeal Orthodox Church.

The smaller **Pelişor Palace** (Palatul Pelişor; same hours as Peleş; admission charge) a few hundred metres/yds uphill from Peleş was built from 1899–1903 for Carol I's nephew and heir Ferdinand, and his wife Marie. Reportedly, Ferdinand found both Peleş and his uncle's brooding company too austere. Although the exterior is also in the German Renaissance style that was all the rage in Sinaia at the time (many fine examples remain), the interior is Art Nouveau, with exquisite examples of Tiffany and Lalique glassware and Viennese furniture. As at Peleş, guided tours are mandatory, although groups are slightly smaller.

Slightly further uphill, the alpine-style **Foişor Lodge** (Foişorul) dates from 1878 and was most famously the place where King Carol II met his Jewish mistress Magda Lupescu, a liaison that scandalised 1920s Romanian society (it occurred at a time when anti-Semitism was rife, and Lupescu was reputed to have several shady financial investments). The lodge and several other buildings in the vicinity are closed to the public and guarded by sentries.

Bușteni

Surrounded by the Caraiman, Coştila and Zamora peaks, **Bușteni** ❽ (Bustény; pop. 9,700), 10 km (6 miles) north of Sinaia, at an altitude of 885 metres (2,904 ft), is a small resort that makes a good base for hiking in the Bucegi Mountains. The town itself, however, is not a patch on Sinaia and is blighted, like Predeal (*see below*), by the extremely busy main road running right through its centre. The main attraction, the **Cezar Petrescu Memorial Museum** (Muzeul Memorial Cezar Petrescu; Str. Tudor Vladimirescu 2; open Tues–Sun 9am–5pm; admission charge) occupies a fine, early 20th-century construction in Romanian peasant style at the northern edge of town. Novelist Cezar Petrescu (1892–1961), who lived here, is best known for his children's book, *Fram the Polar Bear (Fram, ursul polar)*. The starting point for many trails, most well-indicated, is the top of the cable-car line. Maps are widely available. One popular and easy trail goes to the **Urlătoarea waterfall** (Cascada Urlătoarea), while a harder one leads to a couple of unusual and much-photographed geological formations called the **Sphinx** (Sfinxul) and the **Old Ladies** (Babele).

Predeal

At the head of the Prahova Valley at the top of the pass of that name, the skiing resort of **Predeal** ❾ (pop. 5,200; www.primariapredeal.org) has less obvious appeal than the competition, both aesthetically and in terms of skiing. At 1,033 metres (3,388 ft), this is the highest town in Romania, but despite its mountainous setting Predeal lacks the wow factor of Sinaia or the facilities of Poiana Brașov. It may appeal to those looking for somewhere quieter to stay or for less arduous hiking or very easy skiing, although the busy main road and railway line dissecting it is a major disadvantage. Getting from one half of Predeal to the other can mean scrambling over railway lines, going through

the litter-strewn railway tunnel or taking the long road, while arriving there after dark can be a disorienting experience. The Predeal Tour room booking agency (tel: 0268-455304) at the train station is theoretically open Mon–Sat 9am–5pm. There is a map of the area at the station, while the tourist office, also at the station, gives foreigners free maps. Romanians have to pay.

Diagonally opposite the train station and resembling a modern-day fortress, the spanking-new **Orthodox Church** has some extraordinarily vibrant modern-day icons and a soaring glass and wooden interior. It was built in 2000 and looks more like a Baptist or Catholic church than an Orthodox one.

Hiking in the Bucegi

The **Bucegi Massif ⑩** towers over the Prahova Valley in a dramatic series of gigantic precipices – the highest conglomerate cliffs in Europe. Cable cars at Sinaia and Busteni give quick access. The Sinaia cable car (Teleferic) terminal is a short walk up the hill opposite the town hall and tourist information office (by the Hotel Anda). The first stage

reaches Kota 1400 (at 1,400 metres/4,592 ft), which is also accessible by road, then the second stage proceeds all the way up to Kota 2000 (actually at 2,100 metres/6,890ft) at the top of the slope. From here the terrain levels out onto an alpine plateau, with numerous marked trails for hikes of varying length. Buy a copy of the Dimap (1:70,000), which has recommended routes and estimated times. An even better option for those with limited time, or wanting just a short hike, is the cable car from Busteni. There is one stage only but it takes you even higher, and within a couple of hours' walk of some of the most dramatic viewpoints.

For those with more time, and plenty of stamina, the two-day hike over the mountains to Bran is recommended (stay overnight in a *cabana*, a basic mountain hut with bunk beds and hot food – but book ahead; *see page 361 for details*). Beyond Bran, the **Piatra Craiului** range is wilder than most of the Bucegi, and a favourite with hikers. It is also one of the best places in the country to see bears and chamois. Access is via the town of Zărnești. ❏

Map on pages 178-9

TIP

The Sinaia cable car (Telerific) operates from 8.30am–4pm, with the last trip at 3.45pm. Although there isn't a proper timetable – it only starts moving when there are sufficient passengers – you won't have to wait more than 15–20 minutes. The Bușteni cable car operates similar hours.

BELOW: the Piatra Craiului range from the village of Moeciu.

RESTAURANTS & CAFÉS

Braşov

Altstadt
Piaţa Sfatului 1
Tel: 0268-476945
Despite the German name and vaguely Teutonic theme, this restaurant has a mainly Romanian menu. The food and service are good, and the covered terrace overlooks one of Romania's finest squares. €€€

Bella Muzica
Hotelul Bella Muzica,
Piaţa Sfatului 19
Tel: 0268-477946
Occupying the catacombs of the Black Church on the main square, this ludicrously romantic venue offers Hungarian, Mexican and Romanian dishes. The service is extremely good. €€€

Bistro de l'Arte
Piaţa Enescu 1bis
Tel: 0268-473994
Doubling as an art gallery, this German-owned bistro on one of Braşov's prettiest squares is a delight. While the menu may be on the short side, daily specials help add variety. €€

Blue Corner
Piaţa George Enescu 13
Tel: 0268-478590
Top-class modern Transylvanian food and a friendly, hands-on owner who makes a point of greeting every diner. €€€€

Butoiul Sasului
Str. Republicii 53–5
Tel: 0268-410499
Done up like a Saxon ethnography museum, this restaurant is the best place in town for Saxon specialities, and shockingly cheap to boot. Live piano music every night. €€

Casa Pădurarului
Aleea Tiberiu Brediceanu 2
Tel: 0268-415619
Just below Mt Tâmpa's lower chairlift station, this upmarket wooden shack specialises in game. Friendly service and tasty food make this a winner. €€

Deane's Irish Pub & Grill
Str. Republicii 19
Tel: 0268-411767
Haydn Deane, the singing doctor who owns this place, is the former proprietor of Northern Ireland's first Michelin-starred restaurant. The eccentric menu features "Irish pizzas", enchiladas and Ulster fry among other dishes. Service can be erratic. There is music of some sort every night, either karaoke or Deane and his big band. €€€

Gustări "Sirena"
Piaţa Sfatului 14
Tel: 0268-475365
Given the elegant neoclassical interior, swanky contemporary terrace and one of the best locations in town, you might expect this to be expensive, or a tourist trap, or both. Somehow it manages to avoid being either, with excellent value and friendly service. The *specialitate braşoveană* (Braşov speciality: beef, pork and potatoes in a piquant sauce) is worth trying. €€

Irish House
B-dul. Carol I 18
Tel: 0244-310060
While this may be a Romanian take on an Irish pub, it's a stylish and cosy one. The soundtrack veers between lift music and authentically Irish, while the menu has a few vaguely Irish dishes, such as Dublin chicken liver, Irish chicken and "Irish cocktail", and pizzas such as Pizza Dracula, the Romanian options are the safest bet. Draught Guinness is on tap. €€€

Lotus Express
Str. Mureşenilor 20
Tel: 0268-412037
By far the better of Braşov's two Chinese restaurants, with friendly service and food authentic enough to satisfy. Regular Chinese diners here recommend the seafood soup, the Yang Zou rice, the meat-stuffed aubergines and ants in a tree *(furnici în copac)*. €€

LEFT: typically hearty Transylvanian fare.

Morgana
Str. Republicii 7
Tel: 0268-418117
Largely Romanian or Italian, with a few oddities such as Jamaican jerk chicken and tandoori chicken. The food is as beautifully presented as it is tasty. €€€

Pub Rossignol
Str. Mureșenilor 24
Tel: 0268-414145
While most come to this stylish cocktail bar to drink, the food is excellent. In almost any Romanian establishment, ordering a dish like *roastbeef anglais* with tuna salad would be a recipe for disaster, but here it's superb, as are the pizzas. €€€

Șirul Vămii
Str. Mureșenilor 18
Tel: 0268-477725
The adventurous menu does not disappoint and the service is exemplary. Relatively pricey but worth every leu. €€€€

Taverna
Str. Politehnicii 6
Tel: 0268-474618
A legend. Try the grilled chicken rolled around its own liver, or the *pane* mushrooms dipped in a wicked garlic sauce. The best and most popular restaurant in town, so you'll need a reservation to eat here. €€€

Poiana Brașov

Pub Rossignol
Poiana Brașov
Tel: 0268-262470
Next to the lower chairlift station, this popular offshoot of the successful Brașov bar-cum-restaurant makes a perfect après-ski hangout. The Mini sticking out of the wall adds a surreal touch. Winter only. €€

Șura Dacilor
Poiana Brașov
Tel: 0268-262327
No effort has been spared with the Dacian-warlord-themed decor at this rustic inn. Most of the ingredients for the meat-heavy traditional menu come from the restaurant's farm next door. Live Gypsy music in the evenings. €€€€

Bran

Vila Bran
Str. Sohodol 271A
Tel: 0268-236866
While the service is nothing to write home about, the spicy home-made sausages and tasty local specialities at low, low prices are reason enough to seek out this semi-rural ecotourism hideaway. €€

Sinaia

Economat
Str. Peleșului 2
Tel: 0244-311151
Once a *nomenclatură* establishment, this restaurant enjoys a fantastic setting in the Peleș Castle compound, and the terrace is wonderful in summer. However, anyone dazed by the extraordinarily grand exterior may be surprised at how plain and unpretentious the interior is. The food is merely adequate. €€

Taverna Sârbului
Calea Codrului
Tel: 0244-314400
Half of Sinaia regularly descends on this impossibly lively Serbian restaurant above the town on the new road to Cota 1400, making reservations essential. The servings are big enough to sink a ship. €€€€

Predeal

Hollidays Pub
B-dul. Mihail Săulescu 117
Tel: 0268-455276
If ever the style police found out about this establishment – a mix of dungeons-and-dragons fantasy, hunting lodge and fake molten lava – it would be instantly behind a crime scene cordon with helicopters flying above. But if you ignore the decor – which is almost impossible – the pub-cum-restaurant has excellent Romanian dishes and obliging service. €€

Vila Rouă
Str. Nicolae Bălcescu 10
Tel: 0268-457030
This tranquil villa restaurant halfway up the hill may occupy a basement with restricted views but still somehow feels bright and airy. The food too is surprisingly light. Child-friendly. €€

Cafés

Brașov

The Auld Scots Pub
Str. Apollonia Hirscher 2
Tel: 0268-470183
Brașov's little piece of Hibernia and Romania's only Scottish pub is a popular hangout. While most come to enjoy the selection of imported drinks, including malt whiskies, the authentically Scottish pub menu is another good reason to come.

Cafeneaua Graft
Aleea după Ziduri
Tel: 0749-221224
Inside the Graft Bastion, this garret-like café is an agreeable place to rest your legs after the steep climb up to the Black and White Towers.

Ceainăria Teehaus
Str. Gheorghe Barițiu 28
Tel: 0268-473005
Highly likeable teahouse just off the main square with the usual eclectic range of brews.

Sinaia

Brutaria Deutschland
B-dul. Carol I nr. 8
Tel: 0244-312552
Complex of six places including the agreeable Café Marlene Dietrich, with a German-inspired choice of pastries, in a bright modern setting. Old film posters, some of Dietrich herself, line the walls. The ice-cream is excellent. Beware that the table service is only theoretical.

THE DRACULA INDUSTRY

The name Dracula is synonymous with Transylvania. And while much of the legend is based on myth or creative licence, the truth behind it is as fascinating as it is gruesome

In the folklore of Romania and neighbouring lands, vampires share little with the Dracula image familiar from horror flicks. Far from being suave, handsome and aristocratic, they are mean shuffling creatures with red cheeks, unkempt hair and a foul stench.

Eastern Orthodox followers once believed that renouncing their religion could lead to vampirism, and those seeking links between Vlad Țepeș *(see far right)* and vampires sometimes ascribe his conversion to Catholicism as the catalyst. Some suggest a medical explanation, arguing that he may have had porphyria; symptoms include pallid skin, light sensitivity and receding gums – giving the impression of oversized teeth – sometimes accompanied by neurological disturbances. Others point to the fact that, historically, vampire scares often coincide with rabies epidemics. However, little hard evidence exists to suggest any popular association between Vlad Țepeș and vampirism before Bram Stoker wrote his famous novel.

It was Hollywood, of course, that created the image of Dracula familiar internationally. In contrast to the film industry, Romanians have been remarkably slow to latch onto the economic potential it presents. Many find foreigners' association of their country with Dracula puzzling at best, and although the authorities were always willing to accommodate curious foreign tourists, there was little active promotion.

All that looked about to change in 2002, when plans to build a Dracula theme park overlooking Sighișoara were announced. They were dropped after relentless opposition at home and abroad, even from UNESCO and Prince Charles.

Nowadays it doesn't take long in major tourist centres to track down tacky Dracula souvenirs or even Dracula-themed attractions. Many Romanians would prefer that visitors came for the country's other, more authentic, draws.

LEFT: while coach-loads of gullible tourists descend daily upon Bran Castle in search of spooky thrills, hard-core Dracula fans head instead for the less accessible ruins at Poienari, in Wallachia, where the Impaler spent years in refuge.

BELOW: the Dracula tale has endured many adaptations, few quite as fanciful as Hammer's *Dracula AD 1972*, with the count resurrected in swinging London. Critics mauled it for its flimsy plot; others revere it as a camp classic.

The count is back, with an eye for London's hot pants... and a taste for everything.

DRACULA A.D.1972

CHRISTOPHER LEE · PETER CUSHING
CHRISTOPHER NEAME · MICHAEL COLES
And Starring STEPHANIE BEACHAM

VLAD ȚEPEȘ, THE IMPALER

The real Dracula was born in Sighişoara around 1431, taking the name of his father, Vlad. In recognition of his prowess in fighting the Ottomans, Vlad senior was awarded the Order of the Dragon by the Holy Roman Emperor, Sigismund of Nuremberg; it was this that led to the epithet Dracul ("the dragon") for the father and Drăculea (son of Dracu) for the son.

When his father became Wallachia's ruler in 1436, the family moved to Târgovişte, but just six years later the young Vlad was sent for political reasons to Anatolia as a hostage of the Ottomans. Five traumatic years in captivity gave him both a hatred of the Turks and a taste for inventive methods of torture and execution. Having taken control of Wallachia in 1456 (after a brief period in 1448), he ruled with a harshness unusual even for the times, with execution the most usual punishment for almost any crime or affront to his dignity. His favourite method of execution was impaling, a particularly grisly affair in which the victim would have a sharpened stick slowly forced up the rectum and then be hoisted up to die a slow, excruciating and humiliating death. He would visit merchants incognito and execute any found short of his exacting standards of honesty. Vlad was constantly feuding with the Saxons, who represented a threat to his expansion plans.

Romanians remember him for his heroic resistance to the Turks. Defeating the Ottomans at battle in 1462, he impaled 20,000 captive troops alongside the road to Târgovişte. When the remaining forces attempted a second attack, the scare tactics proved effective: they retreated in horror.

Although the exact circumstances of Vlad's death in 1476 remain a mystery, many believe he was assassinated on the order of scheming nobles. Romanians tend to gloss over his excesses, revering him as a hero of the independence struggle and an effective law-maker. Moreover, many argue that his reputation for brutality was exaggerated, as most accounts were the work of his enemies. It was only after death that he acquired the name Țepeș (Impaler).

OVE: vampire myths go back to at least 3000 BC and span many tures, species and forms, with the legend of a blood-sucking human rticularly strong in eastern Europe, not just Romania. The most popular age we have today, of a vampire as a fanged, cape-wearing, light-shunning member of the undead aristocracy who sucks human blood and can change to a bat, is largely the creation of Bram Stoker and the film industry.

LOW: the fabulously spiky and spooky Bran Castle is many people's idea of at a Transylvanian vampire's lair should look like. However its real purpose as more prosaic: it originally served as a customs-post and defensive fort. most historians agree Vlad never lived there.

RIGHT: Irish writer Abraham "Bram" Stoker (1847–1912) is best known for his vampire novel *Dracula*, published in 1897. Although much of it was set in Transylvania, which he describes remarkably accurately, he never went there. He based the story on research he carried out into European folklore and vampirology at the British Library.

SIBIU, SIGHIȘOARA AND THE WESTERN SAXON LANDS

These Transylvanian heartlands are full of interest. Wild mountains, the compelling city of Sibiu and quiet rural backroads leading to the romantic town of Sighișoara

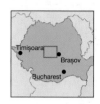

T his chapter covers the tradition- ally Saxon heart of Transylvania from the Făgăraș Mountains in the south to the splendidly time- warped medieval town of Sighișoara in the north. Inbetween is the equally medieval yet more vibrant Sibiu, the first of the Saxon *Siebenbürgen*, and chosen as the European City of Cul- ture for 2007. There are also some fas- cinating Saxon villages and fortified churches to be discovered in the folds of the hilly landscape, while the lofty mountains forming the border with Wallachia to the south make a fantastic hiking destination.

The Făgăraș Mountains

The grimy industrial town of **Făgăraș** has little to recommend it except as a base for exploring the mountains to the south. The tallest (and lengthiest) range of the Southern Carpathians, the **Făgăraș Mountains ⓫** offer hikers an almost continuous ridge, although some trails are only for experienced mountaineers with specialist equip- ment. To walk the entire length of the ridge, some 70 km (44 miles) is a pop- ular target and one that does not require experience or expertise; reckon on four to six days if you are reasonably fit (staying overnight in *cabana – see page 361)*. Maps are widely available (the 1:60 000 Dimap is good) and the trail is clearly marked with degrees of difficulty indicated.

Towards the western end of the Făgăraș, past Moldoveanu – Romania's highest peak at 2,544 metres (8,346 ft) – the **Transfăgărașan Highway** cuts through the ridge. It is so high that it is only open for a few weeks each year – usually from early July until the begin- ning of September *(see page 142)*.

On the main Brașov–Sibiu road, the village of **Avrig ⓬** (Felek, Freck) is a handicrafts centre, a base for trekking in the mountains, and the seat of **Bruken- thal Palace** (Palatul Brukenthal). The

Maps on pages 178, 207

LEFT: Sibiu's old town. **BELOW:** the grandiose Făgăraș Mountains.

*Cascading waters
close to the
Transfăgărașan
Highway.*

BELOW: the
great outdoors.

summer residence of Baron Samuel von Brukenthal (1721–1803), it belongs to the charitable Brukenthal Foundation, and is undergoing long-term restoration. It was once noted for its fine gardens, which are also under renovation.

Although he was the representative of an occupying power, people from Sibiu revere von Brukenthal as a patron of the arts, philanthropist and – unusually – one of their own. Born near Sibiu into a Saxon noble family, he rose through the ranks of the Habsburg administration, which at the time had a policy of trying to recruit representatives of subject nations. Habsburg Empress Maria Theresa was so taken with his fearless defence of the rights of his people that she appointed him her protégé. A series of high positions in the Transylvanian administration followed. Appointed governor of the principality in 1777, Brukenthal was the first and only Transylvanian Saxon to reach such a lofty position.

He also had an important role in medical history as patron of Samuel Hahnemann, whose homeopathic lab was the world's first when founded in 1797.

SIBIU

Named after the River Cibin running through it, **Sibiu** ⑬ (Nagyszeben, Hermannstadt; pop. 155,000; www.sibiu.ro) has somehow managed to fuse a strong element of the Middle Ages with the shock of the new, and to do it sublimely well. One of the most important of the Saxon *Siebenbürgen*, it dates from the late 12th century. The old city centre has retained a largely Saxon aspect, and bears a strong resemblance to a southern German or Austrian town. Today, Sibiu has some of Romania's best museums and best-preserved architecture, as well as an increasingly lively restaurant and nightlife scene.

Anyone who visits the official website, let alone Sibiu itself, will soon conclude that the town has got the hang of public relations better than most places in Romania. When it won the EU vote to be named European City of Culture 2007, alongside Luxembourg, the city launched into an orgy of building, renovation and self-promotion beyond anything ever seen in Romania. As late as October 2006 the train station was a difficult-to-

negotiate pile of mud-strewn rubble, with passengers picking their way over piles of stones for two blocks before finding a road.

While the results were not entirely clear at the time of writing, the pace of change has been impressive. Certainly, it's a good time to work in the construction or heritage industry in Sibiu. Going into 2007, a significant amount of renovation work remained unfinished. The official website for the City of Culture year is www.sibiu2007.ro, with a list of planned events in English, German and Romanian.

The upper town

Sibiu's upper town (Oraşul de sus) lies within the third and final layer of city fortifications laid out from 1357–66. It centres around three main squares, Piaţa Mare, Piaţa Mică and Piaţa Huet.

Lined with historical monuments, **Piaţa Mare** is Sibiu's historic centre and the showcase of its European City of Culture status. First recorded as the site of Sibiu's corn market, it later became a place of public meetings and executions, although the Infamy Pillar (Stilpul infamiei), to which wrongdoers would be strapped, no longer exists. Lining the square is a harmonious and largely restored blend of 15th–17th-century houses. Many have roofs featuring curiously shaped windows, known as the "city's eyes" (ochiuri ale orasului).

One of the main buildings on the square, the Baroque **Roman Catholic church** (Biserica Romano-Catolică) Ⓐ dates from 1726–33. The first Roman Catholic church allowed to function in Sibiu after the Reformation, it was originally a Jesuit foundation serving Austrian troops and administrative officials stationed here. Catering to its ethnically mixed congregation, the church has services in Romanian, Hungarian and German. The vibrant stained-glass windows are from 1901.

The parish house next door, built in 1739 as a Jesuit monastery, has an interesting, if crumbling, old statue in the courtyard. In 1948 it was removed by the communists from its original site outside the church and only returned decades later after persistent lobbying by the priest.

The figure it represents, St John Nepomuk, was tortured to death by King Wenceslas IV of Bohemia, possibly because he refused to reveal his queen's confession. The patron saint of Bohemia, he now lies buried in Prague's St Vitus Cathedral.

Situated at Nos 4–5, the magnificent, Baroque **Brukenthal Museum** (Muzeul Brukenthal; open Tues–Sun 9am–5pm; admission charge; www.brukenthalmuseum.ro) Ⓑ was originally a palace belonging to Baron Samuel von Brukenthal, Austrian Governor of Transylvania from 1777–87.

Built on a rectangular plan, the palace is laid out around two inner courtyards and its carved stone facade still bears Brukenthal's gold coat of arms. In 1817, when it opened as Romania's first museum, many of the artworks came from Brukenthal's extensive private collection. Nowadays, Transylvania's richest art collec-

Maps on pages 178, 207

TIP

Romanian state institutions are not always very good at public relations – tellingly, there is no Romanian word for marketing. But Sibiu is very much an exception. Starting off with a list of 10 reasons to visit the city, and including a what's-on listing for local nightlife, Sibiu City Hall's multilingual website (www.sibiu.ro) is one of the best of its kind in the country.

BELOW: the "eyes" of Sibiu.

Sibiu's Imparatul Romanilor Hotel, lavishly renovated in 2006 and the top place to stay in the city.

BELOW: colonnades in the Saxon centre of Sibiu.

tion is here. In addition to Western paintings from the 15th–18th century and Romanian examples from the 19th–20th century, there is a valuable collection of furniture and Oriental carpets. Sections of the museum were closed for renovations as part of the sprucing-up for the 2007 City of Culture year.

Lovingly restored and vibrantly painted in various shades of yellow, the **town hall** (primăria; Str. Brukenthal 2; www.sibiu.ro) opposite the museum provides a suitably lavish base for one of Romania's highest-profile mayors. Built as a bank in 1906, it is an eclectic Art Nouveau treat. It also houses Sibiu's **tourist office** (open Mon–Fri 9am–5pm, Sat 10am–1pm).

Slightly to the west, the **History Museum ☉** (Muzuel de Istorie; Str. Mitropoliei 2; open Tues–Sun 8.30am–4.30pm; admission charge) was the town hall from 1549–1923, and is an impressive blend of Gothic and Renaissance styles. A plaque in Latin commemorates a visit here in 1773 by Emperor Joseph II. The museum has recently been undergoing renovation.

Piața Mică

The prettiest street in the upper town, and one of its oldest, dating from the early 14th century, **Strada Avram Iancu** leads northeast from Piața Mare. One of the least-changed buildings is Casa Böbel, at No. 16. At the northeast corner of Piața Mare, Strada Magheru also retains a medieval feel. At the junction of the two streets, the Ursuline Church (Biserica Ursulinelor) was originally Dominican, built in 1474, and combines original Gothic features with Baroque additions. It served as an Ursuline nunnery from 1755–1949.

Smaller than Piața Mare, **Piața Mică ☉** (Little Square, Kleiner Ring) is connected to it by narrow passageways, while the Liars' Bridge links it to Piața Huet and Strada Ocnei leads to the lower town. Although still magnificent in its medieval splendour, it has a less monumental air than Piața Mare because from the start it has mainly housed commercial buildings. These days it is also one of Sibiu's liveliest nightlife areas.

Dating from the early 13th century, the **Council Tower** (Turnul Sfatului;

open daily 10am–6pm; admission charge) at No. 1 links Piaţa Mică with Piaţa Mare and originally served as the entrance gate to the second layer of fortifications. The name arose because the building next door was then Sibiu's town hall. The tower partly collapsed in the 1586 earthquake, and was reconstructed two years later; the roof and top floor date from 1829.

At various times it has served as a jail, a warehouse, a fire observation tower and a museum. There's not much to see inside except the clock mechanism on the sixth floor. The seventh floor, reached via 141 steps, has an observation platform.

In the pink building at No. 26, the **Pharmacy Museum ⓔ** (Muzeul Farmaciei; open Tues–Sun 9am–5pm; admission charge) occupies the site of one of Sibiu's earliest pharmacies, opened in 1600. The building dates from 1568 and combines Gothic and Renaissance styles. As well as the original collection, it has many exhibits salvaged from old pharmacies around Romania, Austria and Germany. With bottles of everything from cannabis to

valerium, the last room covers the history of homoeopathy.

It is also a tribute to Dr Samuel Hahnemann (1755–1843), the founder of homoeopathy, who lived in Sibiu from 1777–9. As Baron Samuel von Brukenthal's physician and secretary, he based many of his treatments on folk cures used in Transylvania.

In keeping with its commercial origins, Piaţa Mică's most splendid building, the **Arts House ⓕ** (Casa Artelor) at No. 21 was originally a guild house. Built in 1370, it is the oldest such structure in Transylvania and was originally known as the Butchers' House (Casa macelarilor). Guild meetings took place upstairs, while the ground floor, behind a loggia with eight arcades, served as a market. The shield on the first floor facade represents the coat of arms of Sibiu. Renovated with funding from the German Government, the building is now functioning as the **Saxon Ethnographic Museum** (Muzeul de Etnografie Săsească Emil Sigerus, Museum für Sächsische Volkskunde; open Tues–Sun 9am–5pm; admission charge), with collections

Map below

Sibiu cleaned itself up to mark its selection as the 2007 European Capital of Culture.

BELOW: a white stork's nest on top of a house is said to bring good luck.

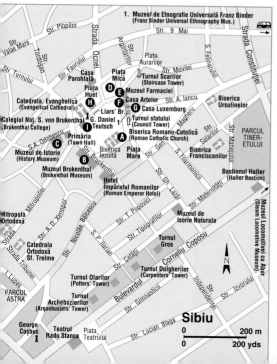

1. Muzeul de Etnografie Universală Franz Binder (Franz Binder Universal Ethnography Mus.)

Sibiu

0   200 m
0   200 yds

Sibiu is the only place in Romania where you can sample bere tăiată – "cut beer" – a two-tone mix prepared to a secret recipe. Sibiu has one of Romania's few brewery pubs, Trei Stejari, offering a range of beers rarely found elsewhere. The local beer industry goes back to 1717.

BELOW: painted easter eggs.

moved from other, smaller museums.

Another beneficiary of foreign funding, the splendidly restored **Casa Luxemburg** (Luxembourg House) is at No. 16. The building was intended to be Luxembourg's consulate in Sibiu, but the plan was later dropped: at first sight Sibiu would have seemed an odd location for the consulate of one of Europe's smallest countries, which doesn't even have an embassy in Bucharest. The decision to restore the building, went back to the two venues' joint selection, in 2004, as European Cities of Culture 2007. More tenuously, the Luxembourg Government claims historical ties because many of the Saxons who settled in Transylvania came from the Mosel area of Germany that borders the Grand Duchy of Luxembourg. To honour their visit in 2004, Sibiu granted the Grand Duke and Grand Duchess of Luxembourg honorary citizenship. Nowadays the 15th-century building has guestrooms for rent, a souvenir shop and a cellar bar. Its ground-floor loggia makes a fine setting for a café, but sadly one without any Luxembourg delicacies on offer.

Occupying a 19th-century, neo-Gothic building at No. 11, the **Franz Binder Universal Ethnography Museum** (Muzeul de Etnografie Universală Franz Binder; open Tues–Sat 10am–6pm; admission charge) was originally known as Casa Hermes – Piaţa Mică was the medieval commercial quarter and Hermes is the god of commerce. The first floor has a collection of mostly African ethnographic relics – some presented to Ceausescu – while the ground floor houses temporary exhibitions. The ground floor and basement also have good handicrafts shops.

Cathedral and college

At No. 24, the 18th-century **Staircase Tower** (Turnul Scărilor, Fingerling-ßteige) nows houses a café. From here a picturesque passageway leads down to Piaţa Aurarilor, beyond which lies one of Sibiu's prettiest and oldest residential areas, full of narrow, winding cobbled streets straight out of the Middle Ages.

Leading from Piaţa Mică to Piaţa Huet, over a passage linking the upper and lower towns, the **Liars' Bridge** (Podul Minciunilor) is Romania's first such cast-iron structure, built in 1859. It is said the bridge will collapse under anyone who tells an untruth when they are on it.

Piaţa Huet (Huetplatz) is the smallest of the three main squares and the least architecturally uniform. However, the massive **Evangelical Cathedral** (Catedrala Evanghelică Evangelische Stadtpfarrkirche; open Mon–Sat 9am–5pm, Sun 11.30am–7pm; free) dominating it lends a heavy Gothic air. Built between the early 14th century and 1520 on the site of a much earlier basilica, the cathedral has an impressive length of 78 metres (256 ft) and Romania's largest church organ built in 1914 with 6,002 pipes, 85 main registers and 75 auxiliary registers. The smaller, older organ (1672) has a Baroque frontispiece lined with figurines. Concerts take place here a

Map on page 207

6pm on Wednesday from June to September. The mainly Gothic interior is richly decorated with carved friezes and Baroque funerary monuments designed to put the fear of God into you. One even incorporates a skeleton. On the north wall of the choir, the cathedral's sole surviving medieval painting is a giant fresco by Johannes von Rosenau, representing the Crucifixion, and dating from 1445. English-speaking guides are on hand to explain the cathedral's history in more detail. The 73-metre (240-ft) tower is open on request and offers fine views. Four small, spiky towers around its spire are a symbol that in medieval times Sibiu enjoyed *ius gladii* – the right of the sword – the power to sentence criminals to death.

Outside the cathedral the **statue of Georg Daniel Teutsch** commemorates the first Lutheran bishop of Sibiu (1817–93). Previously the bishop's seat was in Biertan *(see page 212)*.

On other side of the cobbles, the sedate **Brukenthal College** ❶ (Colegiul Naţional Samuel von Brukenthal; www.brukenthal.ro) is the square's other main building. One of Romania's most venerable educational establishments, it was founded in 1380 or earlier, and became a boarding school in 1471, although the current building largely dates from 1779–86. It is the only school in Sibiu – and one of only five in Romania – where German remains the sole medium of teaching. Since 1990, however, most of its pupils have been Romanian.

Opposite the northern flank of the cathedral, the handsome **Parochial House** (Casa Parohială, Pfarrhaus) at No. 2 has a carved Gothic entrance dating from 1502. A lane next to the cathedral leads to the 16th-century **Stairs Tower** (Turnul Scărilor), built on 11th–12th-century foundations of the old basilica's fortifications. Beneath it, a vaulted passageway, added in 1860, takes you from the upper to the lower town, if you can resist the temptations of its ludicrously romantic wine cellar.

The lower town

The **lower town** (oraşul de jos) grew up inside Sibiu's outer fortifications. While it has fewer recognised monuments and is largely residential, it has

Souvenir stalls are easy to find; anywhere with any tourist presence is likely to have a surfeit.

BELOW: Piaţa Mare after a summer storm.

Home-grown rural technology on display at the Astra Museum.

BELOW: a typical Transylvanian village dwelling.

some of the oldest houses in town and amply rewards a stroll. Its oldest streets, Strada 9 Mai, Strada Faurului and Strada Turnului, possibly date back to the late 12th century and still give strong hints of Sibiu's earliest days.

Leading southwest from Piaţa Mare, the pedestrianised Strada Nicolae Bălcescu has a more modern feel to it and is Sibiu's main shopping drag. Although the street was first laid out in 1492, most of the buildings date from the late 19th century and are in a neo-Renaissance style. The street has borne several names over the years, including that of Stalin from 1947–70.

At No. 4, its most splendid building, **Hotel Împăratul Romanilor** (Roman Emperor Hotel; *see page 346*), oozes opulence and exclusivity. The hotel started life in 1773, although the current building, richly ornamented in a vibrant mix of styles, dates from 1895. Partially closed for renovation in 2006, it is destined to become once again one of Romania's most splendid places to stay. The high point is the lavish restaurant with its sliding roof.

The building at No. 12 once belonged to Baron Michael von Brukenthal – governor Samuel's nephew – who rebuilt it in 1786. The inner courtyard has some interesting original features.

At its far end, Bălcescu gives way to Piaţa Unirii, focal point of a more modern and aesthetically challenged Sibiu. At its southern edge, the highrise, communist-era Hotel Continental towers over a couple of monuments to the events of 1989.

Most of the surviving remains of the old city walls lie further south, between Strada Cetăţii and Bulevardul Coposu. From west to east, the ramparts incorporate the **Arquebusiers' Tower** (Turnul Archebuzierilor), **Potters' Tower** (Turnul Olarilor) and **Carpenters' Tower** (Turnul Dulgherilor), all well-preserved and dating from the 14th and 15th centuries. Further along, the sturdy 16th-century **Haller Bastion** (Bastionul Haller) guards the southeast corner of the original city wall.

The open-air **Steam Locomotive Museum** (Muzeul Locomotivei cu Abur; Str. Dorobanţilor 22; open daily 8am–8pm; admission and photo charge) is in the depot *(depoul)* of the train station. The collection of 40 trains goes back to 1885, and includes two steam cranes and three snow ploughs.

Astra open-air museum

Just outside Sibiu in Dumbrava Sibiului, the **Astra Museum of Traditional Folk Civilisation** ⓴ (Muzeul Astra; open May–mid-Oct Tues–Sun 9am–6pm; admission, photo and video charge; www.muzeulastra.ro) is the largest open-air museum in Europe and one of Romania's finest. It is located 3 km (2 miles) south of town on the road to Răşinari; to get there take bus No. 1 from Sibiu.

Laid out like a village in a rural setting, albeit one with elements from various regions of Romania, the museum is large and interesting enough to merit a whole day's visit. Helpfully, it also has two rustic restaurants and even offers overnight accommodation

(see page 346). While you are likely to find similar exhibits at other museums in Romania, or still in use in villages, you will not find them all in the same place. That fact and the sylvan setting make this museum a winner.

On the lake, some of the most unusual exhibits are the floating water mills and the fishing pavilion. Although all the exhibits have English labels, explanations are in Romanian only. It is therefore worth picking up a printed guide at the entrance or arranging a guided tour, at extra cost. The museum also hosts various folk festivals, while the church makes a popular wedding venue.

AROUND SIBIU

The region between Sibiu and Sighișoara is the old Saxon heartland and one of the most beautiful parts of the country; for those who have the time, its quiet backroads are ideally suited to exploration by bicycle, or on foot.

North to Mediaș

In extreme contrast to the bucolic countryside on its doorstep, the town of **Copşa Mică** ⓯ (Kiskapus, Kleinkopisch; pop. 5300; www.copsa-mica.ro), between Sibiu and Mediaş, is so famous as Romania's most polluted place that even the town's official website makes no secret of the fact. In communist days it was equally famous for the regularity with which its citizens would resolutely repaint their houses in the brightest colours, in defiance of the grime that settled everywhere. The carbon-black (lamp-black) factory which spewed it out closed in 1993, but the smelter continues to seriously pollute the atmosphere.

Put off by its reputation for pollution, many tourists avoid **Mediaş** ⓰ (Medgyes, Mediasch; pop. 52,000; www.primariamedias.ro), just 12 km (7 miles) up the road from filthy Copşa Mică. However, despite the gasworks and heavy industry at its fringes, Medias combines one of the best-preserved old towns in Romania with a refreshing absence of tourists. The settlement dates back at least to 1267, and as one of the *Siebenbürgen* became the administrative centre for the surrounding Saxon villages in

Maps on pages 178, 207

The attractive Saxon centre of Mediaş – not unlike Sibiu, but with barely any tourists.

BELOW: shepherd and flock in midwinter, Biertan.

The church at Viscri has been awarded UNESCO World Heritage status, and has benefitted from the patronage of the Mihai Eminescu Trust – an important force not only in renovating churches but also in revitalising the area's rural communities. (www.mihaieminescu trust.org)

BELOW: the fortified church at Biertan.

1552. It still has a Saxon population of over 1,000. Since 2004, it has also, like Sibiu, had a Saxon mayor, Daniel Thellmann.

Fringed with Saxon buildings from the 16th–18th century, the partially renovated **Piaţa Ferdinand** at the centre of town has a park and is due for pedestrianisation. Two of its oldest and finest buildings are the 16th-century **Schuller House** (No. 25), now a concert and exhibition hall, renovated with German Government funding; and the 17th-century **Rosenauer House** (No. 22), built in Transylvanian Renaissance style.

Lying just north of the square and dominating the town, the Evangelical **St Margaret's Church** (Biserica Sfânta Margareta; open Mon–Fri 10am–3pm; free) forms the heart of its citadel. It was built between the early 14th and late 15th centuries and has a 74-metre (243-ft) clock tower. The altar, the highlight of the interior, dates from 1485 and is a fine example of medieval Saxon art. It also has a 14th-century baptistery font, Gothic murals from 1420, and a 17th-century organ.

To see inside, ask for the key at the parish office next door.

The **Town Museum** (Muzeul municipal; Str. Mihai Viteazul 46; open Tues–Sun 9am–5pm; admission charge) is mainly of interest for the building it occupies, a late 15th-century former Franciscan monastery.

Of the city's fortifications, the best-preserved remains lie around the **Forkesch Gate Tower** (Turnul porţii Forkesch; open Mon–Fri 9am–5pm; admission charge), just off the main square along Strada Nicolae Iorga. The nearby Schmiedgasser Tower (Turnul Schmiedgasser) at Strada I G Duca 44 now houses an atmospheric café.

Biertan and Viscri

The village of **Biertan ⑰** (Berethalom, Birthälm) was one of the first Saxon settlements in Transylvania and has a famous, early 16th-century **Saxon fortified church** (Biserica fortificată), probably the most impressive in Romania. High on a hill and surrounded by three walls and six towers, it was the seat of a Lutheran bishop from 1572–1867, before the bishopric

The Fortified Saxon Churches

The territory between Sibiu, Sighişoara and Braşov contained the bulk of Transylvania's Saxon population, and their legacy can be seen in the remarkable fortified churches. In the years following the Mongol attacks of 1241–42, the Saxons used their skills in stonemasonry and carpentry to build structures that would withstand heavy, prolonged assault and shelter an entire village, sustaining them with supplies kept in the large storage spaces within.

Unusually for medieval Europe, the fortifications were built by the ordinary people to defend themselves with little or no assistance from the ruling classes. This meant that the churches themselves were very plain, with a bare minimum of ornamentation. Many are in poor condition following years of neglect and, while some long-term restoration plans exist, progress is slow. On the positive side, some are in villages given World Heritage status by UNESCO, while the Prince of Wales' well-publicised interest has brought investment to Viscri (*see page 213*). Three organisations working to preserve the churches are the Mihai Eminescu Trust, of which Prince Charles is a sponsor; the UNESCO World Heritage Centre; and Projects Abroad (www.archaeology-romania.org). There is also a movement of returnee Saxons from Germany who are pumping funds into these old villages.

moved to Sibiu. The highlight of the interior is a fabulous painted altarpiece with multiple panels depicting the life of Christ. Couples seeking a divorce would first have to spend two weeks in a room attached to the church, known as the prison. With only one bed and one set of cutlery to share, few couples were not reconciled.

Ecotourism options are available all year round, but the place truly comes to life for the annual reunion of Saxons from Romania and abroad, held on the second or third Saturday of September. Biertan is also a base for trekking in the region.

The area around Biertan, indeed all the small valleys south of Sighişoara, is a bit like something out of a fairy-tale, with compact villages, many with fortified churches, nestling snugly beneath gentle wooded hills.

Besides Biertan, the most spectacular fortified church is some way to the east, near the main Sighişoara–Braşov road, at **Viscri** ⓲ (Szászfehéregyháza, Weisskirch). The white-washed walls of this impregnable-looking fortress tower over the village; its foundations are 13th-century, but the massive walls were added two centuries later. Viscri has become famous since Prince Charles bought property here (*see margin*).

SIGHIŞOARA

A higgledy-piggledy huddle of sloping roofs, pastel facades and cobbled streets, **Sighişoara** (Segesvár, Schäßburg; Latin: Castrum Sex; pop. 31,000; www.sighisoara.org.ro) ⓳ is so redolent of the Middle Ages that even the Ceauşescu regime was sensible enough to leave its centre well alone.

Of all the *Siebenbürgen*, none has preserved its medieval Saxon origins as well or as picturesquely as Sighişoara. It is the only inhabited fortified citadel in Romania, and one of only a few in Europe. Sadly, the Saxons themselves have largely gone (although some are returning), but still the town has a cared-for air, partly thanks to the efforts of various NGOs such as the Mihai Eminescu Trust.

On the downside, Sighişoara is far from undiscovered and is bursting to the seams in July and August, when its

Maps on p178 & below

A 2006 report in a British newspaper that the Prince of Wales was planning to take "a bite of Dracula country" by negotiating the purchase of a ruined farmhouse in the "timewarp" Saxon village of Viscri, partly to live in and partly to rent out to tourists, took many by surprise. However, Prince Charles has long taken an interest in Transylvania, and is a patron of the Mihai Eminescu Trust (see opposite).

BELOW: Sighişoara's clock tower.

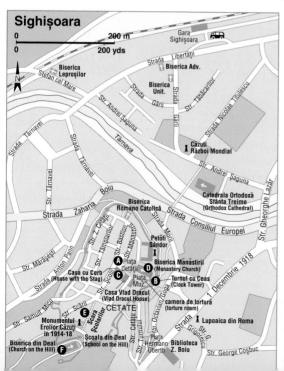

Sighişoara map: Gara Sighişoara; Strada Libertăţii; Biserica Leproşilor; Biserica Adv.; Str. Stefan cel Mare; Strada Gării; Biserica Unit.; Str. Andrei Şaguna; Str. Tăbăcarilor; Strada Nicolae Titulescu; Strada Tárnavei; Tárnava; Căzuti Război Mondial; Str. Tárnavei; Strada Tárnavei; Str. Andrei Şaguna; Boiu; Catedrala Ortodoxă Sfânta Treime (Orthodox Cathedral); Biserica Romano Catolică; Str. Zaharia; Strada; Strada Consiliul Europei; Str. Gheorghe Lazăr; Str. Z. Cetăţii; Str. Mănăstirii; Str. Bastion; Petöfi Sándor; Str. Mărăşeşti; Str. Ánton Pann; Str. Scolii; Str. Tâmplarilor; (A) Piaţa Cetăţii; Casa cu Cerb (House with the Stag); (C); (D) Biserica Mănăstirii (Monastery Church); (B) Turnul cu Ceas (Clock Tower); Piaţa Muz.; Str. 1 Decembrie 1918; Casa Vlad Dracul (Vlad Dracul House); camera de tortură (torture room); (E) Scara Scolarilor; CETATE; Lupoaica din Roma; Str. Samuil Micu; Str. Scării; Monumentul Eroilor Căzuti in 1914-18; Scoala din Deal (School on the Hill); Piaţa Hermann Oberth; Biblioteca Z. Boiu; Str. Turnului; Strada Mănăstirii Goga; Str. G. Grigorescu; Str. George Coşbuc; (F) Biserica din Deal (Church on the Hill); 0 — 200 m / 200 yds

narrow streets are (at least by Romanian standards) packed with tourists and accommodation becomes scarce.

The citadel

At the heart of Sighişoara's citadel, the dreamy, diminutive **Piaţa Cetăţii** Ⓐ (Citadel Square) seems designed as a perfect place to write a postcard. Certainly there is no shortage of terraces or benches to sit and do so, nor places to buy postcards. Lined with two- or three-storey buildings at jaunty angles and painted in pastel shades, it's arguably Romania's finest medieval square. The pace of life is still tranquil despite the occasional car negotiating the cobbles. Few places in Romania cry out more for pedestrianisation.

Despite a slightly grubby exterior in need of repainting, the craggy **clock tower** Ⓑ (Turnul cu Ceas) makes a suitably imposing main entrance to the square. Rebuilt after a fire in 1556 on earlier foundations, it features a series of exterior figurines representing the days of the week – Diana (Mon), Mars (Tues), Mercury (Weds), Jupiter (Thu), Venus (Fri), Saturn (Sat) and the Sun

(Sunday). As elsewhere in Romania, the four small towers around the spire indicate that Sighişoara had *ius gladii* (the power to pass death sentences) in medieval times. The history museum inside is currently closed for renovation.

The small **torture room** (camera de tortură; open daily 9am–3.30pm; admission charge) at the base of the tower was once the military prison. The small collection of torture implements includes a 6-kg (13-lb) stone worn by those accused of cheating, who were tied to the **Infamy Pillar** in the Fortress Square.

One of the oldest buildings on Piaţa Cetăţii, **House with the Stag** Ⓒ (Casa cu Cerb) dates back to 1300 and incorporates a stag's antlers on one corner. Recently restored by the Messerschmidt Foundation, it now functions as a hotel. If you see unusual levels of security in town, Prince Charles is probably staying there.

At Piaţa Muzeului 6, under the clock tower, the **Vlad Dracul House** (Casa Vlad Dracul) is one of Sighişoara's oldest houses and was probably home to Vlad Dracul and the birthplace of his

The Evangelical cemetery, next to the Church on the Hill, is one of Romania's prettiest. Dating from 1700 it mainly serves the Saxon community. The most desirable part, closest to the church, bears witness to past bishops and mayors of Sighişoara.

BELOW: the scholar's stairway.

son, Vlad the Impaler. It now houses a medieval-themed restaurant. Behind it, the **Museum of Medieval Weapons** (open Tues–Sun 10am–3.30pm; admission charge) has a small collection of harquebuses, crossbows and battle-axes from the Middle Ages, as well as more recent weapons.

North of the clock tower, the **Monastery Church** ⓓ (Biserica Mănăstirii) was originally a Dominican foundation, much rebuilt and now Lutheran. As in other medieval Saxon churches, the Oriental rugs lining it are a highlight of an otherwise somewhat austere interior. Organ recitals take place on Friday evenings in summer.

Leading south from Piaţa Cetăţii, Strada şcolii takes you to the covered **Scholars' Stairway** ⓔ (Scara Şcolarilor). So-named because it made reaching the School on the Hill less hazardous for pupils in winter, it has 175 steep steps and a wooden roof. It was built in 1642 behind a rather ornate Renaissance-style facade.

Near the top of the staircase, one of the most venerable schools in Romania, the **School on the Hill** (Şcoala din Deal) originates from 1522, but the current building is from 1729, with later additions. Although the school still has a German-language section, it long ago stopped catering exclusively to the Saxon population.

Slightly higher up, the **Church on the Hill** ⓕ (Biserica din Deal; open summer daily 10am–6pm; admission charge; free multilingual guides) looks out over the town and dominates the whole citadel. Originally the final line of defence, it was built and rebuilt many times between the 13th and 16th centuries, and is a fine example of Gothic architecture. The Messerschmidt Foundation paid to restore it in the 1990s, and in 2004 it won the European Cultural Heritage prize for the best restoration. Its carved stone pulpit dates from 1480. Look out for the painted medieval chests brought here from other Saxon churches. All made without glue or metal fittings, they were restored between 2003 and 2006 by students of Germany's Hildesheim College. Its atmospheric **cemetery** *(see margin opposite)* is a genuinely scary place after dark. ❏

Local people are understandably keen to cash in on the Dracula legend, even if witches are not strictly connected to it.

BELOW: Sighişoara's lively Medieval Arts Festival takes place in late July.

RESTAURANTS, CAFÉS AND BARS

Restaurants

Sibiu

Bolta Rece
Aleea Mihai Eminescu 3
(Parcul Sub Arini)
Tel: 0269-216306
Good and plentiful Italian trattoria food served in a fantastic renovated house in the middle of one of Sibiu's best parks. Decor is splendid, with fine wooden tables adding to the splendour of the whole establishment. €€€€

Crama Ileana
Piața Teatrului 2
Tel: 0269-434343
This rustic restaurant makes a very good second best if the tiny Crama Sibiul Vechi happens to be full, as it often is. While the setting behind a car park may not be the loveliest, the establishment does its best to look like it has been transplanted here from Maramureș, with wooden alcoves lined with folk costumes. Good value and service. €€

Crama Sibiana
Str. Avram Iancu 1–3
Tel: 0729-614260
Rustic-themed restau-

rant that has the advantage of a terrace overlooking Piața Mică. Superb for admiring the audacity of fashion-conscious local women braving the cobbles in high heels. €€€

Crama Sibiul Vechi
Str. Alexandru Papiu Ilarian 3
Tel: 0269-210461
The best place in town for traditional Romanian food in a rustic atmosphere, this small and cosy exposed-brick cellar is rarely quiet, hence the need for reservations. Live folk music in the evenings. So renowned for its soups that a perfect meal could consist of nothing else. Delightful. €€

Gallery
Str. Nicolae Bălcescu 37
Tel: 0748-224807
This is a smart restaurant on Sibiu's main street serving slightly above-average international cuisine to a clientele of both locals and visitors. Try to get a table by the window. €€€

Gasthof Clara
Str. Raului 24
Tel: 0269-222914
As the name suggests, you can expect a warm, buxom Saxon girl to bring huge portions of steaming Transylvanian food to your table with a smile and a wink. Not in the city centre, so you will need to take a taxi down here. €€€

La Turn
Piața Mare 1
Tel: 0269-213985
There is no better location in Sibiu to enjoy simple but homely food than this legendary venue on the main square. Enjoy a pizza on the vast and popular terrace in summer, or a warming *ciorba* inside when there's snow on the ground. €€€

Pivnita de Vinuri (Crama Weinkeller)
Str.Turnului 2
Tel: 0269-210319
Genuine wine bar and bistro serving hearty portions of Transylvanian and Hungarian dishes in a superb cellar close to the centre. Note that overdoing it on the better wines can make this an expensive place. It's best to reserve ahead. €€€€

Mediaș

Select
Hotelul Select,
Str. Petöfi Sándor 3
Tel: 0269-834874
Dependable if not terribly exciting choice on one of Mediaș's prettiest Saxon streets, although the relentless lift music may grate on the many non-fans of the genre. Good value and generous helpings. €€

Traube
Piața Regele Ferdinand I 16
Tel: 0269-844898
Secluded by net curtains from the main

square, this place suggests more than a dash of *fin-de-siècle* refinement, with wood panels and Impressionist oil paintings lining the walls. The menu sticks to a very delicate and tasty rendition of Romanian traditional dishes. The best bet in town. €€

Around Sibiu

Cârciuma din bătrâni
Muzeul Civilizatiei Populare Traditionale (ASTRA)
Pădurea Dumbrava
Tel: 0269-242267
As the ASTRA Museum amply repays a whole day's visit, somewhere to stop for a bite is in order. And this mid-19th-century *cârciumă* (pub) transplanted from Prahova county certainly feels like part of the experience, with tasty peasant food washed down with *țuică* in a blissfully sylvan setting. Slow service. €€

Sighișoara

Casa cu cerb
Str. Scolii 1
Tel: 0265-774625
This superb place – situated on medieval Sighișoara's main square – has some interesting things on its menu, such as a divine cauliflower and cream soup, and a goulash of game, rich in tomatoes and pepper and made with venison. €€

Casa Wagner

Str. Piața Cetatii 7
Tel: 0265-506014
Great little place that gets one black mark for having no terrace. Other than that it is good news all the way as the food – mainly local specialities – is hearty and tasty. Friendly and cheap. €€

Perla

Str. Herman Oberth 15
Tel: 0265-771900
Though looking old and uncared for from the outside, fear not. This place – on lower Sighișoara's main square – has a divine, split-level interior and serves great pizza, coffee and cocktails. €€

Rustic

Str. 1 Decembrie 1918 58
Tel: 0265-775294
Rustic indeed, this charming little restaurant just below the citadel serves great-tasting Transylvanian food at ridiculously cheap prices. The service can be slow but the atmosphere and cheap goulash override that. €

Sighișoara

Hotel Sighișoara
Str. Școlii 4-6
Tel: 0265-771000
Classy without being pretentious, this is one of the best places in the citadel and offers the chance of eating as cheaply or expensively as you like. The menu is more encyclopaedic than usual with a wide range of Transylvanian and Romanian dishes.

The wonderfully secluded bower-like terrace at the back is the loveliest in town. Excellent service. €€€

Vlad Dracul

Str. Cositorarilor 5
Tel: 0265-771596
If the novelty of eating in Dracula's living room is not enough, the overpriced, but good, food (lots of red meat, unsurprisingly) will be. It can be full with coach parties so reserve ahead. €€€€

Cafés and pubs

Sibiu

Berăria Trei Stejari

Str. Fabricii 2
Tel: 0269-430631
One of Romania's few brewery pubs, this is a later addition to the Trei Stejari beer factory next door, founded in 1889 and still independent. Offers a range of hoppy tipples rarely found elsewhere, including *bere tăiată* ("cut" beer), with a meat-heavy menu. €€

Classic Café

Piața Mică 16
Tel: 0269-242000
Behind Casa Luxemburg, this piano bar has the kind of hip décor that would not look out of place in London, Paris or New York. Surprisingly friendly service.

Café del Sol

Piața Mică 24
Tel: 0788-974525
Decorated with imitation French Regency furniture and Impressionist paintings, this bright and breezy café makes a refreshing change from the exposed-brick walls almost ubiquitous in Sibiu. French café music and soothing pop.

Go in Caffe

Piața Mică 9
Tel: 0745-654576
Livelier and open a bit later than most places, this café offers upbeat tunes at night and Hungarian and Celtic music in the daytime.

Kulturcafe

Piața Mică 16
Tel: 0269-213088
Under Casa Luxemburg, this diminutive cellar-bar has Sibiu's café society distilled to just six tables and keeps the midnight burning long after most places have closed. A great place to enjoy some of Sibiu's most clued-up service.

Eclectic music ranging from reggae to smooth jazz.

Mediaș

Art Café

Turnul Schneidmässer
While perhaps it ought by rights to be a museum, and feels a little bit like one, this café in the citadel's Schneidmässer Tower has at least the advantage of being open longer hours. The three interior floors may be gloomy but the sunny balcony offers good views.

Sighișoara

ArtCafé

Str. Ilarie Chendi 28
Intimate vaulted venue under Hotelul Claudiu playing blues and jazz. Decorated with photos of legends of both genres.

RIGHT: the Vlad Dracul restaurant in Sighișoara.

THE SZÉKELY LANDS

Home to the ethnically Hungarian Székler people, this corner of Transylvania lies off the tourist trail, but nonetheless has plenty of scenic and cultural interest

The Székely lands, or Székelyföld as the region is known to the Hungarians, forms the eastern quarter of Transylvania – the counties of Covasna and Harghita, and the eastern portion of Mureş – within which the Székely (pronounced *sek-ey*) population is concentrated. Romanians call this region Tara Secuilor – and the name "Secuiesc" means "of the Székely" in Romanian. *For more on the Székely people and their history, see page 231.*

For the tourist, this part of Transylvania may lack major sights, but is rewarding to visit nonetheless. The rolling wooded countryside is beautiful, the villages often picturesque. The three Székely capitals (Sfântu Gheorge, Miercurea Ciuc and Odorheiu Secuiesc) are nothing special, although the latter is an agreeable enough place.

Sfântu Gheorghe

Sfântu Gheorghe ㉠ (Sepsiszentgyörgy, Sankt Georgen; pop. 60,000; www.sfantugheorghe.ro) lies on the right bank of the Olt River in the valley of the same name. One of the Székler's oldest towns, it dates back at least to 1332, but most of it collapsed in the 1802 earthquake and the current centre dates from the rebuilding after that catastrophe. Despite an abundance of prosaic concrete around the edges, the centre remains pleasant. Sfântu Gheorghe is an important cultural hub where numerous Székely writers have lived.

A major health spa, it has mineral-water springs and a treatment centre.

Much to the anger of Sfântu Gheorghe's Romanian minority, the former county museum has been transformed into the **National Székler Museum** (Muzeul Naţional Secuiesc; Str. Kós Károly 10; open Tues–Sun 9am–5pm; admission charge), in a striking building designed by Kós Károly in 1911, just south of the central park. Inside, exhibits are divided into history, archaeology, ethnography, natural history and art sections. In response, the Romani-

Map on pages 178-9

LEFT: a traditional carved Székler gateway.
BELOW: the National Székler Museum at Sfântu Gheorghe.

The National Székler Museum in Sfântu Gheorghe devotes plenty of space to the 1848 revolution in Transylvania, when the Hungarian population sought independence from the Habsburg Empire (see page 32).

BELOW: the Székely gateway near Sândominic.

ans opened a **Museum of Romanian Spirituality** (Muzeul Spiritualității Românești; Str. ficolii 2; no fixed hours; admission charge), containing various relics from old churches, in the basement of the Orthodox cathedral.

Covasna

In the foothills of the Bretcul Mountains, 31 km (20 miles) east of Sfântu Gheorghe, **Covasna ㉑** (Kovászna, Kowasna; pop. 11,000; www.kovaszna.ro) is one of Romania's most famous spas. Surrounded by more than 1,000 mineral-water springs and with air rich in negative ions, it offers treatment for ailments ranging from rheumatism to male genital diseases. Thanks to unusual volcanic emissions in the area, one popular cure is carbon-dioxide treatment – claimed to be effective against cardiovascular conditions. The thickly forested setting makes it popular with hunters and walkers.

Halfway to **Comandău** on the railway line that runs southeast into the mountains, is the world's sole surviving gravity-operated inclined-plane railway line. Built in 1892 to link the main railway with the forestry railway 330 metres (1,085 ft) higher up, it worked on a simple principle. Attached by a cable, the laden wagon would pull the lighter, unladen one with its own weight. The line mainly carried freight rather than passenger trains. It was last used in 1999, following the closure of the Comandău sawmill, but there is talk of reviving it for tourists.

Târgu Secuiesc

Târgu Secuiesc ㉒ (Kézdivásárhely, Székler Neumarkt; pop. 20,000; www.kezdi.ro) was first settled in Roman times, but the current town dates back to 1407. The centre is largely 19th century but was originally based around a number of guilds, the first of which was founded by leather dressers in 1572, followed by bootmakers and potters. The obvious place to find out more is the **Guilds Museum** (Muzeul Breselor, Céhtörténeti Muzeum; Str. Curtea 10; open Mon–Fri 8am–4pm, Sat–Sun 9am–1pm; admission charge). The museum also has an unusual collection of wooden dolls in folk costume, mostly Hungarian.

The **Roman Catholic Church** (Biserica Romano-Catolică, Római Katolikus Templom) is a fine 18th-century Baroque structure. Built in neoclassical style, the **Officers' Training College** (Şcoala Militară de Subofiţeri) dates from 1817–23 and is treasured by Romanians because of the role its teachers and pupils had in the revolution of 1848.

Băile Tuşnad and St Anne's Lake

The main road from Sfântu Gheorghe to Miercurea Ciuc cuts through the forested Harghita Mountains, which are volcanic in origin and home to several spa towns. **Băile Tuşnad** ㉓ is one of the more scenic, set in the narrow defile carved by the River Olt. It has a reasonable range of accommodation, although its position right on the highway detracts somewhat from the appeal. The development of this spa goes back to the mid-19th century.

Reached via a long and winding side road off the main road, or a two-hour walk from Băile Tuşnad through beautiful beech, birch and conifer forests, **St Anne's Lake** (Lagu Sfântu Ana; Szt. Anna-to) is eastern Europe's only volcanic crater lake, high up in the Harghita Range at an altitude of 950 metres (3,117 ft). It is very popular on summer weekends, with visitor numbers reaching a peak around 26 July (St Anne's Day) when there are festivities. A fee is charged for cars entering the park. It is possible to drive to within 100 metres/yds or so of the lake, which has grassy banks, picnic tables and a couple of small jetties, and is surrounded by the dark forests of the Mohoş Natural Reserve (Rezervaţia Naturală Tinovul Mohoş, Mohos-hegyiláp).

Baraolt and Miclosoara

Across the main ridge west of Băile Tuşnad, the Székler town of **Baraolt** ㉔ (Barót; pop. 9,400) has a small but burgeoning agrotourism sector – as well as a factory making clothes for Hugo Boss. The surrounding hills are teeming with bears, pine martens, wild boar, deer, wolves and otters, and the rivers with trout and grayling. The town is surrounded by a large number of mineral-water springs used to treat

Map on pages 178-9

Some believe the Pied Piper legend to be based on events surrounding the emigration of Saxons to Transylvania. The cave (see page 222) from which the children emerged in the tale is north of Baraolt.

Székely Gateways

You'll know when you are entering the Székely lands when you first notice the distinctive carved wooden gateways (Székelykapu). They symbolise the entrance to life, as well as the Székely identity, and are also part of the rich Transylvanian tradition of woodcarving. All are carved, but some feature colourful paintwork as well. Typical motifs include the sun (on the upper part of the smaller doorway), stars, flowers and birds, while in Calvinist areas vines are a common addition. Practically speaking, they open onto courtyards and normally have one large entrance roomy enough for a hay cart, and a smaller entrance to the side for people.

The village of Satu Mare (Maréfálva), 8 km (5 miles) along the Miercurea Ciuc road from Odorheiu Secuiesc, is one of the best places to see them. Here they are particularly abundant, large, and some are colourfully painted. There is also a collection – the Orbán Balázs Monument – of these gateways at Baile Seiche (Szejke), a small spa village on the Târgu Mureş road 4 km (2½ miles) north of Odorheiu Secuiesc. The unusual road-straddling gate pictured left is near the village of Sândominic, just off the main road between Miercurea Ciuc and Gheorgheni. More typical Székely gates are pictured on pages 218 and 229.

When Count Tibor Kálnoky decided to return to Romania after spending 50 years in exile, his family castle was a ruin. Determined to restore it and the whole village of Micloşoara, in the process he set up one of Romania's most adventurous and high-profile eco-tourism projects.

BELOW: a Kálnoky guesthouse.

rheumatism. Deep in the mountains to the north of Baraolt is the fabled **Vârghiş (Almasch) Cave**, where the lost children of Hamelin emerged in the Pied Piper legend. (An alternative version replaces the cave with the Trumpeters' Tower in Braşov.)

In the opposite direction on the banks of the River Olt, the sleepy little village of **Micloşoara** (Miklósvár) would probably attract few visitors were it not for the efforts of Count Tibor Kálnoky *(see margin)*. While Castle Kálnoky (tel: 0742-202586; www.transylvaniancastle.com) remains a work in progress, paying guests stay in one of two guesthouses in the village, decorated with antique Székler and Saxon furniture and enjoying organic local food and drink. The project employs only local people and all profits go to restoring the castle and village. All-inclusive tours are also available.

Miercurea Ciuc

The Székely centre of **Miercurea Ciuc** ㉕ (Csíkszereda, Széklerburg; pop. 41,000; http://clmc.topnet.ro) at the eastern edge of the Harghita Mountains isn't immediately appealing – lots of grey concrete blocks, weird-looking modern churches, and a barren central area around Soviet-style Piaţa Libertăţii. It also has a reputation as Romania's coldest town. On the plus side, concerted efforts have been made to spruce up Strada Florilor, one of the main shopping streets, which is well-supplied with bars and restaurants.

In terms of sights, the main attraction is the **Mikó Citadel** (Cetatea Mikó), which houses a **museum** (open Tues–Sun 9am–5pm; www.csszm.ro) of regional and Székely history and culture. The interior covers history, archaeology, painting, sculpture and old books. Behind the castle, the open-air section of the museum has houses from six villages in the region as well as a display of Saxon costumes.

Originally built in Italian Renaissance style, the castle itself dates back to the 1620s, taking its name from its founder Ferenc Mikó. It was burnt down during the Turco-Tatar attack of 1661, then rebuilt during the 18th century. It first served as barracks for Austro-Hungarian troops, but from 1764

until the revolution of 1848 the commander of the newly formed First Székler Regiment was based there. Mikó then became the property of the Romanian Army, but was restored in 1970 and opened as the Székler Museum of Ciuc.

Odorheiu Secuiesc

The pleasant, medium-sized town of **Odorheiu Secuiesc** ㉖ (Székelyudvarhely, Oderhellen; pop. 36,000; www. udvph.ro) is regarded as the cultural capital of the Székely lands as well as its western hub, and is a better place to stay than grimy Miercurea Ciuc, its eastern counterpart on the other side of the Harghita Mountains. Most Transylvanian towns have their fair share of lovely old buildings and churches, but here they seem to be more cared for, freshly painted and attractive.

Having said that, there isn't an enormous amount to see. The centre is the long sloping **Piata Primâriei** (Szabadság tér) and adjoining Piata Márton Áron (Márton Áron tér), with three 18th-century churches – Roman Catholic up the steps at the top, Hungarian Calvinist in the middle and the Franciscan church lower down opposite the Târnava-Küküllo Hotel. The 15th-century **Tamad Castle** (Cetatea Tamad, vár) lies a short distance to the northeast along Str. Cetâtii – the site is now occupied by a college, but you can still wander around the walls. The **tourist office** (open summer Mon–Sat 9am–8pm, winter 9am–5pm; tel: 0266-218383; www.tourinfo.ro) at the lower end of Piata Márton Áron can suggest activities and trips out of town. This is one of the most staunchly Hungarian communities in Transylvania, as the sculpture park outside the Târnava-Küküllo Hotel, the coffee house opposite the handsome town hall, and distinct lack of spoken Romanian all bear witness.

There are a few restaurants along Strada Kossuth Lajos (the Sighişoara road) as well as the local **Ethnographic Museum** (Muzeul Haáz Rezső, Haáz Rezső Múzeum; open Tues–Fri 9am–3pm, Sat–Sun 9am–1pm, admission charge; www.hrmuzeum.ro) with captions in Hungarian only. Around 2 km (1½ miles) further along the road on the

Map on pages 178-9

The Romanian language appears to have no indigenous word for Transylvania. Transilvania, meaning "beyond the forest", is medieval Latin, while Ardeal derives from the Hungarian Erdély. Some Hungarian nationalists see this as evidence Hungarians first settled the region, an argument strongly contested by Romanians (see page 51).

BELOW: birch woods near St Anne's Lake.

Just outside Odorheiu Secuiesc, the Jesus Chapel is a tiny fortified church-ette dating from the 13th century – one of the oldest buildings in this neck of the woods – and was built to commemorate a Székely victory against the Tatars.

BELOW: the town hall at Odorheiu Secuiesc.

edge of town is the **Jesus Chapel** (Jésus Kapolná; *see margin).*

Dârjiu (Székelyderzs, Darsch; pop. 1200) is 16 km (10 miles) south-west of Odorheiu Secuiesc off the Sighişoara road. Its fortified Lutheran church is noteworthy because the villagers have maintained the tradition of storing their grain as well as their ham and bacon within the defensive walls (as in times of siege); you may well be offered a sample during your visit. Inside the church there are murals dating from 1419 that illustrate the Hungarian legend of St László. One of Hungary's national heroes, László (1040–95) was the son of King Béla, and became king himself in 1077. No one could accuse him of being an under-achiever. Apart from establishing Christianity as the state religion and building numerous religious foundations, he was responsible for expanding Hungary's borders in the face of constant threats of invasion by the Cumans. He died just as he was about to lead the First Crusade, precipitating three years' national mourning. He was canonised in 1192.

Corund and Praid

The Targu Mureş road (Route 13a) runs north from Odorheiu Secuiesc through pleasant scenery to **Corund** (Korond), famous throughout Romania for its ceramics, with plates, jars and vases lined up in their thousands on the stalls that flank the main street. There are also baskets and other wickerwork, as well as the usual tacky gift items.

Just 10 km (6 miles) to the north is one of the region's most unusual sights, **Praid Salt Mine** (Salina Praid, Parajd Sóbánya; www.salinapraid.ro). The mining of salt in this area dates back to Roman times, and has been an important economic resource ever since. To reward their loyalty and encourage them to stay, King Andrew II of Hungary gave Saxon and Székely settlers rights to access the salt in a famous document called the *Guarantee of Freedom (Goldenen Freibrief)* in 1224.

The salt is some 3 km (2 miles) thick in places, and there is said to be enough here to supply all Europe for more than 100 years. Although the idea of spending time in a salt mine isn't likely to be on your list of priorities, this is a surreal experience and highly recommended. Buy a tour ticket from the office prominently marked "tourist" just opposite the mine entrance, and a bus will drive you down through the tunnel (tours 8am–1pm; admission charge). As soon as you disembark you'll notice the saline air, said to be of great benefit to those suffering from respiratory problems. Romanian doctors prescribe week-long stays in Praid so that patients can spend as much time as possible below ground inhaling the curative properties.

Once you've passed through a small entrance hall and descended a long flight of stairs, open the small wooden door and enter a vast rectangular chamber, some 15 metres (50 ft) tall by 24 metres (80 ft) across, with side channels branching off, rows of picnic tables and – bizarrely for such an unearthly setting – a children's playground. All this is to keep the patients entertained during their four-hour underground ses-

sions a day. Branch off to the left and you'll come to the chapel, cathedral-like in its grandiose, rocky setting (the echoing acoustics of the chamber reinforce the effect). Close by is a museum with captions in English explaining the long history of the mine, which continues to operate today on another part of its extensive site.

East to Gheorgheni

A winding road heads eastwards from Praid across the Gurghiu Mountains. On the far side, in the broad valley of the upper Mureş, the small, predominantly Hungarian town of **Gheorgheni** ❸⓪ (Gyergyószentmiklós, Niklasmarkt) feels like an outpost, its central square surrounded by forlorn-looking Habsburg-era buildings with peeling paint and faded facades. It's not far from here to Lacu Roşu and the Ceahlău Massif *(see page 301)*, though, so it can be useful as a base from which to explore those exceptional beauty spots.

The 15th-century **Lăzarea Castle** lies 5 km (3 miles) north of Gheorgheni *(see margin, page 227)*, from where the road continues to **Topliţa** (Maroshévíz), a logging town with an attractive monastery.

TÂRGU MUREŞ

Despite Ceauşescu's best efforts to dilute its ethnic and architectural purity, **Târgu Mureş** ❸❶ (Maros vásárhely, Neumarkt am Mieresch; pop. 150,000; www.tirgumures.ro), on the left bank of the Mureş River, remains a noticeably Hungarian town. While the fringes follow a concrete Soviet blueprint, the historic centre has survived largely intact, with some of Romania's finest examples of the Secessionist style. Dating back at least to the 14th century, it has long been an important commercial centre, earning the lucrative right to hold fairs all the way back in 1405. It also has a history as a major academic centre, first for the Széklers and then for the Romanians, and was the site of Romania's pioneering public library in 1802.

Whereas many parts of the Székely lands remained overwhelmingly Hungarian throughout the Ceauşescu years, Târgu Mureş was the target of a deliberate policy to dilute its ethnicity, and Hungarians are now a minority (of 47 percent) here, compared with 89 percent in 1910. In 1990 the town was the scene of some of Romania's worst ethnic violence. Things have calmed down since then, but the two communities remain polarised.

Big enough to have its own railway station, the Azomureş factory billowing out smoke on the southern edge of town is not the best introduction, although things have improved since communist times when the river was notoriously smelly from chemical sewage.

The Administrative Palace

Târgu Mureş' main square, **Piaţa Trandafirilor** (Square of the Roses) is the best place to start exploring. Most of the town's main attractions are here or just to the south. At the square's western end, the Secessionist **Administrative Palace** (Palatul Administrativ, Königazgatási Palota) looks like the

Map on pages 178-9

The ceramics workshops in Corund produce a vast array of pottery. For the best bargains, an annual market takes place on the second weekend of August.

BELOW: Corund pottery.

Praid salt mine has playground facilities to keep the kids entertained.

BELOW: the Great Temple synagogue, Târgu Mureş.

winner of a Legoland competition. Few countries are quite so liberal with the use of the word palace as Romania but this one truly merits the description, decorated with multi-coloured roof tiles, stained-glass windows and floral motifs. It dates from 1906–07 when it comprised the first stage of a scheme to modernise the centre of town – much of the current centre is the result of that project. The palace is now the seat of the county council.

Although rubbernecking in the lavish lobby is just about tolerated, the rest of the interior is off limits except on official business. The 60-metre (195-ft) **Clock Tower** (Turnul cu Ceas) is open to visitors (Tues–Sun 9am–4pm on the hour; admission charge). Tickets are available from the Hall of Mirrors in the Palace of Culture next door. A controversial plaque outside the tower commemorates ethnic Romanians imprisoned here for defending the use of their language and faith under Hungarian rule.

The **Latinity Monument** (Monumentul Latinităţii, Latinság Emlékmü) outside the Administrative Palace is a pointed reminder of the supposedly Roman origins of the Romanians. It is a copy of an original that was one of five donated by Italy to Romania after World War I. During World War II it was moved to Turda and the current copy was unveiled in 1991, at a time of high ethnic tension in Târgu Mureş.

The Palace of Culture

In eastern Europe the term Palace of Culture conjures up images of Stalinist wedding-cake architecture and young pioneers enduring indoctrination classes. In Târgu Mureş, however, nothing could be further from the truth. One of the most sumptuous buildings in Romania, the **Palace of Culture** (Palatul Culturii, Kultúrpalota Luni; open Tues–Fri 9am–4pm, Sat–Sun 9am–1pm; free) truly lives up to the meaning of both words. Completed in 1913, when Târgu Mureş was enjoying a cultural boom, the building overwhelms visitors with the vibrancy of its architecture and decor, inside and out.

The architects successfully fused Art Nouveau with folk-art elements, as well as Oriental and pre-Christian motifs. Polychromatic tiles cover the roof, while the main features of the facade are carved porticos, a mosaic by frescoist Aladár Körösföi-Kriesch and bas-reliefs in bronze and stone by sculptor Ede Kallós. The dominant colour is pale purple.

On the ground floor the 45-metre (150-ft) main entrance hall is decorated with Carrara marble and two Venetian mirrors. However, the key interest lies in the two mythological frescoes, also the work of Körösföi-Kriesch. Hungary's leading Art Nouveau artist, who was inspired by the Pre-Raphaelite movement. In keeping with the building's general theme, the frescoes combine Art Nouveau and Oriental styles with Székler folk motifs.

Two grand marble staircases lead up to the balcony overlooking the splendid **Great Hall** (Sala Mare), passing stained-glass windows depicting famous Hungarians. They were the

work of Miksa Roth, who was also responsible for the windows in Budapest's Parliament building. The hall is home to Târgu Mureş State Philharmonic Orchestra (Filarmonica de stat; www.filarmonicams.ro), and an enormous organ, with its 4,463 tubes and 63 registers, dominates the room (which is only open for concerts).

To reach an even more impressive space, take the right staircase from the entrance hall. The **Hall of Mirrors** (Sala Oglinzilor; open Tues–Sun 9am–4pm; admission charge) takes its name from the three Venetian mirrors on either side, giving the illusion of infinity. The 12 stained-glass windows, a masterpiece of their genre, were originally meant to represent Europe at the 1914 San Francisco World Exhibition before the outbreak of war scuppered the plans. They depict Székler folklore and ethnographic scenes. A recorded commentary is available in English.

The Palace of Culture also hosts the **County Library** (Biblioteca Judeţeană; www.bjmures.ro; open Tues–Fri 10am–6pm, Sat–Sun 10am–1pm), with nearly a million volumes. There are several

museums here, too, and tickets to the Hall of Mirrors cover entry to them all.

The **History and Archaeology Museum** (Muzeul de Arheologie-Istorie; open Tues–Fri 9am–4pm, Sat 9am–2pm, Sun 9am–1pm) on the second floor has a particularly rich collection of Roman bronzes.

On the third floor, the **Art Museum** (Muzeul de Artă; open Tues–Fri 9am–4pm, Sat–Sun 9am–1pm) has more than 2,000 works by Romanian and Hungarian artists from the 18th century onwards. There is also a hall for temporary exhibitions, with a balcony that offers fine views.

Around Piaţa Trandafirilor

Along the square from the Palace of Culture, the **Ethnography and Folk Art Museum** (Muzeul de Etnografie şi Artă Populară; Piaţa Trandafirilor 11; open summer Tues–Sun 9am–5pm, winter Tues–Sat 9am–2pm, Sun 9am–1pm; admission charge) was originally the Toldalagi Palace (Palatul Toldalagi), built in French Baroque style. The folk costumes are the highlight. However, the constant espousal

Map on pages 178-9

Lazarea Castle, north of Gheorgheni, dates back to 1532. It was the seat of the Lázár clan, one of the most powerful Hungarian noble families of Transylvania.

BELOW: the facade of Târgu Mures' splendid Palace of Culture.

PALATUL CULTURII KULTÚRPALOTA

of the Daco-Roman Continuity Theory *(see page 52)* can get a bit tiresome, as can the sidelining of Transylvania's minorities.

Behind the Ethnography Museum on Strada Aurel Filimon, the **Great Temple** (Marele templu, Ortodox Zsinagóga) is one of Romania's most gloriously extravagant synagogues. Set beneath three cupolas in Moorish style tempered with Romanian and Gothic elements, it dates from 1899. The eclectic interior is, if anything, even more lavish. To see it you need to contact the local Jewish community (tel: 0265-261810), today numbering a mere 270.

Piața Teatrului

The nearest thing Târgu Mureș has to a civic centre, **Piața Teatrului** (Theatre Square) takes its name from the **National Theatre** (Teatrul Național, Nemzeti Színház), a strikingly futuristic work from 1973 by leading architect Constantin Săvescu. Looking like a prehistoric flying reptile about to take off, the building won Săvescu a prize from the Architects' Union. The lavish interior has a staircase shaped like a snail shell as well as a fine tapestry in the foyer. Uniquely in Romania, the theatre hosts two companies, one Romanian, one Hungarian.

The creation of the square required the partial demolition of a Franciscan church and monastery. All that survives is the Baroque **Franciscan Church Tower** (Turnul Biserici Franciscane), now looking thoroughly out of place in its modern setting. Originally the Franciscans occupied the citadel church but were forced out after the Diet of 1556, only returning in Habsburg times, when they built a monastery here. The tower dates from 1745–47 and contains an ossuary.

The cathedral

An ecclesiastical battleship of a building, the massive **Orthodox Cathedral** (Catedrala Ortodoxă, Ortodox Székesegyház) dominates the eastern end of Piața Trandafirilor in its own traffic island. Its scale and style quite out of kilter with the Baroque, neoclassical and Secessionist architecture surrounding it, it's anything but a subtle statement of Romanian culture. Funded by public subscription, the cathedral took nine years to build before completion in 1934. In Byzantine style in the shape of a Greek cross, the overall impression from outside is very militaristic (that's certainly how Hungarians see it). The interior, with its rich frescoes, is contrastingly vibrant.

Just inside, look out for icons of various Orthodox monasteries and a communist-era inscription lavishing praise on the Socialist Republic of Romania and its president – a reminder of how close the church was to the government in communist days. The inscription now has Ceaușescu's name rubbed out. Another plaque beneath, dedicated to Carol II, clearly had his name removed in communist times and later restored.

Just across the road, the **Roman Catholic Church** (Biserica Romano-Catolică, Római-Katólikus Templom) is a serene example of the Baroque style. Built by Jesuit monks, it dates

Farkas (1775–1856) and his son János Bolyai (1802–1860) were mathematical geniuses. For centuries mathematicians had been trying to solve Euclid's fifth postulate, a somewhat complicated theorem about parallel lines: Bolyai published his ground-breaking treatise in 1832, demonstrating that not everything in geometry could be explained in Euclidian terms. His discoveries later laid the ground for Einstein's Theory of Relativity.

BELOW:
the folk musician Ada Milea hails from Târgu Mures.

from 1728–64 with neo-Renaissance additions from the 1930s. The interior features some exquisite paintings and a fine, gold-plated wooden pulpit.

The **Small Cathedral** (Biserica Mică) at the other (ie western) end of Piața Trandafirilor dates from 1926–36 and is a miniature version of St Peter's in Rome. It housed the Greek Catholic (Uniate) church until 1948, when it was handed over to the Romanian Orthodox Church.

The Bolyai legacy

One of Târgu Mureş's proudest boasts is that Romania's first public library was established here. Founded by Count Samuel Teleki, former chancellor of Transylvania, it opened in 1802 and remains to this day, complete with the original bookshelves and furniture. It is housed in a building dating from 1799–1803, on Strada Bolyai, which leads southeast off Piața Trandafirilor and is one of Târgu Mureş's prettiest streets, retaining a thoroughly bourgeois air. The **Teleki-Bolyai Library** (Biblioteca Teleki-Bolyai, Teleki-Bolyai könyvtár; Str. Bolyai 17; open Tues–Fri 10am–6pm, Sat–Sun 10am–1pm) contains more than 200,000 volumes, many of great rarity. Around 40,000 date back to the original Teleki collection, while 80,000 come from the Bolyai Library, which originally belonged to the Reformed Church College over the road. The two collections merged in 1955. The collection includes the first Tibetan-English dictionary (by Sándor Kőrösi Csoma, 1831) as well as a valuable collection of maps by Joannes Janssonius. In the same building, the **Bolyai Memorial Museum** (same hours; admission charge) commemorates Farkas Bolyai and his son János *(see margin page 228)*, whose collection of manuscripts formed the basis of the Bolyai Library.

The **Bolyai Farkas High School** (Liceul Teoretic Bolyai Farkas, Bolyai Farkas elméleti líceum), across the road on Piața Bolyai, has a pretty yellow-and-white Secessionist facade with floral stucco mouldings. Previously the Reformed Church College, the school continues a tradition dating back to 1557, although it moved to the current location at the start of the 17th century.

Map on pages 178-9

Street kiosks are the places to buy newspapers, phone cards and bus tickets.

BELOW: a typical Székely gateway.

Map
on pages
178-9

Hungarian sweet pastries at a Târgu Mureş street stall.

Around the citadel

Behind the Orthodox Cathedral on Piaţa Bernády, the mustard-and-white **Teleki House** (Casa Teleki, Teleki Ház) was originally home to Count Domokos Teleki, although it's now a rather desirable Reformed Church rectory. Built from 1797–1803, it largely retains its original late-Baroque facade. Its other famous resident, General József Bem, was a Pole who briefly served as commander of the Székler army fighting against the Habsburgs. This building served as his headquarters in January 1849. The **statue** outside, unveiled in 1994, commemorates György Bernády (1864–1938). One of Târgu Mureş's best-loved mayors, he was responsible for building the Palace of Culture and modernising much of the town centre.

On the hill opposite, the **Medieval Citadel** (Cetatea Medievală, Középkori vár) was built in stone on a pentagonal plan in 1492 for *voievode* Stefan Bathory. The 900-metre (2,950-ft) outer wall was a 17th-century addition, along with the seven forts, five named after guilds. The gate tower has a small **exhi**-bition (Expoziţie de Istoria Oraşului şi a Cetăţii; open Tues–Fri 9am–4pm, Sat 10am–2pm, Sun 10am–1pm; admission charge) of items tracing the history of the citadel and Târgu Mureş as a whole.

Within the citadel itself are various municipal offices, a photo gallery, a summer theatre, a café, a funfair and a bandstand. Annual events held here include Târgu Mureş Days and beer and wine festivals.

At the citadel's southwest edge, the **Reformed Church** (Biserica Reformată, Vártemplom) peers sedately over town with its 65-metre (214-ft) clock tower and 1,600-kg (30-cwt) bell. Although the Gothic stone church originally dates from 1316, and stands on the site of an even older Franciscan wooden monastery, it required extensive rebuilding after damage from the Turks in the 17th century. The Franciscans who originally occupied the site had to leave after the religious reforms of 1556, when the Reformed Church took it over. Târgu Mures is one of Romania's major academic centres, and the **university district** lies northeast of the citadel. ❑

RESTAURANTS

Odorheiu Secuiesc

Opium Café Restaurant
Str. Kossuth Lajos 11
The trendiest place in town, this bar-cum-restaurant has a good line in salads and grills. €€

Târgu Mureş

Concordia
Piaţa Trandafirilor 45
Tel: 0265-260602
Târgu Mureş's classiest and priciest joint has designer touches galore – from the china to the loos. High prices, although the midweek business lunches offer good value. The menu trots the globe although is light on local specialities. €€€€

Continental
Piaţa Teatrului 6
Tel: 0265-250416
There is a strongly old-style communist-era whiff to this place, but the tasty Transylvanian food and competent service make this a reliable option. €€€

Crama la Mitica
Strada Revoluţiei 11
Tel: 0265-219061
While stuffiness defines many Târgu Mureş restaurants, this unpretentious wine-cellar offers a Transylvanian hotpot of lively company, hearty food and homely service. Not to mention the best value in town. So popular is this place with the chattering classes that you may feel like multilingual table-hopping. Infectious. €

Emma Vendeglo
Str. Horea 6
Tel: 0265-263021
Hungarian cuisine at its best; the food surpasses the modest surroundings, with game, goulash and Budapest steaks all on the menu – and all good. €€

Leo
Piaţa Trandafirilor 43
Tel: 0265-214999
Good Hungarian restaurant serving great little somlyoi (gorgeous Hungarian dumplings which come topped with cream), though only if you have room after the huge main portions. €€€

Rosen Garden
B-dul. 1 Dec. 1918 163/a
Tel: 0265-266881
Café and restaurant serving a mix of international dishes – mainly steaks, schnitzels and the like – whose main attraction is the splendid garden: a great place in summer. €€€

• • • • • • • • • • • • • • • •
Prices per person for a 3-course meal with wine: € under 30 lei, €€ 30–45 lei, €€€ 45–60 lei, €€€€ over 60 lei.

The Széklers

The origin of the Székely people has long been a matter of dispute, with various theories linking them to the Huns, Avars or Scythians, or to the Magyars themselves. The latter idea is that they were separated from the main westward expansion during the 9th century, making their way from Bessarabia to Transylvania directly over the Carpathian passes, while the other Magyars took different routes. When the Magyars moved back eastwards into the region, it is thought that they found Székely communities already established. Whatever their ancestry, it does seem that they enjoyed fraternal relations with the Magyars from the start.

The present-day Széklers, for their part, consider themselves ethnic Hungarians, speaking the language and retaining a strong affinity with Hungary. Nothing is ever straightforward in the Transylvanian ethnic maze, though, and there are differences of opinion as to what constitutes a modern Székler: some people seem to think that simply being born in this part of Transylvania qualifies. Many regard themselves as simultaneously Székely, Hungarian and Romanian (and Transylvanian).

Historically held in high esteem as warriors, the Széklers traditionally guarded the mountain passes from the threat posed by the tribes from the steppe lands to the east. Some theories even suggest that they were deliberately settled here for that purpose, much like the Saxons (see page 55).

In the convoluted strands of Transylvanian history, they remain a constant presence. In medieval times when Hungarian kings held sway over the region, the Széklers, together with the Hungarian noble class and the Saxons, held a privileged status and were largely self-governing. But this didn't last. Hungarian power in the region was reduced after a series of calamitous defeats to the Ottomans in the 16th century. Transylvania remained under Ottoman influence until the late 17th century when the Habsburgs conquered a large part of the Hungarian lands; the Hungarian princes who had continued to rule Transylvania were replaced, and life for the Széklers deteriorated significantly.

The emergence of Romanian nationalism in the latter half of the 19th century soured relations with ethnic Romanians, and then came 1920 and the traumatic sundering from the newly diminutive Hungary. Suddenly it was the Romanians who had power – Hungarian landowners were dispossessed and estates redistributed amongst the Romanian peasantry. There were also concerted efforts to establish a Romanian identity and the gradual removal of the Hungarian language in education. After a period of relative respite during the early communist years (embodied by the creation of the so-called Hungarian Autonomous Province – largely meaningless though this was – encompassing the Székely lands) the situation worsened again when Ceaușescu began to implement a nationalist policy that actively oppressed the Hungarian minority.

Post-1989, the Hungarian identity – Székely or otherwise – has resurfaced with gusto as EU membership, with its guarantees of protection for minority peoples, has helped ease tensions. And driving through this part of the country today, you can hardly fail to notice the presence of Hungarian language road signs, shop names, and, above all, the distinctive carved wooden gateways (see page 221).

As part of the Székely cultural revival, you'll also see plenty of patriotic green, white and red (the Hungarian colours). The region is very popular with Hungarian tourists, who come here to reconnect with what is perceived as a traditional Magyar culture largely lost back home. There have even been some political moves towards establishing a formal autonomy for the region within Romania. ❑

RIGHT: ties with Hungary remain strong.

CLUJ, WESTERN AND NORTHERN TRANSYLVANIA

This swathe of territory centered on the large, cosmopolitan city of Cluj, encompasses wild mountains, Roman ruins, remote villages and castles

Although most people only make it as far as the lively city of Cluj, the western and northern parts of Transylvania have some interesting folk traditions and plenty of chances to get off the beaten track. Throughout the region the villages are largely unexplored and offer excellent scope for hiking, listening to folk music or appreciating rustic architecture.

CLUJ-NAPOCA

An important academic, cultural and commercial centre, **Cluj-Napoca** ㉜ (Kolozsvár, Klausenburg; pop. 320,000; www.primariaclujnapoca.ro) is the unofficial capital of Transylvania, a role it enjoyed officially under Austro-Hungarian rule. The addition of "Napoca" to the name reflected the determination of Ceausescu to affirm the Daco-Roman heritage of Transylvania. Everyone knows the city simply as Cluj.

Long known for its café society and bohemian intellectual air, Cluj has one of Romania's highest student populations and one of its most renowned universities. It also has some of the region's most imposing and vibrant architecture, its centre retaining a largely Hungarian identity. Mercifully, Cluj escaped the imposition of a *centru civic* in the Ceauşescu era, although, like much of Transylvania, it was the target of the state-sponsored Romanianisation programme. The Hungarian population decreased from 53 percent in 1930 to 19 percent in 2002.

On the downside, Cluj has a more weatherbeaten air than many Transylvanian cities. Thanks partly to its ultra-nationalist "mad mayor" Gheorghe Funar, in power until 2002, money that could have been spent on restoring old monuments went on erecting controversial new ones. The city also suffers from some of the worst traffic jams in Romania.

Cluj was originally a Roman legionary settlement, Napoca, established by Trajan in the 2nd century AD but destroyed after the legions with-

Maps on pages 178, 234

LEFT: the Sambra Oilor festival, held all over Romania, marks the departure of the shepherds with their flocks into the mountains.
BELOW: ornate architecture in Cluj.

St Michael's Church is one of the finest Gothic buildings in Transylvania.

drew from Dacia in 271. Arising anew in 1272, it became one of the Saxon *Siebenbürgen*. As Klausenburg, it steadily increased in prosperity and importance as a free city inhabited equally by Saxons and Hungarians, and by the 16th century it had become the cultural centre of Transylvania. The rapid rise of the Unitarian Church in the 16th century, with Cluj at its heart, caused many Saxons to move away – as Lutherans, they found the Unitarian belief heretical. Among Magyars, the city is revered as the birthplace of one of Hungary's greatest kings, Mátyás, in 1440. Under Habsburg rule, Cluj became the seat of the Translvanian Diet, the political capital and the seat of many Hungarian nobles.

In 1974 the communist authorities renamed the city Cluj-Napoca as a reminder of its Roman origins, a move interpreted by some as a provocation to the Hungarian community.

Piața Unirii

The main square, **Piața Unirii** (Union Square), is an attractive jumble of architectural styles. Despite some clumsy efforts in communist and post-communist times to dilute it, the overall impression remains largely Hungarian with some Saxon elements.

Dominating the square, the majestic, Saxon-built **St Michael's Church** Ⓐ (Biserica Sfântul Mihail, Szent Mihály-templom, Sankt-Michaels-kirche) dates back to the 14th century, although the neo-Gothic clock tower was completed only in 1860. One of Transylvania's finest Gothic buildings, it features three equal-sized naves. The stained-glass windows and statues are particularly fine.

Outside the church is the imposing equestrian **statue of King Mátyás Corvinus** (Statuia lui Mátyás Corvinus; Mátyás király Szoborcsoportot), the work of János Fadrusz, unveiled in 1902. While King Mátyás stands aloof on a pedestal, the figures beneath represent his generals. In 1994 the precincts were dug up, ostensibly in search of archaeological remains. Although nothing very much was found, it was only government intervention that stopped the former mayor, Gheorghe Funar, removing the statue

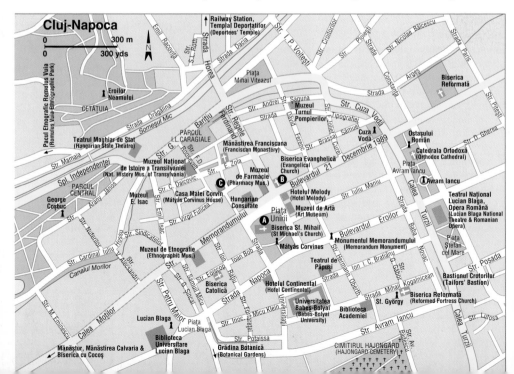

altogether as an unwanted symbol of Hungarian national identity. However, in a sign that ethnic tensions are easing, the city authorities announced plans to renovate the statue in 2006.

The magnificent, eclectic **Hotel Continental** (Hotelul Continental, Continental Szálloda; Str. Napoca 1) on the corner of Piața Unirii dates from 1896. Originally known as the New York Hotel, it attracted glowing reviews from both Patrick Leigh Fermor in *Between the Woods and the Water* and Walter Starkie in *Raggle Taggle*. During World War II the hotel served as German military headquarters in Transylvania. After a long period of neglect under state ownership, it closed for much-needed long-term renovation in 2005.

Built from 1816–29 in a graceful fusion of Baroque and neoclassical styles, the **Evangelical Church** ❸ (Biserica Evanghelică; Lutheránus Templom; B-dul 21 Decembrie 1989 1) on the corner of Piața Unirii was the work of George Winkler and incorporates a 43-metre (141-ft) tower. Diagonally opposite, the renovated **Hotel Melody** (Hotelul Melody; Piața Unirii 29) opened in 1891.

One of only two such institutions in Romania (the other is in Sibiu), the delightful **Pharmacy Museum** (Muzeul de Farmacie; Gyógyszerész-Történeti Múzeum; Piața Unirii 28; open Mon–Sat 10am–4pm; admission charge; www.museum.utcluj.ro) occupies the site of the former St George's Pharmacy, the town's oldest. It functioned from 1573 until 1949, when it became a museum. The basement has a whole laboratory furnished with apothecary and pharmaceutical items from the Middle Ages to the early 19th century, and there is also a display devoted to the history of homeopathy.

At Piața Unirii 23, the **Hungarian Consulate** survived attempts by Gheorghe Funar to close it down. At No. 30, the **Art Museum** (Muzeul de Artă; Szépmıvészeti Múzeum; open Wed–Sun 11am–6pm; admission charge) has one of the finest collections of its kind in Romania, although not every period is covered and only Romanian artists are represented. The building it occupies was originally the Bánffy Palace,

Map on page 234

A large student population makes Cluj one of the liveliest cities in Romania.

BELOW: one of Cluj's many downtown bars.

One of Romania's most famous beers, Ursus (marketed as the king of beers) is brewed in Cluj.

BELOW:
a busy street in downtown Cluj.

built in Baroque style from 1774–85. Although the overall collection is arranged chronologically over 30 rooms, starting with church icons from the 17th century, several rooms are devoted to particular artists. These include Nicolae Grigorescu, Ştefan Luchian and Nicolae Tonitza.

Cluj's oldest domestic building, the cosy 14th-century **Mátyás Corvinus House ⊙** (Casa Matei Corvin, Mátyás Király Szülőháza; Str. Matei Corvin 6) lies on a picturesque little square, Piaţa Teatrului, just northwest of Piaţa Unirii. This was the birthplace of Mátyás, one of Hungary's greatest monarchs, in 1440. These days it houses the Ion Andreescu Fine Arts Academy (Academia de Arte Vizuale Ioan Andreescu) and is closed to the general public.

North of Piaţa Unirii

Just northwest of Piaţa Unirii, Piaţa Muzeului is another small, picturesque square. Archaeologists have unearthed Roman remains here, although excavations are now covered over again. On the eastern side, the building cur-

rently housing the Sigismund Toduţă Music School (Liceul de Muzică Sigismund Toduţă) was previously the **Franciscan Monastery** (Mănăstirea Franciscană, Ferencesrediek Epületegyüttese; Str. Victor Deleu 4). It was founded in 1270, although the current Gothic building dates from the 15th century onwards. At the southern end of the monastery, the **Franciscan Church** (Biserica Franciscană) is a later, Baroque addition (1728–45). A highlight of the lavish interior is the pulpit, decorated with images of Jesus and the Four Evangelists. The communist authorities banned the Franciscan Order in 1949, and the church and part of the monastery only returned to their former owners in 1990.

Relocated from Piaţa Unirii in 1898, the Franz I obelisk (Obeliscul Francisc I) outside the church commemorates the 1817 visit to Cluj of the Austro-Hungarian emperor and empress. The bas-relief depicts various scenes from their trip, as well as the city's coat of arms.

Just west of the square, the **National History Museum of Transylvania** (Muzeul Naţional de Istorie a Transilvaniei, Erdély Nemzeti Történelmi Múzeuma; Str. Constantin Daicoviciu 2; open Tues–Sun 10am–4pm; admission charge; www.museum.utcluj.ro) occupies an early 19th-century building. Tracing Transylvania's history to prehistoric times, the museum has a particularly good collection of Dacian relics, as well as a medieval lapidarium and an ethnographic section.

Close to the Someşul Mic River, the **Hungarian State Theatre** (Teatrul Maghiar de Stat, Állami Magyar Színház; Str. Emil Isac 26–28; www.huntheater.ro), with its stark modernist facade, has accommodated the Hungarian Opera (Opera Maghiară de Stat; Magyar Opera; www.opera-maghiara-cluj.ro) since 1948. To broaden their appeal, both the theatre and opera house offer simultaneous translations of most performances into Romanian.

Close to the railway station, the 19th-century **Deportees' Temple** (Templul Deportaţilor) at Strada Horea 21 was originally known as the Neo-logue Synagogue (Sinagoga Neologă; Neológ Zsinagóga). The current name – together with the plaque outside – commemorates the Jews deported from Cluj to Auschwitz in 1944. On 3 May 1944 one of the shortest-lived Jewish ghettos was established in Cluj. Its population peaked at 18,000, before a wave of deportations emptied it. Only about 15 percent of the city's Jewish population survived the war. Today, it totals 510, a small number but still the fifth largest in Romania. To visit, call the Jewish community on tel: 0264-596600.

The university area

South of Piaţa Unirii, the **Babeş-Bolyai University** (Universitatea Babeş-Bolyai, Babes-Bolyai Tudománye-gyetem; Str. Mihail Kogălniceanu 1; www.ubbcluj.ro) is Romania's largest – and one of its most renowned – acade-mic institutions. It started as a Hungar-ian-language institution in 1872, although its origins date back to a 16th-century Jesuit college. After the Romanian university took it over in 1919, the Hungarian university moved to Szeged (in Hungary), only returning in 1940. Five years later, the Roman-ian university was re-established under the name Babeş, while the Hungarian adopted the name Bolyai. Both were forcibly merged in 1959, to the contin-uing resentment of Hungarians. Nowa-days it also offers its 46,000 students courses in German and English.

Romanians have a talent for funer-ary architecture and one of the best places to appreciate it is the **Hajon-gard Cemetery** (Cimitirul Hajongard, Házsongárdi Temető, Hasengarten; Str. Avram Iancu 24). The name comes from the German *Haselgarten*, mean-ing hazelnut garden. The largest grave-yard in Transylvania, it dates from 1585 when a series of plagues created a demand and the existing cemetery by St Michael's Church was full. Ever since, Hajongard has been Cluj's main cemetery, with Jewish, Lutheran and military sections added later in the immediate vicinity. The oldest surviv-

Map on page 234

Cluj University was considered subversive in communist times – in part because of the city's long tradition of independent thinking, and also because of its sizeable Hungarian community. In the summer months, the university's trade union would rent rooms from people in the Black Sea village of Vama Veche (see page 163), which goes some way to explaining the resort's bohemian character.

BELOW LEFT: the Orthodox Cathedral.
BELOW: National Folk Festival.

ing grave dates from 1599, but few other early tombs remain.

On a hill at the top of Strada Republicii – one of Cluj's grandest streets – the **Botanical Gardens** (Grădina Botanică, Botanikus Kert; Str. Republicii 42; open daily 9am–7pm; admission, photo and video charge) offer respite from the noise and bustle of one of Romania's most congested cities. Crossed by a stream and covering 14 hectares (35 acres), the gardens contain an 83-step observation tower – still a lot lower than many of the trees. The Japanese garden, with a teahouse overlooking a lake, is a delight, as is the Roman Garden, containing plants grown in Roman times and scattered with Classical sculptures. Throughout the gardens, however, a surfeit of concrete detracts slightly from the beauty of the trees and plants.

At the brow of the hill, there are three greenhouses open to the public (daily 9am–5pm; admission charge). There is also a **botanical museum** (theoretically open 9am–5pm; admission charge). Belonging to the University of Cluj, the gardens were founded in 1872 and opened to the public in 1925.

East to Piaţa Ştefan cel Mare

Whereas Piata Unirii has retained a largely Hungarian feel despite Gheorghe Funar's efforts, **Piaţa Ştefan cel Mare** to the east has a more Romanian character and hosts some of the main state institutions. The northern extension of the square, **Piaţa Avram Iancu**, is dominated by the Romanian Orthodox Cathedral. To reinforce the nationalistic message, both squares are lined with more towering Romanian flags than seem strictly necessary.

Built to commemorate Romania's 1918 union with Transylvania, the massive neo-Byzantine **Orthodox Cathedral** (Catedrala Ortodoxă, Ortodox Katedrális; open daily 6am–1pm, 5–8pm; free) was built from 1921–33 by Constantin Pomponiu and George Cristinel, and modelled on Istanbul's Aya Sofia, but with many Romanian decorative elements. It was funded by national subscription.

Outside the cathedral, the oversize **statue of Avram Iancu** (Statuia lui

BELOW: street café on Piaţa Unirii.

Avram Iancu), dating from Funar's time as mayor, is a controversial addition. Its militaristic gunmetal-grey matching the cupolas of the cathedral, the statue commemorates the leader of the 1848 rebellion against Hungarian rule. It aroused protests not just for its provocative theme but for its colossal expense. A memorial on the other side of the cathedral in socialist realist style commemorates Romania's fallen in World War II.

Restored from 1957–59, the **Tailors' Bastion** (Bastionul Croitorilor, Szabók Bástyája; Strada Baba Novac) south of Piaţa Ştefan cel Mare is the only tower of the medieval citadel to have survived. The Tailors' Guild paid for its construction and maintenance. Built in the 15th century, it was destroyed by an accidental gunpowder explosion in 1627. Its current design is the result of two subsequent rebuildings (1627–29 and 1718). The inside of the bastion is closed pending the resolution of a dispute over what to do with it. Fragments of the citadel's crenellated wall survive to the north of the bastion.

Behind the Tailors' Bastion and resembling a massive medieval stone castle, the **Reformed Fortress Church** (Biserica Reformată, Biserica-cetate Reformată, Református Vártemplom; Str. Mihail Kogălniceanu) is one of the most important as well as largest Gothic buildings in Transylvania. It was originally built as a monastery for Franciscans, but they were forced to abandon it in 1536 following religious reforms. Some 40 years later it passed into the hands of Jesuits, but they too were forced out after Unitarians sacked the church in 1603. Then in 1622 it passed to the Reformed Church, who finished rebuilding it in 1646. The interior is richly decorated with the coats of arms of Transylvanian noble families. The carved wooden pews and pulpit are 17th century; the enormous rococo organ dates from 1766.

The equestrian **statue of St George** killing the dragon outside the church is a copy of a 1373 work by brothers Márton and György Kolozsvári. Commissioned by Karoly IV, the original now stands in Prague fortress.

At the eastern end of Bulevardul Eroilor, the **Memorandum Monument** (Monumentul Memorandumului) is another controversial and hugely expensive addition to the city's public architecture by Gheorghe Funar. Widely known for obvious reasons as the Guillotine (Ghilotina), it commemorates Romanian victims of Hungarian oppression.

In front of the cathedral, the magnificent **Lucian Blaga National Theatre** (Teatrul Naţional Lucian Blaga, Színház Lucian Blaga román; www.teatrul-lucian-blaga.ro) was the work of Viennese architects Ferdinand Fellner and Hermann Helmer from 1906–07, and combines Secessionist and Eclectic elements. The building also houses the **Romanian Opera** (Opera Română, Román Opera; www.opera-cluj.com), founded in 1919.

West of Piaţa Unirii

A short distance west of Piata Unirii, the **Ethnographic Museum** (Muzeul de Etnografie, Népmıvészeti Múzeum;

Map on page 234

The controversial statue of Avram Iancu overlooks the Orthodox Cathedral. Iancu was an important figure in the 1848 rebellion and is revered by ethnic Romanians.

BELOW: Piaţa Unirii is Cluj's principal square.

The Memorandum Monument, well known as "the Guillotine" is another controversial city landmark bearing the stamp of former mayor Gheorghe Funar.

BELOW:
Turda Gorge.

Str. Memorandumului 21; open Mon–Fri 8am–4pm; admission charge; www.muzeul-etnografic.ro) occupies the 16th-century Reduta Palace. Rebuilt in the 18th–19th century, it was an important inn, then became a seat of the Transylvanian Diet as well as one of Cluj's main concert halls. Musicians who performed here include Bartók, Brahms, Liszt and Enescu. Pending long-term renovation, the museum is currently open only for temporary exhibitions. It also houses one of Cluj's most atmospheric restaurants, the Etno Club and Grill *(see page 252)*.

In the Romulus Vuia Ethnographic Park (Parcul Etnografic Romulus Vuia) at Strada Tăietura Turcului, Pădura Hoia, the **open-air section** of the museum (secăia in aer liber, szabadtéri részlege; open Mon–Fri 8am–4pm, Sat–Sun 10am–4pm; admission charge) was the first such collection in Romania, opened in 1922. Laid out like a Transylvanian village, it has an interesting collection of homesteads, wooden churches and technical installations including oil presses and mills of various types.

The curiously named **Cock Church** (Biserica cu Cocoș, Kakasos Templom; Str. Moților 88) is so called because its architect, Károly Kós (1883–1977) incorporated crowing cockerels into almost every conceivable interior surface, along with other Transylvanian Hungarian folk motifs. A prominent member of the Hungarian National Romantic School, Kós drew inspiration from the village architecture of the region. The building serves as the Reformed church; if it is closed, ask for the key at the parochial office next door.

In the west of Cluj, the district of **Mănăștur** (Kolozsmonostor, Abtsdorf, Appesdorf) was once a village with an important Benedictine fortified abbey. On the hill of the same name, **Calvaria Monastery** (Mănăstirea Calvaria; Str. Mănășturului 60) was founded in the late 11th century, rebuilt in 1263 and again from 1470–1508, but demolished in 1787 following damage during the war with the Turks. The only surviving part is the Gothic altar, which was transformed into a chapel, and a statue of the Virgin Mary with Jesus under a canopy. From 1930–48 the building was used by the Greek Catholics (Uniates), then handed over to the Romanian Orthodox Church. In 1994 it became Roman Catholic. The particularly hideous communist-era blocks of the surrounding district were designed by North Korean architects.

THE APUSENI MOUNTAINS

Alhough not the highest in Romania, the **Apuseni Mountains** (Munții Apuseni, Erdélyi-Szigethegység) are some of the most dramatic in the country. Certainly, kilometre for kilometre, there are more natural wonders – especially caves – squeezed into these steep hills than anywhere else in Romania.

These uplands are quite extensive; around two-thirds lie within Transylvania, but they also extend west into Crișana – these more westerly areas are described on pages 265–7.

Turda

The ancient town of **Turda** ❸❸ (Torda, Thörenburg; pop. 56,000; www.prim-turda.ro) lies on the River Arieş 32 km (20 miles) southeast of Cluj. It may seem hard to believe today, but this was once one of the richest places in Transylvania, with a lucrative salt mine *(see below),* and is also famed for the 1568 Edict of Turda, which granted equality to Calvinist, Lutheran, Roman Catholic and Unitarian denominations (but not to Orthodoxy). As so often in Romania, there is a pleasant old centre to be explored once you have made it past the grim industrial outskirts. The town **museum** (open Tues–Sun 9.30am–5pm; admission charge) details ethnic and religious history.

Visiting the **Turda Salt Mine** (Salina Turda; open May–Oct daily 9am–5pm; Nov–Apr 9am–3pm; admission charge) in the northern end of town is a surprisingly enjoyable experience. It cannot have been so pleasant to have worked there as extraction has always been purely manual. The mine was first exploited commercially in Roman times, and by the Middle Ages was one of Transylvania's main salt mines. Its galleries commemorate members of the Austro-Hungarian imperial family, with names like the Theresa Mine. Mining stopped in 1932, but deep galleries made a perfect bomb shelter in World War II.

In 1992 the mine re-opened as a tourist attraction. Needless to say, Romanians ascribe many health-giving properties to its saline air, especially for people with breathing problems, and the Rudolph Mine even has a treatment centre. The excellent acoustics also make it an unusual concert venue. It's worth bringing a torch. As temperatures are around 11°C (52°F) whatever the weather is doing outside, wear warm clothes, too.

Turda Gorge

At the eastern edge of the Apuseni Mountains, the **Turda Gorge** (Cheile Turzii), just to the west of Turda, is one of Romania's most dramatic natural attractions. Three km (2 miles) long and 300 metres (985 ft) high, the sheer, almost vertical, limestone cliffs host about 1,000 species of plants, as well

The Apuseni region is popular with Cluj residents for various leisure pursuits.

BELOW:
an Apuseni resident.

Many of Romania's minor roads are unsurfaced, and, particularly in mountain areas such as the Apuseni, in poor condition. A 4X4 vehicle (or an off-road motorbike) are essential.

BELOW: hay is still manually harvested in Transylvania. This non-mechanised agriculture is of great benefit to plants and animals.

as various types of butterflies and more than 100 species of birds, including a pair of golden eagles. With hundreds of climbs to choose from, the gorge also makes an exciting destination for rock climbers. Maps are available at the entrance.

The Padiș Plateau

In the heart of the Apuseni Mountains, the **Padiș Plateau** ❸ is one of Romania's most popular hiking destinations. The usual starting place for trails, the Padiș Cabin (Cabana Padiș) can be reached most easily by four-wheel-drive from Huedin to the north via Răchițele. From Răchițele there is a narrow but passable forestry road. There are poorer roads, difficult in wet weather, from Poiana Horea to the east and Pietroasa to the west.

Taking five hours and marked by blue circles, the most popular trail leads southwest from the Padiș Cabin via Cetățile Ponorului Cabin to the **Ponor Citadels** (Cetățile Ponorului). An amazing fortress-like complex, this is Romania's most impressive karst formation, with the River Ponor gushing

dramatically through it into deep sink-holes. In places the caves reach a height of 200 metres (650 ft). From the Cetățile Ponorului Cabin another trail leads an hour's walk east to the colourfully named **Live Fire Ice Cave** (Peștera Ghețarul Focul Viu). Illuminated by a small gap in the roof, the cave has two chambers filled with an enormous ice block and numerous stalagmites, viewable from a platform.

It is possible to hike south to **Scărișoara Ice Cave** ❸ (Ghețarul Scărișoara; open Tues–Sun 10am–4pm; admission charge). Discovered in 1863, the cave comprises three caverns, of which one contains a block of ice thought to be 3,500 years old. It is up to 22 metres (72 ft) deep and 16 metres (52 ft) thick: that is around 75,000 cubic metres (40,612 cubic ft) of solid ice. The cave sits at an altitude of 1,150 metres (3,772 ft), and its size, together with a maximum temperature of 0.80°C (33°F), prevents it from melting. Icicles, on the other hand, can melt and re-form from year to year, depending on the mean temperature in the cave.

Approaching from Turda and Route

75, the village of **Gârda de Sus**, home to a fine wooden church, is the access point to the cave. Take the road from here to Sfoartea, from where you follow signs for Dealul Ordâncuşii. A shorter route, inaccessible to vehicles, can be hiked by the fit and healthy in around two hours. From Garda de Sus the Vartop Pass leads into Crişana *(the attractions of the western Apuseni are described on pages 265–7)*.

NORTHERN TRANSYLVANIA

North of Cluj

The village of **Bonţida** ❸❻ (Bonczhida, Bonisbruck), 30 km (18 miles) north of Cluj off the main Gherla road, is the site of the Baroque **Bánffy Castle** (Castelul Bánffy; open daily 9am–7pm; admission charge), built between the 16th and 19th centuries. Seat of the Bánffy family, one of the most powerful of Hungarian noble clans, it was one of the most important historical monuments in Transylania, but was almost completely destroyed by the retreating German Army in 1944 in revenge for Count Miklós Bánffy's attempts to sue for peace with the Soviet Union. Apart from being a politician, Miklós Bánffy was also a novelist and author of the *Bánffy Trilogy*, set in Transylvania before World War I. A café on the site of the castle is open daily from 10am–6pm.

On the other side of the hill to the east, the small town of **Sic** (Szék, Marktstuhl, Secken; pop. 2700; www.sic.rural-portal.ro) was at the centre of an important salt-mining area. Largely Hungarian, it is well known for its folk music and the colourful traditional costumes that are still in everyday use. The annual **Sic Days** (Zilele Sicului; around 17–24 August) is a lively celebration of music and local cuisine.

Few places have quite so many alternate names as **Gherla** ❸❼ (Szamos-újvár, Ormenyvaros, Neuschloss, Armenierstadt; Armenian: Hayak-aghak; pop. 24,000), reflecting its historical mix of ethnicities. Gherla dates back to at least the 13th century, although the current city was largely the work of Armenian Catholics who settled here from the early 18th cen-

Map on pages 178-9

TIP

Listed in 1999 as one of the world's 100 most endangered monuments, Bánffy Castle has benefited from a long-term restoration project and is the site of a training centre for architects and craftsmen (www.heritagetraining -banffycastle.org), supported by various NGOS.

BELOW: landscape near Dej. Hilly areas are snow-covered for much of the winter.

Many of these so-called Gypsy palaces were built in the 1990s, when building regulations were loosely enforced. The ostentatious style includes a lavish use of metal roof adornments.

BELOW: villagers in Sic, a centre of Hungarian folk tradition.

tury. While the town preserves many Armenian architectural motifs, the population is now largely Romanian. On the main square, Piaţa Libertăţii, the **Armenian Catholic Church** (Biserica Armenească) dates from 1748–1804 and was built in Baroque style with neoclassical elements. The church's main draw, however, is a painting by Peter Paul Rubens, the *Descent from the Cross* (*Coborârea de pe cruce*), although some dispute its authenticity. Gherla's **History Museum** (Muzeul de Istorie; Str. Mihai Viteazul 6; open Sun–Fri 7am–3am; admission charge) occupies a baroque building and contains a rich collection of Armenian manuscripts and religious items, as well as ethnographic and archaeological exhibitions.

Further north, at the junction of the Someşul Mic and Someşul Mare rivers as well as major roads and railway lines, **Dej** ❸ (Dés; Desch; pop. 38,000; www.primaria.dej.ro) was another salt-mining town, and can trace its origins back to the 11th century. There was once a large Saxon population here. The late-Gothic 15th-century **Reformed Church** (Biserica Reformată), with its 71-metre (232-ft) tower, dominates the main square, Piaţa Bobâlna. On the same square, the **City Museum** (Muzeul Municipal; open Mon–Fri 9am–3pm; admission charge) covers the history of salt mining in the area, and has a large numismatic collection. On the same square the Baroque **Franciscan Church and Monastery** (Biserica şi Mănăstirea Franciscană) date from the 18th century.

Zalău and around

In the valley of the same name 80 km (50 miles) northwest of Cluj, the mainly industrial town of **Zalău** ❸ (Zilah, Waltenberg; pop. 63,000; www.zalausj.ro) largely owes its apppearance to the communist era, when it expanded rapidly. However, the settlement goes back to the 13th century and was once an important station on the Salt Route, an ancient trading route linking Transylvania with central Europe.

The **County Museum of History and Art** (Muzeul Judeţean de Istorie şi Artă; Str. Unirii 9; open Tues–Sun 10am–6pm; admission charge) has a particularly good collection of Dacian and Roman artefacts, including finds from the ruins of **Porolissum**, which lies near the village of **Moigrad**, 7 km (4½ miles) east of Zalău. Founded by Trajan in AD 106, this was a major Roman defence at the northern edge of Dacia, and became an important commercial centre. It remained under Roman occupation until 271. The best-preserved part of the site is the amphitheatre, while the entrance gate is a recent reconstruction. The site is currently under excavation by a joint team of Americans and Romanians.

Bistriţa and the north

Famed as the setting for Bram Stoker's *Dracula*, the quaint little town of **Bistriţa** ❹ (Beszterce, Bistritz; pop. 81,000; www.primariabistrita.ro) is likely to attract fans of the novel for that reason alone, and there is a low-key Dracula industry catering to curious

visitors: almost inevitably, the town's **Coroana de Aur Hotel** came into being to cater for tourists wanting to stay under the same roof as *Dracula's* Jonathan Harker. It is, however, completely fake, built long after Bram Stoker wrote the novel.

However, there are other reasons to visit Bistriţa. One of the *Siebenbürgen*, the town dates back at least to 1264 and its centre remains largely Saxon in style. Dominating the main square, Piaţa Centrală, with its 76-metre (250-ft) tower, the Gothic **Evangelical Church** (Biserica Evanghelică) dates from the 14th century, with later Renaissance additions. The arcaded row of 13 merchants' buildings (**Şugălete**) opposite are a remarkably well-preserved Renaissance ensemble (15th–16th century). South of the centre, the **Coopers' Tower** (Turnul Dogarilor) is the main surviving vestige of the 14th-century citadel, largely sacked in Turk and Tartar invasions. Bistriţa is also a good base for exploring the scenic Bârgău Valley to the east. The road follows the valley deep into the Carpathians,

passing Piatra Fântânele with its Dracula hotel before crossing the **Tihuţa Pass** and descending to the town of Vatra Dornei *(see page 313)*.

On the other side of the Bârgău Mountains north of Bistriţa, the Someş Mare Valley (Valea Someşului Mare) is known for its strong folkloric traditions and has a growing tourism industry. The run-down spa town of **Sângeorz-Băi** ④ (Oláhszentgyörgy; pop. 10,000) provides the best choice of accommodation and makes a good base for hiking in the Rodna Mountains *(see page 329)*. A smaller but more picturesque place to stay is the large village of **Şanţ**, further up the road and renowned for its colourful, traditional wedding celebrations, which last all weekend in summer. It is also a base for little-explored trails leading to the Bârgau Pass, the Rodna Mountains and the Rotunda Pass.

The British-run Ştefan cel Mare Riding Centre (www.riding-holidays.ro) at Lunca Ilvei south of Şanţ offers experienced riders an enticing combination of ecotourism and equestrianism in a remote mountain location.

Map on pages 178-9

The kitsch Count Dracula Hotel in the tiny village and ski resort of Piatra Fântânele, just below the Tihuţa Pass, dates from 1983.

BELOW: a shepherd prepares *mămăligă* (polenta) by mixing it with sheep's cheese.

SOUTHWEST TRANSYLVANIA

Alba Iulia

Romanians treasure **Alba Iulia** 🕸 (Gyulafehérvár, Karlsburg, Weißenburg; Latin: Apulum; pop. 66,000; www.apulum.ro) as a symbol of national unity. Transylvania's capital from 1541–1690, it briefly became capital of a united Romania under Michael the Brave (1600–1; *see page 26*). This was where the Act of Reunification of Romania and Transylvania was signed in 1918, following reunion with Bessarabia and Bukovina. However, Alba Iulia's origins date back to the Dacians, who called it Apulon. Later the Romans had an important legionary base here – Apulum.

The main attractions lie in the upper town; the somewhat grim lower town mainly dates from modern times. Built from 1715–38 on 13th-century foundations, the imposing **Habsburg citadel** (open access) is star-shaped with seven bastions and successive walls. The main entrance is from the east, past a triumphal arch (under restoration). An Austrian double-

headed eagle perches on top. The gangway providing a temporary detour is rickety and poorly lit.

The path leads to the fortress's main entrance through an ornately carved Baroque gateway. Opposite, a slender obelisk (1937) commemorates Vasile Horea, Ioan Closca and Marcu Crisan, leaders of the 1784–85 revolt against their Austro-Hungarian overlords (*see page 30*). Their demands included equality for ethnic Romanians and the abolition of serfdom. Although they initially defeated the Austrians, the revolt was crushed at Forks' Hill (Dealul Furcilor), just south of the citadel.

The three leaders were sentenced to death by breaking on the wheel at the same site, but Crisan cheated the executioner by hanging himself the night before. Another stone obelisk marks the actual execution site. Ultimately, the revolt wasn't in vain: Emperor Joseph II abolished Romanian serfdom later the same year. Horea's death cell is above the gateway opposite.

Inside the citadel you enter a square. To the left, the **Three Fortifications Route** (Traseul Celor Trei Fortificaţii;

Alba Iulia's citadel is a fine example of the Vauban style, which was named after the 17th-century French military engineer, Marshal Vauban.

BELOW: Alba Iulia.

open daily 10am–8pm; admission charge) has some insubstantial remains of the Roman military camp and restored parts of the citadel, linked by underground tunnels. On Saturday, guards in period costume stage a parade at 11am, followed at noon by salvos from three cannons. The site has an outdoor tavern replicating an 18th-century military camp, with waiters sporting period costume. Barbecued *virsli* (sausages) are the speciality.

The centrepiece of one of Romania's finest religious ensembles, the **Reunification Cathedral** (Catedrala Reîntregirii; open Mon–Sat 6.30am–9pm, Sun and hols 7am–9pm; free) at the citadel's western edge is as much a political as a religious statement. Built for King Ferdinand I and Queen Marie's coronation in 1922, it was originally the Coronation Cathedral (Catedrala Încoronării), but it also symbolises Romanian unity. Although the cathedral is Orthodox, the coronation service itself was non-denominational because Ferdinand was Catholic, and Marie (Queen Victoria's grand-daughter) Anglican.

The neo-Brâncoveanu complex was the work of architect Victor Stefănescu. Modelled on Târgoviște's Princely Church, the cathedral itself has the shape of an inscribed Greek cross. Inside, neo-Byzantine frescoes commemorate Ferdinand and Marie, Michael the Brave, his wife Stanca and various Transylvanian saints. Ornately carved cloisters link buildings on the complex's four sides, around a pretty flower garden. In addition to the archbishop's residence these include a pilgrimage agency and offices, while a 58-metre (190-ft) bell tower tops the portal. Throughout, the floral stone carvings are of remarkable quality.

Originally the cathedral doubled as the seat of the bishop to the Romanian army, a position abolished in 1948. Since 1975, when the See was upgraded, it has been the seat of Alba Iulia's archbishop. In 2006, after the archives were belatedly released for the first time, a national scandal broke

when current incumbent Andrei Andreicuț was exposed as a Securitate collaborator. He refused to resign, and downplayed his involvement.

Behind, the splendid **National Museum of Unification** (Muzeul Național al Unirii; Str. Mihai Viteazul 12–14; open Tues–Sun 10am–5pm; admission charge) presents Romanian history as a long quest for unity. The building, a crenellated combination of neo-Gothic and Renaissance styles, looks militaristic because it was originally a barracks.

In a complementary cream-and-white colour scheme, the **Union Hall** (Sala Unirii; same hours and ticket) opposite is where delegates from both territories, honoured by solemn statues outside, assembled to sign the Act of Unification between Romania and Transylvania on 1 December 1918. This date is now Romania's national holiday. The collection includes original documents relating to that momentous event.

The small park behind the hall was the rallying point for troops. On the west side an obelisk commemorates

Map on pages 178–9

This obelisk at Alba Iulia remembers the leaders of the 1784–5 revolt against Transylvania's Habsburg overlords.

BELOW: a guard at Alba Iulia's citadel.

Corvin Castle's popularity as a film set has tended to dilute its authenticity. One section, converted into a dungeon for filming purposes, was originally a store room, but there are no signs to explain and visitors are left none the wiser as to what is and what isn't original.

BELOW: the dramatic approach to Corvin Castle.

Romanian soldiers killed in the Battle of Custozza (1866) in the Austro-Italian War. To the east, a weather-beaten Gothic monument honours Colonel Ludwig von Losenau, Alba Iulia's commander, who fell in 1848 in the Battle of Simera, between imperial and revolutionary Hungarian troops.

South of Strada Mihail Viteazul, the **Roman Catholic Cathedral** (Catedrala Romano-Catolică; open daily 8am–8pm; free entry and multilingual group tours) largely dates from the late 12th–early 13th century and is a somewhat stark fusion of Gothic and Romanesque. Two 16th-century Renaissance additions are the Lászai and Várday chapels. Fine funerary monuments to famous Transylvanian personalities line the austere interior. The most notable is John Hunyadi (c.1387–1456), defender of Hungary from the Turks. When the Turks did successfully invade in the following century, they disinterred his grave (and others) and scattered the bones.

Next door, the splendid Roman Catholic **Bishop's Palace** combines late-Renaissance and Baroque elements. Just south of here, the building housing the Military Circle (closed to visitors) was originally the **Princely Palace** (Palatul Princiar), home to Transylvania's rulers, but has housed the army since 1700. The facade's bas-relief (1975) depicts the palace's foremost resident, Michael the Brave, receiving homage. His bronze statue outside is from 1968.

Hunedoara and around

Those with a specialist interest in the communist era will find much of interest in **Hunedoara** ㊸ (Vajdahunyad, Eisenmarkt; pop. 68,000; www.primaria hd.ro). Iron has been extracted here since the Iron Age, and the Romans first exploited it on a commercial scale. Hunedoara became heavily industrialised in the 1800s, and the pace of development was especially aggressive during communist times.

Today, with the demise of COMECON and its guaranteed markets, many of Hunedoara's factories and steel mills appear long abandoned, although Mittal Steel now runs two of its biggest mills. Unemployment is high.

Despite being one of Romania's unloveliest towns, Hunedoara has one of its most memorable buildings – **Corvin Castle** (Castelul Corvinilor; open May–Aug Tues–Sun 9am–6pm, Sept–Apr 9am–4pm, Mon 9am–3pm all year; admission, photo and video charge; www.castelulcorvinilor.ro). Interestingly juxtapositioned next to a gigantic rusting factory and linked to the town by a high, narrow bridge, this fine example of secular Gothic architecture is a spiky, spooky fantasy topped with assymetrical pointed towers and turrets. The structure has its origins in the 14th century, but was later rebuilt and enlarged by Iancu de Hunedoara (Hunyadi János) and, later, by his son Mátyás. It is also known as Hunyadi Castle (Castelul Huniazilor).

Built around a central courtyard, the interior has been clumsily (sometimes speculatively) restored in places, but is still a joy to explore with its winding staircases, a Renaissance loggia, Gothic vaults and Knights' Hall. The Diet Hall (Sala Dietii), briefly seat of the Transylvanian Diet, is a fashionable wedding venue for Romania's élite.

Deva and around

While not especially scenic, the mining town of **Deva** ㊿ (Déva, Diemrich; pop. 67,000; www.e-deva.ro), 18 km (12 miles) north of Hunedoara, makes a more pleasant base for exploring nearby attractions. Its main sights lie on or immediately beneath **Citadel Hill** (Dealul Cetății), a nature reserve with nearly 1,500 plant species and horned adders (although you're unlikely to see any snakes, long trousers and long socks are advisable).

An attraction in its own right, the state-of-the-art **funicular railway** (telecabina; open 8am–8pm; last trip at 7.45pm) whizzes to the top of two gradients – the higher one alarmingly steep. Opened in 2005, it was the work of the Austrian company that built Mamaia's Telegondolă chair lift. Once you reach the top, there's no longer much to see of the **citadel** (cetatea; open access), and nothing is labelled in any language, but the views – and the ride – make the ascent worthwhile.

In the park below, the gorgeous purple-and-pink **Bethlen Palace** (Palatul Bethlen), housing a history

Map on pages 178-9

Dinosaur eggs discovered in the Hateg Geopark (see page 250).

BELOW: King Mátyás I (Matthias Corvinus).

The Corvin Dynasty

Known as the seat of the mighty Corvin (aka Hunyadi) family, Corvin Castle occupies the site of a small royal citadel donated to Vojk Hunyadi by King Sigismund of Luxembourg in 1409. It was Vojk's son John (Romanian: Iancu de Hunedoara, Hungarian: Hunyadi János), *voievode* of Transylvania from 1441–56 and a Hungarian national hero for vanquishing the Turks at Belgrade in 1456, who began work on the current castle. Over the years it was enlarged by his descendants, including his son Mátyás (Matthias) Corvinus. Mátyás became one of the Hungarians' most revered kings (he was coronated in 1457, partly in tribute to John, following the death of King László). In 1605 the castle passed to the Bethlen family, who added many late-Renaissance touches.

The church at Densuş occupies the site of a 4th-century mausoleum, probably of a Roman soldier. When it was built (11th–13th century) stone from other Roman buildings in the area was used in its construction.

BELOW: the area has strong Roman links. **BELOW RIGHT:** Sarmizegetusa.

museum but currently closed for restoration, dates from the 16th century and combines Renaissance with Baroque elements. Also known as Magna Curia, it was home to the Bethlen family, spawning several *voievodes*.

The heavily guarded **Cetate Sports Academy** (Clubul Sportiv Şcolar Cetate) next door is where Romania's sporting elite receive training. In 1976, Nadia Comăneci, its most illustrious alumna, was the first Olympic gymnast to achieve a perfect score. It is unclear if the guards are there to stop intruders spying on Romania's training secrets, or to keep pupils in. Cut off from the outside world, with a gruelling schedule, students have one week's annual holiday.

Haţeg and around

Palaeontologists have unearthed some of Europe's best-known dinosaur remains around **Haţeg** ㊺ (Hatszeg, Wallenthal; pop. 11,000; www.primaria-hateg.rdslink.ro), 20 km (13 miles) south of Hunedoara. Their unusually small size has given rise to theories that the area was an island in Cretaceous times,

their isolation – and consequent food shortages – leading to dwarfism.

In a stunning location overlooking the Silvaşului Valley, the serene Wallachian-style **Prislop Monastery** (Mănăstirea Prislop), 16 km (10 miles) northwest of Haţeg (the turning is off the main Hunedoara road), is one of Romania's oldest convents, dating from around 1404.

Haţeg makes a possible base for exploring the Retezat Mountains or Sarmizegetusa *(see opposite)* to the south, although public transport is poor. Without a car, hitching or walking is the only option.

The unusual little church of **Densuş**, 12 km (7 miles) west of Haţeg, was built between the 11th and 13th centuries, and retains 15th-century frescoes. It is surrounded by an attractive graveyard, with some Roman artefacts in evidence. Three villages nearby – Clopotiva, Râu de Mori and Sântamaria Orlea – have a large Italian population, descendants of forestry workers who settled here in 1850 (Italian architects were also brought in for the construction of Densuş Church centuries earlier).

Sarmizegetusa

Romania's foremost Roman archaeo-logical site, **Sarmizegetusa** ⑯ (open daily 9am–7pm; admission, photo and video charge) lies 16 km (10 miles) southwest of Hațeg, in the eponymous village on the main Reșița road. Many of the remains are insubstantial, but the forum and amphitheatre – with gladiator school attached – are well preserved. The site also has a Roman temple with an almost complete column. Originally a Dacian settlement known as Sarmis, it fell to the Romans in AD 106, when they established their Dacian capital here. If your idea of an archaeological site is one shared with peasants grazing their flocks, Sarmizegetusa is heaven.

The site lies on the Hațeg–Reșița, Deva–Zaiceni and Hunedoara–Craiova minibus routes. It is possible to stay overnight, with several agro-tourism options – the ticket office (tel: 0744-984613) has information.

Retezat mountains

The rocky **Retezat Mountains** ⑰ (Munții Retezat; Retyezát-hegység), ascending to 2,509 metres (8,230 ft) at Peleaga peak, form part of the southern Carpathians. With an alpine landscape and one of Romania's richest concentrations of flora and fauna, including chamois, brown bear, lynx, boar and golden eagles, the range is one of Europe's most unspoilt wildernesses. Since 1935 much of it has formed the **Retezat National Park** (Parcul Național Retezat; www.retezat.ro). To visit, you'll need a permit, obtainable at the entrance. There are more than 80 glacial lakes, including Romania's largest (Bucura) and deepest (Zănoaga).

Access to the mountains is harder than to many other Romanian ranges but the scenery more than compensates. The easiest way to get here is by train to Ohaba de Sub Patria or any station between Pui and Subcetate on the Târgu Jiu-Petrosani–Simeria line, followed by a hike south. Another access route is from Sarmizegetusa via Râu de Mori and along the Râul Mare Valley to the Gura Zlata Cabin (Cabana Gura Zlatna). The best map available (scale 1:50,000) is published by Budapest's Dimap, which lists 35 trails as well as accommodation options. ❑

Map on pages 178-9

The lax flowered orchid is a common species in the well-watered hay meadows of the region.

BELOW: high in the Retezat Mountains.

RESTAURANTS & CAFÉS

Restaurants

Cluj

Agape
Iuliu Maniu 6
Tel: 0264-406523
Spacious dining room with great big wooden tables, and chairs that could double as thrones. The food is hardly fit for a king, but it is decent international fare, and there is a cheaper self-service restaurant next door if you are on a budget. **€–€€€**

Etno Club & Grill
Str. Memorandumului 21
Tel: 0264-590501
In the courtyard of the ethnography museum, this rustic-themed restaurant, bar and club rolled into one is an excellent choice for Transylvanian country food. Some of the dishes are alarmingly cheap, although the drinks are not. Anyone interested in tracing the origins of pastrami should try the *pastramă de vită* (beef pastrami), which is good – but nothing like the better known New York variety it inspired. **€€**

PRICE CATEGORIES

Price categories are per person for a three-course meal with wine:
€ = under 30 lei
€€ = 30–45 lei
€€€ = 45–60 lei
€€€€ = 60–75 lei
€€€€€ = over 75 lei

Ernesto
Piața Unirii 23
Tel: 0264-596909
Probably the best restaurant in the city centre. At Ernesto's you will find modern international cuisine given a slightly Romanian touch and crafted into a culinary experience unusually good for Romania's provinces. **€€€**

Hey Mamma
Str. Republicii 35
Tel: 0264-439354
Offering "food like Mother makes" it is difficult to fault either the food or the portions here, though service can be a bit slow. The great prices and knockabout atmosphere make for a cheap, fun meal however. **€€**

Noblesse
Str. Ioan Ratiu 12
Tel: 0264-592464
You can try any number of international and European dishes here, though the house overdoes the choice slightly, meaning standards are a little lower than they could be with some more discipline. Nevertheless a classy place, great for a romantic meal or business dinner. **€€€€**

Red House
Str. Constantin Brâncuşi 114
(Andrei Mureşanu)
Tel: 0264-450452
In a well-to-do residential area, this cosy converted house, painted red, is one of the best places for Transylvanian Hungarian food. Obliging service. **€€€**

Roata
Str. Al. Ciura 6A
Tel: 0264-592022
A Cluj legend, this place has been serving high-quality Transylvanian and Romanian dishes for a generation. The terrace is fantastic, and the location, a short walk west of Piața Unirii, is good too. Prices are a bit steep. **€€€€**

Shanghai
Str. Constantin Brâncuşi 98
(Andrei Mureşanu)
Tel: 0264-442027
Near the Red House restaurant in the Andrei Mureşanu district, this small unassuming place is your best bet for Chinese food, with more than 180 dishes on offer. The pagoda-themed garden is a delight in summer. **€€€**

Tokyo Sushi
Str. Marinescu 5
Tel: 0264-598662
Really rather good sushi and Japanese food in a lovely building to the south east of the city centre (a taxi or car is needed to get here). Two Japanese chefs keep standards high (and prices, too) and the people of Cluj appear to love the place: reservations are necessary at weekends. **€€€**

Alba Iulia

Pub 13
Poarta a III-a cetății
Tel: 0258-839555
In a bastion of the citadel, this atmospheric beer cellar and restaurant is one of Alba Iulia's most popular meeting places. For an excellent local take on fish and chips, try the *peşte file*. Thirsty travellers will appreciate the beer sold in metres, although also available by the glass and in bottles. Poor service. **€€**

Trattoria
Str. Frederick Mistral 3
(between Hotelul Parc and Hotelul Transylvania)
This lively intimate venue has a comprehensive menu with Italian and a few Romanian dishes, as well as *sperips* (spare ribs). An appealing place. **€€**

Zhong Yi
Str.Morii 5
Tel: 0258-811557
In the gloomy basement of a gulag-style concrete pod on an otherwise attractive residential street, this restaurant offers above average, if not spectacular, Chinese food. A good option for vegetarians. **€€**

Hunedoara

Corviniana
Str. Constantin Bursan 1
Tel: 0254-749998
If the pollution hasn't put

RIGHT: café life on Cluj's Piața Unirii.

you off your food, this medieval-themed restaurant offers one of the few reasons to linger in Hunedoara. Offers wholesome food at shockingly low prices. €

Deva

Motel Maestro

Calea Zarandului 1
Tel: 0254-212821
The location in an out-of-town development dominated by a McDonald's DriveThru may look unpromising, but this welcoming place is a far cry from your usual motel diner. An excellent choice of salads and plenty of dishes featuring that unusual Romanian ingredient, curry sauce. €€

Wien

Calea Zarandului 55
Tel: 0254-233320
Featuring a truly globe-trotting menu with a heavy emphasis on Austrian, Romanian, Hungarian and Italian specialities, this is far and away Deva's best restaurant. Has a touch of class not easily found elsewhere in town. Exquisite food and flawless service. €€€

Cafés

Cluj

Café Bistro Tango

Str. Gheorghe Bilascu 35
If exploring Cluj's expansive botanical gardens has proven too exerting, this delightfully laid-back café nearby is an excellent place to rest over a drink. Basic bistro menu available. Excellent range of milkshakes, alcohol-free cocktails as well as alcoholic drinks.

Crema

Piața Unirii 25
Tel: 0723-161002
Café-cum-club decked out in French Regency style with designer chairs and supposedly based on an upmarket London lounge. Attracts yuppies and fashionistas, who won't mind that you can easily spend more on drinks here than on a meal elsewhere. Lively at night.

Flowers Teahouse

Piața Unirii 24
Down-to-earth venue in Art Nouveau pastel shades attracting a Bohemian crowd. Free Wi-fi.

Alba Iulia

Chic Café

Str. Avantului 1
Tel: 0747-355775
Anyone worried about the future of Romanian folk music should come to this lively café opposite Hotelul Cetate at night and watch the young crowd enthusiastically dancing the *horă* to it, although purists may disapprove of the house beat. Despite a slightly gangsterish feel, this is a thoroughly enjoyable place to spend the evening.

Deva

Mio Delicio

B-dul. Decebal bl. G
As well as the temptation of beautifully-presented cakes made on the premises, this quiet café is an excellent choice for families as it includes a children's play area, something normally found in Romania only at McDonald's.

WESTERN ROMANIA

Being historically and geographically close to
central Europe, Crişana and Banat are quite
different from the rest of the country

When Romania is divided up, be it for historical, geographical or merely descriptive purposes, it is usually split into the three former principalities of Transylvania, Moldavia and Wallachia. Yet there are parts of the country which do not easily fall into any of these divisions; the Crişana (the area north of the Mureş River) and the Banat (to the south), on Romania's western fringes, and for many the most civilised portions of the country, are two such regions.

While both have their own charms, their individual traits and their own traditions, the history of the two is intertwined. Both escaped all but the briefest periods of Ottoman domination, and as neither land was viewed by the Magyars as historically Romanian, Hungarian (later Habsburg) rule here was by and large just, fair and in many cases benevolent. Indeed, it is the many legacies of Hungarian and Habsburg rule that make the whole region a treat for the visitor. Communications are unusually good, and the architecture of the Baroque and the Secession eras is everywhere.

There are natural wonders in abundance too. The beautiful Apuseni Mountains are crisscrossed by hiking trails, and the caves of the Padiş Plateau are some of Romania's richest treasures. The numerous thermal-

bath complexes that dot the region are another highlight: at Băile Herculane, south of Timişoara, vistors will find a lost paradise of style and grandeur – albeit faded – amongst grand scenery. The southern fringes of the Banat, which touch the Danube and the dramatic Iron Gates, should also be explored.

For all the region's natural charms however, it remains the cities of the Crişana and Banat that people come for. Nowhere in Romania matches Timişoara for swagger, and the fact that the people of this western city kick-started the Romanian Revolution of 1989 was not a coincidence. Likewise, Oradea and Arad have an attitude that is as infectious as their architecture is captivating. ❏

PRECEDING PAGES: a hot day in Timişoara.
LEFT: bringing in the harvest.

CRIȘANA

Fans of the Secession are in for a treat in
Crișana, where the rich architectural legacy
of the region's benevolent Magyar rulers
ensures that its main cities, Oradea and
Arad, are among the finest in Romania

While the term Crișana
(Körösvidék) today refers
merely to the Romanian coun-
ties of Bihor and Arad, study of its past
betrays the eventful history of the
region and of Romania. For much of
the second millennium AD Crișana
formed the western part of the Principality of Transylvania, an apparently
inseparable realm of the Habsburg
Empire. Today, some of the region
remains Hungarian territory: the counties of Hajdu-Bihar and Bekes, including the second-largest city in Hungary,
Debrecen, are considered to be part of
historic Crișana.

The vast majority (around 80 percent and 95 percent in urban areas) of
the population was Hungarian until
1920, when the Treaty of Trianon
awarded the bulk of Crișana to Romania. A long period of migration then
began: Hungarians left and Romanians
arrived to take their place.

Although its ethnographic make-up
may have changed over the past century, modern Crișana – along with the
Banat to the south – remains, perhaps,
the fairest part of Romania. Its towns
are smart and overflowing with glorious, well-preserved architectural wonders (the Secessionist movement was
particularly strong here), and its booming thermal-spa resorts are reminders
of when the rich of central Europe
came to take the waters. With good
public-transport links, decent roads
and a fair smattering of pleasant hotels,
the region is one of the easiest in
Romania to explore.

ORADEA

While the population shifts of the communist period changed the ethnic
make-up of **Oradea ❶** (Nagyvárad;
pop. 207,000; www.oradea-online.ro) for-
ever, reducing the city's Magyar population to a minimum, there is no
mistaking that this is a Hungarian, or at
the very least Habsburg, town. Secessionist architecture defines its streets
and public squares, and even the large

Map
on page
262

LEFT: Pasajul
Vulturul Negru,
Oradea.
BELOW: taking a
stroll in the city.

The Black Vulture Palace (Palatul Vulturul Negru) on Piaţa Unirii is one of the most spectacular buildings in Crişana.

BELOW: Oradea's town hall dates from 1902.

Orthodox Moon Cathedral, seat of the Bishop of Oradea, is a classic piece of late-Baroque design.

Until 1920, the Romanian share of the city's population never reached more than 6 percent. Today, the figure is around 65 percent.

Oradea was founded in the late 11th century, at the same time that its pentagonal **Citadel** (Cetatea Oradea) was constructed. Built by the Magyar king Ladislaus I, it was then the largest citadel in the land, and is today a UNESCO-listed World Heritage Site. Standing south of the river, the citadel is home to Oradea University's Faculty of Arts, and is not considered a tourist attraction. You can walk around the grounds, however, and the views of the town centre from some of the look-out points are splendid.

Besides building the citadel, Ladislaus I also made Oradea a centre of Catholicism, much of his power residing in the goodwill of the Pope, with whom he had sided following the Great Schism of 1054. He founded a monastery nearby (now entirely destroyed), and created the Bishopric

of Oradea. Over the next three centuries the city served as one of the key eastern outposts of Catholicism, a bulwark against Byzantium and Orthodoxy. With Latin the language of the Hungarian court at the time, the city was known as Varadinum.

The citadel was never taken. The Tatars tried and failed in 1241, while the Turks negotiated their way into Oradea, negating the need for military conquest. Indeed, fearful of losing the power the citadel represented, the Turks were kind to Oradea, which enjoyed far greater freedom than almost any other city during their occupation. Oradea's golden age came after it was ceded by the Turks to the Habsburg Empire in 1692. The city enjoyed its first modern system of urban administration, and benefited from a prolonged period of civic construction.

Around Piaţa Unirii

One of the finest squares in Romania, Oradea's **Piaţa Unirii** is somewhat spoilt by the main road that passes through it, but otherwise radiates ele-

gance with its splendid buildings. The finest of all, and the largest, is the **town hall** (primaria municipiului Oradea), built in 1902–3 and possessing a superb facade, not dissimilar to Budapest's Opera House. Containing both Secessionist and neoclassical features, the building was designed by Kalman Rimanoczy, and is perhaps best known for its 50-metre (164-ft) **Bell Tower** (Turnul cu Ceas) overlooking the River Criș. The tower has become as much a symbol of the city as the citadel.

Opposite the town hall is the enormous and astonishing **Black Vulture Palace** (Palatul Vulturul Negru), built from 1907–9 on the site of a medieval inn and today home to an inexpensive and rather disappointing hotel that cries out for a five-star makeover. Occupying an entire block the building has three facades: the finest is that on Piața Unirii, which is all sculpture and stucco, although the pure contours and squiggles of the Vasile Alecsandri facade are more recognisably Secessionist. The building is split into three wings by a glass-covered arcade (Pasajul vulturului negru), which links Piața Unirii with Vasile Alecsandri and Strada Independenței. The arcade contains shops and cafés, and just below the central dome is a stained-glass window featuring a soaring black vulture.

A short walk from the arcade along Strada Independenței will bring you to the city's main **synagogue** (Sinagoga Israelita Neologa, Str. Vasile Alecsandri; open Sun–Thur 9am–5pm; admission charge), completed in 1890 to designs by Ferenc Knapp. Both inside and out it betrays the distinctly Moorish tastes of the architect. A black-marble monument to the Oradea Jews killed in the Holocaust (almost all of them) stands in front of the synagogue.

The Moon Church

Oradea's **Moon Church** (Catedrala Episcopală Biserica cu Lună, Piața Unirii; open 7am–7pm) is a late-Baroque, Orthodox church built in 1784–8. It was one of the few buildings on this side of the river to have survived a great fire in 1836 that destroyed much of the city. The interior is more classi-

Map on page 262

Secessionist splendour inside the Pasajul Vulturul Negru.

BELOW: the synagogue.

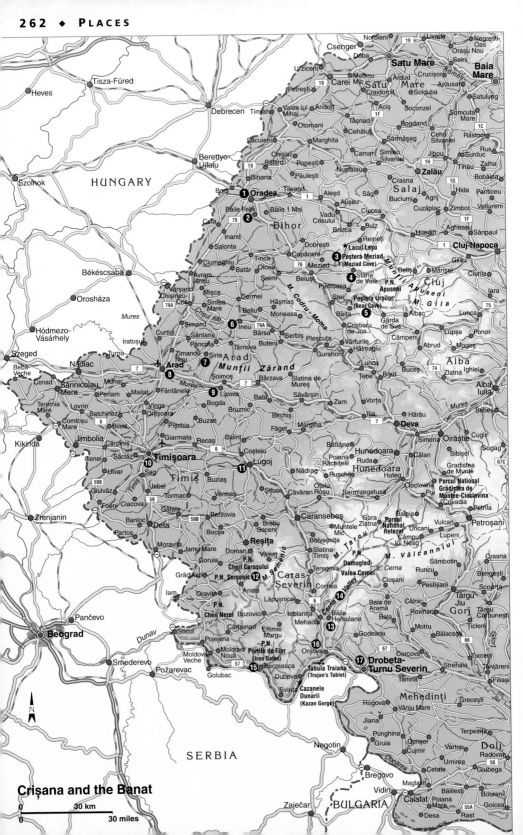

Crişana and the Banat

cally Romanian Orthodox than the exterior, with brightly painted icons in the wooden iconostasis, and decorative altars carved in wood. Look out for the church's prize exhibit: a bible from 1784, one of the last to be produced in Old Church Slavonic. The local Orthodox church began preaching exclusively in Romanian shortly afterwards. The unusual *antimis* – icons painted on fine silk – are worthy of admiration, too. The church takes its name from an unusual mechanism in its tower that keeps track of, and displays, all the phases of the moon.

In front of the church the equestrian statue of Michael the Brave (Mihai Viteazul), who brought the three Romanian principalities together into a single, unitary state for a brief period in 1600, was planted in the centre of the square in 1924 to remind everyone that this was now Romania. On the other side of Piaţa Unirii is the **county library** (Biblioteca Judeteana Gheorghe Şincai), a neo-Renaissance construction from 1903; and behind that is the more sober Catholic **Church of St Ladislaus** (Biserica Romano-Catolică sf. Ladislau), built in 1739 in late-Baroque style, and worth visiting for its frescoes, which were added by local artist Gyula Tury in 1909.

Oradea Veche

Oradea Veche (Old Oradea), as it is known, refers to the clutch of streets that surround Piaţa Republicii. The square is home to the **City Theatre** (Teatru de Stat, Piaţa Republicii 4–5; tel: 0259-236592; box office open Tues–Sun 10am–1pm, 5–7pm), a grand neoclassical building designed by Viennese architects Ferdinand Fellner and Hermann Helmer. The theatre has both Romanian and Hungarian sections, which stage alternating productions. Between Piata Republicii and Strada Republicii is the bazaar. Built in 1908 and originally called the Edison Theatre, it was one of the first cinemas to open in Romania. Today it is home to shops, bars and cafés.

Strada Republicii itself is a Secessionist showcase. Entirely pedestrianised, and lined with cafés and restaurants, it is preceded by the Hotel Crişul Repede, built in 1900 complete with a public bath on the ground floor. The building also hosts the Oradea Restaurant, opened at the same time as the hotel and still a favourite for weddings and christenings, despite its faded grandeur. Among other buildings on Republicii worth looking out for is the **Apollo Palace** (Palatul Apollo, Str. Republicii 12–14), one of the last Secession buildings to go up in Oradea. In a small park behind the palace is the **Ady Endre Museum** (Muzeul Ady Endre, Parcul Traian 1; open Tues–Sun 10am–3pm; admission charge), dedicated to a Hungarian Romantic poet born close by. Behind the museum is the **Great Church of Gheorghe Mucenic** (Biserica Mare Mucenic Gheorghe; open 7am–7pm), built in 1858 as a Catholic seminary.

Petofi Park

Two of Oradea's most worthwhile attractions are a 10-minute walk north

Oradea's football team, FC Bihor, is one of the world's few sides to have won championships in two countries. In 1943 (when the team was known as CAO Oradea) it won the Hungarian league title (much of western Romania having been annexed by Hungary in 1940), before taking the Romanian league championship title in 1949.

BELOW: *oina* is a Romanian sport similar to baseball.

BELOW: The Strandul Felix is the largest public bath in Romania.

of Strada Republicii, in **Parcul Petofi** (Petofi Park). The first is the **Roman Catholic Cathedral** (Catedrala Romano-Catolică, Parcul Petofi 1; open 8am–7pm), the largest Catholic church in Romania. Designed by Franz Hillebrandt and completed in 1764, it is pure Baroque; its most famous features are the two towers, set at an obtuse angle from the main building.

An interesting sight on the other side of the park is the **Roman Catholic Bishop's Palace** (Palatul Episcopului Romano-Catolică), with 365 windows. Built 1762–77, also to designs by Hillebrandt, it was confiscated by Romania's communist government in 1948, and until recently housed the Museum of Crișana. In 2005, however, after a prolonged court case, the building was returned to the Roman Catholic Church, which promptly closed the museum. This is a shame because, although the museum was dull, it allowed visitors to see the wonderful interior of the palace, where almost every room is decorated with fine frescoes.

Felix & 1 Mai: Oradea's baths

Băile Felix ❷ is a popular spa resort 9 km (5 miles) south of Oradea, whose thermal waters flow from the ground at a constant temperature of 39°C (102°F). Roman soldiers allegedly discovered the Felix spring, but the waters have been attracting visitors only since the 18th century. Even then local people missed a trick, as no charge was made either for bathing in or drinking the waters until 1857, and only then for stays of more than four days.

Today, Felix is the largest spa resort in the country, and second in fame only to Băile Herculane (*see page 276*). There are more than 50 hotels here, although many people come on day trips from Oradea: note that on summer weekends it can get oppressively crowded. Although situated at a modest altitude of 140 metres (460 ft), the resort has an enviable microclimate that is as attractive to visitors as are the thermal waters. Summers aren't too hot, and the distinctly mild winters make it is a popular place to spend Christmas and New Year's Eve.

Most hotels have their own swim-

ming pools and health centres, offering treatments for skin complaints and digestive problems. There are also two large public baths, both in the open air. The largest is the **Strandul Felix** (Str. Strandului; open Apr–Oct daily 7am–8pm; admission charge). Encompassing 4 sq. km (1½ sq. miles), this is the largest public baths in the country. Far more pleasant is the smaller but warmer **Strandul Apollo** next door (open Apr–Oct daily 8am–8pm; admission charge), surrounded by a 1950s replica of the resort's original 19th-century pavilion.

At **Băile 1 Mai**, just to the east of Felix, the thermal waters are slightly cooler (32°C/89°F), but are considered perfect for the treatment of rheumatism. There are two pools here (open Apr–Oct daily 8am–8pm; admission charge). The large one is called Venus, the other – far smaller – is known as Valuri, which means waves: it features an antiquated but working wave machine, allegedly the first ever installed in a swimming pool in Romania. For many people, however, the biggest attraction at 1 Mai is the

Water Lily Lake (Lac cu Nuferi), which contains rare white water lilies. 1 Mai is a far smaller resort than Felix, with more *pensiones* than hotels, and is far better suited to families.

In the neighbouring village of **Haieu** there is a delightful, 19th-century Orthodox church, built in 1856 but renovated in 1982, when the impressive interior paintings were added. There is also a romantic little Roman Catholic chapel. Built in 1884 but closed down in 1950, it was restored and reopened in 2004.

THE APUSENI MOUNTAINS

The lowlands around Oradea quickly give way to higher ground as you travel east towards central Romania, and the main road to Cluj (Route 1) winds across the northern edge of the Apuseni, a sparsely populated region of limestone hills most of which lies in Transylvania. *For details on the Transylvanian parts of the Apuseni, see pages 240–243.*

The Apuseni are famous for their caves. Approached from the main Oradea–Hunedoara road (Route 76),

Map on page 262

Swathes of vivid red poppies are a wonderful sight in early summer, thriving on patches of temporarily uncultivated land.

BELOW: taking the waters at Băile Felix.

A sign appeals to people to protect the forest. The Apuseni region has retained a healthy population of brown bears.

BELOW: the Apuseni is one of the best places in Romania for horse-riding. **RIGHT:** inside the Bear Cave.

the first of these is at **Meziad**, a tiny village 22 km (14 miles) northeast of Beiuş (take the road marked Aleşd from Beiuş and turn right at Remetea). The **Meziad Cave** ❸ (Peştera Meziad; Comuna Meziad; open Tues–Sun 9am–4.30pm; admission charge), 2.5 km (1½ miles) beyond the village, was discovered in 1849 by a local mountaineer, and was one of the first great Romanian caves to be developed for tourism. Almost 5 km (3 miles) long, it possesses a number of galleries, all of which contain impressive stalactites and stalagmites. Look out also for the fossilised remains of prehistoric bears.

Past the cave, along the unsurfaced road (all but impassable in wet weather), is **Lake Leşu** (Lacul Leşu), a stunning serpentine lake set amid steep hills that promises adventure at every turn. There is a large motel offering basic accommodation in these glorious surroundings, as well as a couple of more homely *pensiones*. The lake is popular with fishermen, and its trout are said to taste divine. Driving south from the lake, follow a narrow road through the breathtaking Iad Valley

that climbs to the minor ski resort of Stâna de Vale. Below the road on the left-hand side, look out for the **Iadolina Waterfall**, about 6 km (4 miles) past the tail of Lake Leşu.

Stâna de Vale ❹ itself is a bit of a disappointment. Although the setting, at 1,100 metres (3,600 ft), is gorgeous, the choice of hotels here is poor, and the skiing very limited. The Peter and Paul Monastery (Mănăstirea sf. apostoli Petru şi Paul), founded in 1992, is one of the newest in Romania. Despite the lack of good places to stay, the village makes a reasonable hiking base, with routes heading off in all directions. One trail leads over to **Pietroasa**, around 14 km (9 miles) to the south, where there is an 18th-century wooden church, and from where it is just a short walk to the Bear and Măgura caves *(see below)*. Those with a car will have to head back to Beiuş and rejoin the main road.

Visiting the caves

The **Bear Cave** ❺ at Măgura (Peştera Urşilor; open Tues–Sun 10am–5pm; admission charge) is so called because

fossilised remains of prehistoric bears – the *Ursus spelaus,* which became extinct about 15,000 years ago – have been found inside. It was discovered by accident in 1975, when miners at a marble quarry at nearby Chișcău went a little too wild with their dynamite. Although far smaller than others in the region, the Bear Cave is spectacular for the number of stalactites, stalagmites, rocks and pools inside: at times the whole place resembles a scale model of a futuristic city. The cave can be explored only as part of a guided tour, which takes around 45 minutes.

Măgura Cave (Peștera Măgura) is a 30-minute walk futher on, inaccessible by car. Much smaller than Bear Cave, it is open only sporadically to experienced cavers on specialist organised tours.

Back on the main Oradea–Hunedoara road, take a left turn at Lunca (Route 75; follow the signs for Turda), and make your way to **Băița** (Little Mine), one of the oldest mining communities in Romania. The Romans mined silver here, before abandoning the region, but the Hungarians resurrected the mine after finding gold and copper here. The place became notorious in the 1950s as the site of Romania's largest uranium mine. Tens of thousands of forced labourers and soldiers mined up to 30,000 tons of prime uranium a year and all of it was shipped to the Soviet Union. Radiation sickness remains a problem for many of the inhabitants of Nucet, a town built to house mine workers: there continue to be cases of malformed and premature births.

Over the scenic **Vârtop Pass** (1,140 metres/3,740 ft), marking the boundary of Transylvania, a pleasant descent leads through the small town of Arieșeni, a budding ski resort with an unusual wooden church dating from 1791 (Biserica din lemn din Arieșeni Inalțarea Domnului). Its short belfry looks rather haphazardly placed atop the steep roof. More striking, if less aesthetically pleasing, is the newly built, five-spired stone church that towers above it.

From Oradea to Arad

There is nothing to amuse even the most curious tourist travelling the main

 Map on page 262

TIP

The karst region of the Apuseni is the best place for caving in Romania. Various operators offer trips, such as Apuseni Experience (www.apuseni experience.ro) and Green Mountain Holidays (www.greenmountain holidays.ro).

BELOW: livestock is given plenty of space in which to graze.

The abundance of butterflies is an indicator of the wildlife-friendly farming tradition in the region. Numerous species thrive in the flower-rich meadows.

BELOW: children join in with the work of harvesting.

road from Oradea to Arad, as the towns of Salonta, Ciumeghiu and Chişineu-Criş are as dull as they come.

If you are not in a hurry to get to Arad, it is worth turning off the main road at Chişineu-Criş, and heading for **Ineu** ❻, a small town at the head of the Crişul Alb Valley. The town is surrounded by a number of small lakes, all popular with anglers, and the Poiana Narciselor (Oasis of Narcis) is a protected area of abundant flora a short walk from the town centre.

Ineu is best known for its **citadel** (Cetataea Ineului; open Tues–Sun 10am–4pm; admission charge?), which dates back at least as far as 1295. It was the scene of a heroic but ultimately futile siege in 1566, when Transylvanian troops held out for months against the Turks. The fortress was reconquered in 1595 and then strengthened, although it functioned only as a border post and customs house for much of the 17th and 18th centuries. In 1870 it was extensively rebuilt by the Habsburgs. Impressive in size, the fortress is low on frills. It does occasionally host concerts in its inner courtyard, but otherwise stands empty and neglected.

Heading towards Arad via Mocrea, Seleuş and Pancota, there is another fortress waiting to be discovered at **Şiria** ❼, but only ruins remain. Built in the 15th century on the orders of Mátyas Corvinus, it was destroyed in 1784 by the Habsburgs, keen not to see it fall into the hands of Hungarian rebels. Far more impressive is Şiria's **Bohus Castle**, an extravagant neo-Baroque pile constructed in the early 19th century for the Bohus merchant family. Today it houses the **Ioan Slavici and Emil Monţia Museum** (Str. Castelului 1; open Tues–Sun 10am–4pm; admission charge) dedicated to Ioan Slavici (1848–1925), an essayist and journalist, and Emil Monţia (1882–1965), a pianist and composer, both born in the town.

ARAD

The story of **Arad** ❽ (pop. 175,000; www.arad.info.ro) is not dissimilar to that of Oradea. Founded in the Middle Ages, it was primarily a Hungarian town until 1920, when the Treaty of Trianon awarded Crişana and the Banat to Romania. In 1920 three-quarters of the town's inhabitants were Hungarian. Where history differs is in the role played by the two towns in the Hungarian Wars of Independence; while Oradea was by and large a Habsburg stronghold, Arad was a hotbed of Hungarian rebellion.

Arad's six-pointed star of a **citadel** (Cetatea Aradului) occupies a peninsula that juts into the rest of the city where the Mureş River takes a southerly turn. It was built on the orders of Empress Maria Theresa and completed in 1783. Unfortunately, what should be the city's primary attraction is currently closed to visitors as it hosts a military base.

The park in front of the fortress (which has a *strand* with open-air swimming pools in summer) can be visited, however, and Arad's new tourist train takes curious visitors up

to the gates and around part of the perimeter, including the monument to the Hungarian generals executed here by the Habsburgs after the failed rebellion of 1848.

Around Piața Avram Iancu

Piața Avram Iancu is Arad's largest public square, named for the 19th-century Romanian nationalist born nearby. A fine bronze statue of Iancu stands in the centre of the square, overlooking the **State Theatre** (Teatrul de Stat; B-dul. Revoluției 103). This is a glorious study in neoclassicism – complete with high loggia and six Corinthian columns – built from 1872–4, but almost entirely reconstructed after a devastating fire in 1957. Opposite is the equally dashing **Hotel Ardealul** (Hotel Transylvania), originally a concert hall built in 1841, with Baroque touches and a wonderful pre-Secessionist balcony.

A short walk east along Strada Mețianu is Arad's **Orthodox Cathedral** (Catedrala Ortodoxa Romana sf. Ioan Botezatorul; Piața Catedralei 1), a twin-towered Baroque church built in

the 1860s, although the towers were not added until 1906, and the interior frescoes came much later, in 1966. In the square in front of the cathedral is Arad's busiest **market** (open 7am–8pm). Past the market is the 25-metre (82-ft) fortress-like **Old Water Tower** (Vechiul Turn cu Apa, Str. Ceakovski), built in 1896 to ensure the city a steady supply of fresh water.

Arad once had a large Serb community, and its church is due south of the market, on Piața Sârbeasca. The oldest surviving church in the city, it was built in rococo style in 1698. Arad's impressive Byzantine **synagogue** (Sinagoga Neologă; Str. Dobra 10; open Sun–Thur 10am–4pm; admission charge) is south of Piața Avram Iancu. It serves a small Jewish population, the vast majority of Arad's Jews having perished in the Holocaust.

Bulevardul Revoluției

Arad's main thoroughfare is **Bulevardul Revoluției**, which drives a wide wedge between the tight streets of the old town, and provides a showcase for a number of fine palaces and public

Map on page 262

Arad's elegant State Theatre is a masterpiece of neoclassical simplicity.

BELOW: the war memorial on Piața Avram Iancu.

BELOW: the Administrative Palace and Bulevardul Revolutiei.

buildings. Known to local people simply as *Bulevardul* (The Boulevard), it is an absolute gem, and to walk its length is one of the highlights of a visit to Arad.

Starting at the corner of Strada Unirii (whose tightly packed 19th-century houses are characteristic of much of old Arad), admire the 1904 **Roman Catholic Church** opposite, with its replica of Michelangelo's *Pieta* above the portico. From here it is a short, pleasant walk past cafés and shops to the vast public square, Piaţa Primariei, that houses the city's majestic **Administrative Palace** (Palatul Administrativ a Municipului Arad). Occupying three sides of the square the building is home to Arad's town hall, and was built from 1872–4 by Viennese architect Francisc Pekar. An eclectic building, it mixes late-Baroque with neo-Renaissance, although its defining feature, the clock tower, is starkly medieval. The clock is from Switzerland.

On either side of the palace are what is known as the Twin Buildings (Două Clădiri Surori): on the right is the **Cenad Palace** (Palatul Cenad, B-dul. Revoluţiei 73), built in 1894 for a railway company and today used by the city council. On the left is the **Palatul Finanţelor** (1896), once the city's treasury and today the seat of Arad's prestigious Aurel Vlaicu University. On the other side of Revoluţiei is the Neumann Palace, once the home of two local factory-owning brothers, today part of the university.

Behind the boulevard and the Administrative Palace is the **House of Culture** (Casa de cultura, Piaţa George Enescu 1), an eclectic mix of Secessionist and neoclassical architecture, completed in 1913, and home to Arad's philharmonic orchestra. The **Museum of Arad** (Muzeul de Arheologie şi Istorie; open Tues–Sun 10am–4pm; admission charge) stands close by. The museum has interesting exhibitions of archaeology, history and natural science, although the real treat is being able to view the stately interior of the building.

Back on the boulevard, Arad's **Reform Church** (Biserica Luterană) stands on Piaţa Martin Luther. It was

built in 1906 in neo-Gothic style, and its steep spire is the highest in the city, reaching 46 metres (150 ft). Built mainly in red brick it is known as the Biserica Roşie (Red Church).

Lipova

Straddling the Mureş River 31 km (19 miles) to the east of Arad on the main Hunedoara road (Route 7), the small town of **Lipova** ❾ is best known for its thermal baths, lying 3 km (2 miles) from the centre (follow the road for Şiştarovăţ), and for the spectacular, atmospheric ruins of the **Şoimos Fortress** (Cetatea Şoimos).

First built in the 13th century the fortress was rebuilt and extended by János Hunyadi at the end of the 15th century, and changed hands regularly over the next 200 years before being abandoned in 1788, when the new fortress at Arad rendered its continued defence pointless. It has recently been the subject of much renovation work, and is well worth an afternoon's trip from Arad. It is currently open to all comers free of charge, and is a popular spot for picnics and gentle walks. To

get there, follow the signs for the *Cetate* from the main road. A little further along the main road, beneath the hill on which the fortress stands, is a glorious little 19th-century **Orthodox church** (Biserica Buna Vestire), complete with sensational interior frescoes painted by local genius Nicolae Popescu (1835–77).

In the centre of Lipova another Orthodox church (Biserica Adormirea Maicii Domnului) dates from 1338, although most of what remains today was built in the early 1700s. Inside, rich frescoes from various eras (including fragments from the original church) compete with the breathtaking iconostasis for the visitor's attention. The rather run-down shopping arcade opposite is in fact an original Ottoman bazaar, built around 1615. Lipova's **Town Museum** (Muzeul Orăşenesc din Lipova, Str. Nicolae Bălcescu 21; open Tues–Sun 9.30am–noon, 2–5pm; admission charge) houses a prize collection of bibles and religious art alongside finds from the Şoimos Fortress in a splendid 19th-century manor-house setting. ❏

A recent investment of 20 million euros has helped ensure that Arad has a good network of trams and buses.

RESTAURANTS & BARS

Oradea

The Bridge
Str. E. Gojdu 2
Tel: 0259-472644
Great Romanian and Hungarian restaurant serving no-nonsense portions of goulash, *gyros* and even pizza. Sit yourself down at one of the large tables and wonder why the stars and stripes is displayed so predominantly behind the bar. €€€

Royal
Al.Strandului nr.14
Tel: 0259-474241
The terrace is most peo-

ple's favourite part of this great little Hungarian restaurant, but the low-ceilinged cellar provides atmosphere and intimacy. €€€

Taverna
Str. Mihai Eminescu 2
Tel: 0745-144604
Classic Romanian dishes cooked and served by experts in a great setting a short walk north of the city centre. Look out for the stuffed chicken in breadcrumbs, and the superb *ciorba*. The pancakes *(clatite)* are great if you have room left. €€€

Arad

Ambiente
Str. Avram Iancu 11
Tel: 0257-284688
The game dishes are the pick of the menu here, with wild goose, duck, venison and even boar sometimes on offer. Otherwise it is standard Romanian fare at good prices. €€

Ca la Mama Acasa
Str. Horia 2
Tel: 0720-430206
The name means "As good as Mum makes" though we doubt anyone has a mother who cooks Romanian and Hungarian favourites like *tocanita* and goulash as well as

this. *Ciorbas* are great too, and it all costs very little. €€

Lake Grove
B-dul. Revoluţiei 20B,
Piaţa Podgoria
Tel: 0744-147781
Wonderful terrace on the shore of the small lake in Arad's biggest park. Serving a wide variety of food, from simple sandwiches to large steaks cooked on an open grill, it is popular and deservedly so. €€€

● ● ● ● ● ● ● ● ● ● ● ● ● ● ● ●

Prices per person for a 3-course meal with wine: € under 30 lei, €€ 30–45 lei, €€€ 45–60 lei, €€€€ over 60 lei.

THE BANAT

The Banat has long been regarded as the most civilised part of Romania; history has been far kinder to it than to almost all the other Romanian lands, making this southwestern corner of the country a welcoming place to visit

Banat translates as "a land ruled by a ban" (*ban* means "lord" or "ruler" in Serbo-Croat). Much of the historic Banat, including the city of Pančevo, is now in Serbia. Although there were several *banats* in the old kingdom of Hungary, use of the term today generally refers to the Romanian Banat.

Part of Simeon the Great's Bulgarian Empire, the Banat become part of the Kingdom of Hungary as early as the 11th century. It was ruled by the Ottomans for a century, beginning in 1552, becoming a quasi-autonomous province within the Habsburg Empire after the Treaty of Pozărevac (1718), when the Turks were forced to cede much of the western part of their empire. The southern part of the Banat, along the Danube, served as a *krajina* (military boundary) until 1871. Like Crisana and Transylvania, it was incorporated into Romania in 1920. Much of the Banat is sparsely populated marshland, and the only city of any size is Timișoara. The population is mainly Romanian, although pockets of Serbs remain. Away from Timișoara, there are fewer Hungarians than in Crișana to the north.

TIMIȘOARA

Timișoara ❿ (Temesvár; pop. 317,000; www.timisoara.ro) came to the world's attention in 1989 when the first sparks of Romania's revolution ignited here on 16 December. Demonstrating at first against the expulsion of a Hungarian priest, protestors soon turned their anger on the regime that had deprived them of so much. After the army killed numerous protestors – the number remains unclear – but failed to quell the protests, other towns and cities in Romania followed the protestors lead. Within the week Nicolae Ceaușescu and his regime were gone.

It is not coincidence that the revolution began in Timișoara. The city has long surpassed the rest of the country

BELOW: Timișoara has a large number of pavement cafés.

in terms of development, both cultural and political, and its population has a deserved reputation for forward thinking (for example, two lamps in front of the Hunyadi Palace mark the spot where in 1884 Timişoara became the first city in Europe to have electric streetlights).

The city was founded by Serbs in the 13th century (the Serb name for the city is Temişvar) but there is archaeological evidence of a Dacian settlement here as long ago as 1000 BC. The city grew quickly after Charles Robert of Anjou built a palace here shortly before naming himself King of Hungary, and Timişoara as Hungary's capital, in 1316. It also served as a power base for János Hunyadi (1387–1456), who rebuilt and extended Charles Robert's palace.

Timişoara is the fourth-largest city in the country and poses the most important challenge to the commercial supremacy of the capital. The city is well-linked by air to Italy, Germany, Austria and a number of other European countries, and by rail to Belgrade, less than 200 km (125 miles) away.

Today the centre is roughly split in two: Downtown, encompassing the area around Piaţa Victoriei, where the revolution began; and the old town, focused on Piaţa Unirii, whose twin Catholic and Serb Orthodox churches are a reminder of the city's rich history.

Around Piaţa Victoriei

The modern heart of Timisoara is the large, rectangular **Piaţa Victoriei A**, dominated at one end by the green and gold domes of the grand cathedral, and at the other by the more sedate Opera House. The astonishing neo-Byzantine **Orthodox Cathedral B** (Catedrala Ortodoxă din Timişoara, Catedrala mitropolitană; open 8am–6pm) was built from 1936–46, and the main dome, at 83 metres (276 ft), is among the largest in the country. Inside, the four columns of the central dome are decorated with superb frescoes of the apostles. A small but excellent selection of religious iconography, spanning the centuries, can be seen in the basement. At the main entrance to the cathedral, on the left-hand side, is a plaque set

Maps on p262 & below

The view along Piaţa Victoriei to the Orthodox Cathedral.

BELOW: inside the Orthodox Cathedral.

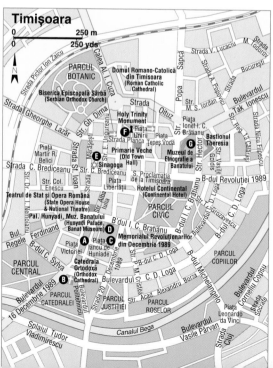

Timişoara

0 — 250 m
0 — 250 yds

N

PARCUL BOTANIC

Domul Romano-Catolica din Timisoara (Roman Catholic Cathedral)

Biserica Episcopală Sârbă (Serbian Orthodox Church)

Strada Pictor Ion Zaicu
Calea Al. Cura
Strada Gheorghe Lazăr
Str. Gh. Dima
Strada Ungureanu

Holy Trinity Monument

Strada
Strada Planca
Piaţa Uniri F
Piaţa Tepes Vodă

Oituz
Str. E. Brătianu

Strada V. Lucaciu
Strada M. Todorov
Sapcă
Popa
Str. M. S. Iordan
Str. A. Popoviu
Strada
Bucureşti
Bulevardul Tak Ionescu
Str. Rea.13 Călăraşi
Strada Nicu Filipescu

Piaţa Martir R. Belici
Str. Mărăşeşti
Str. Gh. Dima
Str. Col. I. Enescu
Str. C. Brediceanu
Strada C. Brediceanu
Str. C. Brediceanu

Primarie Veche (Old Town Hall)
Sinagoga E
Piaţa Libertăţii

Piaţa Ionel I. C. Brătianu
Bastionul Theresia
Str. Hector
Str. Vasile Goldiş

Muzeul de Etnografia a Banatului G

S. Proclamaţia de la Timişoara
Hotelul Continental (Continental Hotel)

B-dul Revoluţiei 1989

B-dul I. C. Brătianu

Teatrul de Stat şi Opera Română (State Opera House & National Theatre)

Pal. Hunyadi, Muz. Banatului (Hunyadi Palace) Banat Museum) D

Strada St. O. Iosif
Strada Alba Iulia
Str. D. I. Memorand

PARCUL CIVIC

Memorialul Revoluţionarilor din Decembrie 1989

B-dul I. C. Brătianu
B-dul C. Grozavescu
B-dul C. D. Loga

Bul. Regele Ferdinand
B-dul C. Sylva
Piaţa A Victoriei
Piaţa Iancu de Huniade
Piaţa C

Str. B-dul C. D. Loga

PARCUL COPIILOR

PARCUL CENTRAL

Catedrala Ortodoxă (Orthodox Cathedral) B

Bulevardul Cetăţei
Str. M. Cristea
Bulevardul 20
Strada Michelangelo
Str. Acad. Alexandru Borza

PARCUL CATEDRALEI
Bulevardul 16 Decembrie 1989
Bulevardul Politehnicii
PARCUL JUSTIŢIEI
PARCUL ROSELOR

Piaţa Leonardo da Vinci

Splaiul Tudor Vladimirescu
Canalul Bega

Bulevardul Vasile Pârvan

Strada Cluj
Bulevardul Cornelia Copşu
Bulevardul Socrate

Detail in the courtyard of the Hunyadi Palace, home to the Banat Museum.

BELOW: Piata Unirii, the Golden Trinity Monument and the Roman Catholic Cathedral.

into the wall commemorating those who were killed in front of the building during the revolution.

Close by is another memorial, the **Monument to the Revolutionaries of 1989 ❸** (Memorialul Revoluţionarilor din Decembrie 1989). A modern and striking structure, it sits in a well-kept garden, overlooked by rather bleak apartment blocks on one side, and more attractive Habsburg-era buildings on the other. In the middle of the garden is a column topped by Romulus and Remus, a familar sight in all large Romanian cities. Street cafés and lively terraces line two sides of the square, while at the far end, directly opposite the cathedral, is the modernist **State Opera House and National Theatre** (Teatrul de Stat şi Opera Română, Piaţa Victoriei).

Across the road, to the right of Piaţa Victoriei, is the **Hunyadi Palace ❹** (Palatul Hunyadi), which hosts the **Banat Museum** (Muzeul Banatului, Piata Huniade; open Tues–Sun 10am–4.30pm; admission charge). The palace was built in the early 14th century and served as the home of Robert of Anjou.

Destroyed by an earthquake in 1443 it was rebuilt by János Hunyadi. It exhibits a collection of artefacts and informative displays from the Geto-Dacian, Roman, medieval and 19th-century eras, but – given Timişoara's role in the 1989 revolution – is disappointingly weak on modern history.

Historic role

South of the Orthodox Cathedral, bordering the river, lie a number of large parks, many with restaurants whose terraces fill up early during the summer. On the other side of the river is the **Hungarian Reformed Church** (Biserica Reformata), which played a major role in the 1989 revolution. Its priest, László Tőkés, was due to be removed and sent to a small parish outside the city as punishment for preaching anti-regime sermons. To prevent his eviction, parishioners surrounded the church in greater and greater numbers. Overnight, the number of protestors became so great that they spilled into Piaţa Victoriei, and a local demonstration quickly became a nationwide revolution.

The old town

To the right of the Opera House, the pedestrianised **Strada Alba Iulia** is a short but attractive street lined with trendy cafés and shops, which leads to Piaţa Libertăţii. North of here, past the modern commercial district, is the old town (or Cetate as it is known locally), much renovated of late and looking better than ever.

Your first stop should be the enormous **synagogue** ❸ (Sinagoga din Cetate, Str. Mărăşeşti), built in 1865, just a year after Jews had been given land rights by Emperor Franz Joseph. Although exterior renovation will be on-going until at least 2008, the synagogue is once again operational, having hosted its first service for 20 years at the end of 2005.

A short walk north is **Piaţa Unirii** ❻, the centrepiece of the old town. The first sight you will see is the yellow **Serbian Orthodox Church** (Biserica Episcopală Sârbă; Str. Ungureanu), built 1744–8. The interior is superb, with fine frescoes added in the 19th century by Constantin Daniel. On the other side of the square is the Baroque **Roman Catholic Cathedral** (Domul Romano-Catolică din Timişoara), designed by the influential Austrian architect Fischer von Erlach. The interior is simple, brightened only by a spectacular golden altarpiece. Besides holding services in Hungarian, Romanian, Serb and Latin, it also hosts regular organ concerts.

In the centre of the square stands the **Holy Trinity monument**, erected in 1740 (although originally found in Piaţa Transylvania) to give thanks for the passing of the bubonic plague, which ravaged Timişoara in 1738–9. Dominating the southern side of the square is the recently restored and gloriously Baroque **old town hall** (Primarie Veche), built on the site of a former Turkish bath between 1731 and 1754. It has been empty since 1958, when the Soviet Army – who used it as their headquarters when stationed in the city – left Romania. Interior renovation continues, but the building will eventually reopen as a Museum of Art.

The rest of the old town's streets, laid out on a simple grid system during an urban renewal programme in the

Map on page 273

The former home of the Serb bishop on Piata Unirii now houses some very desirable apartments. The building was remodelled in 1912 in Secessionist style.

BELOW: Timişoara's faded grandeur.

The attractive railway station at Băile Herculane.

1890s, are well worth exploring, with hidden cellar bars and cafés at every turn. At No. 2 Strada Episcop Augustin Pacha, a plaque on the wall commemorates the fact that Prince Ioan Cuza – the first ruler of a united Romania – spent his last nights in Romania in the building before fleeing into exile in 1868. Further east is Timișoara's 18th-century bastion, around which the city originally grew. Inside is the **Banat Ethnographical Museum** (Muzeul de Etnografie a Banatului; Str. Popa Sapca 30; open Tues–Sun 10am–4.30pm; admission charge), which has exhibitions of traditional crafts and costumes and an excellent gift shop.

SOUTH TO THE DANUBE

Sixty km (37 miles) southeast of Timișoara, **Lugoj** ⓫ must once have been a lovely town, but the building of some of Romania's dreariest suburbs around its core has made it one of the ugliest. Its main square remains mercifully untouched, however.

Its centrepiece is the **Roman Catholic Cathedral** (Catedrala Catolică din Lugoj Coborârea Spiritului Sfânt), built in neoclassical style from 1843–54, with a tower that is one of the most simple and beautiful in Romania.

Ignoring Caransebeș, 42 km (26 miles) south of Lugoj, follow the signs to **Reșița**, from where a number of hikes into the **Semenic Mountains** begin. Much of this mountain region is covered by the **Semenic National Park** ⓬, the most spectacular part of which is the Cheile Carasului, where rocky outcrops hide a number of caves formerly inhabited by hermits. A good hiking map of the mountains is available in bookshops in Reșița, or at the mountain resort of Semenic, 30 km (18 miles) away. There is some good skiing at Semenic, although nothing to detain experts for too long.

Those not up to hiking will be pleased to know that the road from Reșița to Anina, and on to Băile Herculane, offers more than 120 km (75 miles) of quite spectacular scenery. Look out for the ruins of a Roman fort at **Mehadia** (Ad Medium), 6 km (4 miles) north of Băile Herculane. Fans of mountain railways are catered for in the Semenic Mountains, too: an old mining railway still carries passengers from Anina to Oravița twice a day; it occasionally continues on to Iam on the Serbian border.

Băile Herculane

Băile Herculane ⓭ (Hercules' Baths) is two very different places: the modern resort of high-rise hotels that was built in the 1960s, and the neglected Habsburg resort of the 1860s and 1870s further up the valley. Legend has it that Hercules bathed here and the Romans, who certainly *did* bathe here, named the thermal spring after him. A fine bronze statue of Hercules has taken pride of place in the historic centre of the resort since 1874.

Alas for the son of Jupiter, the resort named in his honour – once the most fashionable place to take the waters in central Europe – is now a rather run-down place in dire need of renovation. Most of its older hotels, the casino and

the best restaurants have been abandoned, and a sense of faded grandeur hovers uncomfortably over the place. It is to be hoped that the recent renovation and reopening of the Hotel Ferdinand on Piața Hercules will act as a catalyst for a revival.

Even so, there is still plenty to enjoy. There is the resort's main bathhouse, the **Roman-built baths** in the basement of the Hotel Roman (open daily 7am–8pm; admission charge), which offer every kind of aquatic medical treatment imaginable; and there are seven long hiking trails that begin at the resort. Simply arriving here by train is a pleasure, too, as Herculane is home to one of Romania's most attractive **railway stations**: it has a brightly coloured, tiled dome, built in 1879 in the style of an extravagant Turkish bath. Even if you are not stopping here, make sure you look out for it: Băile Herculane is on the main line from Bucharest to Timișoara.

Running northeast from Băile Herculane, the **Cerna Valley** ⑭ is one of Romania's many natural highlights – a long, narrowing defile leading up to the high Carpathian ridges. Warm air from the southwest is funnelled up the valley, making it one of the warmest places in the country which, combined with plenty of rainfall, makes for unusually lush vegetation.

The Iron Gates

While this far south you should not miss a chance to visit the **Iron Gates** ⑮ (Porțile de Fier), a 117-km (73-mile) stretch of the Danube from Moldova Veche to the (Serbian) Djerdap Dam Hydroelectric Power Station, which passes through four sensational gorges. The first is the **Golubac** (Defileul Golubac), 14 km (9 miles) in length. The town of Golubac (on the Serb side of the river) was flooded during construction of the dam, but nine massive towers – the ruins of a castle that was, for more than two and a half centuries, a base for the Turks for their raids to the north and west until they left in 1688 – can still be seen. On the Romanian side is the tiny town of Coronini.

After a broader section, the second gorge is the Gospodin Vir (Defileul Gospodin), which extends for a further

Maps on pages 262, 273

The construction of the Iron Gates Dam, and subsequent raising of the water levels, has made this formerly turbulent stretch of the Danube far safer for shipping.

BELOW LEFT: the Hotel Cerna in Băile Herculane.
BELOW: fishing by the Kazan Gorge.

Map on page 262

All that remains of the Roman bridge across the Danube are two pillars, one on either side of the river a short distance upstream from Turnu Severin.

BELOW: the Tabula Traiana.

15 km (10 miles), and narrows to 220 metres/yds in places. Beyond is the famous **Kazan Gorge** (Cazanele Danării), 19 km (13 miles) long, where the river flows between towering cliffs soaring 700 metres (2,300 ft) through a chasm only 150 metres (492 ft) across.

The **Tabula Traiana** (Trajan's Tablet) is a monument from Roman times that was laid to commemorate the construction of the Roman military road to the colony of Dacia. The stone plaque, which is on the Serb side of the Kazan Gorge, marks the place where he began to construct his 40-km (25-mile) road around the treacherous cliffs of the Danube, a few miles upstream from the point where work on a remarkable bridge commenced in AD 103. Before the gorge was flooded with the creation of the hydroelectric plant, the plaque was located 40 metres (130 ft) lower. Today, it is set in a rocky cliff, just above the water level of the Danube. The original Latin inscription can still be seen, although the words "Tabula Traiana" are a more recent addition.

On the Romanian side, a 40-metre (130-ft) **image of Decebal**, the Dacian

chief, is carved into the rock. The carving was the idea of the nationalist businessman and financier Iosif Constantin Dragan, and took twelve sculptors ten years (1994–2004) to complete. The inscription underneath immodestly declares in Latin that "Dragan Made This" (Facet Dragan).

The old town of **Orşova** ⑯, jutting beyond the Kazan Gorge, was flooded by the rise in water levels, and largely rebuilt higher up the hill. From here to the dam, 10 km (6 miles) downstream, is the true Iron Gates, once the most dangerous stretch for shipping.

It was here that Trajan built his **bridge**. The river is 800 metres/yds wide here and the bridge measured more than a kilometre from end to end. It was the first across the Danube, and the longest in the world. It was dismantled by Emperor Aurelian when the Romans abandoned Dacia in 271.

Just upstream of here used to be **Ada Kaleh**, a small island on which a mainly Turkish population of 4,000 people lived relatively independently of both Yugoslavia and Romania for much of the 20th century. The island was home to an immense fortress, built by the Habsburgs in 1699 but the property of Turkey from 1738 to 1923, when the island's inhabitants voted to join Romania. With the completion of the dam, Ada Kaleh disappeared underwater in 1968, but only after the fortress had been moved brick by brick to Simian Island, about 10 km (6 miles) downstream. In 2006 Mehedinţi County Council announced it intended to fully restore the fortress, having been awarded an EU grant to do so. The work will continue for up to five years.

Drobeta-Turnu Severin ⑰ itself is a bleak industrial town, though it does have the **Iron Gates Museum** (Muzeul Porţile de Fier; Str. Independenţei 1; open Tues–Sun 9.30am–1pm, 2–5.30pm), a startling **water tower** from 1904 (Castelul de apa; Str. Criflan 1) and the ruins of a 13th-century **Magyar fortress** (Cetatea Severinului; B-dul. Dunarii) on the river front. ❑

RESTAURANTS

Restaurants

Timișoara

Arcade
Str. Hector 4
Tel: 0256-293095
Contemporary European food at good prices in a smart location next to the former bastion and close to the city centre. Part of the clientele can be a little snobbish but the food merits putting up with them. €€€

Beciul Sarbesc
Str. E. Ungureanu 14
Tel: 0256-437151
Great portions of Serb classic dishes – not altogether very different from Romanian – are brought to your table by super-friendly staff in this enjoyable cellar restaurant. €€€

Camelot
Str. Barbu Iscovescu 2
Tel: 0256-221187
Medieval-themed restaurant where huge platters of meat, meat and side dishes of meat are placed unceremoniously in front of you by staff in period costume. Kitsch but great fun. €€€€

Casa cu Flori
Str. Alba Iulia 1
Tel: 0256-430785
Specialities from the Banat – with their strong Austro-Hungarian influences – dominate the menu at this refined little place close to the city centre. €€€

Crama Bastion
Str. Hector 1
Tel: 0256-221199
This lively restaurant is inside the old bastion, the space having been converted at great cost a couple of years ago. Food takes second place to the history of the building, but it is decent enough Romanian fare. €€€

Cucina Moderna
Str. Socrate 12B
Tel: 0256-202405
An intimate yet spacious place where there are just a few tables. Very good Italian food. €€€€

Goethestrasse
Str. Ianos Paris 17
Tel: 0256-270170
Though this great German restaurant is a taxi ride from the city centre it is well worth the effort. It may not look much, but the food is terrific: the bratwurst are genuine and made on the premises. €€€

Intermezzo
Piața Unirii 3
Tel: 0256-432429
Of all the Italian places in the city this is probably the best. The great location, cavernous cellar setting and good-value food make it a must. €€€

Lloyd
Piața Victoriei 2
Tel: 0256-203752
It may be past its best, but there is still a joy to

dining here, especially in summer on the little terrace. Food is decent if not outstanding. €€€€

Taco Loco
Spl. T. Vladimirescu 9
Tel: 0256-204333
Good-value Tex Mex food. You can still get remarkably good burritos and nachos however, and if you want things hot the chef will oblige. €€€

Baile Herculane

Ferdinand Hotel
Piața Hercules 1
Tel: 0255-206073
Home to the finest dining room in the resort, with fine modern European cuisine. Gives hope that Băile Hercu-

lane may soon revive some of its former glory. €€€€

Pensiunea Floare de Colt
Str. Florilor 7
Tel: 0721-252854
There are only a handful of tables in the restaurant here, but the food is fantastic: Romanian specialities are cooked and served by notably obliging staff. €€

PRICE CATEGORIES

Price categories are per person for a three-course meal with wine:

€ = under 30 lei
€€ = 30–45 lei
€€€ = 45–60 lei
€€€€ = over 60 lei

RIGHT: inside the Lloyd restaurant, Timișoara.

EASTERN AND
NORTHERN ROMANIA

Parts of Moldavia, Bukovina and Maramureş are
some of the most isolated regions in Romania,
famous for their remarkable monasteries
and uniquely preserved folk traditions

Comprising Romania's eastern quarter, Moldavia – if Bukovina is counted as a separate entity – lies well and truly removed from the main tourist routes. Originally much larger, various parts were cleaved off as victims of history, including the present-day Republic of Moldova across the River Prut. As a medieval principality, Moldavia enjoyed a golden age period of political and cultural glory in the late 15th century under Stephen the Great, who succeeded in keeping the Ottomans at bay while expanding its borders and building many of its finest monasteries. A later high point came in 1859 when Alexandru Ioan Cuza united it with Wallachia to form the first united Romania. While the capital Iaşi remained an important political, cultural and educational centre, Moldavia as a whole has fared badly ever since: many of its towns were scarred by the communist era, and rural areas are among the country's poorest. Outside of Iaşi, the main attractions are the superb monasteries around Piatra Neamţ, and hiking in the Carpathians along the border with Transylvania.

While historically part of Moldavia, and still often called northern Moldavia (nordul Moldovei), Bukovina (Bucovina) has a distinctive identity from its long period of Habsburg rule (1775–1918). Spread out across thickly-wooded hills dotted with picturesque villages, it is one of Romania's most joyfully bucolic regions. Visitors come to see its gorgeous painted churches, which rank among Romania's greatest gifts to world culture.

Not so much a step as a hop, skip and jump back in time, Maramureş is Romania's living open-air museum of ethnography, a hauntingly scenic and remote region of mountains and forests that has pre-

served its folk traditions better than almost anywhere else in Europe. Best known for its inspirational carved wooden churches, eight of which are on the UNESCO World Heritage List, this sleepy backwater makes other parts of the country look recklessly avant garde. One of the few places in Europe where every day is an occasion to wear folk costume, it casts an irresistible spell over even the most amateur of ethnologists. ❏

PRECEDING PAGES: view of Suceviţa Monastery. **LEFT:** the road through Bicaz Gorge.

MOLDAVIA

Although lacking the recognition of Bukovina's famous painted monasteries, Moldavia has several superb monasteries of its own. This eastern region also offers fabulous Carpathian scenery, peaceful wine-growing areas and the historic city of Iași

What defines "Moldavia" is a source of confusion to many, so first of all some definitions may help. The historic province of Moldavia was split into two parts in 1812, and has remained so ever since. The name Moldavia, as used in the West, refers to the western half of this area, now a province of Romania (Bukovina is sometimes included within its borders). The eastern half, across the River Prut and formerly known as Bessarabia, is these days the Republic of Moldova *(see page 292)*.

Moldavia is strongly associated with the unification of Romania, and with one of it most revered historic figures, Stephen the Great (Ștefan cel Mare*; see page 25)*. It is one of the poorest and least visited parts of the country, but there is plenty to see – the cultural centre of Iasi, the monasteries around Piatra Neamt and, in the west, Carpathian scenery *par excellence* – all with a pleasing absence of tourists.

IAȘI

The historical capital of Moldavia and Romania's second most populous city, **Iași ❶** (pop. 322,000; www.primaria-iasi. ro) is a major pilgrimage centre and a hub of learning and culture.

Scholars are unsure about the origins of the name Iași (pronounced *yash*). It may come from the name of one of the ancient tribes in the area (the Sarmatian Iazyges or the Alanic Jassi) or it may have a connection with the Roman

Iassii legion based nearby. In any case, the first historical reference to the city dates from 1408, although it is probably much older. Iași became the Moldavian capital in 1565 and soon developed into an important religious, artistic and cultural centre. However, thanks to its location, Iași has suffered more than its fair share of invasions and occupations, being ravaged variously by the Tatars, Ottomans and Russians.

To Romanians the city is a symbol of national unity: after the election of local noble Alexandru Ioan Cuza in

Maps
on pages
286, 288

LEFT: the Moldavian countryside near Cotnari.
BELOW:
local heroes
Ștefan cel Mare
and Mihai Viteazul
are commemorated
in Iași.

STEFAN CEL MARE   MIHAI VITEAZUL

Moldavia and Bukovina

1859 as *voievode* of Moldavia, the principalities of Moldavia and Wallachia united. Iași then shared the status of capital with Bucharest until 1862.

The city jealously guarded its position of cultural capital of the "old kingdom" (ie unified Moldavia and Wallachia, sometimes called the Regat), with a strong tradition of poetry, art, literature and publishing. Romania's first university was founded in Iași in 1860, and between 1867 and 1885 many of Romania's prominent writers belonged to its Junimea (The Youth) literary circle. Iași was also home to the country's first literary magazine, and the tradition of Romanian-language theatre came to life here.

But the location, away from the main trading axes, led to a lack of investment throughout the 20th century and today Iași is the capital of the poorest region in Romania, with high unemployment and social problems. What is more, the city was heavily bombed in World War II and in the communist era many of the old buildings in the centre and the Jewish district were demolished and replaced with tower blocks. Many local people partly blame Ion Iliescu, party secretary of Iași county in the 1970s, for the city's neglect.

These days, while it remains a rough diamond of a city, Iași is beginning to lose some of its sharpest edges, partly thanks to a massive influx of EU investment. It is also becoming an important IT centre, with companies such as Amazon and Siemens basing their software development here. The city also has some very good restaurants and an increasingly lively nightlife.

Exploring the town

Iasi's main square, **Piața Unirii** Ⓐ (Union Square) has a hugely symbolic significance for Romanians, as it was here that the ceremony marking the unification with Wallachia – and thus the creation of Romania – took place in 1859 *(see margin)*. Standing in a small garden in the centre of the square, the bronze **statue of A.I. Cuza** is

another symbol of union; the work of Italian sculptor Rafaello Romanelli (1856–1928), it was erected here in 1912.

Iasi's little bit of Paris, and Piața Unirii's most interesting building, is the splendid **Traian Hotel** (Hotelul Traian), dating from 1882. The work of Gustav Eiffel, it may seem to have no obvious connection to his famed metal constructions. However, beneath the elegant *fin-de-siècle* facade it has just such a metal structure, which was then unique in Iași. The hotel is now under extensive renovation, but still open.

Sadly, the rest of the pigeon-infested square is largely an untidy jumble of communist-era monstrosities. Most notable is the drab, 13-storey **Unirea Hotel** (Hotelul Unirea) at No. 5. While the brutalist concrete facade may be an architectural slap in the face to its aristocratic neighbour, a redeeming feature for many will be the splendid socialist-realist murals and mosaic forecourt. Whether their fate is preservation or demolition is anyone's guess.

Slightly north, behind Cinema Republica, the **Union Museum** Ⓑ

Map on page 288

The Traian Hotel overlooking Piața Unirii. Following unification with Wallachia in 1859, Alexandra Ioan Cuza made his inaugural speech in the square. The occasion is marked each year on 24 January (Union Day).

BELOW: a hunters' steak assortment.

(Muzeul Unirii; Str. Lăpușneanu 14) is housed in a building dating from 1806. The ornate orange exterior combines Baroque elements with the Empire style. After the 1859 union, it became Cuza's palace and from 1917–18 it was briefly a royal seat – for King Ferdinand – after the capital shifted temporarily to Iași. The museum contains valuable collections of documents and other items belonging to Cuza and his family. However, the building is in an advanced state of disrepair, and has been closed for renovation since 1997. The main stumbling block is a lack of funds for the costly repairs, and it shows no immediate signs of reopening any time soon.

Leading south, **Bulevardul Ștefan cel Mare și Sfânt C** (Stephen the Great Boulevard) starts off inauspiciously. The northern half combines the worst of the old with the worst of the new. It is like a communist-era extension to Piața Unirii but, if anything, it has worsened since 1989.

On the right, outside Universitatea Petre Andrei at No. 10, the **Green Cube** (Cubul Verde), a large metal cage plonked diagonally into the ground, is an arresting example of public art by sculptor Cristian Constantinescu. Placed there in the 1980s it was originally intended to be the focal point of a new square. However, the project was never completed because of the discovery of the **ruins of a 17th-century palace** (ruinele palatului) just behind the cube. The future both of the original development and the insubstantial ruins remains unresolved.

Shortly afterwards you reach a finely landscaped park, and southwards from here the boulevard is pedestrianised at weekends. Dominating the park, the colossal **city hall D** (primăria) at No. 11 was originally the Roznovanu Palace (Palatul Roznovanu). Initiated in 1832 by Iordache Roznovanu, who was both treasurer of Moldavia and Russia's state counsellor, it followed the designs of Gustav Freywald – also responsible for the cathedral opposite. Following a fire in 1844, Iordache's son Nicolae Rosetti-Roznovanu rebuilt it. With marble exterior statues representing figures from mythology, and exquisite interior

BELOW: Alexandru Ioan Cuza, first ruler of Romania.

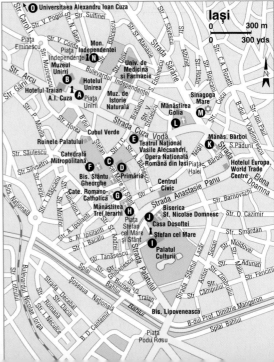

frescoes, the current building combines neoclassical and Baroque elements.

In 1891 the government purchased the building and used it as the city hall. Since then it has changed hands several times. From 1916–18, when the city was temporary capital of Romania, it doubled as offices for ministers displaced from Bucharest; during World War II it became the headquarters of the Romanian and German forces, then the seat of the local communist party after 1944. It was reinstated as the city hall in 1970.

Behind the park, the **Vasile Alecsandri National Theatre E** (Teatrul National Vasile Alecsandri; Str. Agatha Bârsescu 18) is one of Romania's finest. Its Viennese architects Fellner and Helmer had an impeccable pedigree, having designed similar buildings in Vienna, Prague and Salzburg, as well as the national theatres in Cluj, Oradea and Timişoara. Built from 1894–1896 in a French eclectic style, the theatre has 1,000 seats. Its staggeringly beautiful auditorium has a curtain by Austrian painter Maximilian Lenz incorporating various Romanian emblems and sym-bolic motifs as well as a Viennese chandelier. This was the first building in Iaşi with electricity.

The theatre commemorates playwright, poet and politician Vasile Alecsandri *(see page 73)*, the original architect of Romania's theatrical tradition. It is currently closed for renovation but the troupe still performs at other venues.

The building's rear section houses Iaşi's 740-seat **Romanian National Opera House** (Opera Naţională Română din Iaşi; www.opera-iasi.ro), which is still open. It has officially housed the Iaşi National Opera since 1956, although the first operatic performance here was in 1942. There have been sporadic attempts to establish a permament opera house in the city.

Religious buildings

Back on Ştefan cel Mare, at No. 16, the **Metropolitan Cathedral F** (Catedrala Mitropolitană din Iaşi) opposite the City Hall is a huge, pale grey building set in a landscaped garden. It was built from 1833–39 in a neoclassical style to designs by Viennese architects

Map on page 288

Taxis are quite easy to find in Iaşi. See page 338 for a list of companies.

BELOW: A.I Cuza University was Romania's first. Iaşi is traditionally the academic capital of the country.

The Metropolitan Cathedral is Romania's largest Orthodox place of worship and the seat of the Metropolitan See of Moldavia and Bukovina.

Johann and Gustav Freywald. Alas, the central vault was not strong enough to support the building's colossal mass and it soon started to crumble. Rebuilding did not start until 1880.

Of more interest than the somewhat plain exterior are the interior paintings by Gheorghe Tattarescu. However, what really pulls in visitors – on a gigantic scale – is the fact the building contains the relics of Moldavia's patron saint, Parascheva *(see margin, page 291)*. The remains, which are in a fabulous silver casket, cost *voievode* Vasile Lupu the equivalent of a year's national budget when he bought them in 1641.

For the faithful, the investment was worth every penny. Anyone witnessing the masses descending on the cathedral every year for the saint's feast day, 14 October, may wonder if the Second Coming is taking place. With around a million pilgrims from throughout the Orthodox world, Iaşi 's population roughly quadruples and you can forget completely about finding a hotel room unless you booked well in advance. However, it's a fascinating time to be in Iaşi: the feast day is the culmination of a week of festivities.

Immediately south, **St George's Church** (Biserica Sfântu Gheorghe), the former Metropolitan Cathedral, dates from 1761–69. Restored in 1999, it has Byzantine frescoes and an iconostasis in Balkan Baroque style.

With its tapering spire and stark dome shaped like a cross of thorns, the thoroughly modern **Roman Catholic Cathedral ❻** (Catedrala Romano-catolică) at No. 26 is a striking example of a new breed of religious buildings springing up throughout Romania. It was consecrated in 2005. The **old cathedral** (Catedrala veche) in the same complex was built from 1782–89.

At No. 28, the **Three Ierarchs Monastery ❼** (Mănăstirea Trei Ierarhi; open Mon–Sat 9am–noon, 3–5pm admission charge) is one of Iaşi's most popular attractions. Founded by Vasile Lupu and built from 1635–39, it was also home, from 1641–1889, to the relics of St Parascheva, before they were moved to the Metropolitan Cathedral. Its fabulously intricate exterior mouldings feature a riot of geometrical patterns that wouldn't look out of place

on the finest mosques of the same period. Like a weaving in stone, every available inch of its exterior is elaborately carved into 30 bands of interlocking zigzags and circles, interspersed with roses in arches and trellises.

Inside the church the remains of Vasile Lupu and his family lie beneath black marble tombstones in the north of the pronaos, while niches set symmetrically in the southern wall shelter the tombs of Dimitrie Cantemir and Alexandru Ioan Cuza. Ironically, it was because of Cuza's secularisation laws that the monastery was dissolved in 1863. It did not reopen until 1994.

Despite housing Moldavia's patron saint for so long, the monastery hasn't had the best of fortunes. It suffered repeated devastation by Tatar and Polish troops in the late 17th century, followed by an earthquake in 1802 and a fire in 1827. Lecomte de Noüy and Nicolae Gabrielescu restored the church in the 1880s, remaining faithful to the original exterior design. The extravagant gold-plated iconostasis and interior furniture were the gift of Carol I and Queen Elisabeth, while the paintings display a distinctively flamboyant Lecomte de Noüy touch.

The monastery is also famous as the site of Moldavia's first printing press, established by Vasile Lupu in 1640, and its first academy, dating from 1641. A statue in the grounds commemorates the poet Mihai Eminescu, who lived on the premises in 1874.

Palace of Culture

Majestically guarding the southern end of Bulevardul Ştefan cel Mare, the ludicrously grandiose **Palace of Culture** ❶ (Palatul Culturii, Piaţa Ştefan cel Mare 1; open Tues–Sun 10am–5pm; free) is one of Romania's most impressive buildings. Its construction, in a flamboyant neo-Gothic style, took almost 20 years (it was completed in 1925) and both the exterior and interior are richly decorated with heraldic motifs. The clock tower plays *Hora unirii*, the unionist anthem, every hour.

Inside are four museums. Entrance to the Voievodes' Hall or wandering around the interior is free, but each museum has a separate admission charge. All share the palace's opening hours.

The vaulted **Voievodes' Hall** (Sala Voiezovilor) on the first floor is decorated with medallions containing portraits of Moldavian rulers and the kings of Romania. It houses temporary art exhibitions. On the ground floor the **Gothic Hall** (Sala Gotică) features a mosaic representing a medieval bestiary, with griffons, lions and double-headed eagles.

On the ground floor, the **History Museum of Moldavia** (Muzeul de Istorie al Moldovei; same hours as Palace of Culture; admission charge) deals mainly with archaeology. It has a particularly good collection of ceramics from the Cucuteni, an ancient culture which is thought to have lasted in this region from 3700–2500 BC. The Cucutenians had a gift for pottery, adorned with symmetrical geometrical patterns – the only aspect of their decorative art to survive. There are

Map on page 288

The feast day of St Parascheva on 14 October attracts around a million pilgrims from throughout the Orthodox world to Iaşi. As well as the patron saint of Iaşi and Moldavia, St Parascheva is one of the most venerated saints of the Orthodox Church; one reason for her popularity is her reputation for having the power to help families, the sick and the poor.

BELOW: lighting candles during mass.

The Romanians of Moldova

Having to a large degree resolved the Magyar question, Romania now faces a very similar problem on its eastern border: what to do with the 2.6 million ethnic Romanians who live in the Republic of Moldova (or Bessarabia), the eastern half of the historic land of Moldavia.

After the partition of the province in 1812, Bessarabia became part of the Russian Empire. Following the Russian Revolution of 1917, Bessarabia proclaimed independence from Russia, and united with the Kingdom of Romania the following year. Transnistria (a tiny sliver of Bessarabia east of the River Dniestr) did not join Romania, and became the Moldavian ASSR within the Soviet Union in 1924. The Soviet Union occupied the whole of Bessarabia in 1944, and the pro-Soviet government in Bucharest after World War II did not oppose the province's annexation by Moscow.

Over the next 40 years, the Soviet authorities tried to drive a wedge between the Romanians of Moldova and their ethnic and linguistic kindred across the River Prut in Romania. Attempts were made to create a separate literary language called "Moldavian", which according to Soviet linguistics was lexically, phonologically, even grammatically distinct from standard Romanian. In reality, only the alphabet (Moldavian was written in the Cyrillic script) differed, and one of the first acts of the Moldovan government after independence from the Soviet Union, in August 1991, was to reintroduce the Latin alphabet.

In those first throes of independence the notion of reunification was a popular one throughout Bessarabia, though support for the idea has waned over the past decade. The idea has always been less popular in Romania, where reunification is considered an expensive, sentimental luxury that the country simply cannot afford. Moldova is, for one thing, Europe's poorest country. It also has internal problems with the breakaway, unrecognised Republic of Transnistria, which unilaterally declared independence just as Moldova was declaring its own from the Soviet Union.

Perhaps the closest historical parallel would be that of the two Germanies after the fall of the Berlin Wall. When East Germany, one of the Soviet Bloc's most advanced economies, united with West Germany – one of Europe's richest countries – the cost proved hard to bear. Likewise, South Koreans and North Koreans may dream of reunification but few south of Panmunjom would relish the expense of rebuilding a bankrupt economy.

Yet none of these factors has stopped various Romanian politicians – including current president Traian Băsescu – from proposing reunification when politically convenient to do so. Băsescu has often spoken of the Romanian people being "divided between two states." His predecessor Ion Iliescu said in 1995 that there were "two Romanian states, with a joint birth, culture and history".

Reunification is unlikely anytime soon, however. While, in the 1990s Moldova and Romania both firmly occupied Europe's economic poop-scoop, Romania has nudged its way into a club that looks suddenly reluctant to expand its membership list. Before EU membership changed everything, Moldovans could enter Romania without a visa and many did so, some opening businesses there. In early 2007 so many visa applicants overran the Romanian consulate in Chișinău that the Romanian foreign ministry asked the Moldovan government for permission to open two new consulates in Moldova. In the post-Cold War era, many applicants complained about the indignity of having to grapple with one of Europe's most formidable bureaucratic borders to pass from one part of their historic country to another. The subject is likely to remain Romania's biggest unresolved foreign-policy issue for the foreseeable future. ❏

LEFT: casting a vote in the Republic of Moldova.

also some mammoth bones on display.

On the first floor, the **Ethnographic Museum of Moldova** (Muzeul Etnografic al Moldovei; same hours as Palace; admission charge) features a range of improbably oversized mechanical implements used in food production as well as folk costumes and carpets. A shop inside sells handicrafts. On the same floor, the **Art Museum** (Muzeul de Artă; same hours as Palace; admission charge) has two sections as well as a temporary exhibition in the Voievodes' Hall. The first deals with Romanian modern and contemporary art and has Theodor Aman's famous painting *Union of the Principalities (Unirea principatelor)* depicting two women in regional dress holding hands in union. The other section covers European art.

Perhaps most fun – especially for children – is the **Ştefan Procopiu Science and Technology Museum** (Muzeul Ştiinţei şi Tehnicii Ştefan Procopiu; same hours as Palace; admission charge) on the ground floor. It has a weird and wonderful collection of mechanical musical instruments from the 19th and 20th centuries, which the staff will demonstrate. Another section has models of various inventions, many little known outside Romania. One is a curious photocopier called Moldaprint MO3, dating from 1982, a time when access to such machines was tightly restricted.

Outside the palace a large equestrian **statue of Stephen the Great** (statuia lui Ştefan cel Mare), unveiled by Carol I in 1883, points with a sceptre to the road named after him. Panels on either side of the marble pedestal commemorate scenes from the battles of Dumbrava Roşie and Valea Albă, in which he fought.

In the park opposite, the **Dosoftei House ❶** (Casa Dosoftei; Str. Anastasie Panu 54; open Tues–Sun 10am–5pm; admission charge) was the 17th-century residence of Metropolitan Dosoftei, one of Romania's greatest scholars. It also held his printing press, which operated from 1679–86. Nowadays it contains a collection of old Moldavian literature.

Next door, the **Princely St Nicholas Church** (Biserica Sfântu Nicolae Domnesc*;* Str. Anastasie Panu 65) was founded by Stephen the Great and almost every Moldavian *voievode* was anointed here. It was rebuilt from 1888–1904 by Lecomte de Noüy, with a gold-plated iconostasis carved from linden wood and paintings in a neo-Byzantine style.

From here, Strada Anastasie Panu leads east past the **centrul civic** (civic centre), originally a Ceauşescu-style shopping centre. Nowadays, post-communist developments mean that the architecture lacks uniformity, the food hall has moved underground beneath a glass cupola and the new Moldova Mall houses Pizza Hut, KFC and the other usual suspects.

At the end of the street the **World Trade Centre** and the **Europa Hotel** *(*Hotelul Europa) are a glittery, mirror-glass replica on a smaller scale than Bucharest's World Trade Centre and Sofitel Hotel.

Map on page 288

The Princely St Nicholas Church dates from 1491 – making it Iaşi's oldest religious building.

BELOW: Iaşi's Palace of Culture.

The largest massacre of Romanian Jews in World War II took place in Iaşi from 29 June to 6 July 1941. Until 2003 the issue was generally glossed over in Romania, but after Ion Iliescu had made some foolish remark essentially denying it, a huge international backlash and ensuing enquiry confirmed the culpability of the wartime Antonescu government. A plaque on Strada Vasile Alecsandri commemorates the spot where hundreds were shot dead.

BELOW: Golia Monastery.

In a walled garden behind the Europa, the **Bărboi Monastery** (Mănăstirea Bărboi) is in better shape. Built from 1613–15, it was damaged in the 1829 earthquake and rebuilt. Inspired by the architecture of Mount Athos, the church features four spires with semi-spherical domes and is the only one in Iaşi with a Greek cross design. Prince Sturdza *(see pages 30–31)* and his family are buried here.

About 200 metres/yds northwest, the **Golia Monastery** (Mănăstirea Golia; Str. Cuza Vodă 51; www.golia.ro) sits in a rose garden behind a tall stone wall. Originally at Iaşi's northeastern edge, it was founded by boyar Ioan Golia in the early 16th century and rebuilt and enlarged from 1650–53. A successful synthesis of Greek, Russian and Moldavian styles, the church has a neoclassical exterior and a Baroque cornice, while the elaborate roof with differently sized steeples is more Russian in design, and impressed Peter the Great when he visited in 1711. Visitors can climb the 120-step, 30-metre (98-ft) bell tower.

Just to the east, in the once Jewish district of Târgu Cucului, the **Great Synagogue** (Sinagoga Mare; Str. Sinagogilor 7) is Romania's second oldest, dating from 1671. However, the low, tin-roofed building is no longer much to look at, following several restorations, most recently in 1977. Iaşi once had one of Romania's largest Jewish minorities – nearly half the population in 1900 – but now the community numbers a mere 540. A simple obelisk outside commemorates victims of the 1941 massacre *(see margin note)*.

Independence Boulevard

From the synagogue, the generally colourless Bulevardul Independentei leads back to the Union Museum. The **Natural History Museum** (Muzeul de Istorie Naturală; open Tues, Thurs, Sat 8am–3pm; Wed, Fri, Sun 9am–4pm; admission charge; www.bio.uaic.ro/muzeu) is at No. 16, occupying an impressive late-18th century neoclassical pile once known as Casa Roset. The museum is as famous for the fact A.I. Cuza was elected ruler of Moldavia here in 1859 as for any of its 350,000 specimens.

At No. 12, the **University of Medicine and Pharmacy** (Universitatea de Medicină şi Farmacie; www.umfiasi.ro) occupies a fine Baroque building that once housed Iaşi University. Look out for the tableau on the facade depicting a pathology class. In the courtyard, a group-hug statue and an eternal flame commemorate heroes of unification.

A fantasy of kitsch, the **Independence Monument** (Monumentul Independentei) at the end of the same boulevard dates from 1980. It features an androgynous woman with shrunken head and gravity-defying banner. Bronze tableaux around the base commemorate scenes from the War of Independence. With their bristling moustaches, stuffy suits and starched uniforms, the figures here seem totally at odds with the socialist realism above. The murals of the nearby Student House of Culture also display some glorious examples of this genre. Behind it, and a park full of crumbling

statues, Bulevardul Carol I leads uphill through the university district.

In a street lined with imposing mansions, none comes more impressive than the **Alexandru Ioan Cuza University**  (Universitatea Alexandru Ioan Cuza; www.uaic.ro) at No. 11. Romania's oldest university moved to this absurdly magnificent building (dating from 1893–97; *see picture on page 289)* when its previous home – now the University of Medicine and Pharmacy – proved not quite up to scratch. Combining neoclassical and Baroque styles, it was built around eight interior courtyards. Quite appropriately, it's also known as the University Palace (Palatul Universității).

In an exquisite peach-and-white building just east of Bulevardul Carol I, **Pogor House** (Casa Pogor; Str. Vasile Pogor 4; open Tues–Sun 10am–5pm; admission charge) was writer Vasile Pogor's house, where the Junimea literary circle held weekly meetings. Statues in the garden commemorate its members.

Further uphill on Bulevardul Carol I, **Copou Park** (Parcul Copou) contains the ponderously-named Monument of the Organic Regulation (Monumentul Regulamentului Organic), known as the **lion obelisk** (obeliscul leilor). A 15-metre (48-ft) stone column, flanked by four lions, it was built to commemorate the 1831–32 Constitution that helped pave the way for the union with Wallachia.

Eminescu's lime tree (teiul lui Eminescu) in the centre of the park is the one under which the poet used to sit and meditate. Also in the park, the **Mihai Eminescu Museum** (Muzeul Mihai Eminescu; open Tues–Sun 10am–5pm; admission charge) displays exhibits relating to his life, while **Aleea Junimea** (Junimea Alley) has a series of busts of members of the literary circle.

Straddling the top of the hill, Iaşi's fine **Botanical Gardens** (Grădina Botanică Anastasie Fatu; Str. Dumbrava Roşie 7–9; open daily 9am–8pm; admission charge) are Romania's oldest, dating from 1856.

Three monasteries

In semi-rural tranquillity, three monasteries on Iaşi's southern edge make a

Map on page 288

A family attempts to flee from the USSR to Romania across the frozen River Dniester in 1932. From 1918 to 1940, Romania extended east to encompass the present-day Republic of Moldova.

BELOW: the Jewish cemetery.

*Wine tastings
and tours of
Cotnari Vineyard
(Podgoria Cotnari;
tel: 0232-730296;
www.cotnari.ro) are
available with
English-speaking
guides. Telephone
first to make an
appointment.*

BELOW: workers
on the Cotnari
vineyards.

worthwhile excursion. Atop one of the city's seven hills, **Cetăţuia Monastery** (Mănăstirea Cetăţuia; Str. Cetăţuia 1; open daylight hours; free) enjoys a setting so restful it feels quite cut off from the city. Built from 1668–72 by *voievode* Gheorghe Duca, the cloistered monastery is remarkable for having survived largely intact behind its tall stone walls, 7 metres (22 ft) high and 1.4 metres (4½ ft) thick. The church itself, like a simpler version of Trei Ierarhi *(see page 290)*, retains original frescoes by local artists, as well as by three Aromanian brothers from Ioannina.

From here, a 20-minute walk downhill back towards town, across Bulevardul Poitiers, leads to **Frumoasă Monastery** (Mănăstirea Frumoasă; Str. Radu Vodă 1; free). Although the setting below Cetăţuia hill is less dramatic, its lovely gardens alone make it worthy of its name – Beautiful Monastery. Founded in the 16th century as a church by Meletie Balica, it became a monastery in 1618 under Gavril Movilă and then from 1726 held Grigore Ghica's princely court.

With strong Russian and Ukrainian influences in its architecture, the current church dates from 1836.

On the hill of the same name, the **Galata Monastery** (Mănăstirea Galata; Str. Mănăstirii 4; open Mon–Sat 10am–noon, 1–4pm, Sun and holidays 2–4pm; free) was founded by Peter the Lame from 1582–84 and has an imposing bell tower. The only original part is the typically Moldavian church, while the other buildings were extensively rebuilt in 1960. More isolated than Frumoasă, but less so than Cetăţuia, it has a walled garden where the nuns graze their cows and a workshop where they make liturgical vestments and embroidered items.

Cotnari Vineyard

One of Romania's most famed vineyards, **Cotnari ②**, 54 km (34 miles) northwest of Iaşi, dates back to 1448. Its wine was a favourite of Stephen the Great, and in more recent times it has won numerous awards. Its most distinguished products are the white dessert wine *Grasă de Cotnari* and semi-sweet *Tămâioasă românească*.

The Grasă de Cotnari grape will grow nowhere else because it needs Cotnari's unique soil and climate.

WESTERN MOLDAVIA

Târgu Neamţ

The main reason to stop in **Târgu Neamţ ❸** (pop. 20,000; www.primariat-gneamt.ro), some 50 km (30 miles) west of Cotnari and 45 km (28 miles) north of Piatra Neamţ, is to visit its fine castle. Built in the 14th century, **Neamţ Citadel** (Cetatea Neamţ; Str. Arcaşului 1; open Tues–Sun 10am–6pm; admission charge) towers impressively atop Plesului Hill overlooking the town.

It was built in the late 14th century by Peter I Musat during the consolidation of the feudal Moldavian state, and functioned originally as a customs post. Stephen the Great expanded the fortifications, adding four bastions and the access bridge high above a moat. It survived the siege of Mohammed II in 1476 and another siege, this time by the Poles, in 1691, but was then largely destroyed by Mihai Racoviţa in 1717 on the orders of the Turkish sultan, and never repaired. An extensive renovation programme took place in the 1960s.

Access is still by the vertigo-inducing bridge. Note that if you are coming here by car, vehicles are only allowed part of the way up the hill. Surrounding a deep well, the ruins comprise the main 15th-century entrance, the mint, a bathhouse, food warehouses, and the armoury. Children will love exploring.

Monasteries around Piatra Neamţ and Târgu Neamţ

While less famous than those of Bukovina, the monasteries of the region around Piatra Neamţ and Târgu Neamţ offer great tranquillity and are well worth a visit. Very much working monasteries, they are also excellent places to watch Orthodoxy in action. Although theoretically open daily from 8am–8pm, it is unlikely that any will turn you away whatever time you visit.

Neamţ Monastery ❹ (Mănăstirea Neamţ; admission charge), 15 km (9 miles) northwest of Târgu Neamţ, was originally a hermitage, founded in the 12th century. It became a fortified monastery under the reign of Petru I

Maps on pages 286, 288

The viewing point at Târgu Neamţ Citadel.

BELOW LEFT: the 15th-century belfry at Neamţ Monastery.
BELOW: overlooking Lake Izvorul.

TIP

Although there is some public transport along the Târgu Neamț–Piatra Neamț route, the only way to reach all the monasteries on a day trip is by car. The tourist office in Piatra Neamț can help arrange car hire. There is a fast-growing agrotourism sector in the Neamț Valley and it is easy to find rooms for rent advertised along the main road.

BELOW: nuns at Agapia making artificial flowers.

Mușat (1376–92) and was refounded by Alexander the Good (1400–32), who added the belfry, which has survived in good condition to this day. It became the most important religious, artistic and cultural centre of medieval Moldavia, famous for its miniature paintings.

Today, with more than 70 monks, it is the largest monastery for men in Romania, as well as having the largest monastery library in Romania and one of its most important seminaries.

Entered through a large white gate tower with a wooden balcony on either side, the monastery is surrounded by high stone walls. Its church dates from 1497, during the reign of Stephen the Great, and contains the relics of an unknown saint.

Near the village of Agapia, 4 km (2½ miles) south of Târgu Neamț, **Agapia Monastery** ❺ (Mănăstirea Agapia; www.agapia.neamt.ro; open daylight hours; admission charge) dates back at least to 1429 – according to a manuscript preserved in Oxford's Bodleian Library – although is probably much older. There are two communities here.

In a lovely rose garden behind a wall, the first, larger establishment, Agapia din Vale (Agapia of the Valley), is at the edge of the village and houses 360 nuns. Being rather less well-fortified than Neamț, it suffered from repeated robberies and attacks. The painter entrusted to decorate the church was the then unknown Nicolae Grigorescu, aged only 20, who later became one of Romania's most famous artists. The exceptional murals here helped make his reputation, although he was later to be better known as a portraitist and landscape artist. The monastery also has a museum of old icons and the Alexandru Vlahuță Memorial House, dedicated to the writer who spent his summers here.

The smaller community, **Agapia din Deal**, is 2.5 km (1½ miles) uphill from the main complex – worth it for the setting alone – and is much quieter. Its community of 60 nuns observe a strict vegetarian diet.

Dating from 1715, **Văratec Monastery** ❻ (Mănăstirea Văratec; Comuna Agapia, satul Văratec; open daylight hours; admission charge), just 5 km (3 miles) to the south of Agapia, is a community of 440 nuns. The church dates from 1808–12 and features an eclectic mix of Moldavian and foreign styles, while the interior painting, dating from 1841, is in neoclassical style.

There is an icon museum and an embroidery school, although the main draw, still tugging many a heartstring, is the simple **tomb of Veronica Micle** (mormântul Veronicăi Micle). Eminescu's lover and muse, she took a fatal dose of arsenic a few weeks after his death in 1889.

Pedigrees do not get much more glittering than that of **Bistrița Monastery** ❼ (Mănăstirea Bistrița; Comuna Vișoara; free), 7 km (4 miles) northwest of Piatra Neamț. The foundation of four great *voievodes* – Alexander the Good, Stephen the Great, Petru Rareș and Alexandru Lăpușneanu – it was built around 1400 and houses 50 monks. It is also the monastery where the current patriarch, Teoctist, was ordained in

1935. Alexander the Great and his wife Ana are buried here, as well as Stephen the Great's son Alexandru and daughter Ana. The monastery was renovated in 1984, but preserves much of its original architecture. The tall stone bell tower was built by Stephen the Great in 1498. Romanian pilgrims are drawn to the miracle-working **icon of St Ana**, donated to Alexander the Great in 1401, who in turn gave it to the monastery. The **museum** (open daily 10am–6pm; admission charge) has a collection of old books and tapestries.

On a breathtakingly pretty hilltop midway between Piatra Neamț and Bicaz, **Pângăraţi Monastery** ❽ (Mănăstirea Pângăraţi; Comuna Pângăraţi; free) is worth a long detour for the views alone. Founded during the reign of Stephen the Great and rebuilt by the *voievode* Alexandru Lăpuşneanu in 1560, its church is unusual for being on two levels. Above the old church a newer, larger structure in the style of Bistriţa is under construction and looks extremely impressive. Since few people make it here, the monks are more than usually friendly.

Piatra Neamţ

Piatra Neamţ ❾ (pop. 105,000; www.primariapn.ro) makes a pleasant base from which to explore the region. Although Târgu Neamţ is closer to some of the attractions, Piatra Neamţ is livelier and has a wider range of accommodation, as well as one of Romania's most helpful tourist offices.

While the word *piatră* means stone or rock, theories abound as to the origins of the word Neamţ. One is that it comes from *nemţ*, meaning German, but as far as surviving evidence goes there has never been anything particularly German in the town's history.

Piatra Neamţ is very much a town of two halves. While the developments south of the main square hold little aesthetic appeal, the northern part of town is pleasantly leafy and low-rise.

The historic centre around Piaţa Libertăţii, owes its origins to the princely court built here by Stephen the Great in the 15th century. The **Princely St John the Baptist Church** (Biserica Domnească Sf Ioan Botezătorul; Piaţa Libertăţii 2) was built from 1497–98. Alongside similar buildings in Borzeşti

Map on page 286

Romania's Olympic heroine from 1976, Nadia Comaneci hails from Oneşti. Married in Bucharest's Palace of Parliament in 1996, she now lives in Oklahoma.

BELOW: St John the Baptist Church.

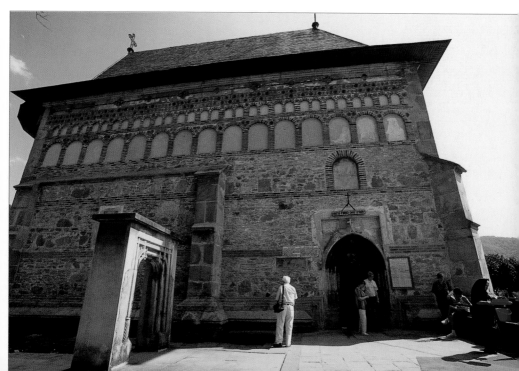

The Bicaz Dam that created Lake Izvorul was built in the 1950s and is an important source of hydro-electric power.

BELOW: crossing the Bistrița River at Broșteni, a small village on the road to Vatra Dornei.

and Războieni, this was one of the earliest examples of what became known as the Moldavian ecclesiastical style. Its pale stone exterior incorporates tiers and arches of bricks of varying colours – red, maroon, bottle-green and orange – while the plan combines rectangular and trefoil elements. Decorated with gaudy modern paintings of Stephen the Great, the interior is less impressive. Built in 1499, a **bell tower** (clopotnița; ask at the church for the key) with a witch's-hat brim stands northwest of the church and once served as a fire observation tower.

Immediately west, in a building that is pure Hansel and Gretel, the **Ethnography Museum** (Muzeul de Etnografie; Piața Libertății; open Tues–Sun 10am–6pm; admission charge) has a small collection of local costumes, carpets and implements as well as several rooms decorated in local peasant style. The **Art Museum** (Muzeul de Artă; Piața Libertății; open Tues–Sun 10am–6pm; admission charge) next door has modern paintings, sculptures and tapestries by Romanian artists.

On the northeast side of the square,

beneath the Petru Rareş school, the **Princely Court Museum** (Muzeul Curtea Domnească; Str. Ştefan cel Mare 4; open Tues–Sun 11am–6pm; admission charge) contains a vaulted cellar of the original princely court and some photographic exhibits. The green ceramic tiles dotting the walls are of exquisite quality and of a colour unique to the princely court. If the door is closed, ask for the keys at the Art Museum.

Next door, Piatra Neamț's finest museum, the **Cucuteni Eneolithic Art Museum** (Muzeul de Artă Eneolitică Cucuteni; Str. Ştefan cel Mare 3; open Tues–Sun 10am–6pm; admission charge) is the only one of its kind in Romania. Opened in 2005, it is dedicated to the Cucuteni culture (*see page 291*). The ground floor has a superb collection of decorated vases, while the first floor displays items of figurative art including anthropomorphic and zoomorphic figurines, most in surprisingly good condition.

Northeast of here, at Strada Dimitrie Ernica 21, the **wooden synagogue** (sinagoga de lemn) is the only one of

its kind in Europe, dating from 1766. The more recent stone synagogue, the **Leipziger Temple** (Templul Leipziger) next door dates from 1839 and is still in use, catering to some 190 Jews. Unfortunately there is not much to see from the street and both buildings are usually locked.

Bicaz and the Ceahlău Massif

The **Bicaz Gorge** ❿ (Cheile Bicazului), on the Gheorgheni road west of Bicaz, is one of the most dramatic defiles in Romania, cutting a swathe through limestone rocks 300 metres (985 ft) high on its narrow route to Transylvania. At the other end of this spectacular stretch of road, and just inside Transylvania, **Lacul Roşu** (Red Lake; Hungarian Gyilkos-tó) is one of Romania's oddest natural phenomena. A natural barrage formed in 1837 after a landslide blocked the Bicaz River; dead tree trunks jauntily stick out of the water, the flooded remnants of a pine forest. Sheltered from strong breezes and refreshingly cool in summer, the resort on its northeastern shore attracts hikers and hedonists alike.

Extending northwest from Bicaz is **Lake Izvorul**, also known as Lake Bicaz, and created by the damming of the Bistriţa River in the 1950s. Rising steeply from its western shores is one of Romania's most rewarding and untrodden hiking and mountaineering areas, the **Ceahlău Massif** (Masivul Ceahlău), where the craggy scenery is rarely less than intoxicating. The national park here, **Parcul Naţional Ceahlău**, shelters some of Romania's richest flora and fauna, including brown bears, lynx and chamois. Since ancient times folk legends have abounded about the range, nicknamed Romania's Olympus.

The principal entry point from the south is via the village of Izvorul Muntelui, 12 km (7 miles) northwest of Bicaz, although this road is frequently closed because of landslides. A better bet is the village and ski resort of **Durău** near the northern end of Lake Izvorul. Picturesque **Durău Monastery** (Mănăstirea Durău; open daylight hours; free entry; accommodation available: tel: 0233-256674) was founded at the start of the 17th century, or earlier, although the current church dates from 1832–5.

Map on page 286

Durău Monastery was once one of many hermitages in the Ceahlău Massif. Two buses run here from Piatra Neamţ daily.

BELOW: the volcanic landscape at Pâclele Mari.

Map on page 286

Russian-style onion domes at Dreptu Orthodox Church on the Vatra Dornei road from Bicaz.

BELOW: Csángó musicians playing the violin and *gardon* cello.

The multiple-tiered **Duruitoarea waterfall** (cascada Duruitoarea) is a popular attraction 2 km (1½ miles) from Durău. As well as the monastery itself, the village offers a number of ecotourism options.

Ghimeş

One of the oldest groups of Hungarians in Romania, the Csángó settled in isolated parts of Moldavia between the 13th and 15th centuries. The most accessible and most visited centre of the Csángó (Ceangăi) culture, the small town of **Ghimeş** ⓫ (Ghimeş-Făget; Gzimesbükk) has a basic, but growing, tourism infrastructure. It is increasingly popular with visitors from Hungary keen to explore – and keep alive – the ancient traditions (since 1997 there has been an annual Csángó Festival held in Budapest).

The main sight is the 19th-century **customs post**, which marks the old border between Transylvania and Moldavia. Above the town, the ruins of **Rácóczi Castle** (Castelul Rácóczi), built in 1626 by Prince Gábor Bethlen, offer a fine view. The appeal, though, is in the chance to experience Csángó folk art, music and dancing.

Vulcanii Noroioşi

Among the strangest of Romania's natural phenomena are the **muddy volcanoes** ⓬ (vulcanii noroioşi) of Pâclele Mari and Pâclele Mici (open access), 12 km (7 miles) north of Berca, just off the main Buzău–Braşov road.

In a series of craters up to about 6 metres (20 ft) deep, the geothermal activity spews methane from deep beneath the earth's surface through a muddy "lava" of various shades of brown and grey. Crystallised salt forms white rings around the brown edge of the craters, while sulphur and other deposits add to the range of colours. The Vrancea region is seismically active and has been at the epicentre of some devastating earthquakes in recent history, not least in 1977 (see page 116).

Brăila & Galaţi

Once an important Danube port, known for its wealth and rich ethnic mix, **Brăila** ⓭ (pop. 217,000; www.pmb.braila.astral.ro) is now something of a backwater and mainly visited by tourists en route to Tulcea and the Danube Delta. On the central square, Piaţa Traian, the **Church of the Archangels Michael and Gabriel** (Biserica sfintii arhangheli Mihail si Gavriil) was originally a mosque which was one of the few buildings in the town to survive the Russo–Turkish War of 1828–29. In 1831 the chief of the Russian Army decided to convert it into a church to commemorate Brăila's liberation from Turkish occupation. However, it retains many Oriental elements, including narrow convex mouldings on the ceiling. It is one of the few churches in Romania without a steeple – the freestanding bell tower is a later addition.

Markedly less attractive than Brăila, **Galaţi** ⓮ (pop. 299,000; www.primaria.galati.ro) is best known as the site of Romania's largest steel mill, and some of the country's worst examples of communist architecture. ❏

RESTAURANTS & CAFÉS

Restaurants

Iași

Casa Bolta Rece
Str. Rece 10
Tel: 0232-212255
Enjoy Moldavian special-
ities such as *parjoale* –
minced-meat croquettes
with a kick – or *ciorbă
de fasole albe* (bean
sour soup). You will find
the Moldavian *ciorbă* to
be far more sour than
elsewhere in the coun-
try. The cellar stocks a
wide range of wine. €€

Casa Lavric
Str. Sfânta Atanasie 21
Tel: 0232-229960
In one of the city's prettiest residential quar-
ters, this delightful villa
exudes hospitality and
atmosphere. It's also a
fine place to watch
Iași's beautiful people.
The mostly Romanian
food is a treat too,
although no better than
at Bolta Rece. Live clas-
sical music in the
evenings. €€€

Dunărea
Str. Panu Anastasie 52
Tel: 0232-272916
Pleasantly old-fashioned
and unpretentious place
specialising in barbe-
cued meat. If Iași's
nightlife has given you a
hangover, head here for
a curative dose of *borș*
or *ciorbă de burtă*. €

Ginger Ale Pub
Str. Săulescu 23
Tel: 0232-276017
Iași's Irish pub looks
very little like an Irish
pub but it does serve
Guinness and offers
some vaguely Irish food,
including chicken pies
and steak sandwiches.
€€

Little Texas
Str. Moara de Vant 31–33
Tel: 0232-272545
On the road out to the
airport you will find this
fantastic Tex-Mex place,
serving food so good
you wonder where the
raw material comes
from: the beef is exquis-
itely tender, for example:
a rarity in Romania.
Lively atmosphere and
great service make it
well worth the taxi ride
out here. €€€€

Pub Baron
Str. Sfântul Lazăr 52
Tel. 0744-543234
In the shadow of
amazon.com's south-
eastern European head-
quarters, this pleasant
music-free TV-free
terrace provides proof
that the art of conversa-
tion is not dead. Apart
from pizza, it serves
Romanian dishes,
mainly grills and roasts.
Open late. €€

Traian
Hotelul Traian, Piața Unirii 1
Tel: 0232-266666
Iași's grandest restau-
rant manages to be
refined and unstuffy at
the same time, with
exemplary service and
implausibly affordable
prices. Romanian and
international dishes. €€

Piatra Neamț

Dao
B-dul. Traian bl. A3
Tel: 0233-228099
Given the lack of any
discernible Oriental com-
munity in Piatra Neamț,
this is a surprisingly
competent Chinese
restaurant, with efficient
service from Romanians
in Chinese costumes.
The inauspicious loca-
tion – by a busy road
surrounded by tower
blocks – wouldn't pass
the *feng shui* test. €€

Central
Hotelul Central,
Piața Petrodava 1–3
Tel: 0233-214530
In contrast to the hotel's
dismal facade and mall-
like annexe, the wood
panels, marble-clad pil-
lars and carved chairs of
its restaurant suggest
an unexpected air of
refinement. Sadly the
food, while passable,
fails to live up to expec-
tations, the menu being
just that little too adventurous for the chef to
cope. €€

Cafés

Iași

Bell Café
Str. Costache Negri 12, bl. G3
Tel: 0232-222101
This stylish place stays
leagues ahead of the
competition, with slick
modern décor and ultra-
efficient service. A per-
fect place to catch up on
e-mails.

Manhattan Café
Str. Hataflul Oilor, Complexul
Tudor Vladimirescu
Tel: 0745-640824
In a district best known
for its student bars, this
venue supplies a rare
dash of sophistication.
The truly international
menu blends equal mea-
sures of imagination
and insanity, with
entries including glazed
unfroggy potatoes,
sesamed hammers and
Shirley Temple Cobbler.
A soothing venue for a
drink or a meal. €€

Moldova
Str. Costache Negri 62
Tel: 0232-256023
Chilled-out café and
pâtisserie near the Trei
Ierarhi church with one
of Iași's tastiest – and
most brightly-coloured –
cake ranges.

Piatra Neamț

Caffè Latino
B-dul. Decebal bl. I4
Tel. 0233-214302
Refreshingly quiet and
civilised, if not terribly
lively, place with eye-
watering choice of tea,
hot chocolate and alco-
holic and non-alcoholic
cocktails, spirits and
liqueurs.

PRICE CATEGORIES

Price categories are per
person for a three-course
meal with wine:
€ = under 30 lei
€€ = 30–45 lei
€€€ = 45–60 lei
€€€€ = over 60 lei

BUKOVINA

Amid steep mountains whose melting snows cause
flooding year after year, the proud people of
Bukovina continue to protect Romania's greatest
cultural legacy: the painted monasteries

First of all, the name, and what it refers to. The term Bukovina implies the whole of the historic region of Bukovina, which includes a large swathe of land annexed by the USSR in 1940 under the terms of the Molotov–Ribbentrop Pact, and which is presently part of Ukraine. Thus Romanian Bukovina is generally called Southern Bukovina, even though it is in the far north of the country. To make things slightly more confusing, it is not a region of Romania in its own right, but merely a northern adjunct of Moldavia. The word probably derives from the Slavic word *buk* (beech).

It is unlikely that the Dacians or the Romans ever settled this far north for any length of time. Although Romanian historians like to suggest otherwise, there is minimal archaeological evidence to support their claims, and the first permanent residents were probably the Slavs, at the end of the 7th century. Later, much of the northern and eastern half of Bukovina formed part of the Kyivan Rus, a prototype Slav state based on the city of Kyiv (Kiev), whose border, from c.900 to 1200, stretched from the Baltic to the Black Sea.

Following the emergence of the principality of Moldavia during the 14th century, Bukovina became the subject of a dispute between this new power and the Polish Empire – the largest successor state to the Kyivan Rus. Under the leadership of Stephen the Great (Ştefan cel Mare; r.

1457–1504) Moldavia staked its claim to the region through a widespread campaign of church building. It is the legacy of this – the famous painted monasteries built in the period immediately after Stephen's death – that is the big draw for visitors.

Suceava and its citadel

Stephen the Great's shadow (in the form of a huge horseback statue on Dealul Ceatate) and his legacy loom large over **Suceava** ⓯ (pop. 106,000; www.e-suceava.com), the only city of any

Map on page 286

LEFT: contemplation outside Voroneţ Monastery.
BELOW: glorious Bukovina scenery.

TIP

For English-language guided tours of Suceava Citadel, call at least 24 hours in advance (tel: 0743-950415).

real size in Bukovina. Situated about 150 km (95 miles) northwest of Iași, it is a fascinating place whose rich history, museums and churches are worth a day or two before moving on to the monasteries.

The city dates to the Middle Ages, its big break coming with the Ottoman invasions of the late 15th century, which necessitated the building of an enormous fortress in the region to protect the newly built churches and monasteries (an earlier fortress – on a hill to the city's northwest – had been abandoned due to subsidence). The extraordinary **Suceava Citadel** (Cetatea de Scaun, Str. Cetății; open Tues–Sun summer 8am–8pm, winter 10am–6pm; admission charge), in the east of the city, was fortified with walls 20 metres (65 ft) high and 2 metres (6 ft) thick. It secured power over all of Moldavia for centuries and has withstood invasions and the passage of time well, although it did need a great deal of reconstruction after an earthquake in 1698.

There is much to see, and a renovation programme has made almost all of it accessible to visitors. The young

BELOW: tourists outside Sucevița Monastery.

can clamber over ramparts and battlements, the less active can walk around the top of the exterior walls on a specially prepared path. A museum is being prepared, and guided tours in a variety of languages are available, offering a full history of the many battles and sieges that took place here. The fiercest were during the Polish–Turkish wars of 1673–4, when a tiny Polish garrison, with local help, held the fortress for six months against a substantial Ottoman force.

Around the Princely Court

The compact little **Church of St John the Baptist** (Biserica Sfântul Ioan Botezatorul; Str. Ana Ipătescu), a short distance west of the citadel, was built in 1643 during the reign of Vasile Lupu. It was originally part of the old Princely Court, the ruins of which are at the end of the same street, and is an impressive late-Gothic construction distinguished by its exquisite exterior decoration and sublime Gothic portico. With no separate belfry, note how the bell was cleverly incorporated into the church's west wall.

Visiting the Monasteries

Despite its treasures, Bukovina is poorly served by public transport. Buses do serve some monasteries, but are irregular and unreliable. Infrequent trains from Suceava to Vatra Dornei stop at Gura Humorului (for Humor and Voroneț) and Câmpulung Moldovenesc (for Moldovița). The best way to see all its towns and monasteries is to fly to Suceava (there are daily flights from Bucharest and Timișoara) and hire a car. Alternatively, there are organised tours to the monasteries from travel agencies in Bucharest and increasingly from abroad, too. If you're doing it yourself, a recommended itinerary is to stay in Suceava for a day or two, visit the monasteries in the immediate area, then go on a longer tour of the northern monasteries, before crossing the Obcina Mountains via the spectacular Ciumârna Pass and heading over to the spa and ski resort of Vatra Dornei.

All the monasteries have nominal opening hours, often from 8am–8pm, with mass at least four times a day, but you are never likely to be refused entry. All have admission charges. There are dress codes for both men and women: neither sex should wear shorts, and women are expected to cover their heads when entering monastery churches. Scarves are usually made available at the entrance for the purpose, although you should be prepared to improvise.

On the other side of the ruins of the Princely Court is the **church of St Dumitru** (Biserica Sfântu Dumitru, Str. Petru Rareş), built in exactly one year from 1534–5 by Ion of Bistriţa. There are interior and exterior frescoes, painted in 1537–8, by Toma of Suceava, the court artist of Petru Rareş, and recently restored with the assistance of wealthy Romanian expatriates in the United States. Even with the recent restoration, however, only small fragments of the exterior frescoes remain, on the southern wall.

Inside, you can get a better idea of Toma's mastery, especially in the portraits of Rareş and his family. The church's separate bell tower, added in 1560, was the tallest tower in medieval Suceava, at 30 metres (98 ft).

The **Princely Court** itself (Curtea Domneasca, Str. Ana Ipătescu) was formed of an L-shaped main building, built of wood during the reign of Petru Muşat, which burnt down in the late 15th century. It fell to Stephen the Great to rebuild it, this time in stone, with heavy fortifications. For the next 250 years the court was the seat of power in Moldavia, but for reasons that remain mysterious was abandoned around 1700. It quickly fell into disrepair and although archaeologists have recently done excellent work, excavating foundations, parts of the northern wall and even remnants of Gothic-style *sobe* (rudimentary but effective radiators), it is difficult to believe that the site was once the seat of power over such a vast principality. A re-creation of part of the court can be found in Suceava's History Museum *(see page 308)*.

The **Mirăuţi Church of St George** (Biserica Mirăuţi Sf. Gheorghe; Str. Mirăuţi), 300 metres/yds to the northeast, was for over a century the coronation church of Moldavian princes and the seat of the Moldavian patriarch (until the Church of St John the New took over both roles). It was built around 1370, but destroyed by the Tatars in 1513. It then lay in ruins until Bogdan III rebuilt it in the first half of the 16th century, but was once again levelled – this time by an earthquake – in 1698. Another two hundred years would pass before restoration was again undertaken.

Map on page 286

Wayside crosses are a common sight in the Romanian countryside.

BELOW:
Suceava Citadel.

For the hundreds of thousands of pilgrims who visit Suceava's Monastery of St John, the remains of St John the New are the biggest draw. The saint was a 14th-century icon painter from Asia Minor, whose work did much to spread the word of Christianity throughout Moldavia. The west wall, which depicts scenes from St John's life, was painted in 1895 by Vladimir Mironescu.

In the centre of town, a 20-minute walk west from the Mirăuți church, is Suceava's last remaining **synagogue** (Sinagoga Hevra Gah; Str. Dimitrie Onciul; open Mon–Fri 10am–4pm), a somewhat dowdy, pre-cubist construction from the late 19th century, brightened inside by a stunning Ark of the Covenant.

The city's **Ethnographic Museum** (Muzeul de Etnografie al Orasului Suceava; Str. Ciprian Porumbescu 5; open Tues–Sun 9am–5pm; admission charge) is housed in downtown Suceava's oldest building, a 15th-century inn and hunting lodge located just to the south of the busy Strada Bălcescu. It features four separate exhibitions of arts, crafts and religious art from the regions of Humor, Radauți, Câmpulung and Putna.

Further south, beyond the rather run-down and unappealing central square, Piața 22 Decembrie, **Suceava History Museum** (Muzeul de Istorie Suceava; Str. Ștefan cel Mare 33; open Tues–Sun 10am–5pm; admission charge) is housed in a glorious little Secessionist palace – partly hidden, alas, behind advertising hoardings. Besides a decent but poorly labelled collection of religious art, treasure and weapons, it also features a full-scale re-creation of the Princely Court of Suceava, complete with life-size waxworks.

Suceava's monasteries

The **Monastery of St John the New** (Mănăstirea Sfântul Ioan cel Nou, Str. Mitropoliei), 400 metres/yds east of Suceava History Museum, is the most important religious building in the city. From its consecration in 1522 its church served as the seat of the Moldavian patriarch for more than 150 years. The church – a mixture of neo-Romanesque and Baroque – is worth visiting for its stunning depiction of the crucifixion above the main altar, painted in 1523 by an unknown artist and given a new lease of life by careful restoration in 2000.

To the northwest of the city, the **Armenian Monastery of Zamca** (Mănăstirea Zamca Armenească) was founded in 1606 by Armenian immigrants on the site of the Suceava's original fortress, which had been abandoned. The monastery was then fortified by Polish troops around 1700, when the battlements were added and the name *zamca* (fortress) first used. Its current state is precarious: the outer walls need renovation work for which there are currently no funds. The Romanesque tower and the 17th-century neo-Byzantine Sfântul Axinte Church are both impressive, however.

THE PAINTED MONASTERIES

One of Romania's main tourist attractions, the extraordinary painted monasteries of Bukovina leave a lasting impression on all who visit. Most people focus on the great triumvirate of Voroneț, Sucevița and Moldovița, but Putna and Humor are also magnificent and there are plenty of lesser-known monasteries, such as Dragomina, to explore too. *See also pages 314–5.*

BELOW: the Monastery of St John the New.

Dragormina Monastery

A short drive north of Suceava is the enchanting **Dragomirna Monastery** (Mănăstirea Dragomirnai; open daily 7am–8pm, admission charge), the last of the painted monasteries to be built. Set spectacularly on the banks of the Dragomirna River, a tributary of the Suceava, Dragomirna is a typical fortress-monastery, surrounded by high, thick bulwarks. It was founded in 1602 by the polymath Anastasie Crimca shortly after he had been named Archbishop of Moldavia. With the help of his brothers he built the tiny church that is now part of the cemetery. The main monastery church is the tall, slim and elegant red-brick Biserica Mare, added in 1627. It is topped with a glorious belfry, which, at 42 metres (138 ft), is one of the highest in the region.

Inside it is covered in frescoes, painted in the 17th century by four artsists known simply as Craciun, Maties, Gligorie and Ignat: we know nothing else about them other than they had considerable talent. The monastery's museum houses a vast collection of medieval art, much of which was donated by Anastasie Crimca himself. It includes some of the earliest Romanian-language bibles ever produced.

Voroneț, Humor and around

A scenic drive of 28 km (18 miles) west from Suceava leads to **Gura Humorului**, a small town traditionally recognised as the gateway to the painted monasteries. From here, the pious usually walk the 4 km (2½ miles) south to **Voroneț Monastery** ⑰ (Mănăstirea Voroneț; open 8am–8pm; admission charge), one of the earliest, probably the most celebrated and certainly the most visited monastery in Bukovina. Stephen the Great himself oversaw its construction in 1488, after a local hermit, St Daniel of Voroneț, promised him victory in an upcoming battle against the Turks should he order the building of a monastery. The battle was duly won.

The frescoes for which the stark, Gothic church is famous were added later. Given that the blue used in the most famous fresco, *The Last Judgement* (considered to be the finest of all the Bukovina paintings) has become known as Voroneț blue, as much a part of the artistic lexicon as Titian red, it is surprising that we know nothing of the fresco's creator, not even a name. A close second to *The Last Judgement* is *Jesse's Tree*, on the south wall, showing the genealogy of Christ.

Five km (3 miles) north of Gura Humorului is **Humor Monastery** ⑱ (Mănăstirea Humor; open 8am–8pm; admission charge) founded in 1530. Humor was painted five years later by Toma Zugravul (Thomas the Painter). Alas, the exterior frescoes have not aged well here, and the devastating scenes of Christian martyrdom, including both the 626 and 1453 sieges of Constantinople, are badly faded. On the other hand, Humor was as well painted inside as out, and the portrayals of torture, salvation and rebirth on the interior walls are in excellent shape. Humor was stripped of

Map on page 286

There are admission charges to the painted monasteries but no fee is charged for photography.

BELOW: souvenir stalls are easy to spot around the monasteries.

Detail from the 1453 Siege of Constantinople fresco at Humor.

BELOW: Voroneţ Monastery.

monastery status by the Habsburgs in 1786, a standing only restored in 1990. The monastery is currently populated entirely by nuns.

Further north, via a forested route along some tricky stretches of road, is the enormous, brilliant-white 16th-century monastery church at **Solca** ⓳ (Mănăstirea Solca). It is often deserted, and the overgrown fortress walls give the impression it has been abandoned, although its church continues to serve the village of Solca. The church lost monastery status a year before Humor suffered the same fate, shortly after the Habsburg annexation of Bukovina. The interior is somewhat bare, its iconostasis having been carted off to Dragomirna.

Ironically, the brewery next door – which occasionally threatens the existence of the monastery and inappropriately uses its former cellars as storage – was founded by the monastery's monks in the 17th century. In the centre of Solca is an 18th-century wooden house, now serving as a small but delightful **village museum** (open Tues-Sun 10am–4pm, admission charge).

The area around **Arbore Monastery** (Mănăstirea Arbore; open 8am–4pm; admission charge), which lies in the Radauţi Depression 6 km (4 miles) downhill (northeast) from Solca, has suffered repeated flooding in recent years. The "monastery" – which is merely a small, beautiful painted church – has survived: a miracle say local people. It was built in a hurry, in five months from April to August 1503, on the orders of Luca Arbore, a confidant of Stephen the Great. The frescoes, which date from 1541, were added by Dragoş of Iaşi. Only those on the western facade, telling the story of the life of St George, remain in good shape.

The northern loop

Starting back in Suceava, a 5-km (3-mile) drive north along the Siret road (Route 2; the main route to the Ukraine) brings you to the turn off for **Pătrăuţi**. This is the site of the monastery of the same name (Mănăstirea Pătrăuţi; open daily 8am–6pm, admission charge), founded by Stephen the Great himself in 1487. It is considered by some to predate

Voroneț, which would make it the second-oldest monastery in Bukovina, having accommodated the community of nuns treating the wounds of Stephen's soldiers. Small in size, the church is large in impact, notably the exterior decoration featuring apocryphal scenes of Turks being defeated – this time in ceramics, not frescoes.

Nine km (5 miles) from Siret (the last town before reaching the Ukraine, and hardly worth the detour except for its Catholic cathedral), take a left turn to **Rădăuți 20**. The city's pride and joy is the Romanesque, single-nave **St Nicholas** (or Bogdana) **Church** (Biserica Sfântul Nicolae, Str. Bogdana Voda 6). Built in 1359, it is the oldest stone church in Moldavia. Interestingly, the church predates the city: it stood alone in a forest until buildings were constructed around it half a century later. Inside it is covered in frescoes painted by Epaminonda Bucevschi in 1880

Rădăuți is infamous as the site of one of the first World War II mass deportations of Romanian Jews (to Transnistria), in 1941. Jews had settled in the city on the invitation of the Habsburgs

after the annexation of Bukovina in 1772. According to the Yad Vashem Centre for Holocaust Research, at least 10,000 were deported – one third of the city's population. Few survived the dreadful conditions they were forced to endure after arrival in Transnistria.

Anyone interested in pottery might like to stop off at **Marginea**, where a workshop on the main road to Sucevița displays the traditional, unmechanised techniques used in the village for centuries. However, most travellers head northwest to the most remote, and earliest, of the great monasteries, at **Putna 21** (Mănăstirea Putna; open 10am–6pm; admission charge). Located in the most picturesque setting of all the painted monasteries, surrounded by the mountains of the Obcina Mare Range, Putna is semi-sacred to Romanians as the resting place of Stephen the Great, who ordered its construction in 1466 to give thanks for victory against the Turks in a nearby battle. Of that original monastery, only the **Treasury Tower** (Turnul Tazaurilor) remains, the rest having been lost in a great fire in the 16th century. It was rebuilt from

Map on page 286

Romania has a long tradition of bee-keeping. Small, rural producers are under threat from stricter sanitary regulations brought in by the EU.

BELOW: locally-produced honey *(miere)* is sold at roadside stalls.

Intricate handmade lace and embroidery can be a good buy in Romania.

BELOW: scenery near Câmpulung Moldovenesc.

1653–72 during the reign of Vasile Lupu, and the original layout – a large church surrounded by fortified outbuildings – was preserved. Further extensions were added after the Austrians took Bukovina in 1772, and much of what we see today carries the flourish of Karl Romstorfer, who renovated much of the monastery complex in the early 20th century.

Stephen the Great's **tomb** is in the burial chamber below the church, alongside that of his wife and two of his children. There is an exhibition of sacred medieval relics in the monastery **museum**. Saint Daniel of Voroneț lived in a cave (which he carved out of the rock himself) 2 km (1 mile) from the monastery. The path to the cave is signposted *Daniil Sihastru*.

From Putna it is a five-hour hike over to Sucevița: those with a car will have to go back to the main road via Marginea. The fabulous **Sucevița Monastery** ㉒ (Mănăstirea Sucevița; open 8am–8pm; admission charge) is just a short walk out of the village of Sucevița, at the foot of a long winding road that leads over the Ciumârna Pass. It is the largest of

the monasteries, surrounded by an imposing fortress with four turrets. Its main church, built between 1582 and 1600, is covered entirely in frescoes, save for the western wall. The *Staircase of Virtue* mural on the northern wall depicts the 30 steps from Hell to Heaven, allegedly the journey taken by Orthodox monks on their deaths. Inside there are more frescoes, this time depicting the Orthodox calendar, and featuring innumerable Orthodox saints. The monastery's founders, Simion and Movila, are buried in the ossuary.

There are few mountain passes in the country more spectacular than the **Ciumârna Pass** (1,109 metres/3,640 ft), both for the hair-raising nature of its serpentine bends and the glorious views it offers of the Obcina Range. Over the other side of the pass is the pretty little village of **Vatra Moldoviței**, from where a road forks off to the right to reach the last of the great monasteries, **Moldovița Monastery** ㉓ (Mănăstirea Moldovița; open 7am– 6pm; admission charge). A fortified church in splendid grounds, whose exterior walls, like those at Humor, depict the 626 siege of

Map on page 286

Constantinople, Moldoviţa was founded in 1532, and the frescoes were painted shortly afterwards, making them among the oldest in Bukovina *(see page 315)*.

Vatra Dornei

From Vatra Moldoviţei another mountain pass, the Paşcanu, leads over the Obcina Feredeului Mountains to **Câmpulung Moldovenesc**. From here there are two routes to Vatra Dornei: the main road takes a circular path around the Rarău Mountains; the second, a minor and much potholed road often impassable in winter, winds its way south through the mountains, passing the Pietrele Doamnei (the Lady's Rocks), a spectacular cave, en route. The **Rartu Mountains** are fine hiking territory, and a number of walks start in Câmpulung Moldovenesc. The best is a full-day hike taking in the Giumalău peak (1,856 metres/6,090 ft), and from there down to Vatra Dornei.

Vatra Dornei ㉔ has long been known for its mineral water, sought after as long ago as Roman times and today one of the most popular in the country, sold nationwide under the brand name *Dorna*. Visitors to the spa town can taste the waters for free, as there are several drinking fountains. It was the Habsburgs who first developed the spa, during the period in the late 18th and 19th centuries when Bukovina was viewed by the Viennese bourgeoisie as being excitingly exotic.

It has since developed into a well known ski resort, and although the town itself sits at a modest altitude of 800 metres (2,625 ft), it is sufficiently far north that snow cover is almost guaranteed from early December to late April. There are two (rather slow) chairlifts and two drag lifts, and although there are only four ski runs all are long, up to 4 km (2½ miles). The chairlifts also run in summer for walkers and hikers. So remote is the resort that queues are never a problem, even at weekends.

West of Vatra Dornei the Tihuţa Pass (1,200 metres/3,936 ft) marks the boundary of Bukovina with Transylvania. Just over the pass is the village and ski resort of **Piatra Fântânele**, where Jonathan Harker came face to face with Count Dracula in the Bram Stoker novel *Dracula (see page 245).* ❏

Carved gate detail at a homestay in the Moldoviţa Valley. Homestays are becoming increasingly popular in Romania; the agro-tourism agency Antrec has details; see www.antrec.ro

---

RESTAURANTS

Suceava

Cetate
B-dul. 1 Decembrie 1918 2
Tel: 0230-513395, 0744 779757
Two km outside town on the way to the Fortress, this beautifully located restaurant serves a decent range of Romanian and international cuisine, and has a very good wine list. €€

Office's Club
Str. Corneliu Coposu
Tel: 0230-209279
Forgive them the grammar mistake, for the food here is terrific. It is classic Romanian cuisine given a very contemporary twist, both in terms of taste and in presentation. There is a popular nightclub and cocktail bar on the same premises. €€€€

Taco Loco
Str. Stefan cel Mare
Tel: 0230-220032
Good Tex Mex, with great burritos, *quesadillas*, tacos, and chilli con carne all bringing in a local and foreign crowd bored with Romanian food. It is open in the mornings too (from 8am) for croissants, coffee and Mexican-style eggs (fried, with peppers). €€€

Vatra Dornei

Les Amis
Str. Luceafarului 19
Tel: 0230-375280
In the centre of the resort, this small café, restaurant and terrace is a great place to eat or just relax with a coffee. The name may be French but the food is mainly Romanian, but fine. Cheap for the location. €€€

Maestro
Str. Republicii
Tel: 0230-375288
At the head of Strada Republicii this terrace café in front of the Maestro hotel is a great venue – and open year round, as long as the weather is good. €€

Valea Dornelor
Str. Mihai Eminescu 28
Tel: 0230-371134
On the first floor of a once gorgeous building this is a restaurant serving standard international cuisine by day, and a rather tacky disco by night. For snacks, the patisserie downstairs serves take away pizza, *plăcinte* (pies) and sandwiches. €€

● ● ● ● ● ● ● ● ● ● ● ● ● ● ●

Prices per person for a 3-course meal with wine: € under 30 lei, €€ 30–45 lei, €€€ 45–60 lei, €€€€ over 60 lei.

THE PAINTED MONASTERIES

In the lush countryside of far northeastern Romania, the medieval painted monasteries of Bukovina are the country's richest cultural legacy

In all there are 15 monasteries in Bukovina, but when referring to the painted monasteries of legend people usually infer the big five: Voroneţ, Humor, Moldoviţa, Suceviţa and Putna. As a group they have been on UNESCO's World Heritage List since 1993, and to many visitors, as well as locals, they represent the very best that Romania has to offer. They are remote, and a car is the only practical way to see them all, but the effort needed to make it up here is rewarded when confronted by these coruscating wonders.

The earlier monasteries were built and painted at a time when Moldavia had only recently shaken off the shackles of Slavic – be it Kyivan or Polish – domination, and its new found independence, achieved under the still-revered Stephen the Great (Ştefan cel Mare), was under constant threat from Ottoman expansion. A key figure in the remarkable flowering of fresco art on the monastery walls was Stephen's illegitimate son, Petru Rareş (c.1486–1546): at the time, the liturgy inside the churches was carried out in Slavonic, and the Moldavian peasants who formed the basis of the principality's army were unable to understand it. Illiterate, they could not read the bible either. From this situation came the idea, encouraged by Petru Rareş, of painting the *outside* walls of the monasteries, to inspire the peasants and soldiers. Some of the scenes showing christians defeating their foes are historically inaccurate.

The survival of the paintings provides the Bukovina with an anchor in the past – important for a region that has changed hands so many times as to render many of its cultural references obfuscated and blurred. The monasteries however are unmistakably Orthodox, and Romanian. With an importance and meaning that is both religious and secular, they are a source of pride for the entire country.

ABOVE: with its fortress-like walls complete with turrets, Suceviţa Monastery commands respect long before its magnificent frescoes have even come into view. Dating from 1582, it is the largest of the monasteries.

LEFT: Suceviţa Monastery is surrounded by formidable fortifications; the best way to appreciate their grandeur is to approach them from the hills – the hike over from Putna takes around 5 hours.

RIGHT: this fresco detail – part of *Jesse's Tree*, a large and colourful holy genealogy – is found on the main church at Voroneţ, generally considered have the finest art of all the Bukovina monasteries.

ABOVE: the exterior frescoes of the monasteries are mostly in excellent condition, and the protection of UNESCO patronage should ensure that further damage and deterioration is limited. Though there are a few restrictions on viewing distances, visitors can still get incredibly close to the paintings.

PILGRIMAGES

Given that the layer of paint applied to any of Bukovina's monasteries never exceeded one quarter of a centimetre, it is unsurprising that locals believe the continued, often pristine condition of the exterior frescoes to be little short of a miracle. This fact has contributed to the monasteries' enduring popularity.

Since Romanians began to once again embrace religion after the collapse of communism in 1989, pilgrimages to the country's religious sites have become an important part of the Orthodox ritual. While all of the country's great churches attract pilgrims, the monasteries of Bukovina are the most popular destination, and receive tens of thousands of pilgrims throughout the year, mostly in groups and always accompanied by the groups's home priest. Pilgrimage in Romania is a collective way of reconnecting with God, requiring the services of a priest; it is not the solo endeavour it can often be in western Europe. Also, it does not have to be an act of sacrifice: many pilgrims arrive in air-conditioned tour buses. Indeed. Orthodox teachings state that pilgrimage should in fact be a period of calm and rest.

Pilgrimages to the monasteries take place throughout the year, but the busiest time is in the run-up to Easter, and in the days preceding the feast day (2 July) of Stephen the Great (Ştefan cel Mare), ruler of Moldavia for almost 50 years in the 1400s and under whose patronage the first churches in the principality were raised. Buried at Putna Monastery on the northern monastery loop, his remains attract tens of thousands of pilgrims each year.

Other popular pilgrimage days include 6 January (St John the Baptist), 15 August (Mary, Mother of God), and Christmas Day (Crăciun).

RIGHT: an Orthodox priest at Voroneţ Monastery. All of the painted monasteries are remain fully functioning religious centres.

BELOW: painted in 1530, the exterior frescoes at Humor have faded more than at the other monasteries, but the depictions of the 626 and 1453 sieges of Constantinople remain vivid.

ABOVE: inside the Church of the Anunciation at Moldoviţa Monastery. Carved in wood and given golden trim, the iconostasis is pious and imperial, but was carefully designed not to outdo the power of the church's exterior. Moldoviţa is almost as solidly fortified as Suceviţa, but some 50 years older, and has some of the best frescoes of all the monasteries. It also has a beautiful setting at the foot of the Obcin Mountains.

MARAMUREȘ

A land of pride and heartbreak, hidden valleys and centuries-old rural ways of life, Maramureș is a fiercely independent land where tradition serves as the basis for renewal

Timișoara · Brașov · Bucharest

Modern Maramureș – if that is not an oxymoron – generally refers to the counties of Satu Mare and Maramureș (Máramaros) in the far north of Romania. Historically it also included what is today the Zakarpattia Oblast of southwestern Ukraine, and was traditionally delineated to the south by the Someș River, and to the north and west by the upper Tisza. Within Romania, Maramureș stretches from the Hungarian border in the west across to the Prislop Pass in the east, where in 1717 the Habsburgs defeated the Tatars in one of the last great battles of the age.

Yet geography does not define Maramureș. That is a role reserved for people (the Moroșenii) and tradition, and for the tall, steep belfries of the wooden churches that dot the landscape, often referred to as a land that time forgot. There are planes and trains from the rest of the country – and abroad – to Satu Mare and Baia Mare, but once in this part of Romania public transport is hopeless, so a car is crucial if you wish to explore the mountains and valleys, forests and villages of this remote area.

Satu Mare

Split by the Someș River, **Satu Mare** ❶ (Szatmár; pop. 115,000; www.satu-mare.ro) has been unfairly dubbed by some the ugliest town in Romania. While such accusations are harsh – and do not reflect the eclectic nature of the town, nor its troubled and eventful his-

tory – it must be admitted that Satu Mare is by no means typical of the rest of Maramureș. It remains a pleasure to visit, however, and for anyone willing to scratch below its surface, the wealth of sights and some splendid architecture will make a day or two here well spent.

While local scholars would have you believe that the Geto-Dacians lived in the area both before and after the Roman occupation of Dacia, history does not acknowledge the existence of Satu Mare until the publication of the

Map on pages 318-9

LEFT: the Wooden Church on the Hill at Ieud is the oldest in the region.
BELOW: Maramureș is famous for its traditional folk costumes.

Ornately carved gateways are a feature of Maramureș.

Gesta Hungarorum, a kind of Magyar Domesday Book, written by the scribe usually known as Anonymous P around 1200. P writes of a great fortress of Zotmar, which formed part of the kingdom of Ménmarót, a pre-Magyar ruler of the Someș basin who was defeated by Árpád – the first king of Hungary – in 907. Romanians insist that Ménmarót was of Dacian descent, although it is far more likely that he was of Bulgar extraction; he may even have been a renegade Magyar tribal leader. Either way, he is never mentioned in history again, and his kingdom was effortlessly absorbed into Hungary.

In subsequent centuries the Zotmar fortress became a key bulwark in this dangerous corner of Europe, and was reinforced and extended many times. In the mid-16th century a moat was built around it. Besieged but never taken by the Ottomans, it was then destroyed by the Habsburgs following the departure of the Turks, who did not want it to become a focus of dissent. Not a single rock remains, and the site of the fortress, on Strada Eminescu, is today occupied by a 20th-century Catholic church.

Traditionally a Hungarian town (in 1910, 95 percent of the population claimed Magyar descent), social engineering and forced migration during the communist years have brought the Romanian share of the town's present population (around 110,000) to just over half. Hungarians are now in the minority, and the Jews, once the second-largest population group in the city, have all but disappeared. Most were deported and killed in the final throes of the Holocaust.

The sights

It is a heart of stone that does not melt at the sight of the **Hotel Dacia** (Piaţa Libertăţii 8; www.hoteldacia.ro), Satu Mare's crowning landmark, on the northern side of the central square, Piaţa Libertăţii. Built in 1902 on the site of the town's former city hall and magistrates' court, it is a Secessionist masterpiece whose facade is a riot of colour and squiggles, towers and motifs. Although now merely a three-star hotel *(see page 351)*, which cries out for an extensive renovation, the faded interiors hint at former glory, not

least the divine Corinthian columns of the foyer and the split-level ballroom-cum-restaurant. The Filarmonica Dinu Lipatti occupies a gorgeous auditorium in the hotel's east wing.

Satu Mare's **Roman Catholic Cathedral** (Catedrala Romano-Catolică din Satu Mare; Piaţa Libertăţii 24) is on the east side of the square. It is a fine example of neo-Baroque architecture, begun in 1786 but not completed until 1838 when the interior decoration (much of it in Carrara marble by Tomán Felix) was completed. The main painting above the altar depicts the Ascension, and was painted by Pesky Gabor.

The town's **Museum of Art** (Muzeul de Arta; Piaţa Libertăţii 21; open Tues–Sun 10am–6pm; admission charge) is opposite, a delightful orange neo-Gothic building constructed in the second half of the 19th century. The exhibitions inside feature a number of contemporary and 20th-century Romanian artists, including local painters Aurel Popp and Paul Erdos.

Behind the museum is the **synagogue** (Sinagoga; Str. Decebal 6; open Tues–Thur 8am–6pm, Fri 8am–noon),

Traffic police seem to be in every village. They may pull you over and fine you an excessive amount if you exceed the speed limit – the problem being that the limit isn't always clear. Generally it's 50 kmh (31 mph) in towns, 70 kmh (44 mph) along semi built-up stretches and 100 kmh (62 mph) on the open road.

built in Moorish style at the beginning of the 20th century, and still serving what remains of the much-depleted Jewish community. Most services are now held in the smaller prayer hall next door. Both buildings are immaculately preserved, a legacy of the personal interest in their survival taken by Joel Teitelbaum, a high-profile local rabbi who emigrated to the US after World War II.

South of the synagogue is the modern centre of Satu Mare – based on Piaţa 25 Octombrie – the part of town that gives the rest a bad name. Built at considerable cost during the 1980s – many old houses and churches were demolished for the purpose – the highlight is the abominable skyscraper that still houses the town's administrative headquarters.

North of Piaţa Libertăţii, past the Hotel Dacia along a leafy open passage, is the **Firewatch Tower** (Turnul Pompierilor) built in 1904 and fully restored in 2005. It stands 45 metres (150 ft) high and has a viewing deck that affords great views over the old part of the town. Unfortunately, it is currently open on one day of the year only – Firemen's Day (Ziua Pompierilor), 13 September. A few metres further on, the passage opens out into Piaţa Păcii, in which the striking **Chain Church** (Biserica Reformata cu Lanţuri; Piaţa Păcii 6; open daily 9am–7pm) catches the eye. Built over nine years from 1793–1802, it gets its name from the pillars that surround it, joined together by wrought-iron chains. It is a single-spire neo-Baroque church with a fine Galli organ from 1814, and houses the oldest bell in the town, cast in 1633. The Hungarian writer Ferenc Kölcsey (1790–1838) briefly preached here, and the school next door carries his name. He is also honoured with a statue in the centre of the square.

Given the come-lately nature of Satu Mare's Romanian population, it is no surprise that the town's Orthodox churches are situated away from the city centre. The largest is the **Church of the**

Maramureş

```
0          20 km
0          20 miles
```

UKRAINE

Farcău
▲1956

Munţii Maramureşului

Poienile de Sub Munte

cova

Viseu de Jos

Viseu de Sus ⑫

Mocăniţa de pe Valea Vaser

Moisei

Borşa

Parcul Naţional Munţii Rodnei

stea Sus

Săcel ⑬

Parcul Naţional Munţii Rodnei

Statiunea Borşa

Prislop
1416 ⑭

Pietrosul 2302

Romuli

Munţii Rodnei

Rotunda
1271

Parcul Naţional Munţii Rodnei

Valea Vinului

Telciu

Şanţ

buc

Parva

Rodna

Ilva Mare

17C

17D

Sângeorz-Băi

Bistriţa-Năsăud

Rebrişoara

Someşul Mare

Tihuţa
1200

Piatra Fântânele

Headscarves are part of the traditional costume for women, and are much in evidence at various ceremonies and festivals.

Cheese seller at Strâmtura village in the Iza Valley. As in much of rural Romania, a large proportion of what people eat is locally produced.

BELOW: the Measurement of the Milk Festival is one of several springtime rituals in the hills.

Archangels Gabriel and Michael (Biserica Sf. Arhangheli Mihail şi Gavril; Str. 1 Decembrie 4). Built from 1932–7 in neo-Brâncovenesque style, it houses a superb collection of icons and other religious art from the Satu Mare diocese. Close by, the contemporaneous neo-Byzantine **Mother of God Cathedral** (Catedrala Ortodoxă Adormirea Maicii Domnului; B-dul. Vasile Lucaciu) sits rather brutally in the middle of a small public square.

The Oaş Land

From Satu Mare to the Ukrainian border, a sparsely populated depression known as the **Oaş Land** (Ţara Oaşului) extends over 600 sq. km (230 sq. miles), before giving way abruptly to the Oaş Mountains. Local people believe that the name Oaş is derived from *Awas*, the name by which this territory was first referred to (in 1270, when the King of Hungary awarded nobles land in the *Terra Awas*). The great Moldovan chronicler and polyglot Grigore Ureche (c. 1590–1647), who recorded stories and legends from all the Moldovan and neighbouring lands, was the first to record the name Oaş.

The area, which is unfairly associated with bandits and lawlessness, has a rich legacy of culture and handicrafts. Some of the traditions of the local people – many of whom wear traditional dress – are among the strongest in Romania. There are some regional linguistic peculiarities, especially when it comes to food: potatoes (*cartofi* in the rest of the country) are *piciouci*, and that Romanian staple *mămăligă* is known in these parts as *tocană*.

The largest village in the Oaş Land is **Negreşti-Oaş ❷**, 46 km (30 miles) northeast of Satu Mare. It is preceded by the tiny village of **Vama** (whose name, simply meaning customs point, gives an idea of this region's borderland credentials), famous throughout Romania for its brightly coloured household pottery. Today, alas, there is just one potter left in the village (in 1950 there were 22), officially employed by the open-air Oaş Land Museum in Negreşti-Oaş, where his wares are on sale.

For a potted history of the region and its people, the **Oaş Land Museum** (Muzeul Ţării Oaşului, Sat Negreşti-Oaş; open Tues–Sun 10am–5pm; admission charge) is the best place to come. Spread over half a hectare (1½ acres) in the centre of the village, it was set up in 1966 and features a 17th-century wooden church brought here from Lechinţa, and houses dating back to the 17th century brought from Moişeni, Negreşti and Gherţa Mică. The village is also home to a monumental Orthodox church, the recently completed **Church of the Birth of the Holy Mother of God** (Biserica Orto-doxa Naşterea Maicii Domnului). On 8 September (St Mary's Day in the Orthodox calendar) the village comes out en masse to take part in an enormous festival of traditional dancing, music, singing and feasting.

Luna Şes, 8 km (5 miles) south of Vama, is the starting point for hikes up to the summit of Pietroasa (1,201 metres/3,940 ft) and Muntele Mic (1,013 metres/3,322 ft) – both routes take about three hours. From the top you can gaze north into Ukraine, as well as south to the taller buildings of Baia Mare. Two rather old ski lifts operate on the mountain in winter. Further south is the aptly named **Băile Puturoasa** (quite literally, Smelly Baths), where the stinking sulphurous waters are claimed to be a cure for almost everything. North of Negreşti-Oaş there are more thermal baths, and a fine 17th-century monastery, at the village of **Bixad**. The monastery's stone church dates from 1771, although it was heavily restored in the 1970s.

Baia Mare: the big mine

Capital of Maramureş country, **Baia Mare ❸** (Nagybánya; the Big Mine) (pop. 138,000; www.baiamare.ro) was first mentioned, under the grand name of Rivulus Dominarum, by Charles Robert of Anjou in 1329. Less than a century later, gold was being mined here, and the name Baia (mine) was first used. In 1446 the mines were among the booty given by the Hungarian king to János Hunyadi, father of Mátyás Corvinus, for services to the Hungarian crown. It continued to flourish on the back of the gold, and

TIP

It is possible to enter Ukraine by road from Maramureş and Bukovina, as well as by rail (although the latter is time-consuming as the track gauge differs between the two countries). As of 2005, EU citizens no longer require a visa.

BELOW LEFT: view of Borşa. **BELOW:** folk costume at a herdsman festival in the Oaş Land.

Map on pages 318-9

remained a wealthy town within the Habsburg Empire for much of the 16th, 17th and 18th centuries. In 1889, one of the first Romanian newspapers, *Gutinul* (a weekly literary review), was published here.

The modern town, however, is an ugly place, much of it resembling a vast 1980s study in concrete, but there is much to see, including some fine museums. It is also the best gateway to the eastern Maramureș, and its stock of hotels is the best in the area.

Around Piața Libertății

What's left of old Baia Mare is centered on Piața Libertății, an eclectic and appealing mix of multicoloured houses, mostly dating from the 17th century, spoilt only by the fact that much of the square is used as a car park. It is dominated by **St Stephen Tower** (Turnul Ștefan; Str. Turnului), but note that the Stephen in question is the great Hungarian king Stephen (István), not the Moldavian Ștefan cel Mare. Just over 40 metres (130 ft) high, it was raised in the 15th century by János Hunyadi, and was originally the bell tower of a

large church, destroyed in the 16th century. Today the site of the church is occupied by the Baroque **Church of the Holy Trinity** (Biserica Sfânta Treime), built in 1707 and featuring fine exterior sculpture and well-preserved interior frescoes.

Hunyadi's former house, at Piața Libertății 8, is the largest in the square. It was built in 1446, shortly before Hunyadi became the Governor Royal of Hungary, and was originally part of a much larger building constructed for Hunyadi's scheming wife, Erszebet. Part of the Maramureș History Museum *(see below)*, it occasionally houses temporary art exhibitions.

Far more interesting to art lovers, however, will be the town's **Museum of Art** (Muzeul de Artă; Str. 1 Mai 8; open Tues–Sun 10am–5pm; admission charge), which is home to a fine body of work produced by the Baia Mare Art Colony, founded in 1896 by painter Simion Hollosy (1856–1918).

Hunyadi, also known by his Romanianised name Iancu de Hunedoara, is well represented at Baia Mare's splendid **Maramureș History Museum**

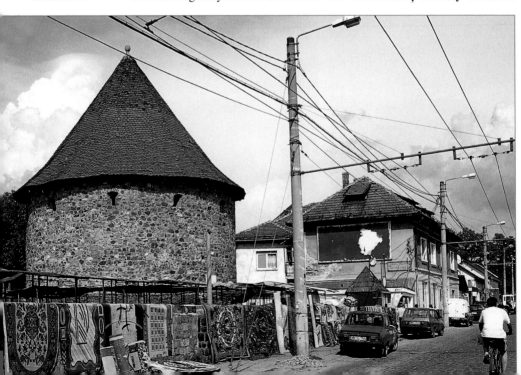

(Secția Istorie a Muzeului Judetean Maramureș; Str. Monetariei 1–3; open Tues–Sun 9am–5pm; admission charge; www.maramuresmuzeu.ro), a short walk north. The museum is housed in an 18th-century mint *(monetariei)*, which used the gold from the city's mines. There are hundreds of coins on display in a collection that dates back to the 14th century, featuring the heads of every ruler of these lands right up to the present day. There is also an outstanding exhibition of antique clocks, and a room dedicated to what passed as technology in the mining industry in centuries past.

Baia Mare's **village museum** (Muzeul de Etnografie și Artă Populară Baia Mare; Str. Deaulul Florilor 1; open Tues–Sun 9am–5pm; admission charge) lies on the other side of the river, behind the stadium. There are two sections to the museum: one is a conventional pavilion hosting arts and crafts from the region, including ceramics from Vama and the Iza Valley, religious art and a room chock full of traditional costumes; the other section comprises houses and other buildings brought here from the surrounding area.

The church is particularly worthy of note: wooden, and sporting the characteristic Maramureș belfry, it dates from 1566, and was originally located in the village of Chechiș, 14 km (8 miles) away. It was brought here in 1984.

Along Strada Lucaciu to the east of Piața Libertății, the 14th-century **Butchers' Bastion** (Bastionul Măacelarilor) is one of the few structures remaining from the original fortress.

The Gutâi Pass and the Mara Valley

Barely 10 km (6 miles) east of Baia Mare is the mining town of **Baia Sprie** ❹, the site of copper and lead mines since the 13th century. Passing through in 1540, the German traveller Joerg Vagner wrote that the miners in Baia Sprie were "the most skilled I have ever seen." Less manually skilled were the thousands of intellectuals sent here – usually without trial – to perform hard labour at the beginning of the 1950s. Most died of starvation and overwork. The moving – albeit fictional – story of one such survivor (unable to find work after being freed

Map on pages 318-9

Baia Mare's Maramureș History Museum.

BELOW: cycling is a great way to see the rural backwaters.

At festivals and fairs, seemingly every Moroşenii (person from Maramures) appears in their colourful embroidered costumes.

BELOW: Maramures shepherd. **BELOW RIGHT:** a primitive trumpet.

from captivity) forms the basis of Romania's greatest post-war novel, Marin Preda's *Cel Mai Iubit Dintre Pământeni (Most Beloved of the Earth Dwellers; see margin, page 322)*. Close to the entrance of the mine is a small memorial to those who died here. The town also has a superb Baroque town hall from 1739, and an Eastern-style Orthodox church, complete with onion domes, built in 1793. There is a good little ski resort close by, at Mogoşa, whose one hotel is perfectly located on the edge of a small lake.

At **Surdeşti** and **Plopiş**, twin villages 6 km (4 miles) south of Baia Sprie, two enormous UNESCO-protected wooden churches make a short detour worthwhile. The church at Surdeşti has a 72-metre (235-ft) spire, reputed to be the tallest in the country. It dates from the early 18th century.

The **Gutâi Pass** ❺ (987 metres/3,240 ft) between Baia Mare and Sighetu Marmaţiei, is sensational, a roller coaster of hairpin bends and fine views. About 2 km (1¼ miles) over the top – where there is a good café – a minor road leads to the mountain

retreat at **Izvoare**, which offers some tame skiing in winter, a decent spa, and good walks in the surrounding forests.

Beyond the pass is truly the land that time forgot. Every village has charm and something to admire. Wooden houses, some with intricately carved doors, are a feature in **Mara**, the first village at the foot of the mountain. Another superb, UNESCO-protected wooden church dominates the next village, **Deseşti**. Its roof is covered in fading frescoes, many dating from the 17th century, when the church was built. It was heavily reconstructed and renovated in the late 1990s, and now forms part of a small village museum.

At **Ocna Şugatag** ❻, just east of the main road, there are two more impressive wooden churches, while the villages east of here: **Breb**, **Budeşti**, **Sârbi** and **Călineşti**, are among the most remote and untouched in all Romania. All have classic Maramureş churches, and all have been restored over the past decade. At Sârbi there is an old wooden (and working) water mill, where women still use the mill's overflow to wash their laundry, as they have for centuries.

From Călineşti it's a short drive to **Vadu Izei ❼**, where the Iza and Mara rivers merge. The village is a living museum renowned for the number and intricacy of its wooden doors. It plays host to a number of festivals throughout the year, including the Maramuzical, a week-long extravaganza of traditional Maramureş music and dancing held every July since 1997. Held at the same time as the festival is the Târg (market), which showcases the many handicrafts made by local artisans. At the **Maramureă Information Centre** (Fundatia OVR Agro-Tur; Vadu Izei 161 – there are no street names in rural Maramureş) you can arrange tours of the region (in a variety of languages), as well as car hire and accommodation in private homes. As the information centre is someone's house, there is usually somebody in, night or day.

Sighetu Marmaţiei

Sighetu Marmaţiei ❽ (pop. 37,000; www.sighetumarmatiei.alphanet.ro) is one of the oldest towns in Maramures, founded in the 12th century. The name derives from the Hungarian *Máramarossziget*, meaning Maramureş Island. Known simply as Sighet to most Romanians, as Sihot to the Ukrainians on the other side of the border, and as hell to those imprisoned here in the 1950s, the town is infamous as the site of Romania's most secure and dreaded communist-era prison, where almost every leading member of the interwar aristocracy and political élite was held and, in many cases, executed by the regime.

If you visit one museum in Romania, it should be this one. Standing in the centre of the city, occupying the former prison buildings, it is today officially known as the **Museum of Arrested Thought and Memorial to the Victims of Communism and to the Resistance** (Muzeul al Gândirii Arestate şi Memorialul Victimelor Comunismului şi al Rezistenţei; Str. Corneliu Coposu 4; open summer Tues–Sun 9.30am–6.30pm, winter 10am–4pm; admission charge; www.memorialsighet.ro). It represents Romania's best attempt to get to grips with its communist past.

That the museum exists at all is only because of the tireless efforts of poet

Map on pages 318-9

Romania's fairly extensive rail network offers access to various points across Maramureş. Services on the minor lines tend to be outstandingly slow, however.

BELOW: Sighet's Museum of Arrested Thought.

Remembering the victims of political oppression at the Sighet Museum of Arrested Thought.

BELOW: the Merry Cemetery at Săpânța.

Ana Blandiana and her Foundation for a Civil Society, formed in 1993 by intellectuals and historians committed to telling the true story of the country's past, however damaging that may be to some who still have a hold on power. Besides the museum, the foundation also operates the Bucharest-based International Centre for the Study of Communism.

The prison building at Sighet was constructed in 1896 as a common jail, with the first political prisoners – a group of anti-Soviet students – being brought here in April 1948. The location was considered by the communist regime to be perfect: the most isolated part of Romania, almost within touching distance of what was then the Soviet Union. The sense of hopelessness felt by the inmates on arrival must have been acute.

The men brought here were the cream of Romanian intellectual and political society, including former ministers Iuliu Maniu, Gheorghe Bratianu, Constantin Bratianu and Contantin Tataranu. Many died of starvation, while others went insane in the tiny cells, where absolute silence was enforced 24 hours a day. The inmates (almost all of whom were well into their sixties) were forbidden to lie on their beds during the day, and those unable to stand upright for so long were punished by being placed in even smaller, pitch-black cells.

The museum opened first as a simple place of remembrance in 1997, but subsequent donations by generous individuals and the European Council (which lists Sighet as one of Europe's most important memorials, alongside Auschwitz) has allowed the quality and quantity of exhibitions to grow, and the prison building to be fully restored. Most recently the Cimitirul Saracilor (Paupers' Cemetery), 2 km (1¼ miles) west of the town, where the 52 inmates who died were, allegedly, buried in secret, has been converted into a permanent memorial. Each summer the Foundation for a Civil Society organises summer schools and academic conferences at the museum, bringing together students from all over the former communist world. The biggest shame is that the museum is so far

The Merry Cemetery

Those interested in the unusual will enjoy the village of Săpânța, to the west of Sighet, famous for its so-called Merry Cemetery (Cimitir Vesel). All the crosses and headstones here are brightly painted with happy scenes from the dead person's life, complete with jolly epitaphs. The predominant colour is blue, which traditionally represents freedom and hope. Despite the pleas of many visitors to be buried here, the cemetery is currently taking only the deceased of the village.

The original creator of this unusual line in woodcarving, Stan Ion Patraș, has passed away, but his old house is now a museum – it is behind the cemetery, signposted, and worth seeking out for the carved portraits of the Ceaușescus (amongst others).

from Bucharest, which means it receives only a fraction of the visitor numbers it deserves.

Elsewhere in Sighet

In the Middle Ages, Sighet grew wealthy as a trading post for the metals extracted nearby, but as it was not itself a mining town, Jews were allowed to settle here *(see margin)*, and did so in great numbers: for centuries almost half the town's population was Jewish. Most were deported in 1944, and almost all died at Auschwitz. Writer Elie Wiesel, who is said to have first coined the term Holocaust, was a survivor of this late deportation. Just one of eight synagogues in Sighet remains, on Strada Bessarabia, and it has recently been renovated.

Wiesel's house is on the corner of Dragos Voda and Tudor Vladimirescu, just north of the town's pleasant central square, **Piaţa Libertăţii**, surrounded on all sides by Baroque town houses. The oldest building is the Hungarian Reformed Church on the northern side, built in the 15th century.

At No. 15, in a superb Baroque mansion built in 1730, the **Maramures Ethnographic Museum** (Muzeul Etnografic al Maramuresului; open Tues– Sun 9am–5.30pm; admission charge) is home to a wide variety of exhibits, which, aside from costumes and handicrafts, also includes carved doors, window frames, painted glass icons and stuffed animals.

Part of the same museum, and accessible on the same ticket, is the complex of 30 houses – some from the 14th century – set around a 17th-century church a short drive south of town, about 300 metres/yds off the main road to Baia Mare. This is the **Village Museum** (Muzeul Satului; Str. Dobăieş 40; open Tues–Sun 9.30am– 5.30pm; admission charge).

To the west of Sighet, a road follows the Tisza River, the border with Ukraine. Fifteen km (9 miles) along the road is the village of **Săpânţa ❾** with its famous cemetery *(see panel, page 326).*

The Iza Valley

From Sighet there are two parallel valleys leading southeast, the Iza and the Vişeu, and the land between them is known as the Maramureş Depression (Depresiunea Maramureşului). The **Iza Valley** is known for its pretty villages with their wooden churches. Even more than elsewhere in Maramureş, this is a place that makes you feel as if you have slipped back in time 100 years or so.

Heading along the Iza from Sighet, one of the first places you'll come to is **Bârsana ❿**, a village dating to 1326, where a monastery (Mănăstirea Bârsana) features two wooden churches. The oldest of the pair was built in 1720, and was restored beam by beam in the 1990s, its interior frescoes given new life. The all-female monastery is a popular place for the Easter pilgrimage, and has a new church, built to rival that at Surdeşti *(see page 324).* At a towering 56 metres (185 ft) in height it dwarfs the original. Its construction respected the tradition of Maramureş church building: no material was used except wood.

Map
on pages
318-9

The 14th-century edict forbidding Jews from mining towns all over the Hungarian and Hapsburg Empires remained more or less in place until 1783. Anti-Semitic prejudice made people consider Jews capable of sabotage, and with mining so important to the economy of the Empire successive rulers kept the ban in place.

BELOW: Maramureş has an ageing population.

Rodna National Park protects an area of pristine montane forest.

BELOW: vast swathes of forest still survive in Romania, but uncontrolled logging presents a growing threat.

Six km (4 miles) past Bârsana, a poor road branches off southwards towards **Glod** (not to be confused with the village that controverisally appears in the film *Borat, see page 79)*, from where there are hiking routes up to the peaks of Semerteş (1,306 metres/4,284 ft) and Secului (1,310 metres/4,397 ft). An equally poor road branches off at **Rozavlea** (whose own wooden church dates from 1720) and leads up to **Poienile Izei**, a fantastic spot high above the valley, and home to yet another UNESCO-listed wooden church. It was built in 1730 and is famous for its frescoes, which depict the devil torturing the sinful in the most graphic and awful detail.

Built in 1364 the **Wooden Church on the Hill** (Biserică de Lemn din Deal) at **Ieud** ⓫ (take a right turn 4 km/2½ miles past Rozavlea) is the oldest in Maramureş. Its interior frescoes were fully restored in 1999. More spectacular still is the newer of the village's churches, the **Uniate Church**, built in 1707 and decorated with a rich number of naïve icons painted on glass. Note the (mainly empty) urban blocks in the centre of the village: under

Ceauşescu's notorious Systemisation programme, Ieud had been designated as an agro-industrial centre, and many of the residents of the Iza Valley whose own homes were due for demolition were to be shipped here to live in the blocks. The revolution saved their homes.

The Vişeu Valley

The 16-km (10-mile) stretch of the Sighetu Marmaţiei–Vişeu de Sus road between Rona de Jos and Petrova, where the **Vişeu Valley** begins, is one of the most scenic routes in Romania. Hugging the hill side, it climbs gently up to 665 metres (2,185 ft) just before Petrova, before plunging down into the valley. However, the villages of the Vişeu lack the charm and the wooden churches of the Iza, and the main interest for visitors will be the **hiking routes** into the mountains.

There are starting points for hikes at Ruscova, Vişeu de Sus and, at the end of a minor road from Ruscova, Poienile de Sub Munte. There are routes from the latter over to Borşa, but note that, unlike in other mountain ranges

in Romania, in these parts cabins are few and far between, and careful planning is needed before setting out.

A narrow-gauge steam train – the tracks are just 760 mm wide – runs the length of the Vaser Valley from **Viseu de Sus** ⑫, 60 km (38 miles) up to the logging town of Comanu (*see margin*).

Between Vişeu de Sus and Borşa, **Moisei** ⑬ was the scene of a massacre in 1944, when the retreating Hungarian Army (which had occupied Maramureş since 1940) killed 29 villagers for no particular reason, before setting the rest of the village ablaze. A memorial to those killed stands in front of the only house that survived the fire, today a small museum displaying photos of those who died.

Borşa is a dull former mining town, famous for its mineral water (sold under the *Borsec* label) and is often confused with **Borşa Resort** (Staţiunea Borşa) further east near the head of the valley. The resort sits at an altitude of 850 metres (2,790 ft), and snow is all but guaranteed up here from December to April. The skiing on the **Rodna Massif**, looming large to the south, is challeng-

ing, and although the slopes are serviced by just two old and very slow chairlifts, the lack of queues and the middle-of-nowhere feel of the place can make it a great place to ski. In summer there are dozens of hiking routes from the resort up into the Rodna, a couple passing through the **Rodna National Park** (Parcul Naţional Munţii Rodnei), a sanctuary for lynx, brown bears and wolves as well as a number of large birds including capercaillies and various eagles.

Further east, a 14-km (8-mile) road of the most vicious twists and hairpin bends imaginable leads up, mainly through woods, to the **Prislop Pass** ⑭ at 1,416 metres (4,645 ft), the historic border between Maramureş and Bukovina. At the top, the Hora de la Prislop (Prislop Circle Dance), a day of singing, dancing and mainly drunken revelry, takes place on the second Sunday of August. A small monument at the roadside marks the spot where the Tatars were defeated in 1717. Hikers can follow a longer route over the pass, taking in Lake Bila-Mare, at 2,279 metres (7,397ft) one of the highest in Romania. ❏

Map on pages 318-9

Vişeu de Sus steam railway is one of the most isolated lines in Europe. It was built from 1930-3 to serve the forestry industry.

RESTAURANTS

Satu Mare

Crama Periniţa
Str. 1 Decembrie 11
Tel: 0788-328200
Traditional Romanian food served in a pleasant environment. They often have locally made goat's cheese, which covered in salt makes the perfect appetiser. **€€**

Corso
Piaţa Libertatii nr. 6
Tel: 0261-714726
Ordinary Romanian and international food at over-the-odds prices, but for location this is as good as it gets in Satu

Mare. The terrace is the hotspot in town and is full to overflowing during the summer. **€€€**

Pub No Pardon
Str. Corvinilor 11
Tel: 0261-768206
You couldn't make a name like that up, but fear not for this is the best place to eat and drink in the city. A great selection of pub food, loads of different beers, booth-like tables and prompt service make it popular year round. What's more, it looks like a real pub. **€€€**

Baia Mare

Oaza Italiana
Str. Culturii 3
Tel: 0262-216302
Not the best Italian food in the world but for a remote regional town it is as good as it gets. There is little more than standard tourist trattoria fare: pasta, pizza and salads, but it is a warm, friendly, and attractive place. **€€€**

Select
Str. Progresului 54
Tel: 0262-222223
The food will not change your life, but given the dearth of places to eat in Baia Mare, it might save it. Good Romanian and international cuisine,

though note that almost every tempting extra placed on your table has to be paid for (bread, butter, etc.) **€€**

Sighetu Marmatiei

Pizzeria Primavera
Str. Traian 9
Tel: 0262-318980
Possibly the only pizzeria in Maramureş which cooks its pizzas on a genuine wood-fired oven. You can expect thin, crispy and delicious pizzas, costing next to nothing. **€€**

● ● ● ● ● ● ● ● ● ● ● ●

Prices per person for a 3-course meal with wine: € under 30 lei; €€ 30–45 lei, €€€ 45–60 lei, €€€€ over 60 lei.

INSIGHT GUIDES

TRAVEL TIPS

ROMANIA

TRAVEL TIPS

TRANSPORT

GETTING THERE AND GETTING AROUND

GETTING TO ROMANIA

By Air

From the UK/Ireland

British Airways (tel: 0870-850 9850; www.ba.com) and the much-improved **Tarom**, 27 New Cavendish Street, London W1G 9UE (tel: 020-7224 3693; www.tarom.ro) have daily direct flights from Heathrow to Bucharest Otopeni. Return fares start at around £190. No-frills Polish carrier **Wizz Air** (tel: 00 48 22-351 9499; www.wizzair.com) offers Luton–Bucharest Băneasa return fares from about £60 (€90). From summer 2007 **Carpatair** (www.carpatair.ro; tel: 020-8602 7077) flies between Stansted and Timişoara. A useful fare comparison website is www.skyscanner.net.

From Ireland, airlines with connections to Romania include **Air France** (tel: 01-814 4060), **Alitalia** (tel: 01-677 5171), **British Airways** (tel: 1800-626747), **LOT** (tel: 1890-200514), **Lufthansa** (tel: 01-844 5544), **Malév** (tel: 01-844 4303) and **Sky Europe** (tel: 00 44 905-722 2747; www.skyeurope.com). Return fares start at about €280.

From the US/Canada

From Jun 2007 Delta and Tarom resume direct flights between New York JFK and Bucharest Otopeni. Fares will start at about US$1090 return. No other airlines fly direct from the USA or Canada to Romania, but there are connections from various cities in North America to Bucharest. Some of the best links are with **Lufthansa** (tel: 1800-645 3880; www.lufthansa-usa.com); **British**

Airways (tel: 1800-247 9297; www.britishairways.us); **Alitalia** (tel: 1800-223 5730; www.alitaliausa.com); and **Austrian** (tel: 1800-843 0002; www.aua.com) from the USA, and **Air France** (tel: 1800-667 2747; www.airfrance.ca); and **Alitalia** (www.alitalia.ca) from Canada.

Return fares from New York to Bucharest start at about US$620 in low season, US$1,070 in high season, and from Montreal C$940 and C$1,720 respectively.

By Rail

Reaching Romania by train is significantly more expensive than flying. However, it offers more adventure for your money, lets you stop off more or less where you want and gives you a chance to absorb the landscape and culture of half of Europe en route. If you get an Inter-rail or one of the many other passes available *(see page 335)* it can even work out to be good value.

From the UK, several routes are possible. All involve at least three changes. Taking the Eurostar to Paris, one option is to change at Munich and then either Vienna or Budapest. Another is to go via Zurich and Budapest. Alternatively, take the Eurostar to Brussels, then change at Cologne, Munich, Vienna and Budapest.

Budapest–Bucharest trains follow different routes, all via Arad. Depending on the train, there are also stops at least daily at Alba Iulia, Braşov, Craiova, Drobeta-Turnu Severin, Ploieşti, Sighişoara, Sinaia, Târgu Jiu and Timişoara, as well as various local trains between the two countries.

The shortest London–Bucharest journey takes about 36 hours.

Second-class fares start at £179 (€267)/£299 (€446) single/return, based on taking the Eurostar to Paris, the overnight express to Vienna (still called the Orient Express, but not the real thing), a day train to Budapest, then an overnight train to Bucharest, with couchettes both nights. More expensive sleeper accommodation is also available, usually via Paris, Munich and Vienna.

An essential companion for anyone planning a European rail trip is the *Thomas Cook International Timetable*. The best online timetable is at www.bahn.de: use local or German spellings for stations. An excellent website for planning a train trip to Romania is www.seat61.com.

The following agencies are experienced at selling tickets to Romania. **Deutsche Bahn UK** 18 Conduit Street, London W1R 9TD (tel: 0870 243 5363; www.deutsche-bahn.co.uk) **European Rail** Tavistock House, North Tavistock Square, London WC1H 3HR (tel: 020-7387 0444; www.europeanrail.com) **Ffestiniog Travel** Harbour Station, Porthmadog, Gwynedd LL49 9NF (tel: 01766-516050; www.festtravel.co.uk) **Transylvania Uncovered** 1 Atkinson Court, Fell Foot, Newby Bridge, Cumbria LA12 8NW (tel: 01539-531258; www.beyondtheforest.com) **Iarnród Éireann (Irish Rail)** 35 Lower Abbey Street, Dublin 1 (tel: 01-703 1885; www.irishrail.ie) **Rail Europe** 44 South Broadway, White Plains, NY 10601 (tel: 1888-382 7245 (1800-361 7245 from Canada); www.raileurope.com)

In Romania, international train tickets and passes are available from **CFR** offices or **Wasteels** (www.wasteels

travel.ro) at Bucharest Gara de Nord (tel: 021-317 0369), Braşov train station (tel: 0268-424313) and Piaţa Libertăţii, 2, Sfântu Gheorghe (tel: 0367-312899).

Passes

Various railway passes are available. Whether it's worth getting one depends on how far – or frenetically – you want to travel within a rigid time slot. Rail passes often aren't the cheapest way of getting around eastern Europe, as point-to-point fares are significantly lower than in western Europe and the passes don't always take account of this fact.

Even with a pass, you'll still need reservations on most trains in Romania and pay extra for couchettes or sleepers and sometimes for Intercity services. Eligibility depends on country of residence. Passes are not available in the country in which the pass was purchased. On all passes, children count as 4- to 11-year-olds (younger children travel free). Youth fares are for 12- to 25-year-olds and seniors are over-60s.

Passes valid for Romania include InterRail, Eurodomino Romania Pass, Balkan Flexipass, Eurail Romania Pass, Eurail Romania-Hungary Pass, Eurail Selectpass, Eurailpass Youth and Eurailpass Youth Flexi.

By Coach

There are few obvious advantages in taking a coach to Romania. From London to Bucharest the journey takes a muscle-stiffening 49 hours via Cologne. Single fares start at £96, return fares at £165 and open returns at £216 (€142, €248 and €322). In the UK tickets are available from **National Express** (tel: 08705-808080; www.nationalexpress.com). In Romania coach tickets to the UK and much of Europe are available from **Touring Europabus Romania**, Str. Buzeşti 44, Bucharest (tel: 0801-000888; www.eurolines.ro); or any international coach station (autogară internaţională).

Possibly of more interest, a Eurolines Pass (www.eurolines.com) offers unlimited coach travel between 40 major cities across Europe (including London, Dublin and Bucharest) for 15 or 30 consecutive days. Fares depend on the starting date. Low season is from 8 Jan–31 Mar and 4 Nov–17 Dec; middle from 1 Apr–22 June and 11 Sept–3 Nov; high from 1–7 Jan, 23 June–10 Sept and 18–31 Dec. For low, middle and high season respectively, fares are £115, £135

and £189 (€172, €202 and €282) for 15 days, and £159, £175 and £249 (€237, €261 and €372) for 30 days. Under-26s receive a 19 percent discount. Passes are invalid for internal travel within any country.

Driving to Romania

Driving may make sense if you are going for a few weeks, as part of a longer trip or if you plan to travel to remote parts of Romania badly served by public transport. Car rental in Romania is fairly expensive (from £30/€50 per day), while hire companies elsewhere often don't allow their vehicles to be driven into Romania.

The most direct route from the UK to Romania crosses France, Belgium, Germany, Austria and Hungary. From Budapest, one route, the E60, goes through Debrecen and the Romanian border post of Borş to Oradea, Cluj, Târgu Mureş, Sighişoara, Braşov, Ploieşti and Bucharest. Another route takes the E75 from Budapest to Szeged, then the E68 via the Romanian border post of Nădlac to Braşov. Other, quieter, crossing points mostly serve local traffic.

Documents & Equipment

EU, US and Canadian driving licences are valid in Romania for up to 30 days, UK licences for 90 days if they are of the EU-type and incorporate a photograph. However, it is advisable to carry an international driving permit as well. The minimum driving age is 18.

At customs, you need to show the vehicle registration papers, proof of insurance and a national driving licence. Although insurance is available at the border, a Green Card is preferable.

A first-aid kit and warning triangle are compulsory, while a fire extinguisher and spare headlamp bulbs are recommended. If bringing a right-hand-drive car, you'll need external rear view mirrors on both sides of the car.

On entry motorists must buy a Rovinietă permitting use of national roads for a fixed period. This must be displayed on the windscreen and can be extended at most petrol stations. Fees are nominal and payable in euros. There is also a toll to cross the Danube between Giurgiu and Ruse.

Sea/River Cruises

The lower Danube is a moderately popular cruise destination. The longest sailing, from Amsterdam to

Olteniţa, lasts up to 26 days and takes in eight countries. Shorter cruises run from Munich to Constanţa and to Bucharest from Vienna, Budapest and Prague. A cruise combining the Danube and Danube Delta starts at Passau and ends at Tulcea (11 days). Different operators have slight variations on the above routes. Some include guided excursions.

Ferries

Hourly car ferries cross the Danube between Calafat (Romania) and Vidin (Bulgaria). Single fares are €3 (plus €17 per car). Frequent car ferries also ply between Giurgiu (Romania) and Ruse (Bulgaria). The twice-weekly Istanbul–Constanţa ferries operated by Med Lines have been suspended indefinitely.

GETTING AROUND

To/From Major Airports

Bucharest

The best way to get to and from Bucharest's international airport, Otopeni Henri Coanda (15 km/9 miles north of town), is by taxi. On exiting arrivals you will be greeted by seemingly friendly taxi drivers offering rides at knock-down prices: ignore them, they are after all of your money. Instead head for the right-hand exit where a fleet of smart Fly Taxis are waiting. A ride to the centre of the city will cost around €25 – not cheap but worth it to avoid hassle.

There is a bus (No. 783) which departs from underneath the arrivals hall, in front of the domestic flights terminal. It runs from 5.30am to 11pm, stopping at Piaţa Victoriei, Piaţa Universitatii and Piaţa Unirii, from where it makes the return journey. Tickets have to be bought before boarding from the silver booth next to the bus stop at the airport. Valid for two trips they cost around €2.

Bucharest's second airport, Baneasa Aurel Valicu, is used mainly by budget airlines, and is closer to the city centre; bus Nos 131 and 301 run between the airport and Piaţa Romana from 4.30am to 11.30pm, the journey taking around 25 minutes. Standard Bucharest transport tickets (approx €0.30) are valid, and can be bought at RAB booths opposite the airport exit. Avoid taking a taxi from Baneasa unless you are sure of its provenance.

Other Cities

Buses run to the city centre from airports at Timișoara (No. 26), Cluj (No. 8) and Bacău (Nos 18 and 22). From Sibiu airport there's a choice: bus No. 11 or trolleybus No. 8. In Cluj, Constanța, Iași, Oradea and Târgu Mureș, **Tarom** runs shuttle buses between its city office and the airport. From other airports a taxi may be required. Estimated taxi fares between the airport and the city centre are: Arad, €2.50; Bacău, €1.50; Cluj, €1.50; Constanța, €9; Iași, €4.50; Oradea, €3; Sibiu, €1.50; Târgu Mureș, €6; Suceava, €5; Timișoara, €6. Avoid accepting a lift from the first driver who approaches you. If in doubt, ask someone to order one by telephone (*Puteți să-mi comandați un taxi*). For a list of recommended taxi companies in Bucharest and other cities see page 338.

Domestic Flights

Tarom flies from Bucharest to Bacău, Baia Mare, Cluj, Iași, Oradea, Satu Mare, Sibiu, Suceava, Târgu Mureș and Timișoara. It has discounted its domestic flights, with single fares to/from all destinations except Timișoara (from 136 RON) and Cluj (from 154 RON) starting at 108 RON, double for return flights.

Carpatair connects Timișoara with Bucharest Otopeni, Constanța, Craiova, Iași and Suceava, and Bucharest Otopeni with Constanța. Tickets are available from travel agencies, in Romania on tel: 08008-300900, in the UK on tel: 0208-602 7077 or by e-mail from the www.carpatair.com website. Fares are similar to Tarom's.

Romanian Railways

Romania has a reasonable railway network. The first railway service on current Romanian territory started in 1854 and during the communist period the railways, already well developed, received more investment than other means of transport.

With a pedigree dating to 1880, the national railway operator, Căile Ferate Române (CFR), runs all passenger services in Romania except forestry lines. Since the 1990s it has invested heavily in new stock, some Romanian, some foreign. Whatever your schedule and budget, it would be a shame not to experience at least one train journey in Romania. While Bucharest is the network hub, some long-distance routes link regional centres, eg Timișoara–Suceava.

On all internal trains, smoking is forbidden in trains and undercover inspectors make sure the rule is enforced. Be aware that platforms are much lower then the train, making alighting difficult for anyone with heavy baggage or a disability. For information about railway tourism see www.turismferoviar.ro/en

Categories

Romanian trains come in a variety of categories, with progressively higher fares payable on the premium services. The difference between best and worst is dramatic, while prices overall are very low by west European standards. It's definitely worth paying extra for a higher category of train if you value your comfort. Except on Intercity services, trains are often under-heated in winter and stifling in summer. It's advisable to bring toilet paper and soap on *accelerat* and *personal* trains.

The pride of CFR, **Intercity** trains (IC on the timetables) usually stop only in major cities and provide an air-conditioned express service on main routes from Bucharest to Sinaia, Predeal, Brașov, Timișoara, Iași and Constanța. Two types of train run on Intercity routes: *Classic* and *Săgeata albastră* (Blue Arrow), the first being faster and more comfortable. All accommodation is in modern, open-plan carriages. Between Bucharest and Iași, the Intercity has only second-class seating and no dining car and is barely faster than the Rapid.

Rapid trains (R) run on modernised stock and serve the busiest routes, stopping in major towns and cities. First-class carriages have six seats per compartment while second-class have eight. First-class carriages are often air-conditioned. Dining cars, couchettes and (on overnight services) sleepers are often available. The latest Siemens RM trains have mother-and-baby areas and four types of recycling bins. What happens to the waste is another matter.

Noticeably slower, less modern, dirtier and less comfortable, **Accelerat** (A) trains stop more often but only at major stations. They have compartments and are often very crowded. Some longer-distance services have couchettes but rarely sleepers.

Finally, **Personal** (P) trains give you the chance to get up close with villagers on a grindingly slow crawl along rural routes via every sleepy halt (*haltă*). Most only have second-class carriages. Some rolling stock dates back to the 1930s. There are no compartments and some trains are double-decker. Linking nearby towns or towns with villages, Personal trains are often the only option for reaching remoter communities.

Sample routes:
Bucharest (Nord and Obor)–Constanța (7 daily; 3 hours 30 minutes–5 hours 20 minutes).
Bucharest (Nord)–Brașov (26 daily; 2 hours 20 minutes–2 hours 50

Rail Fares from Bucharest

Supplements are payable on any train except Personal trains. Rates depend on distance and category. Return tickets carry a 10 percent discount. Under-5s travel free and under-10s pay half. Some one-way fares from Bucharest follow:

	Personal		Accelerat		Rapid		Intercity	
	1st class	2nd class	1st class	2nd class	1st class	2nd class	1st class	2nd class
Arad	€12	€8	€19	€13	€23	€18	€24	€19
Brașov	€5	€3	€9	€6	€10	€7	€10	€7
Cluj	€10	€6	€15	€10	€20	€13	€21	€14
Constanța	€6	€4	€11	€7	€12	€8	€13	€9
Iași	€10	€6	€15	€10	€20	€13	€20	€13
Oradea	€12	€8	€19	€13	€23	€18	–	–
Ploiești	€1.50	€1	€3	€2	€5	€3	€5	€4
Satu Mare	€13	€8	€20	€13	€24	€18	–	–
Timișoara	€11	€7	€17	€11	€21	€15	€22	€16
Tulcea	€7	€5	€12	€8	€17	€11	€17	€11

Choose your Speed

According to CFR, in 2004 trains averaged: Intercity 87 kmh (54 mph), Rapid 85 kmh (53 mph), Accelerat 67 kmh (41 mph) and Personal 35 kmh (21 mph).

minutes)
Bucharest (Nord)–Sibiu (4 daily; 5 hours–5 hours 50 minutes)
Bucharest (Nord)–Timişoara (6 daily; 7 hours 30 minutes–8 hours 20 minutes)
Bucharest (Nord)–Cluj (6 daily; 7 hours 20 minutes–8 hours)
Bucharest (Nord)–Iasi (6 daily; 5 hours 40 minutes–7 hours).
Bucharest (Nord)–Oradea (3 daily; 9 hours 55 minutes–11 hours).
Bucharest (Nord)–Satu Mare (3 daily; 11 hours 40 minutes–13 hours 30 minutes).
Braşov–Cluj (6 daily; 4 hours 40–5 hours 20 minutes)
Cluj–Timişoara (2 daily; 6 hours 30 minutes)
Timişoara–Sibiu (3 dail; 5 hours 10 minutes–6 hours 10 minutes)

Tickets

At Bucharest Gara de Nord and some other major stations, tickets are computerised. However, most stations still issue one or more cardboard slips, depending on whether a supplement or reservation fee is payable. Don't lose these.

On the day of travel, tickets requiring a reservation are available only at the station, a maximum of one hour before departure. Allow extra time to find the right window and for queues. To book tickets in advance go to a CFR office, usually at least 24 – although officially up to five – hours before departure. It's usually not a problem to buy tickets at the station, but safer to book ahead through a CFR office, especially on Black Sea services in the summer or for longer journeys. Tickets are not yet available online.

Train tickets come in three types. The *bilet* is the basic second-class *personal* fare, the *supliment* the supplementary fare for first class, a faster train or sleeping accommodation, and the *tichet* the reservation. From stations with no ticket office you can buy tickets on the train immediately after boarding.

Timetables

The confusing if indispensable CFR timetable comes out every May and is sometimes for sale at CFR offices. Otherwise, timetables are displayed at stations (marked *plecări* for

departures and *şosiri* for arrivals), available on tel: 952 from most towns and cities (tel: 9521 from Bucharest) or online at www.infofer.ro. At stations, departure boards indicate the terminus and the line *(linia)* or platform *(peronul)*. Online, remember to use pre-reform Romanian spellings for stations (â instead of î), without the diacriticals (eg Tirgoviste, not Târgovişte), and be aware that many places have several stations.

Reservations

All Intercity and Rapid and nearly all Accelerat trains require reservations. On timetables an R in a box indicates compulsory reservations. Tickets indicate train number *(trenul)*, carriage number *(vagonul)* and seat number *(loc)*.

Dining Cars

Most Intercity and long-distance Rapid services have a *wagon-restaurant* or *bar-bistro* serving a basic menu of a reasonable standard. However, most passengers bring their own food and use the dining cars just for drinking.

Sleepers and Couchettes

For a small supplement, these are available on some Intercity and most long-distance Rapid routes. Some longer-distance Accelerat services have couchettes but rarely sleepers. Sleeping cars are comfortable and can be an excellent option on long journeys. Costs compare favourably with hotel accommodation. Compartments have one or two berths in a first-class sleeping car *(vagon de dormit clasa întâi)*, three in a second-class sleeping car *(vagon de dormit clasa a doua)* and six in a couchette car *(vagon-cuşetă)*. There's generally a sink with hot and cold water in each compartment. Soap, towels and bedding are provided. Although sleeping cars have attendants, it's advisable to lock or chain compartment doors. Supplements are €11 for a first-class sleeper (€22 for sole use); €8 for a second-class sleeper and €5 for a couchette.

Pets may travel on trains and buses, but large dogs must be muzzled.

Bus & Minibus (Long-distance)

Compared with trains, the long-distance bus network in Romania isn't very developed. Although buses are sometimes the only way of reaching villages, they aren't

recommended for long-distance transport. Run by a panoply of competing companies and owner-drivers, services are poorly coordinated and information can be elusive. Driving can also be hazardous and comfort standards poor. Bus stations are most commonly next to train stations, although many towns have more than one bus terminal *(autogară)*.

Minibuses (known as *maxitaxiuri* or *microbuze*) compete with trains and buses on many routes and generally leave from the same stations. On some routes they're the only option. They're often faster and more frequent than the competition but usually crowded to the gills and neither particularly comfortable nor safe. Air conditioning is rare. Travelling by maxitaxi sometimes feels like a world-record attempt to cram the maximum number of people into a vehicle. It's not surprising some Romanians call them *transport african*. Fares are around €1 per 100 km (62 miles), payable on board.

Taxi drivers and hotel receptionists are usually knowledgeable about local bus and maxitaxi services.

At a bus terminal departures are listed on *programul plecărilor*. Larger stations usually have an information desk. On buses it's best to book a ticket in advance if you want to be sure of a seat. Buses are generally a better option than maxitaxis, although some buses are very decrepit. If you're going to a remote location, always ask the time of the last return or onward service.

Hitching

Hitching *(autostop)* has long been an established part of the public-transport system. It's normal to offer to pay the driver – roughly twice the equivalent bus fare – but sometimes this will be refused. Of course, hitching isn't always safe, but neither is taking a maxitaxi. In rural areas you may be offered lifts on horse carts.

Driving

Fantastic scenery and relatively empty roads (outside of Bucharest, which has a chronic traffic problem – *see page 338*) can make touring by car an excellent way to see the country, and if your time is limited and you want to delve into the splendour of the Romanian countryside, there is little alternative.

The disadvantage is that there are certain hazards which those who have only driven in western Europe or North America will be unfamiliar with. Even

see page 338

TRANSPORT | ACCOMMODATION | ACTIVITIES | A – Z | LANGUAGE

Getting Around Bucharest and Other Large Cities

By Rail/Underground

Bucharest's underground railway, the Metro, was built in the 1970s to ferry workers from the housing estates of Militari and Titan out to the huge industrial complexes at Industriilor, Pipera, IMGB and Republica; visitor requirements were not in the plan. As such it is of limited use to tourists, and gaps between trains are usually more than ten minutes.

Those arriving or departing from Gara de Nord, which has a direct connection with Piața Victoriei, may find it useful, however, and the main north–south line does offer access between Piața Unirii in the south via Piața Universitatii and the Bulevardul Bălcescu–Magheru shopping area to the museums on Șoseaua Kiseleff in the north.

Should you feel the urge, tickets cost next to nothing (€0.25) and are valid for two trips. They can be bought from the booths at station entrances.

By Bus, Tram and Trolleybus

As a rule, bus/trolleybus and tram routes in Bucharest run east–west and north–south, and the frequency of services is impressive. That does not mean they are not crowded, however; be extra careful of pickpockets on all public transport in the city, but especially on bus No. 85 which runs to and from Gara de Nord. There are no bus lanes, which means buses get caught up in the all-too-frequent gridlocks. Note that public transport in the capital is completely inaccessible to the disabled.

Public transport in other Romanian cities offers a choice between buses, trolleybuses and trams, and is generally reliable and easy to use.

Buy tickets, valid for one or two trips, in advance at a kiosk (casă de bilete) and punch them on board. Fares are about €0.25 per trip. For

longer stays, an *abonament* (season ticket) is worthwhile. In all cities tickets are valid for all kinds of public transport, except in Bucharest where the Metro requires a separate ticket.

Taxis

Taxis in Romania are widely available and inexpensive. Fares vary according to location and company but usually range from 1–1.5 lei per km, often with a similar starting fare. Rates can double outside urban limits.

However, there are many cheats who will charge foreigners many times the going rate. The best way to avoid trouble is to book a taxi by telephone from a reputable company (see below), or ask a Romanian to do it for you. *Puteți să-mi comandați un taxi, vă rog?* is the magic expression. You should be especially careful in Bucharest, where cheats are notorious at Baneasa Airport, Gara de Nord, outside all five-star hotels (always ensure the concierge orders you a taxi), the shopping malls and at the airport.

If you want to hail a taxi on the street or outside an airport or station, check that the vehicle displays the name of the taxi company as well as the telephone number and rate per km. Before boarding ask if the meter is working (Merge taximetrul?) and check the rate is the same as advertised. If the meter isn't working, agree a fare in advance or look for another taxi. For longer trips, taxis often work out cheaper and easier than car hire. It's normal to round up fares to the nearest leu.

At the end of the journey, the driver should print out a receipt.

Taxis in Bucharest: Prof Taxi (tel: 9422), Taxi AS (tel: 9435), Meridian (tel: 9444), Perrozzi (tel: 9631)
Arad: Arad Taxi (tel: 244244), Diesel Star (tel: 212222),
Brașov: ETAX (tel: 953); Bratax (tel: 333232); Martax (tel: 944).
Cluj: Diesel Rapid (tel: 946); Mesagerul (tel: 947); Pritax (tel: 942)
Constanța: Mondial (tel: 693333); Romaris (tel: 940).
Iași: Delta (tel: 222222); Euro (tel: 217217); For You (tel: 222444).
Oradea: Start (tel: 940); VIP (tel: 444444)
Sibiu: EuroTotal (tel: 948); Negoiu (tel: 444444); Sibiu (tel: 953).
Timișoara: Prompt (tel: 942); Auto Ravi (tel: 940); Tudo (tel: 945).

Driving

Driving in Bucharest is best avoided. The city's drivers pay practically no attention to the rules of the road, and accidents are common. Traffic congestion is appalling as the city's dated street network fails to cope with more and more cars (more new cars appeared on the city's streets in 2006 than there were cars in the city in 1989). Parking is problematic, as there are few car parks (exceptions are at Piața Unirii and Piața Revolutiei).

In other main cities, congestion is rarely a problem. Major roads are usually in reasonable condition, but watch out for trams and tramlines and faded paint on street lanes. Throughout Romania, drivers toot horns more than strictly necessary. Most cars on the road are beaten-up old Dacias, a 1970s Renault design, recently superseded by the new Logan model.

On Foot

Due in the main to the carelessness of the city's drivers, being a pedestrian in Bucharest is not a wholly enjoyable experience. Streets are wide, noisy and invariably busy, while potholes and randomly parked cars make even walking on pavements hazardous. Crossing the road is best attempted only at traffic lights, as designated pedestrian crossings are generally ignored by drivers.

Walking around towns elsewhere in the country is less fraught with dangers, but again be aware of potholes, randomly parked cars on the pavement, pickpockets and street hustlers. Icy pavements present a danger in winter.

Throughout Romania, but especially Bucharest (see page 125), stray dogs can be a menace. A dog alarm, available from pet shops – or online from www.canineconcepts.co.uk or www.pets pantry.tv – is very effective. Alternatively, stooping down to pick up a stone or – in extremis – actually throwing one, usually does the trick.

Useful Websites

Arad: www.ctparad.ro
Brașov: www.geocities.com/cosmas_ro/transpt/aztbz.htm
Bucharest: www.ratb.ro/eng
Cluj: www.ratuc.ro
Constanța: www.ratc-constanta.ro
Sibiu: www.sibiu.ro/en/transport.htm
Timișoara: www.ratt.ro

on the main Bucharest to Brasov road traffic can be held up by tractors and horse-drawn carts. Few roads have more than two lanes and many are in poor shape. Outside towns, driving at night is perilous. Road lighting is poor and there's no end to the number of unlit obstacles. These include drunks, horse carts and animals, as well as cars, since many Romanian drivers don't use their headlamps. Even in daylight people and animals on the road are a constant danger as many national roads go straight through the centre of villages.

Villages can be large, and you can be driving for 4 or 5 km (2–3 miles) or more within the 50 kmph (30 mph) limit. This, combined with the twisting roads and lack of motorways, means journey times are long – reckon on an average of around 60–70 kmph (38–45 mph), but more like 50 kmph (30 mph) in mountain areas.

Types of Road and Road Conditions

Nearly all roads have only two lanes. Romania has a lower motorway density than almost any other European country – the only fully fledged motorway in the country, the A1, links Bucharest with Pitești. The A2 from Bucharest to Constanta is due for completion in 2007. Others in various stages of construction will eventually link Romania with pan-European corridors, but progress is slow. In 2005 work on the planned Transylvanian motorway linking Brașov, Târgu Mureș, Cluj and Oradea halted because of unpaid bills.

Apart from motorways, public roads in Romania fall into three categories: national (**drum național**, DN), county or secondary (**drum judeţean**, DJ) and communal or country (**drum communal**, DC). Roads on European corridors (nearly all national roads) have an E number (eg E60).

National roads are mostly in reasonable condition, thanks to massive post-Ceaușescu investment, but secondary roads are generally poor, often covered in mud and horse dung so very slippery. Most village roads only have, at best, a loose gravel surface with many little better than rutted tracks passable only on foot, or by horse or 4X4.

In winter, ice can make driving conditions even more perilous than usual. Some mountain roads become impassable without snow chains.

Romanian drivers are, on the whole, not quite as aggressive as some people would have you believe. However, the main message is *drive slowly*.

Regulations

Driving is on the right and overtaking on the left, although trams can be passed on the right. Except where indicated otherwise, traffic coming from the right has priority, including vehicles entering at roundabouts.

Traffic police are everywhere (*see margin, page 319*), so always observe the speed limits: unless road signs state otherwise, these are 50 kmph (31 mph) in built-up areas, 90 kmph (56 mph) on main roads and 110 kmph (70 mph) on motorways.

Front-seat passengers must wear seat belts and under-12s sit in the back. Driving when using a mobile phone, except a hands-free set, is illegal and there's a zero alcohol limit. Fines are severe. Parking is on the right side of the street and in the direction of traffic.

After many years of abuses, traffic police no longer have powers to issue on-the-spot fines. Instead, they must be paid at a bank or local tax administration office and can be disputed.

Fuel

Petrol stations are generally on main roads out of towns and are scarce elsewhere, especially in the mountains. Many cities have 24-hour stations. Diesel (*motorină*) is widely available. Prices are around 3.5 lei a litre – only a little cheaper than in western Europe and therefore extremely expensive for Romanians.

Emergency Assistance

In an accident call and await the police (tel: 112). Ask for a copy of any report. Romania's national automobile association, Automobil Clubul Român (ACR; tel: 021-222 2222) has reciprocal arrangements with many national automobile associations.

Car Hire

This is widely available in main cities and at major airports. International agencies such as Avis, Budget, Europcar and Hertz have offices across Romania, although local companies such as Autonom (www.autonom.ro) are usually cheaper. To hire a vehicle you need to be between 21 and 70 and to have held a licence for a year. A large deposit is necessary unless you pay by credit card. Restrictions apply on driving locally hired vehicles into other countries. Ask when booking. For day trips, hiring a taxi at an agreed price often works out cheaper.

Car hire is available from the following companies:

Brașov: Avis, Suntours, Str. Mureșenilor 15 (tel: 0268-413775); Budget, Hotelul Aro Palace, Bulevardul Eroilor 27 (tel: 0268-474564)
Cluj: Avis, Hotelul Victoria, Str. 21 Dec 1989 54–6 (tel: 0264-439403)
Constanța: Avis, Tarom, B-dul Ștefan cel Mare 15 (tel: 0241-616733); Budget, Str. Ferdinand 70 (tel: 0241-639713); Hertz, B-dul Tomis 65 (tel: 0241-661100)
Iași: Cliven Rent-A-Car, Str. Ștefan cel Mare 8–12 (tel: 0232-258326)
Neptun: Budget, Hotelul Belvedere (tel: 0722-504394)
Oradea: Hertz, Str. Mihai Viteazul 2–8 (tel: 0259-437947)
Sibiu: Avis, Hotelul Bulevard, Piața Unirii 10 (tel: 0729-800393)
Timișoara: Avis, Hotelul Boavista, Str. Sportivilor 7a (tel: 0723-623309); Europcar, Str. Gheorghe Lazăr 9 (tel: 0256-303486); Hertz, Schela de Petrol, Str. Popa Șapcă 2 (tel: 0256-492211)

Motorcycling

Although much less common than in western Europe, motorcycling is increasingly popular and is a great way to see the country. However, spare parts can be elusive and other motorists rarely show much consideration for motorcyclists. In cities tramlines can be a hazard. In the countryside watch out for livestock and all kinds of slippery substances on the roads. Helmets are compulsory.

Motorcycle tours are available from Transylvania Motorcycle Tours, Str. Ion Mester 3, bl. G, ap. 42, Cluj-Napoca (tel: 0740-472259; www.tmtours.net).

Ferries

Ferries and hydrofoils are the main means of transport in the Danube Delta (*see page 166*) but little used for passenger traffic elsewhere.

Cycling

With a network of quiet backroads, cycling is a joy in many rural parts of Romania and a good way for the fit to experience the country's sights and beautiful landscapes. Mountain-biking is also popular, and several companies are getting in on the act (*see page 361*).

Many towns have a bicycle repair shop (*atelier de reparat biciclete*), but it's wise to be prepared for emergency repairs on the road. Bicycle hire (*închiriat de biciclete*) is possible in the more touristy destinations.

A CCOMMODATION

HOTELS, HOSTELS & HOMESTAYS

Choosing a Hotel

Hotels will almost certainly be your biggest expense when travelling in Romania. While good accommodation is relatively easy to find these days, it is rarely, if ever, cheap – at least in comparison with most other things in Romania. There is a wide selection of hotels in most of the country's major cities, such as Bucharest, Braşov, Timişoara, Cluj and Constanţa, but note that some places are still paying catch-up and have a poor selection of hotels (Sibiu and Iaşi are especially guilty here).

Hotels have to be prepared to take disabled guests, to meet EU requirements. Some, however, have done only the absolute minimum.

The Black Sea Coast

Many hotels along the coast especially outside Constanţa and Mangalia, are open only in season, and a few in Mamaia are only fully open in July and August. Exact periods depend partly on the weather. Those that are open outside the main summer season have lower prices. In the main resorts it is generally best to book accommodation through a travel agency, in advance or on arrival. If you are planning to spend most of your trip on the coast, it can work out a lot cheaper to book the whole trip through an agency abroad. Many agencies have highly discounted rates for stays of five days or more, often including full board. You're also likely to be approached by people offering rooms, at the station, on the streets or even on the train (this can also be the case at places like Braşov and Sinaia). Look out for *cazare* or *camere* signs. In high

season, there are accommodation booking *(dispecerat cazare)* booths in operation next to train stations along the coast.

Costs

As with so many things in Romania, price and quality in the accommodation sector do not always go hand in hand. In most places location is still the main factor in determining a hotel's rack rates, with service and comfort coming a poor second. As such do not think for one minute that paying 150 euros will guarantee you a value for money room for the night, especially in peak season (Christmas and New Year) in the ski resorts. Instead shop around as much as possible and use our listings which follow to choose a recommended hotel. By and large you should always be able to find a good hotel within your price range, though when checking-in do not be shy to ask to see a room before agreeing to take it.

In most cases – even in the big five star hotels in the capital – the rack rates can often be negotiated, especially at weekends, while for hotels on the coast and in the ski resorts you are far better booking through a web discounter or travel agent than turning up on spec. Try the hotel bookings accumulator www.bookings.net

Apartments, Hostels and Homestays

Fully equipped apartments can often be a good alternative to hotels, and there is a proliferation of companies offering them in Bucharest. The website of local city guide Bucharest In Your Pocket (www.inyourpocket.com) has a long list of these companies.

Outside of the capital those on a budget can try a growing number of hostels (most major towns now have at least one, see www.hihostels.com or www.gomio.com). However, only six hostels in the entire country are affiliated to the Hostelling International Association. Two are in Bucharest (the best known is the Vila Helga, at 2 Str. Salcâmilor, tel: 021-610 2214), two are in Cluj, and there is one in each of Costineşti, Sighişoara and Mangalia.

Alternatively you can stay with a Romanian family. Most inter-city trains are met at stations by a gaggle of old ladies who will offer *cazare* (rooms) in their own homes for small amouts of money (usually around 10 euros). While you are usually guaranteed warmth and generosity, heating and hot water may be optional extras.

In the countryside agro-tourism is taking off, with pensions and homestays popular amongst foreign and local visitors alike. Here you are usually guaranteed comfort, and great home cooking featuring local delicacies. **Antrec**, the Romanian agro-tourism agency (www.antrec.ro), has details of thousands of village pensions and homestays. The French B&B network **OVR** is now defunct but has left a legacy of good-quality B&Bs and homestays (the name OVR is still sometimes used).

Monasteries and Camping

For a different experience, consider staying in a Romanian monastery – see page 350 for details.

Camping is also possible, although facilities are pretty basic in most campsites. Mountain huts *(cabane)* are used by hikers *(see pages 360–1).*

ACCOMMODATION LISTINGS

Hotels are listed in alphabetical order within price categories.
Towns and cities are listed in the order in which they appear in the book.

BUCHAREST

Athenée Palace Hilton
Str. Episcopiei 1–3
Tel: 021-303 3777
www.hilton.com
The best hotel in the country. Nowhere else comes close to matching the supreme luxury, history and overwhelming sense of occasion that flows through the marble halls of this 100-year old building. Enormous rooms, ostentatiously plush bathrooms, outstanding service and none of it as expensive as you may think. €€€€€

Crowne Plaza
B-dul. Poligrafiei 1
Tel: 021-224 0034
www.bucharest.crowneplaza.com
This figure-of-eight-shaped hotel with glorious interior gardens and courtyards is a luxury establishment that has a single failing: its non city-centre location. Great if you do not mind continually taking taxis into town. €€€€€

Howard Johnson Grand Plaza
Calea Dorobantilor 5–7
Tel: 021-201 5000
www.hojoplaza.ro
A 1970s high-rise, recently renovated. This is a four star-plus hotel that holds its own well in its battle with the big five stars. The superb views from the rooms help, as does the free Wi-Fi, the two outstanding restaurants, and a high-class breakfast. €€€€€

InterContinental
B-dul. Nicolae Bălcescu 2–4
Tel: 021-310 2020
www.intercontinental.com
Though some of the common areas have indeed seen better days, the views from the balconies cannot be matched, and recent renovation of most rooms has returned them to luxury status. Underrated. €€€€€

JW Marriott Grand Hotel
Calea 13 Septembrie 90
Tel: 021-403 1000
www.jwmarriott.ro
If it weren't for the location – some way south of the city centre – the Hilton Athenée Palace would have a genuine rival. The neoclassical building is a gem, and the interior is pure luxury. €€€€€

Novotel Bucharest City Centre
Calea Victoriei 37B
Tel: 021-312 5114
www.novotel.com
The feature of this new glass monster is the entrance: a replica of the neoclassical Romanian National Theatre which stood here in the 1920s and '30s. Inside, the hotel is luxuriously furnished and vividly decorated, though prices are a touch too high. €€€€€

Sofitel
Piaţa Montreal 10
Tel: 021-318 3000
www.sofitel.com
One of several hotels in the north of the city, this is the most luxurious: a lavish treat for tired businessmen with charge accounts. Some of the weekend deals are tempting for tourists too, though the lack of a swimming pool keeps it at four, and not five stars. €€€€€

El Greco
Str. Jean Louis Calderon 16
Tel: 021-315 8131
www.hotelelgreco.ro
This is an outstanding villa conversion in the heart of a residential district within walking distance of the city centre. Rooms are huge, common areas grand and the Greek restaurant superb. €€€€

Golden Tulip Bucharest
Calea Victoriei 166
Tel: 021-212 5558
www.goldentulipbucharest.com
The best of the three Golden Tulip hotels in Bucharest occupies a purpose-built glass tower block on the city's historic north–south avenue. With most of the well-sized rooms having good views and more extras than you would expect, the prices are just about merited. €€€€

Helvetia
Piaţa Charles de Gaulle 13
Tel: 021-223 0566
A charming place to stay, opposite Bucharest's largest park. Quiet rooms with a hint of luxury make up for the rather disappointing breakfast, while the friendly owners will do all they can to make you welcome. €€€€

K+K Hotel Elisabeta
Str. Slanic 26
Tel: 021-311 8631
www.kkhotels.co.ro
The Koller brothers have been opening fine, understatedly luxurious hotels all over central Europe for years, and in 2006 they finally brought their magic to a villa in Bucharest. Expect rooms decorated individually with the finest furnishings, high art, and high prices. €€€€

Lido
B-dul. Magheru 5–7
Tel: 021-314 4930
www.lido.ro
Bucharest's second Art Deco gem of a hotel is opposite the other (the Ambasador) on the city's busiest road. The more luxurious of the two, this place falls a little short of five-star status, though the large bathrooms make it a close call. Staff can be a little surly. €€€€

Ramada Majestic
Calea Victoriei 38–40
Tel: 021-310 2720
www.ramadamajestic.ro
Well located in the city centre, the wooden fittings that greet you at reception may betray its 1970s roots, but this is now a fully renovated, thoroughly modern hotel which besides large comfortable rooms also has the smallest swimming pool in town in the basement. €€€€

Ambasador
B-dul Magheru 8–10
Tel: 021-315 9080
www.ambasador.ro
While the interior is looking a little dated, and the rooms have seen better days, the Ambasador is still a good place to stay, with decent prices, central location and glorious, signature Art Deco architecture, of which there are flourishes at every turn. €€€

Central
Str. Ion Brezoianu 13
Tel: 021-315 5635
www.centralhotel.ro
Small and welcoming, the location is great, on one of the city's main east–west thoroughfares. Far better than the entrance (or prices) would have you believe. €€€

Duke
B-dul Dacia 33
Tel: 021-317 4186
www.hotelduke.ro
Offering one of the best buffet breakfasts in Bucharest, some of the bedrooms can be a bit pokey, but the prices are good and the city centre location great. €€€

Minerva
Str. Gheorghe Manu 2–4
Tel: 021-311 1550
www.minerva.ro
Glorious, high-ceilinged

PRICE CATEGORIES

Price categories are for a double room without breakfast unless mentioned:
€ = under €50
€€ = €50–75
€€€ = €75–100
€€€€ = €100–150
€€€€€ = more than €150

rooms – all with free Wi-Fi – in a great city centre location. A favourite with businessmen the breakfast is commendable, though it is perhaps the only hotel breakfast in the world served in a Chinese restaurant (the Nan Jing, Bucharest's oldest). €€€

NH Bucharest
B-dul. Mircea Voda 21
Tel: 021-300 0545
www.nh-hotels.com
Excellent-value hotel opposite Bucharest's thriving Jewish Theatre. Though the look and feel of the place is a little more tended towards the business traveller than the tourist, it offers cheap weekend rates which includes breakfast. €€€

Professional Realty
Str. George Valentin Bibescu 33, bl, 10/2, sc. A, ap. 6
Tel: 021-232 0406
www.accommodation.com.ro
High-class self-catering apartments with luxury furnishings in city centre locations. Can be rented short- and long-term. €€€

Rembrandt
Str. Smardan 11
Tel: 021-313 9315
www.rembrandt.ro

For under €100 you can do no better in Bucharest. A cracking hotel where staff go to the ends of the earth to make you fell welcome, and the rooms, with their original wooden floors, make you feel right at home. Great location in the Lipscani district. €€€

Tania
Str. Selari 5
Tel: 021-104 2083
www.taniahotel.ro
The second hotel to open in Lipscani is as welcome as the first. As with the Rembrandt expect the great location to be matched with excellent services and rooms with a unique view of Bucharest life. Can be noisy outside in summer. €€€

Ibis Gara de Nord
Calea Grivitei 143
Tel: 021-300 9100
www.ibishotel.com

Ibis Palatul Parlamentului
Str. Izvor 82–84
Tel: 021-401 1000
There are two Ibis hotels, one by the railway station and a smaller establish-ment close to the Parlia-ment building. Expect the same in both: gleaming bathrooms with showers only (no bath tub) and

smiley professional service. Breakfast costs extra. €€

Hanul lui Manuc
Str. Franceză 62–4
Tel: 021-313 1411
www.hanulmanuc.ro
If you want to try sleeping in a genuine piece of the city's history, try a room at Hanul's Inn. Feeling distinctly monastic, the rooms are basic but clean, though a tad overpriced. €€

Opera
Str. Ion Brezoianu 37
Tel: 021-312 4855
www.hotelopera.ro
Big on value the rooms here are a little small in size. They are well equipped however, and the place is bright and breezy, with happy multilingual staff. It is well located close to the city centre. €€

Piccolo Mondo
Str. Clucerului 9
Tel: 021-260 0682
www.piccolomondo.ro
Another three-star hotel in a northern residential district, the rooms here have great little touches, such as the superb wrought-iron beds. Downstairs is the best kebab house in the city,

and a genuine Lebanese restaurant. €€

Cerna
B-dul. Dinicu Golescu 29
Tel: 021-311 0535
Cheap and cheerful, the Cerna is simple, basic and close to the railway station. There are rooms with and without private bath and toilet, tiny singles and a couple of good-value triples. The best budget choice in the city. €

Vila 11
Str. Institutul Medico Militar 11
Tel: 0722-495900
Super little hostel close to the railway station run by a friendly American-Romanian couple. Expect a warm reception, simple but clean rooms and dorms and any help you need during your stay to be forthcoming in an instant. €

Youth Hostel Villa Helga
Str. Salcâmilor 2
Tel: 021-610 2214
www.rotravel.com/hotels/helga
Legendary hostel (the first to open in the city, back in 1996) where a relaxed atmosphere and no curfew, along with a great breakfast, keeps guests coming back time and time again. €

WALLACHIA

Ploieşti

Hanul Găzarilor
Str. Mihai Bravu 45
Tel: 0244-597577
www.rotaru.com.ro
This family-run rustic-style inn oozes charm and character in a town sorely lacking in either. The prices are truly excellent considering the free internet access in every room. The hotel is also equipped with a cosy wine-cellar and a pleasant restaurant. €€

Târgovişte

Cazare Dracula
Calea Dumnească
Tel: 0245-620013
This pension has unbeatable views Târgovişte's Princely Court

directly opposite – make sure you ask for one – but somewhat small and gloomy rooms. Still, the price is right. €

Dâmboviţa
B-dul Libertăţii 1
Tel: 0245-213370
www.hoteldambovita.ro
With a central location overlooking the main park, this communist-era hotel is comfortable without overdoing it on the character front. Many rooms have pleasant balconies with fine park views. The beer-can opener attached to the keys is an unusual touch. €€

Piteşti

Carmen
B-dul. Republicii 84
Tel: 0248-222699

www.hotel-carmen.ro
Noisy and slightly overpriced hotel redeemed by its central location and the presence of some unusually helpful service. The quality of the rooms varies wildly according to price – some are modernised, others It's definitely best to ask to see a few before deciding. €€

Metropol
Str. Panselelor 1
Tel: 0248-222407
This basic hotel offers noisy and small rooms in a conveniently central location, and is distinguished mainly by its unfeasibly well-stocked minibar (which comes complete with question-naire asking what you think of it). €

Curtea de Argeş

Posada
B-dul. Basarabilor 27–29
Tel: 0248-721451
www.posada.ro
Agreeably old-fashioned hotel with some of the best service in Wallachia. While the dead hand of state control still appears to lingers over the place, it is of a more benign sort than elsewhere. Ask for a room at the front with a balcony and view of the mountains. €€

Târgu Jiu

Brâncuși
B-dul. Constantin Brâncuși 10
Tel: 0253-215981
Next to Brâncuși Park,
this hotel features a bright
blue-and-white glass
framed facade with
spacious modernised
rooms in a matching colour
scheme. €

Europa
Calea Eroilor 22
Tel: 0253-211810
www.hotelrestauranteuropa.ro
A restored interwar villa,
this comfortable hotel has
modern facilities together
with more aesthetic
satisfaction than any of the
competition. Unusually,
smoking is banned in all
rooms. €

Miami Energeticianul
Str. Eroilor 21
Tel: 0253-218407
Known as the Miami – even
Romanians find the full
name a bit of a tongue
twister – this centrally
located hotel offers
excellent value with
spacious comfortable rooms
and staff who go out of their
way to help guests. €

Craiova

Bavaria
Str. Caracal 3
Tel: 0251-414449
www.hotelbavaria.ro
Claiming to be Craiova's
only business-class hotel,
this swish contemporary
establishment adds a
dose of sophistication

and efficiency. Popular
with expats and business
travellers. €€€

Green House Hotel
Str. Frații Buzești 25
Tel: 0251-411352
www.greenhousehotel.ro
A hotel so lovely it makes
a destination in its own
right – which is probably
just as well in Craiova. This
gorgeously-restored villa in
eclectic style has more
romance than some can
handle. The huge rooms are
elegantly decorated with
wooden panels in the same
Art Deco style as the rest of
the hotel, right down to the
reproduction telephones.
Unmissable. €€€

Jiul
Calea București 1–3
Tel: 0251-414166

www.jiul.ro
Huge communist-era
monolith in the centre
that once served as a
Communist Party guest-
house. Although both
modernised and
unmodernised rooms
are on offer, there is
little difference between
them except that the first
have air conditioning.
Reasonable value. €€

Parc
Str. Bibescu 16
Tel: 0251-417257
Situated outside of the
centre, this featureless
building has the main
advantage of a pretty park
location. Reasonable value
for money. In some rooms
smoking is not permitted.
€€

DOBROGEA

Constanța

Royal
B-dul Mamaia 191
Tel: 0241-545570
www.hotelroyal.ro
Plush and comfortable
hotel decorated in an
elegant contemporary style.
The location in the northern
part of town (well on the
way to Mamaia) is probably
best suited to those with
their own transport. €€€€

Guci
Str. Răcoalei din 1907 nr 23
Tel: 0241-695500
www.hotel-guci.ro
Constanța's swankiest
modern hotel offers more
mod cons than the

competition and a
convenient location
behind the central post
office, as well as sea
views. €€

Ibis
Str. Mircea cel Batran 39–41
Tel: 0241-508050
www.ibishotel.com
On the promenade
overlooking the main
beach, this well-managed
hotel is everything you
would expect from this
competitively priced
French chain. Breakfast
not included. Wi-fi is
available but not free.
Ask for a room with a
sea view. €€

Kleyn
Str. Primăverii 63A
Tel: 0241-656622
www.kleynturism.ro
This welcoming and
comfortable hotel
enjoys a quiet if slightly
remote location in a
well-to-do residential
quarter near Lake
Tăbăcărului, surrounded
by the villas of the
nouveaux riches. The
abstract art throughout
gives a tasteful contem-
porary touch. Free Wi-fi.
A good choice, especially
for families, if you don't
mind not being near the
centre. €€

New Safari
Str. Karatzali 1
Tel: 0722-322461
www.rolitoral.ro/newsafari
Offering some of the
best-value rooms in the
centre of Constanța,
this decor-conscious
"minihotel" enjoys a fine
seafront location. The
rooms are spacious and
comfortable, but the
receptionists could take
some lessons in customer
service. €€

Mamaia

*If you don't have any
accommodation booked in
advance, your best bet is
the Romanian Seaside
Accommodation Booking
Office (tel: 0241-831200)
in the Cazino complex.*

Iaki
(no street address)
Tel: 0241-831025
Local boy made good
Gheorghe Hagi has put
some of his wealth on
display in Mamaia's largest
and swankiest new hotel, a
palatial lilac building offering
a stylish contemporary foil
to the identikit communist-
era blocks elsewhere in the
resort. The complex
incorporates a spa centre,

plus numerous other
facilities to pamper the
most demanding guest.
(July–Aug only). €€€€€

Rex
(no street address)
Tel: 0241-831595
A majestic wedding cake of
a building *(pictured, left)*,
the legendary Rex has
been oozing Art Deco
elegance and exclusivity
since it opened in 1906,
and is one of the few
pre-communist buildings
remaining in Mamaia.
Reservations are
essential. (Summer only.)
€€€€€

PRICE CATEGORIES

Price categories are for a
double room without
breakfast unless mentioned:
€ = under €50
€€ = €50–75
€€€ = €75–100
€€€€ = €100–150
€€€€€ = more than €150

Agigea/Eforie Nord

Europa Hotel
Str. Republicii 13
Tel: 0241-741710
www.ana.ro
Dominating the town, this complex injects a dash of luxury into the Eforie Nord tourism scene. Almost any part of you that requires pampering will find it here. **€€€€**

Vila Honiara
Str. Alexandru Cuza
Tel: 0241-741388
If this welcoming villa on a quiet street behind the Hotel Grand feels like a family house, that's because it is. Four comfortable rooms, and a resident cook who will prepare guests meals on request to be served in the gardens. **€**

Neptun-Olimp

Neptun-Olimp has several accommodation booking agencies, including one at

Neptun haltă and Agenţia de Turism Neptun (tel: 0241-701858) in the Bazar next to the Doina Hotel (summer only).

Hotel Cocor
Olimp (no street address)
Tel: 0241-701042
www.hotelcocor.ro
In a quiet location at the southern end of Olimp, this large modern hotel is the best in the twin resorts. Features an outdoor heated swimming pool, bar and restaurant, and great facilities for children. (Mar–Oct only.) **€€**

Doi Mai

Hanul Balcanic Hellios Inn
Doi Mai (no street address)
Tel: 0241-732929
www.hellios-inn.ro
With a quaint caravanserai layout, this place claims to be the only traditional Balkan-style *han* left in Dobrogea. Rooms vary hugely, the cheapest being

quite basic, but the blissful setting, delightful swimming pool and friendly service compensate for any lack of amenities. Drainage can be an issue, as the signs everywhere warn. (May to mid-Oct only.) **€**

Tulcea

Delta
Str. Isaccei 2
Tel: 0240-514720
Good location on Piaţa Republicii a stone's throw from the harbour, the Delta isn't anything to write home about but is comfortable and the lobby is pleasant. Price includes breakfast. **€€€**

Europolis
Str. Păcii 20
Tel: 0240-512443
A reasonable budget option near the centre of town, with well-equipped air-conditioned rooms. Operates various trips into the Delta. **€**

Danube Delta

The agrotourism organisation Antrec has information on homestays and pensiones in the Delta: there are several in Crişan, as well as Caraorman, Murgihiol and Mila 35. See www.antrec.ro/ro for details.

Casa Coral
Str. a-l-a 195, Sulina
Tel: 0742-974016
Pleasant pension with 15 rooms, restaurant, and an attractive terrace. **€–€€**

Mareea
Sfântu Gheorghe, no street address
Tel: 0744-306384
An extremely agreeable place to stay in this remote fishing village. **€**

Pensiunea Oprişan
Crişan, no street address
Tel: 0240-547034
One of several pensiones on the long narrow strip that is Crişan village. Close to the pier.

TRANSYLVANIA

Braşov

Aro Palace
Str. Mureşenilor 12
Tel: 0268-477664
www.aro-palace.ro
Founded in 1939, this large brutalist hotel is Braşov's largest and a particularly stark example of the Leninist-Stalinist architectural style already becoming vogueish in Romania. It stands on what used to be part of the city walls. The interior has largely been renovated to a modern standard although some parts still look decidedly communist-era. The hotel has a swimming pool. **€€€€**

Bella Muzica
Piaţa Sfatului 19
Tel: 0268-477946
www.bellamuzica.ro
This fine small hotel offers an unbeatable setting in a Saxon building on Braşov's main square, although only the two apartments offer views of it. While the

service and atmosphere are top-notch, the rooms are a little small for the price. **€€€**

Capitol
B-dul Eroilor 19
Tel: 0268-418920
Opposite Central Park, just north of Strada Republicii, this large communist-era hotel squarely occupies the middle ground. While the rooms are slightly more aesthetically pleasing than those in the cheaper Coroana, also in the same chain, they are smaller and the location is slightly less central. **€€**

Coroana
Str. Republicii 62
Tel: 0268-477448
Dating from 1910, this lovely period building more than makes up what it lacks in mod cons with copious lashings of character and original features. While the hotel is in obvious need of renovation, the rooms are exceptionally spacious

and many enjoy superb balcony views over Braşov's liveliest street. Excellent value and very friendly service. Wi-fi. **€€**

Postăvarul
Str. Republicii 62
Tel: 0268-477448
In the same building as the Coroana and sharing a reception, its no-frills sister hotel offers the same period features but much smaller rooms with shared baths. For the price however, it's the best deal in town. **€**

Aro Sport
Str. Sfântul Ioan 3
Tel: 0268-478800
www.aro-palace.ro/arosport.html
Behind the Aro Palace and part of the same state-owned chain, this shabby one-star place is a world away in terms of facilities, with no-frills accommodation and shared bathrooms and loos. A centrally located bargain for the cash-strapped. **€**

Poiana Braşov

Accommodation here is often cheaper if booked through an agency, in Romania or abroad. Very busy at Christmas, New Year.

Hotel Alpin
(no street address)
Tel: 0268-262343
www.hotelalpin.ro
In terms of facilities and location, this large alpine-style hotel stands head and shoulders over the competition, with a swimming pool, sauna, disco, garden, children's playground and even a funky cigar club. The views are magnificent. Ask for a

room with a balcony overlooking the resort. Although it may feel a little impersonal because of its size, the friendly service helps compensate. €€€ (winter €€€€)

Vila Alexandra
(no street address)
Tel: 0268-262203
Surrounded by fir trees and decked with hanging baskets, this friendly villa has almost as perfect a setting as the Hotel Alpin next door but further uphill. Very adequate rooms, although views vary considerably. Ask for one with a balcony at the back of the building. The excellent apartments (€€€) offer good value for groups of three or four. Friendly service. €€

Pub Rossignol
(no street address)
Tel: 0268-262470
Poiana Braşov's popular après-ski bar also has some cosy wooden rooms available all year round, with beds on a mezzanine level reached by a ladder. Just below the lower chairlift station, this is very convenient for the ski slopes. €

Bran

For information about homestays in and around Bran, ask at the ecotourism office (Birou de cazare centrul agroturistic Bran; tel: 0682-36592, www.turism-bran.go.ro) just outside the entrance to the castle.

Casa Medievală
Str. Principală 293A
Tel: 0788-070777
www.casamedievala.ebran.ro
On the right bank of the river Ponita, 200 metres/yds from the castle on the Braşov road, this vaguely medieval-themed wooden villa has lovely rooms, a friendly owner and a delightful garden with a pavilion. €€

Vila Bran
Str. Sohodol 271A
Tel: 0268-236866
www.vilabran.ro
Although the idea of an

agrotourism complex may sound somewhat artificial, this rustic-themed spot 800 metres/yds from the castle on the Braşov road offers semi-rural tranquillity in a hill-top location and a wide enough range of indoor and outdoor facilities from tobogganing to paintball to keep almost anyone occupied. Spread out over eight villas, the complex has 69 rooms varying in size and comfort, some with balconies. Excellent choice for families. €–€€€

Sinaia

Accommodation at Sinaia is often cheaper if booked through a travel agency, either in Romania or abroad. Over Christmas and the New Year Sinaia is a very popular destination, with prices increasing correspondingly with lack of availability.

International
Str. Avram Iancu 1
Tel: 0244-313851
www.international-sinaia.ro
This plush trapezium-shaped tower incorporates wood-lined corridors and the latest word in designer fittings. A fine place for a splurge, especially for lovers of pastel shades. Free access to the swimming pool, fitness centre and sauna. Smoking not permitted in some rooms. Price includes breakfast and access to swimming pool, fitness centre and sauna. €€€€

New Montana
B-dul Carol I, nr. 24
Tel: 0244-312751
www.newmontana.ro
Unfortunate concrete slab blocking off the horizon, this large communist-era hotel has, however, a thoroughly modern interior with some of the most stylish rooms in town. Setting the tone for the whole hotel, the imposing chrome-and-marble lobby with its swish horseshoe-shaped bar is a popular meeting place. Rooms facing the street have

balconies. Guests enjoy free access to the hotel's fitness centre and swimming pool. €€€

Rowa Dany
B-dul. Carol I nr. 46
Tel: 0244 310629
www.rowadany.ro
More intimate and cosy than other top hotels in Sinaia, this cube of a building offers well-decorated and very comfortable rooms cocooned from the noise of the main street by double-glazing. While not enormously aesthetically pleasing from the outside it's on a smaller scale than the communist-era behemoths nearby. €€€

Sinaia
B-dul. Carol 1, nr. 8
Tel: 0244-302900
www.hotelsinaia.ro
Aesthetically way out of proportion with its surroundings, this big communist-era block dominates the main street. The not especially large rooms feel a bit tired and sterile, although the fine balcony views help to compensate. Swimming pool (additional charge for entry). €€

Palace
Str. Octavian Goga 11
Tel: 0244-310122
Dating from 1911, this elegant hotel was originally built to serve gamblers at the now defunct casino nearby. It still retains much period charm alongside stylishly restored and comfortable rooms in muted pastel shades. Ask for a room with views over the park. €€

Caraiman
B-dul. Carol I nr. 4
Tel: 0244-313551
Inside Dimitrie Ghica Park, this lovely neo-Brâncovenesc pile is Sinaia's second-oldest, dating back to 1880, although restored in 2005. Although not the most luxurious in town, the rooms are comfortable and most have splendid park views. All rooms on the first floor have balconies. The hotel has only two stars – hence the

shockingly reasonable prices – because not all rooms have fridges and the management doesn't have the money to install them. €

Casa Noastră
B-dul. Republicii 9
Tel: 0244-314556
www.casanoastrasinaia.ro
Built like a Viking ship, this wooden chalet-type building offers highly affordable accommodation just south of the centre. €

Cerbul
B-dul. Carol I nr. 19
Tel: 0244-312391
On the main street opposite Dimitrie Ghica Park, this vaguely neo-Brâncovenesc hotel offers perfectly adequate if small rooms and is one of the best deals in town. Breakfast not included. €

Economat
Str. Peleşului 2
Tel: 0244-311151
http://hoteleconomat.apps.ro
With an impossibly romantic setting inside the Peleş Castle complex, this breathtakingly pretty hotel manages to be mock-Tudor in a way that could not be less like British 1930s suburbia. In terms of location, it is the next best thing to staying in Peleş Castle, although the rooms are surprisingly spartan, more like the servants' quarters than the royal lodging the exterior would suggest. The hotel also has four villas with similar or lower prices. €

Irish House
B-dul. Carol I nr. 18
Tel: 0244-310060
www.irishhouse.ro
Sinaia's Irish pub also offers homely accommodation next door in a pink wooden villa. However, the neon lights trailing around the entrance

PRICE CATEGORIES

Price categories are for a double room without breakfast unless mentioned:
€ = under €50
€€ = €50–75
€€€ = €75–100
€€€€ = €100–150
€€€€€ = more than €150

and balcony may put some people off, not to mention the offensively cheesy music from loudspeakers outside the building. €

Păltiniş
B-dul Carol I 67
Tel: 0244-314651
www.paltinish.ro
While the lobby and exterior of Sinaia's oldest hotel hint at long-lost *fin-de-siècle* elegance, the rooms are gloomy and have all the elegance of a 1950s council block due for demolition. It is largely the hotel's balneary treatments that keep the place going. No doubt this shabby hotel will be renovated one day to reveal its potential. A plaque outside commemorates US prisoners of war who received care in the building in World War II. Breakfast not included. €

Predeal

Carmen-Ana
B-dul. Mihail Săulescu 121
Tel: 0268-456517
www.carmen-ana.ro
While the aesthetic appeal of this hotel opposite the railway station is negligible, the value for money and convenient location are mitigating factors. The rooms are adequate for a short stay but visually very unappealing. €

Vila Rouă
Str. Nicolae Bălcescu 10
Tel: 0268-457030
www.vilaroua.ro
Lovely villa halfway up the hill offering a wide range of soothing facilities, some at an extra charge, from a sauna and gym to hydro-

massage, ozonotherapy and water treatment. Oddly, only the cheapest rooms have balconies, while the better ones are much bigger with hydromassage baths. €

Sibiu

Continental
Calea Dumbravii 2–4
Tel: 0269-218100
Fourteen-storey communist-era hotel in a pedestrian-unfriendly location cut off from the old town by a busy road. Although the rooms are comfortable, the atmosphere has a somewhat sterile chain feel and the decor is stuck in the 1980s. Popular with business travellers. €€€

Împăratul Romanilor
Str. Nicolae Bălcescu 4
Tel: 0269-216500
Lavishly renovated in preparation for Sibiu's year as European City of Culture in 2007, its grandest hotel is a riot of opulence. As well as an improbably rich array of period features, the hotel offers reproduction furniture and original oil paintings in each room. The highlight, however, is the absurdly lavish restaurant with sliding roof. Rooms vary and not all have a view of any interest. Ask to see a few before deciding. €€€

Casa Baciu
Str. 9 Mai 29
Tel: 0269-214701
www.casa-baciu.ro
In an old town house with a courtyard, this pension offers spacious rooms with large en-suite bathrooms and is one of the best

deals in town. The main drawback is the traffic noise. Breakfast not included. €

Old Town Hostel
Piaţa Mică 26
Tel: 0269-216445
www.hostelsibiu.ro
In a 16th-century Saxon building where homeopathy was founded, this estab-lishment enjoys a setting that would be the envy of most luxury hotels, although the facilities are fairly standard for a modern hostel. One dorm sleeps eight, the other 12, both with fine views over the square. The one single room is rarely available and there is one bathroom for the whole hostel. Friendly laid-back atmosphere. €

Pensiunea Podul Minciunilor
Str. Azilului 1
Tel: 0269-217259
www.ela-hotels.ro
With six rooms around an inner courtyard, this welcoming pension enjoys an excellent location just below the Liars' Bridge. The rooms are narrow and not very light but otherwise represent some of the best value in town. The reception is open from 8am–11pm only. Breakfast not included. €

Sport Tineret
Str. Octavian Goga 2
Tel: 0269-233673
This somewhat austere youth sports hotel next to the stadium is worth a try if everywhere is full, as is often the case in summer. Breakfast not included at weekends, when the room prices are lower to compensate. €

11 Euro
Str. Tudor Vladimirescu 2
Tel: 0269-222041
So named because originally the cheapest room cost 11 euros, this hotel just over the river from the centre offers a choice of economy class and business class rooms, the cheapest being up three flights of stairs. All the rooms are clean, individually decorated and perfectly adequate. €

Mediaş

The Saxon Lutheran community offers simple guesthouse (Gästzimmer) accommodation (€) through Pfarrer Reinhart Guib (tel: 0269-846902; e-mail kastell@logon.ro) or Pfarrant Sekretärin Brigitte Both (tel: 0269-841962).

Traube
Piaţa Regele Ferdinand I nr 16
Tel: 0269-844898
www.dafora.ro
In a historic building on Mediaş's main square, this lovingly restored hotel feels every bit like the house of a rich Saxon merchant with the addition of the usual mod cons. Decorated with old and new Saxon furniture, it certainly packs in the wood factor. The size of a guest wing, the enormous apartment (€€€€), laid out with a mezzanine level, has to be seen to be believed. Most rooms have views over the courtyard; a few, including the apartment, over the square. Enchanting. €€

Select
Str. Petöfi Sándor 3
Tel: 0269-834874
This moderately successful coach house conversion offers reasonably comfortable if slightly cramped accommodation on a cobbled Saxon street that is one of the finest in town. €

Astra (Dumbrava Sibiului)

Muzeul civilizaţiei populare tradiţionale Astra
www.muzeulastra.ro/oferta/servicii_divertisment_cazare.php
If you find it hard to tear yourself away from the rural bliss of Romania's finest open-air museum, simple overnight accommodation is available here. Beds costs 45 lei a night per bed in a cabin and 25 lei a night in a bedroom. €

Sighişoara

In summer beware that accommodation is in short supply and should be

reserved in advance if possible. During the medieval festival it is common for people to offer private rooms or space in barns, etc. The most atmospheric places to stay are within the citadel, although cheaper options exist and distances are nothing to worry about. There are not many hotels in town and most are quite small. Best to book ahead, especially in July and Aug.

Casa cu Cerb
Str. Şcolii 1
Tel: 0265-774625
www.casacucerb.ro
In a lovingly restored historic building on the main square, the House with the Stag still has some features from the 13th century, including original frescoes. Restored by Germany's Messer-schmitt Foundation, which owns the building, it is surprisingly light and airy inside, with an impressive attention to detail. Although the rooms are comfortable rather than regal, it's not hard to see why The Prince of Wales stays here when he is in town. €€

Casa Wagner
Str. Piaţa Cetăţii 7
Tel: 0265-506014
www.casa-wagner.com
Yet another tastefully restored Saxon building on the main square, this one has comfortable rooms and enough Saxon furniture and fittings to set up an ethnography museum. Like the hugely romantic restaurant, this is understandably popular with couples of a certain age. €€

Sighişoara
Str. Şcolii 4–6
Tel: 0265-771000
www.sighisoara.com/hs/
Highly agreeable historic hotel just off the citadel's main square, with spacious rooms sharing a balcony overlooking the inner courtyard. However, while the general theme is understated medieval the rooms are relatively decor-free. Friendly service. A good deal but often full. €€

Burg Hostel
Str. Bastionului 4–6
Tel: 0265-778489
www.ibz.ro
Head and shoulders above most other hostels in terms of location and character, this one in the centre of Sighişoara dates from the early 14th century. Originally known as the House with the Wooden Roof (Casa cu şindril), it is one of the oldest buildings in the citadel and was restored in 2000–1 with the help of the German Government. €

Casa Costea
Str. Libertăţii 27
Tel: 0265-771237
In a house dating from 1903, this family-run pension near the train station has five very different rooms set around a lovely walled garden, with shared access to a kitchen and barn. Giving the hotels not so much a run for their money as a good thrashing, this is an excellent choice, especially for groups. The friendly owner cooks local specialities for guests and washes clothes as part of the service. €

Casa Sasească
Piaţa Cetăţii 12
Tel: 0265-772400
www.casasaseasca.com
Saxon-owned medieval building on the main square with spacious rooms superbly fitted out with specially commissioned Saxon furniture. No restaurant, although there are plenty to choose from nearby. €

Claudiu
Str. Ilarie Chendi 28
Tel: 0744-823101
www.hotel-claudiu.com
Just below the citadel, this small hotel is an odd combination of medieval-looking exterior and chalet-style interior. Comfortable if not especially spacious rooms. €

Steaua
Str. Gheorghe Doja 12
www.hotelsteaua.go.ro
The day grunge becomes the latest fashion in hotels, this sprawling place in the lower town will be packed. For now however, the

threadbare fusty carpets, a general fusty air and an exterior so crumbly there should be protective netting in place are the epitome of decay. Still, the rooms are better than you might expect, with high ceilings and more recent fittings. €

Odorheiu Secuiesc

Kükullo-Târnava
Piaţa Primăriei 16
Tel: 0266-213963
www.kukullo.ro
Good three-star hotel, with comfortable rooms, a pleasant lobby and Jacuzzi and sauna facilities. €€

Târgu Mureş

Concordia
Piaţa Trandafirilor 45
Tel: 0265-260602
www.hotelconcordia.ro
Heavy on designer features, Târgu Mureş's swishest hotel offers the last word in comfort and refinement – as well as room service by waiters dressed like Ruritanian monarchs – but at a price. Perfect for fashionistas. €€€€

Continental
Piaţa Teatrului 6
Tel: 0265-250416
www.continentalhotels.ro
Part of a communist-era set piece on Piaţa Teatrului, this place now has a slightly old-fashioned feel combined with the impersonality of a chain hotel. Although designed as a focal point, the square around it seems eerily quiet after dark. €€

Transilvania
Piaţa Trandafirilor 46
Tel: 0265-265616
www.unita-turism.ro
Although the rooms are basic, many with shared bathrooms or loos, the central location and value for money are unbeatable, and for all its mustiness the building manages to retain bags of period charm. €€

Voiajor
Str. Gheorghe Doja 143
Tel: 0265-250750
www.voiajor.ro
Decked out in psychedelic

colours, this strikingly futuristic hotel enjoys the improbable location of Târgu Mureş's bus station, which belongs to the same company. The rooms are as bright, pleasant enough and unlike anything you would expect at a Romanian bus station – as is the exterior. €€

Cluj-Napoca

Vila Bethlen Kata
Str. Ponorului 1
Tel: 0265-440510
Part of an ecumenical centre belonging to the Hungarian Reformed Church, this guesthouse in a well-to-do residential area offers the best value in town. While the accommodation is somewhat monastic and there are house rules to observe, the place is spotless, well-run and friendly. Smoking is not permitted and breakfast is at 8am sharp. Price includes breakfast. €€€

Melody
Piaţa Unirii 29
Tel: 0264-597465
www.hcm.ro
With an enviable location on the main square, this period hotel has comfortable if strangely divided rooms, all with balconies. For those overlooking the square, noise is a trade-off for the views. Reasonable value for such a central location, although less so for single rooms. €€

Victoria
B-dul. 21 Decembrie 1989 54–6
Tel: 0264-197963
http://pages.astral.ro/victoria
This thoroughly renovated hotel now looks almost alarmingly modernist, with a towering glass pod and circular galleries on

PRICE CATEGORIES

Price categories are for a double room without breakfast unless mentioned:
€ = under €50
€€ = €50–75
€€€ = €75–100
€€€€ = €100–150
€€€€€ = more than €150

the upper floors. While expanding into the former balconies has made the rooms larger they also have an odd shape as a result. A good choice for lovers of modern architecture. **€€**

Vila Meteor
Str. Meteor 37 A
Tel: 0264-438572
Despite the central location, this villa has a somewhat motel-like feel. But the rooms are comfortable, quiet and very good value for the centre. The entrance is through a passageway past the restaurant kitchen. Price includes breakfast. **€**

Alba Iulia

Parc
Str. Primăverii 4
Tel: 0258-811723
www.hotelparc.ro
Unlike the similarly communist-era Transilvania nearby, this hotel benefits from a thoroughly funky facelift that seems almost too hip for Albia Iulia,

with red and white stripes the theme. Inside the lobby, think flower power with a contemporary twist. The rooms show a similar flair. **€€€**

Cetate
Str. Unirii 3
Tel: 0258-815833
With a lift so decrepit many guests prefer to take the badly lit stairs, this place has clearly seen better days. The rooms are comfy if slightly cramped. Although decorated in a vaguely French-revival style, the clashing carpets somewhat spoil the effect. **€€**

Transilvania
Piața Iuliu Maniu 22
Tel: 0258-812546
Its communist-era concrete facade resembling a barbed-wire fence with jagged glass on top and bloodcurdlingly red almost runic script on the sign, makes this place look uninviting. But the rooms are comfortable and renovated and the service is friendly. **€€**

Hanul cu Berze
Str. Republicii 179
Tel: 0258-830129
Near the river, this inn offers simple but adequate accommodation, all with private bathrooms, and welcoming service. Some rooms are windowless. **€**

Deva

Wien
Calea Zarandului
Tel: 0254-233320
www.hotelwien.ro
The latest addition to Deva's hotel scene exudes Viennese style, mixed with Italian Renaissance art, sadly not original. Real character and panache marred only by a noisy location beside a busy road. **€€€**

Deva
B-dul 22 Decembrie 110
Tel: 0254-211290
Communist-vintage hotel on the main drag that has little to recommend it except a central location. Rooms at the Wien are

much better for only a fraction more. The rooms at the front have very narrow concrete balconies from which you can enjoy the traffic whizzing past. **€€**

Motel Maestro
Calea Zarandului 1
Tel: 0254-212821
www.oge.ro
Unusually welcoming motel a short distance south of the centre that is popular with expats, not least for its restaurant. **€€**

Pensiunea Sub Cetate
Str. Barbu Ștefanescu
Delavrancea 6A
Tel: 0254-212535
www.subcetate.ro
Beneath the citadel in the prettiest residential part of town, this lovely family-run pension makes a perfect home from home and is closer to the main attractions than most of the hotels. Unusually, breakfast is included in the price, giving a chance to chat with the friendly landlady. An excellent choice. **€**

CRIȘANA

Arad

Best Western Central
Str. Horia 8
Tel: 0257-256636
www.bestwesternarad.ro
Located next to Arad's town hall, this place is a decent enough hotel, with simple but clean and bright rooms in a friendly atmosphere. The fair rates include a good buffet breakfast. **€€€**

Continental Astoria
B-dul. Revolutiei 79–81
Tel: 0257-281700
www.continentalhotels.ro
Like most of the Continental hotels around Romania there is little to remark about this non-descript high-rise than the good service and large comfortable rooms. It does have its own small bowling alley, however, which we are fairly certain is unique in Romania. **€€€**

Marem
Calea Victoriei 2c
Tel: 0257-256110
www.maremhotel.com
Wonderfully eccentric little pension, with crazily painted exterior and garish but somehow delightfully charming rooms. About 15 minutes from the city centre, it costs peanuts to stay here and is highly recommended. **€**

Parc
B-dul. General Dragalina 25
Tel: 0257-282255
http://arad.inext.ro/websites/parc
Brilliantly located on the river with views to the citadel, this concrete box has enough going for it to overlook its ugliness: great prices, a good breakfast and large clean rooms (furnished in unmistakable socialist-era style). **€€**

President
Calea Timisorii 164
Tel: 0257-278804
www.hotel-president.ro

Expect bright big rooms, all of whose en-suite bathrooms have Jacuzzis, and super extras: a great outdoor swimming pool, tennis court and garden. The only problem is the location: some way out of the city centre on the road to Timișoara. **€€**

Băile Felix

President
no street address
Tel: 0259-318381
The best of Felix's hotels, this place is a resort within a resort offering – besides excellent rooms – thermal baths, indoor and outdoor swimming pools and a lovely garden. A great choice for families. **€€**

Termal
no street address
Tel: 0259-318214
Close to the large Felix strand in the northern part of the resort, the Termal is

a step above the majority of Felix's high-rises, and so is a little more pricey. **€€**

Oradea

Vulturul Negru
Str. Independentei 1
Tel: 0259-450000
www.vulturulnegru.ro
The city's finest hotel. This historic pile (see page XXX) has long been the choice of the great and good while visiting Oradea, and after years of state-run decline its recent privatisation and renovation has restored it to full luxury. From the lobby, with its

Titanic-esque staircase and retro reception desk, to the sublime rooms, this is the real deal. €€€

Atlantic
Str. Iosif Vulcan 9
Tel: 0259-426911
www.hotelatlantic.ro
The four floors of rooms and apartments at the four-star Atlantic all have a different theme: rustic, modern, colour, simple. The colour floor is the best, though costs slightly more, as the rooms are large. Good breakfast included, and the location close to the city centre is great. €€

Continental Dacia
Aleea Strandului 1
Tel: 0259-418656
www.continentalhotels.ro
On the banks of the Crisul River, this ugly concrete

block is home to some decent rooms and its own thermal bath, open year round and free to guests. Good buffet breakfast. €€

Eden
Str. Cantacuzino 4
Tel: 0259-433222
www.hoteleden.ro
Modern, well-furnished – if a little small – rooms in a smart little building about 15 minutes walk from the city centre. The location is quiet, except when FC Bihor is playing at the stadium opposite. €€

Elite
Str. I.C. Bratianu 26
Tel: 0259-414924
While the building itself is not without charm, it is the classy interiors of this surprisingly good four-star hotel that make it stand

out from much of its competition in Oradea. Well located – you'll find it opposite the large central Bratianu Park. €€

Parc
B-dul. Republicii 5
Tel: 0259-411699
Good-sized, cheap and generally clean rooms that will please bargain hunters looking for a city centre location. A touch noisy and a bit, dare we say, stuffy however. Families should steer clear of the place. €

Stana de Vale

Vilele Izvorul Minunilor
Tel: 0259-407285 (Turist Center Agency)
www.turistcenter.ro
Situated close to the ski

lifts, these seven lovely little villas each have two bedrooms, a living room, a bathroom complete with Jacuzzi and a small kitchen. At a push they can sleep six. You'll have to reserve in advance, and can only do so through Turist Center. €€

Iadolina
Tel: 0259-407285 (Turist Center Agency)
www.turistcenter.ro
Large, recently refurbished hotel that, with its restaurant, bar and hydro-therapy treatment centre, serves as the centre of the resort. The best rooms here are those on the top floor, which have gently and attractively sloping ceilings. Also convenient for the ski lifts. €€

THE BANAT

Băile Herculane

Ferdinand
Piaţa Hercules 1
Tel: 0255-561121
www.hotel-ferdinand.ro
It is to be hoped that the recent renovation of this Habsburg-era hotel is to be a catalyst for the revival of the entire historic centre of Baile Herculane. It is certainly a great start, with its luxurious rooms and wonderful summer garden terraces and restaurant. €€€

Claudia
Str. Complexelor 9
Tel: 0255-560170
www.hotelbaileherculane.ro
Perched rather precariously halfway up the side of a mountain in the upper part of the resort, the Claudia offers simple rooms of which those at the front have quite

stunning views (and which cost a little extra). €€

Roman
Str. Romana 1
Tel: 0255-560390
Monolithic and entirely no-frills establishment (usually full with Romanian pensioners on packages) that nevertheless gets a recommendation for its access to the vast Roman thermal-bath complex in the basement: free to guests. €

Vila Belvedere
Str. N. Stoica de Haţeg 6–8
Tel: 0255-560886
More rooms with a view in the upper part of Herculane. Though a little on the small side the place is well cared for, staff are friendly and there is a nice garden. €

Drobeta Turnu Severin

Continental
B-dul. Carol I 2
Tel: 0252-306730
www.continentalhotels.ro
If fate takes a turn for the worse and you find yourself facing a night in Turnu Severin, you will at least spend it in comfort in this ugly but pleasant

hotel. It has great rooms, a decent terrace with café and children's play area. €€

Semenic

Dusan si Fiul
no street address
Tel: 0742-044944
www.dusansifiul.ro
Though it looks a little strange from outside, this red and orange beast is the best hotel in this small ski resort, with large rooms and apart-ments, a sauna and gym, besides quad bike and ski hire. €€

Timişoara

Boavista
Aleea FC Ripensia 7A
Tel: 0256-309409
www.hotelboavista.ro
The name? Strange, yes, but this place is owned by a former footballer who used to play in Portugal for Boavista. Tastefully decorated with generously sized rooms, the only complaint is the lack of bathtubs in the bath-rooms. It is located a 20-minute walk from the city centre. €€€

Boca Junior
Str. Simion Barnutiu 29
Tel: 0256-400222
www.hotelbocajunior.ro
Another hotel named after a football team, this is a decent four star offering good value and really rather large rooms in a quiet setting on the road out to the airport. Sauna and fitness centre free for guests, as is a great breakfast spread. €€

BW Ambasador
Str. Mangalia 3
Tel: 0256-306880
www.ambassador.ro
About 10 minutes from the historic centre of Timişoara, this is a nice enough place noteworthy for its integral art gallery: most of what you see on the walls, either in the lobby or on the wall of your room is a work by a local artist, and is for sale. €€

TRANSPORT
ACCOMMODATION
ACTIVITIES
A – Z
LANGUAGE

Casa del Sole
Str. Romulus 12
Tel: 0256-306433
www.casadelsole.ro
Super pension with eight
rooms individually furnished
in the most elegant style, it
has a large outdoor pool and
terrace – which hosts great
barbecues in summer – and
a good bistro. It is a fair walk
from the centre. €€

Continental
B-dul Revolutiei 1989 2
Tel: 0256-194144
www.hotelcontinental.ro

If you want to be close to the
city centre then this is as
good as it gets. A
nondescript high-rise, this
hotel has good rooms and
service. The buffet breakfast
is a treat, though the seedy
nightclub in the basement is
to be avoided. €€

Timişoara
Str. Marasesti 1–3
Tel: 0256-498852
www.hoteltimisoara.ro
Looking far better on the
inside than out, this is a
decent city centre hotel

though the rooms are a bit
too expensive for what you
get – rates are lower at
weekends. €€

President
Str. D. Lipatti 25
Tel: 0256-293797
www.hotelpresident.ro
A tremendously good-value
and modern hotel with big,
spacious rooms, a great
restaurant and terrific
staff that loses some of
its appeal when you
discover it is in the far
north of the city. €€

Tresor
Aleea Ghirodei 32
Tel: 0256-228755
www.hoteltresor.ro
Refinement, marked by a
grand lobby and staircase
leading up to some super
rooms with enormous high
ceilings, is the byword for
this superb pension. Add
in decent prices, a large
outdoor pool and terrace,
and a good little bistro and
you have a great package.
It is a taxi ride from the
city centre though. €

MOLDAVIA

Iaşi

*Beware that accommo-
dation becomes almost
unobtainable during the
St Parascheva Festival in
early October unless
booked months ahead.*

Europa
Str. Atanasie Panu 26
Tel: 0232-242000
www.hoteleuropa.ro
Comfortable if sterile option
in the same complex as
Iaşi's World Trade Center.
Popular with business
travellers, although rooms
are not significantly better
than in the much cheaper
Unirea or Astoria. €€€

Little Texas
Str. Moara de Vânt 31 (halfway out
to the airport)
Tel: 0232-272545
www.littletexas.org
This stylish ranch-like hotel
combines Texan architecture
with some of the best views
– and balconies to enjoy
them – in town. Under
US ownership, this place
offers a strong feeling of
exclusivity and class in a
tranquil semi-rural location.
It may, however, be a little
too far from the centre
for some people. If the
architecture seems out of
place in Iaşi, it is interesting
to see how many of the
modern villas in the
neighbouring district are
in a similar style. €€€

Traian
Piaţa Unirii 1
Tel: 0232-266666
www.grandhoteltraian.ro

The *grande dame* of Iaşi's
hotels, this Eiffel-designed
place on the main square
harks back to the *belle
époque* and is slowly being
restored to its former glory.
For a dash of elegance it's
hard to beat. Very spacious
rooms, all decorated with
reproduction period French
furniture. €€€

Astoria
Str. Lăpuşneanu 1
Tel: 0232-233888
www.hotelastoria.ro
Although overshadowed by
its grander sister hotel, the
Traian next door, this
elegant hotel offers an
excellent combination of
location, comfort and value
for money. The transparent
glass and metal lift is
about as state-of-art as you
can get. Beware, however,
that the fitness centre
advertised in the hotel
brochure doesn't yet exist.
Discounts available on
Sat and Sun nights. €€

Unirea
Piaţa Unirii 5
Tel: 0232-205000
www.hotelunirea.ro
Although this communist-
era building is such an ill-
mannered addition to Iaşi's
main square that it could
almost have been placed
here as a practical joke,
the interior has been
extensively and fairly
tastefully renovated with all
manner of state-of-the art
facilities. For location and
value, this place takes
some beating. Beware that
the hotel basement hosts a

disco on Saturday nights
and the noise can carry to
lower floors. €€

Continental
Str. Cuza Vodă 4
Tel: 0232-211846
Beneath the shabby facade
of this crumbling behemoth
there lurks an even
shabbier interior, with
spartan accommodation,
Formica decor, tiny old
Omega TVs in the rooms
and a lift lined with old
carpet castoffs of 1950s
pedigree. Still, for cheap
accommodation in a central
location, this place is hard
to beat. €

Apartment Rental
Comfortable rooms are
available to hire from Travis
Turism (tel: 0232-237171;
www.travis.ro) at B-dul Ştefan
cel Mare 1. Rents vary
from €19–42 per day
depending on the location
and length of stay.

Piatra Neamţ

Ceahlău
Piaţa Ştefan cel Mare 3
Tel: 0233-219990
www.welcome.to/grandhotel
Looking like 1960s council
housing on the demolition
list, this carbuncle seems
to have been designed
specifically to mar the
hillscape overlooking Piatra
Neamţ. The hotel offers
both renovated and
unrenovated rooms. The
first have an almost funky
decor, while the second are
very tired aesthetically but

offer the bonus of a fridge.
Ask for a room with a view
at the back. Much better
value than the Central. €€

Central
Piaţa Petrodava 1–3
Tel: 0233-216230
www.hotelcentral.ro
Although not quite as
unsympathetic to its
surroundings as the
Ceahlău, this high-rise
concrete monstrosity is of
similar architectural
pedigree with all the
charm of a secret-police
headquarters. Inside, the
rooms are badly in need of
a makeover. Some rooms
have air conditioning at an
extra cost. Despite its
name, the Central is
slightly less close to the
main tourist attractions
than the Ceahlău. €€

Monasteries
Anyone looking for a
spiritual retreat or simply
an unusually tranquil place
to stay should enquire
about accommodation in a
monastery. In Moldavia,
monasteries offering rooms
(€) to paying guests in
often unbeatable locations
include **Agapia Monastery**
(Mănăstirea Agapia; Com.

Agapia; tel: 0233-244618, 0233-244736) and **Pângărați Monastery** (Mănăstirea Pângărați;

Com. Pângărați; tel: 0233-240337). Smoking isn't permitted within monastery grounds and food is not

usually provided. Although it's possible to arrange accommodation on the spot, advance booking is prefer-

able, especially in the height of summer. The tourist office in Piatra Neamț can provide more information.

BUKOVINA

Gura Humorului

Best Western Bucovina
Piața Republicii
Tel: 0230-207000
www.bestwesternbucovina.ro
The best hotel in the region, this is an enormous, 10-storey building that manages to blend in with the surroundings given its somewhat daring design. There are a variety of rooms to choose from, from rustic to modern. There is a large health spa on site with sauna, Jacuzzi, massage and gym. €€€€

Sucevita

Dagida
Sucevita
Tel: 0744-139335
www.dagida.ro
A great base from which to explore the monasteries, this is a modern, comfortable hotel with a back-to-nature remoteness that will

appeal to those looking for peace and quiet. Good double rooms, or a separate four-bedroom cabin out the back. €€

Suceava

Balada
Str. Mitropoliei 3
Tel: 0230-522146
www.balada.ro
Close to Suceava Fortress, a longish walk from the city centre, the Balada is a good little hotel with large and well-appointed rooms which all have superbly decorated bathrooms. €€€
Continental
Str. Mihai Viteazul 4–6
Tel: 0230-210944
www.continentalhotels.ro
Simple but large and well-appointed rooms in a fine, leafy setting make this a decent, good-value choice. The terrace is a lovely place to take breakfast in summer. €€€€

Câmpulung Moldovenesc

Eden
Calea Bucovinei 148
Tel: 0230-314733
www.hotel-eden.ro
Halfway between Suceava and Vatra Dornei, this complex is a perfect spot from which to explore the monasteries. There is a bright, simple hotel, colourfully painted bungalows and a wooden villa to choose from. €€

Vatra Dornei

Carol
Str. Republicii 3
Tel: 0230-374690
www.hotelcarol.ro
Looking like an imperial castle from outside, rooms at this grand establishment are modern and surprisingly reasonably priced. The best thing about the place, however, is the great restaurant serving a variety of local delicacies. €€

Complex Bradul – Calimani
Str. Republicii 5A
Tel: 0230-375314
Smart but well-priced hotel at the foot of the Vatra Dornei pistes. For what you are paying you get an awful lot of room, and a buffet breakfast the envy of most other hotels in the resort. €
Maestro
Str. Republicii
Tel: 0230-375288
Situated in the centre of the resort, this place is cheap and cheerful, though check out the room you are offered before taking it: many have two single beds placed end to end, not side by side. €

MARAMUREȘ

Sarasau

Pensiunea Alisa
Sarasau 729
Tel: 0262-371136
Probably the most comfortable place to stay in Maramureș. This is a gorgeous pension in Sarasau, halfway between Sighetul Marmatiei and the Merry Cemetery at Sapânța. There are just three rooms, as well as a garden, a farm, and the Sopron restaurant, serving a variety of local dishes. €

Sighetul Marmației

Coroana
Piața Libertatii 21

Tel: 0262-311610
On Sighet's central square this is a recently renovated two-star hotel with modern if simple and cheap rooms, all of which have en-suite bathrooms and come equipped with televisions. €
Perla Sigheteana
Str. Avram Iancu 65/A
Tel: 0262-310613
A not altogether unpleasant-looking motel and restaurant about 2 km (1 mile) from the historic centre of Sighet, on the road to Sarasau and Sapânta. Rooms might be a bit garish for some, but service is good and friendly and prices are cheap. €

Satu Mare

Aurora
Piața Libertatii 11
Tel: 0261-714946
www.aurora-sm.ro
This 1970s concrete hulk in the middle of town was recently renovated and now offers eight floors of reasonable, good-value rooms and apartments. €€
Dacia
Piața Libertatii 8
Tel: 0261-715774
www.hoteldacia.ro
This place has been hosting guests since 1902, and though most rooms have been modernised since then, the lobby retains a real sense of the past. It is the best place in Satu

Mare, and is well located on the city's central square. €

PRICE CATEGORIES

Price categories are for a double room without breakfast unless mentioned:
€ = under €50
€€ = €50–75
€€€ = €75–100
€€€€ = €100–150
€€€€€ = more than €150

A CTIVITIES

THE ARTS, NIGHTLIFE, CHILDREN'S ACTIVITIES, FESTIVALS, SHOPPING, SPORTS AND TOURS

THE ARTS

Theatre

Bucharest is the main hotbed of theatrical activity, with more than 30 state-financed and independent theatres vying for the patronage of the city's theatre-goers. The National Theatre (see page 115) on Piața Universității is the largest in the country, and besides a mainstream repertoire of Romanian and foreign pieces, it also hosts musicals and the occasional concert. Other, more intimate, theatres include the Small Theatre (Teatrul Mic), an auditorium so tiny it will make you curious to visit the even more miniscule Very Small Theatre (Teatrul Foarte Mic). The Bulandra, Comedy Theatre (Teatru de Comedie) and the Odeon are also known for the quality of their performers. You will rarely find a performance in a language other than Romanian, however.

Outside the capital, Sibiu's Radu Stanca National Theatre (Teatru Național Radu Stanca) hosts a theatre festival every September, while Timișoara's State Opera House and National Theatre (Teatrul de Stat și Opera Română) is a gorgeous auditorium in which to enjoy quality theatre. Oradea's State Theatre is a grand neoclassical building designed by the Viennese pair, Ferdinand Fellner and Hermann Helmer, and stages lavish productions in both Romanian and Hungarian; while there is a dedicated Hungarian language theatre in Cluj, the Hungarian State Theatre (Teatrul Maghiar de Stat). The city's Romanian theatre (Teatrul Național) is equally celebrated. Cluj is also home to the very good Puppet Theatre (Teatrul de Papuși).

For open-air theatre try the Sighișoara Medieval Arts Festival (see page 358).

Bucharest

Teatrul Național
B-dul. Nicolae Bălcescu 2
Tel: 021-313 9175
http://tnb.kappa.ro
Puts on just about everything from musicals to Shakespeare. Details of what's on from the box office on the ground floor, open daily 10am–4pm.
Teatrul Mic
Str. Constantin Mille 16
Tel: 021-314 7081
www.teatrulmic.ro
The domain of Florin Calinescu, one of the country's best actors and a well-known television presenter.
Teatrul Foarte Mic
B-dul. Carol 21
Tel: 021-314 0905
Intimate and enchanting; watching a play here is a personal and rewarding experience.
Teatrul Bulandra
Sala Toma Caragiu, Str. Calderon 76A
Tel: 021-212 0527
www.bulandra.ro
Features a courageously experimental repertoire.
Teatrul Odeon
Calea Victoriei 40–42
Tel: 021-314 7234
www.teatrul-odeon.ro
Mainstream Russian classics and Shakespeare in a wonderful Secessionist playhouse.
Teatrul de Comedie
Str. Sfântul Dumitru 2
Tel: 021-315 9137
www.comedie.ro
Comedy, Romanian style, although many productions are local interpretations of foreign classics.

Cluj

Teatrul Național
Piața Stefan cel Mare 24
Tel: 0264-591799
Cluj's Romanian theatre.
Teatrul Maghiar de Stat
Str. E. Isac 26–28
Tel: 0264-593469
www.huntheater.ro
Those who call the city Kolosvar (see page 233) take in their culture here.
Teatrul de Papuși PUCK
Str. Ion I. C. Bratianu 23
Tel: 0264-595992
www.teatrulpuck.ro
Romania's best puppet theatre will be a hit with kids whatever language they speak.

Oradea

Teatrul de Stat
Piața Ferdinand 4–6
Tel: 0259-236592
Classical and quite lavish productions take place in this gorgeous auditorium.

Sibiu

Teatrul Național Radu Stanca
Str. Corneliu Coposu 2
Tel: 0269-210092
www.sibfest.ro
German and Romanian plays are performed at this large and impressive theatre. It also attracts the occasional touring troupe from western Europe, including the UK.

Timișoara

Teatrul de Stat
Str. Marasesti 2
Tel: 0256-201291
www.infotim.ro/tgst
A good theatre company performs contemporary Romanian work in Timișoara's opera house.

Opera and Ballet

The Romanian National Opera shares the 1950s neoclassical Bucharest Opera House with the country's national ballet company. They stage decent, well-performed productions, although relatively low-budget. There's a rather unadventurous repertoire, with the Puccini classics given a thorough outing every season (September to June). Ticket prices are extraordinarily cheap.

In the provinces the best opera companies are to be found at Cluj (where it occupies the wonderful Opera Română din Cluj-Napoca), Timișoara, Brașov, Iași and Oradea. Opera in Romania is performed in the original language with Romanian subtitles projected above the stage. The Teatru Național in Târgu Mureș sometimes stages the Hungarian epic *Bank Ban*. George Enescu's *Oédipe* is almost never performed in Romania's opera houses as it is not considered a mainstream work.

The national ballet company in Bucharest usually sticks to an equally classical repertoire, rarely performing anything more challenging than *Swan Lake*, *Coppelia* and *The Nutcracker*. However, a daring new production of *Cassanova* in early 2007 does herald promise of more adventurous productions.

Bucharest

Opera Naționala Română
B-dul. Mihail Kogălniceanu 70–72
Tel: 021-3146980
www.operanb.ro
The box office is open daily from 10am–noon. All performances begin at 6.30pm and latecomers are not admitted. No sports shoes or jeans.

Brașov

Opera Brașov
Str. Bisericii Romane 51
Tel: 0268-415990
www.opera-brasov.ro
The weakest of the regional operas, but, as elsewhere, ticket prices are cheap and performances are, at least, worthy.

Cluj

Opera Naționala Română
Piața Cel Mare 24
Tel: 0264-597175
www.operacluj.com
Decent performances from a company that spends much of its time touring.

Iași

Opera Naționala Română
Str. Agatha Barsescu 18
Tel: 0232-211144

Probably the best opera company in the country, after Bucharest. It regularly features guest sopranos from the Moldovan State Opera in Chișinău.

Târgu Mureș

Teatru Național
Piața Teatrului 1
Tel: 0265-164848
The theatre occasionally stages Hungarian operas.

Timișoara

Opera de Stat
Str. Marasesti 2
Tel: 0256-433020
www.opera-timisoara.ro
A good repertoire of mainly Italian operas keeps the large Italian expat community of the city coming back for more.

Concerts

Fans of classical music are in for a real treat in Romania, especially those spending any time in the capital. The Ateneu Român hosts the George Enescu Philharmonic Orchestra, quite simply one of the greatest orchestras in the world. Seeing one of their concerts, led by head conductor Cristian Mandeal, under a ceiling adorned with Costin Petrescu frescoes, is a highlight of any trip to Romania. Concerts usually take place here every Thursday, Friday and Saturday evening at 7pm. During September the George Enescu Philharmonic is the host orchestra for the Enescu Festival, a three-week celebration of the life and work of Enescu, which attracts some of the finest musicians in the world.

There is also high-quality music on offer in the capital at the Sala Radio, the auditorium of Romanian Radio. There are concerts and recitals most evening, with matinee performances at 11am on Saturday.

The Sibiu Philharmonic is the second most important in the country, closely followed by the State Philharmonic in Cluj-Napoca. Up in Iași the city's State Philharmonic puts on performances

Buying Tickets

In most cases theatre tickets can only be purchased from the theatres themselves, although in Bucharest the bigger productions sometimes offer tickets for sale via the website www.bilete.ro. There is no central booking agency anywhere in Romania.

every evening. In all Romania's concert halls you will be able to hear a mixture of music far more adventurous and daring than you would perhaps expect. One piece you will almost certainly *not* hear however is Enescu's *Romanian Rhapsody*.

Bucharest

Philharmonic George Enescu
Ateneu Român
Str. Franklin 1
Tel: 021-315 6875
www.bucharest-philharmonic.ro
Societate Română de Radiodifuziune
Studioul de concerte Mihail Jora
Str. Genereal Berthelot 60–64
Tel: 021-222 2241
www.srr.ro

Cluj

State Philharmonic
Piața Stefan cel Mare 4
Tel: 0264-430060
www.cluj-philharmonic.org

Sibiu

Sibiu Philharmonic
Str. Filarmonicii 2
Tel: 0269-210264
www.filarmonicasibiu.ro

NIGHTLIFE

No city in Romania can match London, Paris or Berlin for nightlife, but Bucharest and – in the summer – Mamaia are endeavouring to hold their own against smaller European destinations as far as nightlife is concerned. Bars, pubs and clubs all compete with casinos and live music venues to bring in those looking for night-time adventure, with more and more places now splashing out serious money to bring over big-name DJs. The top clubs in the capital offer at least one well-known DJ every week, while local DJs, some of whom, such as Rhadoo, Magda and Vali Barbulescu, have big followings, can be seen from time to time in the provinces. The website www.inyourpocket.com/romania has plenty of information on the capital's nightlife scene.

Live music is still limited to local bands, of which there has been an explosion since 1990. Most are of the forgettable Europop variety (the Eurovision Song Contest is taken very seriously in Romania) but there are notable exceptions. *Zdob si Zdub* (from the Republic of Moldova), *Sarmalele Reci*, *Vama Veche* and *Sistem* are all worth catching if you get the opportunity. Live concerts in Romania are often free, public affairs, paid for by local councils and held in town squares. Big Western pop and rock names rarely perform in Romania. When Depeche Mode came to Bucharest in the summer of 2006 it was the biggest music event in the country's history. Romania likes jazz, and there are two very good jazz clubs in Bucharest.

Romanians mostly develop a taste for late nights from an early age (notice how local people steadfastly refuse to send their children to bed at a reasonable hour) and wherever you are in the country you will never be short of a place to either shake your thing or just sit and enjoy a late drink or coffee. You will be amazed, in the Transylvanian countryside, to find that the local bar owner may readily get out of bed to open up his bar if he hears foreigners want a drop of his ţuică.

There is also a seedy side to nightlife in Romania that merits a word of warning. Prostitution is illegal, despite any appearances to the contrary. Also take care if you are tempted by one of the many strip clubs that can be found easily in Bucharest, Timişoara, Iaşi and Constanţa: many are merely front operations for illegal brothels and all should be avoided. At the very least you will be ripped off by paying over the odds for drinks. In a nutshell, if you are thinking of coming to Romanian for a bout of sin, forget it.

Bucharest

Clubs & Discos

Bamboo
Str. Ramuri Tei 39
Tel: 0723-226266
www.bamboosportingclub.ro
On a hot summer's evening in the capital this open-air venue fills up with the trendiest and best-dressed clubbers in the city.
Cuba
Str. Oltetului 30
Tel: 0744-305503
Another open-air venue that succeeds in being just a little less posey than Bamboo, and is nowhere near as expensive or exclusive.
Embryo
Str. Ion Oteteleseanu 3a
Tel: 0727-379023
www.embryo.ro
Achingly cool bar and club with futuristic decoration and a crowd that comes to see and be seen. It might be a bit too trendy for some tastes.
EXIT
Str. Covaci 6
Tel: 021-313 7580

www.amsterdam.ro
Great club where good DJs play excellent music to a mainstream crowd on Thursday, Friday and Saturday night. You'll find it under the Amsterdam café *(see below)*.
Kristal
Str. J. S. Bach 2
Tel: 021-231 2136
www.clubkristal.ro
The best club in Bucharest, and the venue that really got the ball rolling with imported DJs. Open Friday and Saturday night only; you will need to take a taxi out here.
Oldies
Calea Mosilor 91
Tel: 0723-666551
If you want oldies – both in terms of 1970s and '80s music and a more mature crowd – then this is the place to come.
Salsa III
Str. Mihai Eminescu 89
Tel: 0723-531841
Latino rhythms every night of the week keep Romanians dancing and making it all look so very easy.
Studio Martin
B-dul. Iancu de Hunedoara 41
Tel: 0722-399228
The most serious rival to Kristal's title as club king. You'll find a top international DJ spinning records here every Friday and Saturday night.
Stuf
Str. Berzei 25A
Tel: 0745-694791
Another down-to-earth place where an older crowd dances to a mix of music, mainly from decades long gone.
Twice
Str. Sf. Vineri 4
Tel: 021-313 5592
Fun and sexy, this place brings in a teenybopper set looking for some Friday night action. Hot and sweaty, you should dress down.

Jazz & Music Clubs

Art Jazz Club
B-dul. N. Bălcescu 23A
Tel: 0723-52043
As cool as you like, this place brings in a knowing, jazz-loving crowd that enjoys listening to the more experimental stuff performed here.
Green Hours
Calea Victoriei 120
Tel: 021-314 5751
www.green-hours.ro
A more mainstream jazz club and garden where you can expect to hear decent music every night except Monday, when there is usually a play.
Laptaria Enache/La Motor
B-dul. Nicolae Bălcescu 2
Tel: 021-315 8508

www.laptaria.totalnet.ro
On the roof of the National Theatre, this place is a legend. During winter the action takes place inside: a long bar with a stage at one end hosting local rock bands most evenings. In summer, everyone sits on the vast rooftop terrace.
Music Club
Str. Baratiei 31
Tel: 021-314 6197
A big hit ever since it opened in 2006, this is where Romania's musical stars come to party and let their hair down. As a result the resident band is often joined on stage by well-known local performers.

Pubs & Bars

Amsterdam
Str. Covaci 6
Tel: 021-313 7580
www.amsterdam.ro
Single-handedly, this place helped make the Lipscani area a great place to be once more. Eat great goulash and bar food by day, mingle with hip young people by night.
Backstage
Str. Gabroveni 14
Tel: 021-312 3943
www.backstage.ro
Student-centred bar and club with few pretensions except making sure everybody enjoys themselves.
Bavaria Pub
Str. Orhideelor 19
Tel: 021-316 6403
www.bavariapub.ro
Rather tawdry kind of place with mud wrestling, male strippers and all sorts of goings-on, but the loud young student crowd that flocks here loves it.
Café & Terrace
Str. Franklin 12
Tel: 021-310 1017
www.cafeterrace.ro
Bucharest's best terrace, looking out on Piata Revolutiei. Enjoy decent food and drink and live sports on the big screens.
Coyote Café
Calea Victoriei 48–50 (Pasajul Victoriei)
Tel: 021-311 3487
Cavernous cellar bar and rock club where you can enjoy live, bang-them-out classics most evenings from a very good house band.
Déjà vu
B-dul. Nicolae Bălcescu 25
Tel: 021-311 2322
For the best cocktails in the city and the most lively good-time crowd you could hope for, this outstanding undergound bar is the place to come. Expect to make new

friends and stay until very late.
Dubliner
B-dul. N. Titulescu 18
Tel: 021-222 9473
www.irishpubs.ro
Romania's original expat pub is still
bringing in a crowd of local ne'er do
wells to watch football, rugby and
cricket via satellite on the big
screens. Guinness and great steak
and kidney pies.
English Bar
Str. Epicopiei 1–3 (Athenee Palace
Hilton)
Tel: 021-303 3777, ext. 3962
Legendary bar in a legendary hotel.
Little has changed since Olivia
Manning set much of the *Balkan
Trilogy* in its intrigue-filled nooks and
crannies.
Harp
Str. Bibescu Voda 1
Tel: 021-335 6508
Another large Irish pub serving
Guinness and pies to a mainly local
crowd. Superb location on Piața
Unirii.
Planters
Str. Mendeleev 8–10
Tel: 0723-559908
Loud and proud, this place is not
exactly sophisticated and attracts a
few rowdies, but it remains a life-
affirming kind of pub where anything
could happen and quite often does.
Terminus
Str. George Enescu 5
Tel: 021-318 1667
Basement pub that must be one of
the city's fire hazards. That doesn't
stop local people flocking here to
enjoy Guinness, clouds of cigarette
smoke and loud music.
Temple
Splaiul Independentei (Colț cu Selari)
Tel: 0727-297610
An all-female staff of bartenders (the
Bar Goddesses, they call
themselves) and a great cocktail list
make this a popular favourite.
The Office
Str. Tache Ionescu 2
Tel: 021-211 6748
www.theoffice.ro
The most exensive and pretentious
bar in town it may be, but you cannot
help having a good time here: just
make sure you check with your bank
manager before going inside.
Turabo Café
Str. Episcopiei 6
Tel: 0748-110000
www.turabo-cafe.ro
Trendy café serving a great selection
of pastries and cakes in a superb
location behind Piața Revoluției.
Via Café
Str. Bibescu Voda 1
Tel: 021-337 2978
www.viacafe.ro

With tremendous views out across
Piața Unirii from its upper level, this
café and bar is a great place to stop
for a break.
White Horse
Str. George Călinescu 4A
Tel: 021-231 2795
Another of the original expat bars,
still attracting a loyal following. The
restaurant upstairs serves a good
selection of hearty international fare.
Yellow Bar
Str. Edgar Quinet 10
Tel: 021-310 1351
Great little cellar cocktail bar with the
comfiest, reddest and downright
sexiest sofas in the city. The cocktail
list runs to many pages.

Outside the Capital

Brașov

Deane's
Str. Republicii 19
Tel: 0268-411767
www.deanes.ro
Every night of the week there's
something fun going on at Deane's,
from the owner – singing doctor
Haydn Deane and his Big Band – to
the most boisterous karaoke in the
land.
Festival 39
Str. Muresenilor 23
Tel: 0722-470129
Small but relaxing and eternally
popular bar famed for its top
selection of coffee, cognac and
cigars.
Hush Hush Club
Str. Avram Iancu 76
Tel: 0723-521375
www.hushhush.ro
Brasov's top club buzzes on weekend
nights until very late, as Romania's
best DJs spin the latest club sounds.

Cluj

Autograf
Str. Memorandumului 23
Great club for a more mature crowd
that enjoys listening and dancing to
classic tunes, or taking in one of the
regular folk and rock concerts that
are held here.
Diesel
Piața Unirii 17
Tel: 0264-58441
www.dieselclub.com
A smart lounge, bar and club in the
centre of Cluj, the current favourite of
the city's hip set. Expect high prices,
high times and some fantastic dance
music from the resident DJ.
King Club
Str. Roosevelt 12
Tel: 0264-591605
Rough-and-ready rock club where
there are live bands almost every
night of the week. When the band

isn't playing, great music from
decades past and present is.

Iași

Byblos
B-dul. Carol 48
Tel: 0232-757575
www.byblosclub.ro
Serious dance-music venue for
serious clubbers. You will find a top-
name Romanian DJ here every Friday
and Saturday night.
XS Club
Piața Unirii 5 (Hotel Unirea)
Tel: 0740-55426
www.xsclub.ro
If you stick around long enough you
will find something for everyone in
this eclectic club: dance music with
international DJs, rock concerts and
experimental theatre.

Mamaia

La Mania
Hotel Lido
Tel: 0241-611716
www.lamania.ro
This is where Bucharest's rich set
comes to party in August. It's the
best club on the coast but it gets
very busy and you may have to show
up early – or with a local celebrity.
Ultima Playa
North Mamaia
A more laid-back, fully open-air club
on one of Mamaia's best private
beaches. It really *is* the last beach:
take the last left turn before exiting
the northern side of the resort.

Sibiu

Art Café
Str. Filarmonicii 2
Tel: 0722-265992
As smoky as hell, but this place is a
great late-night drinking venue full of
cool and trendy art-house types.
Club Chill Out
Piața Mica 23
Tel: 0722-246640
www.chilloutsibiu.ro
A huge indoor/outdoor venue that
manages to combine trendy decor with
an unpretentious atmosphere. Great
DJs playing serious dance music.
Cotton Club
Str. Dr. Ion Ratiu 9
Tel: 0269-211516
www.cottonclub.ro
The best late-night option in Sibiu.
Don't be put off by the less-than-
welcoming entrance: this
subterranean bar/disco is immensely
popular.
Imperium Pub
Strada Nicolae Bălcescu 24
Tel. 0269-226744
Sibiu's best live music venue.
Music every night jazz, blues
and rock.

What's On Listings

Throughout Romania two heavily competing weekly free sheets provide information on the latest bar and club openings, concerts and events. One is called *Șapte Seri*, the other *B24 Fun*. While both are in Romanian, listings such as the cinema programme or concert information should be relatively simple to understand.

For details of bars, pubs and clubs in Bucharest turn to a copy of *Bucharest In Your Pocket (see maps, page 367)*, or head for the gossip website www.psst.ro. For a full schedule of what's on at Romania's cinemas go to www.cinema.ro.

Timișoara

Escape
Parcul Justitiei 1
Tel: 0256-493097
Timișoara's top venue is an eclectic place and you never quite know what you are going to get. It could be Italo-disco, it could be a Sinatra night, or it could be cutting-edge house music. Just go and enjoy it.

Park Place
Str. Mihai Viteazul 1
Tel: 0256-296323
Another large, multi-purpose venue that hosts concerts and club nights. Weekends are mainly given over to DJs, including the odd star name from abroad.

Tunnel
Str. Maraseşti 12
Tel: 0256-295318
Vast cellar pub in the heart of the old town, which offers a great atmosphere from lunch time until early the next morning. Always a lively crowd, and the music is good but never loud enough to prevent conversation.

Casinos

Casinos are a big fixture on Bucharest's nightscape, and gambling is one of the city's main attractions for an increasing number of visitors. The city has a great selection of casinos, some of which are as plush and exclusive as you could wish for. They all offer black-jack, roulette and a vast array of slot machines. You need to be over 21 to gamble at a casino in Romania, and you will need to take your passport. Chips can be bought with lei, dollars and euros.

Bucharest

Casino Bucharest
B-dul. Nicolae Bălcescu 4

(InterContinental Hotel)
Tel: 021-310 2020, ext 7592
www.casinobucharest.ro
Casino Palace
Calea Victoriei 133
Tel: 021-311 9744
www.casinopalace.ro
Grand Casino
Calea 13 Septembrie 90
(JW Marriott Grand Hotel)
Tel: 021-403 0801
Princess Casino
B-dul. Regina Elisabeta 13
Tel: 021-310 3910
Queen Casino
(Howard Johnson Grand Plaza)
Calea Dorobantilor 5–7
Tel: 021-201 5000
www.queen-casino.ro

Timișoara

Casino Caesar
Str. 1 Mai 2 (Hotel Timișoara)
Tel: 0256-430931
Casino Senitor
Calea Lugojului
Tel: 0256-230270

Cinema

The good news for foreign visitors is that movies are shown in their original language with Romanian subtitles. The majority of major cities and towns have modern multiplex cinemas, showing films just a few weeks after their release in the US or western Europe. Some are even released in Romania simultaneously.

Romania itself has a burgeoning film industry, both producing its own feature films and as a location for international films. The vast Media Pro Studio complex at Buftea, close to Bucharest, has recently been the chosen location for a number of first-rate international films, including *Sex Traffic*, the Film Four winner of nine BAFTAS in 2005. The studios are vast and the management has recently begun opening them up to visitors, eager to show what the Romanian film industry is capable of. Tours of the studios are free; you just need to book a day or two in advance (Str. Studioului 1, Buftea, tel: 031-825 1840, www.mediaprostudios.ro).

Local films that have met with international acclaim include 2005's *The Death of Mr Lazarescu*, which won its director Cristi Puiu a clutch of awards, and two 2006 films dealing with the 1989 revolution: *Was it or Wasn't it?* and *What I Did During the End of the World*. Romania was also featured (most unflatteringly) in the 2006 film *Borat*, when a poor Romanian village (Glod, in Dâmbovița county) was used as the setting of

fictional Kazakstani journalist Borat's home village *(for more on cinema see pages 77–79)*.

Bucharest

Hollywood Multiplex
Calea Vitan 55–59
Tel: 021-327 7020
www.hmultiplex.ro
Excellent multi-screen cinema inside the Bucharest Mall showing all the latest local fims and Hollywood blockbusters. Entrance costs around 90 lei.

Movieplex
B-dul. Timisoara 26 (Plaza Romania)
Tel: 021-407 8300
www.plazaromania.ro
The country's best cinema complex is inside the Plaza Romania shopping centre, on the second floor.

Iași

Glendale Multiplex Moldova Mall
Str. Palat 1
Tel: 0232-248040
Flash new multi-screen cinema that has become something of a badge of honour for local people.

Oradea

Hollywood Multiplex Mall
Str. Olteniei 80
Tel: 0259-420002/3
This was the first multi-screen cinema to open in Romania, back in 1999.

CHILDREN'S ACTIVITIES

Romania offers plenty of thrills for children, and they will be made to feel especially welcome wherever you take them. The main problem with travelling with children in Romania is the poor transport infrastructure that makes getting from one town to another difficult and time-consuming. Try to plan your travel well.

Practicalities

Children under seven travel free on the country's railways. From that age onwards they have to pay, but at a reduced rate if sitting in second class. For first-class travel there is no reduction. Children below the age of 12 receive a small reduction on Tarom internal flights.

When travelling around the countryside make sure you bring all you need, such as formula milk, nappies or medicine, especially if touring with babies or very young children. Do not expect to find much in the way of baby-changing facilities anywhere in the country. Public breast feeding, no matter how discreet, is a definite no-no.

Bucharest

Bucharest is not a great place to stay with kids for any length of time. There is a water park (called simply Water Park) just outside the city, opposite the airport, but it is in the open air and functions only during the summer. Bucharest also has a zoo, but it is a rather sorry affair, and your time – certainly with younger children – is probably better spent in the plentiful playgrounds in its large parks. In Herăstrău Park there are pleasure boats that cruise around the large lake, as well as a go-kart track for older children, and the veritable paradise that is Insula Copiilor (Children's Island): all bouncy castles, slides and other inflatables. If it is raining try the Arlechino Club or Kids' Planet, both large indoor playgrounds. There is a very good circus with shows every Saturday and Sunday at 3pm and 6.30pm. Tickets are cheap.

Arlechino Club
B-dul. Unirii 9
Tel: 021-335 4399
www.arlechinoclub.ro
Circus Globus
Aleea Circului 15
Tel: 021-2105152
Insula Copiilor (Children's Island)
Parcul Herăstrău
Tel: 021-2322128
www.insulacopiilor.ro
Kid's Planet
Piața Alba Iulia 2
Tel: 021-326 6046
www.kidsplanet.ro
Water Park
Șos București-Ploiești
www.waterpark.ro
Open summer only 10am–8pm.

The Mountains

The ski resort of Poiana Brașov has specialist children's ski schools, ice rinks, gentle slopes for sledging, and swimming pools. There are also horse-drawn sleigh rides through the snow available at the resort's equestrian centre. In summer the same place organises children's horse-riding courses, and pony trekking *(see below)*. It really is a great destination for active children. Predeal, too, has a special children's ski slope, and a winter playground in front of the town hall. Heading off on ambitious mountain walks with children is not recommended, as they can quickly become cold, wet and bored.

Centrul de Echitatie Speranta
Poiana Brasov
Tel: 0268-262161

The Seaside

In the summer the resort of Mamaia has a fantastic water park at its southern end, as well as a gondola ride that links the centre of the resort to the water park. It offers great views of the resort, of Constanța, and far out to sea. The beach at Mamaia is tremendous: wide, sandy and perfect for children. Most of the other Black Sea beaches are less child-friendly.

Older children might be tempted to try out some water sports, or banana-boat rides, and there are places all along Mamaia beach where they can do so. Such pursuits are expensive in Romania, however.

Eating Out With Children

When it comes to eating out with children you will find that few restaurants turn children away, but equally few are well prepared for them. High chairs are rare, except in the best hotels and international chain restaurants, like Pizza Hut and Ruby Tuesday. Public baby-changing facilities are likewise very difficult to find. Food in general in Romania should not be a problem. Romanians are not fond of spicy foods, while universal children's favourites, such as omelettes, or steak with fries, are found on every menu in the country. The eternal children's favourite, McDonalds, is ubiquitous.

SHOPPING

It is doubtful that anywhere in Romania will ever be a shopper's paradise on the level of London, Paris or Milan. However, things have certainly improved since 1989, and shiny new shopping centres, full of international chains, now ring the centres of most cities. A good number of select designers have also opened stores along the posher boulevards of Bucharest. As a rule, however, expect to find little you wouldn't get elsewhere, and most things will cost considerably more than at home.

What to Buy

There are a number of locally produced items that are worth looking out for. You will probably not be able to avoid buying an Orthodox icon, or at least a modern replica of one (originals form part of the national patrimony and are next to impossible to export). Look out for modern glass icons, which make better souvenirs than the rather predictable wooden reproductions. Painted eggs make another great gift. They are especially prominent at Easter but available from souvenir shops throughout the year. These eggs are the most bright and visible example of the country's rich cultural legacy, and were originally painted by village women and children on Good Friday. It is said that the patterns would often contain coded messages from one village to another. The eggs for sale in most shops are wooden, but you can usually get hold of genuine hollowed-out egg shells at Easter time.

Romanian pottery is well worth seeking out, as it is by and large still made using a traditional foot-powered wheel. The tradition remains strongest in the Maramureș, but there are pottery centres in other places around the country, for instance at Corund in Transylvania (*see page 224*). Romanians are also very good at working with wood (the centuries-old wooden churches of the Maramureș are evidence of that), and wooden toys, cutlery and walking sticks can make superb gifts.

Textile weaving remains the most common of Romania's traditional crafts, and you will see beautifuly embroidered tablecloths, blouses, waistcoats and headscarves for sale in most parts of the country. The best stuff comes from Transylvania, especially around Sibiu. Look out, too, for small, simple but elegant rugs, a speciality of Moldavia.

Romanian wine (*see page 63*) can be good, but you should know what you are buying; there is much chaff among the wheat. Generally, stick to red wines, especially the cabernet sauvignon and merlot grapes. Specialist wine shops have popped up in a couple of cities recently and will be able to help you select the perfect wine.

Most shops are open 9am–6pm,

Romania's Festivals (folk, religious, arts and music)

A large number of traditional festivals are still celebrated in Romania. Most of them mark saints' feast days, or traditional rural dates such as the departure of shepherds for the summer grazing pastures in the mountains. Due to constraints of space, we cannot provide details on the dozens of small local festivals that take place throughout the year, but the following list highlights the major events of interest to travellers. Contemporary arts and music festivals are included.
See also pages 80–81

January

New Year's Day (Revelion) is celebrated all over Romania – though especially in central Transylvania, around Făgăraș – by groups of young men who wander through cities and villages in goatskins, sheepskins and even bearskins singing, dancing and banging drums, collecting money from onlookers.
St John's Day (Sf. Ioan) on 7 January sees churches all over the country packed with the faithful waiting to receive blessed water from priests.

February

At Târgu Jiu musicians from all over Oltenia gather for a two-day **Festival of Traditional Music** on the middle weekend of February. In Bucharest, the **Spring Gift Fair** is held at the Peasant Museum from late February into March.

March

1 March is **Mărțșor**, when all females are presented with a *mărțșor* – usually a brooch tied with red and white thread – which symbolises the coming of spring. In the weeks before *mărțșor*, vendors can be seen in city centres.
8 March is **International Women's Day**, celebrated in Romania by men giving women flowers.
On the last Sunday before Lent the **Inmormantarea Farsangulu** (Burial of Fun) festival takes place in Rimitea, near Alba Iulia. Other pre-Lenten festivals include the spectacular **Roata de Foc** festival in Sinca Noua, close to Făgăraș.

April/May

Orthodox Easter (Paște) – which often falls in May according to the Gregorian calendar – is the most important event of the year.

Lamb is the traditional meal, always eaten very early on Sunday after people return from Saturday's midnight mass. There are **Easter craft fairs and markets** over the Easter weekend at all of the Bukovina monasteries, and at the Peasant Museum in Bucharest. In Sfântu Gheorghe (Székely Land) the three-day **St George Festival** from 28–30 April has dancing, local music and traditions.
The **Stâna** (the Measurement of the Milk Festival) is held after Easter across the Carpathians.

May

1 May is a national holiday. The first weekend in May is the **Juni** festival in Brașov.
Also at the beginning of May, the **Târgul Fetelor** (Girl Fair) is held at Gurghiu, Mureș county.
There are **wine festivals** every weekend in May in Iași, Constanța, Cluj and Bucharest. In Bucharest the **Jeunesse Musicales** is an international competition for young musicians, with most events held at the Atheneu Roman.
The **Sibiu Jazz Festival** takes place in mid-May, and has been a fixture on the international jazz calendar since 1970. It attracts top international names, as well as the cream of Romania's jazz scene. At Târgu Lapus, in the Maramureș, there is a **Festival of Țuică** (plum brandy) at the end of every May.

June

The **Transylvania Film Festival** in Cluj showcases Romanian cinema. On 21 June, concerts in Bucharest celebrate **Fête de la Musique**, part of a worldwide international Francophile music festival.
Sibiu's **International Theatre Festival** is in the first week of June.

July

The **feast day of Stephen the Great** (2 July) at Putna Monastery *(see page 315)*.
At Vadul Izei in Maramureș a **Wedding Fair** is held on the first Sunday in July, the same day as a **Cherry Festival** takes place in Brâncovenesti, near Târgu Mureș. In Piața Sfatului, Brașov, the **Cerbul de Aur** (Golden Stag) pop festival has been held every year since the 1960s.
The **Mt Gaiana Girl Fair**, near Avram Iancu in the Apuseni Mountains, takes place on the

weekend preceding 20 July. The **Sighișoara Medieval Arts Festival** takes place in late July.

August

At the Astra Museum near Sibiu the **Festivalul National al Traditiilor Populare din Romania**, a festival of arts and crafts, is held over the first week of August. On the second Sunday of August people from Maramureș, Transylvania and Moldavia meet for a large-scale **Hora** (traditional dance) at the Prislop Pass.
At the seaside, the Romanian Navy is honoured with **fireworks and parades** on 15 August.
The **Callatis Festival** at Mangalia is Romania's largest music festival, mainly featuring Europop.
The **Mamaia Music Festival** takes place in late August.

September

The alternative rock festival **Stufstock** *(see page 162)* at Vama Veche has taken place in early September, but the date may move to July or August.
The **George Enescu Music Festival** – held every odd-numbered year – attracts artists and music lovers from all over the world. It is held over three weeks at the Ateneul Român in Bucharest.
Sibiu's philharmonic orchestra hosts an **Opera Festival** at the end of the month.

October

Bucharest hosts a **Jazz Festival** throughout October, while Sibiu is home to the **Astra Film Festival**, a showcase for documentary film makers held every even year.
14 October is the **feast day of St Parascheva** in Iași.

December

Romania celebrates its **National Day** on 1 December to mark the unification of Transylvania with Wallachia and Moldavia. There is usually a military parade in Bucharest and a religious service at Alba Iulia (where the unification treaty was signed).
Christmas (Crăciun) is celebrated by sacrificing a pig a week or two before 25 December. Carol singing is very popular on Christmas Eve.
On **New Year's Eve** almost every town in Romania holds open-air concerts, regardless of the weather. The biggest is in Bucharest at Piața Revoluției.

although those in the city centre or in shopping centres stay open much later. On Saturday some shops (even those in the city centre) close at 2pm, and many do not open at all on Sunday. Shopping centres and supermarkets remain open until late seven days a week *(see page 365)*.

Where to Buy

In Bucharest the main shopping areas are Bulevardul Magheru, the central part of Calea Victoriei, and around Piaţa Unirii and Lipscani. In Braşov there are some enjoyable shops all along Strada Republicii and around Piaţa Sfatului. In Sibiu, Strada Nicolae Bălcescu is lined with the weird and wonderful. Sighişoara's old town shelters souvenir shops and art galleries galore, but other than that you will be limited to out-of-town shopping centres.

Department Stores and Shopping Centres

The only real *magazin universal* (department store) left in Romania is the wonderfully eccentric Star in Braşov. Elsewhere, the communist-era universals have been converted into shopping centres. The largest is Unirea, in Bucharest.

Bucharest
Bucureşti Mall
Calea Vitan 55–59
Tel: 021-327 6100
www.bucurestimall.com
Plaza Romania
B-dul. Timisoara 26
Tel: 021-319 5050
www.plazaromania.ro
Unirea
Piaţa Unirii 1
Tel: 021-303 0307
www.unireashop.ro

Braşov
Eliana Mall
Str. Bazaltului 2
www.elianamall.ro
Star Magazin Universal
Str. Nicolae Balcescu 62

Constanţa
Tomis Mall
Str. Stefan cel Mare 36–40
Tel: 0241-616018
www.tomis.ro

Iaşi
Iulius Mall
B-dul. Tudor Vladimirescu
Tel: 0232-208500
www.iuliusmall.com
Mall of Moldavia
Str. Palat 1
Tel: 0232-256031

Oradea
Lotus Market
Str. Nufarului 30
Tel: 0259-43622
www.lotusmarket.ro

Ploieşti
Omnia Shopping Center
B-dul. Republicii 15
Tel: 0244-541414

Timişoara
Iulius Mall
Str. Demetriade 1
Tel: 0256-401604
www.iuliusmall.ro

Book Stores in Bucharest

Carturesti
Str. Pictor Arthur Verona 13
Tel: 021-317 3459
www.carturesti.ro
Book shop and café – we think the only one of its kind in Romania – where you can browse at leisure while enjoying a great espresso.
Libraria Noi
B-dul. Nicolae Bălcescu 18
Tel: 021-311 0700
www.librarianoi.ro
Superb book store selling a good range of English-language books about Romania, besides an unmatchable map section.
Salingers
DN 1 Bucuresti – Ploiesti 44A
(Feeria Commercial Centre)
Tel: 021-319 4268
www.salingers.ro
Great English-language bookshop selling a wide range of fiction, travel guides and maps. There is also an outlet in Otopeni airport.

Craft Markets in Bucharest

You will find three craft markets, selling a wide variety of traditional Romanian handicrafts, strung along the side of the road between Sinaia and Predeal. There is also a very good craft market at the foot of Bran Castle *(see page 191)*. Throughout December, and in the weeks running up to Easter, a gift market selling some exquisite little knick-knacks (including painted Easter eggs) is held at the Librăria Noi gallery in Bucharest.
Librăria Noi
B-dul. Nicolae Bălcescu 18
Tel: 021-311 0700
www.librarianoi.ro
Hanul cu Tei
Str. Lipscani 63–65
Tel: 021-315 5663
An entire street of antiques shops, craft workshops and art galleries. Look out for glass icons, communist memorabilia and reproduction

furniture. It's all here and you could easily spend half a day just looking around.
Piaţa Obor
The country's largest outdoor market sells everything from fine porcelain to fruit and vegetables, live chickens and ducks. It is an enjoyable morning out just to come here and watch Romanians bargaining and arguing.

Fashion

Dan Coma
Str. Franklin 5
Bucharest
Tel: 021-314 0196
Custom-designed shoes with matching handbags from Dan Coma, a shoe designer whose reputation stretches way beyond Romania's borders.
Irina Schrotter
Outlets at Bucureşti Mall, Plaza Romania, Iulius Mall Iaşi and Iulius Mall Timişoara.
www.irinaschrotter.ro
Schrotter is the biggest name in Romanian women's fashion, and designs tasteful, elegant clothes for ladies who lunch.

Glass

Sticerom
Str. Selari 9–11
Bucharest
Outstanding examples of hand-blown glass. Much of it is made in the workshop at the back of the shop. Expensive but superb gifts.

Ski Hardware

Ascent
Piaţa Sfatului 17
Braşov
Large selection of skis, snowboards and winter clothing. In summer the shop becomes a good outlet for hiking and climbing gear.
Rossignol
Str. Mureşenilor 20
Braşov
Romania's best ski store. All the latest Rossignol hardware, often

available at prices far cheaper than you would expect, especially from the end of February onwards when the ski season begins to tail off.

Souvenirs & Romanian Handicrafts

Although souvenirs are found everywhere, the best places to pick up good-quality gifts are the many museums around Romania that have souvenir shops. The best is at the Muzeul Ţaranului in Bucharest, but all those listed here have a good range of arts and handicrafts.

Muzeul Satului
Şos. Kiseleff 28
Bucharest
Tel: 021-222 9110
Muzeul Ţaranului
Şos. Kiseleff 3
Bucharest
Tel: 021-312 9875
Artizana
Str. Sf. Ioan 26
Braşov
Tel: 0268-477549
Muzeul Astra
Sibiu
Tel: 0269-218195
www.muzeulastra.ro
Galeria Helios
Piaţa Victoriei 6
Timişoara
Tel: 0265-208659

Wine

Vinexpert
Piaţa Unirii 1 (Unirea Shopping Centre)
Bucharest
Tel: 021-303 0280
www.vinexpert.info
Vinalia
Str. Mureşenilor 27
Braşov
Vinoteca Bolyai
Str. Bolyai Janos 1–3
Cluj
Tel: 0264-450460

SPORTS

Winter Sports

Romanians are big on skiing, and there are as many as 15 resorts of one description or another dotted all over the country, from the well-known destination of Poiana Braşov to the tiny, one-chairlift resort of Durău in the Ceahlău Massif. As a rule, skiing is a less than satisfying experience in Romania, given the long queues and crowds that assemble on ski slopes every weekend of the season. Snow care is also poor, meaning that even after a fresh fall of snow pistes are often icy and even rocky.

The best skiing in Romania is at Sinaia, where the wide, open pistes of the Valea Dorului offer great skiing. Alas, the snow up here is not at all reliable, as the exposed nature of the area means that high winds often blow the slopes bare. Access to the Sinaia ski area is via a rather old two-stage cable car, for which queues at weekends are long. Catch some great snow on a weekday, however, and skiing in Sinaia is wonderful. The run from the top of the cable car down to the resort, a 15-km (10-mile) roller coaster, is as good as skiing gets.

Best known outside the country is Poiana Braşov, the main destination for western European package tourists. A short drive from the city of Braşov it buzzes – especially at the weekend – with the new Romanian rich who flock here in massive numbers. Queues can be very long at weekends, although the new high-speed gondola – installed at the start of the 2006–7 season – has eased the queuing problem slightly.

Besides Sinaia and Poiana Braşov the Prahova Valley is also home to Predeal, which offers decent but limited skiing (there are just three pistes, all around 4 km (2½ miles) in length, but these are better cared for than elsewhere).

Snow can usually be relied upon from the beginning of December until the end of March; the highest slopes at Sinaia often stay open as late as mid-May, and the season is often slightly prolonged in the more northern resorts around Ceahlău and Vatra Dornei. Lift tickets are sold on a points basis, and are relatively expensive. A day's skiing at Poiana Braşov can cost as much as 100 lei. The toughest skiing is at Sinaia, while Poiana Braşov has gentle slopes for beginners, and nothing at all challenging for experts. There are other skiing options in Romania, notably in the north at Borşa and Vatra Dornei, at Paltiniş near Sibiu, and at Semenic near Reşiţa in the southwest. None has more than one or two ski runs, however.

Ski Equipment Hire

Most hotels in Romanian ski resorts arrange ski and boot hire for around 40 lei per day. Equipment can sometimes be a bit old, however, so if you can it is best to pay more and to go to a specialist ski hire store. In Poiana Braşov the best place is *Club Rossignol*, at the foot of the Postavarul Express gondola lift, in Sinaia, try the New Montana Hotel (which rents out great equipment and is right next to the cable car); in Predeal the best place is the Fulg de Nea *pension* and ski shop at the foot of the slopes. In all these places the equipment is usually new and very good, and you should expect to pay as much as 75 lei for a day's hire.

Hiking

Hiking in the hills and mountains is about the most popular physical activity in Romania. The season begins properly in June, as the unpredictable mountain weather makes hiking dangerous any earlier in the year (this does not stop some people taking to the hills in March and April, however, and stories of injury and disappearance are not uncommon). The most popular areas for hiking are the Bucegi *(see page 197)* and Făgăraş *(see page 203)* ranges, where hundreds of well-marked routes of all difficulties and lengths crisscross the mountains. A vast network of *cabane* – basic mountain huts with bunk beds, basic

toilets and hot food and *ţuica* – provide overnight shelter for the legions of local and international hikers who head for the hills every summer. The most popular cabins on the most popular routes are often full. Try booking in advance if possible, although in theory these cabins are not allowed to turn anyone away. Camping high up in the mountains is not a good idea, as bears can be a danger. The website www.infomontan.ro has details of routes and cabins (currently in Romanian only, however), and can take reservations for the larger ones.

Although all hiking routes in Romania are well marked, before setting off you will need a good map. The tourist information office in Predeal has an excellent selection of specialist hiking maps, as do most good book stores in Bucharest *(see page 359)* and Braşov. There is also a decent map of the hiking routes in the Bucegi Mountains on sale at the cable-car ticket office in Sinaia. Always take warm and waterproof clothing with you on any hike, as the weather can change quickly.

Horse Riding

Horse riding is popular in the Romanian countryside, where the horse and cart can still often be the primary form of transport. Considered a bourgeois sport under the communist regime, riding was not encouraged, but one excellent equestrian centre, **Centrul de Echitaţie** (tel: 0268-262161), at Poiana Braşov, remains open. You will find it around 2 km (1 mile) from the entrance to the resort of Poiana on the right-hand side of the access road. You can go pony trekking, hire a horse and cart, learn how to ride and, in winter, take superb horse-drawn sleigh rides through the surrounding countryside.

The **Ştefan cel Mare Riding Centre** (www.riding-holidays.ro) in northern Transylvania *(see page 245)* is recommended for relatively experienced riders. Elsewhere there are few public opportunities for riding, although most villagers with a horse will happily hire you his stallion or mare for a few euros. Show jumping is popular in Transylvania, and there are regular contests at Oradea, where there is a professional show-jumping school.

Mountain Biking

Mountain biking is a relatively new pursuit in Romania, as indeed is cycling of any sort, but it is catching on fast for organised tours with companies such as Adventure Transylvania (www.adventuretransylvania.com). There are a number of marked tracks laid out especially for mountain bikers at Poiana Braşov, one of the few places you can hire quality equipment (from the Club Rossignol bar and hotel). A couple of hotels in Sinaia and Predeal also hire out mountain bikes, although both resorts lack any real biking facilities. You will struggle to find anywhere in the cities where you can hire a bike – cycling is simply not popular, although that does not mean cycling the quiet rural roads is not a pleasure.
Club Rossignol
Str. Sulinar
Poiana Braşov
Tel: 0268-262470

Golf

Romania does not currently possess a full 18-hole golf course. The nearest you can get to a round of golf is at Lac de Verde, in Breaza, a short distance south of Sinaia. Here, a rather easy nine-hole course in superb surroundings is complemented by a fabulous country club, complete with hotel and restaurant, spa, health club, driving range and tennis courts.
Lac de Verde
Breaza
Tel: 0244-343525
www.lacdeverde.ro

Spectator Sports

Romanians are crazy about football (soccer), although recently there has been very little to celebrate. The national team has not qualified for a major championship for years, and a dearth of talent means they could be out of the international limelight for

some time to come. The few stars the country does produce play abroad, in Spain, Italy and Turkey. Although the standard of the local league (Divizia A) is poor, it still has a pull among fans, and big games are well worth attending.

It is a long time since Steaua Bucharest won the European Cup (1986) but it did qualify for the Champions League in 2006 (for the first time in a decade) and was able to bring big names such as Lyon and Real Madrid to Bucharest. It remains the biggest club in the country, and local derbies with eternal rivals Dinamo and Rapid draw big crowds. Tickets for these derbies are hard to come by via normal channels, although their relatively low face value (from 10 lei upwards) means you can pick one up from a tout outside the stadiums for as little 50 lei. The best supported teams in the country are in the provinces: Politechnica Timişoara and Universitatea Craiova sometimes play in front of crowds that top 30,000. The Romanian national team plays most of its home matches in Constanţa, avoiding Bucharest where it often gets a frosty reception. The Romanian football season runs from July to June, with a four-month break from November to March.

Other popular spectator sports include handball – male and female. Romania's women's team was the runner-up at the 2006 World Cup. Rugby – once very popular – has lost its appeal since the Romanian team, a force in the 1980s, began losing most of its matches by large margins. Ice hockey is popular in the provinces. The strongest team is from the Transylvanian city of Miercurea Ciuc, and is backed by a wealthy Hungarian businessman.

The Romanian and Moldovan sport of oina *(see picture on page 263)* bears more than a passing resemblance to baseball, although it evolved from a game traditionally played by shepherds. A national league has existed since the 1930s.

TOURS AND AGENCIES

Bicycle Tours

You'll be stared at by almost everyone you pass, but the meandering roads of much of Transylvania, the Maramureş and Bukovina were almost tailor-made for cycling holidays, and most of the companies listed on the following page now arrange accompanied tours.

TRANSPORT

ACCOMMODATION

ACTIVITIES

A – Z

LANGUAGE

Danube Delta and Bird-watching Tours

Home to more than 300 species, the Danube Delta is a dream for ornithologists, and bird-watching in the region is one of the fastest-growing areas of Romanian tourism. Many areas of the Delta are protected, getting around can be difficult, and even experienced bird-watchers will get far more from a trip to the Delta by joining an organised tour. Make sure you use a reputable company, and one that avoids using motorboats (the engine scares off the wildlife).

Dracula Tours

The whole Dracula business may be something of a cliché, but there is a back story to the legend, and travelling Transylvania on a Dracula Tour is a great way to find out more about it. It is also a superb way to see some fantastic castles and learn a great deal about Transylvania's troubled and eventful history.

Fishing

Fishing is allowed in any river or pond at any time of year except 1 April to 31 May. The sport is popular all over Romania. Freshwater fishing is especially good in the Apuseni Mountains, where you will be able to find (depending on the season) carp, mullet, pike and pike-perch. The Danube Delta is probably the best fishing destination, however, with huge carp the prime attraction.

Hiking Tours

There are two kinds of hiking tour on offer. The first is for serious walkers looking to cover as much ground as possible, the second is for those who want to take it a bit easier and enjoy the flora and fauna of Romania's uplands. Both are popular, although local people prefer to do their own thing, and see an organised hike as utterly defeating the object.

Hunting

Hunting is big business in Romania and popular with local people. You can shoot bear, boar, deer, pheasant and duck, but there is a wide-ranging list of restrictions on how, how much and where you can shoot. The only way to be sure of not breaking the law is to go on a specialised hunting tour, with a company that will take care of permits, licences and temporary importation of firearms.

Skiing

Those looking for wild skiing in Romania should forget the resorts of the Prahova Valley and head for Balea Lac, an unmarked ski area in the Făgăraș Mountains above the Transfăgărașan Highway. You can ski here as late as June on fantastic snow. You will need a guide, and an organised tour is the best option.

Tour Operators

UK-based

Balkan Holidays
Sofia House, 19 Conduit Street
London W1S 2BH
Tel: 0845-130 1114
www.balkanholidays.co.uk
With more than 20 years' experience in the region, Balkan Holidays organises standard ski and beach packages, besides mountain tours, city breaks and twin-centre holidays (Romania and Bulgaria).

Beyond the Forest
1 Atkinson Court
Fell Foot, Newby Bridge
Cumbria LA12 8NW
Tel: 01539-531258
www.beyondtheforest.com
Eco-friendly tours of Transylvania and Bukovina. Tour themes include wildlife, Dracula, Gypsies, crafts and folklore, monasteries and the Maramureș.

Responsible Travel
www.responsibletravel.com
Online travel agent offering eco-friendly tours of Transylvania on foot and horseback, as well as more general cultural tours.

Romanian Affair
www.romanianaffair.com
Monastery and Dracula tours, as well as accompanied sightseeing of the Maramureș, fishing holidays and bird-watching tours.

Romanian Travel Centre
33 Mount Pleasant
Tunbridge Wells
Kent TN1 1PN
Tel: 01892-673437
www.romaniantravelcentre.com
A one-stop shop for every imaginable kind of tour. It organises custom-designed ski holidays, Dracula tours, monastery tours, Danube Delta and bird-watching expeditions and can help with hunting and fishing trips.

US-based

Bike Tours Direct
1638 Berkley Circle
Chattanooga, TN 37405
Tel: 1-877 462 2423
www.biketoursdirect.com
Specialises in bike tours of Transylvania, ranging from two to eight days. For those not coming from the US it is possible to join the tours at Bucharest's Otopeni Airport.
Quest Tours & Adventures
P.O. Box 1060
Fairview, OR 97024
Tel: 1-800 621 8687
www.romtour.com
An expert in specialised Romanian holidays, Quest can help with hunting, fishing, hiking, monastery and art tours.

Wilderness Travel
1102 Ninth Street
Berkeley, CA 94710
Tel: 1-510 558 2488
Wilderness offers a wide variety of tours to Romania, including medieval villages, mountains and legends and hiking in the Făgăraș range.

Romania-based

Apuseni Experience
Piata 1 Decembrie
Oradea
Tel: 0259-472434
www.apuseniexperience.ro
Tailor-made nature and cultural tours of the Apuseni region.

Carpathian Nature Tours
Magura 139
Moeciu
Tel: 0268-223098
German-Romanian tour operator specialising in bear-tracking in the Southern Carpathians.

Delta Travel
Str. Scarletescu 7
Bucharest
Tel: 021-311 2203
www.traveldelta.ro
Responsible ecotourism specialist to the Danube Delta.

Jolly Tours
Athenee Palace Hilton
Str. Episcopiei 1–3
Bucharest
Tel: 021-303 3796
www.jollytours.ro.
Arranges excellent-value tours of Bucharest and the Carpathian Mountains and can arrange private cars with driver and guide for tailor-made trips, starting at around €70 per day.

Marshal Turism
B-dul. Magheru 43
Bucharest
Tel: 021-319 4455
www.marshal.ro
Specialists in vineyard and monastery tours.

Roving Romania
Tel: 0724-348272/0744-212065
Email: roving@deltanet.ro
www.roving-romania.co.uk
Tailor-made tours for small groups, hosted by a British Romania expert who is a resident of Brașov.

The **Association of Ecotourism in Romania** (**AER**) has a list of responsible local tourist agencies on its website: www.eco-romania.ro

Romania's National Parks, Natural Parks and Other Protected Areas

Apuseni Natural Park
Protects the core area of the Apuseni limestone plateau, with rocky habitats and montane meadows. Area: 758 sq. km.
www.parcapuseni.ro

Balta Mic a Brăilei Natural Park
An important expanse of wetland south of the city of Brăila on the Danube. Area: 175 sq. km.
www.bmb.ro

Bucegi Natural Park
The dramatic Bucegi Mountains are the most accessible and visited in the country. The Natural Park seeks to limit the impact of this popularity on the environment. Area: 327 sq. km.
www.bucegipark.ro (no English)

Buila Vânturarita National Park
On the southeastern flank of the Carpathians, Buila Vânturarita is a limestone massif with impressive cliffs popular with rock climbers. Area: 96 sq. km.

Călimani Natural Park
The largest massif in the Eastern Carpathians, this volcanic area is noted for its rare plants, bears, wolves, lynx and pine martens. Area: 240 sq. km.
www.calimani.ro

Ceahlău National Park
Romania's "Mount Olympus", the Ceahlău Massif is a spectacular sight. The rocky peaks and ledges are a good place to see chamois. Area: 84 sq. km.
www.parculnational.ceahlau.ro

Cheile Bicazului-Hăşmaş National Park
The Bicaz Gorges-Hăşmaş Mountain National Park incorporates picturesque Lacu Roşu and fantastic gorge scenery. Area: 66 sq. km.
www.cheilebicazului-hasmas.ro

Cheile Nerei-Beuşniţa National Park
Just to the north of the Portile de Fier National Park, the Cheile Nerei gorges are Romania's longest. Area: 371 sq. km.
www.cheilenerei-beusnita.ro

Comana Natural Park
Wetland area between Bucharest and Giurgiu. Area: 250 sq. km.
www.comanaparc.ro

Cozia National Park
Midway along the Southern Carpathians, the forested massif overlooks Cozia Monastery. Area: 171 sq. km.
www.cozia.ro (no English)

Danube Delta Biosphere Reserve
This UNESCO reserve protects the world's largest reedbed and its rich birdlife and other wildlife. Area: 5,800 sq. km.
www.ddbra.ro, www.deltadunarii.ro

Defileul Jiului National Park
This new national park, opened in 2005, is located in the forested hills overlooking the narrow Jiu Valley between Petroşani and Târgu Jiu. Area: 110 sq. km.

Domogled-Valea Cernei National Park
The Cerna Valley, with its warm microclimate, has an extremely rich biodiversity; the park is home to many species not found elsewhere in Romania. Area: 601 sq. km. www.domogled-cerna.ro

Grădiştea Muncelului Cioclovina Natural Park
Surrounding the Roman ruins at Sarmizegetusa and other Dacian relics in the Grădiştea Mountains east of Haţeg. Area: 100 sq. km.
www.gradiste.ro (no English)

Lunca Joasa a Prutului Inferior Natural Park
A new park north of Galaţi on the the border with the Republic of Moldova. Protects a wetland and meadow area by the Prut River. Area: 80 sq. km.

Lunca Mureşului Natural Park
The Mureş River floodplain west of Arad close to the Hungarian border. Area: 172 sq. km.
www.luncamuresului.ro

Maramureşului Mountain Natural Park
Right on the Ukraine border, these wild mountains harbour plenty of wildlife and also caving opportunities. Area: 1,490 sq. km.
www.muntiimaramuresului.ro

Munţii Măcin National Park
The Măcin Mountains near Tulcea feature some significant steppe vegetation, and are a great place to see birds of prey. Area: 113 sq. km.
www.parcmacin.ro (no English)

Munţii Rodnei National Park
These mountains in north-central Romania are some of the wildest in the country, with the highest peak in the Eastern Carpathians (2,300 metres). Area: 464 sq. km.
www.parcrodna.ro

Piatra Craiului National Park
One of the country's richest parks for wildlife, known for its bears, wolves and lynx. The scenery is magnificent. Area: 148 sq. km.
www.pcrai.ro

Platoul Mehedinţi Geopark
Adjoining the Portile de Fier and Domogled-Cernei parks to form a sizeable protected area in the southwest of the country. Area: 1,060 sq. km.

Portile de Fier Natural Park
One of Romania's largest protected areas, the famous Iron Gates along the Danube reach their climax at Kazan Gorge. Area: 1,156 sq. km.
www.portiledefier.ro (no English)

Putna-Vrancea Natural Park
Another new protected area, Putna-Vrancea is located in the volcanically active southeastern Carpathians. Area: 382 sq. km.

Retezat National Park
This fabulous park, Romania's oldest, protects over 50 species of mammal including the 'big three' as well as chamois. Area: 380 sq. km. www.retezat.ro

Semenic-Cheile Carasului National Park
Best known for its magnificent beech forest, this park also features some interesting caves and other karst features. Area: 366 sq. km. www.semenic.online.ro

Tara Haţegului Dinosaurus Geopark
This large park in the Haţeg area of western Transylvania is known for its dinosaur finds. Their excellent website tells you all you need to know. Area: 1,024 sq. km.
www.geopark.go.ro

Vânători-Neamţ Natural Park
In the north of Neamţ county, this forested park in the foothills of the Eastern Carpathians is best known for its European bison breeding project. Area: 308 sq. km. www.vanatoripark.ro

A – Z

A HANDY SUMMARY OF PRACTICAL INFORMATION, ARRANGED ALPHABETICALLY

A ddresses

Romanian addresses can take on the appearance of complicated equations when an apartment block in a big city is involved (in this book we have used simplified forms). An address such as *Str. Eminescu Nr. 15, Bl. T24, Sc. 3, Et. 9, Ap. 16* for example may leave you not knowing where to start. Usually the street name comes before number, though often with the actual first word such as *strada* (street) or *bulevardul* (boulevard, often abbreviated to *b-dul*) omitted. Next comes the number of the building: if it is a house the address stops there. If it is a block, the address will contain the following: *Bl.* block number, *Sc.* entrance, *Et.* floor, and *Ap.* apartment number.

Many street names have changed since 1990, but despite this, the old name is often still used in the vernacular. In Bucharest for example Bulevardul 1 Mai is officially called Bulevardul Ion Mihalache, yet few people acknowledge the fact. Likewise Strada Lascar Cartagiu is still referred to by its communist-era name, Ana Ipatescu.

Admission Charges

Almost all Romania's museums, art galleries and other attractions charge an admission fee, but it is usually nominal; even the most popular museums charge no more than 3 lei. Children, students and pensioners usually pay even less. The only exceptions are places that require a compulsory guided tour, such as the Parliament Palace in Bucharest, or Peleş Castle in Sinaia. Even here, charges are far lower than in other parts of Europe. The once common practice of charging foreign tourists more than locals has now officially ended: if anyone tries to charge you more you should hold your ground and refuse to pay the extra. Many places charge fairly high fees for photography.

B udgeting for Your Trip

While certain things such as public transport and train travel, taxis, museum admission fees and snacks remain ridiculously cheap, Romania is becoming increasingly expensive, especially the Black Sea coast, the ski resorts and Bucharest.

The biggest expense, anywhere in the country, is accommodation. Good cheap hotels can be hard to come by, and the mid-range sector is very much in its infancy. The choice is between luxurious, expensive hotels and cheaper but less satisfactory places. You should budget on at least €50 per day. A good option for larger groups or families is to rent an apartment: a couple of companies in Bucharest offer fully equipped one-bedroom apartments from €40 per night. The cheapest option is to take up the offers of old ladies who greet trains at railway stations, offering *cazare*, usually a room in their home with meals if wanted (between 75–100 lei per night).

Public transport is very cheap. Even first-class train travel will be within the budget of most travellers. A ticket from Bucharest to Braşov costs between 40–75 lei, depending on the type of train. Flights are a faster but more expensive option. Single fares from Bucharest to Cluj, Satu Mare and Sibiu start at around €50. Within cities, public transport is chaotic but cheap. Taxis are inexpensive, as long as you ensure the taxi is from a

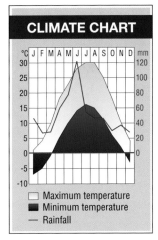

CLIMATE CHART

°C J F M A M J J A S O N D mm
30 — 120
25 — 100
20 — 80
15 — 60
10 — 40
5 — 20
0 — 0
-5
-10

☐ Maximum temperature
■ Minimum temperature
— Rainfall

reputable company *(see page 338)*. Even a cross-city ride in Bucharest should not cost more than €7–10.

Eating well is affordable, and even a top-class dinner in one of Bucharest's flashy restaurants should cost no more than €50 a head. A meal in a standard restaurant, serving hearty portions of decent, simple local fare, will usually work out at around €10 per head. Romanian wine is cheap and can be good, but quality matches price so pay as much as you can afford; imported wine is expensive. Food in supermarkets is cheap if it is produced locally, but imported food is much more expensive.

Business Hours

Opening hours in Romania are famously fickle. The tradition is for **shops** to be open 9am–6pm on weekdays and until 2pm on Saturdays, but there are plenty of exceptions to this rule. In large city centres and shopping malls, many are open Mon–Sat 8am–8pm (sometimes 10pm), and often 9am–1pm on Sunday, while **supermarkets** are usually open 9am–9pm. Most grocery shops and **markets** open from dawn to 8pm or later. Kiosks selling cigarettes, alcohol and soft drinks can stay open until 11pm or even all night. **Bank** hours are Mon–Thur 9am–5pm, Fri 9am–3pm.

Bars and pubs open around lunch time and stay open until at least 2am at weekends. **Restaurants** open for lunch at noon and take their last orders around 10.30pm. They do not as a rule close during the afternoon, but this varies across the country.

Generally **museums** are open Tues–Sun (in the bigger cities a few are open on Mondays), at least from

10am–5pm. Whatever their official opening hours, visitors are unlikely to be turned away from **monasteries** within daylight hours, or in many even at night, because some offer accommodation. **Church** opening hours are erratic, especially ones that are not major tourist attractions. It is sometimes a case of being there when the cleaner comes or waiting for a service or asking at the parish office for the key.

C limate and Clothing

Romania has a continental climate with hot summers and cold winters. Winter begins in November, and snow can cover much of the country for weeks on end; unless you are skiing it is not a recommended time to visit. Spring is brief and can be beautiful, before the hot season sets in before May is out – although there is considerable variation from year to year. June, July and August see temperatures climb to over 30°C (86°F), with numerous days reaching 35°C (95°F) or higher, and nights are sticky. September is warm and usually sunny, before temperatures begin to fall away sharply in October. Rainfall is erratic, but spells of rain lasting for several days can occur in spring and autumn. Torrential downpours are most common in early summer.

The best months for visiting are May, June and September, when the weather is warm but not too hot, although early summer thunderstorms are common. July and August in the south is too hot for most people, but in the mountains temperatures are often perfect. The seaside is great all summer due to the cooling breezes off the Black Sea. Skiers will usually find snow in the resorts from December to March, with skiing possible at the top of Sinaia as late as April or even May.

What to Wear

Even if visiting in midsummer, bring a windcheater or waterproof, and something a bit warmer if you want to go walking or hiking in the mountains: temperatures there can plummet from one hour to the next. During winter, wrap up very warm: thick jumpers, a good hat and gloves are essential. Remember that spring and autumn can be fickle, so bring clothing for warm and cold weather.

Crime and Safety

By and large Romania is a safe country. Violent crime is almost non-existent, and the biggest threat is the

street dogs in Bucharest *(see page 125)*. On the other hand, pickpockets are common on public transport, especially in railway stations and on buses and trams to and from airports. Backpackers are seen as a particularly good target. The Black Sea beaches are notorious for thieves. Aggressive begging on the Bucharest Metro and outside five-star hotels is common.

In an emergency, call the general emergency number for police, fire and ambulance, tel: 112. To report a petty crime for insurance purposes go to the police station nearest to the place where the incident happened. Try to make sure that you take someone who speaks Romanian, as Romania's policemen are almost all monoglot. You should carry some form of ID at all times, as this is law, though random checks are not common. A photocopy of your passport will suffice if you do not wish to carry the original.

Another danger is Romanian drivers: even on a pedestrian crossing you will not be given the right of way. Traffic lights are the best places to cross the road.

Customs Regulations

Romanian customs procedures and regulations have been greatly relaxed since the country joined the EU. Visitors from other EU and EEA countries can now come and go as they please, importing or exporting more or less anything. Cash in excess of €10,000 (or an equivalent value in any currency) must be declared on entry. Nationals of non-EU countries should check with the Romanian Embassy before travelling. For a full list of Romanian embassies abroad go to the Romanian Foreign Ministry's website www.mae.ro.

If travelling to another EU country note that while Romania places no restrictions on what you can export, the country you are going to often will (for instance, the UK restricts cigarette imports from certain EU member states – including Romania). The only restrictions Romania places on exports to EU states are of national treasures and original religious iconography (usually more than 50 years old). If you buy an antique or icon from a respected dealer then he or she should do the paperwork for you. This takes time, however, and may often mean that you will have to leave before your antique.

If arriving from outside the EU, or travelling outside the EU when you leave, the following allowances apply both ways: two bottles of alcohol, 200 cigarettes or 50 cigars or 25 grams of tobacco. Gifts and souvenirs totalling more than €1,000 in value should be declared on leaving, as should all electrical items bought while in Romania.

Visas and Passports

EU and EEA citizens may stay in Romania as long as they like; they do not even need a passport: national ID cards are enough. For stays of up to 90 days, citizens of Canada, Croatia, Chile and the US don't need a visa, though they may be asked to show a return or onward ticket. Almost everybody else needs a visa, which must be procured at a Romanian Consulate abroad. For a full list of countries who are visa-exempt, see www.mae.ro. If non-EU citizens wish to stay longer than 90 days, they must go to a local police station to obtain an extension.

D isabled Travellers

Romania is making giant strides towards accommodating travellers with disabilities, but getting around the country remains difficult. Sibiu and Timișoara are leading the way, installing rudimentary wheelchair ramps in many public places and tourist attractions. Bucharest, too, is making an effort, though the capital's notoriously potholed pavements and streets make negotiating them dangerous.

Public transport is problematic: although new buses have been purchased by many city authorities to meet EU requirements, they are generally too crowded for anyone to think about lowering the vehicle to allow a disabled person to board. The new Intercity trains are the most disabled-friendly form of transport. Public toilets for the disabled are still a rarity, but can be found in shopping centres, cinemas, and all branches of McDonalds.

E lectricity

Romania uses the 200 volts AC system. Visitors from the UK and the US will need a socket adaptor for electrical appliances; US visitors need a transformer for 120-volt equipment. The power supply these days is good.

Embassies and Consulates

Romanian Embassies Abroad

Australia
4 Dalman Cres., O'Malley, ACT 2606, Canberra, tel: 61-26 286 23 43
Canada

655 Rideau St, Ottawa, Ontario K1N 6A3, tel: 1-613 789 37 09.
Ireland
26 Waterloo Rd, Dublin 4, tel: 353-1 668 12 75.
South Africa
117 Charles St, Brooklyn 0181, P.O. Box 11295, Hatfield 0028, tel: 27-12 460 69 41.
UK
Arundel House, 4 Palace Green, London W8 4QD, tel: 44-20 7937 9666.
US
1607 23rd St NW, Washington DC 20008, tel: 1-202 232 36 94.

Embassies in Bucharest

Australia B-dul. Unirii 74, tel: 021-320 9826.
Canada Str. Nicolae Iorga 36, tel: 021-307 5000.
Ireland Str. Vasile Lascăr 42–44, tel: 021-212 2136.
UK Str. Jules Michelet 24, tel: 021-312 0303.
US Str. Filipescu 26, tel: 021-210 4042.

Etiquette

Romanians are marvellous hosts, but suffer from a lack of diplomatic skills. If invited to a Romanian home you should bring a gift: flowers for the hostess, a good bottle of whisky for the host. On entering, take off your shoes (or at least offer to). Conversation will depend on the situation and surroundings, but do not be surprised to be asked some very direct questions on your opinions of Romania, homosexuality and the church. You will also probably be asked about your income.

When entering Orthodox churches dress as modestly as the season allows; shorts are not forbidden (for men at least) but are frowned upon. Women should wear long dresses and cover their shoulders.

G ay and Lesbian Travellers

Romania is not a gay- and lesbian-friendly country. Homosexual activity between consenting adults was only legalised in 2002, after much badgering from the EU. Bucharest's first Gay Pride march in June 2005 ended in violence. There are few gay bars and clubs. Public displays of affection among members of the same sex will attract stares, which may be accompanied by threats.

For more information, visit Romania's one gay and lesbian organisation, Accept (www.accept-romania.ro); the site www.gaybucuresti.ro has details of gay clubs and bars.

H ealth and Medical Care

There are no specific health risks particular to Romania, but you should take out adequate health insurance before travelling. General standards of health care in urban areas are satisfactory, but in the countryside it is often ad hoc. Emergency medical treatment is free, but you may have to pay for some medicines. You will also be expected to tip doctors and nurses, who are underpaid.

Tap water is safe to drink, but the low cost of the bottled variety means that hardly anyone actually does. Mosquitoes are a problem in most parts during the summer, and repellent is a must. Stray dogs (see page 125) can be a problem.

Medical Treatment

Bucharest
Emergency Clinic Hospital
Calea Floreasca 8, tel: 021-317 0121
Euroclinic
Calea Floreasca 14 A, tel: 021-200 6800, www.spitaluleuroclinic.ro
Medicover
Calea Plevnei 96, tel: 021-310 4410, www.medicover.ro
Unirea Medical Centre
B-dul. Unirii 57, bl. E4, tel: 021-327 1188, www.cmu.ro
Brașov
Medo
Str. M. Kogalniceanu 14, tel: 0268-412421, www.medo.ro
Cluj
Medicover
Str. Gheorghe Bilascu 75, tel: 0264-414545, www.medicover.com.ro
Constanța
Medicover
Str. Stefan cel Mare 133, tel: 0241-661602, www.medicover.com.ro
Iași
Medicover
Str. Closca 10, tel: 0232-219977, www.medicover.com.ro
Timișoara
Omnisan
Str. Diana 7, tel: 0256-220950, www.omnisan.ro

Dental Treatment

Bucharest
BB Clinic
Str. Ionescu Gion 4, tel: 021-320 0151, www.germandentist.ro

Emergencies

For ambulance, police or fire you can call one number throughout the country: **112**. As long as you speak clearly you should be understood. Most operators speak some English and French.

Dent-A-America
Str. Varsovia 4, tel: 021-230 2608,
www.dent-a-americainc.ro
Velvet Medical
Str. Sf. Vineri 29 (Bectro Center),
tel: 021-322 3787, www.velvetdental.ro

Pharmacies

Chemists are ubiquitous in Romania,
and many remain open 24 hours a
day. Two major chains, Senisblu and
Help Net, dot the country and stock a
wide range of medicines. You can buy
a number of drugs over the counter
that you cannot in many other
countries, including antibiotics. Most
pharmacists speak English and are
happy to answer questions. If you
have a minor ailment, you may just
as well go a chemist as to a doctor.

Internet

You are never far from an internet
café. They are cheap, charge by the
hour, open round the clock and
English is usually spoken by
personnel. However, they are usually
simply a bunch of computers in a
small, smoky room. Few sell drinks.
Bucharest
Atena
B-dul. Regina Elisabeta 25
Brit Café
Calea Dorobantilor 14 (British
Council), www.britishcouncil.ro
Cybercafe
Str. Franklin 14
Baia Mare
Internet Planet
B-dul. Republicii 22
Oradea
Karomas
Str. Gen Magheru 13
Sinaia
Green Point
B-dul Carol 1
Suceava
Assist Internet Café
Piața 22 Decembrie
Timișoara
3D
Popa Sapca 20b

Most major hotels offer some form of
internet connection in their rooms,
but it is rarely free. Check the rates.
Wi-Fi is limited to Bucharest and a
few places on the Black Sea coast.

Left Luggage

Every railway station in Romania has
a left-luggage counter (there are no
lockers), but outside the major cities
opening hours can be erratic. Make
sure you check that you will be able
to collect your bag when you want to.
Prices for leaving luggage are dirt
cheap, no more than 2 lei per day.

Maps

Most hotel concierges will be able to
provide you with some kind of town
map, but few of these are any good.
One exception is the city guide
Bucharest In Your Pocket, which has
an excellent map of central Bucharest.
The best city map is published by AGC
and shows all transport lines and
points of interest. It is obtainable in
supermarkets, book stores and petrol
stations. Elsewhere, look out for maps
published by Amco Press, which are
clear and easy to use.

An excellent road map of
Romania, including maps of every
major town centre, is published by
Karpatia JIF Szarvas (obtainable at
most petrol stations and good book
shops) and costs around 40 lei.
Other good road maps are produced
by Cartographia and Freytag &
Berndt. The excellent *Librăria Noi*
bookstore in Bucharest stocks most
of these.

The Hungarian publisher Dimap
has an excellent range of hiking maps
(and also an extremely good map of
Transylvania). You should also be able
to pick up these and other hiking
maps at most book stores in
Bucharest and other cities.
Librăria Noi
B-dul. Nicolae Bălcescu 18,
Bucharest, tel: 021-311 0700.

Media

Newspapers

You can find the English-language
press at news kiosks in the five-star
hotels in Bucharest, and the most
central newsstands. French, German
and Italian newspapers are also
available in Bucharest, usually a day
late. You are unlikely to find any
foreign press outside the capital.

Local English publications are
limited to the *Bucharest Daily News*,
written in questionable English, and
the weekly *Business Review*, a glossy
freesheet. You will find it in hotels,
banks, bars and restaurants.

For restaurant and entertainment
listings in the capital, try *Bucharest
In Your Pocket*, free at all hotels. The
website, www.inyourpocket.com/romania/en,
has general information on Romania,
and specific coverage of Brașov and
Poiana Brașov. Elsewhere in the
country look out for the English-
language free guides called *What,
Where, When*. They are published in
Timișoara, Constanța, Brașov and
Cluj, and carry listings and city maps.

Television and Radio

Local television is generally poor,
though there are plenty of imported
programmes, shown in their original
language with Romanian subtitles. The
most popular channel is state-run TVR
1, while the most popular commercial
station is Pro TV. There are three
dedicated news channels, Realitatea
TV, National 24 and Antena 3.

Most hotels offer cable or satellite
TV, with a wide variety of foreign
news channels, usually including BBC
World, CNN and EuroNews.

BBC World Service radio
broadcasts in Bucharest on 88.0 FM,
with a mix of Romanian and English
programming.

Money

Romania's currency is the *leu*, plural
lei. It is usually written in full *(lei)* but
sometimes appears as RON or ROL.
The exchange rate is normally around
5 RON to £1 sterling, 3.3 to 1 euro.
Banknotes come in denominations of
500, 200, 100, 50, 10, 5 and 1.
One leu is subdivided into 100 *bani*,
in coins of 50, 20, 10, 5, 2 and 1.
You may find old banknotes in
circulation, the same as the new
ones but slightly larger and with four
extra zeros. Since 1 January 2007,
these have no longer been legal
tender, but can be exchanged in
banks. The leu is freely convertible
but it is difficult to change it, so try
not to end up with too much at the
end of your trip. The best place to
change money is in a bank.

Cheques and Credit Cards

Visa/MasterCard credit and debit
cards are accepted in most hotels,
shops and restaurants; you may be
asked to input your PIN. Note that
many places that display the Visa or
MasterCard signs will turn their noses
up when presented with plastic.
Check in advance. American Express
and Diners Club cards are not
particularly welcome, and traveller's
cheques are notoriously difficult to
get rid of.

There are Roman Catholic churches in all cities, and in Bucharest there is an Anglican church that holds services, in English, every Sunday at 10am. **Anglican Church of the Resurrection**, Str. Xenopol 2, tel: 021-210 2937.

S tudent Travellers

Most museums offer a student reduction. There are no discounts on trains for international students. For hostelling information, *see page 340.*

T elecommunications

There are public phones (usually blue and orange) almost everywhere in Romania; all need a phone card. You can buy them from kiosks, newsstands and small shops – look for the sign *Avem cartele Romtelecom.* Simply insert the card (your available credit will be displayed on the screen), and then dial. You can make calls from most hotel rooms, but usually at great cost.

The country code for Romania is +40. The city code for Bucharest is 021, and for Braşov is 0268. Other important city codes include: Cluj 0264, Constanţa 0241, Sibiu 0269, Sinaia 0244 and Timişoara 0256. As usual, the first "0" is dropped if calling from abroad. Within Romania the city code is used in full, unless you are dialling from the same city or area. For international calls, dial 00, the country code, then the number.

Most mobile phones work in Romania, but roaming charges mean that costs are high. For longer stays it may be worth buying a local pay-as-you-go SIM card from one of the local companies, Orange (www.orange.ro) or Vodafone (www.vodafone.ro). They cost around 35 lei, include a few free

P hotography

Many museums and attractions charge a fee for taking photographs, and in some places, such as the Parliament Palace in Bucharest, this can be quite high (up to 30 lei).

Postal Services

Post offices can be found in even the smallest village, but if you are posting something abroad, it is best do so from Bucharest. Even from there, post can take ages to reach its destination. Getting served in a Romanian post office is time consuming; it's worth asking at your hotel if they can buy stamps for you. **Central Post Office** (Oficiul Poştal 1), Str. Matei Millo 10, Bucharest (open 24 hrs).
DHL, Calea Buzesti 65–69, tel: 021-222 1771, www.dhl.ro
Federal Express, tel: 021-201 4822, www.fedex.com/ro
TNT, tel: 021-303 4567

Public Toilets

There are very few decent public toilets in Romania. In Bucharest the best ones are in the Unirea, Bucharest Mall and Plaza Romania shopping centres. Those at most Romanian railway stations are less hygienic. In the mountains even restaurant and retreat toilets can leave a lot to be desired. When travelling on trains it is advisable to carry some toilet paper, as there is often none supplied.

R eligious Services

Orthodox services are held daily, usually at 11am and 5pm. The best-attended religious service takes place at midnight on Easter Saturday, and is a genuine spectacle.

Public Holidays

Romania has few national holidays. Orthodox Easter is the biggest celebration, and usually falls a week or two after the Western Easter. Note that if a holiday falls on a weekend, so be it: the Western practice of taking the next working day off is not yet a Romanian one.
1 January New Year's Day
April/May Orthodox Easter
1 May Labour Day
1 December National Day (Commemorating the union of Transylvania with Wallachia and Moldavia in 1919)
25–26 December Christmas

minutes, and can be bought from newsstands, public-transport ticket booths and phone dealerships.

Tipping

You are expected to tip waiters and waitresses (but check your bill to ensure that service is not included), domestic hotel staff and doormen. A 10 percent tip is seen as obligatory. Unusually, taxi drivers do not expect a tip. If you need medical treatment, you should tip everybody at the clinic or hospital, from the

Time Zone

Romania is two hours ahead of GMT: noon in Bucharest is 5am in New York, 10am in London. As in the rest of the EU, clocks are advanced one hour from late March to late October.

receptionist to the doctor.

Tour and Travel Agents

see Activities, page 362.

Tourist Information

There are few tourist information offices in Romania. Two notable exceptions are the mountain resort of Predeal, which has an excellent information centre in the forecourt of the railway station, open daily 10am–4pm, and the Transylvanian city of Sibiu, which has a tourist office on the main square. In Bucharest there is no tourist information office whatsoever, although this is expected to change.

Romanian Tourist Offices Abroad
UK: 22 New Cavendish Street, London WIM 7LH, tel: 44-20 7224 3692.
US: 355 Lexington Avenue, 19th Floor, New York, NY 10017, tel: 1-212 545 8484

W ebsites

see Further Reading, page 375.

What to Bring

Toiletries in Romania are expensive, so bring what you need from home. Baby formula milk and nappies are also expensive. Batteries and camera film are likely to cost more than at home. If planning on visiting a Romanian family at home a bottle of spirits from your home country is always appreciated.

L ANGUAGE

UNDERSTANDING THE LANGUAGE

While the grammar can at first appear daunting, Romanian *(limba română)* is generally considered one of the easiest eastern European languages for English-speakers to learn. And if you ever struggled over Latin conjugations at school and wondered what the earthly point was, a head start on learning Romanian could well be the answer – grammatically this is the closest living language to Latin, although there are many Slavic, French and, more recently, English influences in the vocabulary. Linguists believe there is also a core of about 400 words of ancient Dacian origin, for example the word *brânză* for cheese.

Having the only Romance language in the region has always made Romanians feel culturally removed from their neighbours. Rather superior in fact, although the feeling has never been reciprocated. For historical and cultural reasons, Romania belongs to La Francophonie, the league of French-speaking countries. Bucharest even hosted the Francophone summit in 2006 (with road blocks that brought the city to a standstill). However, young Romanians are far more likely to speak English than French.

Romanian is the sole official state language and is also the state language of the Republic of Moldova (although officially known there as Moldovan). However, in communities where they make up at least 20 percent of the population, linguistic minorities enjoy official recognition of their language. This includes dealings with local authorities, street signs and the right to state-funded education in that language. The best-known examples are Hungarian minorities in Transylvania but there is also a town (Budeşti, in Călăraşi County) where Gypsies enjoy official recognition of their language.

Romanian has a number of oddities. It is the only Romance language to have preserved three genders and the vocative. It is the only language to use the letters ă, ş (with a comma, not cedilla) and ţ, hence the fact that most fonts and keyboards cannot render Romanian correctly. It is also unusual for having so many variants of "you" *(see panel, left)*.

You

In French correctly navigating between *tu* and *vous* can be a social minefield. Romanian, however, offers double the opportunity for confusion and offence. Romanian has four ways of saying you: *tu, dumneata, voi* and *dumneavoastră*. To confuse matters, usage is different according to region and the rules are so nuanced that even many Romanians are unable to explain them adequately.

Tu is the informal singular, used between friends, relatives and young people, or to children and teenagers. *Tu* is more common in big cities than in the countryside. *Voi* is the plural version of *tu*. *Dumneata* (colloquially *mata*) is a more formal version of the singular, used when talking to colleagues or people much younger than yourself but generally best avoided. In current usage *dumneata* is generally considered disrespectful except when addressing someone a

lot younger (for example someone in their 50s speaking to someone in their 20s).

Most formal of all however is *dumneavoastră*, the plural of dumneata. It can be used to address one person or several people but it always takes a second person plural verb. If in doubt, it's safest to use this form when addressing strangers or older people, or to use the plural form without any pronoun altogether, but *tu* if someone about the same age uses it when speaking to you. There are also polite forms for the third person, but that's another story.

When addressing strangers, it's polite to use the word *domnule* (sir), *doamna* (madam) or *domnişoara* (miss). Under communism, *tovarăşe* (comrade) became the prescribed form of address and is now, somewhat ironically, creeping back as a greeting within street gangs.

Nouns

The indefinite article is *un* for masculine and neuter nouns and *o* for feminine in the singular, and *nişte* for all genders in the plural, for example: *un băiat* (a boy, masculine), *un tren* (a train, neuter), *o fată* (a girl, feminine), *nişte băiaţi* (boys, some boys), *nişte trenuri* (trains, some trains), *nişte fete* (girls, some girls).

However, instead of using a separate word like *the*, Romanian forms the definite with a suffix. This oddity is a legacy from medieval Latin when *ille* (that) became in common use to mean *the* (for example, *homo ille*, the man, becoming *omul* in Romanian). The form of the suffix depends on the gender and final letter of the noun. Nouns ending in a consonant or *u* are usually masculine or neuter and those ending in a vowel except *u* usually feminine. In the singular, the most usual definite ending is *-ul* in the masculine and neuter and *-a* (replacing final *ă* or *e*) in the feminine. In the plural masculine nouns take *-i* and feminine and neuter nouns end in *-le*. Some typical examples are: *un leu* (a lion), *leul* (the lion); *o casă* (a house), *casa* (the house); *o cafea* (a coffee), *cafeaua* (the coffee); *o expresie* (an expression), *expresia* (the expression)

Plural forms also vary depending on gender and word ending. Generally masculine nouns end in *-i* (eg *lei*, lions), feminine in *-e* (eg *case*, houses) and neuter in *-uri*, *-e* or *-i* (eg *plicuri*, envelopes; *fructe*, fruits; *ochelari*, spectacles).

Pronouns

In Romanian you can usually omit the personal pronoun if it's the subject of a verb. For example, the most usual way of saying "I'm at home" is *Sunt acasă*, not *Eu sunt acasă*.

I *eu*
you (sing.) *tu* (familiar), *dumneata* (polite), *dumneavoastră* (very polite)
he/she *el/ea* (familiar),

dânsul/dânsa (polite), *dumnealui/dumneaei* (very polite)
it *el* (masc. and neut.), *ea* (fem.)
we *noi*
you (pl.) *voi* (familiar), *dumneavoastră* (polite)
they *ei* (masc. and mixed), *ele* (fem. and neut.) (familiar), *dânsii/dânsele* (polite), *dumnealor* (very polite)
Who? *Cine?*
What? *Ce?*
Which (one)...? *Care...?*

Words and Phrases

Hello *Salut/Bună*
Good morning *Bună dimineaţa*
Good afternoon *Bună ziua*
Good evening *Bună seara*
Good night *Noapte bună*
Bon voyage! *Drum bun!*
Welcome! *Bine aţi venit!*
Goodbye/Bye *La revedere/Pa*
Good luck!/Cheers! *Noroc!*
How are you? *Ce mai faceţi?*
Very well, thanks *Foarte bine, mulţumesc*
And you? *Şi dumneavoastră?*
So so *Aşa şi aşa*
What is your name? *Cum vă numiţi?*
My name is... *Mă numesc...*

I am British/American *Sunt britanic(ă)/ american(ă)*
I don't understand *Nu înţeleg*
Please speak more slowly *Vorbiţi mai rar, vă rog*
Please can you help me *Puteţi să m-ajutaţi, vă rog?*
I am looking for... *Caut...*
Where is...? *Unde este...?*
I don't know *Nu ştiu*
Here it is *Aici e*
There it is *Acolo este*
Let's go *Să mergem*
At what time? *La ce oră?*
When? *Când?*
What time is it? *Cât e ceasul?*
yes/no *da/nu*
please (requesting something) *vă rog*
please (offering something) *poftiţi*
thank you (very much) *mulţumesc (foarte mult)*
excuse me *nu vă supăraţi/scuze*
OK *bine*
here *aici*
there *acolo*
today *azi/astăzi*
yesterday *ieri*
tomorrow *mâine*
now *acum*
(a bit) later *(un pic) mai târziu*
right away *imediat*

The Romanian Alphabet

The Romanian alphabet has 31 letters, some with diacritical marks. Three are unique to Romanian (*ă, ş* and *ţ*). The first of these is correctly written with a semicircle, the last two with a comma, not a cedilla. In an alphabetical list such as a telephone directory *ă* follows *a*, *â* follows *ă*, *ş* follows *s* and *ţ* follows *t*. The letters *k, q, w, x* and *y* are recent additions to Romanian and only found in words of foreign origin, for example *watt, quasar* and *whisky*. Letters generally have the same value regardless of their position in a word. The main exception is that a single *i* at the end of a word is usually almost silent, pronounced like a very brief *y* as in dockyard.

Consonants

b = as **b** in **b**at
c = when followed by *i* or *e*, as **ch** in **ch**ick; otherwise as **c** in s**c**an
ch = (only found before *e* or *i*) as **c** in s**c**an
d = as **d** in **d**esk, but dental (with the flat of the tongue touching the roof of the mouth just behind the teeth)
f = as **f** in **f**it
g = when followed by *i* or *e*, as **g** in **g**em; otherwise as **g** in **g**ood
gh = (only found before *e* or *i*) as **g** in **g**ood

j = as **s** in trea**s**ure
k = as **c** in s**c**an
l = as **l** in **l**ove
m = as **m** in **m**ake
n = as **n** in **n**ote but dental
p = as **p** in s**p**eak
q = as **c** in s**c**an
r = as **r** in **r**at but trilled as in Scottish or Italian
s = as **s** in **s**moke
ş = as **sh** in ru**sh**
t = as **t** in s**t**ay but dental
ţ = as **ts** in bi**ts** but dental
v = as **v** in **v**oice
w = as **v** in **v**at or **w** in **w**ater
x = as **ks** in boo**ks** or as **gs** in ba**gs**
y = as **ee** in s**ee**
z = as **z** in **z**oo but dental

Vowels

a = as **u** in b**u**t
ă = as **er** in sist**er** but without any *r* sound
â = exactly the same as **î** below (this only occurs in the middle of words)
e = as **e** in p**e**n
i = as **i** in mach**i**ne; if unstressed at the end of a word a single *i* is barely pronounced, but softens the previous consonant
î = no exact English equivalent; similar to the **o** in kingd**o**m (since the latest spelling reforms this

nearly always occurs only at the start or end of a word)
o = as **or** in f**or**t but without any *r* sound
u = as **u** in p**u**t

Diphthongs

Romanian is rich in vowel combinations, all pronounced as one syllable. The most common diphthongs follow. There are also triphthongs (eg *ioa* in *creioane*, crayons, in which the middle letter is pronounced as a vowel and the first and last as semivowels).
ai = as **igh** in h**igh**
au = as **ow** in n**ow**
ău = as **o** in n**o**
ea = no exact English equivalent; similar to **a** in c**a**t. At the end of a word like **ayer** in pl**ayer** but without any *r* sound
ei = as **ay** in p**ay**
eu = no English equivalent; starts with **e** as in p**e**t then with brief **oo** sound as in l**oo**
ia = as **ya** in **ya**rd but without any *r* sound
ie = as **ye** in **ye**s
io = as **yo** in **yo**nder
iu = as **ew** in p**ew**
oa = as **wha** in **wha**t
oi = as **oy** in t**oy**
ua = as **wa** in **wa**sh
uă = similar to **ue** in infl**ue**nce

this morning *azi dimineață*
tomorrow morning *mâine dimineață*
this afternoon *azi/astăzi după amiază/masă*
this evening *diseară*
yesterday evening *aseară*
tonight *la noapte*
the day after tomorrow *poimâine*

Accommodation

I'd like a (single/double/twin) room *Aş vrea o cameră (cu un pat/două paturi/pat dublu)*
...with shower *cu duş*
...with bath *cu baie*
...with a view (towards the road/lake/sea) *cu vedere către stradă/lac/mare*
...with disabled access *cu acces pentru persoane invalide*
Is breakfast included? *Prețul include şi micul dejun?*
I have reserved a room *Am rezervat o cameră*
May I see the room, please? *Pot să văd camera, vă rog?*
washbasin *chiuvetă*
key *cheie*
bed *pat*
lavatory *toaletă/W.C.*
lift/elevator *lift/ascensor*
air conditioning *aer condiționat*
hot water *apă caldă*

Emergencies

Help! *Ajutor!*
Fire! *Foc!*
Stop thief! *Opriți hoțul!*
Call a doctor, quickly *Chemați un doctor, repede*
Call an ambulance *Chemați o salvare*
Call the police *Chemați poliția*
Call the fire brigade *Chemați pompieri*
Where is there a telephone? *Unde se găseşte un telefon?*
Where is the nearest (emergency) hospital? *Unde este cel mai apropiat spital (de urgență)?*
I am sick *Sunt bolnavă*
I have lost my passport/bag *Mi-am pierdut paşaportul/sacul*

Shopping

How much does it cost (per kilo)? *Cât costă (un kilogram)?*
It's (too) expensive *E (prea) scump*
Where can I buy...? *Unde pot să cumpăr...?*
I'm just looking *Mă uit doar*
Have you got...? *Aveți...?*
Is there...? *Există...?*
I'll take it *Îl cumpăr*
A kilo/500 grammes, please *Un kilo/cinci sute de grame, vă rog*
shop *magazin*
kiosk *chioşc*

open/shut *deschis/închis*
post office *poştă*
stamp *timbru*
letter *scrisoare*
envelope *plic*
ATM *bancomat*
marketplace *piață*
bookshop *librărie*
fresh/frozen *proaspăt/înghețat*
organic *organic (not a common word yet, except in some supermarkets)*
bakery *brutărie*
cake shop *patiserie*
chemist's (drugstore) *farmacie*
fishmonger's *pescărie*
grocery *băcănie*
greengrocer's *zarzavagiu*
tobacconist's *tutungerie*
wine merchant's *magazin de vinuri*
What is this? *Ce este asta?*
antiques shop *anticariat*

Getting Around

General/Public Transport/Taxis

I want to get off at... *Vreau să cobor la...*
Is there a bus to the centre? *Există un autobuz către centru?*
What is the name of this street? *Cum se numeşte această stradă?*
How far is...? *Cât e până la...?*
How can I get to...? *Cum se ajunge la...?*
airport *aeroport*
customs *vamă*
train station *gară*
bus terminal *autogară*
bus station/stop *statie (de autobuz)*
ticket office *casa de bilete*
left-luggage office *birou depozit bagaje de mână*
Metro station *staţie de metrou*
bus *autobuz*
bus stop *staţie de autobuz*
train *tren*
tram *tramvai*
trolleybus *troleibuz/trolebuz*
boat *barcă*
coach *autocar*
platform *peron*
ticket *bilet*
I want... *Aş vrea...*
a single/return ticket to Iaşi *un bilet dus/dus-întors pentru Iaşi*
a couchette *o cuşetă*
a sleeper *un loc la vagon de dormit*
1st/2nd class *clasa întâia/clasa a două*
What time does the train/bus depart/arrive? *La ce oră pleacă/ajunge trenul/autobuzul?*
hitchhiking *autostop*
Please could you order me a taxi *Puteţi să-mi comandaţi un taxi, vă rog?*
How much does it cost to the Continental Hotel? *Cât costă până la hotelul Continental?*
Is the taximeter (not) working? *(Nu) merge taximetrul?*

False Friends

Romanian has many false friends for English-speakers. Examples include *email* (enamel), *librărie* (bookshop), *cald* (hot) and *prezervativ* (condom).

Railway Station Signs

bagaje de mană **left-luggage office**
camera mama şi copilul **mother-and-baby room**
casa (case) de bilete **ticket office(s)**
informaţii **information**
linia **line**
mesagerie **parcel office**
obiecte găsite **lost property**
plecări **departures**
sala de aşteptare **waiting room**
sosiri **arrivals**

Driving

Where's the road to...? *Unde este drumul spre...?*
left/right *la stânga/la dreapta*
straight ahead *drept înainte*
I'm lost *M-am rătăcit*
near/far *aproape/departe*
in front of/behind... *în faţa.../în spatele...*
next/near to... *lângă...*
car park *(loc de) parcare*
over there *acolo*
at the end of... *la sfârşitul...*
on foot *pe jos*
by car *cu maşina*
town map *hartă a oraşului*
(national) road map *hartă a drumurilor (naţionale)*
street *stradă*
square *piaţă*
motorway *autostradă*
no parking *parcare interzisă*
petrol (gas) station *benzinăria*
Where's the nearest garage? *Unde este cel mai apropiat service?*

Sightseeing

art gallery *galerie de artă*
beach *plajă*
castle *castel*
cathedral *catedrală*
chapel *bisericuţă*
church *biserică*
cinema *cinema*
citadel/fortress *cetate*
city *oraş*
convent *mânăstire*
exhibition *expoziţie*
fountain *fântână*
garden *grădină*
hill *deal*
lake *lac*
monastery *mănăstire*
mountain *munte*
museum *muzeu*
nave *naoş*

Market Shopping

Supermarkets (supermarketuri) and, increasingly, hypermarkets (hypermarketuri) are self-service and full of imported goods. However, often the freshest, cheapest and best produce is to be found at the market (piaţă). The food has rarely travelled very far and is usually organic. Prices are generally by the kilo (un kilo) or hundred grams (o sută de grame), but not always displayed. Haggling is in order and part of the fun. Take your own bag (pungă).

old town/quarter oraş vechi
opera operă
palace palat
park parc
river râu
ruin ruină
statue statuie
swimming pool piscină/ştrand
synagogue sinagogă
theatre teatru
ticket office casa de bilete
tourist information office oficiu de turism
tower turn
town oraş
town hall primărie
travel agency agenţie de voiaj
valley vale
village sat
zoo grădină zoologică
free entry intrare gratuită
open/closed deschis/închis
every day in fiecare zi
all year tot timpul anului
all day toată ziua

Eating Out

restaurant restaurant
menu meniu
breakfast mic dejun
lunch prânz
dinner cină
meal masă
starters antreuri
main course fel principal
set menu meniu fix
vegetarian dishes mâncăruri pentru vegetarieni
diet food mâncare de regim
wine list listă de vinuri
fork furculiţă
knife cuţit
spoon lingură
plate farfurie
glass pahar
bottle sticlă
napkin şerveţel
ashtray scrumieră
Waiter/Waitress! Chelner/Chelneriţă!

I'd like to pay Aş vrea să plătesc
Keep the change Păstraţi restul
house speciality specialitatea casei,
chef's speciality specialitatea şefului

Drinks

coffee house cafenea
terrace terasă
coffee cafea
  Turkish turcească
  black neagră
  with milk cu lapte
  decaffeinated decafeinizată
instant coffee ness
sugar zahăr
tea ceai
  with lemon cu lămâie
herbal tea ceai din plante
milk lapte
mineral water apă minerală
  sparkling gazoasă
  still negazoasă/plată
fruit juice suc natural
lemonade limonadă
hot cald(ă)
beer bere
  bottled îmbuteliată
  Romanian românească
  imported importată
  draught la halbă
soft drink băutură nealcoolică
with ice cu gheaţă
wine vin
  red roşu
  white alb
  rosé roze
  dry sec
  sweet dulce
  sparkling spumos
house wine vin de casa
glass pahar
a bottle of... o sticlă de...
half bottle jumătate de sticlă
carafe carafă
with/without water cu/fără apă
brandy, cognac coniac
gin gin
vodka vodcă
whisky whisky
rum rom
tonic water apă tonică
soda water sifon
Cheers! Noroc!

Menu Decoder

Breakfast and Snacks

brânză cheese
gem jam
iaurt yoghurt
măsline (verzi/negre) (green/black) olives
mezeluri cold meats
ouă eggs
  fierte (moi) (soft-)boiled
  jumări scrambled
  ochiuri fierte în apă poached
  moi soft
  prăjite fried

pâine bread
pâine prăjită toast
piper pepper
roşii tomatoes
salam salami
sare salt
slănină şi ouă bacon and eggs
şuncă şi ouă ham and eggs
unt butter

Meat/Carne

afumat smoked
antricot entrecôte steak
biftec beefsteak
bine prăjit well done
cabanos sausages (long and dry, served fried)
carne de căprioară venison
carne de miel lamb
carne de oiae mutton
carne de porc mistreţ wild boar
carne de porc pork
carne de vacă beef
carne de viţel veal
caşcaval pane fried breaded cheese
cârnaţi sausages
chiftele meatballs
copt baked
cotlet chop
cu puţin sânge rare
cu sos in sauce
ficat liver
fiert boiled
fiert înăbuşit stewed
filet Chateaubriand tenderloin
frigărui kebabs
friptură de... fried/roast...
friptură de vacă beefsteak
iepure rabbit
iepure de câmp hare
în sange very rare
la grătar barbecued/grilled
mici/mititei small spicy skinless sausages
muşchi de vacă sirloin steak
muşchi filet fillet steak
potrivit medium
prăjit fried
prăjit la cuptor roast
pulpă de miel leg of lamb
rinichi kidneys
sarmale în (foi de) varză cabbage leaves with rice and minced meat
sarmale în (foi de) viţă vine leaves stuffed with rice and minced meat
şniţel (pane) schnitzel
şuncă gammon/ham
tocană/tochitură stew/casserole
umplut stuffed

Poultry/Păsări

aripă wing
curcan turkey
fazan pheasant
găină chicken
gâscă goose
piept breast
prepeliţă quail
pulpă leg
raţă duck

Fish and Seafood

afumat **smoked**
caviar **caviar**
crap **carp**
creveți **prawns/shrimps**
file **fillet**
homar **lobster**
icre **roe**
icre negre **caviar**
la cuptor **baked**
langustă **crab, lobster**
morun/nisetru **sturgeon**
păstrăv **trout**
prăjit **fried**
raci **crab**
rasol **boiled**
saramură de/în saramură **in brine**
sardele **sardines**
scrumbii **kippers**
somon **salmon**
stridii **oysters**
șalău **pike**
ton **tuna (tunny)**

Vegetables/Cereals/Salads

ardei (grași) roșii/galbeni/verzi **red/yellow/green peppers**
ardei iuți **chilli peppers**
brocoli **broccoli**
cartofi **potatoes**
castravete/castraveți **cucumber(s)**
ceapă/cepe **onion(s)**
ciuperci **mushrooms**
conopidă/conopide **cauliflower(s)**
dovlecel **courgette/zucchini**
fasole **beans**
fasole verde **green beans**
ghiveci **stewed vegetables**
legume **vegetables**
linte **lentils**
mazăre **peas**
mămăligă/mămăliguță **polenta**
morcovi **carrots**
murat **pickled**
murături **pickles**
orez **rice**
paste făinoase **pasta**
roșie/roșii **tomato(es)**
salată asortată **mixed salad (usually cucumbers and tomatoes)**
salată verde **lettuce**
spanac **spinach**
tăiței **noodles**
ulei de măsline **olive oil**
usturoi **garlic**
varză/verze **cabbage(s)**
vânătă **aubergine/eggplant**

Fruit and Desserts

ananas **pineapple**
banană **banana**
caise **apricots**
căpșuni **strawberries**
cireșe **cherries**
clătite **pancakes**
coazăce negre **blackcurrants**
desert **dessert**
fructe (proaspete) **(fresh) fruit**
grepfrut **grapefruit**
înghețată **ice cream**

lămâie **lemon**
mandarine **tangerines**
măr/mere **apple(s)**
pară/pere **pear(s)**
pepene galben **melon**
pepene verde **watermelon**
piersic/piersici **peach(es)**
plăcintă **flaky pastry pie**
portocală/portocale **orange(s)**
prăjitură **cake/torte**
prună/prune **plum(s)**
struguri **grapes**
zmeură **raspberries**

Herbs and Spices

arpagic **chives**
busuioc **basil**
cimbru **thyme**
măcriș **watercress**
mentă **mint**
muștar **mustard**
paprica **paprika**
pătrunjel **parsley**
rozmarin **rosemary**
salvie **sage**
scorțișoară **cinnamon**
sovârv **oregano**

Numbers, Days and Dates

Numbers

Used before a noun, numbers from 20 upwards (or compound numbers ending in 20–99, eg 457) are followed by *de*, for example: *douăzeci de cărți* (20 books). Below 20 there is no *de*: *trei cărți* (three books). Numbers ending in 1 or 2 change according to gender but all others are invariable. Commas indicate decimal points and points indicate thousands, eg: *1,25 lei, 2.600 km* (2,600 km).

one *unu* (masc. and neut.), *una* (fem.) (used independently); *un* (masc. and neut.), *o* (fem.) (preceding a noun)

two *doi* (masc.), *două* (fem. and neut.);
three *trei*; **four** *patru*; **five** *cinci*;
six *șase*; **seven** *șapte*; **eight** *opt*;
nine *nouă*; **ten** *zece*
11 *unsprezece* (pronounced *unșpe*)
12 *doisprezece* (masc.), *douăsprezece* (fem. and neut.) (pronounced *doișpe* and *douășpe*)
13 *treisprezece* (*treișpe*)
14 *paisprezece* (*paișpe*)
15 *cincisprezece* (*cinșpe*)
16 *șaisprezece* (*șaișpe*)
17 *șaptisprezece* (*șaptișpe*)
18 *optsprezece* (*optișpe*)
19 *nouăsprezece* (usually pronounced *nouășpe*)
20 *douăzeci*
21 *douăzeci și unu* (masc. and neut.), *douăzeci și una* (fem.)
22 *douăzeci și doi* (masc. and neut.), *douăzeci și două* (fem.)
30 *treizeci*
40 *patruzeci*
50 *cincizeci*
60 *șaizeci*
70 *șaptezeci*
80 *optzeci*
90 *nouăzeci*
100 *o sută*
150 *o sută cincizeci*
200 *două sute*
300 *trei sute*
400 *patru sute*
1,000 *o mie*
2,000 *două mii*
1 million *un milion*

Saying the Date

10 May 2007 *zece mai două mii șapte*

Days of the Week

Romanians consider Monday the first day of the week.
Monday *luni*
Tuesday *marți*
Wednesday *miercuri*
Thursday *joi*
Friday *vineri*
Saturday *sâmbătă*
Sunday *duminică*

Seasons

spring *primăvară*
summer *vară*
autumn *toamnă*
winter *iarnă*

Months

January *ianuarie*
February *februarie*
March *martie*
April *aprilie*
May *mai*
June *iunie*
July *iulie*
August *august*
September *septembrie*
October *octombrie*
November *noiembrie*
December *decembrie*

Table Talk

I'm a vegetarian *Sunt vegetarian(ă)*
I'm on a diet *Țin regim*
What do you recommend? *Ce îmi recomandați?*
Do you have local specialities? *Aveți specialități locale?*
I'd like to order *Aș vrea să comand*
That's not what I ordered *Aceasta nu este ce am comandat*
May I have another glass/bottle of wine? *Aș mai vrea un pahar/ o sticlă cu vin, vă rog*
Enjoy your meal *Poftă bună*
Where's a good place to hear folk/house music? *Unde este un bun loc pentru muzică folclorică/ house?*

FURTHER READING

History

The Balkans. Mark Mazower. Phoenix Press (2000). A concise and lucid account of the history of southeastern Europe, it only occasionally touches on Romania but is good on the Ottoman period and the (mis)perceptions of the region by the West.

Ceauşescu and the Securitate: Coercion and Dissent in Romania, 1965–89. Dennis Deletant. M.E. Sharpe (1996). Written by a Romania expert with long experience of Ceauşescu's Romania and a Romanian wife, this excellent book is an authoritative blend of personal experiences and thorough research into the travails of life under Ceauşescu.

The Holocaust in Romania. Radu Ioanid, foreword by Elie Wiesel. Ivan R Dee (2000). Account of the destruction of Romania's Jews and Gypsies under the Antonescu regime between 1940 and 1944. Using archival materials made available since the 1990s, Ioanid examines the rise of anti-Semitism in the years leading up to World War II.

Kiss the Hand You Cannot Bite: The Rise and Fall of the Ceauşescus. Edward Behr. Villard (1991) Taking its name from an old Romanian proverb, this gripping book explains Romania's sorry plight under Ceauşescu as the culmination of a historical process going back to ancient times, helping explain how he was able to get away with such excesses by abusing power and developing a personality cult. It can make for depressing reading.

Michael of Romania: The King and the Country. Ivor Porter. Sutton Publishing (2005). Affectionate and authoritative biography of Romania's king written by a former SOE officer based in Romania in World War II. Describing his brave but ultimately futile efforts to save Romania from foreign domination, it makes fascinating reading for anyone interested in the royal family or Romania's 20th century, not to mention a strong case for Michael's restoration.

Red Horizons: The True Story of Nicolae and Elena Ceauşescus' Crimes, Lifestyle, and Corruption. Ion Pacepa. Regnery Publishing (1990). Written by the former head of Romania's foreign intelligence service, the DIE, who defected to the USA in 1978, this lurid exposé covers several months in that year inside Romania's inner circle. Many however have questioned the accuracy of some of the allegations and Pacepa's own complicity.

Romania in Turmoil. Martyn Rady. I.B. Tauris (1992). A meticulously-researched one-stop shop for anyone wanting to understand the events leading up to the downfall of the Ceauşescus in a 20th-century context.

Theft of a Nation: Romania Since Communism. Tom Gallagher. C Hurst (2005). Detailed coverage of Romania's turbulent post-communist period leading up to the accession talks for EU membership.

Art & Architecture

Romanian Folk Art: A Guide to Living Traditions. Karsten McNulty. Aid to Artisans Inc (1999). Lavishly illustrated rundown of the subject with practical information for souvenir hunters. The author spent two years in Romania with the US Peace Corps.

Transylvania: Its Products and its People. Charles Boner. Longmans, Green, Reader, and Dyer, 1865. Long out of print, this somewhat rambling Victorian narrative was an inspiration for Bram Stoker's Dracula and gives some fascinating descriptions of the region's Saxon fortified churches. It is also available online at http://depts. washington.edu/cartah/text_archive/boner/toc_pag.shtml.

Travel Literature

The Balkan Trilogy. Olivia Manning. Penguin, 1988. Semi-autobiographical trilogy covering the adventures of a Communist-leaning itinerant British lecturer posted to Bucharest at the start of World War II, based closely on her experiences living there with her husband, a Communist-leaning itinerant British lecturer. A highly entertaining romp through Balkan

history, depicting Bucharest as a hotbed of decadence, debauchery and espionage.

Between the Woods and the Water. Patrick Leigh Fermor, John Murray (1986). One of the best travel books ever written, Leigh Fermor's luminous account of pre-war Romania evokes a lost world but remains essential reading for anyone visiting the country. It forms the second part of an unfinished trilogy covering the author's 1930s journey on foot from the Hook of Holland to Istanbul (A Time of Gifts, which traces his route as far as Esztergom in Hungary, is also recommended).

Transylvania and Beyond. Dervla Murphy. Overlook Press (1995). The intrepid über-traveller's account of Transylvania and its people in the aftermath of the events of 1989. Murphy explains the sense of alienation felt by the Hungarian population, and accurately describes Romania as "one of Europe's least European countries".

Winds of Sorrow; Travels in and around Transylvania. Alan Ogden, Orchid Press (2004). A rambling collection of essays and musings on Transylvania, with a good history chapter and plenty of background on the various peoples of the region.

Literature

Dracula. Bram Stoker. Penguin Classics (2003). It goes without saying that the theme has been done to death, and that the links with Romania are tenuous, but this is still a wonderfully realised gothic fantasy and of interest to anyone travelling to the Romanian countryside.

Hour of Sand. Ana Blandiana. Learning Links, 1990. The first translation in English of works by one of Romania's most revered poets, giving a tender yet uncompromising analysis of contemporary issues. In the 1980s Blandiana wrote a number of protest poems about life under Ceauşescu, including most famously Totul (Everything), which became a samizdat favourite for its bleak portrayal of everyday shortages.

The Land of Green Plums. Herta Müller. Northwestern University Press

(1998). The author is a Transylvanian Saxon who grew up in Ceaușescu's Romania and based this powerful novel on the everyday horrors of life there.

Night Elie Wiesel. Penguin (2006). Harrowing account of the Holocaust from the perspective of a Hungarian Jew, beginning at the Sighetul Marmației camp.

Refuges Augustin Buzura. Editura Fundatiei Culturale Române (1993). One of the most importnat works of modern Romanian literature, Refuges takes totalitarianism and the role of ideology to task.

Romanian Culture

Taste of Romania: Its Cookery and Glimpses of Its History, Folklore, Art, Literature and Poetry. Nicolae Klepper. Hippocrene, 1999. An excellent instruction to Romania's cuisine and wine, interspersed the recipes with colourful titbits about Romanian culture in general.

The Wedding of the Dead: Ritual, Poetics and Popular Culture in Transylvania. Gail Kligman. University of California Press (1992). Describes the life of Ieud village, in deepest Maramureș, from an anthropological perspective. Kligman has also written an interesting book on Ceaușescu's ill-advised attempts to raise Romania's birth-rate – an initiative that led to the "orphan" crises of the 1990s.

Natural History

Birding in Eastern Europe. Gerard Gorman, WildSounds (2006). This guide covers the best birding sites in eleven eastern European countries. Over 230 sites are described, each with a map. Eleven country context maps are also provided.

Romania – a Birdwatching and Wildlife Guide. James Roberts, Burton Expeditions (2000). The most comprehensive guide, covering birds, mammals, reptiles, amphibians, invertebrates and plants. The detailed coverage of dozens of bird- and wildlife-watching sites, including maps, is tremendous.

Trekking

Trekking in Romania. Tim Burford. Bradt Travel Guides (1996). While some of the practical information is in need of an update, this remains a dependable companion to Romania's great outdoors.

For maps, see page 367.

Useful Websites

Romanian National Tourist Office
www.visitromania.com. A decent overview of the country and its main attractions, plus a directory of useful phone numbers and addresses.

In Your Pocket
www.inyourpocket.com. Detailed and packed with up-to-the-minute information on Bucharest, Brasov and Poiana Brasov.

BBC Romania
www.bbc.ro. The BBC's Romanian-language service.

Blog Bucharest
http://blogbucharest.blogspot.com. An unofficial and opinionated insight into Romania and its people.

HotNews
http://english.hotnews.ro/. For news and current affairs, the English-language pages of this website are excellent.

Online Tickets
www.bilete.ro. Online ticket and event information.

Romanian Railways
www.cfr.ro/mersultrenurilor. The full Romanian train schedule.

Southeast European Times
www.setimes.com. A good site for news

Feedback

We do our best to ensure the information in our books is as accurate and up-to-date as possible. The books are updated on a regular basis, using local contacts, who painstakingly add, amend and correct as required. However, some mistakes and omissions are inevitable and we are ultimately reliant on our readers to put us in the picture.

We would welcome your feedback on any details related to your experiences using the book "on the road". Maybe we recommended a hotel that you liked (or another that you didn't), as well as interesting new attractions, or facts and figures you have found out about the country itself. The more details you can give us (particularly with regard to addresses, e-mails and telephone numbers), the better.

We will acknowledge all contributions, and we'll offer an Insight Guide to the best letters received.

Please write to us at:
Insight Guides
PO Box 7910
London SE1 1WE
United Kingdom
Or send e-mail to:
insight@apaguide.co.uk

from the region, with a useful database of background information on Romania and its neighbours.

Tarom
www.tarom.ro. Book internal and external flights online at the website of Romania's national airline.

The Association of Ecotourism in Romania
www.eco-romania.ro. A useful resource for anyone interested in trekking, bird-watching, caving, cycling, etc, with links to eco-friendly tour operators.

Vivid
www.vivid.ro. Excellent site with plenty of information and analysis of Romanian issues: news, politics culture and the economy.

Other Insight Guides

Titles which highlight destinations in this part of Europe include:

Insight Guide: Bulgaria, captures the essence of this fascinating country with incisive text and memorable photography.

Insight Guide: Hungary surveys the entire country with insightful text and superb photography. There's also a Pocket Guide to Budapest.

The **Pocket Guide to Slovakia** is the perfect on-the-spot companion to one of eastern Europe's most exciting destinations. Text, photographs and maps are all carefully cross-referenced for maximum practicality in this superbly portable format.

GLOSSARY OF ROMANIAN AND HISTORICAL TERMS

ACR (Automobil Clubul Român) Romanian Automobile Club
agenție de voiaj travel agency
alimentară food shop, grocery
ambasadă embassy
Aromanians ethnic minority spread throughout the southern Balkans, closely related to Romanians
autogară bus station

bacșiș bakhsheesh (a bribe or tip)
băile (eg Băile Herculane) bath, spa
berărie beer hall
Bessarabia historical term for the present-day Republic of Moldova
biserică church
biserică de lemn wooden church
bloc (eg blocul or bl. B) block
boyar historical term for a member of the ruling aristocracy
brâncovenesc architectural style named after Constantin Brâncoveanu, mainly found in Wallachia and Moldavia; a fusion of Oriental and Baroque influences, it incorporates ornate stone carvings and lavish painting
bulevard (abbr. b-dul) boulevard

cabană chalet or mountain refuge; cabin (in the mountains)
câine rău/pericolos dangerous dog
calea (eg Calea Victoriei) avenue
casă (eg Casa Vernescu) house
cazare accommodation (available)
căsuțe wooden hut
centru civic civic centre: Ceaușescu-era town centre characterised by wide boulevards and tower blocks
cetate citadel or fortress
CFR (Căile Ferate Române) Romanian Railways
chei (eg cheile Turzii) gorge
ciorbă sour soup
ciubuc bribe, backhander, tip
comună (eg comuna or com. Golești) commune (administrative unit comprising several villages)
cramă wine cellar, often serving basic traditional food

Danubian Principalities historical name for Wallachia and Moldavia
deal (eg dealul Spirii) hill
deschis open
doamnă (eg doamna or D-na or Dna. Popescu) lady, (as a title) Mrs
domn (eg domnul or Dl. Popescu) gentleman, (as a title) Mr
domnișoară young or unmarried lady, (as a title) Miss
drum road

episcop bishop
etaj (eg etajul or et. 10 or X) floor, storey (Romanian follows British usage: the ground floor is parterul and the first floor is etajul I or 1)

gară railway station
horă traditional round or circle dance
hospodar lord; alternate form of voievode used by the rulers of Wallachia and Moldavia

interzis forbidden

intrarea (Int.) entrance
închis closed

județ (eg județul or jud. Neamț) county

Lipovani descendants of the Old Believers who rejected Peter the Great's religious reforms and left Russia to avoid religious persecution; almost all live in Dobrogea
luncă meadow

Magyars a name for ethnic Hungarians
Mahala Ottoman administrative unit: district, suburb or slum
mămăligă polenta made with yellow cornmeal: a Romanian staple
mănăstire (eg Mănăstirea Durău) monastery or convent
mic dejun breakfast
moară hill
Muntenia historical province forming the western half of Wallachia, divided from Oltenia by the Olt River

neo-Brâncoveanesc architectural style common in Wallachia and Moldavia in the early 20th century reviving elements of the Brâncoveanu style
neo-Romanian architectural style fusing elements of Art Nouveau and Romanian folkloric motifs
nu atinge do not touch
număr (eg numărul or nr. 3) number

Oltenia historical province forming the eastern half of Wallachia, divided from Muntenia by the Olt River
Ottomans the Turkish dynasty that ruled much of southeastern Europe from the 15th–19th centuries

palat (eg palatul Cantacuzino) palace
parter ground floor (floors are numbered as in Britain)
pasaj (eg pasajul Victoriei) passage(way)
patriarh (eg patriarhul Teoctist) patriarch: (title of) head of the Romanian Orthodox church
pădure forest, wood
pericol de moarte danger of death
peștera (eg peștera Comarnic) cave
Phanariots Ottomans of Greek origin who occupied high positions in the administration of Wallachia and Moldavia between 1711 and 1821
piatră stone, rock
piața (eg Piața Victoriei) square, marketplace
plajă (eg plajă Neptun) beach
pod (eg podul Grant) bridge
poiană (eg Poiană Brașov) glade, clearing
primărie (eg primăria Brașov or Brașovului) town hall

râu (eg râul Dâmbovița) river
Regat name for the united provinces of Wallachia and Moldavia from 1859 until 1920 when Transylvania was awarded to Romania after World War I
rege (eg regele Ferdinand) king

Regină (eg regină Maria) queen
Roma Gypsy (many prefer the term Roma), Romany
Romania Mare (Greater Romania) name given to the enlarged state of Romania that existed between 1920 and 1940
Roma Gypsy (many prefer the term Roma), Romany
Roumania, Rumania alternate spellings for Romania, largely historical

sarmale favourite Romanian dish of seasoned minced meat and rice wrapped in a cabbage or vine leaf
sat (eg satul Bistrița) village
Saxons (Romanian: sași) ethnic Germans who settled in Transylvania from the 12th century
Secessionism, -ist decorative architectural style, similar to Art Nouveau, popular in areas of Romania under Habsburg rule
Securitate secret police service in communist times
sfânta (eg Sfânta or Sf. Ana) saint (female)
sfântu (eg Sfântul or Sf. Gheorghe) saint (male)
Siebenbürgen German name for Transylvania, after the "seven towns" populated by Transylvanian Saxons
smântână (smetana) Romanian staple, similar to crème fraîche but sourer; frequently stirred into borș
Stână (eg Stână de Vale) sheepfold
stradă street
sus, de sus up, upper
Swabians Germans (mostly not actually from Swabia) who settled in the Banat in the 18th century
Széklers, Székely Hungarian ethnic minority largely found in Covasna, Harghita and Mureș counties
Șosea (eg Șoseaua or Șos. Kiseleff) avenue, highway, street

târg (eg Târgu or Târgul Mureș) fair, market, small town
Țară Românească usual historical term for Wallachia, literally the Romanian Land, distinguished from Țară Unghurească (the Hungarian Land), ie Transylvania
Tatars a collective term for all the Mongol and Turkic-speaking peoples of Asia who over the course of several centuries spread westwards into parts of Europe. Mongols, Turks and Cumans can all be referred to as Tatars. Often misspelled "Tartar"
țuică potent plum brandy, usually home-made

Uniates Greek-Catholics: semi-autonomous Eastern Rite church using the Byzantine liturgical rite in the Romanian language but in full communion with the Roman Catholic church

vârf peak, summit
Vlachs ethnic Romanians, derived from Wallachia, mostly historical use
voeivode (also voievod, voivode) governor of a province

ART & PHOTO CREDITS

INDEX